Lecture Notes in Computer Science 11704

More information about this series at http://www.springer.com/series/7411

Mohamed Faouzi Atig ·
Alexander A. Schwarzmann (Eds.)

Networked Systems

7th International Conference, NETYS 2019
Marrakech, Morocco, June 19–21, 2019
Revised Selected Papers

 Springer

Editors
Mohamed Faouzi Atig (iD)
Uppsala University
Uppsala, Uppsala Län, Sweden

Alexander A. Schwarzmann
Augusta University
Augusta, GA, USA

ISSN 0302-9743   ISSN 1611-3349   (electronic)
Lecture Notes in Computer Science
ISBN 978-3-030-31276-3   ISBN 978-3-030-31277-0   (eBook)
https://doi.org/10.1007/978-3-030-31277-0

LNCS Sublibrary: SL5 – Computer Communication Networks and Telecommunications

This Springer imprint is published by the registered company Springer Nature Switzerland AG
The registered company address is: Gewerbestrasse 11, 6330 Cham, Switzerland

Preface

This volume contains the papers presented at the 7th International Conference on NETworked sYStems (NETYS 2019) held during June 19–21, 2019, in Marrakech, Morocco.

The aim of the NETYS conference series is to bring together researchers and engineers from both the theory and practice of distributed and networked systems. The scope of NETYS 2019 covered all aspects related to the design and development of these systems, including, but not restricted to, concurrent and distributed algorithms, parallel/concurrent/distributed programming, multi-core architectures, formal verification, distributed databases, cloud systems, networks, security, formal verification, etc. NETYS provides a forum to report on best practices and novel algorithms, results, and techniques on networked systems.

The Program Committee (PC) of NETYS 2019 included researchers from 16 countries. There were 60 papers submitted to the conference (in addition there were 14 abstract-only submissions). The PC selected 23 contributions out of the 60 full paper submissions for regular presentations at the conference (which represents an acceptance rate of 38,33%). Every submitted paper was read and evaluated by at least three members of the PC. The PC was assisted by more than 29 external reviewers. Revised and expanded versions of several selected papers may be considered for publication in the Springer journal *Distributed Computing*.

The program also included invited talks by Parosh Abdulla (Uppsala University, Sweden), Paul Attie (Augusta University, USA), Suresh Jagannathan (Purdue University, USA), Somesh Jha (University of Wisconsin, USA), Dariusz Kowalski (Augusta University, USA), and Marc Shapiro (Inria Paris, France).

The Best Paper Award was presented to "Recoverable Mutual Exclusion with Abortability." The Best Student Paper Award of NETYS 2019 was presented to the papers "Checking Causal Consistency of Distributed Databases" and "Liveness in Broadcast Networks."

NETYS is coupled with the METIS Spring School which aims at introducing young researchers to the domain of distributed and networked systems through tutorials on basics, as well as talks on new research topics and current trends in this domain. This year, VDS 2019, the Workshop on Verification of Distributed Systems, was also co-located with NETYS.

We are grateful to all members of the Program and Organizing Committees, to all referees for their cooperation, and to Springer for their professional support during the production phase of the proceedings.

Finally, we would like to thank the sponsoring institutions without whom NETYS 2019 could not have been a reality. We are also thankful to all authors of submitted papers and to all participants of the conference. Their interest in this conference and contributions to the discipline are greatly appreciated.

August 2019

Mohamed Faouzi Atig
Alexander A. Schwarzmann

Organization

ENSIAS, Mohammed V University in Rabat, Morocco

rs

as, Université Paris Diderot, France
EPFL, Switzerland

irs

ig Uppsala University, Sweden
rzmann Augusta University, USA

ittee

Chennai Mathematical Institute, India
Augusta University, USA
Augusta University, USA
EMI, Mohammed V University, Morocco
Cedric - Le Cnam, Paris, France
FS, Mohammed V University in Rabat, Morocco
USMBA, Morocco
University of Ottawa, Canada
Université Paris Diderot, France
Microsoft Research Redmond, USA
Academia Sinica, Taiwan
Université Paris Diderot, France
Inria Paris, ENS, France
University of California, Santa Barbara, USA
IBM Research, Switzerland
Université Paris Diderot, France
The University of Sydney, Data61-CSIRO, Australia
SICS, Sweden
Brown University, USA
University of Sfax, Tunisia
c Mediego, France
oulali Uiversité Mohammed V Souissi, Morocco
University of Liverpool, UK
Microsoft Research, India
MPI-SWS, Germany

Roland Meyer	TU Braunschweig, Germany
Tarik Moataz	Brown University, USA
Nicolas Nicolaou	University of Cyprus, Cyprus
Guevara Noubir	Northeastern University, USA
Ruzica Piskac	Yale University, USA
Andreas Podelski	University of Freiburg, Germany
Sergio Rajsbaum	Instituto de Matematicas, UNAM, Mexico
Michel Raynal	Irisa Rennes, France, and Hong Kong Polytech University, SAR China
Ahmed Rezine	Linköping University, Sweden
Riadh Robbana	LIP2, INSAT, University of Carthage, Tunisia
Paul Spirakis	University of Liverpool, UK, and University of Greece

Organizing Committee

Khadija Bakkouch	IRFC, Morocco
Yahya Benkaouz	FS, Mohammed V University, Morocco
Abdellah Boulouz	FS, Ibn Zohr University, Morocco
Rachid Guerdaoui	Mohammed VI Polytechnic University, Morocco
Zahi Jarir	FS, Cadi Ayyad University, Morocco
Abdellatif Kobbane	ENSIAS, Mohammed V University, Morocco
Mohammed Ouzzif	EST, Hassan II University, Morocco

Students Committee

Maryem Ait El Hadj	ENSIAS, UM5 Rabat, Morocco
Rachid Zennou	ENSIAS, UM5 Rabat, Morocco

Additional Reviewers

Mohammad Javad Amiri
Imen Ben Hfaiedh
Saoussen Cheikhrouhou
Peter Chini
Argyrios Deligkas
Giorgio Delzanno
Sanae El Hassani
Hugues Fauconnier
Ghofrane Fersi
Amal Ghorbel
David Ilcinkas
Marijana Lazic
Hsin-Hung Lin
Sujaya Maiyya
Braham Lotfi Mediouni

Themistoklis Melissourgos
Mohammed Anisse Moutaouekkil
Sebastian Muskalla
Prakash Saivasan
Arnaud Sangnier
Ocan Sankur
Marouane Sebgui
Wael Sellami
Lilia Sfaxi
Io Taxidou
George Turkiyyah
Sebastian Wolff
Xin Xu
Victor Zakhary

Sponsors

Mohammed VI
Polytechnic University

OCP Group

Springer

King Abdullah
University of Science
and Technology

اوطوهول
Auto Hall

Auto Hall

Fondation Hassan II

Fondation Hassan II

thinline

Thinline

Microsoft Research

Université Mohammed
V de Rabat

ENSIAS

Association Alkhawarizmi de Génie Informatique

Keynote Talks

How to Structure Your Concurrent Program and Its Verification

Paul Attie

Augusta University, USA

Abstract. I present some local methods for both *writing* and verifying large concurrent programs: pairwise normal form, dynamic addition of pairwise interactions, and deadlock-freedom via subsystem checking. In pairwise normal form, a process P_i is a set of actions, where each action is a *conjunction* of smaller pairwise-actions, over the neighbours of P_i (the processes that P_i interacts directly with). Variables are shared among pairs. This provides for locality and modifiability in program design, and for tractability in verification. Mutex among n processes can be expressed as 2-process mutex among every pair. If 2-process mutex is enforced among some pairs only, I obtain generalized dining philosophers. If some 2-process mutexes are replaced by a version which gives priority to one process, I obtain readers-writers. Verification of pairwise safety and liveness can be carried out by model-checking each pair in isolation, thereby avoiding state-explosion. Pairs can be added dynamically, at run time. This enables an infinite-state system to be expressed as a countably infinite number of finite-state processes. I introduce the first sound and complete characterization of deadlock for concurrent programs. Most approaches to deadlock observe that a wait-for cycle is necessary for deadlock. However, a cycle is not *sufficient* for deadlock, since a process in the wait-for cycle can choose to interact with a process outside the cycle. This leads to high degree of *incompleteness* in such methods. My approach analyzes the AND-OR generalization of a wait-for cycle, which is necessary and sufficient for a deadlock. I then impose local conditions (over small subsystems) which prevent the creation of such AND-OR wait-for cycles. My methods have been implemented in the Eshmun tool.

Automated Reasoning for Weak Consistency

Suresh Jagannathan

Purdue University, USA

Abstract. Modern distributed applications often replicate data across geo-graphically diverse locations to enable trust decentralization, guarantee low-latency access to application state, and provide high availability even in the face of node and network failures. Replication complicates program reasoning, however, since not all copies of an object are guaranteed to hold the same state at the same time. Existing verification approaches impose a high cognitive burden on developers to establish necessary invariants and derive sophisticated proof strategies to ensure application correctness in these environments. In this talk, I describe several techniques to enable automated verification of distributed applications in the face of weak-consistency that greatly alleviates this burden. Our solutions employ new logical specification formalisms, novel symbolic execution and model-checking abstractions, and tailored static analyses that collectively enable the construction of trustworthy (geo-replicated) distributed applications, without requiring extensive programmer involvement to enable verification.

Towards Semantic Adversarial Examples

Somesh Jha

University of Wisconsin, USA

Abstract. Fueled by massive amounts of data, models produced by machine-learning (ML) algorithms, especially deep neural networks, are being used in diverse domains where trustworthiness is a concern, including automotive systems, finance, health care, natural language processing, and malware detection. Of particular concern is the use of ML algorithms in cyber-physical systems (CPS), such as self-driving cars and aviation, where an adversary can cause serious consequences. However, existing approaches to generating adversarial examples and devising robust ML algorithms mostly ignore the semantics and context of the overall system containing the ML component. For example, in an autonomous vehicle using deep learning for perception, not every adversarial example for the neural network might lead to a harmful consequence. Moreover, one may want to prioritize the search for adversarial examples towards those that significantly modify the desired semantics of the overall system. Along the same lines, existing algorithms for constructing robust ML algorithms ignore the specification of the overall system. In this talk, we argue that the semantics and specification of the overall system has a crucial role to play in this line of research. We present preliminary research results that support this claim.

Living on the Edge, Safely or: Life without Consensus

Marc Shapiro

Inria Paris, France

Abstract. The centre-of-gravity of cloud is moving towards the edge. At edge scale, the opposition between the requirements of availability and ensuring correctness precludes any single simple answer. Choosing the right trade-off is a most vexing issue for application developers. To address this, we propose an application-driven approach, Just-Right Consistency (JRC). JRC derives a consistency model that is adapted to the specific application, being sufficient to maintain its invariants, otherwise remaining as available as possible.

In order to maintain its invariants, even sequential code follows some standard patterns. We leverage mechanisms that uphold several of these patterns while maintaining availability:

Conflict-Free Replicated Data Types (CRDTs) ensure that concurrent updates can be merged; Causal Consistency preserves relative ordering; Available Transactions preserve grouping. Together, these mechanisms form the TCC+ model. Furthermore, our CISE logic and analysis tools distinguish cases, in the remaining pattern, where the application's semantics requires synchronisation or not. This talk presents the challenges of edge-scale computing and the basics of the JRC approach by following the concrete example of a healthcare network. This research is supported in part by European projects SyncFree and Light-Kone, and by ANR project RainbowFS.

Contents

Security

Concurrency

Networks

Invited Papers

Dynamic Partial Order Reduction Under the Release-Acquire Semantics (Tutorial)

Parosh Aziz Abdulla$^{(\boxtimes)}$, Mohamed Faouzi Atig, Bengt Jonsson, and Tuan Phong Ngo

Uppsala University, Uppsala, Sweden
parosh@it.uu.se

Abstract. We describe at a high-level the main concepts in the Release-Acquire (RA) semantics that is part of the C11 language. Furthermore, we describe the ideas behind an optimal dynamic partial order reduction technique that can be used for systematic analysis of concurrent programs running under RA.

This tutorial is based on the material presented in [5], which also contains the formal definitions of all the models, concepts, and algorithms.

1 Introduction

Concurrent programs are difficult to get correct. The main reasons are the large number of threads that may arise during a given execution of the program, and the intricate nature of interactions among these threads. *Model checking* has been of the most prominent approaches to program verification during the last three decades [16]. Given a formal model of a program and a property to be checked, a model checking algorithm checks *automatically* whether the program satisfies the property or not. A limiting factor in the application of model checking is the *state explosion problem* which occurs since the size of the state space of the program grows exponentially with the number of threads. *Stateless Model Checking* (SMC) [21] has been proposed as a way to reduce the problem at the price of sacrificing the completeness of the analysis. The aim is to exploit the hypothesis that bugs that arise only due to some (usually a small number) of the possible thread schedulings. In contrast to full model checking, SMC algorithms are run under two assumptions on the input program:

- Each thread in the program is assumed to be terminating. To enforce this condition, program loops are unfolded a certain *a priori* decided number of times.
- Each thread is assumed to be data-deterministic, and hence the only source of non-determinism lies in the thread schedulings. To enforce the condition we analyze the program for a given initial value per variable.

Under these two assumptions, SMC systematically explores the set of all thread schedulings that are possible during the runs of the program. The SMC exploration is derived by a special run-time scheduler which derives new thread

© Springer Nature Switzerland AG 2019
M. F. Atig and A. A. Schwarzmann (Eds.): NETYS 2019, LNCS 11704, pp. 3–18, 2019.
https://doi.org/10.1007/978-3-030-31277-0_1

schedulings whenever it detects that such decisions may affect the interaction between threads. In such a manner, it is guaranteed that the exploration covers all possible executions. This also means that the algorithm detects any unexpected program results, program crashes, or assertion violations. Due to the assumptions, we can in general consider SMC as an *under-approximate* verification framework in the sense that all reported errors are true bugs in the program, but certain bugs may remain undetected. Despite not being complete, SMC offers numerous advantages, namely:

- It is completely automatic.
- It has no false positives.
- It does not consume excessive memory.
- It can easily reproduce the concurrency bugs it detects.

Due to these advantages, SMC has along the years been implemented in numerous tools, such as VeriSoft [23], CDSCHECKER [18,31], CHESS [30], Concuerror [14], rInspect [37], and Nidhugg [1], and successfully applied to realistic concurrent programs [22,27].

Notwithstanding, SMC still faces the state space explosion problem, albeit in a less severe manner. To circumvent this problem, different techniques have been proposed to reduce the number of explored executions. The most important one is *partial order reduction*. Partial order techniques were first developed for full model checking [11,12,15,20,32,36]. It was later integrated in the SMC framework, and called *dynamic partial order reduction* (DPOR) [2,3,19,34,35]. DPOR avoids redundant exploration of equivalent executions with the same order between conflicting instructions. Two executions are regarded as equivalent if they induce the same ordering between conflicting events. It is sufficient to explore one execution in each equivalence class. The equivalence classes are sometimes called *Mazurkiewicz traces* [29]. An important goal is to avoid exploring several traces that belong to the same equivalence class since, after all, such traces carry the same information with respect to the property to be verified. Ideally, we would like to design DPOR algorithms that are *optimal* in the sense that they explore *exactly* one interleaving in each equivalence class [2].

In this tutorial, we will consider two issues related to the principles of the DPOR approach:

- Mazurkiewicz traces distinguish executions based on the ordering of conflicting write operations, and on how reads are ordered wrt. the writes. Therefore, Mazurkiewicz traces induce an equivalence relation that is occasionally unnecessarily coarse for checking typical properties such as program crashes or assertion violations. For instance, it includes *coherence order*, i.e., the order in which write events on shared variables reach the memory. Coherence order is irrelevant for checking the above properties, and hence using Mazurkiewicz traces is a source of redundancy, inherently limiting the efficiency that can possibly be achieved in the analysis. In this tutorial, we will consider a weaker equivalence relation that is still sufficiently strong to guarantee full coverage of the state space, and that will therefore potentially achieve efficiency levels that are not possible with current techniques.

Initially $x = 0$

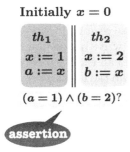

$(a = 1) \wedge (b = 2)?$

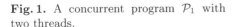

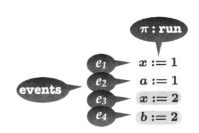

Fig. 1. A concurrent program $\mathcal{P}_1$ with two threads.

Fig. 2. A run of the program $\mathcal{P}_1$.

– The DPOR framework was originally deigned for concurrent program running under the classical model of Sequential Consistency (SC) [2,19,35]. However, nowadays most parallel software run on platforms that do not guarantee SC. More precisely, to satisfy demands on efficiency and energy saving, such platforms implement optimizations that lead to the relaxation of the inter-component synchronization, hence offering only *weak consistency* guarantees. In recent years, DPOR has also been adapted to hardware-induced relaxed memory models, such as TSO and PSO [1,37], and language-level concurrency models, such as the C/C++ memory model [26,31]. In this tutorial, we will describe how to extend DPOR to a particular consistency model, namely the Release-Acquire fragment of C11 [28].

2   Sequential Consistency

We will introduce concurrent programs, define the notions of runs and traces, and describe (optimal) DPOR algorithms.

2.1   Concurrent Programs

Fig. 1 depicts a program $\mathcal{P}_1$ with two threads, namely th_1 and th_2. The threads operate on a set X of shared variables, (in this example, one shared variable x), and a set of local variables (here one variable in each thread, namely a and b in th_1 and th_2 respectively). The code of each thread consists of two instructions, one *writing* the values 1 resp. 2 to the shared variable x, and one *reading* the value of x, and storing the value in the local variables a resp. b.

2.2   Runs and Traces

Fig. 2 depicts a run π of $\mathcal{P}_1$ under the *Sequential Consistency (SC) semantics*. A run is a sequence of *events* each corresponding to the execution of one instruction by a thread. Under SC, instructions are executed in *program-order*, i.e., in the same order as they occur in the code of the thread. A *run* is the interleaving of the executions of the different threads. In particular, the read and write instructions are executed atomically. This means that when a write instruction is executed by a thread, its effect will be immediately visible to all the other threads, and a read instruction on a variable x will get its value from the latest write instruction on x. For instance, in the run π of Fig. 2, the value of x read by thread th_1 is 1 since the latest write instruction on x assigned the value 1 to x. Notice that we represent a read event by the value that it reads from the shared variable.

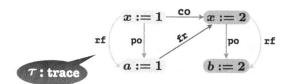

Fig. 3. The trace corresponding to π in Fig. 2.

Next, we define the notion of a *trace* that we will use to represent sets of runs. Traces have three advantages in our framework, namely exactness, efficiency, and abstraction:

- They provide sufficient information for checking different program properties, and therefore they are an *exact* representation of program runs.
- The provide a more compact representation than program runs, and therefore they are more *efficient* when performing verification.
- They are *abstract* in the sense that they can easily be adapted to different memory models.

A *trace* τ, corresponding to the run π in Fig. 2 is depicted in Fig. 3. We write $\pi \models \tau$ to denote that τ corresponds to π. A trace is a graph where the nodes represent events. The edges between the nodes represent four different relations. The *program-order* relation po is the order in which the events are executed by a given thread. The *read-form* relation rf defines the write event from which a read event gets its value. The *coherence-order* relation is defined as $\mathsf{co} = \cup_{x \in X} \mathsf{co}^x$, where co^x is a total order defining the order in which the write events are carried out on the variable x. Finally, the relation fr gives the write event which overwrites the value that is read by a read event. More precisely, if e_1 reads from e_2 and e_3 is the immediate successor of e_2 in the coherence-order relation, then e_1 precedes e_3 in the read-from relation. The relation fr can be derived from the relations rf and co in the sense that $\mathsf{fr} = \mathsf{co}^{-1} \circ \mathsf{rf}$.

Different memory models can be defined by requiring the acyclicity of different fragments of the above relations. For a trace τ, we write $\tau \models SC$ to denote that $acyclic(\mathsf{po} \cup \mathsf{rf} \cup \mathsf{co}\,\mathsf{fr})$ holds, i.e., SC is defined by the constraint that the union of the four relations should be acyclic. We write $\pi \models SC$ to denote that both $\pi \models \tau$ and $\tau \models SC$, i.e., a run is in SC if its trace satisfies the SC condition.

Fig. 4. (Optimal) Partial Order Reduction.

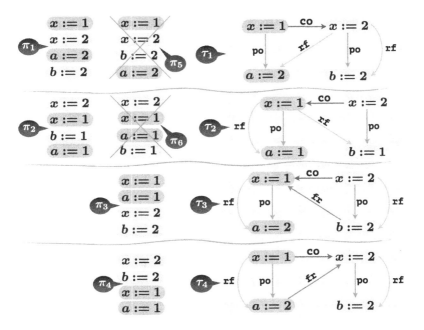

Fig. 5. The runs of the program in Fig. 1, together with their traces.

2.3   DPOR

A DPOR algorithm is represented as a black-box in Fig. 4. The algorithm is given a concurrent program as input and the algorithms generates at least one run per trace. The algorithm analyzes the traces on-the-fly to check for unexpected program results, program crashes, or assertion violations. An important goal for any DPOR algorithm is to generate as a few runs as possible per trace, thus increasing the efficiency of the analysis. An optimal DPOR algorithm generates exactly one run per each trace [2,3]. Fig. 5 shows all the six runs of the program $\mathcal{P}_1$ of Fig. 1, together with the corresponding traces. The runs π_1 and π_5 have the same trace τ_1, and the runs π_2 and π_6 have the same trace τ_2. A possible outcome of an optimal DPOR algorithm is the set $\{\pi_1, \pi_2, \pi_3, \pi_4\}$. The runs π_5 and π_6 are not generated. The algorithm may as well generate π_5 instead of π_1 but not both. The same applies to π_2 and π_6.

We can take one step further by observing that two traces may have identical program-order and read-from relations and differ only in their coherence-order.

In Fig. 5 this applies to the traces τ_3 and τ_4. The coherence-order relation is used to define the memory model, and it has no bearing on the set of assertions that are satisfied by the program. The latter are solely decided by the program-order and the read-from relations. Therefore, we can only generate runs that have different program-order and read-from relations without sacrificing the precision of the analysis. A *super-optimal* DPOR algorithm will only generate one of the runs π_3 and π_4 since their traces have identical program-order and read-from relations [5]. Therefore their traces τ_3 and τ_4 can be "merged" into one trace τ_5 which has the same program-order and read-from relations as τ_3 and τ_4 (Fig. 6).

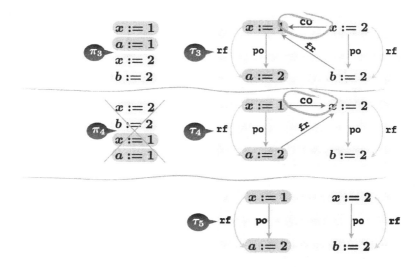

Fig. 6. Super-Optimal Partial Order Reduction.

3 The Release-Acquire Semantics

We will recall the Release-Acquire semantics, and describe the main ideas of a DPOR framework for the analysis of concurrent program running under RA. To that end, we introduce a saturation procedure, and use it to define operations for adding new events to traces, and finally descries the DPOR algorithm.

3.1 Semantics

The Release-Acquire semantics (RA) is defined by the constraint

$$\forall x \in X.\ acyclic(\mathsf{po} \cup \mathsf{rf} \cup \mathsf{co}_x \cup \mathsf{fr}_x)$$

In other words, for each variable $x \in X$, the union of the program-order and reads-form relations, together with the restriction of the coherence-order and from-read relations to x should be acyclic. Fig. 7 shows a program $\mathcal{P}_2$ with four threads, and a trace τ of $\mathcal{P}_2$ that satisfies RA (denoted $\tau \models RA$). In this case, $\tau \not\models SC$ due to the cycle $(x := 1) \xrightarrow{\text{po}} (y := 2) \xrightarrow{\text{co}^y} (y := 1) \xrightarrow{\text{po}} (x := 2) \xrightarrow{\text{co}^x} (x := 1)$. The cycle does not violate the RA semantics since it contains coherence-order relations on different variables (x and y).

$$
\begin{array}{c||c||c||c}
a := x & x := 1 & y := 1 & c := y \\
b := x & y := 2 & x := 2 & d := y
\end{array}
$$

Fig. 7. A concurrent program $\mathcal{P}_2$ with four threads.

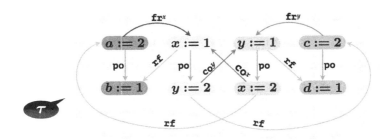

Fig. 8. A trace of the program in the RA-semantics.

3.2 DPOR

We will describe a super-optimal DPOR algorithm for concurrent programs under the RA-semantics. The aim of such an algorithms is to satisfy the following criteria for any input program $\mathcal{P}$:

- *Soundness*: If the algorithm generates a run π then (i) π is a run of $\mathcal{P}$, and (ii) $\pi \models \tau$ for some trace with $\tau \models RA$.
- *Completeness*: For any trace τ where $\pi \models \tau$ for some run π of $\mathcal{P}$ and $\tau \models RA$, the algorithm generates a run π' of $\mathcal{P}$ such that $\pi' \models \tau$.
- *Optimality*: The algorithms never generates two runs π_1 and π_2 such that there are traces τ_1 and τ_2, with $\pi_1 \models \tau_1$, $\pi_2 \models \tau_2$, and τ_1 and τ_2 have identical program-order and read-from relations.

Roughly, the DPOR algorithm operates as follows:

- It builds the traces one after one.
- For a given trace τ:
  - It builds τ incrementally.
  - It *extends* τ by one event e at a time.

We will describe how traces are extended by events. To do that, we will first define the notion of *saturation*.

3.3   Saturation

As mentioned above, coherence-order is not essential for checking assertion violations. On the other hand, coherence-order is part of the definition of the semantics, so it cannot be neglected completely; otherwise we may generate traces
that do not satisfy the semantics, which makes the DPOR algorithm unsound.
The idea is to *saturate traces*, i.e., add coherence-order edges by demand during
the analysis, thus ensuring that we only add edges that are necessary to keep
consistency wrt. the semantics. In fact, in the case of RA, saturation is sufficient
to achieve optimality, i.e., never generating two traces with the program-order
and read-from relations. Under the RA semantics, saturation is simple and be
computed in polynomial time (in the size of the trace). To illustrate how, consider the trace in Fig. 9. The trace contains two write events w_1^x and w_2^x, and
one read event r^x. The three events satisfy two conditions:

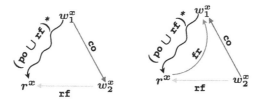

Fig. 9. Saturating a trace under the RA semantics. The coherence-order should point
form the event w_1^x to w_1^x (left part of the figure); otherwise we create a cycle violating
the RA semantics (right part).

- There is a sequence of po- and rf-edges leading from w_1^x to r^x.
- r^x reads from w_2^x.

In such a case, the saturation procedure adds a co-edge from w_1^x and w_2^x (the
left part of Fig. 9). To see why this is necessary, consider the right part of Fig. 9.
If the co-edge is put in the reverse direction, then we get a cycle that violates
the RA-semantics. In general, for write events e_1 and e_2, and a read event e_3,
all on the same variable x, we add an edge $e_1 \xrightarrow{co^x} e_2$ whenever $e_1 \left(\xrightarrow{po \cup rf} \right)^+ e_3$
and $e_2 \xrightarrow{rf} e_3$. The trace is *saturated* if the saturation rule does not add any
new edges. A trace can be saturated in polynomial time, since we can compute
the transitive closure of the relation po $\cup$ rf using, e.g., the Floyd-Warshall
algorithm [17]. The trace in Fig. 10 is not saturated. Due to the path $(x :=$
$2) \xrightarrow{rf} (a := 2) \xrightarrow{po} (b := 1)$, and $(x := 1) \xrightarrow{rf} (b := 1)$, the saturation procedure
will add the edge $(x := 2) \xrightarrow{co^x} (x := 1)$. Analogously, it will add the edge
$(y := 2) \xrightarrow{co^y} (y := 1)$, thus obtaining the trace τ in Fig. 8 which is saturated.

In the DPOR algorithm, all the generated traces are saturated by construction. In Subsect. 3.4 we see how this can be achieved.

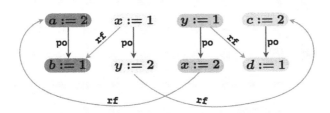

Fig. 10. Unsaturated trace.

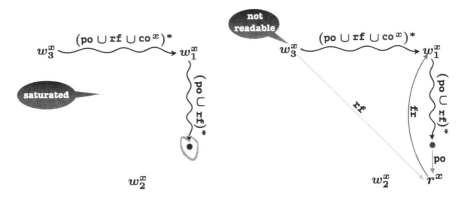

Fig. 11. Part of a trace before adding a new event.

Fig. 12. Reading from the wrong write.

3.4 Adding Events to Traces

Suppose that we are given a trace τ that is saturated. We would like to add a new event e to τ such that the new trace remains saturated. We consider two cases, namely when e is a read resp. write event. Adding a read event amounts to two operations:

- Finding the write events, from which we can read the value of the new variable without violating the RA semantics.
- Adding the necessary (and only the necessary) coherence-order edges to maintain saturation.

To illustrate these ideas, consider a saturated trace partially shown in Fig. 11, with (among others) three write events w_1^x, w_2^x, and w_3^x. Assume that we are about to add a new read event r^x at the marked position. In this example the event r^x is not allowed to read from w_3^x, since this would create a cycle that violates the RA-semantics as shown in Fig. 12. We say that a write event e_1 on a variable x is *readable* if there is no other write event e_2 on x such that e_1 can reach e_2 and e_2 can reach the reading thread through the ($\mathsf{po} \cup \mathsf{rf} \cup \mathsf{co}^x$)-relation.

In Fig. 12, w_3^x is not readable for the read event since w_1^x is "blocking" its path to the reading thread.

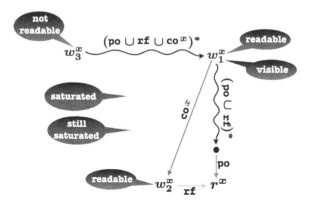

Fig. 13. Adding a new read event.

Assume that w_2^x is readable and that the new event r^x reads its value from w_2^x, as depicted in Fig. 13. Our objective is to make the new trace saturated (assuming that the original trace was saturated). To that end, we add all the new coherence-order edges that are necessary according to the RA semantics. This amounts to applying the saturation rule repeatedly until the trace becomes saturated. To find out where in the trace to apply the saturation rule, we consider the so called *visible events*. These are write events that are readable and can reach the read event through po- and rf-edges. The write event w_1^x is a visible event in Fig. 13. For each visible event, we add a coherence edge the write from which the new event reads (e.g., the edge $w_1^x \xrightarrow{\mathrm{co}^x} w_2^x$ in Fig. 13). If the original trace is saturated, and we add the edges from the visible events (as described above) then the new trace will be saturated.

Adding write events events is a much simpler operation. We only need to add one program-order edge, as depicted in Fig. 14, If the original trace is saturated, then the new trace will be saturated, without the need to add any extra edges.

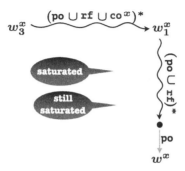

Fig. 14. Adding an new write event.

Fig. 15. A concurrent program with four threads.

Fig. 16. A concurrent program with four threads.

3.5 Algorithm

Our DPOR algorithm generates systematically different runs of the input programs, and uses the operations described in the previous sub-section to build the corresponding traces. At any point of time, the algorithm will be in the middle of generating one particular run, while also scheduling (start segments) of other runs to be considered later. The algorithm is implemented recursively where a new call generates the next node in the recursion tree. The new node may correspond to the next event in the current run in which case we may also schedule parts of new runs to be considered when the recursive call has returned. The new node may also correspond to the start of the execution of one of the scheduled runs. Upon termination, the set of paths in the recursion tree represents the set of program runs that have been generated. The algorithm will not generate the full tree at the same time. Instead, it generates one path (corresponding to one run) at a time.

Figure 15 depicts a concurrent program with four threads. The DPOR algorithm will no-deterministically select a thread and run its next instruction (Fig. 16). In the current scenario it selects the instruction $x := 2$. Next, it selects the instruction $a := x$. Here, there are two choices. The read event may either read the initial value of x which is assumed to be 0, or read from the write event $x := 2$ that has already been generated. The choice is made non-deterministically. In the example, the algorithm will read from the initial value. Since, we only want to generate one run at a time, we *schedule* the event $a := 2$ (which corresponds to $a := x$ reading from $x := 2$), for future execution (Fig. 16). More precisely, we call the algorithm recursively with $a := 0$, and when the recursive call returns, we consider $a := 2$ to generate a new run. We call this *read-branching*, to hint that the tree branches on the different write events that a given instruction can read from. In the next step, the algorithm selects a possible next instruction, which in this case is $b := y$, for which it selects the only possible value, namely 0. Assume that the algorithm next selects the instruction $x := 3$ (Fig. 17). The instruction could have been used by the read instruction $a := x$. However, this was not made part of the schedule since the instruction $x := 3$ had not yet been detected. An event is called a *postponed write* if it is generated by the algorithm

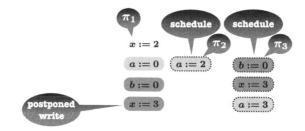

Fig. 17. Postponed writes.

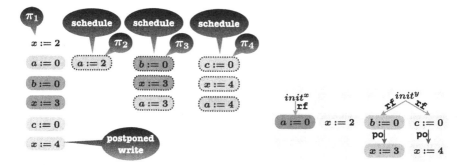

Fig. 18. A complete run π_1.   **Fig. 19.** The trace of π_1.

after a read event that may read it. To get the event $a := 3$, we also need to include the sequence of events that *happen before* it, i.e., the sequence of events that are needed to generate $a := 3$. The happens-before sequence is the sequence of events that proceed the given event by the **po**- and **rf**-relations. In our case, this sequence is $b := 0\ x := 3$. The schedule then will contain the happen-before sequence as well as the event itself.

The run terminates after executing the instructions $c := 0$ (no branching needed), and $x := 4$ which is a postponed write for $a := x$ (the run π_1 Fig. 18). The trace corresponding to π_1 is shown in Fig. 19. The algorithm will now backtrack and considers the schedules. The second schedule $a := 2$ will induce the run π_2 shown in Fig. 20, with the trace of Fig. 21. In particular, it generates the postponed write instruction $x := 3$ for the read instruction $a := x$. However, this write instruction (together with its happens-before event $b := 0$) is already in the set of schedules, and therefore it will not be added to the set of schedules. This feature guarantees that we never generate two traces with identical program-order and read-from relations.

Finally, the two remaining schedules will be considered, resulting in runs two new runs (Fig. 22) whose traces are shown in Fig. 23.

The algorithm has generated all the four traces that belong to the program in Fig. 15 (completeness), has not generated any other traces (soundness), and all the generated traces have different program-order and read-from relations (optimality).

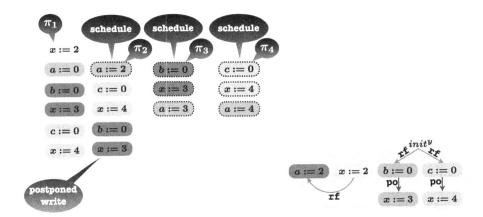

Fig. 20. Another run π_2.

Fig. 21. The trace of π_2.

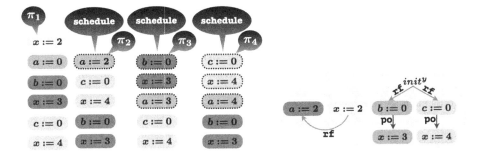

Fig. 22. Two more runs π_3 and π_4.

Fig. 23. The trace of π_3 and π_4.

4   Related Work

This tutorial is based on the material presented in [5].

Stateless model checking (SMC), coupled with (dynamic) partial order techniques, was initiated in the works of Verisoft [21,23] and CHESS [30], and has since been developed in several subsequent works, e.g., [2,19,22,27,33]. The method of [2] is optimal w.r.t. Mazurkiewicz traces under SC.

SMC has been applied to weak memory models such TSO, PSO, and POWER [1,4,18,37]. SMC has been adapted to (variants of) the C/C++11 memory model, which includes RA, and implemented in tools such as CDSCHECKER [31] and RCMC [26].

Several recent DPOR techniques aim at using a weaker equivalence than Mazurkiewicz traces [13,24,25,31]. Maximal causality reduction (MCR) is a technique based on exploring the possible *values* that reads can see, instead of the possible value-producing writes, as in our approach. MCR has been developed for SC [24] and for TSO and PSO [25].

5   Conclusions and Future Work

We have presented the main ideas behind a DPOR algorithm for the analysis of concurrent programs running under the RA semantics. The algorithm is optimal in the sense that it generates at most one trace with a given program-order and read-from relation.

In this tutorial we only consider the RA semantics. It is interesting to extend the approach to other memory models. In particular, the *relaxed* fragment of C/C++11 is challenging since it contains speculative operations that are not covered in the current framework. However, we believe that speculations can be handled using a scheme similar to the postponed write mechanism that we described in this paper.

Other directions for future work include considering probabilistic and game-based models that describe the manner in which a given message will be read by a given process. It might then be possible to analyze the system using techniques for the analysis of probabilistic and game-based extensions of multi-dimension infinite-state systems, e.g., [6,8,9]. It is also relevant to check whether a given platform guarantees a given weak memory, using monitoring techniques such as the one described in [10]. Finally it is interesting to obtain efficient verification frameworks by integrating powerful abstraction techniques for infinite-state systems such as the one in [7].

References

1. Abdulla, P.A., Aronis, S., Atig, M.F., Jonsson, B., Leonardsson, C., Sagonas, K.: Stateless model checking for TSO and PSO. In: Baier, C., Tinelli, C. (eds.) TACAS 2015. LNCS, vol. 9035, pp. 353–367. Springer, Heidelberg (2015). https://doi.org/10.1007/978-3-662-46681-0_28
2. Abdulla, P., Aronis, S., Jonsson, B., Sagonas, K.: Optimal dynamic partial order reduction. In: Symposium on Principles of Programming Languages, (POPL), pp. 373–384. ACM, San Diego (2014)
3. Abdulla, P.A., Aronis, S., Jonsson, B., Sagonas, K.: Source sets: a foundation for optimal dynamic partial order reduction. J. ACM **64**(4), 25:1–25:49 (2017). https://doi.org/10.1145/3073408
4. Abdulla, P.A., Atig, M.F., Jonsson, B., Leonardsson, C.: Stateless model checking for POWER. In: Chaudhuri, S., Farzan, A. (eds.) CAV 2016. LNCS, vol. 9780, pp. 134–156. Springer, Cham (2016). https://doi.org/10.1007/978-3-319-41540-6_8

5. Abdulla, P.A., Atig, M.F., Jonsson, B., Ngo, T.P.: Optimal stateless model checking under the release-acquire semantics. PACMPL **2**(OOPSLA), 135:1–135:29 (2018). https://doi.org/10.1145/3276505
6. Abdulla, P.A., Bertrand, N., Rabinovich, A.M., Schnoebelen, P.: Verification of probabilistic systems with faulty communication. Inf. Comput. **202**(2), 141–165 (2005). https://doi.org/10.1016/j.ic.2005.05.008
7. Abdulla, P.A., Bouajjani, A., Cederberg, J., Haziza, F., Rezine, A.: Monotonic abstraction for programs with dynamic memory heaps. In: Gupta, A., Malik, S. (eds.) CAV 2008. LNCS, vol. 5123, pp. 341–354. Springer, Heidelberg (2008). https://doi.org/10.1007/978-3-540-70545-1_33
8. Abdulla, P.A., Bouajjani, A., d'Orso, J.: Deciding monotonic games. In: Baaz, M., Makowsky, J.A. (eds.) CSL 2003. LNCS, vol. 2803, pp. 1–14. Springer, Heidelberg (2003). https://doi.org/10.1007/978-3-540-45220-1_1
9. Abdulla, P.A., Deneux, J., Mahata, P.: Multi-clock timed networks. In: 19th IEEE Symposium on Logic in Computer Science (LICS 2004), 14–17 July 2004, Turku, Finland, Proceedings, pp. 345–354. IEEE Computer Society (2004). https://doi.org/10.1109/LICS.2004.1319629
10. Abdulla, P.A., Haziza, F., Holík, L., Jonsson, B., Rezine, A.: An integrated specification and verification technique for highly concurrent data structures. In: Piterman, N., Smolka, S.A. (eds.) TACAS 2013. LNCS, vol. 7795, pp. 324–338. Springer, Heidelberg (2013). https://doi.org/10.1007/978-3-642-36742-7_23
11. Abdulla, P.A., Jonsson, B., Kindahl, M., Peled, D.: A general approach to partial order reductions in symbolic verification. In: Hu, A.J., Vardi, M.Y. (eds.) CAV 1998. LNCS, vol. 1427, pp. 379–390. Springer, Heidelberg (1998). https://doi.org/10.1007/BFb0028760
12. Abdulla, P.A., Kindahl, M., Peled, D.A.: An improved search strategy for lossy channel systems. In: Togashi, A., Mizuno, T., Shiratori, N., Higashino, T. (eds.) Formal Description Techniques and Protocol Specification, Testing and Verification, FORTE X / PSTV XVII'97, IFIP TC6 WG6.1 Joint International Conference on Formal Description Techniques for Distributed Systems and Communication Protocols (FORTE X) and Protocol Specification, Testing and Verification (PSTV XVII), 18–21 November 1997, Osaka, Japan, IFIP Conference Proceedings, vol. 107, pp. 251–264. Chapman & Hall (1997)
13. Chalupa, M., Chatterjee, K., Pavlogiannis, A., Sinha, N., Vaidya, K.: Data-centric dynamic partial order reduction. Proc. ACM Program. Lang. **2**(POPL), 31:1–31:30 (2017). https://doi.org/10.1145/3158119
14. Christakis, M., Gotovos, A., Sagonas, K.: Systematic testing for detecting concurrency errors in Erlang programs. In: International Conference on Software Testing. Verification and Validation, (ICST), pp. 154–163. IEEE, Luxembourg (2013)
15. Clarke, E.M., Grumberg, O., Minea, M., Peled, D.A.: State space reduction using partial order techniques. STTT **2**(3), 279–287 (1999)
16. Clarke, E.M., Henzinger, T.A., Veith, H., Bloem, R. (eds.): Handbook of Model Checking. Springer, Cham (2018). https://doi.org/10.1007/978-3-319-10575-8
17. Cormen, T.H., Leiserson, C.E., Rivest, R.L., Stein, C.: Introduction to Algorithms. The MIT Press, Cambridge (2009)
18. Demsky, B., Lam, P.: Satcheck: Sat-directed stateless model checking for SC and TSO. In: Object-Oriented Programming, Systems, Languages, and Applications, (OOPSLA), pp. 20–36. ACM, Pittsburgh (2015)
19. Flanagan, C., Godefroid, P.: Dynamic partial-order reduction for model checking software. In: Principles of Programming Languages, POPL, pp. 110–121. ACM, Long Beach (2005)

20. Godefroid, P.: Partial-Order Methods for the Verification of Concurrent Systems: An Approach to the State-Explosion Problem. Ph.D. thesis, University of Liége (1996). Also, volume 1032 of LNCS, Springer
21. Godefroid, P.: Model checking for programming languages using VeriSoft. In: Principles of Programming Languages, POPL, pp. 174–186. ACM Press, Paris (1997)
22. Godefroid, P., Hammer, B., Jagadeesan, L.: Model checking without a model: an analysis of the heart-beat monitor of a telephone switch using VeriSoft. In: Proceedings of ACM SIGSOFT International Symposium on Software Testing and Analysis. pp. 124–133 (1998)
23. Godefroid, P.: Software model checking: the VeriSoft approach. Formal Methods Syst. Des. 26(2), 77–101 (2005)
24. Huang, J.: Stateless model checking concurrent programs with maximal causality reduction. In: Programming Language Design and Implementation, PLDI, pp. 165–174. ACM, Portland (2015)
25. Huang, S., Huang, J.: Maximal causality reduction for TSO and PSO. In: Object-Oriented Programming, Systems, Languages, and Applications, (OOPSLA), pp. 447–461. ACM, Amsterdam (2016)
26. Kokologiannakis, M., Lahav, O., Sagonas, K., Vafeiadis, V.: Effective stateless model checking for C/C++ concurrency. In: POPL (2018, to appear). http://plv.mpi-sws.org/rcmc/
27. Kokologiannakis, M., Sagonas, K.: Stateless model checking of the linux kernel's hierarchical read-copy-update (tree RCU). In: Symposium on Model Checking of Software, SPIN, pp. 172–181. ACM, Santa Barbara (2017)
28. Lahav, O., Giannarakis, N., Vafeiadis, V.: Taming release-acquire consistency. In: Proceedings of the 43rd Annual ACM SIGPLAN-SIGACT Symposium on Principles of Programming Languages, POPL 2016, St. Petersburg, FL, USA, 20–22 January 2016, pp. 649–662. ACM (2016)
29. Mazurkiewicz, A.: Trace theory. In: Advances in Petri Nets (1986)
30. Musuvathi, M., Qadeer, S., Ball, T., Basler, G., Nainar, P., Neamtiu, I.: Finding and reproducing heisenbugs in concurrent programs. In: OSDI, pp. 267–280. USENIX Association (2008)
31. Norris, B., Demsky, B.: A practical approach for model checking C/C++11 code. ACM Trans. Program. Lang. Syst. 38(3), 10:1–10:51 (2016)
32. Peled, D.: All from one, one for all: on model checking using representatives. In: Courcoubetis, C. (ed.) CAV 1993. LNCS, vol. 697, pp. 409–423. Springer, Heidelberg (1993). https://doi.org/10.1007/3-540-56922-7_34
33. Rodríguez, C., Sousa, M., Sharma, S., Kroening, D.: Unfolding-based partial order reduction. In: CONCUR 2015, pp. 456–469 (2015)
34. Saarikivi, O., Kähkönen, K., Heljanko, K.: Improving dynamic partial order reductions for concolic testing. In: Application of Concurrency to System Design, ACSD, pp. 132–141. IEEE, Hamburg (2012)
35. Sen, K., Agha, G.: A race-detection and flipping algorithm for automated testing of multi-threaded programs. In: Haifa Verification Conference. pp. 166–182 (2007), lNCS 4383
36. Valmari, A.: Stubborn sets for reduced state space generation. In: Rozenberg, G. (ed.) ICATPN 1989. LNCS, vol. 483, pp. 491–515. Springer, Heidelberg (1991). https://doi.org/10.1007/3-540-53863-1_36
37. Zhang, N., Kusano, M., Wang, C.: Dynamic partial order reduction for relaxed memory models. In: Programming Language Design and Implementation (PLDI), pp. 250–259. ACM, Portland (2015)

On the Complexity of Fault-Tolerant Consensus

Dariusz R. Kowalski[1,2] and Jarosław Mirek[2(✉)]

[1] School of Computer and Cyber Sciences, Augusta University, Augusta, USA
[2] Department of Computer Science, University of Liverpool, Liverpool, UK
{D.Kowalski,J.Mirek}@liverpool.ac.uk

Abstract. We consider the problem of reaching agreement in a distributed message-passing system prone to crash failures. Crashes are generated by *Constrained* adversaries - a *Weakly-Adaptive* adversary, who has to fix, in advance, the set of f crash-prone processes, and a *k-Chain-Ordered* adversary, who orders all the processes into k disjoint chains and has to follow this order when crashing them. Apart from these constraints, both of them may crash processes in an adaptive way at any time. While commonly used *Strongly-Adaptive* adversaries model attacks and *Non-Adaptive* ones - pre-defined faults, *Constrained* adversaries model more realistic scenarios when there are fault-prone dependent processes, e.g., in hierarchical or dependable software/hardware systems. In this view, our approach helps to understand better the crash-tolerant consensus in more realistic executions. We propose time-efficient consensus algorithms against such adversaries. We complement our algorithmic results with (almost) tight lower bounds, and extend the one for *Weakly-Adaptive* adversaries to hold also for (syntactically) weaker *Non-Adaptive* adversaries. Together with the consensus algorithm against *Weakly-Adaptive* adversaries (which automatically translates to the *Non-Adaptive* adversaries), these results extend the state-of-the-art of the popular class of *Non-Adaptive* adversaries, in particular, the result of Chor, Meritt and Shmoys [7], and prove separation gap between *Constrained* adversaries (including *Non-Adaptive* ones) and *Strongly-Adaptive* adversaries, analyzed by Bar-Joseph and Ben-Or [3] and others.

1 Introduction

We study the problem of consensus in synchronous message passing distributed systems. There are n processes, out of which at most f can crash. Each process is initialized with a binary input value, and the goal is to agree on a common value (from the input values) by all processes. Formally, the following three properties need to be satisfied: *agreement:* no two processes decide on different values; *validity:* only a value among the initial ones may be decided upon; and *termination:* each process eventually decides, unless it crashes. In case of randomized

Supported by the Polish National Science Center (NCN) grant UMO-2017/25/B/ST6/02553.

M. F. Atig and A. A. Schwarzmann (Eds.): NETYS 2019, LNCS 11704, pp. 19–31, 2019.
https://doi.org/10.1007/978-3-030-31277-0_2

solutions, the specification of consensus needs to be reformulated, which can be done in various ways (cf., [2]). We consider a classic reformulation in which validity and agreement are required to hold for every execution, while termination needs to hold with probability 1. Efficiency of algorithms is measured by the number of rounds (time complexity) until all non-faulty processes decide. This work focuses on *efficient randomized solutions* – time is understood in expected sense.

Randomization has been used in consensus algorithms for various kinds of failures specified by adversarial models, see [1,2]. Reason for considering randomization is to overcome inherent limitations of deterministic solutions. Most surprising benefits of randomization is the solvability of consensus in as small as constant time [7,9,18]. Feasibility of achieving small upper bounds on performance of algorithms solving consensus in a given distributed environment depends on the power of adversaries inflicting failures.

1.1   Previous and Related Work

Consensus is one of the fundamental problems in distributed computing, with a rich history of research done in various settings and systems, cf., [2]. Recently its popularity grew even further due to applications in emerging technologies such as blockchains. Below we present only a small digest of literature closely related with the setting considered in this work.

Consensus is solvable in synchronous systems with processes prone to crashing, although time $f+1$ is required [10] and sufficient [12] in case of deterministic solutions. Chor, Meritt and Shmoys [7] showed that randomization allows to obtain a constant expected time algorithm against a *Non-Adaptive* adversary, if the minority of processes may crash.

Bar-Joseph and Ben-Or [3] proved a lower bound $\Omega(f/\sqrt{n \log n})$ on the expected time for randomized consensus against the *Strongly-Adaptive* adversary and proposed an algorithm reaching consensus in $\mathcal{O}(f/\sqrt{n \log(2 + f/\sqrt{n})})$ for any $f < n$. This solution meets their lower bound, provided that the adversary can fail $f = \Omega(n)$ processes. What is more, for such condition these bounds reformulate to $\Theta(\sqrt{n/(n \log n)})$.

Fisher, Lynch and Paterson [11] showed that for the message passing model consensus cannot be solved deterministically in *asynchronous settings*, even if only one process may crash. Loui and Abu-Amara [17] showed a corresponding result for shared memory. These impossibility results can be circumvented when randomization is used and the consensus termination condition does not hold with probability 1.

Bracha and Toueg [5] observed that it is impossible to reach consensus by a randomized algorithm in the asynchronous model with crashes if the majority of processes are allowed to crash. Ben-Or [4] gave the first randomized algorithm solving consensus in the asynchronous message passing model under the assumption that the majority of processes are non-faulty.

The consensus problem has been recently considered against different adversarial scenarios. Robinson, Scheideler and Setzer [19] considered the synchronous consensus problem under a late ϵ-bounded adaptive adversary, whose observation of the system is delayed by one round and can block up to ϵn nodes in the sense that they cannot receive and send messages in a particular round.

1.2   Our Results

Table 1. Time complexity of solutions for the consensus problem against different adversaries. Formulas with * are presented in this paper.

		Strongly-Adaptive	Weakly-Adaptive and Non-Adaptive	k-Chain-Ordered
Randomized	Upper bound	$\mathcal{O}\left(\sqrt{\frac{n}{\log n}}\right)$ [3]	$\mathcal{O}\left(\sqrt{\frac{n}{(n-f)\log(n/(n-f))}}\right)$ *	$\mathcal{O}\left(\sqrt{\frac{k}{\log k}}\log(n/k)\right)$ *
	Lower bound	$\Omega\left(\sqrt{\frac{n}{\log n}}\right)$ [3]	$\Omega\left(\sqrt{\frac{n}{(n-f)\log(n/(n-f))}}\right)$ *	$\Omega\left(\sqrt{\frac{k}{\log k}}\right)$ *
Deterministic	Upper bound		$f+1$ [12]	
	Lower bound		$f+1$ [10]	

We analyze the consensus problem against restricted adaptive adversaries. The motivation is that a *Strongly-Adaptive* adversary, typically used for analysis of randomized consensus algorithms, may not be very realistic; for instance, in practice some processes could be set as fault-prone in advance, before the execution of an algorithm, or may be dependent i.e., in hierarchical hardware/software systems. In this context, a *Strongly-Adaptive* adversary should be used to model attacks rather than realistic crash-prone systems. On the other hand, a *Non-Adaptive* adversary who must fix all its actions before the execution does not capture many aspects of fault-prone systems, e.g., attacks or reactive failures (occurring as an unplanned consequence of some actions of the algorithm in the system). Therefore, analyzing the complexity of consensus under such constraints gives a much better estimate on what may happen in real executions and, as we demonstrate, leads to new, interesting theoretical findings about the performance of consensus algorithms.

Table 1 presents time complexities of solutions for the consensus problem against different adversaries. Results for the *Strongly-Adaptive* adversary and for deterministic algorithms are known (see Sect. 1.1), while the other ones are delivered in this work. We design and analyze a randomized algorithm that reaches consensus in expected $\mathcal{O}\left(\sqrt{\frac{n}{(n-f)\log(n/(n-f))}}\right)$ rounds against any *Weakly-Adaptive* adversary that may crash up to $f < n$ processes. This result is time optimal due to the proved lower bound $\Omega\left(\sqrt{\frac{n}{(n-f)\log(n/(n-f))}}\right)$ on expected number of rounds.

The lower bound could be also generalized to hold against the (syntactically) weaker *Non-Adaptive* adversaries, therefore all the results concerning *Weakly-Adaptive* adversaries delivered in this paper hold for *Non-Adaptive* adversaries as well. This extends the state-of-the-art of the study of *Non-Adaptive* adversaries done in high volume of previous work, cf., [6, 7, 13], specifically, an $O(1)$ expected time algorithm of Chor et al. [7] only for a constant (smaller than 1) fraction of failures. Our lower bound is the first non-constant formula depending on the number of crashes proved for this adversary. In view of the lower bound $\Omega\left(\frac{f}{\sqrt{n}\log n}\right)$ [3] on the expected number of rounds of any consensus algorithm against a *Strongly-Adaptive* adversary crashing at most f processes, *our result shows a separation between the two important classes of adversaries – Non-Adaptive and Strongly-Adaptive – for the consensus problem, which is one of the most fundamental problems in distributed computing.*

We complement these results by showing how to modify the algorithm designed for the *Weakly-Adaptive* adversary, to work against a *k-Chain-Ordered* adversary, who has to arrange all processes into an order of k chains, and then has to preserve this order of crashes in the course of the execution. The algorithm reaches consensus in $\mathcal{O}\left(\sqrt{\frac{k}{\log k}}\log(n/k)\right)$ rounds in expectation. Additionally, we show a lower bound $\Omega\left(\sqrt{\frac{k}{\log k}}\right)$ for the problem against a *k-Ordered* adversary. Finally, we show that this solution is capable of running against an arbitrary partial order with a maximal anti-chain of size k. Similarly to results for the *Weakly-Adaptive* adversary, formulas obtained for *Ordered* adversaries separate them from *Strongly-Adaptive* ones.

2   Model

Synchronous Distributed System. We assume having a system of n processes that communicate in the message passing model. This means that processes form a complete graph where each edge represents a communication link between two processes. If process v wants to send a message to process w, then this message is sent via link (v, w). It is worth noticing that links are symmetric, i.e., $(v, w) = (w, v)$. We assume that messages are sent instantly.

Following the synchronous model by [3], we assume that computations are held in a synchronous manner and hence time is divided into rounds consisting of two phases:

– Phase A - generating local coins and local computation.
– Phase B - sending and receiving messages.

Adversarial Scenarios. Processes are prone to crash-failures that are a result of the adversary activity. The adversary of our particular interest is an adaptive one - it can make arbitrary decisions and see all local computations and local coins, as well as messages intended to be sent by active processes. Therefore, it can decide to crash processes during phase B. Additionally while deciding that a certain process will crash, it can decide which subset of messages will reach their recipients.

In the context of the adversaries in this paper we distinguish three types of processes:

- Crash-prone - processes that can be crashed by the adversary.
- Fault-resistant - processes that are not in the subset of the *Weakly-Adaptive* adversary and hence cannot be crashed.
- Non-faulty - processes that survived until the end of the algorithm.

- *Strongly-Adaptive and Weakly-Adaptive adversaries.* The only restriction for the *Strongly-Adaptive* adversary is that it can fail up to f processes, where $0 \leq f < n$.

The *Weakly-Adaptive* adversary is restricted by the fact that before the algorithm execution it must choose f processes that will be prone to crashes, where $0 \leq f < n$.

Observe that for deterministic algorithms the *Weakly-Adaptive* adversary is consistent with the *Strongly-Adaptive* adversary, because it could simulate the algorithm before its execution and decide on choosing the most convenient subset of processes.

- *k-Chain-Ordered and k-Ordered adversaries.* The notion of a *k-Chain-Ordered* adversary originates from partial order relations, hence appropriate notions and definitions translate straightforwardly. The relation of our particular interest while considering partially ordered adversaries is the precedence relation. Precisely, if some process v precedes process w or w precedes v in the partial order of the adversary, then we say that v and w are comparable. This means that either process v must be crashed by the adversary before process w or w must be crashed before v, accordingly. Consequently a subset of processes where every pair of processes is comparable is called a chain. On the other hand a subset of processes where no two different processes are comparable is called an anti-chain.

It is convenient to think about the partial order of the adversary from a Hasse diagram perspective. The notion of chains and anti-chains seems to be intuitive when graphically presented, e.g., a chain is a pattern of consecutive crashes that may occur while an anti-chain gives the adversary freedom to crash in any order due to non-comparability of processes.

Formally, the *k-Chain-Ordered* adversary has to arrange **all** the processes into a partial order consisting of k disjoint chains of arbitrary length that represent in what order these processes may be crashed.

By the *thickness* of a partial order P we understand the maximal size of an anti-chain in P. An adversary restricted by a wider class of partial orders of thickness k is called a *k-Ordered* adversary.

We refer to a wider class of adversaries in this paper, constrained by an arbitrary partial order, as *Ordered* adversaries. What is more, adversaries having additional limitations, apart from the possible number of crashes (i.e. all described in this paper but the *Strongly-Adaptive* adversary), will be called *Constrained* adversaries. Note that *Ordered* adversaries are also restricted by the number of possible crashes f they may enforce.

- *Non-Adaptive adversaries.* The *Non-Adaptive* adversaries are characterised by the fact that they must fix all their decisions prior to the execution of the algorithm and then follow this pattern during the execution.

Consensus Problem. In the consensus problem n processes, each having its input bit $x_i \in \{0, 1\}$, $i \in \{1, \ldots, n\}$, have to agree on a common output bit in the presence of the adversary, capable of crashing processes. We require any consensus protocol to fulfill the following conditions:

- Agreement: all non-faulty processes decide the same value.
- Validity: if all processes have the same initial value x, then x is the only possible decision value.
- Termination: all non-faulty processes decide with probability 1.

We follow typical assumption that the first two requirements must hold in *any* execution, while termination should be satisfied with probability 1.

Complexity Measure and Algorithmic Tools. The main complexity measure used to benchmark the consensus problem is the number of rounds by which all non-faulty processes decide on a common value.

Throughout the paper we use black-box fashioned procedures that allow us to structure the presentation better. We now briefly describe their properties and later refer to them in the algorithms' analysis. Details could be found in the full version of this paper [15].

LEADER-CONSENSUS *properties.* We use the LEADER-CONSENSUS procedure as a black-box tool for reaching consensus on a small group of processes, and we require that it satisfies the following properties:

- it is executed by a process and takes two values as input: the time for which it is executed (unless it terminates earlier because consensus was reached) and the current value of a process;
- the output is a tuple (*decided, value*), where *decided* is a boolean variable indicating whether the consensus value has been decided by a process during the procedure and *value* is the current value of a process after the procedure terminates (if the consensus has been decided – it is the consensus value);
- it satisfies termination, validity and *conditional agreement*, defined as follows: for any two processes v, w, if LEADER-CONSENSUS executed by v outputs (*true, x*) and LEADER-CONSENSUS executed by w outputs (*true, y*), then $x = y$;
- LEADER-CONSENSUS($T_{LC}(g), x$) satisfies agreement when run by a group of no more than g processes, with probability at least $\frac{9}{10}$, where T_{LC} is the expected time complexity function of LEADER-CONSENSUS.

We say that an algorithm fulfilling properties above satisfies *Conditional-Consensus*. A candidate solution to serve as LEADER-CONSENSUS is the Ben-Or and Bar-Joseph's SYNRAN algorithm from [3], and we refer the reader to the details therein. In particular, to Lemma 4.2 [3], which proves that SYNRAN assures conditional agreement besides of other typical properties of consensus.

PROPAGATE-MSG *Properties.* We assume that procedure PROPAGATE-MSG propagates messages in 1 round with $\mathcal{O}(n^2)$ message complexity. This is consistent with a scenario where full communication takes place and each process sends a message to all the processes.

3 *Weakly-Adaptive* Adversary

In this section we consider the fundamental result i.e. ALGORITHM A that consists of two main components - a leader election procedure, and a reliable consensus protocol. We combine them together in an appropriate way (cf., Fig. 1), in order to reach consensus against a *Weakly-Adaptive* adversary.

Algorithm 1: ALGORITHM A, pseudocode for process v

---

1 initialize list LEADERS to an empty list;
2 *decided := false*;
3 *value := x_v*;
4 **repeat**
5   LEADERS := ELECT-LEADER;
6   **if** *LEADERS contains v* **then**
7   *(decided, value) :=* LEADER-CONSENSUS$(T_{LC}(|$LEADERS$|), value)$;
8   **if** *decided* **then**
9   execute PROPAGATE-MSG$(value)$ twice;
10   **end**
11   **else**
12   **if** *heard the same consensus value CV_w twice from some process w* **then**
13   *value := CV_w*;
14   *decided = true*;
15   **end**
16   **if** *heard consensus value CV_w once from some process w* **then**
17   *value := CV_w*;
18   **end**
19   **end**
20   **end**
21   **else**
22   idle for T_{LC} rounds;
23   **if** *heard the same consensus value CV_w twice from some process w* **then**
24   *value := CV_w*;
25   *decided = true*;
26   **end**
27   **if** *heard consensus value CV_w once from some process w* **then**
28   *value := CV_w*;
29   **end**
30   **end**
31   clear list LEADERS;
32 **until** *decided*;

Algorithm 2: ELECT-LEADER, pseudocode for process v

---

1 coin $:= \frac{1}{n-f}$;

2 initialize list LEADERS to an empty list;

3 toss a coin with the probability coin of heads to come up;

4 **if** *heads came up in the previous step* **then**

5 | PROPAGATE-MSG("v") to all other processes;

6 | add v to list LEADERS;

7 **end**

8 fill in list LEADERS with elected leaders' identifiers from received messages;

9 return LEADERS;

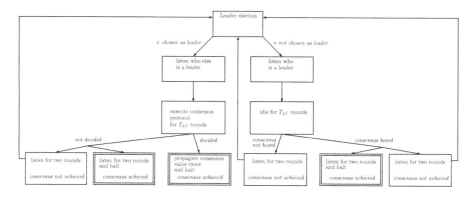

Fig. 1. ALGORITHM A flow diagram for process v.

ALGORITHM A has an iterative character and begins with a leader election procedure in which we expect to elect $\mathcal{O}(\frac{n}{n-f})$ leaders simultaneously. Leaders run the LEADER-CONSENSUS procedure in which they reach consensus within their own group with a certain probability. If they do so, this fact is propagated to all processes via PROPAGATE-MSG so that all processes that were not in the leaders group, know about small consensus being reached and set their consensus values accordingly. Communicating this fact, implies reaching *consensus* by the whole system. There are several subtle points in this intuitive description to be clarified, what we do next.

Let us follow Algorithm 1 from the perspective of some process v. At the beginning of the protocol every process takes part in ELECT-LEADER procedure and process v tosses a coin with probability of success equal $\frac{1}{n-f}$ and either is chosen to the group of leaders or not. If it is successful, then it communicates this fact to all processes.

Process v takes part in LEADER-CONSENSUS together with other leaders in order to reach a *Conditional-Consensus*, what happens with certain probability. Hence, if LEADER-CONSENSUS is successful and the consensus value is fixed, v tries to convince other processes to this value twice. This is because if some process $w \neq v$ receives the consensus value (obtained from LEADER-CONSENSUS) in the latter round, then it may be sure that other processes received this value from v as well in the former round (so in fact every process has the same consensus value fixed from that point). Process v could not propagate its value for the second time if it was not successful in propagating this value to every other process for the first time – if just one process did not receive the value, this would indicate a crash of v.

However, if LEADER-CONSENSUS is unsuccessful in agreeing on a common value, the procedure is terminated after a certain number of rounds, which is fixed as an input value for LEADER-CONSENSUS. Even though *Conditional-Consensus* was not reached, it might happen that some of the processes, including v, terminate the procedure with a decided value. In what follows, these processes propagate this value to all other processes, similarly as in the successful case.

On the other hand, if process v was not chosen to be a leader then it listens to the channel for an appropriate amount of time and afterwards tries to learn the consensus value twice. If it is unable to hear the value twice, then it is consistent with being idle for two rounds. If consensus is not reached, then the protocol starts again with electing another group of leaders. Nevertheless, if process v hears a consensus value once, it holds and assigns it as a candidate consensus value. This guarantees the continuity of the protocol and its validity.

The idea standing behind ALGORITHM A is built on the fact that if just one fault-resistant process is elected to the group of leaders then the adversary is unable to crash it in the course of an execution, and hence consensus is achieved after a certain expected number of rounds.

Theorem 1. ALGORITHM A *reaches consensus in the expected number of rounds equal* $\mathcal{O}\left(T_{LC}\left(\frac{n}{n-f}\right)\right)$, *satisfying termination, agreement and validity.*

Corollary 1. *Instantiating* LEADER-CONSENSUS *with* SYNRAN *from [3] results in* $\mathcal{O}\left(\sqrt{\frac{n}{(n-f)\log(n/(n-f))}}\right)$ *expected rounds to reach consensus by* ALGORITHM A.

Theorem 2. *The expected number of rounds of any consensus protocol running against a Weakly-Adaptive or a Non-Adaptive adversary causing up to f crashes is* $\Omega\left(\sqrt{\frac{n}{(n-f)\log(n/(n-f))}}\right)$.

4 *k-Chain-Ordered* and *k-Ordered* Adversaries

In this section we present ALGORITHM C - a modification of ALGORITHM A specifically tailored to run against the *k-Chain-Ordered* adversary. Then we also show that it is capable of running against a *k-Ordered* adversary.

Algorithm 3: ALGORITHM C, pseudocode for process v

---

1 ALGORITHM A with ELECT-LEADER substituted by GATHER-LEADERS;

The algorithm begins with electing a number of leaders in GATHER-LEADERS. However, as the adversary models its pattern of crashes into k disjoint chains then we would like to elect approximately k leaders.

It may happen that the adversary significantly reduces the number of processes and hence the leader election procedure is unsuccessful in electing an appropriate number of leaders. That is why we adjust the probability of success by approximating the size of the network before electing leaders. If the initial number of processes was n and the drop in the number of processes after estimating the size of the network was *not significant (less than half the number of the approximation)* then we expect to elect $\Theta(k)$ leaders.

Algorithm 4: GATHER-LEADERS, pseudocode for process v

---

1 initialize variable n^*;
2 $n^* :=$ COUNT-PROCESSES;
3 $i = \lfloor n/n^* \rfloor$;
4 coin $:= \frac{k}{2^{i-1} n^*}$;
5 initialize list LEADERS to an empty list;
6 toss a coin with the probability coin of heads to come up;
7 **if** *heads came up in the previous step* **then**
8 $\quad$ PROPAGATE-MSG("v") to all other processes;
9 $\quad$ add v to list LEADERS;
10 **end**
11 fill in list LEADERS with elected leaders' identifiers from received messages;
12 return LEADERS;

Algorithm 5: COUNT-PROCESSES, pseudocode for process v

---

1 PROPAGATE-MSG("v") to all other processes;
2 return the number of ID's heard ;

Otherwise, if the number of processes was reduced by more than half, the probability of success is changed and the expected number of elected leaders is reduced. This helps to shorten executions of LEADER-CONSENSUS because a smaller number of leaders executes the protocol faster. In general if there are $\frac{n}{2^i}$ processes, we expect to elect $\Theta\left(\frac{k}{2^i}\right)$ leaders.

Elected leaders are expected to be placed uniformly in the adversary's order of crashes. If we look at a particular leader v, then he will be present in some chain k_i. What is more, his position within this chain is expected to be in the middle of k_i.

Leaders execute the small consensus protocol LEADER-CONSENSUS. If they reach consensus, then they communicate this fact twice to the rest of the system. Hence, if the adversary wants to prolong the execution, then it must crash all leaders. Otherwise, the whole system would reach consensus and end the protocol.

If leaders are placed uniformly in the adversary's order, then the adversary must preserve the pattern of crashes that it declared at first. In what follows, if there is a leader v that is placed in the middle of chain k_i, then half of the processes preceding v must also be crashed.

When the whole set of leaders is crashed then another group is elected and the process continues until the adversary spends all its possibilities of failing processes.

Theorem 3. ALGORITHM C *reaches consensus in the expected number of rounds equal* $\mathcal{O}(T_{LC}(k) \log(n/k))$, *satisfying termination, agreement and validity.*

Corollary 2. *Instantiating* LEADER-CONSENSUS *with* SYNRAN *from [3] results in* $\mathcal{O}\left(\sqrt{\frac{k}{\log k}} \log(n/k)\right)$ *expected number of rounds to reach consensus by* ALGORITHM C.

4.1 Algorithm C Against the Adversary Limited by an Arbitrary Partial Order

Let us consider the adversary that is limited by an **arbitrary** partial order relation $\succ$ on the set of all processes. Two elements in this partially ordered set are *incomparable* if neither $x \succ y$ nor $y \succ x$ hold. Translating this into our model, the adversary may crash incomparable elements in any sequence during the execution of the algorithm. We assume that crashes forced by the adversary are constrained by some partial order P. Let us recall the following lemma.

Lemma 1 *(Dilworth's theorem [8]).* *In a finite partial order, the size of a maximum anti-chain is equal to the minimum number of chains needed to cover all elements of the partial order.*

Combining Lemma 1 with Theorem 3 and its instantiated form in Corollary 2, we obtain the following.

Theorem 4. ALGORITHM C *reaches consensus in expected* $\mathcal{O}(T_{LC}(k) \log(n/k))$ *number of rounds, against the k-Ordered adversary, satisfying termination, agreement and validity.*

We finish with the lower bound for reaching consensus against the *k-Ordered* adversary.

Theorem 5. *For any reliable randomized algorithm solving consensus in a message-passing model and any integer $0 < k \leq f$, there is a k-Ordered adversary that can force the algorithm to run in $\Omega(\sqrt{k/\log k})$ expected number of rounds.*

5   Conclusions and Open Problems

In this work we showed time efficient randomized consensus against the *Weakly-Adaptive*, *Non-Adaptive* and *Ordered* adversaries generating crashes. We proved that all these classes of *Constrained* adaptive adversaries are weaker than the *Strongly-Adaptive* one. Our results also extend the state-of-the-art of the study of popular *Non-Adaptive* adversaries.

Three main open directions emerge from this work. One is to improve the message complexity of proposed algorithms and make them resistant to (rarely expected, but possible) very long executions resulting from unsuccessful probabilistic events. Another open direction could pursue a study of complexities of other important distributed problems and settings against *Weakly-Adaptive* and *Ordered* adversaries, which are more realistic than the *Strongly-Adaptive* one and more general than the *Non-Adaptive* one, commonly used in the literature. Finally, there is a scope of proposing and studying other intermediate types of adversaries, including further study of recently proposed delayed adversaries [14] and adversaries tailored for dynamic distributed and parallel computing [16].

References

1. Aspnes, J.: Randomized protocols for asynchronous consensus. Distrib. Comput. **16**(2–3), 165–175 (2003)
2. Attiya, H., Welch, J.: Distributed Computing: Fundamentals, Simulations and Advanced Topics. John Wiley & Sons Inc., USA (2004)
3. Bar-Joseph, Z., Ben-Or, M.: A tight lower bound for randomized synchronous consensus. In: Proceedings of the Seventeenth Annual ACM Symposium on Principles of Distributed Computing, PODC 1998, New York, NY, USA, pp. 193–199. ACM (1998)
4. Ben-Or, M.: Another advantage of free choice (extended abstract): completely asynchronous agreement protocols. In: Proceedings of the Second Annual ACM Symposium on Principles of Distributed Computing, PODC 1983, New York, NY, USA, pp. 27–30. ACM (1983)
5. Bracha, G., Toueg, S.: Asynchronous consensus and broadcast protocols. J. ACM **32**(4), 824–840 (1985)
6. Chlebus, B.S., Kowalski, D.R.: Locally scalable randomized consensus for synchronous crash failures. In: Proceedings of the Twenty-First Annual Symposium on Parallelism in Algorithms and Architectures, SPAA 2009, New York, NY, USA, pp. 290–299. ACM (2009)
7. Chor, B., Merritt, M., Shmoys, D.B.: Simple constant-time consensus protocols in realistic failure models. J. ACM **36**(3), 591–614 (1989)
8. Dilworth, R.P.: A decomposition theorem for partially ordered sets. Ann. Math. **51**(1), 161–166 (1950)
9. Feldman, P., Micali, S.: An optimal probabilistic protocol for synchronous byzantine agreement. SIAM J. Comput. **26**(4), 873–933 (1997)
10. Fischer, M.J., Lynch, N.A.: A lower bound for the time to assure interactive consistency. Inf. Process. Lett. **14**(4), 183–186 (1982)
11. Fischer, M.J., Lynch, N.A., Paterson, M.S.: Impossibility of distributed consensus with one faulty process. J. ACM **32**(2), 374–382 (1985)

12. Garay, J.A., Moses, Y.: Fully polynomial byzantine agreement in t + 1 rounds. In: Proceedings of the Twenty-Fifth Annual ACM Symposium on Theory of Computing, STOC 1993, New York, NY, USA, pp. 31–41. ACM (1993)

13. Gilbert, S., Kowalski, D.R.: Distributed agreement with optimal communication complexity. In: Proceedings of the Twenty-First Annual ACM-SIAM Symposium on Discrete Algorithms, SODA 2010, Austin, Texas, USA, 17–19 January 2010, pp. 965–977 (2010)

14. Klonowski, M., Kowalski, D.R., Mirek, J.: Ordered and delayed adversaries and how to work against them on a shared channel. Distrib. Comput. 1–25, September 2018

15. Kowalski, D.R., Mirek, J.: On the complexity of fault-tolerant consensus. CoRR, abs/1905.07063 (2019)

16. Kowalski, D.R., Mosteiro, M.A.: Polynomial counting in anonymous dynamic networks with applications to anonymous dynamic algebraic computations. In: 45th International Colloquium on Automata, Languages, and Programming, ICALP 2018, 9–13 July 2018, Prague, Czech Republic, pp. 156:1–156:14 (2018)

17. Loui, M.C., Abu-Amara, H.H.: Memory requirements for agreement among unreliable asynchronous processes. Adv. Comput. Res. 4(163183), 31 (1987)

18. Rabin, M.O.: Randomized byzantine generals. In: 24th Annual Symposium on Foundations of Computer Science (FOCS 1983), pp. 403–409 (1983)

19. Robinson, P., Scheideler, C., Setzer, A.: Breaking the $\Omega(\sqrt{n})$ barrier: fast consensus under a late adversary. In: Proceedings of the 30th on Symposium on Parallelism in Algorithms and Architectures, SPAA 2018, Vienna, Austria, 6–18 July 2018, pp. 173–182 (2018)

Formal Verification

Checking Causal Consistency
of Distributed Databases

Rachid Zennou[1,2(✉)], Ranadeep Biswas[1], Ahmed Bouajjani[1],
Constantin Enea[1], and Mohammed Erradi[2]

[1] Université de Paris, IRIF, CNRS, 75013 Paris, France
{ranadeep,abou,cenea}@irif.fr
[2] ENSIAS, University Mohammed V, Rabat, Morocco
rachid.zennou@gmail.com, mohamed.erradi@gmail.com

Abstract. Causal consistency is one of the strongest models that can
be implemented to ensure availability and partition tolerance in distributed systems. In this paper, we propose a tool to check automatically the conformance of distributed/concurrent systems executions to
causal consistency models. Our approach consists in reducing the problem of checking if an execution is causally consistent to solving Datalog
queries. The reduction is based on complete characterizations of the executions violating causal consistency in terms of the existence of cycles
in suitably defined relations between the operations occurring in these
executions. We have implemented the reduction in a testing tool for
distributed databases, and carried out several experiments on real case
studies, showing the efficiency of the suggested approach.

1 Introduction

Causal consistency [23] is one of the most implemented models for distributed
systems. Contrary to strong consistency [19] (Linearizability [20] and Sequential Consistency [22]), causal consistency can be implemented in the presence of
faults while ensuring availability. Several implementations of different variants
of causal consistency (such as causal convergence [25] and causal memory [6])
have been developed i.e., [8,12,13,21,24,26,27]. However, the development of
such implementations that meet both consistency requirements and availability
and performance requirements is an extremely hard and error prone task. Hence,
developing efficient approaches to check the correctness of executions w.r.t consistency models such as causal consistency is crucial. This paper presents an
approach and a tool for checking automatically the conformance of the computations of a system to causal consistency. More precisely, we address the problem
of, given a computation, checking its conformance to causal consistency. We
consider this problem for three variants of causal consistency that are used

This work is supported in part by the European Research Council (ERC) under the
European Union's Horizon 2020 research and innovation programme (grant agreement
No. 678177).

M. F. Atig and A. A. Schwarzmann (Eds.): NETYS 2019, LNCS 11704, pp. 35–51, 2019.
https://doi.org/10.1007/978-3-030-31277-0_3

in practice. Solving this problem constitutes the cornerstone for developing dynamic verification and testing algorithms for causal consistency.

Bouajjani et al. [9] studied the complexity of checking causal consistency for a given computation and showed that it is polynomial time. In addition, they formalized the different variations of causal consistency and proposed a reduction of this problem to the occurrence of a finite number of small "bad-patterns" in the computations (i.e., some small sets of events occurring in the computations in some particular order). In this paper, we build on that work in order to define a practical approach and a tool for checking causal consistency, and to apply this tool to real-life case studies. Our approach consists basically in reducing the problem of detecting the existence of bad patterns defined in [9] in computations to the problem of solving a Datalog queries. The fact that solving Datalog queries is polynomial time and that our reduction is polynomial in the size of the computation, allows to solve the conformance checking for causal consistency in polynomial time and match the theoretical complexity bound of the problem. We have implemented our approach in an efficient testing tool for distributed systems, and carried out several experiments on real distributed databases, showing the efficiency and performance of this approach. To the best of our knowledge, this is the first efficient and full-automated testing tool for causal consistency verification.

The rest of this paper is as follows, Sect. 2 presents preliminaries that include the used notations and the system model. Section 3 is dedicated to defining the causal consistency models. Section 4 recalls the characterization of causal consistency violations introduced in [9]. Section 5 presents our reduction of the problem of conformance checking for causal consistency to the problem of solving Datalog queries. Section 6 describes our testing tool, the case studies we have considered, and the experimental results we obtained. Section 7 presents related work, and finally conclusions are drown in Sect. 8.

2   Preliminaries

Notations. Given a set $\mathcal{O}$ and a relation $\mathcal{R} \subseteq \mathcal{O} \times \mathcal{O}$, we use the notation $\mathcal{R}(o_1, o_2)$ to denote the fact that $(o_1, o_2) \in \mathcal{R}$. If $\mathcal{R}$ is an order, it denotes the fact that o_1 precedes o_2 in this order. The transitive closure of $\mathcal{R}$ is denoted by $\mathcal{R}^+$. The reflexive closure of $\mathcal{R}$ is denoted by $\mathcal{R}^*$.

System Model. We consider a distributed system model in which a system is composed of several processes (sites) connected over a network. Each process performs operations on objects (variables) $\mathsf{Var} = \{x, y, \ldots\}$. These objects are called replicated objects and their state is replicated at all processes. Clients interact with the system by performing operations. Assuming an unspecified set of values Val and a set of operation identifiers IdO. We define the set of operations as $\mathsf{Op} = \{\mathsf{read}_i(x, v), \mathsf{write}_i(x, v) : i \in \mathsf{IdO}, x \in \mathsf{Var}, v \in \mathsf{Val}\}$. Where $\mathsf{read}_i(x, v)$ is a read operation reading a value v from a variable x and $\mathsf{write}_i(x, v)$ is a write operation writing a value v on a variable x. The set of read operations is $\mathbb{R}(O)$,

The set of write operations is $\mathbb{W}(O)$. The variable accessed by an operation o is denoted by $\mathsf{var}(o)$.

Histories. We consider an abstract notion of an execution called *history* which includes write and read operations. The operations performed by the same process are ordered by a *program order* po. We assume that histories include a *write-read* relation that matches each read operation to the write operation written its return value.

Formally, a *history* $\langle O, \mathsf{po}, \mathsf{wr} \rangle$ is a set of read or write operations O along with a partial *program order* po and a *write-read* relation $\mathsf{wr} \subseteq \mathbb{W}(O) \times \mathbb{R}(O)$, such that if $\mathsf{wr}(\mathsf{write}(x,v), \mathsf{read}(x',v'))$, then $x = x'$ and $v = v'$. For $o_1, o_2 \in O$, $\mathsf{po}(o_1, o_2)$ means that o_1, o_2 were issued by the same process and o_1 was submitted before o_2. We mention that the *write-read* relation can only be defined for differentiated histories.

Differentiated Histories. A history $\langle O, \mathsf{po}, \mathsf{wr} \rangle$ is differentiated if each value is written at most once, i.e., for all write operations $\mathsf{write}(x,v)$ and $\mathsf{write}(x,v')$, $v \neq v'$.

Data Independence. An implementation is data-independent if its behavior does not depend on the handled values. We consider in this paper implementations that are data-independent which is a natural assumption that corresponds to a wide range of existing implementations. Under this assumption, it is good enough to consider differentiated histories [9]. Thus, all histories in this paper are differentiated. In addition, we assume that all variables are initiated to the value 0, i.e., for all write operations $\mathsf{write}(x,v)$, $v \neq 0$.

3   Causal Consistency

We introduce in the following three variations of causal consistency.

3.1   Weak Causal Consistency

The weakest variation of causal consistency is called *weak causal consistency* (CC, for short). A history is CC if all operations that are in a causal relation (causally-related) are seen in the same order by all processes. The relation of causality is given by the *program order* or the *write-read* relation or any transitive composition of these relations. Formally, a history $\langle O, \mathsf{po}, \mathsf{wr} \rangle$ is CC if $\mathsf{po} \cup \mathsf{wr} \cup \mathsf{rw}$ is acyclic where the *read-write* relation rw is defined as

$$\mathsf{rw}(\mathsf{read}(x,v), \mathsf{write}(x,v')) \text{ iff } \mathsf{co}(\mathsf{write}(x,v), \mathsf{write}(x,v')) \text{ and}$$
$$\mathsf{wr}(\mathsf{write}(x,v), \mathsf{read}(x,v)), \text{ for some } \mathsf{write}(x,v)$$

Example 1. The history Fig. 1d is CC, we can consider that $\mathsf{write}(x,1)$ is not causally-related to $\mathsf{write}(x,2)$.

Example 2. The history Fig. 1e is not CC. The reason is that, we have co(write$(x, 1)$, write$(x, 2)$) by the transitivity which include po(write$(x, 1)$, write$(y, 1)$) and wr(write$(y, 1)$, read$(y, 1)$) and po(read$(y, 1)$, write$(x, 2)$). However, in p_3 we have po(read$(x, 2)$, read$(x, 1)$) which is not allowed by CC.

p_1: p_2:
write$(z, 1)$ write$(x, 2)$
write$(x, 1)$ read$(z, 0)$
write$(y, 1)$ read$(y, 1)$
                 read$(x, 2)$

(a) CCv but not CM

p_1: p_2:
write$(x, 1)$ write$(x, 2)$
read$(x, 2)$ read$(x, 1)$

(b) CM but not CCv

p_1: p_2:
write$(x, 1)$ write$(x, 2)$
read$(y, 0)$ read$(y, 0)$
write$(y, 1)$ write$(y, 2)$
read$(x, 1)$ read$(x, 2)$

(c) CC , CCv and CM

p_1: p_2:
write$(x, 1)$ write$(x, 2)$
                 read$(x, 1)$
                 read$(x, 2)$

(d) CC but not CCv nor CM

p_1: p_2: p_3:
write$(x, 1)$ read$(y, 1)$ read$(x, 2)$
write$(y, 1)$ write$(x, 2)$ read$(x, 1)$

(e) not CC (nor CCv, nor CM)

Fig. 1. Histories illustrating the differences between the causal consistency models CC, CCv, and CM.

3.2 Causal Convergence

Causal convergence (CCv, for short) is stronger than CC. It requires that concurrent operations are observed in the same order by all processes. The definition of CCv is based on a notion of conflict. Intuitively, two writes w_1 and w_2 on the same variable are in conflict, if w_1 is causally-related to a read taking its value from w_2. Formally, the *conflict relation* cf is defined as

$$\text{cf}(\text{write}(x, v), \text{write}(x, v')) \text{ iff } \text{co}(\text{write}(x, v), \text{read}(x, v')) \text{ and}$$
$$\text{wr}(\text{write}(x, v'), \text{read}(x, v')), \text{ for some } \text{read}(x, v')$$

Then a history is CCv if it is CC and po $\cup$ wr $\cup$ cf is acyclic.

Example 3. The history Fig. 1a is CCv, we can set an order in which write$(x, 1)$ is ordered before write$(x, 2)$.

Example 4. The history Fig. 1b is not CCv. In order to read read$(x, 2)$, write$(x, 1)$ must be ordered before write$(x, 2)$. On the other hand, to read read$(x, 1)$, write$(x, 2)$ must be ordered before write$(x, 1)$, thus we get a cycle in po $\cup$ wr $\cup$ cf.

3.3   Causal Memory

The third model we consider is *causal memory* (CM, for short) that is also stronger than CC. It requires that each process should observe concurrent operations in the same order. In addition, this order should be maintained throughout its whole execution, but it can differ from one process to another.

Formally, a history is CM if it is CC and for each operation o in the history, the relation hb_o is acyclic. The hb_o relation is defined as follows.

Let $\langle O, po, wr \rangle$ be a history, for all operation $o \in O$, we define hb_o be the smallest transitive relation such that:

1. if two operations are in causal relation, and each one is causally-related to o, then they are related by hb_o, i.e., if $co(o_1, o)$, and $co^*(o_2, o)$, then $hb_o(o_1, o_2)$ and
2. two write operations w_1 and w_2 are hb_o-related if w_1 precedes in hb_o a read getting its value from w_2, and that read precedes o in the *program order*, i.e., $hb_o(\text{write}(x, v), \text{write}(x, v'))$ if $hb_o(\text{write}(x, v), \text{read}(x, v'))$ and $wr(\text{write}(x, v'), \text{read}(x, v'))$, and $po^*(\text{read}(x, v'), o)$, for some $\text{read}(x, v')$.

As we noticed above, CC is weaker that CCv and CM. For instance, the history in Fig. 1d is CC but not CCv nor CM. It is CC, we can consider that $\text{write}(x, 1)$ is not causally-related to $\text{write}(x, 2)$. On the other hand, for reading the value 1 the process p_2 decides to order $\text{write}(x, 2)$ before $\text{write}(x, 1)$, then it changes this order to read the value 2. This is not allowed under CM nor under CCv.

Both CCv and CM require that each process should observe concurrent operations in the same order. In CM this order can differ from one process to another. It seems that this intuitive description implies that CCv is stronger than CM but these two models are actually incomparable. The following examples illustrate the differences between these models.

Example 5. For instance, the history in Fig. 1b is CM, but not by CCv. It is not CCv because reading the value 1 from x in the p_1 implies that $\text{write}(x, 1)$ is ordered after $\text{write}(x, 2)$ while reading the value 2 from x in p_2 implies that it $\text{write}(x, 2)$ is ordered after $\text{write}(x, 1)$. This is allowed by CM as different processes can observe concurrent write operations in different orders. Then, the history in Fig. 1a is CCv but not CM. CCv requires that concurrent operations should be observed in the same order by all processes. Thus a possible order for concurrent write operations $\text{write}(x, 1)$ and $\text{write}(x, 2)$ is to order $\text{write}(x, 2)$ after $\text{write}(x, 1)$. Under CM, in order to read $\text{read}(z, 0)$, $\text{write}(x, 1)$ should be ordered after $\text{write}(x, 2)$ while to read 2 from x, $\text{write}(x, 2)$ must be ordered after $\text{write}(x, 1)$ ($\text{write}(x, 1)$ must have been observed because p_2 reads 1 from y and the writes on x and y are causally-related).

4   Causal Consistency Violations

4.1   Bad-Patterns

In [9], computations that are violations of CC, CCv or CM are caracterised by the occurrence within them of a finite number of particular (small) sets of ordered events, called bad-patterns. We recall these bad-patterns in this section. The Tables 1 and 2 represent the bad-patterns of each model and their definitions respectively.

Table 1. Bad-patterns for each causal consistency model

CC	CCv	CM
CyclicCO	CyclicCO	CyclicCO
WriteCOInitRead	WriteCOInitRead	WriteCOInitRead
ThinAirRead	ThinAirRead	ThinAirRead
WriteCORead	WriteCORead	WriteCORead
	CyclicCF	WriteHBInitRead
		CyclicHB

Table 2. Bad-patterns definitions

CyclicCO	the causality relation co is cylic
WriteCOInitRead	a $\mathsf{read}(x,0)$ is causally preceded by a $\mathsf{write}(x,v)$ (i.e., $co(\mathsf{read}(x,0),\mathsf{write}(x,v)))$ such that v $\neq 0$
ThinAirRead	there is a $\mathsf{read}(x,v)$ operation that read a value v such that v $\neq 0$ that it is never written before.(it can not be related to any write by a wr relation)
WriteCORead	there exist write operations w_1, w_2 such that $\mathsf{var}(w_1) = \mathsf{var}(w_2)$ and a read operation r_1 such that $\mathsf{wr}(w_1, r_1)$. In addition, $co(w_1, w_2)$ and $co(w_2, r_1)$.
WriteHBInitRead	there exist a $\mathsf{read}(x,0)$ and a $\mathsf{write}(x,v)$ (v $\neq 0$) such that $\mathsf{hb}_o(\mathsf{read}(x,0),\mathsf{write}(x,v))$ for some operation o
CyclicHB	the hb_o relation is cyclic for some operation o
CyclicCF	the union of cf and co (cf $\cup$ co) is cyclic

Fact 1 *([9]). A history h is CC if it does not contain any of the bad-patterns* CyclicCO, WriteCOInitRead, ThinAirRead *and* WriteCORead.

Fact 2 *([9]). A history h is CCv if it is CC and does not contain the bad-pattern* CyclicCF.

Fact 3 *([9]). A history h is CM if it is CC and does not contain any of the bad-patterns* WriteHBInitRead *and* CyclicHB.

Example 6. 1. The history in Fig. 1a contains the bad-pattern WriteCORead so it is not CC. The $\mathsf{write}(x,1)$ is causally ordered before $\mathsf{write}(x,2)$ by the transitivity. On the other hand, the process p_3 read $\mathsf{read}(x,1)$ from $\mathsf{write}(x,1)$ ($\mathsf{wr}(\mathsf{write}(x,1), \mathsf{read}(x,1))$). The read $\mathsf{read}(x,1)$ is also causally-related to $\mathsf{write}(x,2)$ by transitivity. However, the history in Fig. 1c does not contain any one of the bad-pattern so it is CC, CCv and CM.

2. The History in Fig. 1b is not CCv as it contains the bad-pattern CyclicCF. In order to read read$(x, 2)$, write$(x, 2)$ must precedes write$(x, 2)$ in the conflict order. On the other hand, to read read$(x, 1)$, write$(x, 2)$ must be ordered in the conflict order before write$(x, 1)$. Thus lead to CyclicCF bad-pattern.
3. The history 1a contains the bad-pattern WriteHBInitRead so it is not CM. Let's consider $hb = hb_{read(x,2)}$. We have po(write$(z, 1)$, write$(x, 1)$) and $hb($write$(x, 1)$, write$(x, 2))$ (co(write$(x, 1)$, read$(x, 2)$) implies co(write$(x, 1)$, write$(x, 2)$) and po(write$(x, 2)$, read$(z, 0)$), thus by transitivity we have $hb($write$(z, 1)$, read$(z, 0))$

4.2 Algorithm of Causal Consistency Verification

Algorithm 1 verifies whether a given history satisfies a given causal consistency model.

Input: A history $h = \langle O, \text{po}, \text{wr} \rangle$ and a causal consistency model M
Output: SAT iff h satisfies M

1 **if** *a bad-pattern is found* **then**
2 $\quad$ | $\quad$ return *UNSAT*;
3 **else**
4 $\quad$ | $\quad$ return *SAT*;
5 **end**

Algorithm 1: Checking Causal Consistency.

Theorem 1. *Algorithm 1 returns **SAT** iff the input history h satisfies the causal consistency model.*

5 Reduction to Datalog Queries Solving

In this section, we show our reduction of the problem of checking whether a given computation is a CC, CCv or CM violation to the problem of Datalog queries solving. Datalog is a logic programming language that does not allow functions as predicate arguments. The advantage of using Datalog is that it provides a high level language for naturally defining constraints on relations and that solving queries is polynomial time [29].

5.1 Datalog

A rule in datalog is a statement of the following form:

$$r_1(v_1) : -r_2(v_2), ..., r_i(v_i)$$

Where i $\geq$ 1, r_i are the names of predicates (relations) and v_i are arguments. A Datalog program is a finite set of Datalog rules over the same schema [5]. The LHS is called the rule head and represents the outcome of the query, while the RHS is called the rule body.

Example 7. For instance, this Datalog program computes the transitivity closure of a given graph.

```
trans(X,Y) :- edge(X,Y).
trans(X,Y)  :-  trans(X,Z), trans(Z,Y).
```

Where the fact edge(a,b) means that there exists a direct edge from a to b.

In the literature, there are three definitions for the semantics of Datalog programs, *model theoretic*, *proof-theoretic* and *fixpoint semantics* [5]. In this paper, we have considered the *fix-point semantics*.

Fix-Point Semantics. This approach is based on the fix-point theory. A fixed point of a function $f()$ is an element e from its domain which is mapped by the function to itself i.e., $f(e) = e$. An operator called immediate consequence operator is defined from the Datalog program rules. This operator is applied repeatedly on existing facts in order to get new facts until getting a fixed point. It is a constructive definition of Datalog programs semantics.

5.2 Histories Encoding

In our approach, extracted relations from a history (po, wr...) are represented as predicates called facts, while the algorithm for fixed point computation is formulated as Datalog recursive relations called inference rules.

We first introduce all the facts. For instance, consider the fact po(a, b) which represents the program order from the operation a to the operation b (similarly po(b, c)),

```
po(a,b).
po(b,c).
```

We have defined the necessary relations for our approach.

– *rd(X)*, X is a read operation.
– *wrt(X)*, X is a write operation.
– *po(X,Y)*, X precedes Y in the po order.
– *wr(X,Y)*, Y read the value from a write operation X (wr relation).
– *co(X,Y)*, X precedes Y in the causal order.
– *sv(X,Y)*, the operations X and Y accessed to the same variable.

Then, we define the inference rules. For instance, the following rule says that the causal relation co is transitive.

```
co(X,Z) :- co(X,Y), co(Y,Z).
```

5.3 Bad-Patterns Encoding

We have expressed all the bad-patterns as Datalog inference rules, except

ThinAirRead that we verify externally as it contains a universal quantification over all operations. There exist two kinds of bad-patterns. The first type is related to the existence of a cycle in a relation. For instance, the bad-pattern CyclicCO that can be expressed as

```
:- co(X,Y), co(Y,X).
```

Intuitively, this means that there exist no operations X and Y such that X precedes Y in the causal order and Y also precedes X in the causal order. Since co is transitive, we can simply write it as

```
:- co(X,X).
```

The second type is related to the occurrence of some operations in some particular order. For instance, WriteCORead can be expressed as follows

```
:- co(X,Y), co(Y,Z), wr(X,Z), wrt(X), wrt(Y), rd(Z), sv(X,Y), sv(Y,Z).
```

Intuitively, this means that there exist no write operations X and Y on the same variable and a read operation Z which takes the value from X such that X precedes Y in the causal order and Y precedes Z in the causal order.

Example 8. This example represents the history Fig. 1b Datalog program:

```
% Facts
wrt("w(x,1,id0)").
po("w(x,1,id0)","r(x,2,id1)").
sv("r(x,2,id1)","w(x,1,id0)").
sv("w(x,2,id2)","w(x,1,id0)").
sv("r(x,1,id3)","w(x,1,id0)").
rd("r(x,2,id1)").
sv("w(x,1,id0)","r(x,2,id1)").
wr("w(x,2,id2)","r(x,2,id1)").
sv("w(x,2,id2)","r(x,2,id1)").
sv("r(x,1,id3)","r(x,2,id1)").
wrt("w(x,2,id2)").
sv("w(x,1,id0)","w(x,2,id2)").
sv("r(x,2,id1)","w(x,2,id2)").
po("w(x,2,id2)","r(x,1,id3)").
sv("r(x,1,id3)","w(x,2,id2)").
rd("r(x,1,id3)").
wr("w(x,1,id0)","r(x,1,id3)").
sv("w(x,1,id0)","r(x,1,id3)").
sv("r(x,2,id1)","r(x,1,id3)").
sv("w(x,2,id2)","r(x,1,id3)").
initread("r(a,0,ida)").
% Inference rules
co(X,Y) :- po(X,Y).
```

```
co(X,Y) :- wr(X,Y).
co(X,Z) :- co(X,Y), co(Y,Z). % Transitivity
% CC bad-patterns
:- co(X,X). % CyclicCO
:- co(X,Y), wrt(X), initread(Y), sv(X,Y). % WriteCOInitRead
:- co(X,Y), co(Y,Z), wr(X,Z), wrt(X), wrt(Y), rd(Z), sv(X,Y), sv(Y,Z).
% WriteCORead
```

5.4   Complexity

Our reduction is polynomial time in the size of the computation. For a given execution, the relations po and wr can be extracted directly (as all the considered execution are differentiated) and their size is relative to the computation size. Moreover, the size of bad-patterns is constant on the execution and the complexity of evaluating a Datalog programs is PTIME [29]. Thus, the complexity of our approach is PTIME, which meet the complexity shown in [9].

6   Experimental Evaluation

We have investigated the efficiency and scalability of our tool (named *CausalC-Checker*) by applying it to two real-life distributed transactional databases, CockroachDB [1] and Galera [2].

Histories Generation: The Fig. 2 presents the general architecture of the used testing procedure in the next experiments. Histories are generated using random clients with the parameters, the number of sessions, the number of transactions per session, the number of events per transaction (in this paper, we consider one event per transaction), and the number of variables. A client is generated by the generator of histories (Algorithm 2) by choosing randomly the type of operation (read or write) in each transaction, the variable and a value for write operations. That constitutes non executed histories that are the histories which do not contain the return values of read operations. Each client performs a session, communicates with the database cluster by executing operations (read/write) and gets the return values for read operations. The recorded histories are called executed histories in the Fig. 2. We ensure that all histories are differentiated. These histories are the input of our *CausalC-Checker*.

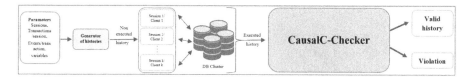

Fig. 2. The General architecture of the histories checking procedure

6.1   Case Study 1: CockroachDB

We have used the highly available and strongly consistent distributed database CockroachDB [1] (v2.1.0) that is built on a transactional strongly-consistent key-value store. Considering one operation per transaction lead to our model. We have examined the effect of the number of operations on runtime for a fixed number of processes (4 processes) and the effect of the number of processes. We have tested 200 histories for each configuration and calculated the average runtime.

Input: nClient, nTransaction, nEvent, nVariable
Output: A non executed history

1   $lastWrite \leftarrow \emptyset$;
2   **foreach** $v \in 1..nVariable$ **do**
3 | $lastWrite(v) \leftarrow 0$;
4   **end**
5   history $\leftarrow \emptyset$;
6   **foreach** $1..nClient$ **do**
7 | Client $\leftarrow \emptyset$;
8 | **foreach** $1..nTransaction$ **do**
9 | | Transaction $\leftarrow \emptyset$;
10 | | **foreach** $1..nEvent$ **do**
11 | | | Event $\leftarrow new$(Event);
12 | | | Event.$operation \leftarrow uniformly\_choose(\{$Read, Write$\})$;
13 | | | Event.$variable \leftarrow uniformly\_choose(\{1..$nVariable$\})$;
14 | | | **if** $Event.operation = Write$ **then**
15 | | | | Event.$value \leftarrow lastWrite($Event.$variable) + 1$;
16 | | | | $lastWrite($Event.$variable) \leftarrow lastWrite($Event.$variable) + 1$;
17 | | | **end**
18 | | | Transaction.$push$(Event);
19 | | **end**
20 | | Client.$push$(Transaction);
21 | **end**
22 | history.$push$(Client);
23   **end**
24   **return** history;

Algorithm 2: The histories generator algorithm

We have checked CC, CCv and CM for all generated histories. Figure 3 shows the results. The graphs 3a, c and d show the runtime while increasing the number of operations from 100 to 600, in augmentations of 100 (with a fixed number of processes, 4 processes). The graphs 3b, e and f report the runtime when increasing the number of processes from 2 to 6, in augmentations of 1. For each number of processes x we have considered $50x$ operations.

The graph 3c resp., graph 3d, shows the evolution of CC and CCv verification resp., CM verification, runtime while increasing the number of operations. The graph 3e resp., graph 3f, shows the evolution of CC and CCv verification resp., CM verification, runtime while increasing the number of processes.

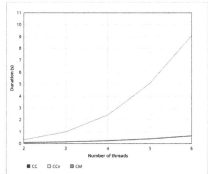

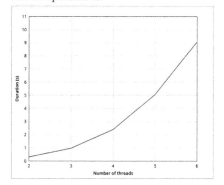

(a) Checking Causal Consistency while varying the number of operations.

(b) Checking Causal Consistency while varying the number of processes.

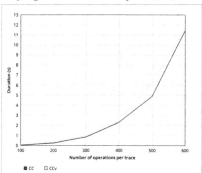

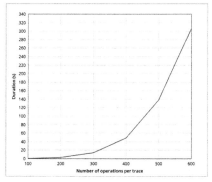

(c) Checking CC and CCv while varying the number of operations.

(d) Checking CM while varying the number of operations.

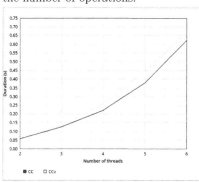

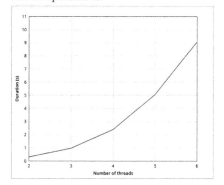

(e) Checking CC and CCv while varying the number of processes.

(f) Checking CM while varying the number of processes.

Fig. 3. Checking Causal Consistency for CockreachDB histories.

Our approach is more efficient in the case of CC and CCv verification compared to the CM case. All the tested histories were valid w.r.t. all the considered causal consistency models.

6.2   Case Study 2: Galera

We have also used the cluster called Galera [2] (v3.20). Galera Cluster is a database cluster based on synchronous replication and Oracle's InnoDB/MySQL. It is expected to implement *Snapshot isolation* when transactions are processed in separated nodes.

Similarly to the first case study, we have studied the evolution of runtime while increasing the number of operations from 100 to 600, in augmentations of 100. We have verified 200 histories for each number of operations and compute the runtime average.

The graphs in Fig. 4 show the impact of increasing the number of operations on runtime while fixing the number of processes (4 processes). The graph 4b reports the evolution of CC and CCv verification runtime. On the other hand, the graph 4c shows the evolution of CM checking runtime.

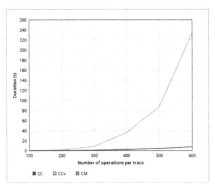

(a) Checking Causal Consistency while varying the number of operations.

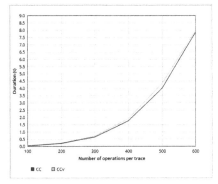

(b) Checking CC and CCv while varying the number of operations.

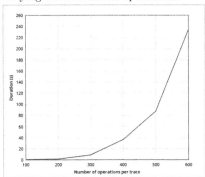

(c) Checking CM while varying the number of operations.

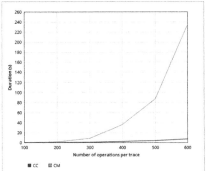

(d) Comparing CM and CC violations runtimes while varying the number of operations.

Fig. 4. Checking causal consistency for Galera histories.

We have found that 1.25% of the Galera tested histories violate causal consistency, that confirms the bugs submitted on Github [3]. We mention that 73.3% of the detected CM violations are also CC violations. The suggested approach scales well and detects violations on the used version of Galera DB.

The experiments show that our approach is efficient for both verification of valid computations and detection of violations, especially in the case of CC and CCv. The gap between CC (CCv) and CM runtimes reported in the graphs 3a, b and 4a is due to the fact that in CM, we compute the hb_o relation and check the bad-patterns for each operation. Since CM costs more compared to CC in terms of runtime (Fig. 4d) and the most CM violations in practice are CC violations (73.3% in the Galera case), one can start by verifying CC first.

7 Related Work

Several works have considered the problem of checking strong consistency models such as *Linearizability* and *Sequential consistency* (SC) [4,7,11,14,16–18,28,30]. However, few have addressed the problem of checking weak consistency models. Emmi and Enea [15] proposes an algorithm to optimize the consistency checking based on the notion of minimal-visibility. However, their work relies on some specific relaxations in those criteria, leading to the naive enumeration in the context of strong consistency models such as SC and TSO (*Total store ordering*). Bouajjani et al. [10] presents a formalization of eventual consistency for replicated objects and reduces the problem of checking eventual consistency to reachability and model checking problems.

Bouajjani et al. [9] considers the problem of checking causal consistency. They present the formalization of the different variations of causal consistency (CC, CCv and CM) we use in this work and a complete characterization of the violations of those models. In addition, they show that checking if an execution is conforme to one of those models is polynomial time. However, this work does not propose any implementation.

8 Conclusion

We have presented a tool for checking automatically that given computations of a system are causally consistent. Our procedure for solving this conformance problem is based on implementing the theoretical approach introduced in [9] where causal consistency violations are characterised in terms of the occurrence of some particular bad-patterns. We build on this work by reducing the problem of detecting the existence of these patterns in computations to the problem of solving Datalog queries. We have applied our algorithm to two real-life case studies. The experimental results show that in the case of CC and CCv our approach is efficient and scalable. In the CM case, the costs grow polynomially but much faster than in the case of CC and CCv. Nevertheless, it turned out that interestingly, most of the CM violations that we found are in fact CC violations, and therefore can be caught using a more efficient procedure. Still, an interesting question for future work is whether CM has an alternative characterization leading to a better conformance checking procedure.

References

1. https://www.cockroachlabs.com. Accessed 15 Nov 2018
2. http://galeracluster.com. Accessed 15 Nov 2018
3. https://github.com/codership/galera/issues/336. Accessed 15 Nov 2018
4. Abdulla, P.A., Haziza, F., Holík, L.: Parameterized verification through view abstraction. STTT **18**(5), 495–516 (2016). https://doi.org/10.1007/s10009-015-0406-x
5. Abiteboul, S., Hull, R., Vianu, V. (eds.): Foundations of Databases: The Logical Level, 1st edn. Addison-Wesley Longman Publishing Co., Inc., Boston (1995)
6. Ahamad, M., Neiger, G., Burns, J.E., Kohli, P., Hutto, P.W.: Causal memory: definitions, implementation, and programming. Distrib. Comput. **9**(1), 37–49 (1995). https://doi.org/10.1007/BF01784241
7. Alur, R., McMillan, K.L., Peled, D.A.: Model-checking of correctness conditions for concurrent objects. Inf. Comput. **160**(1–2), 167–188 (2000). https://doi.org/10.1006/inco.1999.2847
8. Bailis, P., Ghodsi, A., Hellerstein, J.M., Stoica, I.: Bolt-on causal consistency. In: Proceedings of the 2013 ACM SIGMOD International Conference on Management of Data, SIGMOD 2013, pp. 761–772. ACM, New York (2013). https://doi.org/10.1145/2463676.2465279, http://doi.acm.org/10.1145/2463676.2465279
9. Bouajjani, A., Enea, C., Guerraoui, R., Hamza, J.: On verifying causal consistency. In: Castagna, G., Gordon, A.D. (eds.) Proceedings of the 44th ACM SIGPLAN Symposium on Principles of Programming Languages, POPL 2017, Paris, France, 18–20 January 2017, pp. 626–638. ACM (2017). http://dl.acm.org/citation.cfm?id=3009888
10. Bouajjani, A., Enea, C., Hamza, J.: Verifying eventual consistency of optimistic replication systems. In: Proceedings of the 41st ACM SIGPLAN-SIGACT Symposium on Principles of Programming Languages, POPL 2014, pp. 285–296. ACM, New York (2014). https://doi.org/10.1145/2535838.2535877. http://doi.acm.org/10.1145/2535838.2535877
11. Burckhardt, S., Dern, C., Musuvathi, M., Tan, R.: Line-up: a complete and automatic linearizability checker. In: Zorn, B.G., Aiken, A. (eds.) Proceedings of the 2010 ACM SIGPLAN Conference on Programming Language Design and Implementation, PLDI 2010, Toronto, Ontario, Canada, 5–10 June 2010, pp. 330–340. ACM (2010). https://doi.org/10.1145/1806596.1806634
12. Du, J., Elnikety, S., Roy, A., Zwaenepoel, W.: Orbe: Scalable causal consistency using dependency matrices and physical clocks. In: Proceedings of the 4th Annual Symposium on Cloud Computing, SOCC 2013, pp. 11:1–11:14. ACM, New York (2013). https://doi.org/10.1145/2523616.2523628. http://doi.acm.org/10.1145/2523616.2523628

13. Du, J., Iorgulescu, C., Roy, A., Zwaenepoel, W.: GentleRain: cheap and scalable causal consistency with physical clocks. In: Proceedings of the 5th ACM Symposium on Cloud Computing, SOCC 2014, November 2014. https://doi.org/10.1145/2670979.2670983

14. Eiríksson, Á.T., McMillan, K.L.: Using formal verification/analysis methods on the critical path in system design: a case study. In: Wolper, P. (ed.) CAV 1995. LNCS, vol. 939, pp. 367–380. Springer, Heidelberg (1995). https://doi.org/10.1007/3-540-60045-0_63

15. Emmi, M., Enea, C.: Monitoring weak consistency. In: Chockler, H., Weissenbacher, G. (eds.) CAV 2018. LNCS, vol. 10981, pp. 487–506. Springer, Cham (2018). https://doi.org/10.1007/978-3-319-96145-3_26

16. Emmi, M., Enea, C.: Sound, complete, and tractable linearizability monitoring for concurrent collections. PACMPL 2(POPL), 25:1–25:27 (2018). https://doi.org/10.1145/3158113

17. Emmi, M., Enea, C., Hamza, J.: Monitoring refinement via symbolic reasoning. In: Grove, D., Blackburn, S. (eds.) Proceedings of the 36th ACM SIGPLAN Conference on Programming Language Design and Implementation, Portland, OR, USA, 15–17 June 2015, pp. 260–269. ACM (2015). https://doi.org/10.1145/2737924.2737983

18. German, S.M., Sistla, A.P.: Reasoning about systems with many processes. J. ACM 39(3), 675–735 (1992). https://doi.org/10.1145/146637.146681

19. Gilbert, S., Lynch, N.: Brewer's conjecture and the feasibility of consistent, available, partition-tolerant web services. SIGACT News 33(2), 51–59 (2002). https://doi.org/10.1145/564585.564601

20. Herlihy, M.P., Wing, J.M.: Linearizability: a correctness condition for concurrent objects. ACM Trans. Program. Lang. Syst. 12(3), 463–492 (1990). https://doi.org/10.1145/78969.78972

21. Jiménez, E., Fernández Anta, A., Cholvi, V.: A parametrized algorithm that implements sequential, causal, and cache memory consistencies. J. Syst. Softw. 81, 120–131 (2008). https://doi.org/10.1016/j.jss.2007.03.012

22. Lamport, L.: How to make a multiprocessor computer that correctly executes multiprocess programs. IEEE Trans. Comput. 28(9), 690–691 (1979). https://doi.org/10.1109/TC.1979.1675439

23. Lamport, L.: Time, clocks, and the ordering of events in a distributed system. Commun. ACM 21(7), 558–565 (1978). https://doi.org/10.1145/359545.359563

24. Lloyd, W., Freedman, M.J., Kaminsky, M., Andersen, D.G.: Don't settle for eventual: Scalable causal consistency for wide-area storage with cops. In: Proceedings of the Twenty-Third ACM Symposium on Operating Systems Principles, pp. 401–416. ACM, New York (2011). https://doi.org/10.1145/2043556.2043593

25. Mahajan, P., Alvisi, L., Dahlin, M.: Consistency, availability, convergence. Technical report (2011)

26. Petersen, K., Spreitzer, M.J., Terry, D.B., Theimer, M.M., Demers, A.J.: Flexible update propagation for weakly consistent replication. SIGOPS Oper. Syst. Rev. 31(5), 288–301 (1997). https://doi.org/10.1145/269005.266711

27. Preguiça, N., et al.: Swiftcloud: fault-tolerant geo-replication integrated all the way to the client machine. In: Proceedings of the 2014 IEEE 33rd International Symposium on Reliable Distributed Systems Workshops, SRDSW 2014, pp. 30–33. IEEE Computer Society, Washington, DC (2014). https://doi.org/10.1109/SRDSW.2014.33

28. Qadeer, S.: Verifying sequential consistency on shared-memory multiprocessors by model checking. IEEE Trans. Parallel Distrib. Syst. 14(8), 730–741 (2003). https://doi.org/10.1109/TPDS.2003.1225053
29. Vardi, M.Y.: The complexity of relational query languages (extended abstract). In: Proceedings of the Fourteenth Annual ACM Symposium on Theory of Computing, STOC 1982, pp. 137–146. ACM, New York (1982). https://doi.org/10.1145/800070.802186
30. Wing, J.M., Gong, C.: Testing and verifying concurrent objects. J. Parallel Distrib. Comput. 17(1–2), 164–182 (1993). https://doi.org/10.1006/jpdc.1993.1015

Liveness in Broadcast Networks

Peter Chini$^{(\boxtimes)}$, Roland Meyer, and Prakash Saivasan

TU Braunschweig, Braunschweig, Germany
{p.chini,roland.meyer,p.saivasan}@tu-bs.de

Abstract. We study two liveness verification problems for broadcast networks, a system model of identical clients communicating via message passing. The first problem is *liveness verification*. It asks whether there is a computation such that one of the clients visits a final state infinitely often. The complexity of the problem has been open since 2010 when it was shown to be P-hard and solvable in EXPSPACE. We close the gap by a polynomial-time algorithm. The algorithm relies on a characterization of live computations in terms of paths in a suitable graph, combined with a fixed-point iteration to efficiently check the existence of such paths. The second problem is *fair liveness verification*. It asks for a computation where all participating clients visit a final state infinitely often. We adjust the algorithm to also solve fair liveness in polynomial time.

1 Introduction

Parameterized systems consist of an arbitrary number of identical clients that communicate via some mechanism like a shared memory or message passing [3]. Parameterized systems appear in various applications. In distributed algorithms, a group of clients has to form a consensus [29]. In cache-coherence protocols, coherence has to be guaranteed for data shared among threads [10]. Developing parameterized systems is difficult. The desired functionality has to be achieved not only for a single system instance but for an arbitrary number of clients that is not known a priori. The proposed solutions are generally tricky and sometimes buggy [2], which has lead to substantial interest in parameterized verification [7], verification algorithms for parameterized systems.

Broadcast networks are a particularly successful model for parameterized verification [4,6,8,9,11,12,17,20,21,24,36]. A broadcast network consists of an arbitrary number of identical finite-state automata communicating via passing messages. We call these automata clients, because they reflect the interaction of a single client in the parameterized system with its environment. When a client sends a message (by taking a send transition), at the same time a number of clients receive the message (by taking a corresponding receive transition). A client ready to receive a message may decide to ignore it, and it may be the case that nobody receives the message.

What makes broadcast networks interesting is the surprisingly low complexity of their verification problems. Earlier works have concentrated on safety verification. In the coverability problem, the question is whether at least one

© Springer Nature Switzerland AG 2019
M. F. Atig and A. A. Schwarzmann (Eds.): NETYS 2019, LNCS 11704, pp. 52–66, 2019.
https://doi.org/10.1007/978-3-030-31277-0_4

participating client can reach an unsafe state. The problem has been shown to be solvable in polynomial time [11]. In the synchronization problem, all clients need to visit a final state at the same time. Although seemingly harder than coverability, it turned out to be solvable in polynomial time as well [23]. Both problems remain in P if the communication topology is slightly restricted [4], a strengthening that usually leads to undecidability results [4,12].

The focus of our work is on liveness verification. Liveness properties formulate good events that should happen during a computation. To give an example, one would state that every request has to be followed by a response. In the setting of broadcast networks, liveness verification was studied in [12]. The problem generalizes coverability in that at least one client needs to visit a final state infinitely many times. The problem was shown to be solvable in EXPSPACE by a reduction to repeated coverability in Petri Nets [18,22]. The only known lower bound, however, is P-hardness [11].

Our contribution is an algorithm that solves the liveness verification problem in polynomial time. It closes the aforementioned gap. We also address a fair variant of liveness verification where all clients participating infinitely often in a computation have to see a final state infinitely often, a requirement known as compassion [33]. We give an instrumentation that compiles away compassion and reduces the problem to finding cycles. By our results, safety and liveness verification have the same complexity, a phenomenon that has been observed in other models as well [17,19,24,25].

Our results yield efficient algorithms for (fair) model checking broadcast networks against linear-time specifications [32]. If the specification is given as an automaton [37], we compute a product with the clients and run our algorithms.

At the heart of our liveness verification algorithm is a fixed-point iteration that terminates in polynomial time. It relies on an efficient representation of computations. We first characterize live computations in terms of paths in a suitable graph. Since the graph is of exponential size, we cannot immediately apply a path finding algorithm. Instead, we show that a path exists if and only if there is a path in some normal form. Paths in normal form can then be found efficiently by the fixed-point iteration. The normal form result is inspired by ideas presented in [23].

Related Work. We already discussed the related work on safety and liveness verification of broadcast networks. Broadcast networks [12,20,36] were introduced to verify ad hoc networks [28,35]. Ad hoc networks are reconfigurable in that the number of clients as well as their communication topology may change during the computation. If the transition relation is compatible with the topology, safety verification has been shown to be decidable [27]. Related studies do not assume compatibility but restrict the topology [26]. If the dependencies among clients are bounded [30], safety verification is decidable independent of the transition relation [38,39]. Verification tools turn these decision procedures into practice [15,31]. D'Osualdo and Ong suggested a typing discipline for the communication topology [16]. In [4], decidability and undecidability results for reachability problems were proven for a locally changing topology. The case when communication is fixed along a given graph was studied in [1]. Topologies with bounded diameter were considered in [13]. Perfect communication where a sent message is received by all clients was studied in [20]. Networks with communication failures were considered in [14]. Probabilistic broadcast networks were studied in [5]. In [6], a variant of broadcast networks was considered where the clients follow a local strategy.

Broadcast networks are related to the leader-contributor model. It has a fixed leader and an arbitrary number of identical contributors that communicate via a shared memory. The model was introduced in [24]. The case when the leader and all contributors are finite-state automata was considered in [21] and the corresponding reachability problem was proven to be NP-complete. In [9], the authors took a parameterized complexity look at the reachability problem and proved it fixed-parameter tractable. Liveness verification for this model was studied in [17]. The authors show that repeated reachability is NP-complete. Networks with shared memory and randomized scheduler were studied in [8].

For a survey of parameterized verification we refer to [7].

2   Broadcast Networks

We introduce the model of broadcast networks of interest in this paper. Our presentation avoids an explicit characterization of the communication topology in terms of graphs. A *broadcast network* is a concurrent system consisting of an arbitrary but finite number of identical clients that communicate by passing messages to each other. Formally, it is a pair $\mathcal{N} = (D, P)$. The *domain* D is a finite set of messages that can be used for communication. A message $a \in D$ can either be sent, $!a$, or received, $?a$. The set $Ops(D) = \{!a, ?a \mid a \in D\}$ captures the communication operations a client can perform. For modeling the identical clients, we abstract away the internal behavior and focus on the communication with others via $Ops(D)$. With this, the clients are given in the form of a finite state automaton $P = (Q, I, \delta)$, where Q is a finite set of states, $I \subseteq Q$ is a set of initial states, and $\delta \subseteq Q \times Ops(D) \times Q$ is the transition relation. We extend δ to words in $Ops(D)^*$ and write $q \xrightarrow{w} q'$ instead of $(q, w, q') \in \delta$.

During a communication phase in $\mathcal{N}$, one client sends a message that is received by a number of other clients. This induces a change of the current state in each client participating in the communication. We use *configurations* to display the current states of the clients. A configuration is a tuple $c = (q_1, \ldots, q_k) \in Q^k$, $k \in \mathbb{N}$. We use $Set(c)$ to denote the set of client states occurring in c. To access the components of c, we use $c[i] = q_i$. As the number of clients in the system is arbitrary but fixed, we define the set of all configurations to be $CF = \bigcup_{k \in \mathbb{N}} Q^k$. The set of *initial configurations* is given by $CF_0 = \bigcup_{k \in \mathbb{N}} I^k$. The communication is modeled by a transition relation among configurations. Let $c' = (q'_1, \ldots, q'_k)$ be another configuration with k clients and $a \in D$ a message. We have a transition $c \xrightarrow{a}_{\mathcal{N}} c'$ if the following conditions hold: (1) there is a sender, an $i \in [1..k]$ such that $q_i \xrightarrow{!a} q'_i$, (2) there is a number of receivers, a set $R \subseteq [1..k] \setminus \{i\}$ such that $q_j \xrightarrow{?a} q'_j$ for each $j \in R$, and (3) all other clients stay idle, for all $j \notin R \cup \{i\}$ we have $q_j = q'_j$. We use $idx(c \xrightarrow{a}_{\mathcal{N}} c') = R \cup \{i\}$ to denote the indices of clients that contributed to the transition. We extend the transition relation to words $w \in D^*$ and write $c \xrightarrow{w}_{\mathcal{N}} c'$. Such a sequence of consecutive transitions is called a *computation* of $\mathcal{N}$. Note that all configurations appearing in a computation have the same number of clients. We write $c \rightarrow^*_{\mathcal{N}} c'$ if there is a word $w \in D^*$ with $c \xrightarrow{w}_{\mathcal{N}} c'$. If $|w| \geq 1$, we also use $c \rightarrow^+_{\mathcal{N}} c'$. Where appropriate, we skip $\mathcal{N}$ in the index. We are interested in infinite computations, infinite sequences $\pi = c_0 \rightarrow c_1 \rightarrow \dots$ of consecutive transitions. Such a computation is *initialized*, if $c_0 \in CF_0$. We use $\text{Inf}(\pi) = \{i \in \mathbb{N} \mid \exists^\infty j : i \in idx(c_j \rightarrow c_{j+1})\}$ to denote the set of clients that participate in the computation infinitely often. We let $\text{Fin}(\pi) = \{i \in \mathbb{N} \mid \exists^\infty j : c_j[i] \in F\}$ represent the set of clients that visit final states infinitely often.

3 Liveness

We consider the *liveness verification problem* for broadcast networks. Given a broadcast network $\mathcal{N} = (D, P)$ with $P = (Q, I, \delta)$ and a set of final states $F \subseteq Q$, the problem asks whether there is an infinite initialized computation π in which at least one client visits a final state from F infinitely often, $\text{Fin}(\pi) \neq \emptyset$.

Liveness Verification
Input: A broadcast network $\mathcal{N} = (D, P)$ and final states $F \subseteq Q$.
Question: Is there an initialized computation π with $\text{Fin}(\pi) \neq \emptyset$?

The liveness verification problem was introduced as *repeated coverability* in [12]. We show the following:

Theorem 1. *The liveness verification problem is* P-*complete.*

P-hardness is due to [11]. Our contribution is a matching polynomial-time decision procedure. Key to our algorithm is the following lemma which relates the existence of an infinite computation to the existence of a finite one.

Lemma 2. *There is an infinite computation* $c_0 \rightarrow c_1 \rightarrow \dots$ *that visits states in* F *infinitely often if and only if there is a finite computation of the form* $c_0 \rightarrow^* c \rightarrow^+ c$ *with* $\text{Set}(c) \cap F \neq \emptyset$.

If there is a computation of the form $c_0 \rightarrow^* c \rightarrow^+ c$ with $\text{Set}(c) \cap F \neq \emptyset$, then $c \rightarrow^+ c$ can be iterated infinitely often to obtain an infinite computation visiting F infinitely often. In turn, in any infinite sequence from Q^k one can find a repeating configuration (pigeon hole principle). This in particular holds for the infinite sequence of configurations containing final states.

Our polynomial-time algorithm for the liveness verification problem looks for an appropriate reachable configuration c that can be iterated. The difficulty is that we have a parameterized system, and therefore the number of configurations is not finite. Our approach is to devise a finite graph in which we search for a cycle that mimics the cycle on c. While the graph yields a decision procedure, it will be of exponential size and a naive search for a cycle will require exponential time. We show in a second step how to find a cycle in polynomial time.

The graph underlying our algorithm is inspired by the powerset construction for the determinization of finite state automata [34]. The vertices keep track of sets of states S that a client may be in. Different from finite-state automata, however, there is not only one client in a state $s \in S$ but arbitrarily (but finitely) many. As a consequence, a transition from s to s' may have two effects. Some of the clients in s change their state to s' while others stay in s. In that case, the set of states is updated to $S' = S \cup \{s'\}$. Alternatively, all clients may change their state to s', in which case we get $S' = (S \setminus \{s\}) \cup \{s'\}$.

Formally, the graph of interest is $G = (V, \rightarrow_G)$. The vertices are tuples of sets of states, $V = \bigcup_{k \leq |Q|} \mathcal{P}(Q)^k$. The parameter k will become clear in a moment. To define the edges, we need some more notation. For $S \subseteq Q$ and $a \in D$, let

$$post_{?a}(S) = \{r' \in Q \mid \exists r \in S : r \xrightarrow{?a} r'\}$$

denote the set of successors of S under transitions receiving a. The set of states in S where receives of a are *enabled* is denoted by

$$enabled_{?a}(S) = \{r \in S \mid post_{?a}(\{r\}) \neq \emptyset\}.$$

There is a directed edge $V_1 \rightarrow_G V_2$ from vertex $V_1 = (S_1, \ldots, S_k)$ to vertex $V_2 = (S'_1, \ldots, S'_k)$ if the following three conditions are satisfied: (1) there is an index $j \in [1..k]$, states $s \in S_j$ and $s' \in S'_j$, and an element a from the domain D such that $s \xrightarrow{!a} s'$ is a send transition. (2) For each $i \in [1..k]$ there are sets of states $Gen_i \subseteq post_{?a}(S_i)$ and $Kill_i \subseteq enabled_{?a}(S_i)$ such that

$$S'_i = \begin{cases} (S_i \setminus Kill_i) \cup Gen_i, & \text{for } i \neq j, \\ (U_j \setminus Kill_j) \cup Gen_j \cup \{s'\}, & \text{for } i = j \end{cases}$$

where U_j is either S_j or $S_j \setminus \{s\}$. (3) For each index $i \in [1..k]$ and state $q \in Kill_i$, the intersection $post_{?a}(q) \cap Gen_i$ is non-empty.

Intuitively, an edge in the graph mimics a transition in the broadcast network without making explicit the configurations. Condition (1) requires a sender, a component j capable of sending a message a. Clients receiving this message are represented by (2). The set Gen_i consists of those states that are reached by clients performing a corresponding receive transition. These states are added to S_i. As mentioned above, states can get killed. If, during a receive transition, all clients decide to move to the target state, the original state will not be present anymore. We capture those states in the set $Kill_i$ and remove them from S_i. Condition (3) is needed to guarantee that each killed state is replaced by a target state. Note that for component j we add s' due to the send transition. Moreover, we need to distinguish whether state s gets killed or not.

The following lemma relates a cycle in the constructed graph with a cyclic computation of the form $c \rightarrow^+ c$. It is crucial for our result.

Lemma 3. *There is a cycle* $(\{s_1\}, \ldots, \{s_m\}) \to_G^+ (\{s_1\}, \ldots, \{s_m\})$ *in G if and only if there is a configuration c with* $\mathrm{Set}(c) = \{s_1, \ldots s_m\}$ *and* $c \to^+ c$.

The lemma explains the restriction of the nodes in the graph to k-tuples of sets of states, with $k \le |Q|$. We explore the transitions for every possible state in c, and there are at most $|Q|$ different states that have to be considered. We have to keep the sets of states separately to make sure that, for every starting state, the corresponding clients perform a cyclic computation.

Proof. We first fix some notations that we use throughout the proof. Let $c \in Q^n$ be any configuration and $s \in \mathrm{Set}(c)$. By $\mathrm{Pos}_c(s) = \{i \in [1..n] \mid c[i] = s\}$ we denote the positions of c storing state s. Given a second configuration $d \in Q^n$, we use the set $\mathrm{Target}_c(s, d) = \{d[i] \mid i \in \mathrm{Pos}_c(s)\}$ to represent those states that occur in d at the positions $\mathrm{Pos}_c(s)$. Intuitively, if there is a sequence of transitions from c to d, these are the target states of those positions of c that store s.

Consider a computation $\pi = c \to^+ c$ with $\mathrm{Set}(c) = \{s_1, \ldots, s_m\}$. We show that there is a cycle $(\{s_1\}, \ldots, \{s_m\}) \to_G^+ (\{s_1\}, \ldots, \{s_m\})$ in G. To this end, assume π is of the form $\pi = c \to c_1 \to \cdots \to c_\ell \to c$. Since $c \to c_1$ is a transition in the broadcast network, there is an edge

$$(\{s_1\}, \ldots, \{s_m\}) \to_G (\mathrm{Target}_c(s_1, c_1), \ldots, \mathrm{Target}_c(s_m, c_1))$$

in G where each state s_i gets replaced by the set of target states in c_1. Applying this argument inductively, we get a path in the graph:

$$
\begin{aligned}
(\{s_1\}, \ldots, \{s_m\}) &\to_G (\mathrm{Target}_c(s_1, c_1), \ldots, \mathrm{Target}_c(s_m, c_1)) \\
&\to_G (\mathrm{Target}_c(s_1, c_2), \ldots, \mathrm{Target}_c(s_m, c_2)) \\
&\to_G \cdots \\
&\to_G (\mathrm{Target}_c(s_1, c), \ldots, \mathrm{Target}_c(s_m, c)).
\end{aligned}
$$

Since $\mathrm{Target}_c(s_i, c) = \{s_i\}$, we found the desired cycle.

For the other direction, let a cycle $\sigma = (\{s_1\}, \ldots, \{s_m\}) \to_G^+ (\{s_1\}, \ldots, \{s_m\})$ be given. We construct from σ a computation $\pi = c \to^+ c$ in the broadcast network such that $\mathrm{Set}(c) = \{s_1, \ldots, s_m\}$. The difficulty in constructing π is to ensure that at any point in time there are enough clients in appropriate states. For instance, if a transition $s \xrightarrow{!a} s'$ occurs, we need to decide on how many clients to move to s'. Having too few clients in s' may stall the computation at a later point: there may be a number of sends required that can only be obtained by transitions from s'. If there are too few clients in s', we cannot guarantee the sends. The solution is to start with *enough* clients in any state. With invariants we guarantee that at any point in time, the number of clients in the needed states suffices.

Let cycle σ be $V_0 \to_G V_1 \to_G \cdots \to_G V_\ell$ with $V_0 = V_\ell = (\{s_1\}, \ldots, \{s_m\})$. Further, let $V_j = (S_j^1, \ldots, S_j^m)$. We will construct the computation π over configurations in Q^n where $n = m \cdot |Q|^\ell$. The idea is to have $|Q|^\ell$ clients for each of the m components of the vertices V_i occurring in σ. To access the clients belonging to a particular component, we split up configurations in Q^n into *blocks*, intervals $I(i) = [(i-1) \cdot |Q|^\ell + 1 \mathbin{..} i \cdot |Q|^\ell]$ for each $i \in [1..m]$. Let $d \in Q^n$ be arbitrary. For $i \in [1..m]$, let $B_d(i) = \{d[t] \mid t \in I(i)\}$ be the set of states occurring in the i-th block of d. Moreover, we blockwise collect clients that are currently in a particular state $s \in Q$. Let the set $\mathrm{Pos}_d(i, s) = \{t \in I(i) \mid d[t] = s\}$ be those positions of d in the i-th block that store state s.

We fix the configuration $c \in Q^n$. For each component $i \in [1..m]$, in the i-th block it contains $|Q|^\ell$ copies of the state s_i. Formally, $B_c(i) = \{s_i\}$. Our goal is to construct the computation $\pi = c_0 \to^+ c_1 \to^+ \cdots \to^+ c_\ell$ with $c_0 = c_\ell = c$ such that the following two invariants are satisfied. (1) For each $j \in [0..\ell]$ and $i \in [1..m]$ we have $B_{c_j}(i) \subseteq S^i_j$. (2) For any state s in a set S^i_j we have $|\mathrm{Pos}_{c_j}(i, s)| \geq |Q|^{\ell-j}$. Intuitively, (1) means that during the computation π we visit at most those states that occur in the cycle σ. Invariant (2) guarantees that at each configuration c_j there are *enough* clients available in these states.

We construct π inductively. The base case is given by configuration $c_0 = c$ which satisfies invariants (1) and (2) by definition. For the induction step, assume c_j is already constructed such that (1) and (2) hold for the configuration. Our first goal is to construct a configuration d such that $c_j \to^+ d$ and d satisfies invariant (2). In a second step we show to construct a computation $d \to^* c_{j+1}$.

In the cycle σ there is an edge $V_j \to_G V_{j+1}$. From the definition of $\to_G$ we get a component $t \in [1..m]$, states $s \in S^t_j$ and $s' \in S^t_{j+1}$, and an $a \in D$ such that there is a send transition $s \xrightarrow{!a} s'$. Moreover, there are sets $Gen_t \subseteq post_{?a}(S^t_j)$ and $Kill_t \subseteq enabled_{?a}(S^t_j)$ such that the following equality holds:

$$S^t_{j+1} = (U_t \setminus Kill_t) \cup Gen_t \cup \{s'\}.$$

Here, U_t is either S^t_j or $S^t_j \setminus \{s\}$. We focus on t and take care of other components later. We apply a case distinction for the states in S^t_{j+1}.

Let q be a state in $S^t_{j+1} \setminus \{s'\}$. If $q \in Gen_t$, there exists a $p \in S^t_j$ such that $p \xrightarrow{?a} q$. We apply this transition to $|Q|^{\ell-(j+1)}$ many clients in the t-th block of configuration c_j. If $q \in U_t \setminus Kill_t$ and q not in Gen_t, then certainly $q \in U_t \subseteq S^t_j$. In this case, we let $|Q|^{\ell-(j+1)}$ many clients of block t stay idle in state q. For state s', we apply a sequence of sends. More precise, we apply the transition $s \xrightarrow{!a} s'$ to $|Q|^{\ell-(j+1)}$ many clients in block t of c_j. The first of these sends synchronizes with the previously described receive transitions. The other sends do not have any receivers. For components different from t, we apply the same procedure. Since there are only receive transitions, we also let them synchronize with the first send of a. This leads to a computation τ

$$c_j \xrightarrow{a} d^1 \xrightarrow{a} d^2 \xrightarrow{a} \ldots \xrightarrow{a} d^{|Q|^{\ell-(j+1)}} = d.$$

We argue that the computation τ is *valid*: there are enough clients in c_j such that τ can be carried out. We again focus on component t, the reasoning for the other components is similar. Let $p \in \mathrm{Set}(c_j) = S^t_j$. Note that the equality is due to invariants (1) and (2). We count the clients of c_j in state p (in block t) that are needed to perform τ. We need

$$|Q|^{\ell-(j+1)} \cdot |post_{?a}(p) \cup \{p, s'\}| \leq |Q|^{\ell-(j+1)} \cdot |Q| = |Q|^{\ell-j}$$

of these clients. The set $post_{?a}(p) \cup \{p, s'\}$ appears as a consequence of the case distinction above: there may be transitions mapping p to a state in $post_{?a}(p)$, it may happen that clients stay idle in p, and in the case $p = s$, we need to add s' for the send transition. Since $|\operatorname{Pos}_{c_j}(t, p)| \geq |Q|^{\ell-j}$ by invariant (2), we get that τ is a valid computation. Moreover, note that configuration d satisfies invariant (2) for $j + 1$: for each state $q \in S^t_{j+1}$, the computation τ was constructed such that $|\operatorname{Pos}_d(t, q)| \geq |Q|^{\ell-(j+1)}$.

To satisfy invariant (1), we need to erase states that are present in d but not in S^t_{j+1}. To this end, we reconsider the set $Kill_t \subseteq enabled_{?a}(S^t_j)$. For each state $p \in Kill_t$, we know by the definition of $\rightarrow_G$ that $post_{?a}(p) \cap Gen_t \neq \emptyset$. Hence, there is a $q \in S^t_{j+1}$ such that $p \xrightarrow{?a} q$. We apply this transition to all clients in d currently in state p that were not active in the computation τ. In case $U_t = S^t_j \setminus \{s\}$, we apply the send $s \xrightarrow{!a} s'$ to all clients that are still in s and were not active in τ. Altogether, this leads to a computation $\eta = d \rightarrow^* c_{j+1}$.

There is a subtlety in the definition of η. There may be no send transition for the receivers to synchronize with since s may not need to be erased. In this case, we synchronize the receive transitions of η with the last send of τ. This does not change the result.

Computation η substitutes the states in $Kill_t$ and state s, depending on U_t, by states in S^t_{j+1}. But this means that in the t-th block of c_{j+1}, there are only states of S^t_{j+1} left. Hence, $B_{c_{j+1}}(t) \subseteq S^t_{j+1}$, and invariant (1) holds.

After the construction of $\pi = c \rightarrow^+ c_\ell$, it is left to argue that $c_\ell = c$. But this is due to the fact that invariant (1) holds for c_ℓ and $S^t_\ell = (\{s_1\}, \ldots, \{s_m\})$. □

The graph G is of exponential size. To obtain a polynomial-time procedure, we cannot just search it for a cycle as required by Lemma 3. Instead, we now show that if such a cycle exists, then there is a cycle in a certain normal form. Hence, it suffices to look for a normal-form cycle. As we will show, this can be done in polynomial time. We define the normal form more generally for paths.

A path is in *normal form*, if it takes the shape $V_1 \rightarrow^*_G V_m \rightarrow^*_G V_n$ such that the following conditions hold. In the prefix $V_1 \rightarrow^*_G V_m$ the sets of states increase monotonically, $V_i \sqsubseteq V_{i+1}$ for all $i \in [1..m-1]$. Here, $\sqsubseteq$ denotes the componentwise inclusion. In the suffix $V_m \rightarrow^*_G V_n$, the sets of states decrease monotonically, $V_i \sqsupseteq V_{i+1}$ for all $i \in [m..n-1]$. The following lemma states that if there is a path in the graph, then there is also a path in normal form. The intuition is that the variants of the transitions that decrease the sets of states can be postponed towards the end of the computation.

Lemma 4. *There is a path from V_1 to V_2 in G if and only if there is a path in normal form from V_1 to V_2.*

Proof. If $V_1 \to_G^* V_2$ is a path in normal form, there is nothing to prove. For the other direction, let $\sigma = V_1 \to_G^* V_2$ be an arbitrary path. To get a path in normal form, we first simulate the edges of σ in such a way that no states are deleted. In a second step, we erase the states that should have been deleted. We have to respect a particular deletion order ensuring that we construct a valid path.

Let $\sigma = U_1 \to_G U_2 \to_G \cdots \to_G U_\ell$ with $U_1 = V_1$ and $U_\ell = V_2$. We inductively construct an increasing path $\sigma_{\mathrm{inc}} = U_1' \to_G \cdots \to_G U_\ell'$ with $U_j' \sqsupseteq U_i$ or all $i \leq j$ by mimicking the edges of σ.

For the base case, we set $U_1' = U_1$. Now assume σ_{inc} has already been constructed up to vertex U_j'. There is an edge $e = U_j \to_G U_{j+1}$ in σ. Since $U_j' \sqsupseteq U_j$, we can simulate e on U_j': all states needed to execute the edge are present in U_j'. Moreover, we can mimic e such that no state gets deleted. This is achieved by setting the corresponding Kill sets to be empty. Hence, we get an edge $U_j' \to U_{j+1}'$ with $U_{j+1}' \sqsupseteq U_j'$ (no deletion) and $U_{j+1}' \sqsupseteq U_{j+1}$ (simulation of e).

The states in $V_2' = U_\ell'$ that are not in V_2 are those states that were deleted along σ. We construct a decreasing path $\sigma_{\mathrm{dec}} = V_2' \to_G^* V_2$, deleting all these states. To this end, let $V_2' = (T_1, \ldots, T_m)$ and $V_2 = (S_1, \ldots, S_m)$. An edge in σ deletes sets of states in each component $i \in [1..m]$. Hence, to mimic the deletion, we need to consider subsets of $Del = \bigcup_{i \in [1..m]} (T_i \setminus S_i) \times \{i\}$. Note that the index i in a tuple (s, i) displays the component the state s is in.

Consider the equivalence relation $\sim$ over Del defined by $(x, i) \sim (y, t)$ if and only if the last occurrence of x in component i and y in component t in the path σ coincide. Intuitively, two elements are equivalent if they get deleted at the same time and do not appear again in σ. We introduce an order on the equivalence classes: $[(x, i)]_\sim < [(y, t)]_\sim$ if and only if the last occurrence of (x, i) was before the last occurrence of (y, t). Since the order is total, we get a partition of Del into equivalence classes $P_1, \ldots, P_n$ such that $P_j < P_{j+1}$ for each $j \in [1..n-1]$.

We construct $\sigma_{\mathrm{dec}} = K_0 \to_G \cdots \to_G K_n$ with $K_0 = V_2'$ and $K_n = V_2$ as follows. During each edge $K_{j-1} \to_G K_j$, we delete precisely the elements in P_j and do not add further states. Deleting P_j is due to an edge $e = U_k \to_G U_{k+1}$ of σ. We mimic e in such a way that no state gets added and set the corresponding Gen sets to the empty set. Since we respect the order $<$ with the deletions, the simulation of e is possible. Suppose, we need a state s in component t to simulate e but the state is not available in component t of K_{j-1}. Then it was deleted before, $(s, t) \in P_1 \cup \cdots \cup P_{j-1}$. But this contradicts that s is present in U_k. Hence, all the needed states are available.

Since after the last edge of σ_{dec} we have deleted all elements from Del, we get that $K_n = V_2$. This concludes the proof. $\qquad\square$

Using the normal-form result in Lemma 4, we now give a polynomial-time algorithm to check whether $(\{s_1\}, \ldots, \{s_m\}) \to_G^+ (\{s_1\}, \ldots, \{s_m\})$. The idea is to mimic the monotonically increasing prefix of the computation by a suitable post operator, the monotonically decreasing suffix by a suitable pre operator, and intersect the two. The difficulty in computing an appropriate post operator is to ensure that the receive operations are enabled by sends leading to a state in the intersection, and similar for the pre. The solution is to use a greatest fixed-point computation. In a first Kleene iteration step, we determine the ordinary $post^+$ of $(\{s_1\}, \ldots, \{s_m\})$ and intersect it with the pre^*. In the next step, we constrain the $post^+$ and the pre^* computations to visiting only states in the previous intersection. The results are intersected again, which may remove further states. Hence, the computation is repeated relative to the new intersection. The thing to note is that we do not work with standard post and pre operators but with operators that are constrained by (tuples of) sets of states.

For the definition of the operators, consider $C = (C_1, \ldots, C_m) \in \mathcal{P}(Q)^m$ for an $m \leq |Q|$. Given a sequence of sets of states $X_1, \ldots, X_m$ where each $X_i \subseteq C_i$, we define $post_C(X_1, \ldots, X_m) = (X'_1, \ldots, X'_m)$ with

$$X'_i = \{s' \in Q \mid \exists s \in X_i : s \xrightarrow{!a}_{P \downarrow C_i} s'\}$$
$$\cup \{s' \in Q \mid \exists s_1, s_2 \in X_\ell : \exists s \in X_i : s_1 \xrightarrow{!a}_{P \downarrow C_\ell} s_2 \wedge s \xrightarrow{?a}_{P \downarrow C_i} s'\} .$$

Here, $P \downarrow_{C_i}$ denotes the automaton obtained from P by restricting it to the states C_i. Similarly, we define $pre_C(X_1, \ldots, X_m) = (X'_1, \ldots, X'_m)$ with

$$X'_i = \{s \in Q \mid \exists s' \in X_i : s \xrightarrow{!a}_{P \downarrow C_i} s'\}$$
$$\cup \{s \in Q \mid \exists s_1, s_2 \in X_\ell : \exists s' \in X_i : s_1 \xrightarrow{!a}_{P \downarrow C_\ell} s_2 \wedge s \xrightarrow{?a}_{P \downarrow C_i} s'\} .$$

The next lemma shows that the (reflexive) transitive closures of these operators can be computed in polynomial time.

Lemma 5. *The closures $post_C^+(X_1, \ldots, X_m)$ and $pre_C^*(X_1, \ldots, X_m)$ can be computed in polynomial time.*

Proof. Both closures can be computed by a saturation. For $post_C^+(X_1, \ldots, X_m)$, we keep m sets $R_1, \ldots, R_m$, each being the post of a component. Initially, we set $R_i = X_i$. The defining equation of X'_i in $post_C^+(X_1, \ldots, X_m)$ gives the saturation. One just needs to substitute X_i by R_i and X_ℓ by R_ℓ on the right hand side. The resulting set of states is added to R_i. This process is applied consecutively to each component and then repeated until the sets R_i do not change anymore, the fixed point is reached.

The saturation terminates in polynomial time. After updating R_i in each component, we either already terminated or added at least one new state to a set R_i. Since there are $m \leq |Q|$ of these sets and each one is a subset of Q, we need to update the sets R_i at most $|Q|^2$ many times. For a single of these updates, the dominant time factor comes from finding appropriate send and receive transitions. This can be achieved in $\mathcal{O}(|\delta|^2)$ time.

Computing the closure $pre_C^*(X_1, \ldots, X_m)$ is similar. One can apply the above saturation and only needs to reverse the transitions in the client. $\square$

As argued above, the existence of a cycle reduces to finding a fixed point. The following lemma shows that it can be computed efficiently.

Lemma 6. *There is a cycle* $(\{s_1\},\ldots,\{s_m\}) \to_G^+ (\{s_1\},\ldots,\{s_m\})$ *if and only if there is a non-trivial solution to the equation*

$$C = post_C^+(\{s_1\},\ldots,\{s_m\}) \cap pre_C^*(\{s_1\},\ldots,\{s_m\}) \,.$$

Such a solution can be found in polynomial time.

Proof. We use a Kleene iteration to compute the greatest fixed point. It invokes Lemma 5 as a subroutine. Every step of the Kleene iteration reduces the number of states in C by at least one, and initially there are at most $|Q|$ entries with $|Q|$ states each. Hence, we terminate after quadratically many iteration steps.

It is left to prove correctness. Let $(\{s_1\},\ldots,\{s_m\}) \to_G^+ (\{s_1\},\ldots,\{s_m\})$ be a cycle in G. By Lemma 4 we can assume it to be in normal form. Let $(\{s_1\},\ldots,\{s_m\}) \to_G^+ C$ be the increasing part and $C \to_G^* (\{s_1\},\ldots,\{s_m\})$ the decreasing part. Then, C is a solution to the equation.

For the other direction, let a solution C be given. Since C is contained in $post_C^+(\{s_1\},\ldots,\{s_m\})$ we can construct a monotonically increasing path $(\{s_1\},\ldots,\{s_m\}) \to_G^+ C$. Similarly, since $C \subseteq pre_C^*(\{s_1\},\ldots,\{s_m\})$, we get a decreasing path $C \to_G^* (\{s_1\},\ldots,\{s_m\})$. Hence, we get the desired cycle.   □

What is yet open is the question on which states s_1 to s_m to perform the search for a cycle. After all, we need that the corresponding configuration is reachable from an initial configuration. The idea is to use the set of all states reachable from an initial state in the client. Note that there is a live computation if and only if there is a live computation involving all those states. Indeed, if a state is not active during the cycle, the corresponding clients will stop moving after an initial set-up phase. Since the states reachable from an initial state can be computed in polynomial time [11], the proof of Theorem 1 is completed.

The liveness verification problem does not take fairness into account. A client may contribute to the live computation (and help the distinguished client reach a final state) without ever making progress towards its own final state.

4   Fair Liveness

We study the *fair liveness verification problem* that strengthens the requirement on the computation sought. Given a broadcast network $\mathcal{N} = (D, P)$ with clients $P = (Q, I, \delta)$ and a set of final states $F \subseteq Q$, the problem asks whether there is an infinite initialized computation π in which clients that send or receive messages infinitely often also visit their final states infinitely often, $\mathrm{Inf}(\pi) \subseteq \mathrm{Fin}(\pi)$. This requirement is also known as compassion or strong fairness [33].

Fair Liveness Verification
Input: A broadcast network $\mathcal{N} = (D, P)$ and final states $F \subseteq Q$.
Question: Is there an initialized computation π with $\mathrm{Inf}(\pi) \subseteq \mathrm{Fin}(\pi)$?

We solve the problem by applying the cycle finding algorithm from Sect. 3 to an instrumentation of the given broadcast network. Formally, given an instance

$(\mathcal{N}, F)$ of fair liveness, we construct a new broadcast network $\mathcal{N}_F$, containing several copies of Q. Recall that Q is the set of client states in $\mathcal{N}$. The construction ensures that cycles over Q in $\mathcal{N}_F$ correspond to cycles in $\mathcal{N}$ where each participating client sees a final state. Such cycles make up a fair computation. The main result is the following.

Theorem 7. *Fair liveness verification is in* P.

To explain the instrumentation, we need the notion of a good computation, where good means the computation respects fairness. Computation $c_1 \to^+ c_n$ is *good for* F, denoted $c_1 \Rightarrow_F c_n$, if every client i that makes a move during the computation, $i \in idx(c_j \to c_{j+1})$ for some j, also sees a final state in the computation, $c_k[i] \in F$ for some k. The following strengthens Lemma 2.

Lemma 8. *There is a fair computation from c_0 if and only if $c_0 \to^* c \Rightarrow_F c$.*

The broadcast network $\mathcal{N}_F$ is designed to detect good cycles $c \Rightarrow_F c$. The idea is to let the clients compute in phases. The original state space Q is the first phase. As soon as a client participates in the computation, it moves to a second phase given by a copy $\hat{Q}$ of Q. From this copy it enters a third phase $\tilde{Q}$ upon seeing a final state. From $\tilde{Q}$ it may return to Q.

Let the given broadcast network be $\mathcal{N} = (D, P)$ with $P = (Q, I, \delta)$. We define $\mathcal{N}_F = (D \cup \{n\}, P_F)$ with fresh symbol $n \notin D$ and extended client

$$P_F = (\bar{Q}, \tilde{I}, \bar{\delta}) \quad \text{where} \quad \bar{Q} = Q \cup \hat{Q} \cup \tilde{Q}.$$

For every transition $(q, a, q') \in \delta$, we have $(q, a, \hat{q}'), (\hat{q}, a, \hat{q}'), (\tilde{q}, a, \tilde{q}') \in \bar{\delta}$. For every final state $q \in F$ we have $(\hat{q}, !n, \tilde{q}) \in \bar{\delta}$. For every state $q \in Q$ we have $(\tilde{q}, !n, q) \in \bar{\delta}$. Configuration c admits a good cycle if and only if there is a cycle at c in the instrumented broadcast network. Even more, also an initial prefix can be mimicked by computations in the third phase.

Lemma 9. $c_0 \to^* c \Rightarrow_F c$ *in* $\mathcal{N}$ *if and only if* $\tilde{c}_0 \to^* c \to^+ c$ *in* $\mathcal{N}_F$.

We argue that the cycle can be mimicked, the reasoning for the prefix is simpler. A good cycle entails a cycle in the instrumented broadcast network. For the reverse direction, note that in c all clients are in states from Q. As soon as a client participates in the computation, it will move to $\hat{Q}$. To return to Q, the client will have to see a final state. This makes the computation good.

For the proof of Theorem 7, it is left to state the algorithm for finding a computation $\tilde{c}_0 \to^* c \to^+ c$ in $\mathcal{N}_F$. We compute the states reachable from an initial state in $\mathcal{N}_F$. As we are interested in a configuration c over Q, we intersect this set with Q. Both steps can be done in polynomial time. Let s_1 up to s_m be the states in the intersection. To these states we apply the fixed-point iteration from Lemma 6. By Lemma 3, the iteration witnesses the existence of a cycle over a configuration c of $\mathcal{N}_F$ that involves only the states s_1 up to s_m.

References

1. Abdulla, P.A., Atig, M.F., Rezine, O.: Verification of directed acyclic ad hoc networks. In: Beyer, D., Boreale, M. (eds.) FMOODS/FORTE -2013. LNCS, vol. 7892, pp. 193–208. Springer, Heidelberg (2013). https://doi.org/10.1007/978-3-642-38592-6_14
2. Akhiani, H., et al.: Cache coherence verification with TLA%. In: Wing, J.M., Woodcock, J., Davies, J. (eds.) FM 1999. LNCS, vol. 1709, p. 1871. Springer, Heidelberg (1999). https://doi.org/10.1007/3-540-48118-4_62
3. Apt, K.R., Kozen, D.: Limits for automatic verification of finite-state concurrent systems. Inf. Process. Lett. **22**(6), 307–309 (1986)
4. Balasubramanian, A.R., Bertrand, N., Markey, N.: Parameterized verification of synchronization in constrained reconfigurable broadcast networks. In: Beyer, D., Huisman, M. (eds.) TACAS 2018. LNCS, vol. 10806, pp. 38–54. Springer, Cham (2018). https://doi.org/10.1007/978-3-319-89963-3_3
5. Bertrand, N., Fournier, P., Sangnier, A.: Playing with probabilities in reconfigurable broadcast networks. In: Muscholl, A. (ed.) FoSSaCS 2014. LNCS, vol. 8412, pp. 134–148. Springer, Heidelberg (2014). https://doi.org/10.1007/978-3-642-54830-7_9
6. Bertrand, N., Fournier, P., Sangnier, A.: Distributed local strategies in broadcast networks. In: CONCUR. LIPIcs, vol. 42, pp. 44–57. Schloss Dagstuhl (2015)
7. Bloem, R., et al.: Decidability of Parameterized Verification. Synthesis Lectures on Distributed Computing Theory. Morgan & Claypool Publishers, San Rafael (2015)
8. Bouyer, P., Markey, N., Randour, M., Sangnier, A., Stan, D.: Reachability in networks of register protocols under stochastic schedulers. In: ICALP. LIPIcs, vol. 55, pp. 106:1–106:14. Schloss Dagstuhl (2016)
9. Chini, P., Meyer, R., Saivasan, P.: Fine-grained complexity of safety verification. In: Beyer, D., Huisman, M. (eds.) TACAS 2018. LNCS, vol. 10806, pp. 20–37. Springer, Cham (2018). https://doi.org/10.1007/978-3-319-89963-3_2
10. Delzanno, G.: Automatic verification of parameterized cache coherence protocols. In: Emerson, E.A., Sistla, A.P. (eds.) CAV 2000. LNCS, vol. 1855, pp. 53–68. Springer, Heidelberg (2000). https://doi.org/10.1007/10722167_8
11. Delzanno, G., Sangnier, A., Traverso, R., Zavattaro, G.: On the complexity of parameterized reachability in reconfigurable broadcast networks. In: FSTTCS. LIPIcs, vol. 18, pp. 289–300. Schloss Dagstuhl (2012)
12. Delzanno, G., Sangnier, A., Zavattaro, G.: Parameterized verification of ad hoc networks. In: Gastin, P., Laroussinie, F. (eds.) CONCUR 2010. LNCS, vol. 6269, pp. 313–327. Springer, Heidelberg (2010). https://doi.org/10.1007/978-3-642-15375-4_22
13. Delzanno, G., Sangnier, A., Zavattaro, G.: On the power of cliques in the parameterized verification of ad hoc networks. In: Hofmann, M. (ed.) FoSSaCS 2011. LNCS, vol. 6604, pp. 441–455. Springer, Heidelberg (2011). https://doi.org/10.1007/978-3-642-19805-2_30
14. Delzanno, G., Sangnier, A., Zavattaro, G.: Verification of ad hoc networks with node and communication failures. In: Giese, H., Rosu, G. (eds.) FMOODS/FORTE -2012. LNCS, vol. 7273, pp. 235–250. Springer, Heidelberg (2012). https://doi.org/10.1007/978-3-642-30793-5_15
15. D'Osualdo, E., Kochems, J., Ong, C.-H.L.: Automatic verification of erlang-style concurrency. In: Logozzo, F., Fähndrich, M. (eds.) SAS 2013. LNCS, vol. 7935, pp. 454–476. Springer, Heidelberg (2013). https://doi.org/10.1007/978-3-642-38856-9_24

16. D'Osualdo, E., Luke Ong, C.-H.: On hierarchical communication topologies in the π-calculus. In: Thiemann, P. (ed.) ESOP 2016. LNCS, vol. 9632, pp. 149–175. Springer, Heidelberg (2016). https://doi.org/10.1007/978-3-662-49498-1_7

17. Durand-Gasselin, A., Esparza, J., Ganty, P., Majumdar, R.: Model checking parameterized asynchronous shared-memory systems. In: Kroening, D., Păsăreanu, C.S. (eds.) CAV 2015. LNCS, vol. 9206, pp. 67–84. Springer, Cham (2015). https://doi.org/10.1007/978-3-319-21690-4_5

18. Esparza, J.: Some applications of Petri nets to the analysis of parameterised systems (talk). In: WISP (2003)

19. Esparza, J.: Keeping a crowd safe: on the complexity of parameterized verification (invited talk). In: STACS. LIPIcs, vol. 25, pp. 1–10. Schloss Dagstuhl (2014)

20. Esparza, J., Finkel, A., Mayr, R.: On the verification of broadcast protocols. In: LICS, pp. 352–359. IEEE (1999)

21. Esparza, J., Ganty, P., Majumdar, R.: Parameterized verification of asynchronous shared-memory systems. In: Sharygina, N., Veith, H. (eds.) CAV 2013. LNCS, vol. 8044, pp. 124–140. Springer, Heidelberg (2013). https://doi.org/10.1007/978-3-642-39799-8_8

22. Esparza, J., Nielsen, M.: Decidability issues for Petri nets - a survey. Bull. EATCS **52**, 244–262 (1994)

23. Fournier, P.: Parameterized verification of networks of many identical processes. Ph.D. thesis, University of Rennes 1 (2015)

24. Hague, M.: Parameterised pushdown systems with non-atomic writes. In: FSTTCS. LIPIcs, vol. 13, pp. 457–468. Schloss Dagstuhl (2011)

25. Hague, M., Meyer, R., Muskalla, S., Zimmermann, M.: Parity to safety in polynomial time for pushdown and collapsible pushdown systems. In: MFCS. LIPIcs, vol. 117, pp. 57:1–57:15. Schloss Dagstuhl (2018)

26. Hüchting, R., Majumdar, R., Meyer, R.: Bounds on mobility. In: Baldan, P., Gorla, D. (eds.) CONCUR 2014. LNCS, vol. 8704, pp. 357–371. Springer, Heidelberg (2014). https://doi.org/10.1007/978-3-662-44584-6_25

27. Joshi, S., König, B.: Applying the graph minor theorem to the verification of graph transformation systems. In: Gupta, A., Malik, S. (eds.) CAV 2008. LNCS, vol. 5123, pp. 214–226. Springer, Heidelberg (2008). https://doi.org/10.1007/978-3-540-70545-1_21

28. König, B., Kozioura, V.: Counterexample-guided abstraction refinement for the analysis of graph transformation systems. In: Hermanns, H., Palsberg, J. (eds.) TACAS 2006. LNCS, vol. 3920, pp. 197–211. Springer, Heidelberg (2006). https://doi.org/10.1007/11691372_13

29. Konnov, I.V., Lazic, M., Veith, H., Widder, J.: A short counterexample property for safety and liveness verification of fault-tolerant distributed algorithms. In: POPL, pp. 719–734. ACM (2017)

30. Meyer, R.: On boundedness in depth in the π-calculus. In: Ausiello, G., Karhumäki, J., Mauri, G., Ong, L. (eds.) TCS 2008. IIFIP, vol. 273, pp. 477–489. Springer, Boston, MA (2008). https://doi.org/10.1007/978-0-387-09680-3_32

31. Meyer, R., Strazny, T.: Petruchio: from dynamic networks to nets. In: Touili, T., Cook, B., Jackson, P. (eds.) CAV 2010. LNCS, vol. 6174, pp. 175–179. Springer, Heidelberg (2010). https://doi.org/10.1007/978-3-642-14295-6_19

32. Pnueli, A.: The temporal logic of programs. In: FOCS, pp. 46–57. IEEE (1977)

33. Pnueli, A., Sa'ar, Y.: All you need is compassion. In: Logozzo, F., Peled, D.A., Zuck, L.D. (eds.) VMCAI 2008. LNCS, vol. 4905, pp. 233–247. Springer, Heidelberg (2008). https://doi.org/10.1007/978-3-540-78163-9_21

34. Rabin, M.O., Scott, D.: Finite automata and their decision problems. IBM J. Res. Dev. **3**(2), 114–125 (1959)
35. Saksena, M., Wibling, O., Jonsson, B.: Graph grammar modeling and verification of ad hoc routing protocols. In: Ramakrishnan, C.R., Rehof, J. (eds.) TACAS 2008. LNCS, vol. 4963, pp. 18–32. Springer, Heidelberg (2008). https://doi.org/10.1007/978-3-540-78800-3_3
36. Singh, A., Ramakrishnan, C.R., Smolka, S.A.: Query-based model checking of ad hoc network protocols. In: Bravetti, M., Zavattaro, G. (eds.) CONCUR 2009. LNCS, vol. 5710, pp. 603–619. Springer, Heidelberg (2009). https://doi.org/10.1007/978-3-642-04081-8_40
37. Vardi, M., Wolper, P.: An automata-theoretic approach to automatic program verification. In: LICS, pp. 322–331. IEEE (1986)
38. Wies, T., Zufferey, D., Henzinger, T.A.: Forward analysis of depth-bounded processes. In: Ong, L. (ed.) FoSSaCS 2010. LNCS, vol. 6014, pp. 94–108. Springer, Heidelberg (2010). https://doi.org/10.1007/978-3-642-12032-9_8
39. Zufferey, D.: Analysis of Dynamic Message Passing Programs (a framework for the analysis of depth-bounded systems). Ph.D. thesis, Institute of Science and Technology (2013)

Formal Verification of UML State Machine Diagrams Using Petri Nets

Achraf Lyazidi$^{(\boxtimes)}$ (ID) and Salma Mouline (ID)

LRIT - CNRST URAC No. 29, Faculty of Sciences, Rabat IT Center,
Mohammed V University, Rabat, Morocco
lyazidi.achraf@gmail.com, salma.mouline@um5.ac.ma

Abstract. UML State Machine diagrams are widely used for behavioral modeling. They describe all of the possible states of a system and show its lifetime behavior. Nevertheless, they lack of semantics. A State Machine diagram may be interpreted in different manners that can lead to unwanted situations. In this paper, we propose a formal verification phase for UML State Machine diagrams using a formal language. The aim is to ensure UML State Machine diagrams properties to designers and to highlight errors. Petri nets, a formal notation for concurrent systems, are suitable for modeling systems behavior and they are well supported by analysis tools. Based on Model-Driven Engineering, we define a transformation from UML State Machine diagrams to Petri nets. The resulting Petri nets models are formally verified regarding properties. We also define a post-interpretation of the verification results in terms of UML State Machine diagrams.

Keywords: UML State Machine diagrams · Petri nets ·
Formal verification · Model transformation · Model-Driven Engineering

1 Introduction

UML State Machine diagram (UML-SMD) is a behavior model which describes discrete behavior of a system through states and transitions, and expresses its usage protocol. A UML-SMD uses additional information such as textual specification of actions and guards. The exact syntax of actions and guards is not defined within the UML specification. This leads to use languages such as English or more formally, expressions in a programming language (e.g., Java).

UML-SMDs can be interpreted in several ways, which can lead to undesirable situations. Then, a verification phase using a formal language is a necessary step. Another problem when verifying UML-SMDs is the lack of interpretation of the obtained results for designers who are not familiar with formal languages.

Many formal languages are used to formally verify UML-SMDs such as Automata or Petri Nets. In this work, we chose to use Petri Nets (PNs) due to their similarity to system behavior modeling represented with states and transitions. In this work, we present a Model-Driven Engineering approach transforming UML-SMDs to PNs for a formal verification purpose. We first implement a

© Springer Nature Switzerland AG 2019
M. F. Atig and A. A. Schwarzmann (Eds.): NETYS 2019, LNCS 11704, pp. 67–74, 2019.
https://doi.org/10.1007/978-3-030-31277-0_5

mapping between UML-SMDs and PNs. Then we analyse the PNs and present a post-interpretation phase of the verification results in terms of UML-SMDs.

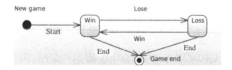

Fig. 1. An example of a UML State Machine diagram

The rest of the paper is structured as follows. Section 2 presents a reminder of UML State Machine diagrams and Petri nets. In Sect. 3 we present our transformation process and an illustration example. In Sect. 4 we conduct a case study with erroneous models to demonstrate our proposal along with the interpretation phase. Section 5 summarizes a brief state of the art while Sect. 6 concludes our paper.

2   Preliminaries

UML State Machine Diagrams: Within the Unified Modelling Language (UML), State Machine diagrams provide a graphical notation for describing dynamic aspects of system behaviour. UML-SMDs depict how an object reacts to different events. Creating a UML-SMD aims to explore the complex behavior of an object, an actor, a subsystem or a real-time system. For an introduction to UML-SMDs, you may refer to [1]. The UML-SMDs notation consists of main elements which are *Events, States, Guard Conditions, Actions, Transitions* and *Pseudo States.* Figure 1 presents a UML-SMD example of a simple game with *States* (New game, Win, Loss, Game end) and *Transitions* (Start, Lose, Win, End). Also, the UML-SMDs use other nodes such as *joins, forks, junctions,* or *choices* to graphically represent the flow of control. A UML-SMD is a graphical state diagram and a textual representation that accurately captures both the states topology and the actions. For that, a formal verification phase is primordial in order to obtain safe UML-SMDs. The objective is to ensure that the modeled system, or a part of it, is valid and satisfy behavioral properties. The properties we want to check concern the soundness (i.e., *Correctness, Safety*) and the vivacity (i.e., *Liveness*) of the desired system. These properties are:

– *Correctness:* System accuracy regarding modeling, elements connection and required properties to define within objects
– *Safety (Deadlock-free):* Non existence of failure behavior of the system or a part of it (system should not crash)
– *Liveness:* Termination of all the possible paths of the system (every path eventually terminates)

Petri Nets: PNs are a graphical mathematical language for modeling distributed systems. They are used to describe and study systems that can be concurrent, distributed, parallel or stochastic. A PN is represented by a directed and valued graph, in which nodes represent *places* (conditions, signified by circles) and *transitions* (events that may occur, signified by bars). Directed arcs (signified by arrows) describe which places are preconditions and/or postconditions for which transitions. Figure 2 shows an example of a PN with *places* (New game, Win, Loss, Game end) and *transitions* (Start, Win, Lose, End). For an introduction to PNs, you may refer to [2].

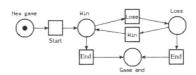

Fig. 2. An example of a Petri net model

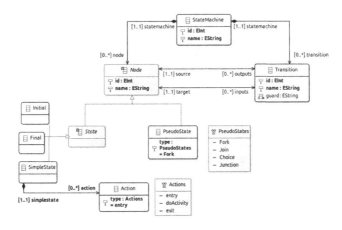

Fig. 3. UML State Machine diagrams metamodel

PNs have formal semantics that allow performing formal analysis and they are very well supported by analysis tools. They offer a graphical notation for stepwise processes that include choice, iteration, and simultaneous execution. The analysis results of a PN model may reveal failure cases and then enable improvement of it. PNs provide a good balance between modeling power and analyzability. They allow to verify structural and reachability properties such as *Liveness*, *Boundedness* and *Safety*.

3 Transforming UML State Machines into Petri Nets

To transform a UML-SMD into a PN model, we use a Model Driven Engineering
approach which supplies concepts, languages and tools to create and transform
models based on their metamodels and transformation rules respectively. Different metamodels exist for UML-SMDs. In order to stick with its specification
and all its elements, and based on the different metamodels we found, we propose and use the metamodel illustrated in Fig. 3. A UML-SMD is composed of
Nodes and *Transitions*. A *Node* can be a *State* or a *PseudoState*. A *State* can
be *Initial*, *Final* or a *Simple State* which is composed of *Actions*. For Petri net,
many metamodels can be found in the literature too. Figure 4 presents the used
metamodel for Petri nets in the transformation process. A Petri net contains
Nodes and *Arcs*. A *Node* can be a *Place* or a *Transition*.

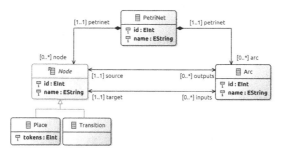

Fig. 4. Petri nets metamodel

Table 1. Mapping UML State Machine diagrams into Petri nets

UML State Machine object	Petri net module	Illustration
Transition	Arc	→
Node→State→Final	Place	○
Node→State→Initial		
Node→State→Simple State	Place + Arc + Transition	○—⊟
Node→PseudoState: Fork		
Node→PseudoState: Junction		
Node→PseudoState: Join	Place* + Arc* + Transition	
Node→PseudoState: Choice	Place + Arc* + Transition*	
Action	Arc + Place + Arc + Transition	→○—⊟

*: many

Our transformation consists in three steps. First, we define the transformation rules that transform UML-SMDs elements to PN elements (cf. Table 1). Then, we applied these rules to a UML-SMD. The obtained result is a PN. This latter is transformed into a textual PN file for analysis and verification. The generated textual PN is conform to TINA (TIme petri Net Analyzer) [3], a toolbox for editing and analysing PNs. The metamodels and the transformations rules (UMLSMD2PN and PN2TPN) are respectively defined using Ecore (a model defining manipulable concepts in Eclipse Modeling Framework (EMF) [4]) and the ATLAS Transformation Language (ATL) [5] within Eclipse IDE. In the next section, we will illustrate our transformation with a case study.

4 Case Study

To illustrate our proposal, we conduct a case study. First, we apply the transformation process to some UML-SMD examples about smart home components with modeling errors as shown in Fig. 5. The example (a) presents an error at the *user* state which will trigger the state *Location* and the UML-SMD will be blocked in the *join* node, and the example (b) presents an error in the transitions between the states *Windows* and *Close* which will run infinitely. Then, we analyse the generated PN shown in Fig. 6 using the TINA toolbox in order to interpret the analysis

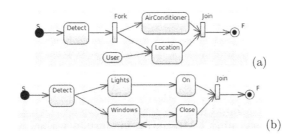

Fig. 5. The UML State Machine diagram examples

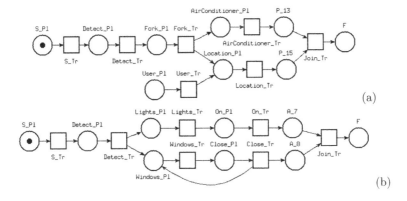

Fig. 6. The generated Petri nets from the UML State Machine diagrams in Fig. 5

results in term of UML-SMDs properties. Note that all The UML-SMDs are valid within the editor (Eclipse), and that we have not listed all experienced examples to respect the page limit.

Table 2. Analysis results of the generated Petri nets (cf. Fig. 6) and their interpretation

Model	Analysis results	UML interpretation
(a)	Bounded; Not live; 1 Dead place; 1 Dead transition	⊗ Liveness ⊗ Safety
(b)	Not bounded; Not live; The marking increases to infinity	⊗ Liveness ⊗ Safety ⊗ Correctness

⊗ Unsatisfied property

The analysis results of the generated PN and their interpretation in term of UML-SMDs are shown in Table 2. The analysis of the model (a) shows that the PN contains 1 dead transition and 1 dead place. Also, the PN is not live. In fact, in the corresponding UML-SMD (a), the Simple State *User* will never be targeted. Note that the syntax checks of all the PNs are successful.

Our approach will allow the detection of expected errors. The aim is to prevent structural errors to the UML-SMDs designers while remaining within the design phase before the delicate implementation phase. The proposed transformation and interpretation phase enable to verify all the required UML State Machines properties cited in Sect. 2.

5   Related Works

Several works exists to formally verify UML-SMDs. We can classify them into two categories: PN-based and non PN-based approaches. Since there is a lot of contributions in transforming UML-SMDs for formal verification purpose, we limit this related works section to transformations that take into account the semantic power of the target language, the consistency of the transformation and the properties to be verified. For the non PN-based approaches, most of the existing approaches use model checking techniques such as [6–9].

Using PNs, many works exist in translating UML-SMDs to PNs derivative and extensions. In [10], UML State Machines are automatically translated into generalized stochastic PNs and a composition of the resulting net models suitable for reaching a given analysis goal (validation, performance evaluation) in order to apply mathematical techniques on UML models for system validation since they lack of formal semantics. The authors of [11] describe a methodology to develop a colored PN of a system. The technic is to derive a system-level colored PN from UML-SMDs then, this system can be analyzed by various formal PN analysis techniques. The goal is the validation of UML behavioral specifications.

A mapping approach between systems specified using UML diagrams and colored PN notations is proposed in [12] to support systematic simulation of such models. Along with a description of a prototype tool, simulation results are provided in form of self-defined trace files and Message Sequence Charts. In order to formalize non-concurrent UML-SMDs, the works in [13] and [14] introduce an algorithm to automatically generate a colored PN model associated with a State Machine description to provide a formal specification. However, the authors do not consider concurrent aspects such as fork and join. They implement this translation in an automated manner using the model-to-text transformation tool Acceleo for the application of model checking techniques that could guarantee the system safety. In [15], a PN based approach to Formally Verify UML State Diagrams is proposed. By translating UML state diagrams into Coloured PNs, desired properties can be checked automatically. The issue is to supply formal verification techniques of UML diagrams that are completely automatic and transparent to the designer.

The works cited above still present limitations such as the lack of verification of the all desired properties. Some approaches aim to check only one or two of these properties while others try to verify all the properties but take into account a limited UML-SMDs elements. Other works only present a transformation process without the analysis phase. Another lack is the absence of interpretation of the results of analysis in terms of the source language (UML-SMDs) to designers.

Our proposal overcomes these limits by taking account all the necessary elements of UML-SMDs, allowing the verification of properties such as Safety, Liveness and Correctness of the modeled diagrams and offering a post interpretation phase in term of UML-SMDs for designers who are not supposed to be familiar with the used target formalism (PNs).

6   Conclusion

In this paper, we present a formal verification phase for UML State Machine diagrams. Using an MDE approach, we transform UML State Machine diagrams into Petri nets for validation and verification of these latter regarding their structures. We also present the interpretation of the verification results to UML designers who are not supposed to be familiar with the used formal languages. This phase that is not taken into account by other existing transformations.

References

1. Drusinsky, D.: Modeling and Verification Using UML Statecharts: A Working Guide to Reactive System Design, Runtime Monitoring and Execution-Based Model Checking. Elsevier, Amsterdam (2011)
2. Murata, T.: Petri nets: properties, analysis and applications. Proc. IEEE **77**(4), 541–580 (1989)
3. Berthomieu, B., Vernadat, F.: Time Petri nets analysis with TINA. In: QEST, vol. 6, pp. 123–124, September 2006
4. Budinsky, F., Steinberg, D., Ellersick, R., Grose, T.J., Merks, E.: Eclipse Modeling Framework: A Developer's Guide. Addison-Wesley Professional, Boston (2004)

5. Jouault, F., Allilaire, F., Bézivin, J., Kurtev, I.: ATL: a model transformation tool. Sci. Comput. Program. **72**(1–2), 31–39 (2008)
6. David, A., Möller, M.O., Yi, W.: Formal verification of UML statecharts with real-time extensions. In: Kutsche, R.-D., Weber, H. (eds.) FASE 2002. LNCS, vol. 2306, pp. 218–232. Springer, Heidelberg (2002). https://doi.org/10.1007/3-540-45923-5_15
7. Latella, D., Majzik, I., Massink, M.: Automatic verification of a behavioural subset of UML statechart diagrams using the SPIN model-checker. Formal Aspects Comput. **11**(6), 637–664 (1999)
8. Knapp, A., Merz, S.: Model checking and code generation for UML state machines and collaborations. In: Proceedings 5th Wsh. Tools for System Design and Verification, pp. 59–64 (2002)
9. Jussila, T., Dubrovin, J., Junttila, T., Latvala, T., Porres, I., Linz, J.K.U.: Model checking dynamic and hierarchical UML state machines. In: Proceedings MoDeV2a: Model Development, Validation and Verification, Genova, Italy, pp. 94–110 (2006)
10. Bernardi, S., Donatelli, S., Merseguer, J.: From UML sequence diagrams and statecharts to analysable Petri net models. In: Proceedings of the 3rd International Workshop on Software and Performance, Rome, Italy, pp. 35–45. ACM, July 2002
11. Saldhana, J., Shatz, S. M.: UML diagrams to object Petri net models: an approach for modeling and analysis. In: International Conference on Software Engineering and Knowledge Engineering, Chicago, IL, USA, pp. 103–110, July 2000
12. Hu, Z., Shatz, S.M.: Mapping UML diagrams to a Petri net notation for system simulation. In: International Conference on Software Engineering and Knowledge Engineering, Anbert, Canada, pp. 213–219, June 2004
13. André, É., Choppy, C., Klai, K.: Formalizing non-concurrent UML state machines using colored Petri nets. SIGSOFT Softw. Eng. Notes **37**(4), 1–8 (2012)
14. André, E., Benmoussa, M.M., Choppy, C.: Translating UML state machines to coloured Petri nets using Acceleo: a report. In: Proceedings of the Third International Workshop on Engineering Safety and Security Systems, Singapore, pp. 1–7 (2014)
15. Choppy, C., Klai, K., Zidani, H.: Formal verification of UML state diagrams: a Petri net based approach. SIGSOFT Softw. Eng. Notes **36**(1), 1–8 (2011)

Synthesize Models for Quantitative Analysis Using Automata Learning

Yu-Fang Chen[1]([✉]), Hsiao-Chen Chung[1], Wen-Chi Hung[1,2], Ming-Hsien Tsai[1], Bow-Yaw Wang[1], and Farn Wang[2]

[1] Institute of Information Science, Academia Sinica, Taipei, Taiwan
yfc@iis.sinica.edu.tw
[2] Graduate Institute of Electronic Engineering, National Taiwan University, Taipei, Taiwan

Abstract. We apply a *probably approximately correct* learning algorithm for multiplicity automata to generate quantitative models of system behaviors with a statistical guarantee. Using the generated model, we give two analysis algorithms to estimate the minimum and average values of system behaviors. We show how to apply the learning algorithm even when the alphabet is not fixed. The experimental result is encouraging; the estimation made by our approach is almost as precise as the exact reference answer obtained by a brute-force enumeration.

1 Introduction

Limited resources such as time and space are crucial factors in system evaluation. Quantitative analysis of system behaviors subsequently has become an important research issue in recent years [12,13]. Usually, models are required to describe system behaviors during analysis. Quantitative model construction, however, can be as difficult as the analysis itself if not more. Consider analyzing the amount of data transmission in web browsing. When a user clicks on a hyperlink, a new page is generated and sent from the server through Internet. Suppose we would like to estimate the average amount of data transmission from a certain website over k hyperlink clicks. Usually, the first thing to do is to construct a system model with a suitable abstraction. However, it is not immediately clear how to build an abstract quantitative model for such system behaviors automatically.

We apply a *probably approximately correct* (PAC) learning algorithm for *multiplicity automata* to generate abstract models for quantitative system behaviors. Multiplicity automata are the class of *weighted automata* over the semiring $(\mathbb{R}, +, \times, 0, 1)$. We model system behaviors by words in the alphabet of a multiplicity automaton. The quantity (such as the amount of data transmission) associated with a system behavior is hence the result of the automaton on the input word. Through a teacher who simulates the system on a given input and measures the quantity of interest, the learning algorithm can infer a multiplicity automaton as an approximation to quantitative system behaviors with a statistical guarantee. Unlike most applications in verification, we do not aim for *exact*

© Springer Nature Switzerland AG 2019
M. F. Atig and A. A. Schwarzmann (Eds.): NETYS 2019, LNCS 11704, pp. 75–92, 2019.
https://doi.org/10.1007/978-3-030-31277-0_6

quantitative models of system behaviors but their *approximations* instead. For quantitative analysis, quantities of system behaviors (such as response time, distance to a target, heat generation, and power consumption) are often measured and hence imprecise. Inferring exact quantitative models is not very meaningful in the presence of measurement errors. Moreover, exact learning is impossible when the target cannot be characterized mechanically or expressed by the model in use. Indeed, approximate quantitative models may suffice for certain quantitative analyses such as average response time. Exact models are not necessary for such analyses even if they are attainable.

After a multiplicity automaton is inferred, we show how to analyze the minimum and average values of system behaviors with a fixed length k in Sect. 5. The transitions of a multiplicity automaton with an alphabet of size n can be represented by a matrix whose entries are polynomials of degree n. For behaviors of length k, they can be represented by a multivariate polynomial of degree kn. The polynomial enables us to perform various quantitative analyses with standard mathematical tools. For instance, we can compute an approximation of the minimum amount of data transmission for k hyperlink clicks in web browsing by *gradient descent*.

Some practical issues on applying learning to quantitative analysis are addressed in Sect. 6. The algorithm assumes a fixed alphabet. In practice, the alphabet may not be known in advance. We give an algorithm which increases the alphabet when necessary. Also, note that the inferred quantitative model is just an approximation, it may give meaningless values (such as a negative amount of data transmission) on certain behaviors due to its inaccuracy. We give a simple amendment to prevent meaningless analysis results.

Our approach has several advantages. For example, once the mapping between words and system behaviors has been decided, the approach runs fully automatically. After the quantitative models are computed, different analyses can be performed on them without further simulation. For instance, suppose we would like to analyze the average amount of data transmission for $1, \ldots, k$ hyperlink clicks from the home page. These k analyses can all be carried out on the same inferred approximate model. The quantitative model can also be reused for other types of analyses (such as the maximum amount of data transmission). The experimental results in Sect. 8 suggest that the estimation produced by our learning-based approach is almost as precise as the exact reference answer obtained by a brute-force enumeration.

Related Works. Exact learning algorithms for classical automata was first proposed by Angluin [2]. The result has been generalized to the class of multiplicity automata in [5,16]. The concept of probably approximately correct (PAC) learning was first proposed by Valiant in his seminal work [19]. The idea of turning an exact learning algorithm to a PAC learning algorithm can be found in [3]. PAC learning has been applied to testing and verification [9,11,20]. The work [20] considers the problem from a theoretical aspect. It focuses on issues such as the lower bound on the number of required queries to infer a system model. The work [11] tests if the output of a graph-manipulating program is bipartite,

k-colorable, etc. The authors of [9] apply PAC-learning to infer a model of a computer program and then verify if any assertion violation can occur in the model. To the best of our knowledge, PAC-learning techniques have not been applied to infer quantitative models of systems before. Both our approach and statistical model checking [14,17,21] provide a statistical guarantee. Statistical model checking assumes a given model while ours generates models with a statistical guarantee. The inferred models can be reused for different properties.

Contributions. The contributions of our work are threefold.

(a) A framework that automatically extracts quantitative models via learning with a statistical guarantee.
(b) Efficient and effective algorithms to check interesting quantitative properties of multiplicity automata.
(c) Careful analysis of the capacity of the learning algorithm when applied to construct quantitative models and suggestions on effective optimizations.

2   Preliminaries

We assume $\mathbb{N}$ is the set of natural numbers. Matrices and vectors are over real numbers $\mathbb{R}$. For a matrix M, $[M]_{(i,*)}$ is the i-th row of M and $[M]_{(i,j)}$ is the entry at row i and column j. For a vector $\boldsymbol{u}$, $\boldsymbol{u}(i)$ is its i-th entry. We assume all vectors in this paper are column vectors. We use $\mathbb{R}^{m \times n}$ and $\mathbb{R}^k$ to denote the sets of matrices of size $m \times n$ and column vectors of size k, respectively. The product of two matrices M_1, M_2 is denoted as $M_1 M_2$ and the product of k copies of M is denoted as M^k. We use a, b, c, d to denote symbols, w, x, y to denote words, λ to denote the empty word, and v to denote variables. The concatenation of two words x, y is denoted as $x \cdot y$. The set of integers $\{k \mid m \le k \le n\}$ is denoted as $[m, n]$ and $[n]$ is a shorthand for $[1, n]$.

A *multiplicity automaton* (MA) $\mathcal{A} = (\mathcal{M}, \boldsymbol{b})$ over a finite alphabet Σ is represented as a set of *transition matrices* $\mathcal{M} = \{M_a \in \mathbb{R}^{n \times n} \mid a \in \Sigma\}$ (one matrix for each symbol in Σ) and an *output vector* $\boldsymbol{b} \in \mathbb{R}^n$. The output of an MA $\mathcal{A}$ corresponding to a word $w = d_1 d_2 \cdots d_m \in \Sigma^+$ is $\mathcal{A}(w) = [M_{d_1} M_{d_2} \ldots M_{d_m}]_{(1,*)} \boldsymbol{b}$ and $\mathcal{A}(\lambda) = \boldsymbol{b}(1)$. Intuitively, the entry $[M_a]_{(i,j)}$ is the *weight of the transition* from state q_i to state q_j with symbol a and $\boldsymbol{b}(i)$ is the *weight of the state* q_i. The initial state is q_1. The output of an MA w.r.t. a word w is the sum of the *weight of all *runs* (sequences of transitions) corresponding to w, where the weight of a run is the product of the weights of the last state and all transitions in the run. An example of an MA from the view of a set of matrices and also the view of a labeled state-transition system is given in Fig. 1.

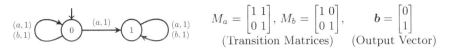

$$M_a = \begin{bmatrix} 1 & 1 \\ 0 & 1 \end{bmatrix}, \quad M_b = \begin{bmatrix} 1 & 0 \\ 0 & 1 \end{bmatrix}, \quad \boldsymbol{b} = \begin{bmatrix} 0 \\ 1 \end{bmatrix}$$
(Transition Matrices)   (Output Vector)

Fig. 1. An MA computes the number of occurrences of symbol a (Example 5.3 of [6]).

The *Hankel matrix* (HM) of a function $f : \Sigma^* \to \mathbb{R}$ is an infinite matrix F indexed with words from Σ^* such that $[F]_{(x,y)} = f(x \cdot y)$. Let $f : \Sigma^* \to \mathbb{R}$ be a function with the corresponding HM F. For short, we use the *rank of f*, denoted $rank(f)$, to mean the rank of the HM corresponding to f. We say an MA $\mathcal{A}$ is *equivalent* to f iff $\forall w \in \Sigma^* : \mathcal{A}(w) = f(w)$. It has been shown in [8,10] that if $r = rank(f)$ is finite then the smallest MA $\mathcal{A}$ equivalent to f has r states. More concretely, let $[F]_{(x_1,*)}, [F]_{(x_2,*)}, \dots, [F]_{(x_r,*)}$ be r independent rows of F with $x_1 = \lambda$. One can construct an equivalent MA $\mathcal{A} = (\mathcal{M}, \boldsymbol{b})$ from F as follows. The output vector $\boldsymbol{b}$ is $([F]_{(x_1,\lambda)}, [F]_{(x_2,\lambda)}, \dots, [F]_{(x_r,\lambda)})$. The transition matrices $M_a \in \mathcal{M}$ can be obtained by solving the following equation for each $a \in \Sigma, i \in [r]$:

$$[F]_{(x_i \cdot a,*)} = \sum_{j \in [r]} [M_a]_{(i,j)} [F]_{(x_j,*)}. \tag{1}$$

Intuitively, Eq. (1) states that the weight from the state represented by the word $x_i \cdot a$ to any state q is equivalent to the sum of the weights from state q_i to all other state q_j via the symbol a multiplies the weight from q_j to q for all $j \in [r]$.

3   Learning Algorithm of Multiplicity Automata

Now we have all the building blocks required to describe the learning algorithm for MA proposed by Beimel et al. [4], under the *minimal adequate teacher* (MAT) model by Angluin [2]. The MAT model assumes the existence of a *teacher* answering two types of queries about a function $f : \Sigma^* \to \mathbb{R}$: (a) On *membership queries* of a word w, denoted $Mem(w)$, the teacher replies $f(w)$. (b) On *equivalence queries* of an MA $\mathcal{A}_h$, denoted $Equ(\mathcal{A}_h)$, the teacher replies true when $\mathcal{A}$ is equivalent to f. Otherwise, it replies false accompanying with a word w s.t. $\mathcal{A}_h(w) \neq f(w)$. Let F be the HM of the target function f. When $r = rank(f)$ is finite, it is sufficient to characterize f using an $r \times r$ sub-matrix of F (with rank r) [4]. The learning algorithm (in Fig. 2) tries to find such an $r \times r$ matrix.

Assume that the rank of the target function f is finite and let $r = rank(f)$. For the MA learning algorithm in Fig. 2, the content of $[F_Y]_{(x,*)}, [F_Y]_{(x \cdot a,*)}$ can be obtained by $r(r + r|\Sigma|)$ membership queries, where Y is the set of current *experiments*. The existence of a prefix satisfying conditions (a) and (b) is guaranteed by Claim 3.1 of [4] and it takes only polynomially many membership queries to find such a prefix. Observe that adding y_{l+1} to Y is sufficient to make the row of x_{l+1} independent with all other rows in X. The learning algorithm will find an MA with r states that is equivalent to f in r iterations.

Probably Approximately Correct Learning
The MA learning algorithm assumes a teacher who can answer equivalence queries. This assumption is invalid in many practical settings. Angluin [3] showed that even if we substitute equivalence testing with sampling, we can still make statistical claims about the difference between the target and inferred model.

Assume the target function for MA learning is $f : \Sigma^* \to \mathbb{R}$ and a probability distribution D over Σ^* is given. We use $\varphi(w)$ to denote that the inferred MA

Input: The alphabet Σ and a teacher answers $Mem(w)$ and $Equ(\mathcal{A})$ about f.
Init: $x_1 \mapsto \lambda; y_1 \mapsto \lambda; X \mapsto \{x_1\}; Y \mapsto \{y_1\}; l \mapsto 1$.
Step(I): Generate a candidate MA $\mathcal{A}_h$:
- The output vector is $(Mem(x_1), \ldots, Mem(x_l))$.
- Let F_Y be a sub-matrix of F obtained by restricting the columns to the index Y. Observe that each row of F_Y has l elements, but F_Y has infinitely many rows. For each $a \in \Sigma$, the transition matrix M_a can be obtained by solving for each $i \in [l]$ the following equation, which is an adaptation of Equation (1):

$$[F_Y]_{(x_i \cdot a, *)} = \sum_{j \in [l]} [M_a]_{(i,j)} [F_Y]_{(x_j, *)}.$$

Step(II): Ask an equivalence query on $\mathcal{A}_h$:
- If the answer is true, halt and output $\mathcal{A}_h$.
- Otherwise, the teacher returns a word w s.t. $\mathcal{A}_h(w) \neq f(w)$.
- Analyze w and find the pair (x_{l+1}, y_{l+1}) as follows:
  * Search for a prefix $d_1 \cdots d_k a$ of w satisfying the conditions:
    (a) $[F_Y]_{(d_1 \cdots d_k, *)} = \sum_{j \in [l]} [M_{d_1} \ldots M_{d_k}]_{(1,j)} [F_Y]_{(x_j, *)}$
    (b) $\exists y \in Y : [F_Y]_{(d_1 \cdots d_k a, y)} \neq \sum_{j \in [l]} [M_{d_1} \ldots M_{d_k}]_{(1,j)} [F_Y]_{(x_j \cdot a, y)}$
  * Assign $x_{l+1} := d_1 \cdots d_k$ and $y_{l+1} := a \cdot y$.
- Reassign $X \mapsto X \cup \{x_{l+1}\}; Y \mapsto Y \cup \{y_{l+1}\}; l \mapsto l + 1$ and goto Step(I).

Fig. 2. The learning algorithm for MA

$\mathcal{A}_h$ and f are consistent on w, i.e., $\mathcal{A}_h(w) = f(w)$. The term $Prob_{w \Leftarrow D}[\neg \varphi(w)]$ denotes the probability that $\varphi(w)$ is false for w chosen randomly according to D. For a hypothesis of the form

$$H : Prob_{w \Leftarrow D}[\neg \varphi(w)] \leq \epsilon,$$

we call ϵ the *error* parameter and use *confidence* to denote the least probability that the hypothesis H is correct. We say that an inferred MA is *probably approximately correct* (PAC) [19] w.r.t. ϵ and δ, denoted $PAC(\epsilon, \delta)$, if H holds with confidence δ. In the example of estimating the amount of data transmission, $f(w)$ denotes the actual amount of data transmission with the input w and $\mathcal{A}_h$ is the inferred MA. Consider the uniform distribution D_k over all words of length k and $(\epsilon, \delta) = (0.1, 0.9)$. We say $\mathcal{A}_h$ is $PAC(\epsilon, \delta)$ if with probability at least 90%, the probability that $f(w)$ and $\mathcal{A}_h(w)$ are different is bounded by 10% when w is chosen uniformly from words of length k.

The task of an equivalence query $Equ(\mathcal{A}_h)$ is changed from checking *exact* equivalence to checking *approximate* equivalence. More concretely, Step(II) in Fig. 2 is replaced with the one in Fig. 3.

The teacher answers the i-th equivalence query by picking n_i samples according to D and testing if $\mathcal{A}_h(w) = f(w)$ for all samples w. The number of samples n_i needed to establish that $\mathcal{A}_h$ is $PAC(\epsilon, \delta)$ is given by Angluin in [3] (page 326). Note that the target function f is not necessary of a finite rank. When f is of an infinite rank, the learning algorithm can still infer an MA $\mathcal{A}$ approximating f with a statistical guarantee.

Step(II): Simulate the equivalence query on $\mathcal{A}_h$ by sampling:

- Let $i = 1; n_l = \left\lceil \frac{1}{\epsilon} \left(\ln \frac{1}{1-\delta} + l \ln 2 \right) \right\rceil$.
- Repeat the following steps until $i > n_l$:
  1: Sample a word w according to D and reassign $i := i + 1$.
  2: If $\mathcal{A}_h(w) \neq f(w)$, analyze w and find a pair (x_{l+1}, y_{l+1}) using the approach in Figure 2, reassign $X \mapsto X \cup \{x_{l+1}\}; Y \mapsto Y \cup \{y_{l+1}\}; l \mapsto l + 1$, and goto (I).
- Halt and output $\mathcal{A}_h$.

Fig. 3. Replacing equivalence query with sampling. It assumes the following additional input: a distribution D over Σ^*, the parameters $0 < \epsilon, \delta < 1$.

4   Overview

The learning algorithm for MA will be applied to construct a quantitative model of system behaviors. Fix an alphabet Σ for system actions. Assume that the system behavior on $w \in \Sigma^*$ can be modeled by the quantity $f(w) \in \mathbb{R}$ for some unknown $f : \Sigma^* \to \mathbb{R}$.

The framework has three components: Teacher, Learner, and Analyzer. The Learner obtains information about the target system by posing queries to the Teacher. The Teacher measures the quantity $f(w)$ by simulating the system on w. On a membership query $Mem(w)$, the Teacher answers the query by measuring the quantity $f(w)$. On an equivalence query $Equ(\mathcal{A}_h)$, the Teacher checks if $\mathcal{A}_h(w)$ and the measured quantity $f(w)$ coincide on a number of randomly chosen w. If so, the Teacher concludes that the MA $\mathcal{A}_h$ represents the unknown function f with a statistical guarantee and the Learner will pass $\mathcal{A}_h$ to the Analyzer for further analysis. Otherwise, the Teacher returns w_0 with $\mathcal{A}_h(w_0) \neq f(w_0)$.

Once an approximation $\mathcal{A}$ to the unknown function f is obtained from the Learner, the Analyzer transforms $\mathcal{A}$ to a multivariate polynomial $g_k(d_1, d_2, \ldots, d_k)$ which encodes $\mathcal{A}(d_1 d_2 \cdots d_k)$ for any $d_1 d_2 \cdots d_k \in \Sigma^k$. The transformation to the polynomial form allows us to perform various quantitative analyses using powerful mathematical tools. Particularly, we are interested in the minimum and average of system behaviors on inputs of length k. Section 5 explains how to analyze such properties based on the polynomial g_k.

Limitations of the learning algorithm are found during our case studies. The learning algorithm presumes a fixed alphabet. The alphabet, however, is not predetermined when we analyze the average amount of data transmission from a website. In the example, the number of hyperlinks per page (the size of alphabet) is not known *a priori*. Moreover, recall that the inferred MA $\mathcal{A}$ is an approximation to the unknown function f. When $\mathcal{A}$ is used to compute the minimum of f, the result can be a value that is not a possible outcome of the system under analysis. For instance, a negative minimum waiting time may be computed from $\mathcal{A}$. We develop approaches to address those practical limitations in Sect. 6.

In Sects. 7 and 8, four examples are used to showcase how to design effective Teachers and evaluate the performance of the proposed approach. The experimental results suggest that the estimation made by our approach is very precise; it is very close to the exact reference answer obtained by enumeration.

5   Analyzing Properties of Multiplicity Automata

When the learning algorithm finds an MA $\mathcal{A}$ for the target system, the next step is to analyze the quantitative properties of $\mathcal{A}$. Two interesting quantitative properties of MA are identified: (1) the minimum/maximum output value of an MA from an input of length k and (2) the average output value of an MA from all inputs of length k. A naive way to compute the minimum/maximum or average output values of a given MA is to enumerate all inputs of length k and compute the corresponding output. It is easy to see that the naive approach cannot scale to a large k. So our goal is to develop more efficient algorithms to compute these values.

Assuming that the Analyzer receives an MA $\mathcal{A} = (\mathcal{M}, \boldsymbol{b})$, where $\mathcal{M} = \{M_a \in \mathbb{R}^{n \times n} \mid a \in \Sigma\}$ and $\Sigma \subset \mathbb{N}$, from the Learner. It will transform $\mathcal{A}$ to a *multivariate polynomial* $g_k(d_1, d_2, \ldots, d_k) : \mathbb{R}^k \to \mathbb{R}$ that outputs the value of $\mathcal{A}(d_1 d_2 \cdots d_k)$ when $d_1 d_2 \cdots d_k \in \Sigma^k$.

The transformation is similar to the one in [4] using interpolation. We first define $p(v)$, an $n \times n$ matrix of polynomials over the variable v, as follows.

$$p(v) = \sum_{a \in \Sigma} \left(\left(\prod_{b \in \Sigma \setminus \{a\}} \frac{v - b}{a - b} \right) M_a \right)$$

Example 1. Consider the MA in Fig. 1. We use $0, 1$ to represent a, b, respectively. Then

$$p(v) = (\frac{v - 1}{0 - 1} M_a) + (\frac{v - 0}{1 - 0} M_b) = \begin{bmatrix} 1 & (1 - v) \\ 0 & 1 \end{bmatrix}.$$

Observe that $\forall a \in \Sigma : p(a) = M_a$. Then $g_k(v_1, \ldots, v_k)$ is defined as $g_k(v_1, \ldots, v_k) = [p(v_1)p(v_2) \ldots p(v_k)]_{(1,*)} \boldsymbol{b}$. Observe that $g_k(v_1, \ldots, v_k)$ is indeed a multivariate polynomial satisfying all requirements specified above. In principle, standard calculus techniques can be applied to analyze properties (such as optimal values or average) of the multivariate polynomial $g_k(v_1, \ldots, v_k)$. However, $g_k(v_1, \ldots, v_k)$ contains many monomials with very large rational coefficients. It takes a lot of time to compute the exact polynomial because all those rational coefficients have to be computed symbolically. On the other hand, approximating those rational coefficients using floating-point numbers gives very inaccurate analysis results due to numerical errors. Although the multivariate polynomial g_k represents $\mathcal{A}$ in theory, it is very costly to compute g_k explicitly and hence is not immediately useful in practice. Below we describe more practical approaches to compute the minimum/maximum and average value of g_k.

Computing the Minimum/Maximum Value of g_k The global optimization problem of multivariate polynomial is known to be very difficult. It is already NP-hard when the degree is 4 [15]. Here we suggest to use the *gradient descent* (GD) algorithm or any similar algorithm[1] to find a local minimum/maximum of g_k instead.

---

[1] In our implementation, we use a similar gradient-based algorithm, called *sequential quadratic programming (SQP)* [7], implemented in the *fmincon* function of Matlab.

Let $V = \{v_i \mid i \in [k]\}$. Intuitively, the GD algorithm begins with an arbitrarily chosen initial assignment $\eta : V \to \mathbb{R}$. It searches in g_k the direction from η leading to the steepest downward gradient and picks another assignment by moving from η toward the chosen direction for a distance. The steeper the gradient is, the longer the distance is. The algorithm repeats the above procedure to obtain better assignments. It terminates when, e.g., the distance to move becomes very small, which indicates that an assignment close to a local minimum/maximum is reached. Note that the GD algorithm does not need the polynomial g_k explicitly. It only requires the values of g_k on the selected assignments. Since $g_k(d_1, \ldots, d_k) = [p(d_1)p(d_2) \ldots p(d_k)]_{(1,*)} \boldsymbol{b}$, we simply use the MA $\mathcal{A}$ to compute the values of $p(d_1), p(d_2), \ldots, p(d_k)$ on given assignments. When the GD algorithm is applied to our analysis, it begins with an arbitrarily chosen assignment from V to the discrete domain Σ^k. However, the GD algorithm may still find an assignment η' outside Σ^k when it terminates. In this case, our procedure searches all "neighboring" assignments to η' over Σ^k and pick the one with the minimum/maximum output w.r.t g_k.

Computing the Average Value of g_k
The average value can be obtained by computing the sum using the following formula and then dividing it by $|\Sigma|^k$.

$$\sum_{d_1 \in \Sigma} \sum_{d_2 \in \Sigma} \cdots \sum_{d_k \in \Sigma} g_k(d_1, \ldots, d_k)$$

$$= \sum_{d_1 \in \Sigma} \sum_{d_2 \in \Sigma} \cdots \sum_{d_k \in \Sigma} [p(d_1)p(d_2) \ldots p(d_k)]_{(1,*)} \boldsymbol{b} \qquad (2)$$

$$= \left[\left(\sum_{d_1 \in \Sigma} p(d_1) \right) \left(\sum_{d_2 \in \Sigma} p(d_2) \right) \cdots \left(\sum_{d_k \in \Sigma} p(d_k) \right) \right]_{(1,*)} \boldsymbol{b}$$

$$= \left[\left(\sum_{d \in \Sigma} M_d \right)^k \right]_{(1,*)} \boldsymbol{b} \qquad (3)$$

Sometimes we are only interested in the average value w.r.t. a subset S of Σ. Such an average value can be computed by replacing Σ in (3) with S. Observe that the computation of (2) is more expensive than (3). The former uses $k|\Sigma|^k$ matrix product operations, while the latter uses only k product operations.

6   Optimizations

In this section, approaches to address some practical limitations of our learning-based algorithm are discussed.

Learning the Alphabet Symbols Incrementally. Recall that the MA learning algorithm assumes a finite alphabet Σ. The assumption does not hold for systems

such as a website. We propose an adaption to the learning algorithm to eliminate the assumption. The main idea is to incrementally build the alphabet Σ.
Initially, we assume $\Sigma = \emptyset$.[2] If a word w sampled according to D contains new
symbols, i.e., $sym(w) \not\subseteq \Sigma$, we reassign $\Sigma := \Sigma \cup sym(w)$ and use **Step(I)** of the
learning algorithm to rebuild $\mathcal{A}_h$. The update of the alphabet Σ will eventually
terminate, provided that the distribution D is over words constructed from a
finite alphabet. The algorithm is obtained by modifying the **Step(II)** in Fig. 2
to the one in Fig. 4. Later we will see in Sect. 8.1 that applying the optimization
improves the overall performance by roughly 10% even for systems where Σ can
be predetermined.

Step(II): Simulate the equivalence query on $\mathcal{A}_h$ by sampling:
- Let $i = 1; n_l = \left\lceil \frac{1}{\epsilon} \left(\ln \frac{1}{1-\delta} + l \ln 2 \right) \right\rceil$.
- Repeat the following steps until $i > n_l$:
    1: Sample a word w according to D and reassign $i := i + 1$.
    2: If $sym(w) \not\subseteq \Sigma$, reassign $\Sigma := \Sigma \cup sym(w)$ and rebuild $\mathcal{A}_h$ using the procedure
       in (I). Here $sym(w)$ denotes the set of symbols in w.
    3: If $\mathcal{A}_h(w) \neq f(w)$, analyze w and find a pair (x_{l+1}, y_{l+1}) using the approach in
       Figure 2, reassign $X \mapsto X \cup \{x_{l+1}\}; Y \mapsto Y \cup \{y_{l+1}\}; l \mapsto l + 1$, and goto (I).
- Halt and output $\mathcal{A}_h$.

Fig. 4. The PAC learning algorithm for MA that does not require to know the alphabet
beforehand. It assumes the following additional input: a distribution D over words
constructed from an unknown finite alphabet, the parameters $0 < \epsilon, \delta < 1$ and the
initial value $\Sigma = \emptyset$.

Double Check the Learned Minimum/Maximum Value. Let $\mathcal{A}$ be the MA inferred
by the learning algorithm and $f : \Sigma^* \to \mathbb{R}$ be an unknown function representing
the behavior of the system under analysis. Assume that our approach finds a
minimum value on $\mathcal{A}$ with the input $\bar{w}$. Since $\mathcal{A}$ is an approximation of f, it can
be the case that $\mathcal{A}(\bar{w}) \neq f(\bar{w})$. Sometimes, a result of this kind is meaningless,
e.g., the result can be a negative amount of people. In such a case, we suggest to
return $\bar{w}$ as a counterexample to the MA learning algorithm to refine the conjecture further. The immediate benefit of the optimization is that we can guarantee
that the model and the system are consistent at the inferred minimum/maximum
value.

7   An Example: Calculator

In this section, we demonstrate how our approach works using a simple but
concrete example, a "calculator" with numeral buttons 0 to 9 and operator
buttons + and −. We want to compute the average and maximal output values
the calculator can produce with an input of length k. Here a natural choice is to

---

[2] The algorithm also works when Σ is a non-empty subset of system actions.

map each button to a symbol in $[0, 11]$ because we have 12 buttons in total. We use the mapping that buttons 0 to 9 are mapped to the corresponding number in $[0, 9]$ and $+, -$ are mapped to 10, 11, respectively. We use an underline to emphasize the segmentation of symbols, e.g., to distinguish $\underline{1}\,\underline{0}$ and $\underline{10}$. A word in $[0, 11]^*$ is evaluated in the same way as Matlab does. For example, $[\![\underline{3}\,\underline{3}\,\underline{4}]\!] = 334$, $[\![\underline{3}\,\underline{10}\,\underline{4}]\!] = 7$ (interpreted as $3+4$), and $[\![\underline{1}\,\underline{10}\,\underline{11}\,\underline{2}]\!] = -1$ (interpreted as $1+(-2)$). Here $[\![w]\!]$ is the evaluation of w in Matlab. For an incomplete expression (e.g., the empty word λ or $\underline{10}\,\underline{11}$, which is interpreted as $+-$), its evaluation is 1.

The PAC-learning algorithm for MA requires a distribution over words in $[0, 11]^*$ that will be used for sampling. We use the so-called *monkey distribution* with a stop probability p. The distribution tries to simulate the behavior of a monkey playing a system. The monkey has no preference on which button to push and hence each symbol is assumed to have the same chance to be pushed. There is a probability p (checked after each button pushing) that the monkey is bored and decides to stop pushing more buttons. A similar idea has been used in software testing under the name "monkey testing", which is included as a standard testing tool in Android Studio [1]. The monkey distribution can be viewed as a generalization of the *geometric distribution* in probability theory to finite words. The average length of word sampled by the monkey distribution is $1/p$.

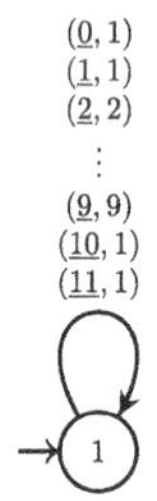

Fig. 5. Iteration 1

We demonstrate the first two iterations of applying the MA learning algorithm to learning the calculator model in Figs. 5 and 6. Assume the parameters $(\epsilon, \delta, p) = (0.05, 0.9, 0.2)$. On the left of Fig. 5, we show the rows of F_Y w.r.t. X and its one step extension. These numbers are sufficient to establish all transition matrices and the output vector. For example, now we have $x_1 = \lambda$, $l = 1$ and consider the case $a = \underline{9}$ and $i = 1$, from the equation

$$[9] = [F_Y]_{(\lambda \cdot \underline{9},*)} = [F_Y]_{(x_i \cdot a,*)} = \sum_{j \in [l]} [M_a]_{(i,j)}[F_Y]_{(x_j,*)} =$$

$$\sum_{j \in [1]} [M_{\underline{9}}]_{(1,j)}[F_Y]_{(x_j,*)} = [M_{\underline{9}}]_{(1,1)}[F_Y]_{(\lambda,*)} = [M_{\underline{9}}]_{(1,1)}[1],$$

we can derive $M_{\underline{9}} = [9]$. On the right of Fig. 5, we show the first conjectured MA $\mathcal{A}_{h_1}$. The teacher returns the first counterexample $ce_1 = \underline{6}\,\underline{8}$. Observe that $\mathcal{A}_{h_1}(ce_1) = 48$ while $f(ce_1) = 68$. By analyzing ce_1, we found its prefix $\underline{6}\,\underline{8}$ satisfies both conditions stated in the step(II) of Fig. 2 with $y = \lambda$ as follows.

(a) $[F_Y]_{(\underline{6},*)} = [6] = [M_{\underline{6}}]_{(1,1)}[F_Y]_{(\lambda,*)} = \sum_{j \in [1]}[M_{\underline{6}}]_{(1,j)}[F_Y]_{(x_j,*)}$
(b) $[F_Y]_{(\underline{6}\,\underline{8},\lambda)} = 68 \neq 48 = [M_{\underline{6}}]_{(1,1)}[F_Y]_{(\lambda \cdot \underline{8},\lambda)} = \sum_{j \in [1]}[M_{\underline{6}}]_{(1,j)}[F_Y]_{(x_j \cdot \underline{8},\lambda)}$

Hence we add $(\underline{6},\underline{8})$ to (X,Y) and proceed to iteration 2. Similarly, on the left of Fig. 6, we show the rows of F_Y w.r.t. X and its one step extension. On the right of Fig. 6 we show the conjectured MA $\mathcal{A}_{h_2}$. The construction of $\mathcal{A}_{h_2}$ is similar to $\mathcal{A}_{h_1}$. Still, $\mathcal{A}_{h_2}$ is incorrect evidenced by the counterexample $ce_2 = \underline{11}\,\underline{11}$. Observe that $\mathcal{A}_{h_2}(ce_2) = \frac{127}{5}$ while $f(ce_2) = 1$. The learning algorithm will analyze ce_2 and extend the sets X and Y. It repeats the above procedure until finds an MA $\mathcal{A}_h$ that is $PAC(\epsilon,\delta)$. That is, with confidence 90%, if a word w is sampled using the monkey distribution, the probability that $\mathcal{A}_h(w) \neq f(w)$ is less than 5%.

	λ	8
λ	1	8
6	6	68
0	1	8
1	1	18
$\vdots$	$\vdots$	$\vdots$
9	9	98
10	1	8
11	1	-8
6 0	60	608
6 1	61	618
$\vdots$	$\vdots$	$\vdots$
6 9	69	698
6 10	1	14
6 11	1	-2

Fig. 6. Iteration 2

8   Evaluation

The evaluation has several objectives: (1) evaluate the precision of the estimated quantitative numbers obtained by our approach, (2) test the scalability of the MA learning algorithm, (3) check effectiveness of the proposed optimizations. We first use the calculator example to perform an in-depth evaluation of our approach from all the aspects mentioned above.

We further examine the generality of the proposed approach in estimation precision using three more examples: "operating system scheduling", "missionaries and cannibals", and "amount of data transmission in a website". Our implementation is in Matlab and Perl and is available at https://github.com/fmlab-iis/ma-learning/wiki.

8.1   Calculator

Precision of the Estimation Made by Our Approach. In Table 1, we compare the approximate average values obtained via learning and the exact values obtained directly from the calculator.

Table 1. Comparing the approximate average computed via learning and the exact answer obtained directly from the calculator. The parameters $(\epsilon,\delta,p) = (0.1, 0.9, 0.2)$.

	Length 5	Length 10	Length 15	Length 20	Length 25	Length 30
Learning	4.8×10^5	4.6×10^{10}	4.4×10^{15}	4.2×10^{20}	4.1×10^{25}	3.8×10^{30}
Exact	4.5×10^5	4.5×10^{10}	4.5×10^{15}	4.5×10^{20}	4.5×10^{25}	4.5×10^{30}
Difference (%)	6%	2%	2%	7%	9%	16%

Recall that the average sample length is $1/p = 5$. We compare the inferred approximation with exact value on length up to 30. To make the result easier to verify, we compute the average of words over the alphabet $[0, 9] \subset [0, 11]^3$. All words in $[0, 9]^k$ are complete Matlab expressions and we can easily compute by hand that the average of a length k word in $[0, 9]^k$ is 4.5×10^k. Still, we want to emphasize that the learning algorithm and also the inferred MA $\mathcal{A}$ is over the complete alphabet $[0, 11]$.

Considerations on the Choice of Alphabet Symbols. Observe that our mapping from buttons to alphabet symbols keeps the natural order of the numeral buttons. Below we evaluate whether such a mapping is helpful to the performance of our approach. We call the mapping we introduced before the *natural* mapping. Here we define the *random* mapping which assign randomly each button to a number in $[0, 11]$. The result of the experiment is in Table 2, which is the summary of 20 runs for each alphabet mapping. The results in the row "Enumeration" is obtained by a brute-force enumeration of all words w of length 5 and then computing the average of their evaluation in Matlab. The column "#Mem. Queries" is partitioned into three parts: "HM","PAC", and "CE", which denotes those for filling the HM, PAC-based sampling, and counterexample analysis, respectively. Observe that more than a half of the membership queries are used for filling the HM.

Table 2. Comparing the performance of natural and random alphabet mappings. The parameters $(\epsilon, \delta, p) = (0.2, 0.8, 0.1)$.

	Time in learning (sec.)	#Equ. queries	#Mem. queries			Length 5	
			HM	PAC	CE	Average	Maximum
Natural	60.01	11	1622	106	615	20152.64	98646.75
Random	122.65	14	2922	168	1038	18460.47	99449.60
Enumeration						20969.34	99999

The analysis using the natural mapping is clearly more efficient than the one with random mapping; with the natural mapping, it takes only 60 s to find a MA with PAC guarantee. We believe the reason is that it is easier for the learning algorithm to find "regularity" when the mapping is natural. This is supported by the fact that the size of the MA learned with the natural mapping is significantly smaller than the one with a random mapping. The lesson learned here is that to use a natural mapping when it is possible for the system under analysis.

Considerations on the Choice of Distribution. We evaluate the impact of choosing different distributions. Beside the monkey distribution, we introduce the other two distributions. (a) A uniform distribution over all words of length 5.

---

[3] Recall that the algorithm in Sect. 5 allows us to focus on a subset of $[0, 11]$.

(b) A uniform distribution over all words of length smaller than or equals to 5. The average result of 20 runs of each distribution is in Table 3. We found that our quantitative analysis is very stable w.r.t. the choice of sampling distributions. Observe that a word of length longer than 5 will never be sampled using the two uniform distributions, but the estimated values on length 7 are still very precise. We believe this is due to the fact the MA learning algorithm is very good in generalizing the collected samples. Note that the HM may still contain entries corresponding to words of length longer than 5.

Table 3. Comparing the performance using different sampling distributions. $(\epsilon, \delta) = (0.2, 0.8)$. We use the random alphabet mapping.

	Length 3		Length 5		Length 7	
	Avg.	Max.	Avg.	Max.	Avg.	Max.
Monkey $(p = 0.2)$	281.93	995	18464.92	99590	1207020.65	9956008
Uniform$(=5)$	281.88	995	18460.63	99477	1206739.71	9920706
Uniform(≤ 5)	281.87	994	18455.93	99510	1206126.91	9949555
Enumeration	301.36	999	20969.34	99999	1456246.39	9999999

Incremental Alphabet Refinement. We use a 10 min timeout period and the parameters $(\epsilon, \delta, p) = (0.2, 0.8, 0.1)$ to evaluate the performance difference of our approach when the incremental alphabet refinement optimization is turned on and off. We execute 100 MA learning tasks for each setting. If a task cannot be completed within the timeout period, we use 600 s as its execution time. The setting when the optimization is turned off has 20 timeouts and the average execution time is 166.96 s. The one with the optimization turned on has only 17 timeouts and the average execution time is 150.99 s. Here we can see that the gain in execution time with the optimization is roughly 10%.

Distribution of the Execution Time. We investigate the performance bottle-neck of MA learning. The top 4 time-consuming component are (1) filling the Hankel matrices, (2) building the transition matrices, (3) processing PAC-based equivalence queries by sampling, and (4) counterexample analysis. The results are presented in Table 4. We set the error rate to almost zero so the learning algorithm will never terminate. The stop probability p is set to 0.1. Beside the standard 12-button calculator, we also tried calculator with 22 and 42 buttons, i.e., with numeral button 0–19 and 0–39, respectively. We list the time spent in iterations 10, 20, 40, and 80. The result indicates that most of the time is spent in (1) and hence should have the highest priority for further optimizations. For the 80-th iteration of the case $|\Sigma| = 12$, the time spent in PAC-equivalence query dominates the total execution time. The reason is that the inferred MA is already very close to the actual behavior of the calculator. So the teacher needs to sample and test a large number of words before preceding to the next iteration. Also observe that if the time budget is one hour, the learning algorithm can find an MA with more than 40 states even if the alphabet size is 42.

Table 4. The time used in different steps of MA learning.

$|\Sigma|$	Iter.	Time in seconds				
		Filling the HM	Building the TM	PAC Equ. query	CE analysis	Total
12	10	11.08	2.91	2.52	11.03	27.60
	20	59.07	15.76	40.74	72.90	188.83
	40	315.00	114.06	241.49	112.90	784.20
	80	1950.94	941.27	2223.31	372.71	5490.04
22	10	19.98	4.91	1.77	8.65	35.36
	20	108.63	28.87	7.10	45.78	160.47
	40	675.50	203.77	38.81	38.67	956.90
	80	5283.39	1725.94	398.66	203.06	7611.33
42	10	46.68	9.19	1.08	5.36	62.33
	20	297.34	57.74	4.79	11.18	371.10
	40	2124.13	412.61	34.18	30.23	2601.25
	80	23672.27	3800.65	263.59	155.37	27892.06

8.2   Operating System Scheduling

An operating system (OS) on a uniprocessor machine maintains a queue of processes that are ready to run. Depending on the scheduling policy, the OS may
deactivate the running process, insert it into the queue, and then remove some
process p from the queue and activate p for a certain time period. In this example,
we assume the first come first serve (FCFS) scheduling policy [18]. We assume
no processes will arrive simultaneously.

We are interested in the *waiting time* of a process (the total time period in
which the process is ready to run but not activated). We assume the maximal
execution time is 10 time units for all processes and define a set of alphabet
$\Sigma = [0, 10]$. Basically, for a word $w = a_0 a_1 \ldots a_l$, the symbol a_i indicates that at
the i-th time unit (1) a new process with execution time a_i is arrived and ready
to run if $a_i > 0$, or (2) no new process arrived if $a_i = 0$. For example, 20053
means jobs that require 2, 5, 3 time units arrive at time 1, 4, 5, respectively. The
output $f(w)$ is computed by simulating the OS under the FCFS policy. Table 5
summaries the results of running the analysis 3 times. The result is surprisingly
promising; our analysis is as precise as the result obtained by enumerating all
words of length k.

8.3   Missionaries and Cannibals

The missionaries and cannibals example is one of the classical river-crossing
problems. In our setting, 3 missionaries and 3 cannibals want to cross a river
using a boat under the following constraints: (1) the boat can carry at most 3
people; (2) at least one person is required to row the boat; (3) if there are more

Table 5. Performance on "Operating System Scheduling". The parameters $(\epsilon, \delta, p) = (0.1, 0.9, 0.2)$. The row "Enumeration" is obtained by enumerating all words of length k.

	Time (sec.)	#Equ. queries	Length 3		Length 5		Length 7	
			Avg.	Max.	Avg.	Max.	Avg.	Max.
Learning	212.08	22.33	4.50	9.00	9.00	18.00	13.50	27.00
Enumeration			4.50	9.00	9.00	18.00	13.50	27.00

cannibals than missionaries present on a bank (or on a boat), then the cannibals will devour the missionaries. To analyze the missionaries and cannibals example with MA, we define the set of alphabet $\Sigma = \{(i, j) \mid i + j \in [3]\}$. For a word $w = (i_0, j_0)(i_1, j_1) \ldots (i_l, j_l)$, the symbol (i_k, j_k) indicates that i_k missionaries and j_k cannibals row the boat (1) from the source bank to the destination bank if k is even, or (2) in the other direction if k is odd. Our goal is to estimate the number of people on the destination bank at the k-th step. We encode the number of people on the destination bank in the power of 2. That is, 2^n denotes there are n people on the destination bank. Then moving one person to the destination bank becomes $\times 2$ and removing one becomes $\div 2$.

Observe that by encoding the number of missionaries and cannibals at each bank and the position of the boat as the states of an MA, one can obtain a deterministic MA that precisely computes the number of people on the destination bank. Each alphabet symbol will move the MA from one state to only one target state and update the number of people on the destination bank accordingly using $\times 2$ and $\div 2$. The number of states are bounded by $3^6 \times 2$. The boat has two positions and each person has at most three statuses: at the source, at the destination, and being devoured. So we know that rank of the target function is finite, although its value can be high.

Table 6 summaries the results of running the analysis 20 times. The output $f(w)$ is computed by simulating the move of the boat according to w. In general, our method produces a very precise estimation on the average output value. In this case, the maximum value we obtained is only sub-optimal. We believe this is caused by a special feature of the example: once we made an incorrect step, some missionaries will be devoured and there is no way to resurrect them. So the imprecision of the model will cause a huge impact to the estimated maximum value. Similarly, we obtain the reference answer by enumeration. We only have results up to length 7 because it takes more than 10 h to compute the reference answer when the length is 7.

8.4   Amount of Data Transmission in a Website

Average and worst-case response time are important measures of the performance of a website. For static web pages, the response time is usually proportional to the size of the page being transmitted. In the experiment, we estimate the average and maximum size of data transmitted during k page visits.

Table 6. Performance on "Missionaries and Cannibals". The parameters $(\epsilon, \delta, p) = (0.1, 0.9, 0.2)$. The row "Enumeration" is obtained by enumerating all words of length k.

	Time (sec.)	#Equ. queries	Length 3		Length 5		Length 7	
			Avg.	Max.	Avg.	Max.	Avg.	Max.
Learning	682.09	32	$2^{2.00}$	$2^{4.74}$	$2^{1.99}$	$2^{4.74}$	$2^{1.97}$	$2^{5.05}$
Enumeration			$2^{2.00}$	2^{5}	$2^{1.99}$	2^{6}	$2^{1.97}$	2^{6}

Define an initial set of alphabet $\Sigma = [2]$. Basically, a symbol $i \in \Sigma$ indicates the i-th hyperlink in the current web page. Whenever a web page containing k hyperlinks with $k > 2$ is detected during sampling, the alphabet is extended to $[k]$. A word $\underline{3}\,\underline{4}\,\underline{2}$ denotes the sequence of actions: click the 3rd hyperlink in the first web page, the 4th hyperlink in the next web page, and then the 2nd link in the last web page. We use the personal web-site of our colleague as the target to analyze. The result is presented in Table 7.

Table 7. Performance on the "Amount of Data Transmission in a Website" problem. The parameters $(\epsilon, \delta, p) = (0.1, 0.9, 0.2)$. Here the numbers are in byte and the size of alphabet of the learned MA is 16.

	Time (sec.)	#Equ. queries	Length 3		Length 5		Length 7	
			Avg.	Max.	Avg.	Max.	Avg.	Max.
Learning	371.58	4.00	35365.04	73398.33	53207.33	122083.67	67766.23	140557.67
Enumeration			35365.04	77757.00	-	-	-	-

We encountered a number of difficulties working on a realistic problem like this. For example, the web server blocks our connection when we make too many requests within a period of time. So we can only send one request per second to avoid being blocked. Subsequently, a membership on a word of length n requires n requests to the website, which costs at least n seconds. Therefore, here we can only offer the exact reference answer for the case of length 3. We could not offer the reference answer of other lengths because it would require months of time.

9 Conclusion

Our work is the first to apply an MA learning algorithm with a PAC guarantee to the context of quantitative analysis. The encouraging experimental results suggest that our approach has tremendous potential. Although the MA learning algorithm terminates only when the target function is of a finite rank, our approach can be applied even when the rank of the target function is infinite. Observe that beside the example "missionaries and cannibals", we do not know if the target function is of a finite or an infinite rank. Currently, our tool can infer an MA model with 50 to 100 states within one hour, provided that the size of alphabet is below 50. Our implementation is in Matlab and Perl. We believe its performance can be improved using a more efficient programming language.

References

1. Android Studio: The Monkey tester (2017). https://developer.android.com/studio/test/monkey.html. Accessed 01 August 2017
2. Angluin, D.: Learning regular sets from queries and counterexamples. Inf. Comput. **75**(2), 87–106 (1987)
3. Angluin, D.: Queries and concept learning. Mach. Learn. **2**(4), 319–342 (1988)
4. Beimel, A., Bergadano, F., Bshouty, N.H., Kushilevitz, E., Varricchio, S.: Learning functions represented as multiplicity automata. JACM **47**(3), 506–530 (2000)
5. Bergadano, F., Varricchio, S.: Learning behaviors of automata from multiplicity and equivalence queries. SIAM J. Comput. **25**(6), 1268–1280 (1996)
6. Berstel, J., Reutenauer, C.: Rational Series and Their Language. Monographs in Theoretical Computer Science. An EATCS Series, vol. 12. Springer, Heidelberg (1988)
7. Boggs, P.T., Tolle, J.W.: Sequential quadratic programming. Acta Numerica **4**, 1–51 (1995)
8. Carlyle, J., Paz, A.: Realizations by stochastic finite automata. J. Comput. Syst. Sci. **5**(1), 26–40 (1971)
9. Chen, Y.F., et al.: PAC learning-based verification and model synthesis. In: ICSE, pp. 714–724 (2016)
10. Fliess, M.: Matrices de Hankel. J. Math. Pures Appl. **53**(9), 197–222 (1974)
11. Goldreich, O., Goldwasser, S., Ron, D.: Property testing and its connection to learning and approximation. JACM **45**(4), 653–750 (1998)
12. Herd, B., Miles, S., McBurney, P., Luck, M.: Quantitative analysis of multiagent systems through statistical model checking. In: Baldoni, M., Baresi, L., Dastani, M. (eds.) EMAS 2015. LNCS (LNAI), vol. 9318, pp. 109–130. Springer, Cham (2015). https://doi.org/10.1007/978-3-319-26184-3_7
13. Kwiatkowska, M.: Quantitative verification: models, techniques and tools. In: ESEC/FSE, pp. 449–458. ACM (2007)
14. Legay, A., Delahaye, B., Bensalem, S.: Statistical model checking: an overview. In: Barringer, H., et al. (eds.) RV 2010. LNCS, vol. 6418, pp. 122–135. Springer, Heidelberg (2010). https://doi.org/10.1007/978-3-642-16612-9_11
15. Nesterov, Y.: Squared functional systems and optimization problems. In: Frenk, H., Roos, K., Terlaky, T., Zhang, S. (eds.) High Performance Optimization. Applied Optimization, vol. 33, pp. 405–440. Springer, Boston (2000). https://doi.org/10.1007/978-1-4757-3216-0_17
16. Ohnishi, H., Seki, H., Kasami, T.: A polynomial time learning algorithm for recognizable series. IEICE Trans. Inf. Syst. **77**(10), 1077–1085 (1994)
17. Sen, K., Viswanathan, M., Agha, G.: Statistical model checking of black-box probabilistic systems. In: Alur, R., Peled, D.A. (eds.) CAV 2004. LNCS, vol. 3114, pp. 202–215. Springer, Heidelberg (2004). https://doi.org/10.1007/978-3-540-27813-9_16
18. Silberschatz, A., Galvin, P.B., Gagne, G.: Operating System Concepts, 8th edn. Wiley Publishing, Hoboken (2008)
19. Valiant, L.G.: A theory of the learnable. CACM **27**(11), 1134–1142 (1984)

20. Walkinshaw, N.: Assessing test adequacy for black-box systems without specifications. In: Wolff, B., Zaïdi, F. (eds.) ICTSS 2011. LNCS, vol. 7019, pp. 209–224. Springer, Heidelberg (2011). https://doi.org/10.1007/978-3-642-24580-0_15
21. Zuliani, P., Platzer, A., Clarke, E.M.: Bayesian statistical model checking with application to stateflow/simulink verification. FMSD **43**(2), 338–367 (2013)

Continuous *vs.* Discrete Asynchronous Moves: A Certified Approach for Mobile Robots

Thibaut Balabonski[1], Pierre Courtieu[2], Robin Pelle[1], Lionel Rieg[3], Sébastien Tixeuil[4], and Xavier Urbain[5(✉)]

[1] LRI, CNRS UMR 8623, Université Paris-Sud, Université Paris-Saclay, Orsay, France
[2] CÉDRIC – Conservatoire national des arts et métiers, Paris, France
[3] Université Grenoble Alpes, Grenoble INP, VERIMAG, 38401 Saint Martin d'Hères, France
[4] Sorbonne Université, CNRS, LIP6, 75005 Paris, France
[5] Université Claude Bernard Lyon-1, LIRIS CNRS UMR 5205, Université de Lyon, Lyon, France
xavier.urbain@liris.cnrs.fr

Abstract. Oblivious Mobile Robots have been studied both in continuous Euclidean spaces, and discrete spaces (that is, graphs). However the obtained literature forms distinct sets of results for the two settings. In our view, the continuous model reflects well the physicality of robots operating in some real environment, while the discrete model reflects well the digital nature of autonomous robots, whose sensors and computing capabilities are inherently finite.

We explore the possibility of bridging results between the two models. Our approach is certified using the COQ proof assistant and the Pactole framework, which we extend to the most general asynchronous model without compromising its genericity. Our extended framework is then used to formally prove the equivalence between atomic moves in a discrete space (the classical "robots on graphs" model) and non-atomic moves in a continuous unidimensional space *when robot vision sensors are discrete* (robots move in straigth lines between positions, but their observations are at source and destination positions only), irrespective of the problem being solved. Our effort consolidates the integration between the model, the problem specification, and its proof that is advocated by the Pactole framework.

Keywords: Formal proof · Proof assistant · COQ · Mobile autonomous robots · Distributed algorithms

A preliminary brief announcement of this work appears in SSS 2018 [2].
This work was partially supported by Project CoPRAH of the *Fédération Informatique de Lyon*, and the CNRS PEPS INS2I project DiDASCaL.

© Springer Nature Switzerland AG 2019
M. F. Atig and A. A. Schwarzmann (Eds.): NETYS 2019, LNCS 11704, pp. 93–109, 2019.
https://doi.org/10.1007/978-3-030-31277-0_7

1   Introduction

Networks of mobile robots captured the attention of the distributed computing community, as they promise new application (rescue, exploration, surveillance) in potentially harmful environments. Originally introduced in 1999 by Suzuki and Yamashita [40], the model has been refined since by many authors while growing in popularity (see [28] for a comprehensive textbook). From a theoretical point of view, the interest lies in characterising, for each of these various refinements, the exact conditions that enable solving a particular task.

In the model we consider, all robots are anonymous and operate using the same embedded program through repeated Look-Compute-Move cycles. In each cycle, a robot first "looks" at its environment and obtains a snapshot containing some information about the locations of all robots, expressed in the robot's own self-centred coordinate system, whose scale and orientation might not be consistent with the other robots' coordinate systems (or even with the same robot's coordinate system from a previous cycle). Then the robot "computes" a destination, still in its own coordinate system, based only on the snapshot it just obtained (which means the robot is oblivious, in the sense that its behaviour is independent of the past history of execution). Finally the robot "moves" towards the computed destination.

Different levels of synchronisation between robots have been considered. The weakest [28] (and most realistic) is the asynchronous model (ASYNC), where each robot performs its Look, Compute and Move actions at its own pace, which may not be consistent with that of other robots. The strongest [40] is the fully synchronous model (FSYNC), where all robots perform simultaneously and atomically all of these three steps. An intermediate level [40] is called semi-synchronous (SSYNC), where the computation is organised in rounds and only a subset of the robots are active at any given round; the active robots in a round performing exactly one atomic Look-Compute-Move cycle.

The general model is agnostic to the shape of the space where the robots operate, which can be the real line, a two dimensional Euclidean space, a discrete space (*a.k.a.* a graph), or even another space with a more intricate topology. To date, two independent lines of research focused on *(i)* continuous Euclidean spaces, and *(ii)* graphs, studying different sets of problems and using distinct algorithmic techniques.

1.1   Continuous *vs.* discrete spaces

The core problem to solve in the context of mobile robot networks that operate in bidimensional continuous spaces is *pattern formation*, where robots starting from distinct initial positions have to form a given geometric pattern. Arbitrary patterns can be formed when robots have memory [13,40] or common knowledge [29], otherwise only a subset of patterns can be achieved [30,42,45]. Forming a point as the target pattern is known as *gathering* [3,16,17,37,40], where robots have to meet at a single point in space in finite time, not known beforehand. The problem is generally impossible to solve [17,37,40] unless the setting is fully synchronous [3] or robots are endowed with multiplicity detection [16]. Recently, researchers considered tridimensional Euclidean spaces [41,43,44], where robots must solve *plane formation*, that is, land on a common plane (not determined beforehand) in finite time. It turns out that robots cannot form a plane from most of the semi-regular polyhedra, while they can form a plane from every regular polyhedron (except a regular icosahedron). In the context of robots operating on graphs, typical problems are *terminating exploration* [15,21–23,26,27,35], where robots must explore all nodes of a given graph and then stop moving forever, *exclusive perpetual exploration* [5,9–11,20], where robots must explore all nodes of a graph forever without ever colliding, *exclusive searching* [8,19,20], where robots must capture an intruder in the graph without colliding, and *gathering* [12,20,32–34], where robots must meet at a given node in finite time, not determined beforehand.

Although some of the studied problems overlap (*e.g.* gathering), the algorithmic techniques that enable solving problems are substantially different. On the one hand, robots operating in continuous spaces may typically use fractional distance moves to another robot, or non-straight moves in order to make the algorithm progress, two options that are not possible in the discrete model. On the other hand, in the asynchronous continuous setting, a robot may be seen by another robot as it is moving, hence at some arbitrary position between its source and destination point within a cycle, something that is impossible to observe in the discrete setting. Indeed, all aforementioned works for robots on graph consider that their moves are atomic, even in the ASYNC setting, which may seem unrealistic to a practitioner.

1.2 Related Works

Designing and proving mobile robot protocols is notoriously difficult. Formal methods encompass a long-lasting path of research that is meant to overcome errors of human origin. Unsurprisingly, this mechanised approach to protocol correctness was successively used in the context of mobile robots [1,3,4,6,7,10, 17,21,36,38,39].

In the discrete setting, model-checking proved useful to find bugs (usually in the ASYNC setting) in existing literature [7,24,25] and formally check the correctness of published algorithms [7,21,38]. Automatic program synthesis [10,36] can be used to obtain automatically algorithms that are "correct-by-design". However, those approaches are limited to small instances with few robots. Generalising to an arbitrary number of robots with similar approaches is doubtful as Sangnier *et al.* [39] proved that safety and reachability problems become undecidable in the parameterised case.

When robots move freely in a continuous bidimensional Euclidean space, to the best of our knowledge the only formal framework available is the Pactole framework.[1] Pactole enabled the use of higher-order logic to certify impossibility

---

[1] https://pactole.liris.cnrs.fr.

results [1,4,17] as well as certifying the correctness of algorithms [3,18], possibly for an arbitrary number of robots (hence in a scalable manner). Pactole was recently extended by Balabonski *et al.* [4] to handle discrete spaces as well as continuous spaces, thanks to its modular design. However, to this paper, Pactole only allowed one to express specifications and proofs with the FSYNC and SSYNC models.

1.3   Our Contribution

In this paper, we explore the possibility of establishing a first bridge between the continuous movements and discrete observation vs. discrete movements and observation in the context of autonomous mobile robots. Our position is that the continuous model reflects well the physicality of robots operating in some environment, while the discrete model reflects well the digital nature of autonomous robots, whose sensors and computing capabilities are inherently finite. For this purpose, we consider that robots make continuous, non atomic moves, but only sense in a discrete manner the position of robots. Our approach is certified using the CoQ proof assistant and the Pactole framework.

In more details, we first extend the Pactole framework to handle the ASYNC model, preserving its modularity by keeping the operating space and the robots algorithm both abstract. This permits to retain the same formal framework for both continuous and discrete spaces, and the possibility for mobile robots to be faulty (even possibly malicious *a.k.a. Byzantine*). Then, as an application of the new framework, we formally prove the equivalence between atomic moves in a discrete space (the classical model for robots operating on graphs) and nonatomic moves in a continuous unidimensional space *when robot vision sensors are discrete* (that is, robots are only able to see another robot on a node when they perform the Look phase, but robots can move anywhere on a straight line between two adjacent nodes), irrespective of the problem being solved. Our effort consolidates the integration between the model, the problem specification, and its proof that is advocated by the Pactole framework.

Pactole and the formal developments of this work are available at https://pactole.liris.cnrs.fr.

2   The Asynchronous Look-Compute-Move Model

The complete lack of synchronisation makes reasoning in the ASYNC model particularly error prone. Nevertheless, being the most realistic model, it is widely used in the literature. In this section, we describe how to include the ASYNC model in the Pactole framework.

The formalisation of the Look-Compute-Move model in Pactole for FSYNC and SSYNC has been described in [1,3,18]. We briefly recall what we need here, and emphasise what characterises the ASYNC model.

2.1 Configurations

Locations. The notion of location is a parameter of the Pactole framework and is left abstract in this section, as it depends on the nature of the space in which the robots operate. In Sect. 3, we present two different spaces based on graphs, one in which the robots are only located on vertices of the graph, and the other in which the robots can also be located on edges.

Configurations associate a conformation to a robot. In the original Pactole model, robots were mapped to locations only. To reflect in ASYNC the lack of synchronisation and of uniformity of robot actions, and to add generality to the model, we enrich configurations to map a robot id to a *conformation* (RobotConf) consisting of the current location, and information about movement: namely source and target locations. We can also add other information relating to individual robots such as their speeds or internal states. This allows for some robots to move while others are looking or computing. Note that integrating more information into the configuration does not give the robots extra power: they only "see" a configuration through their sensors, the result being what we call a *spectrum* in the sequel (see below).

```
Record Info : Type := { source: Location ; target: Location}.
Record RobotConf := { loc :> Location; robot_info: Info }.
Definition configuration := identifier → RobotConf.
```

We may now consider robots to be in two possible states summarised in Fig. 1: an Idle state and a Moving state. An idle robot is ready to start a new cycle with a simple Look/Compute action performing the usual Look and Compute phases. Merging these two actions is justified by the fact that the computation is based on the snapshot taken during the Look action only, thus its result cannot be changed by any other event taking place after the Look action. A robot is considered to be moving whenever its current and target locations are different, and becomes idle again when it reaches its target location (thus an idle robot that decides not to move stays idle).

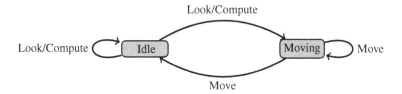

Fig. 1. States and actions of the robots

Spectra and Robograms. We call the embedded program the robots use to define their moves a *robogram*. It consists of a function pgm that simply returns a destination location when given a perception (*spectrum*) of the environment and the robot's perception of its current location. Spectra inhabit an arbitrary type that is part of the description of the model and contributes to its genericity. Indeed, depending on the robots' capabilities, the perception usually contains less information that the complete configuration: anonymous robots cannot see names, they may lack detection of multiplicity, frames of reference may not be shared, vision can be limited, etc. In the case of ASYNC in particular, the robots generally do not perceive the additional information describing the ongoing movements of other robots. The forbidden information is pruned from the configuration, using the function Spect.from_config which returns a *spectrum*, to be given as input to the robogram's pgm.

Depending on the space considered, the destination returned may be restricted, e.g., to locations that are close enough to the starting location. The pack of theses possible constraints with the declaration of the function pgm constitutes what we call a *robogram*.

```
Record robogram := { pgm: Spect.t → Location.t → Location.t;
                     (* + constraints *) }.
```

2.2   ASYNC Executions

For all synchronisation models, an execution is a sequence of configurations, each of which is deduced from the previous one, based on the robogram and on a scheduler (called a *demon*) that assigns a change (or not) of conformation to each robot and which is considered as an adversary. To mimic this behaviour, our formal model does not introduce any extra information: execution steps are completely characterised through a transition function by: *(i)* the current configuration, *(ii)* the demon's choices for the step (a *demonic action*), and *(iii)* the considered protocol. Executions are simply streams of consecutive configurations for that function.

Demonic Actions. Formally, each demonic action can request a moving robot to travel further towards its target, or an idle robot to initiate a new move. In each of these cases the demon provides its choices through the action: either the distance travelled along an ongoing move for a Move action, or a frame of reference for the perception of a robot for a Look/Compute action.

```
Inductive action {A} :=
  | Move (dist: A)                        (* moving distance *)
  | LookCompute (Location.t → Iso.t).  (* change frame of ref *)
```

This choice (Move or LookCompute) is performed by the function step. When relevant, demonic actions also relocate Byzantine robots in an arbitrary way (the regular states and actions being *per se* irrelevant for these robots).

We have no control on the choices made by the demon, which is why we call it an adversary. It must nonetheless still make meaningful choices, which we model by the following constraint: only idle robots (that is, robots that are at their target location) may receive an order to look and compute.

```
step_LookCompute : ∀ robot robot_conf ref_change,
  step robot robot_conf = LookCompute ref_change
  → robot_conf.loc = robot_conf.robot_info.target
```

Transition Function. One obtains successive configurations by running the robogram according to the current demonic action and configuration.

This is done by the function `round` computing new conformations (`RobotConf`) in a configuration, for each robot identifier `r`, according to a demonic action `da`:

1. If `r` is Byzantine, it is relocated directly by `da` on `LookCompute` actions, and ignores `Move` ones.
2. Else, if `r` carries further its ongoing move (`Move` action), its current location is updated to the location it reached during this move (the way this reached location is computed may depend on the underlying space). In the diagram in Fig. 1, this corresponds to:
   - the Move transition from Moving to Idle when `r` reaches its target location,
   - the Move loop around Moving when `r` does not reach its target location,
   - a Move loop (not shown) around Idle if `r` was already at its target location.
3. Else, a new target location is defined as follows:
   (a) The local frame of reference provided by `da` is used to convert the configuration according to the relevant local point of view,
   (b) The resulting local configuration is transformed into a spectrum using `from_config`,
   (c) The obtained spectrum is passed as a parameter to the robogram, which returns the target location.
   (d) The target location is converted from the local frame to the global one.
   The robot's conformation is updated with the obtained location as new target, and with the current location as new source. In the diagram in Fig. 1, this corresponds to:
   - the Look/Compute transition from Idle to Moving when `r`'s current and target locations are different,
   - the Look/Compute loop around Idle when `r`'s current and target location are equal.

To define a full execution, the function `execute rbg d config` iterates `round` starting from configuration `config`, using robogram `rbg` and demon `d`. Note that a step in an ASYNC execution *does not always imply* a change in the multiset of inhabited locations, as some robots may undergo a change of state only.

3   Application: Formal Equivalence Between Discrete and Continuous Models

In a discrete setting, the simplest possible location type is discrete graphs where robots can only be located on vertices. A robogram takes as parameters a spectrum (perception) and a current location based on robots located on vertices, and returns a vertex as destination location. Travel along an edge is unnoticed as the target vertex is supposed to be reached instantaneously. Particularly simple, this model is convenient for reasoning; it may however be considered as rather artificial.

A more realistic point of view is given by continuous models, which take into account the *continuous* movements of the robots. We nevertheless restrict ourselves to *discrete observations*: each robot is only perceived as being close to some reference point. As a consequence, the space can still be seen as a graph (the graph of the chosen reference points) and the robots are always observed on the vertices. The movement of a robot between two vertices however is now continuous. The corresponding edge is parameterised by a travel ratio called threshold, which is compared to the position of a robot along the edge to determine whether the robot is perceived at the source or target vertex. Computed destinations are still vertices.

We propose formalisations for these two models in our formal framework, and prove formally their equivalence in the context of oblivious robots with discrete observations, regardless of their actual observation capabilities.

3.1   Discrete Graphs

A formal model for graphs has been provided, and illustrated for SSYNC in [4] to which we refer for further details. Briefly, a graph is defined as a pair (V, E) of two sets, the vertices and the edges. Each edge has a source vertex and a target vertex, given by functions src and tgt respectively. A change of frame of reference is supported by a graph isomorphism (the type of which is written Iso.t in the formalisation). We want to extend this model by combining it with the ASYNC aspects presented above.

A graph Graph and a set Names of robots of some size N being given, we provide a model DGF in which the ASYNC notions described above are blended.

Module DGF (Graph : GraphDef)(N : Size)(Names : Robots(N)).

The locations are given by the set V of vertices of the graph.

Given a spectrum, a robogram computes as destination a location that must be reachable from (i.e., adjacent to) the current location of the robot. It is thus required that the target is linked through an edge to the current location. This is simply an additional constraint pgm_range to the definition of a robogram.

A moving robot travelling instantaneously between its source and target locations, the notion of travel distance degenerates into a Boolean choice: the robot either jumps to its destination, or stays at its current location. Hence the only effort in defining an ASYNC discrete graph in our formal model is to instantiate the parameter A in the definition of the demonic action with `bool`.

Further note that for technical reasons we will use, in our case study, a version of these discrete graphs enriched with a field `threshold` that will remain unused in the discrete case. This way both kinds of graphs will inhabit the same datatype, thus easing comparisons.

3.2 Continuous Graphs with Discrete Observations

As in the discrete model, a graph and a set of robots being given, we provide a model CGF in which both ASYNC and continuous moves are embedded.

Module CGF (Graph : GraphDef)(N : Size)(Names : Robots(N)).

The type of locations is richer, and distinguishes two cases: a robot is either on a vertex of the graph (`OnVertex`) or at some position along an edge other than its source or target (`OnEdge`). A position along an edge is given by a *position* ratio p of its length such that $0 < p < 1$ (thus making actual lengths unnecessary in the model). We represent these ratios using arbitrary reals and a continuous bijection between reals and the interval $]0, 1[$.

Inductive location := OnVertex (l : Graph.V)
                        | OnEdge (e : Graph.E) (p : R).

Discrete observation is understood as a limitation (capability) of the robots' sensors. As such, it is naturally included in the spectrum. For example, with anonymous robots enjoying multiplicity detection, the spectrum of a configuration is based on multisets of locations, however it does not show robots' locations with accuracy. Instead, each robot is seen at the "nearest" vertex: a robot located at some position ratio p along an edge is perceived at its source if p is less than or equal to the edge `threshold`, and at its target otherwise. For this, it is sufficient to use the following projection function in the construction of a spectrum from a configuration whenever the position of a robot is looked up.

Definition LocC2D (locC : CGF.Location.t) : DGF.Location.t :=
  match locC **with**
    | CGF.OnVertex l ⇒ l
    | CGF.OnEdge e p ⇒ **if** Rle_dec p (Graph.threshold e)
                       then Graph.src e **else** Graph.tgt e
  end.

Thus the type of spectra is exactly the same as in the discrete model. Note that we also require the returned destination to be a vertex in the additional constraints embedded in the definition of a robogram.

The parameter provided by the demonic action in a Move transition is more precise than in the discrete setting: it can be any *moving* ratio m in the interval $[0, 1]$. The transition function then interprets this moving ratio the following way:

– If the robot is on the source vertex of its ongoing move, $m = 0$ means staying there, $m = 1$ means going directly to the destination vertex, and $0 < m < 1$ means going at the corresponding position along the edge between the current vertex and the destination vertex.
– If the robot is at some position p on an edge, then it goes to the position $m + p$ on the same edge. In case $m + p \geq 1$ the robot goes to the target vertex.
– If the robot is already on the destination vertex, then it stays there.

For this model to make sense, the configurations must satisfy the following properties:

– The source and target locations of robots are vertices, with an edge going from the source to the target.
– If a robot is on a vertex, it is either its source or its target vertex.
– If a robot is on an edge, the latter has the same source and target vertices as the robot.

These properties are collected in a good_conf property, which is shown to be preserved by the transition function round.

Lemma good_conf_round: ∀
(config: CGF.Config.t) (rbg: robogram)
    (da: DGF.demonic_action),
    good_conf config → good_conf (round rbg da config).

Hence we restrict our initial configurations to configurations in which these properties hold, and this ensures that the configurations will remain well-formed in any execution.

3.3   Simulation of the Discrete Model in the Continuous Model

To prove that the discrete model and the continuous model with discrete observation are equivalent for oblivious robots, we show that any given robogram produces the same executions in both models. We firstly establish in Theorem graph_equivD2C that for any "discrete" execution, there is a demon such that this execution can take place in the continuous model with discrete observation context.

First remark that any robogram in one of the models can also be read as a robogram of the other model, thanks to the following facts:

– the first parameter of a robogram is a spectrum, and the types of spectra are the same in both models,
– the current position of the robot is always a vertex since the general model assumes that the robogram is applied only for idle robots, which are located on vertices,
– the destination returned by a robogram is a vertex.

Technically the types are different and a translation has to be applied to see a discrete robogram as continuous or a continuous robogram as discrete, but the translation only casts 1 ⟿ CGF.OnVertex 1 in both directions.

We define a translation ConfigD2C from discrete to continuous configurations, and show that this translation relates any execution step in the discrete model with an execution step of the same robogram in the continuous model. Since for any given underlying graph the locations of the discrete model are a subset of the locations of the continuous model, the translation of the configurations is straightforward: mapping each vertex 1 to the (continuous) location CFG.OnVertex 1. The property then reads as follows: for any robogram rbg, demonic action da and configuration c in the discrete model, there is a demonic action da′ in the continuous model such that the diagram in Fig. 2 is satisfied.

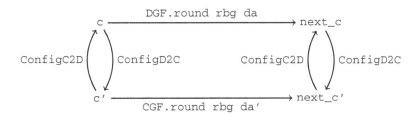

Fig. 2. Bisimulation

Theorem graph_equivD2C: ∀ (c: DGF.Config.t)(rbg: DGF.robogram)
        (da: DGF.demonic_action),
 ∃ (da′: CGF.demonic_action),
   ConfigD2C (DGF.round rbg da c)
           ≡$_{CGF}$ CGF.round (rbgD2C rbg) da′ (ConfigD2C c).

The proof of this lemma requires to provide a demonic action da′ in the continuous model, which is again obtained by quite a simple translation of the discrete action da. In particular, the boolean parameter associated to a move action is canonically translated to either 0 or 1, and the conversion to the local frame of reference needs not be translated (since both models have the same underlying graph). Note that, since demonic actions are associated to constraints (namely step_LookCompute), the definition of a new demonic action requires a proof that these constraints are satisfied. Once this witness is provided, the proof amounts to reasoning by cases on the various parameters of the transition function: is the robot Byzantine or not? is the scheduled action a move or a new activation? is the parameter of the move true or false?

From this, we deduce that any execution in the discrete model can be simulated in the continuous model. The reciprocal property, which is more complex, is detailed in the next section.

3.4   Simulation of the Continuous Model in the Discrete Model

Configurations in the continuous model can also be translated to configurations in the discrete model. The translation ConfigC2D uses the location projection function LocC2D already defined in the description of spectra in the continuous model.

This translation allows us to state a second simulation result, similar to the previous one but relating continuous executions steps to discrete ones (that is, reading the diagram in Fig. 2 from bottom to top).

```
Theorem graph_equivC2D: ∀(c': CGF.Config.t)(rbg: CGF.robogram)
        (da': CGF.demonic_action),
  CGF.good_conf c' →
  ∃ da, ConfigC2D (CGF.round rbg da' c')
                ≡_DGF DGF.round (rbgC2D rbg) da (ConfigC2D c').
```

The definition of the witness da is subtler than in the previous lemma. The case where an idle robot is activated and computes a new destination (LookCompute action) is straightforward, since again we can use the same isomorphism. The Move case however cannot be treated using only the information in the continuous action da': when a continuous demonic action provides a move ratio, we have to translate it into a boolean choice describing whether the move will end in the region of the source vertex or in the region of the target vertex. That is, we have to know whether the movement will pass the threshold or not. This requires knowing not only the demonic action da', but also the configuration c'. The full definition then takes the following form:

```
Definition daC2D (daC: CGF.demonic_action) (confC: CGF.Config.t):
    DGF.demonic_action :=
{| DGF.relocate_byz := fun b ⇒ LocC2D (daC.relocate_byz b);
   DGF.step := fun robot robot_conf ⇒
     (* Here we assume that {robot_conf} is the projection
        of {confC robot} *)
     (* Consider the action given by the continuous demon... *)
     match daC.step robot (confC robot) with
       (* a Look/Compute action is preserved, *)
       | CGF.LookCompute ref_change ⇒ DGF.LookCompute ref_change
       (* a Move action requires checking the current location
          of the robot. *)
       | CGF.Move m ⇒
         match (confC robot).loc with
           (* If the robot is on a vertex, then compare {m} to
              the threshold of the edge to target vertex {e}. *)
           | CGF.OnVertex _ ⇒
             match (Graph.find_edge robot_conf.robot_info.source
                                    robot_conf.robot_info.target)
           with
             | Some e ⇒ if Rle_dec m (Graph.threshold e)
                        then DGF.Move false else DGF.Move true
             | None ⇒ DGF.Move false
           end
```

```
(* If the robot is on an edge do the same after adding
   the current position ratio to {m}. *)
| CGF.OnEdge e p ⇒
  if Rle_dec p (Graph.threshold e)
  then if Rle_dec (m + p) (Graph.threshold e)
       then DGF.Move false else DGF.Move true
       else DGF.Move false
  end
end |}.
```

Again, the proof is by cases on all the parameters of the transition function, which are more numerous than in the previous case since the definition of the demonic action da′ itself distinguishes many more cases.

These two simulation results, taken together, mean that any execution in any of the two models (discrete or continuous) can be related to an equivalent execution in the other model.

4 Concluding Remarks

Our work established the first formal bridge between two previously distinct models for oblivious mobile robots. From a practical point of view, the formal equivalence we provide between the discrete model and the continuous model with discrete sensors sheds new light about what is actually computable in real environments by limited capabilities robots. Furthermore, our work hints at possible new paths for future research:

– The first issue we plan to tackle is that of realistic sensing models for mobile robots. Actual robots endowed with omnidirectional 3D visibility sensors typically use a digital camera with a set of parabolic mirrors [14], which implies that the accuracy of the localisation of a robot varies with the distance to its target robot. In our modeling, the threshold for a given edge e is the same for all participating robots, while a threshold that varies according to the distance of the observing robot to e would be more realistic. Adding this possibility to our framework is not difficult thanks to its modularity, but the equivalence proof is then likely to fail in the extended model.
– Another important long-term open question raised by our work is that of model equivalence beyond oblivious mobile robots. Our approach considers the equivalence of executions and is hence agnostic with regards to the actual problem being solved; it also enables Byzantine robots. It would be interesting to consider model equivalences with other classical distributed computing models (*e.g.* Problem A in robot model m with f faulty robots is equivalent to problem B in asynchronous shared memory model m' with f' faulty processes). A natural candidate case study would be the Consensus *vs.* Robot Gathering problem [31].

References

1. Auger, C., Bouzid, Z., Courtieu, P., Tixeuil, S., Urbain, X.: Certified impossibility results for byzantine-tolerant mobile robots. In: Higashino, T., Katayama, Y., Masuzawa, T., Potop-Butucaru, M., Yamashita, M. (eds.) SSS 2013. LNCS, vol. 8255, pp. 178–190. Springer, Cham (2013). https://doi.org/10.1007/978-3-319-03089-0_13

2. Balabonski, T., Courtieu, P., Pelle, R., Rieg, L., Tixeuil, S., Urbain, X.: Brief announcement continuous *vs.* discrete asynchronous moves: a certified approach for mobile robots. In: Izumi, T., Kuznetsov, P. (eds.) SSS 2018. LNCS, vol. 11201, pp. 404–408. Springer, Cham (2018). https://doi.org/10.1007/978-3-030-03232-6_29

3. Balabonski, T., Delga, A., Rieg, L., Tixeuil, S., Urbain, X.: Synchronous gathering without multiplicity detection: a certified algorithm. In: Bonakdarpour, B., Petit, F. (eds.) SSS 2016. LNCS, vol. 10083, pp. 7–19. Springer, Cham (2016). https://doi.org/10.1007/978-3-319-49259-9_2

4. Balabonski, T., Pelle, R., Rieg, L., Tixeuil, S.: A foundational framework for certified impossibility results with mobile robots on graphs. In: Bellavista, P., Garg, V.K., (eds.) Proceedings of the 19th International Conference on Distributed Computing and Networking, ICDCN 2018, Varanasi, India, 4–7 January 2018, pp. 5:1–5:10. ACM (2018)

5. Baldoni, R., Bonnet, F., Milani, A., Raynal, M.: Anonymous graph exploration without collision by mobile robots. Inf. Process. Lett. **109**(2), 98–103 (2008)

6. Bérard, B., et al.: Formal methods for mobile robots: current results and open problems. Int. J. Inform. Soc. **7**(3), 101–114 (2015). Invited Paper

7. Bérard, B., Lafourcade, P., Millet, L., Potop-Butucaru, M., Thierry-Mieg, Y., Tixeuil, S.: Formal verification of mobile robot protocols. Distrib. Comput. **29**(6), 459–487 (2016)

8. Blin, L., Burman, J., Nisse, N.: Exclusive graph searching. Algorithmica **77**(3), 942–969 (2017)

9. Blin, L., Milani, A., Potop-Butucaru, M., Tixeuil, S.: Exclusive perpetual ring exploration without chirality. In: Lynch, N.A., Shvartsman, A.A. (eds.) DISC 2010. LNCS, vol. 6343, pp. 312–327. Springer, Heidelberg (2010). https://doi.org/10.1007/978-3-642-15763-9_29

10. Bonnet, F., Défago, X., Petit, F., Potop-Butucaru, M., Tixeuil, S.: Discovering and assessing fine-grained metrics in robot networks protocols. In 33rd IEEE International Symposium on Reliable Distributed Systems Workshops, SRDS Workshops 2014, Nara, Japan, 6–9 October 2014, pp. 50–59. IEEE (2014)

11. Bonnet, F., Milani, A., Potop-Butucaru, M., Tixeuil, S.: Asynchronous exclusive perpetual grid exploration without sense of direction. In: Fernàndez Anta, A., Lipari, G., Roy, M. (eds.) OPODIS 2011. LNCS, vol. 7109, pp. 251–265. Springer, Heidelberg (2011). https://doi.org/10.1007/978-3-642-25873-2_18

12. Bonnet, F., Potop-Butucaru, M., Tixeuil, S.: Asynchronous gathering in rings with 4 robots. In: Mitton, N., Loscri, V., Mouradian, A. (eds.) ADHOC-NOW 2016. LNCS, vol. 9724, pp. 311–324. Springer, Cham (2016). https://doi.org/10.1007/978-3-319-40509-4_22

13. Bouzid, Z., Dolev, S., Potop-Butucaru, M., Tixeuil, S.: RoboCast: asynchronous communication in robot networks. In: Lu, C., Masuzawa, T., Mosbah, M. (eds.) OPODIS 2010. LNCS, vol. 6490, pp. 16–31. Springer, Heidelberg (2010). https://doi.org/10.1007/978-3-642-17653-1_2

14. Caron, G., Mouaddib, E.M., Marchand, É.: 3D model based tracking for omnidirectional vision: a new spherical approach. Robot. Auton. Syst. **60**(8), 1056–1068 (2012)
15. Chalopin, J., Flocchini, P., Mans, B., Santoro, N.: Network exploration by silent and oblivious robots. In: Thilikos, D.M. (ed.) WG 2010. LNCS, vol. 6410, pp. 208–219. Springer, Heidelberg (2010). https://doi.org/10.1007/978-3-642-16926-7_20
16. Cieliebak, M., Flocchini, P., Prencipe, G., Santoro, N.: Distributed computing by mobile robots: gathering. SIAM J. Comput. **41**(4), 829–879 (2012)
17. Courtieu, P., Rieg, L., Tixeuil, S., Urbain, X.: Impossibility of gathering, a certification. Inf. Process. Lett. **115**, 447–452 (2015)
18. Courtieu, P., Rieg, L., Tixeuil, S., Urbain, X.: Certified universal gathering in $\mathbb{R}^2$ for oblivious mobile robots. In: Gavoille, C., Ilcinkas, D. (eds.) DISC 2016. LNCS, vol. 9888, pp. 187–200. Springer, Heidelberg (2016). https://doi.org/10.1007/978-3-662-53426-7_14
19. D'Angelo, G., Navarra, A., Nisse, N.: A unified approach for gathering and exclusive searching on rings under weak assumptions. Distrib. Comput. **30**(1), 17–48 (2017)
20. D'Angelo, G., Stefano, G.D., Navarra, A., Nisse, N., Suchan, K.: Computing on rings by oblivious robots: a unified approach for different tasks. Algorithmica **72**(4), 1055–1096 (2015)
21. Devismes, S., Lamani, A., Petit, F., Raymond, P., Tixeuil, S.: Optimal grid exploration by asynchronous oblivious robots. In: Richa, A.W., Scheideler, C. (eds.) SSS 2012. LNCS, vol. 7596, pp. 64–76. Springer, Heidelberg (2012). https://doi.org/10.1007/978-3-642-33536-5_7
22. Devismes, S., Lamani, A., Petit, F., Tixeuil, S.: Optimal torus exploration by oblivious robots. In: Bouajjani, A., Fauconnier, H. (eds.) NETYS 2015. LNCS, vol. 9466, pp. 183–199. Springer, Cham (2015). https://doi.org/10.1007/978-3-319-26850-7_13
23. Devismes, S., Petit, F., Tixeuil, S.: Optimal probabilistic ring exploration by semi-synchronous oblivious robots. Theoret. Comput. Sci. **498**, 10–27 (2013)
24. Doan, H.T.T., Bonnet, F., Ogata, K.: Model checking of a mobile robots perpetual exploration algorithm. In: Liu, S., Duan, Z., Tian, C., Nagoya, F. (eds.) SOFL+MSVL 2016. LNCS, vol. 10189, pp. 201–219. Springer, Cham (2017). https://doi.org/10.1007/978-3-319-57708-1_12
25. Doan, H.T.T., Bonnet, F., Ogata, K.: Model checking of robot gathering. In: Aspnes, J., Felber, P. (edS.) Principles of Distributed Systems - 21th International Conference (OPODIS 2017), Leibniz International Proceedings in Informatics (LIPIcs), Lisbon, Portugal, December 2017. Schloss Dagstuhl-Leibniz-Zentrum fuer Informatik
26. Flocchini, P., Ilcinkas, D., Pelc, A., Santoro, N.: Remembering without memory: tree exploration by asynchronous oblivious robots. Theoret. Comput. Sci. **411**(14–15), 1583–1598 (2010)
27. Flocchini, P., Ilcinkas, D., Pelc, A., Santoro, N.: Computing without communicating: ring exploration by asynchronous oblivious robots. Algorithmica **65**(3), 562–583 (2013)
28. Flocchini, P., Prencipe, G., Santoro, N.: Distributed Computing by Oblivious Mobile Robots. Synthesis Lectures on Distributed Computing Theory. Morgan & Claypool Publishers, California (2012)
29. Flocchini, P., Prencipe, G., Santoro, N., Widmayer, P.: Arbitrary pattern formation by asynchronous, anonymous, oblivious robots. Theoret. Comput. Sci. **407**(1–3), 412–447 (2008)

30. Fujinaga, N., Yamauchi, Y., Kijima, S., Yamashita, M.: Asynchronous pattern formation by anonymous oblivious mobile robots. In: Aguilera, M.K. (ed.) DISC 2012. LNCS, vol. 7611, pp. 312–325. Springer, Heidelberg (2012). https://doi.org/10.1007/978-3-642-33651-5_22

31. Izumi, T., Bouzid, Z., Tixeuil, S., Wada, K.: Brief announcement: the BG-simulation for Byzantine mobile robots. In: Peleg, D. (ed.) DISC 2011. LNCS, vol. 6950, pp. 330–331. Springer, Heidelberg (2011). https://doi.org/10.1007/978-3-642-24100-0_32

32. Izumi, T., Izumi, T., Kamei, S., Ooshita, F.: Mobile robots gathering algorithm with local weak multiplicity in rings. In: Patt-Shamir, B., Ekim, T. (eds.) SIROCCO 2010. LNCS, vol. 6058, pp. 101–113. Springer, Heidelberg (2010). https://doi.org/10.1007/978-3-642-13284-1_9

33. Kamei, S., Lamani, A., Ooshita, F., Tixeuil, S.: Asynchronous mobile robot gathering from symmetric configurations without global multiplicity detection. In: Kosowski, A., Yamashita, M. (eds.) SIROCCO 2011. LNCS, vol. 6796, pp. 150–161. Springer, Heidelberg (2011). https://doi.org/10.1007/978-3-642-22212-2_14

34. Kamei, S., Lamani, A., Ooshita, F., Tixeuil, S.: Gathering an even number of robots in an odd ring without global multiplicity detection. In: Rovan, B., Sassone, V., Widmayer, P. (eds.) MFCS 2012. LNCS, vol. 7464, pp. 542–553. Springer, Heidelberg (2012). https://doi.org/10.1007/978-3-642-32589-2_48

35. Lamani, A., Potop-Butucaru, M.G., Tixeuil, S.: Optimal deterministic ring exploration with oblivious asynchronous robots. In: Patt-Shamir, B., Ekim, T. (eds.) SIROCCO 2010. LNCS, vol. 6058, pp. 183–196. Springer, Heidelberg (2010). https://doi.org/10.1007/978-3-642-13284-1_15

36. Millet, L., Potop-Butucaru, M., Sznajder, N., Tixeuil, S.: On the synthesis of mobile robots algorithms: the case of ring gathering. In: Felber, P., Garg, V. (eds.) SSS 2014. LNCS, vol. 8756, pp. 237–251. Springer, Cham (2014). https://doi.org/10.1007/978-3-319-11764-5_17

37. Prencipe, G.: Impossibility of gathering by a set of autonomous mobile robots. Theoret. Comput. Sci. **384**(2–3), 222–231 (2007)

38. Aminof, B., Murano, A., Rubin, S., Zuleger, F.: Verification of asynchronous mobile-robots in partially-known environments. In: Chen, Q., Torroni, P., Villata, S., Hsu, J., Omicini, A. (eds.) PRIMA 2015. LNCS (LNAI), vol. 9387, pp. 185–200. Springer, Cham (2015). https://doi.org/10.1007/978-3-319-25524-8_12

39. Sangnier, A., Sznajder, N., Potop-Butucaru, M., Tixeuil, S.: Parameterized verification of algorithms for oblivious robots on a ring. In: Formal Methods in Computer Aided Design, Vienna, Austria, October 2017

40. Suzuki, I., Yamashita, M.: Distributed anonymous mobile robots: formation of geometric patterns. SIAM J. Comput. **28**(4), 1347–1363 (1999)

41. Tomita, Y., Yamauchi, Y., Kijima, S., Yamashita, M.: Plane formation by synchronous mobile robots without chirality. In: Aspnes, J., Bessani, A., Felber, P., Leitão, J. (eds.) 21st International Conference on Principles of Distributed Systems, OPODIS 2017. LIPIcs, vol. 95, Lisbon, Portugal, 18–20 December 2017, pp. 13:1–13:17. Schloss Dagstuhl - Leibniz-Zentrum fuer Informatik (2017)

42. Yamashita, M., Suzuki, I.: Characterizing geometric patterns formable by oblivious anonymous mobile robots. Theoret. Comput. Sci. **411**(26–28), 2433–2453 (2010)

43. Yamauchi, Y., Uehara, T., Kijima, S., Yamashita, M.: Plane formation by synchronous mobile robots in the three-dimensional Euclidean space. J. ACM **64**(3), 16:1–16:43 (2017)

44. Yamauchi, Y., Uehara, T., Yamashita, T.: Brief announcement: pattern formation problem for synchronous mobile robots in the three dimensional euclidean space. In: Giakkoupis, G. (ed.) Proceedings of the 2016 ACM Symposium on Principles of Distributed Computing, PODC 2016, Chicago, IL, USA, 25–28 July 2016, pp. 447–449. ACM (2016)
45. Yamauchi, Y., Yamashita, M.: Pattern formation by mobile robots with limited visibility. In: Moscibroda, T., Rescigno, A.A. (eds.) SIROCCO 2013. LNCS, vol. 8179, pp. 201–212. Springer, Cham (2013). https://doi.org/10.1007/978-3-319-03578-9_17

Distributed Systems

Self-stabilizing Snapshot Objects for Asynchronous Failure-Prone Networked Systems

Chryssis Georgiou[1], Oskar Lundström[2], and Elad Michael Schiller[2]([✉])

[1] Computer Science, University of Cyprus, Nicosia, Cyprus
chryssis@cs.ucy.ac.cy
[2] Computer Science and Engineering, Chalmers University Technology,
Gothenburg, Sweden
osklunds@student.chalmers.se, elad@chalmers.se

Abstract. A *snapshot object* simulates the behavior of an array of single-writer/multi-reader shared registers that can be read atomically. Delporte-Gallet *et al.* proposed two fault-tolerant algorithms for snapshot objects in asynchronous crash-prone message-passing systems. Their first algorithm is *non-blocking*; it allows snapshot operations to terminate once all write operations had ceased. It uses $\mathcal{O}(n)$ messages of $\mathcal{O}(n \cdot \nu)$ bits, where n is the number of nodes and ν is the number of bits it takes to represent the object. Their second algorithm allows snapshot operations to *always terminate* independently of write operations. It incurs $\mathcal{O}(n^2)$ messages. The fault model of Delporte-Gallet *et al.* considers node failures (crashes). We aim at the design of even more robust snapshot objects. We do so through the lenses of *self-stabilization*— a very strong notion of fault-tolerance. In addition to Delporte-Gallet *et al.*'s fault model, a self-stabilizing algorithm can recover after the occurrence of *transient faults*; these faults represent arbitrary violations of the assumptions according to which the system was designed to operate (as long as the code stays intact). In particular, in this work, we propose self-stabilizing variations of Delporte-Gallet *et al.*'s non-blocking algorithm and always-terminating algorithm. Our algorithms have similar communication costs to the ones by Delporte-Gallet *et al.* and $\mathcal{O}(1)$ recovery time (in terms of asynchronous cycles) from transient faults. The main differences are that our proposal considers repeated gossiping of $\mathcal{O}(\nu)$ bits messages and deals with bounded space, which is a prerequisite for self-stabilization.

1 Introduction

We propose self-stabilizing implementations of shared memory snapshot objects for asynchronous bounded space networked systems whose nodes may crash.

Context and Motivation. Shared registers are fundamental objects that facilitate synchronization in distributed systems. In the context of networked systems, they provide a higher abstraction level than simple end-to-end communication,

© Springer Nature Switzerland AG 2019
M. F. Atig and A. A. Schwarzmann (Eds.): NETYS 2019, LNCS 11704, pp. 113–130, 2019.
https://doi.org/10.1007/978-3-030-31277-0_8

which provides persistent and consistent distributed storage that can simplify the design and analysis of dependable distributed systems. Snapshot objects extend shared registers. They provide a way to further make the design and analysis of algorithms that base their implementation on shared registers easier. Snapshot objects allow an algorithm to construct consistent global states of the shared storage in a way that does not disrupt the system computation. Their efficient and fault-tolerant implementation is a fundamental problem, as there are many examples of algorithms that are built on top of snapshot objects.

Task Description. Consider a fault-tolerant distributed system of n asynchronous nodes that are prone to failures. Their interaction is based on the emulation of Single-Writer/Multi-Reader (SWMR) shared registers over a message-passing communication system. Snapshot objects can read the entire array of system registers [1,2]. The system lets each node update its own register via write() operations and retrieve the value of all shared registers via snapshot() operations. Note that these snapshot operations may occur concurrently with the write operations that individual nodes perform. We are particularly interested in the study of atomic snapshot objects that are *linearizable*: the operations write() and snapshot() appear as if they have been executed instantaneously, one after the other (*i.e.,* they appear to preserve real-time ordering).

Fault Model. We consider an asynchronous message-passing system in which nodes may crash and packets may be lost, duplicated and reordered. In addition to these failures, we also aim to recover from *transient faults, i.e.,* any temporary violation of assumptions according to which the system was designed to behave, *e.g.,* the corruption of control variables, such as the program counter and operation indices, which are responsible for the correct operation of the studied system, or operational assumptions, such as that at least half of the system nodes never fail. Since the occurrence of these failures can be combined, we assume that these transient faults alter the system state in unpredictable ways. In particular, when modeling the system, we assume that these violations bring the system to an arbitrary state from which a *self-stabilizing algorithm* should recover the system. Therefore, starting from an arbitrary state, the correctness proof of self-stabilizing systems [3] has to show the return to a "correct behavior" within a bounded period. The complexity measure of self-stabilizing systems is the length of the recovery period.

Related Work. We follow the design criteria of self-stabilization, which was proposed by Dijkstra [3] and detailed in [4]. Our overview of the related work focuses on self-stabilizing algorithms for shared-memory objects. Attiya *et al.* [5] implemented SWMR atomic shared-memory in an asynchronous networked system. Delporte-Gallet *et al.* [6] claim that when stacking the shared-memory atomic snapshot algorithm of [1] on the shared-memory emulation of [5] (with some improvements), the number of messages per snapshot operation is $8n$ and it takes 4 round trips. Their proposal, instead, takes $2n$ message per snapshot and just one round trip to complete. Our solution follows the non-stacking approach of Delporte-Gallet and it tolerates any failure (in any communication or operation invocation pattern) that [6] can as well as recover after the occurrence of transient faults that arbitrarily corrupt the system state. The literature on self-stabilization includes a practically-self-stabilizing variation for the work of Attiya *et al.* [5] by Alon *et al.* [7]. Their proposal guarantees wait-free recovery from transient faults. However, there is no bound on the recovery time. Dolev *et al.* [8] consider MWMR atomic storage that is wait-free in the absence of transient faults. They guarantee a bounded time recovery from transient faults in the presence of a fair scheduler. They demonstrate the algorithm's ability to recover from transient faults using unbounded counters and in the presence of fair scheduling. Then they deal with the event of integer overflow via a consensus-based procedure. Since integer variables can have 64-bits, their algorithm seldom uses this non-wait-free procedure for dealing with integer overflows. In fact, they model integer overflow events as transient faults, which implies bounded recovery time from transient faults in the seldom presence of a fair scheduler (using bounded memory). They call these systems *self-stabilizing systems in the presence of seldom fairness.* Our work adopts these design criteria. We are unaware of self-stabilizing algorithms for snapshot objects that can recover from node failures. We note that "stacking" of self-stabilizing algorithms for asynchronous message-passing systems is not straightforward; the existing "stacking" needs schedule fairness [4, Section 2.7].

Contributions. We propose self-stabilizing algorithms for snapshot objects in networked systems. To the best of our knowledge, we are the first to consider both node failures and transient faults. Specifically, we propose:

(1) *A self-stabilizing variation on the non-blocking algorithm by Delporte-Gallet* et al. (Sect. 3). As by Delporte-Gallet *et al.*, each snapshot or write operation uses $\mathcal{O}(n)$ messages of $\mathcal{O}(\nu \cdot n)$ bits, where n is the number of nodes and ν is the number of bits for encoding the object. Our communication costs are slightly higher due to $\mathcal{O}(n^2)$ gossip messages of $\mathcal{O}(\nu)$ bits, where ν is the number of bits it takes to represent the object.

(2) *A self-stabilizing variation on the always-terminating algorithm by Delporte-Gallet* et al. (Sect. 4). Our algorithm can: (i) recover from of transient faults, and (ii) both write and snapshot operations always terminate (regardless of the invocation patterns of any operation). We achieve *(ii)* by choosing to use *safe registers* for storing the result of recent snapshot operations, rather than a *reliable broadcast* mechanism, which often has higher communication costs. Moreover, instead of dealing with one snapshot task at a time, we take care of several at a time. We also consider an input parameter, δ. For the case of $\delta = 0$, our self-stabilizing algorithm guarantees an always-termination behavior (as in the non-self-stabilizing algorithm by Delporte-Gallet *et al.*) that blocks all write operation upon the invocation of any snapshot operation at the cost of $\mathcal{O}(n^2)$ messages. For the case of $\delta > 0$, our solution aims at using $\mathcal{O}(n)$ messages per snapshot operation while monitoring the number of concurrent write operations. Once our algorithm notices that a snapshot operation runs concurrently with at least δ write operations, it blocks all write operations and uses $\mathcal{O}(n^2)$ messages for completing the snapshot operations. Thus, the proposed algorithm can trade communication costs with an $\mathcal{O}(\delta)$ bound on snapshot operation latency.

Moreover, between any two consecutive periods in which snapshot operations block the system for write operations, the algorithm guarantees that at least δ write operations can occur.

The proposed algorithms use unbounded counters. In Sect. 5 we explain how to bound these counters. Due to the page limit, omitted details and proofs appear in [9], together with an explanation on how to extend our solutions to reconfigurable ones.

2   System Settings

We consider an asynchronous message-passing system. The system includes the set $\mathcal{P}$ of n failure-prone nodes whose identifiers are unique and totally ordered in $\mathcal{P}$. Any pair of nodes have access to a bidirectional bounded capacity communication channel that has no guarantees on the communication delays.

Each node runs a program, which we model as a sequence of *(atomic) steps*. Each step starts with an internal computation and finishes with a single communication operation, *i.e.*, message *send* or *receive*. The *state*, s_i, of $p_i \in \mathcal{P}$ includes all of p_i's variables and the set of all incoming communication channels. Note that p_i's step can change s_i and remove a message from $channel_{j,i}$ (upon message arrival) or add a message in $channel_{i,j}$ (when a message is sent). The term *system state* refers to a tuple, $c = (s_1, s_2, \cdots, s_n)$, where each s_i is p_i's state. An *execution* $R = c_0, a_0, c_1, a_1, \ldots$ is an alternating sequence of system states c_x and steps a_x, such that each c_{x+1}, except, c_0, is obtained from the preceding state c_x by the execution of step a_x. Let R' and R'' be a prefix, and resp., a suffix of R, such that R' is a finite sequence, which starts with a system state and ends with a step $a_x \in R'$, and R'' is an unbounded sequence, which starts in the system state that immediately follows step $a_x \in R$. The proof of the algorithms considers the number of *(asynchronous) cycles* of a fair execution, *i.e.*, every step that is applicable infinitely often is executed infinitely often and fair communication is kept. The first (asynchronous) cycle (with round-trips) of a fair execution $R = R'' \circ R'''$ is the shortest prefix R'' of R, such that each non-failing node executes in R'' at least one complete iteration of its do forever loop (and completes the round trips associated with the messages sent during that iteration), where $\circ$ denotes the concatenation operator. The second cycle in execution R is the first cycle in suffix R'' of execution R, and so on.

Fault Model. We assume communication fairness, *i.e.*, if p_i sends a message infinitely often to p_j, node p_j receives that message infinitely often. We note that without this assumption, the communication channel between any two correct nodes eventually becomes non-functional. We consider standard terms for characterizing node failures [10]. A *crash failure* considers the case in which a node stops taking steps forever and there is no way to detect this failure. We say that a failing node resumes when it returns to take steps without restarting its program—the literature sometimes refer to this as an *undetectable restart*. The case of a detectable restart allows the node to restart all of its variables. We assume that each node has access to a quorum service, *e.g.*, [8, Section 13], that deals with packet loss, reordering, and duplication. A failure of node $p_i \in \mathcal{P}$ implies that it stops executing any step without any warning. The number of failing nodes is at most f and $2f < n$ for the sake of guaranteeing correctness [11]. In the absence of transient faults, failing nodes can simply crash, as in Delporte-Gallet *et al.* [6]. In the presence of transient faults, we assume that failing nodes resume within some unknown finite time and restart their program after initializing all of their variables (including the control variables). The latter assumption is needed *only* for recovering from transient faults; in [9] we explain how to remove this assumption. As already mentioned, we consider arbitrary violations of the assumptions according to which the system and the communication network were designed to operate. We refer to these violations as *transient faults* and assume that they can corrupt the system state arbitrarily (while keeping the program code intact). The occurrence of a transient fault is rare. Thus, we assume that transient faults occur before the system execution starts [4]. Moreover, it leaves the system to start in an arbitrary state.

Dijkstra's Self-stabilization Criterion. The set of *legal executions* (LE) refers to all the executions in which the requirements of the task T hold. We say that a system state c is *legitimate* when every execution R that starts from c is in LE. An algorithm is *self-stabilizing* with respect to the task of LE, when every (unbounded) execution R of the algorithm reaches within a bounded period a suffix $R_{legal} \in LE$ that is legal. That is, Dijkstra [3] requires that $\forall R : \exists R' : R = R' \circ R_{legal} \wedge R_{legal} \in LE \wedge |R'| \in \mathbb{N}$, where the length of R' is the complexity measure, which we refer to as the *recovery time*.

Self-stabilization in the Presence of Seldom Fairness. As a variation of Dijkstra's self-stabilization criterion, Dolev *et al.* [8] proposed design criteria in which (i) any execution $R = R_{recoveryPeriod} \circ R' : R' \in LE$, which starts in an arbitrary system state and has a prefix ($R_{recoveryPeriod}$) that is fair, reaches a legitimate system state within a bounded prefix $R_{recoveryPeriod}$. (Note that the legal suffix R' is not required to be fair.) Moreover, (ii) any execution $R = R'' \circ R_{globalReset} \circ R''' \circ R_{globalReset} \circ \ldots : R'', R''', \ldots \in LE$ in which the prefix of R is legal, and not necessarily fair but includes at most $\mathcal{O}(n \cdot z_{\max})$ write or snapshot operations, has a suffix, $R_{globalReset} \circ R''' \circ R_{globalReset} \circ \ldots$, such that $R_{globalReset}$ is required to be fair and bounded in length, but it might permit the violation of liveness requirements, *i.e.*, a bounded number of operations might be aborted (as long as the safety requirement holds). Furthermore, R''' is legal and not necessarily fair, but includes at least $z_{\max}$ write or snapshot operations before the system reaches another $R_{globalReset}$. Since we can choose $z_{\max} \in \mathbb{Z}^+$ to be a very large value, say 2^{64}, and the occurrence of transient faults is rare, we refer to the proposed criteria as one for self-stabilizing systems that their execution fairness is unrequited except for seldom periods. We note that self-stabilizing algorithms (that follows Dijkstra's criterion) often assume fairness *throughout R*.

3   The Non-blocking Algorithm

The non-blocking solution to snapshot object emulation by [6, Algorithm 1] allows writes to terminate regardless of the invocation patterns of any other operation (as long as the invoking nodes do not fail during the operation). However, snapshot operation termination is guaranteed only after the last write operation. We discuss Delporte-Gallet *et al.* [6, Algorithm 1]'s solution before proposing our self-stabilizing variation.

Delporte-Gallet *et al.*'s Non-blocking Algorithm. Algorithm 1 presents [6, Algorithm 1] using our presentation style; the boxed code lines are irrelevant to [6, Algorithm 1]. The node state appears in lines 2 to 4 and automatic variables (which are allocated and deallocated automatically when program flow enters and leaves the variable's scope) are defined using the let keyword, *e.g.*, the variable *prev* (line 19). Also, when a message arrives, we use the parameter name xJ to refer to the arriving value for the message field *x*.

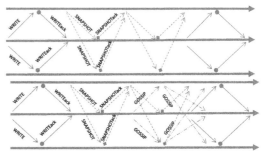

Fig. 1. Examples of Algorithm 1's executions. The upper drawing illustrates a case of a terminating snapshot operation (dashed line arrows) that occurs between two write operations (solid line arrows). The acknowledgments of these messages are arrows that start with circles and squares, respectively. The lower drawing depicts the execution of Algorithm 1's self-stabilizing version for the same case illustrated in the upper drawing. Note that the gossip messages do not interfere with other messages.

Node p_i stores the array *reg* (line 4), such that the k-th entry stores the most recent information about node p_k's object and $reg[i]$ stores p_i's actual object. Every entry is a pair of the form (v, ts), where the field v is an object value and ts is an unbounded object index. The relation $\preceq$ can compare (v, ts) and (v', ts') according to the write operation indices (line 1). Node p_i also has an index for the snapshot operations, *i.e.*, *ssn*.

The write(v) *Operation.* Algorithm 1's write(v) operation appears in lines 12 to 15 (client-side) and lines 17 to 23 (server-side). The client-side operation write(v) stores the pair (v, ts) in $reg[i]$ (line 13), where p_i is the calling node and ts is a unique operation index. Upon the arrival of a WRITE message to p_i from p_j (line 26), the server-side code is ran. Node p_i updates *reg* according to the timestamps of the arriving values (line 27). Then, p_i replies to p_j with the message WRITEack (line 31), which includes p_i's local perception of the system shared registers. Getting back to the client-side, p_i repeatedly broadcasts the message WRITE to all nodes until it receives replies from a majority of them (line 14). Once that happens, it uses the arriving values for keeping *reg* up-to-date (line 15).

The snapshot(v) *Operation.* Algorithm 1's snapshot() operation appears in lines 17 to 23 (client-side) and lines 29 to 31 (server-side). Delporte-Gallet *et al.* [6, Algorithm 1] is non-blocking w.r.t. snapshot operations (in the absence of writes). Thus, the client-side is written as a repeat-until loop. Node p_i tries to query the system for the most recent value of the shared registrars. As said, the success of such attempts depends on the absence of writes. Thus, before each such broadcast, p_i copies reg's value to $prev$ (line 19) and exits the repeat-until loop once the updated value of reg indicates the obscene of concurrent writes.

Algorithm 1: Self-stabilizing algorithm for non-blocking snapshot object; code for p_i. The boxed code lines mark our additions to Delporte-Gallet *et al.* [1, Algorithm 1].

---

1 **Definitions of $\preceq$:** For integers t and t': $(\bullet, t) \preceq (\bullet, t') \iff t \leq t'$; For arrays tab and tab' of $(\bullet, integer)$: $tab \preceq tab' \iff \forall p_k \in \mathcal{P} : tab[k] \preceq tab'[k]$; Also, $a \prec b \equiv a \preceq b \wedge a \neq b$;

2 **local variables initialization (optional in the context of self-stabilization):**
3    $ssn := 0; ts := 0;$ /* indices of the snapshout, resp., write operations */
4    $reg := [\bot, \ldots, \bot];$ /* shared registers ($\bot$ is smaller than any other written value) */

5 **macro** merge(Rec) **begin**
6    $ts \leftarrow \max(\{ts, reg[i].ts\} \cup \{r[i].ts \mid r \in Rec\});$
7   **for** $p_k \in \mathcal{P}$ **do** $reg[k] \leftarrow \max(\{reg[k]\} \cup \{r[k] \mid r \in Rec\});$

8 **do forever begin**
9   **foreach** $ssn' \neq ssn$ **do delete** SNAPSHOTack$(-, ssn')$;
10    $ts \leftarrow \max\{ts, reg[i].ts\};$
11   **for** $p_k \in \mathcal{P} : k \neq i$ **do send** GOSSIP($reg[k]$) to p_k;

12 **operation write(v) begin**
13    $ts \leftarrow ts + 1; reg[i] \leftarrow (v, ts);$ **let** $lReg := reg;$
14   **repeat broadcast** WRITE($lReg$); **until** WRITEack($regJ \succeq lReg$) *received from a majority*;
15   merge(Rec) **where** Rec is the set of reg arrays received at line 14;
16   **return**();

17 **operation snapshot() begin**
18   **repeat**
19   **let** $prev := reg;$ $ssn \leftarrow ssn + 1;$
20   **repeat broadcast** SNAPSHOT(reg, ssn); **until** SNAPSHOTack($\bullet, ssnJ = ssn$) *received from a majority*;
21   merge(Rec) **where** Rec is the set of reg arrays received at line 20;
22   **until** $prev = reg;$
23   **return**(reg);

24 **upon** message GOSSIP($regJ$) arrival from p_j **begin**
25    $reg[i] \leftarrow \max\{reg[i], regJ\}; ts \leftarrow \max\{ts, reg[i].ts\};$

26 **upon** message WRITE($regJ$) arrival from p_j **begin**
27   **for** $p_k \in \mathcal{P}$ **do** $reg[k] \leftarrow \max_{\preceq}(reg[k], regJ[k]);$
28   **send** WRITEack(reg) to p_j;

29 **upon** message SNAPSHOT($regJ, ssn$) arrival from p_j **begin**
30   **for** $p_k \in \mathcal{P}$ **do** $reg[k] \leftarrow \max_{\preceq}\{reg[k], regJ[k]\};$
31   **send** SNAPSHOTack(reg, ssn) to p_j;

The Proposed Unbounded Self-stabilizing Variation. We propose Algorithm 1 as an extension of Delporte-Gallet *et al.* [6, Algorithm 1]. The boxed code lines mark our additions. We denote variable X's value at node p_i by X_i. Algorithm 1 considers the case in which any of p_i's operation indices, ssn_i and

ts_i, is smaller than some other ssn or ts value, say, ssn_m, $reg_i[i].ts$, $reg_j[i].ts$ or $reg_m[i].ts$, where X_m appears in the X field of some on transit message. For the case of corrupted ssn values, p_i's client-side ignores arriving messages with ssn values that do not match ssn_i (line 20). The do-forever loop removes any stored snapshot reply whose ssn field is not ssn_i. For the case of corrupted ts values, p_i's do-forever loop makes sure that ts_i is not smaller than $reg_i[i].ts$ (line 10) before gossiping to every node $p_j \in \mathcal{P}$ its local copy of the shared register (line 11). Also, upon the arrival of such gossip messages, Algorithm 1 merges the arriving information with the local one (line 25). Moreover, when replies from write or snapshot messages arrive to p_i, it merges the arriving ts value with the one in ts_i (line 6). Figure 1's upper and lower drawings depict executions of the non-self-stabilizing algorithm [6], and respectively, our self-stabilizing version (Algorithm 1). The drawings illustrate a write operation that is followed by a snapshot operation and then a second write. We use this example for comparing Algorithms 1, 2 and 3 (the latter two are presented in Sect. 4). The complete discussion for Algorithm 1 and proof details appear in [9].

Theorem 1 (Recovery). *Within $\mathcal{O}(1)$ cycles, a fair execution of Algorithm 1 reaches a state c in which (i) ts_i's value is not smaller than any p_i's timestamp value. Also, if node p_i takes a step immediately after c that includes line 13, then in c it holds that $ts_i = reg_i[i].ts = reg_j[i].ts$ and for every messages m that is in transit from p_i to p_j or p_j to p_i it holds that $m.reg[i].ts = ts_i$. Moreover, (ii) ssn_i is not smaller than any p_i's snapshot sequence number.*

Proof Sketch. Arguments (1) to (3) show invariant (i). (1) *The values installed in ts_i, $reg_i[i].ts$, $reg_j[i].ts$, $reg_i[i]$ and $reg_j[i]$ are non-decreasing,* since their values are never decremented. (2) *Within $\mathcal{O}(1)$ cycles, $ts_i \geq reg_i[i].ts$,* since p_i executes line 10 at least once in every cycle. (3) Within $\mathcal{O}(1)$ cycles, $reg_i[i].ts \geq reg_m[i].ts$ and $reg_i[i].ts \geq regJ[i].ts$ whenever p_j raises SNAPSHOTack($regJ, ssn$) or WRITE($regJ$), where m' is a message on transit from p_j to p_k and denote $reg_{m'}$ as values of the reg filed in m', and $p_i, p_j, p_k \in \mathcal{P}$ are non-failing nodes (and $i = k$ possibly holds). Moreover, $reg_j[i].ts \geq reg_{m'}[i].ts$ and $reg_i[i].ts \geq regJ[i].ts$ whenever p_k raises GOSSIP($regJ$), WRITEack($regJ$) or SNAPSHOTack($regJ, \bullet$). The proof follows by the nodes' message exchange. Invariant (ii) follows by arguments similar to (1) to (3). ∎

4   The Always-Terminating Algorithm

Delporte-Gallet *et al.* [6, Algorithm 2] guarantee termination for any invocation pattern of write and snapshot operations, as long as the invoking nodes do not fail during these operations. Its advantage over Delporte-Gallet *et al.* [6, Algorithm 1] is that it can deal with an infinite number of concurrent write operations. Before proposing our self-stabilizing always-terminating solution, we bring [6, Algorithm 2] in Algorithm 2 using the presentation style of this paper.

Delporte-Gallet *et al.*'s Always-Terminating Algorithm. Delporte-Gallet *et al.* [6, Algorithm 2] use a job-stealing scheme for allowing rapid termination of snapshot operations. Node $p_i \in \mathcal{P}$ starts its snapshot operation by queueing this new task at all nodes $p_j \in \mathcal{P}$. Once p_j receives p_i's new task and when that task reaches the queue front, p_j starts the baseSnapshot(s,t) procedure, which is similar to Algorithm 1's snapshot() operation. This joint participation in all snapshot operations makes sure that all nodes are aware of all on-going snapshot operations. Moreover, it allows the nodes to make sure that no write() can stand in the way of on-going snapshot operations. To that end, the nodes wait until the oldest snapshot operation terminates before proceeding with later operations. Specifically, they defer write operations that run concurrently with snapshot operations. This guarantees termination of snapshot operations via the interleaving and synchronization of snapshot and write operations.

Algorithm 2 extends Algorithm 1 (non-self-stabilizing version, which does not include the boxed code lines) in the sense that it uses all of Algorithm 1's variables and an additional one, array *repSnap*, which snapshot() operations use.

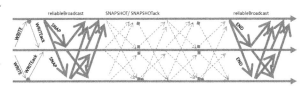

Fig. 2. Algorithm 2's run for the case of Fig. 1's upper drawing.

The entry $repSnap[x,y]$ holds the outcome of p_x's y-th snapshot operation, where no explicit bound on the number of invocations of snapshot operations is given. Note that bounded space is a prerequisite for self-stabilization.

The write(v) *Operation and the* baseWrite() *Function.* Since write(v) operations are preemptible, p_i cannot always start immediately to write. Instead, p_i stores v in $writePend_i$ together with a unique operation index (line 43). It then runs the operation as a background task (line 37) using baseWrite() (lines 47 to 50).

The snapshot() *Operation.* A call to snapshot() (line 45) causes p_i to reliably broadcast, via the primitive reliableBroadcast, a new *ssn* index in a SNAP to all nodes in $\mathcal{P}$. Node p_i then places it as a background task (line 46).

The baseSnapshot() *Function.* As in Algorithm 1's snapshot, the repeat-until loop iterates until the retrieved *reg* vector equals to the one that was known prior to the last repeat-until iteration. Then, p_i stores in $repSnap[s,t]$, via a reliable broadcast of the END message, the snapshot result (line 58 and 65).

Synchronization Between the baseWrite() *and* baseSnapshot() *functions.* Algorithm 2 interleaves the background tasks in a do forever loop (lines 37 to 41). As long as there is an awaiting write task, node p_i runs the baseWrite() function (line 37). Also, if there is an awaiting snapshot task, node p_i selects the oldest task, (*source, sn*), and uses the baseSnapshot(*source, sn*) function. Here, Algorithm 2 blocks until $repSnap[source, sn]$ contains the result of that snapshot task.

Figure 2 depicts an example of Algorithm 2's execution where a write operation is followed by a snapshot operation. Each snapshot is handled separately and the communications of each such operation requires $\mathcal{O}(n^2)$ messages.

Algorithm 2: The non-self-stabilizing and always-terminating algorithm by Delporte-Gallet *et al.* [6] that emulates snapshot object; code for p_i

```
32  local variables initialization: ssn := 0; ts := 0;  /* snapshout, resp., write indices */
33  reg := [⊥,...,⊥];  /* shared registers (⊥ is smaller than any other written value) */
34  foreach k, s : repSnap[k, s] := ⊥;   /* stores p_k's snapshot task result for index s */
35  macro merge(Rec) for p_k ∈ P do reg[k] ← max({reg[k]} ∪ {r[k] | r ∈ Rec});
36  do forever begin
37  |   if (writePending ≠ ⊥) then baseWrite(writePending); writePending ← ⊥;
38  |   if (there are messages SNAP() received and not yet processed) then
39  |   |   let SNAP(source, sn) be the oldest of these messages;
40  |   |   baseSnapshot(source, sn);
41  |   |_  wait until (repSnap[source, sn] ≠ ⊥);

42  operation write(v) begin
43  |_  writePending ← v; wait until (writePending = ⊥); return();

44  operation snapshot() begin
45  |   sns ← sns + 1; reliableBroadcast SNAP(i, sns);
46  |_  wait until (repSnap[i, sns] ≠ ⊥); return(repSnap[i, sns]);

47  function baseWrite(v) begin
48  |   ts ← ts + 1; reg[i] ← (ts, v); let lReg := reg;
49  |   repeat broadcast WRITE(lReg); until WRITEack(regJ ⪰ lReg) received from a
    |     majority;
50  |_  merge(Rec) where Rec is the set of reg arrays received at line 49;

51  function baseSnapshot(s, t) begin
52  |   while repSnap[s, t] = ⊥ do
53  |   |   let prev := reg; ssn ← ssn + 1;
54  |   |   repeat
55  |   |   |   broadcast SNAPSHOT(s, t, reg, ssn);
56  |   |   until (sJ = s, tJ = t, •, ssnJ = ssn) received from a majority);
57  |   |   merge(Rec) where Rec is the set of reg arrays received at line 55;
58  |   |_  if prev = reg then reliableBroadcast END(source, sn, prev);

59  upon message WRITE(regJ) arrival from p_j begin
60  |   for p_k ∈ P do reg[k] ← max_{≺sn}(reg[k], regJ[k]);
61  |_  send WRITEack(reg) to p_j;

62  upon message SNAPSHOT(s, t, regJ, ssnJ) arrival from p_j begin
63  |   for p_k ∈ P do reg[k] ← max_{≺sn}(reg[k], regJ[k]);
64  |_  send SNAPSHOTack(s, t, reg, ssnJ) to p_j;

65  upon message END(s, t, val) arrival from p_j do repSnap[s, t] ← val;
```

An Unbounded Self-stabilizing Always-Terminating algorithm. We propose Algorithm 3 as a variation of Delporte-Gallet *et al.* [6, Algorithm 2]. Algorithms 2 and 3 differ mainly in their ability to recover from transient faults. This implies some constraints. *E.g.*, Algorithm 3 must have a clear bound on the number of pending snapshot tasks. For the sake of simple presentation, Algorithm 3 assumes that the system needs, for each node, to cater for at most one pending snapshot task. We avoid the use of a reliable broadcast, which Delporte-Gallet *et al.* use, and instead, we use a simpler mechanism for safe registers.

Algorithm 3 can defer snapshot tasks until either (i) at least one node was able to observe at least δ concurrent write operations, where δ is an input parameter, or (ii) there are no concurrent write operations. The tunable parameter δ balances between the latency (with respect to snapshot operations) and communication costs. *I.e.,* for the case of δ being a very high (finite) value, Algorithm 3 guarantees termination in a way that resembles [6, Algorithm 1], which uses $\mathcal{O}(n)$ messages per snapshot operation, and for the case of $\delta = 0$, Algorithm 3 behaves in a way that resembles [6, Algorithm 2], which uses $\mathcal{O}(n^2)$ messages per snapshot.

Algorithm Details. Algorithm 3 lets every node disseminate its (at most one) pending snapshot task and use a safe register for facilitating the delivery of the task result to its initiator. *I.e.,* once a node finishes a snapshot task, it broadcasts the result to all nodes and waits for replies from a majority of nodes, which may possibly include the initiator of the snapshot task (see safeReg(), line 70). This way, if node p_j notices that it has the result of an ongoing snapshot task, it sends that result to the node who initiated the task.

The do forever loop. Algorithm 3's do forever loop (lines 73 to 79), includes a number of lines for cleaning stale information, *e.g.,* out-of-synch SNAPSHOTack messages (line 73), out-dated operation indices (line 74), illogical vector-clocks (line 75) or corrupted pndTsk entries (line 76). The gossiping of operation indices (lines 77 and 97) also helps to remove stale information (as in Algorithm 1 but only with the addition of *sns* values). The synchronization between write and snapshot operations (lines 78 and 79) starts with a write, if there is any such pending task (line 78), before running its own snapshot task, if there is any such pending, as well as any snapshot task (initiated by others) for which p_i observed that at least δ write operations occur concurrently with it (line 79).

The baseSnapshot() *Function and the* SNAPSHOT *Message.* Algorithm 3 maintains the state of every snapshot task in the array pndTsk. The entry $\text{pndTsk}_i[k] = (sns, vc, \text{fnl})$ includes: (i) the index sns of the most recent snapshot operation that $p_k \in \mathcal{P}$ has initiated and p_i is aware of, (ii) the vector clock representation of reg_k (*i.e.,* just the timestamps of reg_k, cf. line 68) and (iii) the final result fnl of the snapshot operation (or $\perp$, in case it is still running).

The baseSnapshot() function includes an outer loop part (lines 86 and 93), an inner loop part (lines 86 to 89), and a result update part (lines 90 to 92). The outer loop increments the snapshot index, ssn (line 86), so that it can consider a new query attempt by the inner loop. The outer loop ends when there are no more pending snapshot tasks that this call to baseSnapshot() needs to handle. The inner loop broadcasts SNAPSHOT messages, which includes all the pending snapshot tasks, $(S \cap \Delta)$, that are relevant to this call to baseSnapshot() together with the local current value of reg and the snapshot query index ssn. The inner loop ends when acknowledgments are received from a majority of processors and the received values are merged (line 89). The results are updated by writing to an emulated safe shared register (line 90) whenever $prev = reg$. In case the results do not allow p_i to terminate its snapshot task (line 92), Algorithm 3 uses the query results for storing the timestamps in the field vs. This allows to balance a trade-off between snapshot operation latency and communication costs, as we explain next.

The Use of the Input Parameter δ for Balancing the Trade-off Between Snapshot Operation Latency and Communication Costs. For the case of δ = 0, since no snapshot task is to be deferred, the set Δ (line 69) includes all the nodes for which there is no stored result, *i.e.,* pndTsk[k].fnl = ⊥. The case of δ > 0 uses the fact that Algorithm 3 samples the vector clock value of reg_k and stores it in pndTsk[k].vc (line 92) once it had completed at least one iteration of the repeat-until loop (line 88 and 89). *I.e.,* the sampling of the vector clock is an event that occurs not before the start of p_k's snapshot (that has the index pndTsk[k].sns).

Many-jobs-stealing scheme for reduced blocking periods. Whenever pndTsk[k].fnl ≠ ⊥ and sns > 0, we consider p_k's task as active. To the end of helping all actives tasks, p_i samples the set of currently pending task ($S_i ∩ Δ_i$) (line 86) before starting the inner repeat-until loop (lines 88 to 89) and broadcasting the client-side message SNAPSHOT, which includes the most recent snapshot task information. The server-side reception of this message (lines 102 to 103), updates the local information (line 104) and sends the reply to the client-side (lines 105 to 106). Note that if the receiver notices that it has the result of an ongoing snapshot task, then it sends that result to the requesting processor (line 106).

The safeReg() Function and the SAVE Message. The safeReg() function considers a snapshot task that was initiated by node $p_k ∈ \mathcal{P}$. This function is responsible for storing the results of snapshot tasks in a safe register. It does so by broadcasting the client-side message SAVE to all nodes in the system (line 70). Upon the arrival of the SAVE message to the server-side, the receiver stores the arriving information, as long as the arriving information is more recent than the local one. Then, the server-side replies with a SAVEack message to the client-side, who is waiting for a majority of such replies (line 70).

Figure 3 depicts two examples of Algorithm 3's execution. In the upper drawing, a write operation is followed by a snapshot operation. Note that fewer messages are considered when comparing to Fig. 2's example. The lower drawing illustrates the case of concurrent invocations of snapshot operations by all nodes. Observe the potential improvement with respect to number of messages (in the upper drawing) and throughput (in the lower drawing) since Algorithm 2 uses $\mathcal{O}(n^2)$ messages for each snapshot task and handles only one snapshot task at a time.

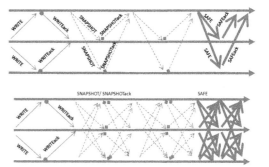

Fig. 3. The upper drawing depicts an example of Algorithm 3's execution for a case that is equivalent to the one depicted in the upper drawing of Fig. 2, i.e., only one snapshot operation. The lower drawing illustrates the case of concurrent invocations of snapshot operations by all nodes.

Algorithm 3: Self-stabilizing always-terminating snapshot; code for p_i

---

66 **input:** δ a number of observed concurrent writes after which writes block temporarily;

67 **variables:** $ts := 0$ is p_i's write operation index; $ssn, sns := 0$ are p_i's snapshot operation indices; $reg[n] := [\bot, \ldots, \bot]$ buffers all shared registers; $\mathrm{pndTsk}[n] := [(0, \bot, \bot), \ldots, (0, \bot, \bot)]$ control variables of snapshot operations; each entry form is (sns, vc, fnl), where sns is an index, vc is a vector clock that time stamps the snapshot operation sns, and fnl is the operation's returned value; (In the context of self-stabilization, variable initialization is optional.)

68 **macro** $\mathrm{VC} := [ts_k]_{p_k \in \mathcal{P}}$ **where** $ts_k := 0$ when $reg[k] = \bot$ **otherwise** $reg[k] = (\bullet, ts_k)$;

69 **macro** $\Delta := \{(k, \mathrm{pndTsk}[k].sns, \mathrm{pndTsk}[k].vc) | p_k \in \mathcal{P} \wedge \mathrm{pndTsk}[k].fnl = \bot \wedge ((\delta = 0 \wedge \mathrm{pndTsk}[k].sns > 0) \vee (\mathrm{pndTsk}[k].vc \neq \bot \wedge \delta \leq \sum_{\ell \in \{1, \ldots, n\}} \mathrm{VC}[\ell] - \mathrm{pndTsk}[k].vc[\ell]))\} \cup \{(i, \mathrm{pndTsk}[i].sns, \mathrm{pndTsk}[i].vc) : \mathrm{pndTsk}[i].sns > 0 \wedge \mathrm{pndTsk}[i].fnl = \bot\}$;

70 **macro** safeReg(A) **repeat** broadcast SAVE(A) **until** majority of SAVEack($AJ = \{(k, s) : (k, s, \bullet) \in A\}$) arrived;

71 **macro** merge(Rec) $\{ts \leftarrow \max(\{ts, reg[i].ts\} \cup \{r[i].ts \mid r \in Rec\}); \textbf{for } p_k \in \mathcal{P} \textbf{ do } reg[k] \leftarrow \max(\{reg[k]\} \cup \{r[k] \mid r \in Rec\})\}$;

72 **do forever begin**

73   **foreach** $ssn' \neq ssn$ **do** delete SNAPSHOTack($-, ssn'$);

74      $(ts, sns) \leftarrow (\max\{ts, reg[i].ts\}, \max\{sns, \mathrm{pndTsk}[i].sns\})$;

75   **for** $k \in \{1, \ldots, n\} : \mathrm{pndTsk}[k].vc \npreceq \mathrm{VC}$, **where line 1 defines the relation** $\preceq$ **do** $\mathrm{pndTsk}[k].vc \leftarrow \bot$;

76   **if** $sns \neq \mathrm{pndTsk}[i].sns$ **then** $\mathrm{pndTsk}[i] \leftarrow (sns, \bot, \bot)$;

77   **for** $p_k \in \mathcal{P} : k \neq i$ **do** send GOSSIP($reg[k], \mathrm{pndTsk}[i].sns$) to p_k;

78   **if** $writePending \neq \bot$ **then** {baseWrite($writePending$); $writePending \leftarrow \bot$; };

79   **if** $\Delta \neq \emptyset$ **then** baseSnapshot(Δ);

80 **operation** write(v) $\{writePending \leftarrow v; \textbf{wait until } (writePending = \bot); \textbf{return}();\}$

81 **operation** snapshot() **begin**

82      $(sns, \mathrm{pndTsk}[i]) \leftarrow (sns + 1, (sns, \bot, \bot)); \textbf{wait until}$ $(\mathrm{pndTsk}[i].fnl \neq \bot); \textbf{return}(\mathrm{pndTsk}[i].fnl)$;

83 **function** baseWrite(v) $\{ts \leftarrow ts + 1; reg[i] \leftarrow (ts, v); \textbf{let } lReg := reg; \textbf{repeat}$ broadcast WRITE($lReg$); merge(Rec) **where** Rec is the received reg arrays} **until** WRITEack($regJ \succeq lReg$) received from a majority;

84 **function** baseSnapshot(S) **begin**

85   **repeat**

86          $ssn \leftarrow ssn + 1; \textbf{let } prev := reg; \textbf{repeat}$

87   broadcast SNAPSHOT($(S \cap \Delta), reg, ssn$);

88   **until** $(S \cap \Delta) = \emptyset$ or majority of (SNAPSHOTack($\bullet, ssnJ = ssn$) arrived);

89   merge(Rec) **where** Rec is the set of reg arrays received at line 87;

90   **if** $prev = reg \wedge (S \cap \Delta) \neq \emptyset$ **then**

91   safeReg($\{(k, \mathrm{pndTsk}[k].sns, prev) : (k, s, \bullet) \in S\}$)

92   **else if** $((i, \bullet) \in (S \cap \Delta)) \wedge (\mathrm{pndTsk}[i].vc = \bot)$ **then** $\mathrm{pndTsk}[i].vc \leftarrow \mathrm{VC}$;

93   **until** $(S \cap \Delta) = \emptyset \vee ((S \cap \Delta) = (i, \bullet) \wedge \mathrm{pndTsk}[i].sns > 0 \wedge \mathrm{pndTsk}[i].fnl = \bot \wedge \delta \leq \sum_{\ell \in \{1, \ldots, n\}} (\mathrm{VC}[\ell] - \mathrm{pndTsk}[i].vc[\ell]))$;

94 **upon** message SAVE(AJ) arrival from p_j **begin**

95   **foreach** $(k, s, r) \in AJ : \mathrm{pndTsk}[k].sns < s \vee \mathrm{pndTsk}[k] = (s, \bullet, \bot)$ **do** $(\mathrm{pndTsk}[k].sns, \mathrm{pndTsk}[k].fnl) \leftarrow (s, r)$;

96   send SAVEack($\{(k, s) : (k, s, \bullet) \in AJ\}$) to p_j;

97 **upon** message GOSSIP($regJ, snsJ$) arrival from p_j **begin**

98      $reg[i] \leftarrow \max\{reg[i], regJ\}; (ts, sns) \leftarrow (\max\{ts, reg[i].ts\}, \max\{sns, snsJ\})$;

99 **upon** message WRITE($regJ$) arrival from p_j **begin**

100   **for** $p_k \in \mathcal{P}$ **do** $reg[k] \leftarrow \max_{\prec_{sn}}(reg[k], regJ[k])$;

101   send WRITEack(reg) to p_j;

102 **upon** message SNAPSHOT($SJ, regJ, ssnJ$) arrival from p_j **begin**

103   **for** $p_k \in \mathcal{P}$ **do** $reg[k] \leftarrow \max_{\prec_{sn}}(reg[k], regJ[k])$;

104   **foreach** $(s, sn, vc) \in SJ : \mathrm{pndTsk}[s].sns < sn \vee \mathrm{pndTsk}[s] = (sn, \bot, \bot)$ **do** $\mathrm{pndTsk}[s] \leftarrow (sn, vc, \bot)$;

105   **let** $A := \{(k, \mathrm{pndTsk}[k].sns, \mathrm{pndTsk}[k].fnl) : (k, \bullet) \in SJ \wedge \mathrm{pndTsk}[k].fnl \neq \bot\}$;

106   send SNAPSHOTack($reg, ssnJ$) to p_j; **if** $A \neq \emptyset$ **then** send SAVE(A) to p_j ;

Correctness. The complete discussion and proof details appear in [9].

Definition 1 (Consistent system states and executions). *(i) Let c be a system state in which ts_i is greater than or equal to any p_i's timestamp values in the variables and fields related to ts. We say that the ts' timestamps are consistent in c. (ii) Let c be a system state in which ssn_i is greater than or equal to any p_i's snapshot sequence numbers in the variables and fields related to ssn. We say that the ssn's snapshot sequence numbers are consistent in c. (iii) Let c be a system state in which sns_i is not smaller than any p_i's snapshot index sns. Moreover, $\forall p_i \in \mathcal{P} : sns_i = \mathrm{pndTsk}_i[i].sns$ and $\forall p_i, p_j \in \mathcal{P} : \mathrm{pndTsk}_j[i].sns \leq \mathrm{pndTsk}_i[i].sns$. We say that the sns's snapshot indices are consistent in c. (iv) Let c be a system state in which $\forall p_i, p_k \in \mathcal{P} : \mathrm{pndTsk}_i[k].vc \preceq VC_i$ holds, where VC_i is the returned value from VC() (line 68). We say that the vector clock values are consistent in c. We say that system state c is consistent if it is consistent with respect to invariants (i) to (iv). Let R be an execution of Algorithm 3 that all of its system states are consistent and R' be a suffix of R. We say that execution R' is consistent (with respect to R) if any message arriving in R' was indeed sent in R and any reply arriving in R' has a matching request in R.*

Theorem 2 (Recovery). *Let R be Algorithm 3's fair execution. Within $\mathcal{O}(1)$ cycles in R, the system reaches a consistent state $c \in R$ (Definition 1). Within $\mathcal{O}(1)$ cycles after c, the system starts a consistent execution R'.*

Proof Sketch. Note that Theorem 1 implies invariants (i) and (ii) of Definition 1 also for the case of Algorithm 3, because they use the similar lines of code for asserting these invariants. For invariant (iii), *sns* and pndTsk in Algorithm 3 follow the same propagation patterns as *ts* and *reg* in Algorithm 1. Moreover, within a cycle, every $p_i \in \mathcal{P}$ executes line 76. Thus, invariant (iii)'s proof follows similar arguments to the ones in Theorem 1's proof. Invariant (iv)'s proof is implied by the fact that within a cycle, $p_i \in \mathcal{P}$ executes line 75. By the definition of cycles (Sect. 2), within a cycle, R reaches a suffix R', such that every received message during R' was sent during R. By repeating the previous argument, it holds that within $\mathcal{O}(1)$ cycles, R reaches a suffix R' in which for every received reply has an associated request that was sent during R.   ∎

Theorem 3 (Algorithm 3's termination and linearization). *Let R be Algorithm 3's consistent execution (Definition 1). Suppose that there exists $p_i \in \mathcal{P}$, such that in R's second system state, it holds that $\mathrm{pndTsk}_i[i] = (s, \bullet, \bot)$ and $s > 0$. Within $\mathcal{O}(\delta)$ cycles, the system reaches $c \in R : \mathrm{pndTsk}_i[i] = (s, \bullet, x) : x \neq \bot$.*

Proof Sketch. Lemma 1 sketches the key arguments of the termination proof.

Lemma 1 (Algorithm 3's termination). *Within $\mathcal{O}(\delta)$ cycles, the system reaches a state $c \in R$ in which either: (i) for any non-failing node $p_j \in \mathcal{P}$ it holds that $i \in \Delta_j$ (line 69) and $\mathrm{pndTsk}_j[i] = (s, \bullet, \bot)$, (ii) $\forall M \subseteq \mathcal{P} : |M| > |\mathcal{P}|/2 : \exists_{p_j \in M} : \mathrm{pndTsk}_j[i] = (s, \bullet, x) : x \neq \bot$ or (iii) $\mathrm{pndTsk}_i[i] = (s, \bullet, x) : x \neq \bot$.*

Proof Sketch. We show that R has a prefix R' that includes $\mathcal{O}(\delta)$ cycles, such that none of the lemma invariants hold during R'.

Claim (a). There is no step $a_i \in R'$ in which p_i evaluate the if-statement condition in line 90 to be true (or one of the lemma invariants holds).

Proof of Claim. Towards a contradiction, suppose that $a_i \in R$ calls $\mathsf{safeReg}_i()$. Arguments (1) and (2) show that this happens for the case of $k = i$, and that invariant (ii) holds. *Argument (1): a_i includes the execution of line 90.* This is because, once in $\mathcal{O}(1)$ cycles, p_i calls $\mathsf{baseSnapshot}_i(S_i)$ (line 79), which does not change the value of S_i. *Argument (2): invariant (ii) holds.* The function $\mathsf{safeReg}_i(\{(\bullet, r) : r \neq \bot\})$ (line 70) repeatedly broadcasts $\mathrm{SAVE}(\{(\bullet, r) : r \neq \bot\})$ until p_i receives $\mathrm{SAVEack}(\{(\bullet, r) : r \neq \bot\})$ from a majority. Theorem 2 and R's consistency imply that every received SAVEack is associated with a SAVE that was sent in R. Invariant (ii) holds due to the majority intersection property. □

Claim (b). Within $\mathcal{O}(1)$ asynchronous cycles, the system reaches a state $c' \in R'$ in which for any non-faulty node $p_j \in \mathcal{P}$ it holds that $\mathrm{pndTsk}_j[i] = (s, y, \bullet) : y \neq \bot$.

Proof of Claim. For the case of $j = i$, we note that claim (a) implies that $(i, \bullet) \in S_i$ holds and the execution of line 92 in every call for $\mathsf{baseSnapshot}(S_i)$. For the $j \neq i$ case, we note that within $\mathcal{O}(1)$ cycles, p_i executes lines 86 and 87 in which p_i broadcasts $\mathrm{SNAPSHOT}(\{(\bullet, \mathrm{pndTsk}_i[i].vc), \bullet\})$, such that $\mathrm{pndTsk}_i[i].vc \neq \bot$ holds by the case of $j = i$. Once p_j receives this message, $\mathrm{pndTsk}_j[i].vc \neq \bot$ holds (line 104). The above arguments for the case of $j \neq i$ can be repeated as long as invariant (iii) does not hold. Thus, the arrival of such a SNAPSHOT message to all $p_j \in \mathcal{P}$ occurs within $\mathcal{O}(1)$ asynchronous cycles. □

Claim (c). Let $c' \in R'$ be a system state in which for any non-faulty node $p_j \in \mathcal{P}$ it holds that $\mathrm{pndTsk}_j[i] = (s, y, \bullet) : y \neq \bot$. Let x be the number of iterations of the outer loop in $\mathsf{baseSnapshot}()$ (lines 86 and 93) that node p_i takes between c' and $c'' \in R'$, where c'' is a system state after which it takes at most $\mathcal{O}(\delta)$ asynchronous cycles until the system reach the state c''' in which at least one of the lemma invariants holds. The value of x is actually finite and $x \leq \delta$.

Proof of Claim. Argument (1): during the outer loop in $\mathsf{baseSnapshot}()$ (lines 86 and 93), p_i tests the if-statement condition at line 90 and that condition does not hold, due to Claim (a). Argument (2): suppose that there are at least x consecutive and complete iterations of p_i's outer loop in $\mathsf{baseSnapshot}()$ (lines 86 and 93) between c' and c'' in which the if-statement condition at line 90 does not hold. Then, there are at least x write operations that run concurrently with the snapshot operation that has the index of s, since the only way that the if-statement condition in line 90 does not hold in a repeated manner is by repeated changes of ts fields in reg_i during the different executions of lines 86 to 89 (due to line 80 of $\mathsf{write}()$). We define the function $\mathcal{S}_i()$ so that whenever p_i's program counter is outside of the function $\mathsf{baseSnapshot}()$, $\mathcal{S}_i()$ returns Δ_i. Otherwise, it returns $(S_i \cap \Delta_i)$. Argument (3): there exists $x' \leq \delta$ for which $(i, \bullet) \in \mathcal{S}_i()$, where x' is the number of consecutive and complete iterations of p_i's outer loop in baseSnapshot() *between c' and c'' in which the if-statement condition at line 90 does not hold.* This is because Argument (2) implies that the number of iterations continues to grow. During every such iteration there are increments of the summation $\sum_{\ell \in \{1,\dots,n\}} \text{VC}_i[\ell] - \text{pndTsk}_i[i].vc[\ell]$ until it is at least δ, and thus, $(i, \bullet) \in \mathcal{S}_i()$ holds (line 69 , for the case of $k = i$). *Argument (4): suppose that p_i has taken at least x' iterations of the outer loop in* baseSnapshot() *(lines 86 and 93) after system state c'. After this, suppose that the system has reached a state c'' in which $i \in \Delta_i$, where c'' is defined in Argument (3). Within $\mathcal{O}(1)$ cycles after c'', the system reaches c''' in which $i \in \Delta_j$ holds for any non-failing $p_j \in \mathcal{P}$.* Within $\mathcal{O}(1)$ asynchronous cycles after c'', it holds that reg_i's ts fields are not smaller than the ones of reg_i's ts fields in c'' (because in every iteration of the outer loop in baseSnapshot(), p_i broadcasts reg_i and these broadcasts arrive within one cycle to p_j, who updates reg_j). The rest of the proof shows that $i \in \Delta_j$ holds (line 69, case of $k = i$), as in Argument (3).   □

This completes the proof of the lemma.   ■

The rest of the theorem's proof considers the case in which (i) in any system state of R, it holds that $\text{pndTsk}_i[i] = (s, \bullet, \bot)$, $s > 0$ and any majority $M \subseteq \mathcal{P} : |M| > |\mathcal{P}|/2$ include at least one $p_j \in M$, such that $\text{pndTsk}_j[i] = (s, \bullet, x) : x \neq \bot$, or (ii) in any system state of R, it holds that $\text{pndTsk}_i[i] = (s, \bullet, \bot)$, $s > 0$ and for any non-failing node $p_j \in \mathcal{P}$ it holds that $i \in \Delta_j$ (line 69) and $\text{pndTsk}_j[i] = (s, \bullet, \bot)$. The idea is to show that within $\mathcal{O}(1)$ cycles, the system is in state $c \in R$ in which $\text{pndTsk}_i[i] = (s, \bullet, x) : x \neq \bot$. For the case (i), the proof shows that p_i receives a SNAPSHOTack message that matches the first condition in line 88 due to a reply to an SNAPSHOT message in line 105. The proof of case (ii) follows by the fact that all non-failing nodes participate in a helping scheme that solves p_i's task and then write the result to a safe register by calling safeReg() in line 90.

Linearizability. We note that the baseWrite(wp) functions in Algorithms 2 and 3 are identical. Moreover, Algorithm 2's lines 53 to 55 are similar to Algorithm 3's lines 86 to 89, but differ in the following manner: (i) the dissemination of the operation tasks is done outside of Algorithm 2's lines 53 to 55 but inside of Algorithm 3's lines 86, and (ii) Algorithm 2 considers one snapshot operation at a time whereas Algorithm 3 considers many snapshot operations. The linearizability proof of Delporte-Gallet *et al.* [6, Lemma 7] is independent of the task dissemination and result propagation. Moreover, it shows a way to select linearization points according to some partition. The proof there explicitly allows the same partition to include more than one snapshot result.   ■

5   Bounded Variations on Algorithms 1 and 3

There is a technique for transforming a self-stabilizing atomic register algorithm that uses unbounded operation indices into one with bounded indices, see [8, Section 10]: [Step-1] once p_i notices an index that is at least MAXINT $= 2^{64} - 1$, it disables new operations and starts gossiping of the maximal indices (while merging the arriving information with the local one). [Step-2] once all nodes share the same maximal indices, the procedure uses a consensus-based global reset procedure for replacing, per operation type, the highest operation index with its initial value, 0, while keeping the values of all shared registers unchanged. After the end of the global reset procedure, all operations are enabled.

Self-stabilizing Global Reset Procedure. The implementation of the self-stabilizing procedure for global reset can be based on existing mechanisms, such as the one by Awerbuch *et al.* [12]. We note that the system settings of Awerbuch *et al.* [12] assume execution fairness. This assumption is allowed by our system settings (Sect. 2). This is because we assume that reaching MAXINT can only occur due to a transient fault. Thus, execution fairness, which implies all nodes are eventually alive, is seldom required (only for recovering from transient faults).

6   Discussion

We showed how to transform the two non-self-stabilizing algorithms of Delporte-Gallet *et al.* [6] into ones that can recover after the occurrence of transient faults. This requires some non-trivial considerations that are imperative for self-stabilizing systems, such as the explicit use of bounded memory and the reoccurring clean-up of stale information. Interestingly, these considerations are not restrictive for the case of Delporte-Gallet *et al.* [6]. As a future direction, we propose to consider the techniques presented here for providing self-stabilizing versions of more advanced algorithms, *e.g.,* [13].

References

1. Afek, Y., Attiya, H., Dolev, D., Gafni, E., Merritt, M., Shavit, N.: Atomic snapshots of shared memory. J. ACM **40**(4), 873–890 (1993)
2. Anderson, J.H.: Multi-writer composite registers. Distrib. Comput. **7**(4), 175–195 (1994)
3. Dijkstra, E.W.: Self-stabilizing systems in spite of distributed control. Commun. ACM **17**(11), 643–644 (1974)
4. Dolev, S.: Self-Stabilization. MIT Press, Cambridge (2000)
5. Attiya, H., Bar-Noy, A., Dolev, D.: Sharing memory robustly in message-passing systems. J. ACM **42**(1), 124–142 (1995)
6. Delporte-Gallet, C., Fauconnier, H., Rajsbaum, S., Raynal, M.: Implementing snapshot objects on top of crash-prone asynchronous message-passing systems. IEEE Trans. Parallel Distrib. Syst. **29**(9), 2033–2045 (2018)
7. Alon, N., Attiya, H., Dolev, S., Dubois, S., Potop-Butucaru, M., Tixeuil, S.: Practically stabilizing SWMR atomic memory in message-passing systems. J. Comput. Syst. Sci. **81**(4), 692–701 (2015)
8. Dolev, S., Petig, T., Schiller, E.M.: Self-stabilizing and private distributed shared atomic memory in seldomly fair message passing networks. CoRR abs/1806.03498 (2018)

 9. Georgiou, C., Lundström, O., Schiller, E.M.: Self-stabilizing snapshot objects for asynchronous failure-prone networked systems. CoRR (2019)
10. Georgiou, C., Shvartsman, A.A.: Cooperative Task-Oriented Computing: Algorithms and Complexity. Synthesis Lectures on Distributed Computing Theory. Morgan & Claypool Publishers (2011)
11. Lynch, N.A.: Distributed Algorithms. Morgan Kaufmann, San Francisco (1996)
12. Awerbuch, B., Patt-Shamir, B., Varghese, G., Dolev, S.: Self-stabilization by local checking and global reset. In: Tel, G., Vitányi, P. (eds.) WDAG 1994. LNCS, vol. 857, pp. 326–339. Springer, Heidelberg (1994). https://doi.org/10.1007/BFb0020443
13. Imbs, D., Mostéfaoui, A., Perrin, M., Raynal, M.: Set-constrained delivery broadcast: Definition, abstraction power, and computability limits. In: 19th Distributed Computing and Networking, ICDCN, ACM (2018) 7:1–7:10

Self-stabilization Overhead: A Case Study on Coded Atomic Storage

Chryssis Georgiou[1], Robert Gustafsson[2,3], Andreas Lindhé[2,3], and Elad Michael Schiller[2(✉)]

[1] University of Cyprus, Nicosia, Cyprus
chryssis@cs.ucy.ac.cy
[2] Chalmers University of Technology, Gothenburg, Sweden
{robg,lindhea}@student.chalmers.se, elad@chalmers.se
[3] Combitech AB, Linköping, Sweden
{andreas.lindhe,robert.gustafsson1}@combitech.se

Abstract. Shared memory emulation on distributed message-passing systems can be used as a fault-tolerant and highly available distributed storage solution or as a low-level synchronization primitive. Cadambe *et al.* proposed the Coded Atomic Storage (CAS) algorithm, which uses erasure coding to achieve data redundancy with much lower communication cost than previous algorithmic solutions. Recently, Dolev *et al.* introduced a version of CAS where transient faults are included in the fault model, making it self-stabilizing. But self-stabilization comes at a cost, so in this work we examine the overhead of the algorithm by implementing a system we call CASSS (CAS Self-Stabilizing). Our system builds on the self-stabilizing version of CAS, along with several other self-stabilizing building blocks. This provides us with a powerful platform to evaluate the overhead and other aspects of the real-world applicability of the algorithm.

In our case-study, we evaluated the system performance by running it on the world-wide distributed platform PlanetLab. Our study shows that CASSS scales very well in terms of the number of servers, the number of concurrent clients, as well as the size of the replicated object. More importantly, it shows (a) to have only a constant overhead compared to the traditional CAS algorithm and (b) the recovery period (after the last occurrence of a transient fault) is no more than the time it takes to perform a few client (read/write) operations. Our results suggest that the self-stabilizing variation of CAS, which is CASSS, does not significantly impact efficiency while dealing with automatic recovery from transient faults.

1 Introduction

Sharing a data object among decentralized servers that provide distributed storage has been an active research topic for decades. We consider the problem of emulating a shared memory in a way that appears atomic (linearizable) [1]. Early solutions [2,3] do not scale well when it comes to larger data objects due to the

© Springer Nature Switzerland AG 2019
M. F. Atig and A. A. Schwarzmann (Eds.): NETYS 2019, LNCS 11704, pp. 131–147, 2019.
https://doi.org/10.1007/978-3-030-31277-0_9

use of full replication of the data to all servers in the system. Cadambe *et al.* [4] proposed the *Coded Atomic Storage* (CAS) algorithm, which uses erasure coding in order to achieve data redundancy but with much lower communication cost compared with algorithms that use full replication. Although CAS provides an efficient solution that tolerates node crashes, Dolev *et al.* [5,6] solve the same problem while considering an even more attractive notion of fault-tolerance since their solution can recover after the occurrence of *transient faults*. Such faults model any violation of the assumption according to which the system was designed to operate. Dolev *et al.* present a self-stabilizing version of CAS, which we refer to as CASSS (CAS Self-Stabilizing). Unlike CAS, their version guarantees recovery after the occurrence of transient faults. The authors suggests that the variant of CAS from [5] has similar communication costs as CAS [4]. Our results validate [5]'s prediction, but more importantly, they demonstrate the system's ability to recover from transient faults efficiently, while tolerating node failures.

Atomic Shared Memory Emulation. The goal of emulating a shared memory is to allow the clients to access via read and write operations a shared storage in the network. By that, the service hides from the user low-level details, such as message exchange between the clients and the servers. As the shared data is replicated on the servers, data consistency between the replicas (data copies) must be ensured. Atomicity (linearizability) [1] is the strongest consistency guarantee and provides the illusion that operations on the distributed storage are invoked sequentially, even though they can be invoked concurrently. A read (resp. write) operation is invoked with a read (resp. write) request and it *completes* with a response (*e.g.*, an acknowledgment). There are two criteria that need to be satisfied for the atomicity property: (1) Any invocation of a read operation, after a write operation is completed, must return a value at least as recent as the value written by that write operation. (2) A read operation that follows another read operation will return a value at least as recent as the value returned by the first read operation. Thus, the operations appear sequential.

Fault Model. *(i) Benign Failures.* We consider message passing systems in which communication failures may occur during packet transit, such as packet loss, duplication, and reordering. However, the studied algorithms assume *communication fairness*, *i.e.*, if the sender transmits a packet infinitely often, the receiver gets this packet infinitely often. The early solutions [2,3] model node failures as crashes and restrict the number f of failing servers (nodes) to be less than half of the nodes in the system. We follow a similar approach but require that in the presence of transient faults, and only then, a crashed node either restarts (we call this a *detectable restart*) or is removed from the system via a reconfiguration service [7]. Moreover, as specified in [5,6], our restriction on the number of crashes f is similar to the one of CAS [4].

(ii) Transient Faults. We also consider violations of the assumptions according to which the system was designed to operate. We model their impact on the system as arbitrary changes of the *state*, as long as the program code stays intact. Since these faults are rare, our model assumes that the system starts after the last occurrence of these transient faults. Transient faults can, for example, be soft errors (which are sometime called, single event upset) or the event of a CRC code failing to detect a bit error in a transmitted packet.

(iii) Self-stabilization. These design criteria, which requires recovery without external (human) intervention, provides a strong fault-tolerance guarantee in that the system always recovers from transient faults. By the definition given by Dijkstra [8], the correctness proof of a self-stabilizing system needs to show recovery within a bounded period after the last transient fault. That is, when starting from an arbitrary system state, the system needs to exhibit legal behavior within a bounded time.

Dolev *et al.* [7] proposed the following refinement of Dijkstra's design criteria of self-stabilization, which we believe to be convenient for dealing with the asynchronous nature of distributed systems. In the absence of transient faults, the environment is assumed to be asynchronous. Moreover, servers and clients may at any time crash. In the presence of transient faults, it is assumed that (a) all failing servers to recover eventually and (b) there is a sufficiently long period (which allows recovery) in which the system run is fair, *i.e.,* each node makes progress infinitely often.

Related Work. Shared memory can support either a *single-writer and multi-reader* (SWMR) context, *e.g.,* ABD [2], or a *multi-writer and multi-reader* (MWMR) context, *e.g.,* MW-ABD [3]. A discussion on such non-self-stabilizing solutions is given in [9].

The term *reconfiguration* refers to a change from one server configuration to another and requires old configuration members to send the data to the new members; the data is replicated to all configuration members. Shared memory emulation has also been studied under such dynamic server participation, *e.g.,* RAMBO [10]. See [11] for a survey on (non-self-stabilizing) reconfigurable solutions to memory emulation. ARES [12] is a recent solution that supports reconfiguration of a shared memory emulation service and is based on erasure coding. The authors also present the first atomic memory service that uses erasure coding with only two rounds of message exchanges for a client operation. While combining these two creates an efficient solution with respect to liveness, even during configuration collapses, such a solution does not consider self-stabilization.

Nicolaou and Georgiou [13] did an experimental evaluation of four non-self-stabilizing MWMR register emulation algorithms on PlanetLab. The algorithms evaluated were *SWF, APRX-SWF, CwFr* and *SIMPLE*. Algorithm SIMPLE is an MWMR version of ABD for quorum systems (quorums are intersecting sets of servers), similar to the one we use in this work (called MW-ABD) to compare its performance with CAS and CASSS.

Our Contributions. We are the first to implement, and evaluate via experiments, a self-stabilizing algorithm for coded atomic MWMR shared memory emulation. We show that the overhead associated with self-stabilization does not really affect the efficiency advantage associated with erasure coding. We have also implemented a (graceful) counter restart mechanism, based on principles from [7]. The counter restart mechanism can perform a (synchronized) global reset of the entire system while keeping the most recently written data object using an agreement protocol. Additionally, we implemented a self-stabilizing reincarnation number service [5], which provides recyclable client identifiers, and by that helps to deal with detectable client restarts.

Our experiments on PlanetLab shows that our pilot implementations of CAS and CASSS have comparable performances with respect to operation latency. Furthermore, the evaluation shows that our implementation of CASSS scales very well when increasing the number of servers and clients, respectively. More importantly, the overhead caused by self-stabilization in our experiments is only greater than the non-self-stabilizing CAS implementation by a *constant* factor. The system evaluation shows almost no slowdown for data objects up to 512 KiB, and is only slightly slower for data objects up to 1 MiB. Last but not least, the evaluation reveals that the counter restart mechanism is fast – it takes about the same amount of time as three or four normal write operations. This demonstrates CASSS's ability to rapidly recover from transient faults. Encouraged by these evaluation results, we believe that our pilots and their building blocks could be used for implementing other self-stabilizing algorithms and prototypes.

2   System and Background

The system includes a network of N nodes. Each node can host clients and/or servers. Servers use a gossip service for communicating among themselves. Clients interact with the shared-memory service using read and write operations. These operations include multiple communication rounds of requests and responses. Every client performs its operations sequentially, but its operations may be interleaved arbitrarily with operations from other clients.

Servers are arranged into pairwise intersecting sets, or *quorums*, that together form a *quorum system*. The intersection property of quorums enables information communicated to a quorum to be passed (via the common servers) to another quorum. Majorities (subsets containing a majority of the servers) form a simple quorum system (used, for example, in ABD [2]). The *self-stabilizing* quorum system considered in this work follows the one proposed in [5,6]. We note that the quorum system needs to be self-stabilizing. This is, for example, because of the fact that client algorithms often include several phases. The clients and the servers needs to be synchronized both with respect to the phases and the associated object version.

Each server has access to a set of *records*, which are tuples of the form *(tag,data,phase)*. A tag has the form of *(number, clientID)*, *i.e.*, a pair with a sequence number and the unique identifier of the client that is writing this version. The data field holds either null, or a coded element of an object that is stored in the system. The tag is used to determine the causal relationship among operations, *e.g.,* when retrieving the object's most up-to-date version. The phase field keeps track of which *phase* of the protocol that the data in the record have reached.

2.1   The CAS Algorithm

Coded Atomic Storage (CAS) is based on techniques for reducing communication costs, such as erasure coding and an earlier algorithm [14], by avoiding full replication, as in ABD and MW-ABD. CAS is a quorum based algorithm, where a quorum is any subset Q of the servers, such that $|Q| \geq k_{threshold} = \lceil \frac{N+k}{2} \rceil$; N is the number of servers and k is the coding parameter deciding the least amount of needed elements to decode the object value. CAS allows for up to f server failures. See [4] for full details.

Writer's Procedure. There are three phases: *query, pre-write* and *finalize*. *Query:* The query phase is based on MW-ABD [15]'s query, but considers only finalized records, *i.e.,* records that has their *phase* field set to 'fin' (rather than 'pre').

Pre-write: p_i's client sends a message, $\langle (x+1,i), m_j,$ 'pre' $\rangle$, to any server p_j and waits for a quorum of replies, where x is the maximum tag number retrieved from the query phase and m_j holds the coded element to the server at p_j.

Finalize: p_i sends a message $\langle (x, i+1), \perp,$ 'fin' $\rangle$, to all servers. After receiving a quorum of acknowledgments, the write operation is finished. The finalize phase hides the write operations that have not been seen by a quorum since the query phase only looks at records with phase 'fin'. Once the client has passed the *pre-write* phase, it knows that at least a whole quorum has enough elements to reconstruct the data and therefore it can be made visible in other operations.

Reader's Procedure. There are two phases: *query* and *finalize*. The query phase is identical to the writer's query phase.

Finalize: client p_i sends out a message $\langle t_{max}, m_j,$ 'fin' $\rangle$ to all servers, where $t_{max} = (x, \bullet)$ is the tag retrieved from the query phase. The client waits until a quorum has responded; each response includes a coded element corresponding to t_{max} (or a null if the server stored no record corresponding to t_{max}). If at least k of the responses include a coded element, the reader decodes the object value and returns it to the application. Otherwise, it just returns as an unsuccessful read.

Server's Events. The servers store different versions of the objects in records of the form $(t, w, label)$, where t is a tag, w is a coded element and *label* is either 'pre' or 'fin'. The server's procedures include the event handlers corresponding to the client requests: query, pre-write and finalize (of both read and write). Note

---

Algorithm 1: A description of CASSS, code for p_i's client and server

---

1 **The client:** For $write(s)$: Query all servers for finalized tags. After hearing from a quorum, get the maximum tag (z, j). Encode the elements $w_1, w_2, \ldots,$ w_N using input s, such $p_i \in P$ hosts a server. Send to all servers $((z + 1, j), w_i,$ 'pre') and wait for a quorum of replies. For each server $p_j \in P$, send $((z + 1, j),$ 'null', 'fin') and wait for a quorum of replies. The algorithm uses the 'FIN' phase label for making sure that at least a quorum of servers store the record $((z + 1, j), w_i,$ 'fin'). This way, the quorum intersection property guarantees the record visibility w.r.t. prospective client operations. Then, send for each p_j's server $((z + 1, j),$ 'null', 'FIN') and wait for a quorum before returning. The algorithm uses the 'FIN' phase label for making sure that any server that has the record $((z + 1, j), w_i,$ 'FIN') knows that there is at least a quorum of servers with the record $((z + 1, j), w_i, label) : label \in \{$'fin', 'FIN'$\}$ regardless of whether the client that invoked this operation has failed or not.;

2 For $read()$: Query all servers for 'pre' tags. After hearing from a quorum, get the maximal tag $t := (z, j)$. For each server, send $(t, \perp,$ 'fin') and wait for a quorum of replies with the requested coded elements that are associated with t. If at least $k_{threshold}$ replies include coded elements so that it is possible to decode them, return the decoded value. Otherwise, return $\perp$;

3 **The server:** *Upon query arrival from p_j's client to p_i's server.* If p_j's client is a reader, acknowledge with $(t, \perp,$ 'qry')), where t is the maximal tag of any finalized stored record. Else, acknowledge using t that is the maxim tag that any stored record.

4 *Upon pre-write $(t, w,$ 'pre') arrival from the p_j's writer.* Make sure that the stored record include the coded element w and acknowledge using $(t, \perp,$ 'pre').

5 *Upon finalize or FINALIZE $(t, \perp, d) : d \in \{$'fin', 'FIN'$\}$ arrival from p_j's client to p_i's server.* If (t, w, d) is stored and p_j's client is a reader, then acknowledge using (t, w, d). Else, acknowledge using $(t, \perp, d)$.

6 *Upon gossip $(pre[j], fin[j], FIN[j])$ arrival from p_j's server to p_i's server.* Integrate the arriving information with the stored one by making sure that $pre[j]$, $fin[j]$ and $FIN[j]$ are not greater than any of the tags of the stored records with 'pre', 'fin', and respectively, 'FIN' phases. In case there is a quorum of gossip records with the phase 'fin', update the phase label to 'FIN'. The updated phase value later allows the servers to consider this record as a candidate for garbage collection (when it becomes not among the δ newest records of phase 'FIN'). Gossip to all servers $(pre[i], fin[i], FIN[i])$, where $pre[i]$, $fin[i]$ and $FIN[i]$ are the greatest stored tags of stored records with 'pre', 'fin', and respectively, 'FIN' phases.

---

that the algorithm clearly tolerates any writer failure (crash) whenever either no server or a quorum receives the finalize message. To the end of establishing the viability of a write operation that only some servers (but not a quorum) store a finalized record, the algorithm employs a reliable gossip mechanism for disseminating among the servers tags of finalized records. This dissemination is invoked once for any arriving finalized message.

2.2 Self-stabilizing CAS

The variation of CAS from [5,6] is both self-stabilizing and privacy-preserving. Our pilot implementation, which we call CASSS (CAS Self-Stabilizing), we only focus on the algorithms self-stabilizing ability (i.e., it's ability to recover after the occurrence of a transient fault). This is modelled by considering transient faults that can corrupt arbitrarily the system state (as long as the program code stays intact). Moreover, it is assumed that the system starts after the last occurrence of these failures [8,16].

1. In the starting system state, the server at node p_i may store tag $t_{\max}$ (in a record that has its phase set to either 'pre' or 'fin'), such that due to the system asynchronous nature, it is not retrieved by any query for an arbitrarily long period. The challenge is to bound the number of write operations in which stale information, such as $t_{\max}$'s record, may reside at the system without having a write that hides $t_{\max}$.
2. Self-stabilizing (reliable) end-to-end communications require that the underlying channels have bounded capacities [16, Chapter 3.2]. Thus, in the context of self-stabilization in asynchronous systems, the quorums that send acknowledgments to the clients might complete write operations at a faster rate than the *reliable* gossip service delivers. Therefore, it is not clear how the writer can avoid blocking in a self-stabilizing system where its channels are bounded (and still deliver all messages).
3. All variables must be bounded, including, for example, the tag values. This means that when the system state encodes the maximum tag values, wrapping around to value zero must not disrupt the algorithm invariants, such as the tags' ability to order events.

Addressing Challenge (1). The servers repeatedly gossips the highest tag value that any server has. Each server includes in these messages the maximum tag that is part of locally stored records, such that their labels are 'pre' and also the maximum tag of records with the labels 'fin' and 'FIN'. Also, any write operation queries for the highest 'pre' tag so that the new tag of this operation is greater than all the (possibly corrupted) pre-write records in the system. (The read procedure is borrowed from CAS.) The correctness proof in [5,6] demonstrates that this modification still preserves atomicity and thus CASSS addresses the first challenge.

Addressing Challenge (2). The proof also shows that the gossip service does not need to guarantee the delivery of all messages and that the message's eventual delivery (or later messages with higher tag values) is sufficient. The server just overwrites the last received message in the buffers when a new gossip message arrives.

Addressing Challenge (3). To bound the storage size for each server, Dolev *et al.* [5] first bound the number of records each server stores and then bound the tag size. (Note that the client state of CAS is easy to bound and the message size is implied by the bound on its fields.)

Bounding the number of stored records is based in the assumptions that failing clients do not restart and that each client invokes at most one instance of the write procedure. This means that at any time, a client can have at most two relevant records in any server storage (regardless of whether it is failing or not). That is, one of these records might be the one that holds the most recent object value (written by an already completed p_i's operation) and the other record could be of an ongoing p_j's write operation. So, any stored record older than the two most recent records from client p_i is irrelevant, because it is either obsolete or stale. Thus, we can bound the number of relevant records by $2N$, where N is the number of clients. Dolev *et al.* [5] reduce this bound to $N + \delta + 3$ by adding to write procedure a fourth round, labeled by 'FIN', where δ is a bound on the number of read operations that occur concurrently with a write operation.

Bounding the maximum label requires to consider the case in which the system state includes a tag that has reached its overflow value, $(\text{MAXINT}, \bullet)$. Note that by choosing MAXINT to be a very high value, say, $2^{64} - 1$, we can guarantee that such an event happens only after the occurrence of a transient fault (because counting from zero to MAXINT takes much longer time than the lifetime of all relevant practical systems). As an extension to Algorithm 1, Dolev *et al.* [5] propose to let the servers detect the presence of this overflow value and then to stop responding to queries while keeping the gossip service running. By that, the servers disseminate the overflow values in the system while abstaining from supporting new operations from installing pre-write records. This continues until the servers detect, via gossip, that all of them have the same maximum finalized tag value, $t_{\max}$. At that point, the algorithm in [5] invokes a self-stabilizing (graceful) counter restart that allows the preservation of the object value using an agreement protocol (Sect. 3.3). During the counter restart, all clients are forced to perform also a local reset, which causes the abortion of all ongoing operations. Once the agreement procedure is terminated, the servers empty their local storages while keeping only the most recent finalized record and replacing its tag $t_{\max}$ with the initial tag value before resuming operation.

3   Implementation

We call our system CASSS, for CAS Self-Stabilizing. The CASSS pilot was implemented as a library in Python, which can be used by applications in order to provide access to the read and write operations. Calls to the functions `read()` and `write(x)` should behave as if the service was an actual shared memory. Calls to these functions block the calling process until the call returns. A successful read operation returns the data object, and a successful write operation blocks until it is done writing the object (and returns nothing). We proceed to describe the building blocks of the system.

3.1   Gossip and Quorum Communications

We used a self-stabilizing version of the token passing algorithm of [16, Figure 4.1] using UDP/IP as the basis for implementing the gossip and quorum services. CASSS requires the use of a self-stabilizing gossip protocol between servers to periodically share the largest tags for each phase. We used UDP/IP and let the arriving gossip messages overwrite the old ones (even if the old ones were not delivered). Our self-stabilizing quorum system follows the one in [5]. For the sake of improved performance, whenever it was required to transfer large data objects, a new TCP/IP connection was established. Our pilot implementation simply used a configuration file for retrieving the list of available storage servers (rather than an external directory service like DNS), for the sake of simple presentation.

3.2   Reincarnation Service

CAS assumes that clients cannot resume after failing. CASSS includes an extension that allows clients to reincarnate [5]. This is based on extending the client identifier to uid, which consists of a unique hardware address and an incarnation number.

The client algorithm performs a periodic task that starts with a query phase to check if its current incarnation number is up to date. It does this by querying all servers and awaits responses from a quorum of servers. The maximum value of all received incarnation numbers is calculated, and if that number differs from the current client incarnation number, a second phase is triggered. During the second phase, the incarnation number is updated both at the client side and in the quorum system. The client takes the maximum of the current incarnation number and all received incarnation numbers, increments that by one and sends it out to all servers. After receiving a quorum of acknowledgements, the client knows that it has been assigned a new valid incarnation number and can thus proceed to operate as usual by updating its uid accordingly.

3.3   Graceful Global Counter Restart

We use a graceful reset mechanism for restarting sequence numbers (of tags and incarnation numbers). The algorithm facilitates a wraparound based on the ability to achieve agreement and thus we assume that all servers are alive, *e.g.,* via a self-stabilizing service for quorum reconfiguration [7]. We further borrow ideas from [7, Algorithm 3.1] for performing a global counter restart while preserving the recent object value and a mechanism for recovering from transient faults. The algorithm can be extended to detect failures, and hence not requiring all servers to be alive in order to restart, in partially synchronous settings using the failure detection mechanism of [7]; including such discussion would make the presentation of the algorithm more difficult to follow, without contributing directly to our experimental evaluation.

4   Evaluation Methodology

To the end of evaluating our implementation, we have experimented on a true-to-life distributed system (rather than injecting faults or simulating the system). The implementation code can be accessed via www.self-stabilizing-cloud.net.

4.1   Evaluation Criteria and Platform

A common evaluation criteria in the field is to measure operation latency—the average time it takes for an operation to complete [13]. This includes both communication delay and local processing time. The operation latency is measured both in isolated settings (where no other client is making any requests), and in settings where we have different levels of base load on the servers. For comparison, we have implemented both CAS and CASSS, as well as a MW-ABD, using a self-stabilizing quorum system. We used the PlanetLab-EU platform (www.planet-lab.eu) to have a true-to-life, large-scale distributed system to run the evaluation on.

4.2   Experiment Scenarios

In this section, we describe the experiment settings, and how we measure performance before the details of each experimental scenario.

Baseline Settings. For unifying the evaluation, we often use the same baseline for each of the experiments (unless otherwise noted). The setting that all experiments proceed from is to have 15 machines in total, ten of which run one server process each and five of which run one client process each. When increasing the number of clients or servers beyond the number of physical machines, multiple instances are put on the same physical machine. In order to guarantee a fair latency between a client and a server instance, clients processes are never placed on the same physical machine as server processes. More clients or servers than available nodes are distributed in a round-robin fashion. Operations of a client are invoked sequentially with a random delay in between.

The system is initialized by a 512 KiB data object with random data being written to the quorum system before the experiments start. Each client repeats the operation 50 times, and the fastest and slowest operations are removed in order to mitigate the effect of outliers (by pre-experiment evaluations we were able to identify 50 as a reasonable number, where experiments would complete in reasonable time, while giving consistent results). The final operation latency result is the average of every client's average operation latency. Taking the average over all clients accounts for local variations, which is important since different PlanetLab nodes have different conditions. PlanetLab servers do not have any uptime guarantees, and we, therefore, want to allow a few servers to fail (*i.e.*, $f > 0$). But because k is bounded to be an integer value, such that $1 \leq k \leq N - 2f$, the value of f cannot be chosen freely. It, therefore, stands clear that if f is constant, N can never be chosen such that k would be forced to be less than one. Therefore, since we want to run an experiment with as few as five servers, we have chosen $f = 2$.

Client Scalability Experiment. This scenario is made to evaluate how the read and write latencies are affected when increasing the number of writers and readers respectively. This tests the servers' ability to handle an increase of concurrent operations. The number of failing nodes tolerated (f) is kept constant, *i.e.*, the quorum size is also constant. Both the reads and writes latency is measured. For reader scalability, we consider 5, 10, 15, 20, 30 and 40 readers, while having 10 writers and 10 servers. Corresponding numbers are used for write operation scalability.

Server Scalability Experiment. The server scalability experiment is constructed to evaluate in what way the read and write latencies are affected when increasing the number of servers. The number of failing nodes tolerated is kept constant, *i.e.*, the quorum grows with the number of servers. So when the servers increase, the number of servers that a client has to access will also increase but the coded elements will be smaller. One interesting aspect to look at when increasing the number of servers is whether the effect of a higher code rate trumps the effects of having a larger quorum. Both read and write latencies are measured. We use 5, 10, 15, 20 and 30 servers while having 10 readers and 10 writers.

Data Object Scalability Experiment. For evaluating how the read and write latencies are affected by the object size, this experiment performs operations using increasingly large data objects. The size is increased to a maximum of 4 MiB, which was found to be enough to demonstrate the scalability. In particular, we consider objects of size 1, 32, 128, 512, 1024, 2048 and 4096 KiB. The number of failing nodes tolerated is kept constant ($f = 2$), as well as the number of servers (10), which means that the quorum size is also constant. The experiment is run in isolation from other client nodes, so that scalability in increasing object sizes can be reliably measured. Both the read and write latencies are measured.

Counter Restart Experiment. This scenario measures how long it takes for the servers to restart their local state after a transient fault. Since this part requires the participation of all servers, we do not allow any server to be unresponsive (*i.e.*, $f = 0$). Because some nodes on PlanetLab were highly unstable, it was hard to run experiments for prolonged stretches of time. Therefore, we limited the number of repetitions for the counter restart experiment (which was expected to take longer than the other experiments) to 20 instead of 50. For the same reason, we restricted the object size to 0.25 KiB. Having to restart the global system state is the worst case scenario when it comes to recovery after a transient fault. The time measured is from a client pre-write phase (with a maximal tag number) until a query ends successfully. As discussed, we set $f = 0$, in order to know that every server has finished the reset phase, meaning the client has to receive responses from all servers before returning.

Overhead Experiment. In this scenario, we compare the overhead of CASSS with our implementation of CAS. In our case, the CAS implementation builds on the CASSS implementation, but does not include the fourth round ('FIN') nor does it perform any gossiping. In other words, this implementation uses the same number of phases and gossip messages as in [4], but, for a fair comparison, it is based on the same software components as the CASSS implementation. Here we use 10 servers (with $f = 2$), one writer and one reader.

5   Evaluation Results

Client Scalability. Figure 1(a) shows the result of the experiment where the number of concurrent readers was changed, and Fig. 1(b) the corresponding experiment for number of concurrent writers. Both charts shows a rather flat curve, which indicates that none of the experiments reached a point where the system was overwhelmed by the number of concurrent operations.

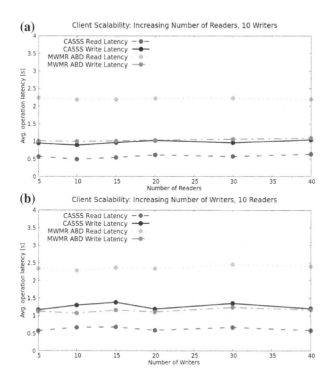

Fig. 1. Operation latency with respect to the number of concurrent (a) readers and (b) writers.

Note the difference between the operations. The fact that MW-ABD read operation is the slowest of the four is not a surprise. Not only does MW-ABD send larger messages, due to the lack of coding, but also its read operation actually transfers data twice: once to fetch the data from the servers, and once during the propagation phase. The MW-ABD and CASSS complete write operations in about the same amount of time. While CASSS writes has two more communication rounds than MW-ABD writes, MW-ABD messages are larger due to the lack of coding. It seems that, with the relatively short RTT between PlanetLab nodes ($\approx$50 ms avg ping time), the cost of two extra rounds seems to be about as expensive as the cost of larger messages. We find that CASSS reads are the fastest ones. This too was expected, since it has as few rounds as MW-ABD writes, but uses coding which decreases the message size.

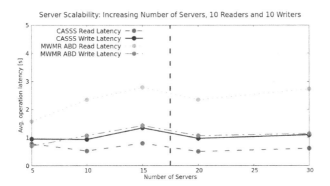

Fig. 2. Operation latency with respect to the number of servers. The vertical dashed line denotes the point where the parameter f had to be changed.

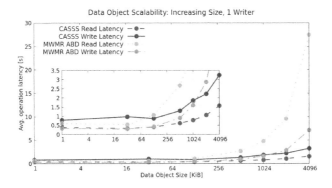

Fig. 3. Operation latency with respect to the size of the data object.

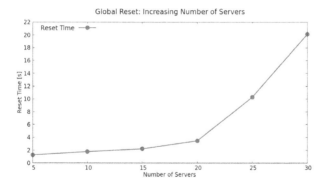

Fig. 4. The time it takes for the Global Reset mechanism to complete, with respect to the number of servers.

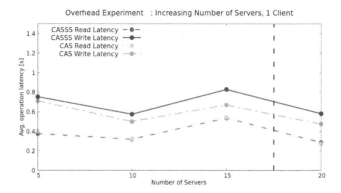

Fig. 5. Comparison between the operation latency of CASSS versus the traditional CAS algorithm. The dashed vertical line denotes the point where the parameter f had to be changed.

Server Scalability. Figure 2 presents the results of the servers scalability experiment. Note that with five servers, both reads and writes of CASSS and MW-ABD writes end up at more or less the same spot. That is because, with only five servers, CASSS effectively performs full replication and the CASSS quorum size is equal to majority quorum. While MW-ABD reads have fewer rounds than CASSS writes, MW-ABD reads transfer more data. This is why it the slowest of all operations.

Looking at the interval between five and ten servers, the operation latency of MW-ABD increases while the operation latency of CASSS decreases or stays the same. That is because when increasing the number of servers, the quorum size grows but so does the code rate. So while both MW-ABD and CASSS waits for responses from more servers, CASSS gains the advantage of decreased message size. The used coding library has a limitation that $k + m \leq 32$. Thus, f could not be kept at 2 for quorum systems with 20 and 30 servers. For 20 servers, f had to be at least 4, and for 30 servers it had to go all the way up to 14. The point where f is changed is marked by the dashed vertical line.

Data Object Scalability. Figure 3 shows the results of the data object scalability experiment. (Existing solutions [14] show how to transform ABD-like algorithms to more suitable implementations for large data objects.) Up to ca 1 MiB, the operation latency is fairly minimal. MW-ABD begins to escalate at 512 KiB, but CASSS is reasonably fast all the way to 4 MiB. This is of course a consequence of the coding, which reduces the message size.

Global Counter Restart. The global counter restart is triggered only after the occurrence of a transient fault, *i.e.,* it is invoked very rarely. Even so, it is still important that the counter restart terminates within a reasonable amount of time. Figure 4 shows that, for up to 20 servers, the time it takes for the counter restart procedure to finish is equivalent to the time it takes to perform two write operations, *i.e.,* it takes only a few seconds. As the number of servers increases, the likelihood of having to wait for slower servers increases too. If the responsiveness for a server at a given time is normally distributed, the likelihood of having one or more slow servers in the system increases exponentially.

Overhead. Figure 5 depicts the overhead that the extra communication round and intensive gossiping have. The figure has a vertical dashed line, which indicates at which point the variable f was changed due to the coding library requirement discussed previously. Note that CASSS reads and CAS reads are nearly identical. This is exactly what one would expect since CASSS has the same number of rounds for the reads as CAS. The write operations differ slightly, and with CASSS needing one extra communication round to complete the write operation, we expected it to be slightly slower than CAS. The average ping time between the PlanetLab nodes was about 50 ms, so the expected cost for one round is consistent with what we observe in Fig. 5.

6   Conclusion

Our case-study is, to the best of our knowledge, the first work to practically evaluate a system based on a self-stabilizing atomic MWMR coded shared memory emulation, with bounded storage size. We have implemented a system that is based on several self-stabilizing building blocks. This includes both a restart mechanism that performs a synchronized global reset of the entire system in a graceful manner, and a reincarnation number service that provides the failing client another chance to participate. We show that the CASSS system scale very well both in terms of the number of servers and number of concurrent clients. It also scales well with respect to the size of the replicated object. We see that CASSS system has a recovery period of only a few client operations.

Furthermore, it only has a constant overhead compared to the traditional CAS algorithm. This shows that the overhead introduced by self-stabilization can be fairly small, and in many cases negligible – especially when considering the upside of handling transient faults. We view this work as a promising first step in developing an efficient self-stabilizing cloud storage service based on atomic coded shared memory emulation.

A natural extension to our work would be the development of a reconfigurable version of CASSS, similar to the proposal in [17]. We see such extensions of the prototype proposed in this paper, as self-stabilizing building blocks for Cloud systems. We note the existence of other such prototypes, *e.g.*, Renaissance [18,19], as well as other algorithms that we propose as prospective candidates for prototyping, such as self-stabilizing Byzantine tolerant replicated state-machine [20] and self-stabilizing (Byzantine tolerant) end-to-end communications [21,22].

References

1. Herlihy, M.P., Wing, J.M.: Linearizability: a correctness condition for concurrent objects. ACM Trans. Program. Lang. Syst. **12**(3), 463–492 (1990)
2. Attiya, H., Bar-Noy, A., Dolev, D.: Sharing memory robustly in message-passing systems. J. ACM **42**(1), 124–142 (1995)
3. Lynch, N., Shvartsman, A.: Communication and data sharing for dynamic distributed systems. In: Schiper, A., Shvartsman, A.A., Weatherspoon, H., Zhao, B.Y. (eds.) Future Directions in Distributed Computing. LNCS, vol. 2584, pp. 62–67. Springer, Heidelberg (2003). https://doi.org/10.1007/3-540-37795-6_12
4. Cadambe, V.R., Lynch, N., Medard, M., Musial, P.: A coded shared atomic memory algorithm for message passing architectures. Distrib. Comput. **30**(1), 49–73 (2017)
5. Dolev, S., Petig, T., Schiller, E.M.: Self-stabilizing and private distributed shared atomic memory in seldomly fair message passing networks. CoRR abs/1806.03498 (2018)
6. Dolev, S., Petig, T., Schiller, E.M.: Brief announcement: robust and private distributed shared atomic memory in message passing networks. In: ACM Symposium on Principles of Distributed Computing, PODC, pp. 311–313. ACM (2015)
7. Dolev, S., Georgiou, C., Marcoullis, I., Schiller, E.M.: Self-stabilizing reconfiguration. In: Networked Systems NETYS, pp. 51–68 (2017)
8. Dijkstra, E.W.: Self-stabilizing systems in spite of distributed control. Commun. ACM **17**(11), 643–644 (1974)
9. Attiya, H.: Robust simulation of shared memory: 20 years after. Bull. EATCS **100**, 99–113 (2010)
10. Lynch, N., Shvartsman, A.A.: RAMBO: a reconfigurable atomic memory service for dynamic networks. In: Malkhi, D. (ed.) DISC 2002. LNCS, vol. 2508, pp. 173–190. Springer, Heidelberg (2002). https://doi.org/10.1007/3-540-36108-1_12
11. Musial, P.M., Nicolaou, N.C., Shvartsman, A.A.: Implementing distributed shared memory for dynamic networks. Commun. ACM **57**(6), 88–98 (2014)
12. Cadambe, V.R., Nicolaou, N.C., Konwar, K.M., Prakash, N., Lynch, N.A., Médard, M.: ARES: adaptive, reconfigurable, erasure coded, atomic storage. CoRR abs/1805.03727 (2018)
13. Nicolaou, N.C., Georgiou, C.: On the practicality of atomic MWMR register implementations. In: 10th IEEE Parallel and Distributed Processing with Applications, ISPA, pp. 340–347 (2012)

14. Fan, R., Lynch, N.: Efficient replication of large data objects. In: Fich, F.E. (ed.) DISC 2003. LNCS, vol. 2848, pp. 75–91. Springer, Heidelberg (2003). https://doi.org/10.1007/978-3-540-39989-6_6
15. Lynch, N.A., Shvartsman, A.A.: Robust emulation of shared memory using dynamic quorum-acknowledged broadcasts. In: 27th Fault-Tolerant Computing, pp. 272–281 (1997)
16. Dolev, S.: Self-Stabilization. MIT Press, Cambridge (2000)
17. Dolev, S., Georgiou, C., Marcoullis, I., Schiller, E.M.: Self-stabilizing reconfiguration. In: El Abbadi, A., Garbinato, B. (eds.) NETYS 2017. LNCS, vol. 10299, pp. 51–68. Springer, Cham (2017). https://doi.org/10.1007/978-3-319-59647-1_5
18. Canini, M., Salem, I., Schiff, L., Schiller, E.M., Schmid, S.: A self-organizing distributed and in-band SDN control plane. In: ICDCS, IEEE Computer Society, pp. 2656–2657 (2017)
19. Canini, M., Salem, I., Schiff, L., Schiller, E.M., Schmid, S.: Renaissance: a self-stabilizing distributed SDN control plane. In: ICDCS, IEEE Computer Society, pp. 233–243 (2018)
20. Dolev, S., Georgiou, C., Marcoullis, I., Schiller, E.M.: Self-stabilizing byzantine tolerant replicated state machine based on failure detectors. In: Dinur, I., Dolev, S., Lodha, S. (eds.) CSCML 2018. LNCS, vol. 10879, pp. 84–100. Springer, Cham (2018). https://doi.org/10.1007/978-3-319-94147-9_7
21. Dolev, S., Liba, O., Schiller, E.M.: Self-stabilizing byzantine resilient topology discovery and message delivery. In: Gramoli, V., Guerraoui, R. (eds.) NETYS 2013. LNCS, vol. 7853, pp. 42–57. Springer, Heidelberg (2013). https://doi.org/10.1007/978-3-642-40148-0_4
22. Dolev, S., Hanemann, A., Schiller, E.M., Sharma, S.: Self-stabilizing end-to-end communication in (bounded capacity, omitting, duplicating and non-FIFO) dynamic networks. In: Richa, A.W., Scheideler, C. (eds.) SSS 2012. LNCS, vol. 7596, pp. 133–147. Springer, Heidelberg (2012). https://doi.org/10.1007/978-3-642-33536-5_14

STAKECUBE: Combining Sharding and Proof-of-Stake to Build Fork-Free Secure Permissionless Distributed Ledgers

Antoine Durand[1], Emmanuelle Anceaume[2(✉)], and Romaric Ludinard[3]

[1] IRT SystemX, Paris-Saclay, Paris, France
antoine.durand@irt-systemx.fr
[2] CNRS, Univ Rennes, Inria, IRISA, Rennes, France
emmanuelle.anceaume@irisa.fr
[3] IMT Atlantique, IRISA, Nantes, France
romaric.ludinard@imt-atlantique.fr

Abstract. Our work focuses on the design of a scalable permissionless blockchain in the proof-of-stake setting. In particular, we use a distributed hash table as a building block to set up randomized shards, and then leverage the sharded architecture to validate blocks in an efficient manner. We combine verifiable Byzantine agreements run by shards of stakeholders and a block validation protocol to guarantee that forks occur with negligible probability. We impose induced churn to make shards robust to eclipse attacks, and we rely on the UTXO coin model to guarantee that any stakeholder action is securely verifiable by anyone. Our protocol works against adaptive adversary, and makes no synchrony assumption beyond what is required for the byzantine agreement.

Keywords: Blockchain · Proof-of-stake · Distributed Hash Table · Sharding

1 Introduction

Permissionless blockchains, also called distributed ledgers, initially appeared as the technological solution for the deployment of the Bitcoin digital cryptocurrency and payment system [23]. Permissionless blockchains aim at achieving the impressive result of being a persistent, distributed, consistent and continuously growing log of transactions, publicly auditable and writable by anyone. Despite the openness of the environment and thus the inescapable presence of malicious behaviors, security and consistency of permissionless blockchains do not demand the presence of a trusted third party.

This is a real achievement, which mainly results from the tight combination of two ingredients: a randomized election of the next block of transactions to be appended to the blockchain and a short latency broadcast primitive. While the latter one relies on the properties of peer-to-peer networks, the former one has so

M. F. Atig and A. A. Schwarzmann (Eds.): NETYS 2019, LNCS 11704, pp. 148–165, 2019.
https://doi.org/10.1007/978-3-030-31277-0_10

far been commonly implemented by solving proof-of-work (PoW), a cryptographic puzzle that is provably secure against a large proportion of participants that may wish to disrupt the system, and allows to keep the rate at which blocks are created parametrizable and independent of the size of the system. This second aspect is important to guarantee that the ratio between the message transmission delay and the block time interval remains low enough whatever the system activity, guaranteeing accordingly an easy management of conflicting blocks, if any.

Unfortunately, resilience of PoW-based solutions fundamentally relies on the massive use of computational resources, which is a real issue today. Lot of investigations have been devoted to find a secure alternative to PoW, but most of them either rely on the intensive use of a large quantity of physical resources (*e.g.*, proof-of-space [5], proof-of-space/time [22]) or makes compromises in their trust assumptions (*e.g.* proof-of-elapsed-time [18], delegated proof-of-stake [14]). In contrast, solutions based on proof-of-stake (PoS) seem to be a quite promising way to build secure and permissionless blockchains. Indeed, proof-of-stake rely on a limited but abstract resource, the crypto-currency, in such a way that the probability for a participant to create the next block of the blockchain is generally proportional to the fraction of currency owned by this participant. It is an elegant alternative in the sense that all the information needed to verify the legitimacy of a stakeholder to create a block (i.e., crypto-currency possession) is already stored in the blockchain. Finally, by being a sustainable alternative (creating a block requires a few number of operations), scalability concerns, exhibited by PoW-based solutions, should be a priori more tractable.

An important condition for a PoS-blockchain to be secure is randomness. The creator of the next block must be truly random, and the source of randomness must not be biaised by any adversarial strategy. So far, this has been achieved by two main approaches: chain-based consensus and block-wise Byzantine agreement with respectively Ourobouros [8] and Algorand [16] as main representatives. In the former approach, a snapshot of the current users' status is periodically taken, from which the next sequence of leaders is computed. In the latter one, a Byzantine agreement per block, relying on the properties of verifiable random cryptographic schemes, is achieved. High robustness against adaptive adversarial strategies results from the dynamic participation of thousands of users, each one participating for a single step of the algorithm.

In this paper we present a new blockchain protocol called STAKECUBE which aims at improving scalability of the block-wise Byzantine agreement approach by combining sharding techniques, users presence and stake transfer to operate in a PoS setting. The key idea of STAKECUBE is to organise users (*i.e.* stakeholders) into shards—such that the number of shards increases sub-linearly with the total number of active UTXOs—and within each shard, to randomly choose a constant size committee in charge of executing the distributed algorithms that contribute to the creation of blocks. Each block at height h in the blockchain is by design unique (no fork), and once a block is accepted in the blockchain, the next one is created by a sub-committee of shards whose selection is random with a distribution that depends on the content of the last accepted block.

To make such a solution correct in presence of a Byzantine adversary, we guarantee that the adversary cannot predict the shards in which users will sit, and that the sojourn time of users in their shard is limited. Doing so is an effective way to protect the system against eclipse attacks [2,6]. We introduce the notion of unpredictable and perishable users' credentials. Then to cope with this induced churn, shards' views are updated, signed and installed once, and this occurs right before the acceptation of a new block. Finally, the creation of blocks is efficiently handled by an agreement among a verifiable sub-committee of shards. We might expect that solely relying on stakeholders (*i.e.*, owners of the coins of the cryptocurrency system) to the secure construction of the blockchain makes sense due to their incentive to be fully involved in the blockchain governance, rather than delegating it to powerful miners. However the analysis against rational players is left as future work.

The remaining of the paper organised as follows. Section 2 presents related work, Sect. 3 details our model and assumptions while Sect. 4 formalises the addressed problem. Section 5 describes an high-level view of the required building blocks of STAKECUBE while Sect. 6 presents the design principles of the proposed solution. A security analysis is provided in Sect. 7 before concluding in Sect. 8.

2   Related Work

Omniledger [20] is the closest work to ours. It is a PoS-compatible, sharded, distributed ledger, resilient against a weakly dynamic adversary that corrupts up to $\frac{1}{4}$ of participants. In contrast to our approach, Omniledger assumes a strongly synchronous setting, and each shard maintains its own ledger and, global synchronisation of transactions is achieved through an atomic commit protocol tailored to their usage. Ouroboros [19], representative of the chain-based approach, is a synchronous PoS protocol resilient against a weakly dynamic adversary that owns $1/2 - \epsilon$ of stake. Moreover, Ouroboros has been recently improved to work in the partially synchronous setting against a dynamic adversary [7,8], but keeping the same design principles as the original one. In Ouroboros, a unique leader is elected at each round to broadcast its block which contrasts with our sharded approach where the block creation process is distributed. Snow White [13] is a synchronous PoS protocol resilient against a weakly dynamic adversary that owns $1/2$ of the *active* stake. This protocol also relies on a leader election. Algorand [16], is a representative of the blockwise Byzantine agreement approach. It provides a distributed ledger against an strongly adaptive adversary without assuming strong synchrony assumptions. However, by its design, agreement for each block of the blockchain is achieved by involving a very large number of stakeholders so that each one needs to effectively participate only for one exchange of messages.

3   Model

We assume a large, finite set of users whose composition may change over time. Users do not have synchronized clocks, but their individual clocks drift at the same rate. Users communicate by propagating messages within the system. The delivery of network messages is at the discretion of the adversary, but subject to synchrony assumptions. Our construction in itself makes no synchrony assumption except for what is required for the Byzantine resilient building blocks. Since our construction uses multiple building blocks, synchrony assumptions may be changed if they are instantiated differently than suggested. Users have access to basic cryptographic functions, including a cryptographic hash function $\mathfrak{h}$, and a CPA-secure signature scheme. Function $\mathfrak{h}$ is modeled as a random oracle. Users own some minimal amount of stake (*i.e.* money), which gives them the right to participate to STAKECUBE. We adopt (a simplified version of) what is commonly known as the Bitcoin Unspent Transaction Output (UTXO) model. An UTXO can be roughly seen as a user's account credited by some stake. An UTXO is uniquely characterized by a public key pk_i and its associated amount of stake s_i. Each public key is related to the digital signature schema Σ with the uniqueness property, which allows stakeholders to use the public keys (or a hash thereof) of their UTXOs as a reference to them, as demonstrated in the "Public Keys as Identities principle" of Chaum [10]. Note that the number of users evolves according to the UTXO set. At any time, a user can own multiple UTXOs. UTXOs can be debited only once, and once debited, an UTXO does not exist anymore. To simplify discussion, transactions outputs do not contain $\mathfrak{h}(pk_i)$ but directly pk_i.

Threat Model: A Weakly Adaptive Adversary. We assume the presence of Byzantine (*i.e.* malicious) users which controls up to $\mu \leq 1/3 - \epsilon$ of the total amount of stake currently available in the system. Here, ϵ quantifies the gain in the effective adversarial power, related to the security parameter. This model, named the "Stake Threshold Adversary" by Abraham and Malkhi [1], is an alternative to the common Threshold Adversary Model, which bounds the total number of parties the adversary controls relative to the total population of the system, and an extension (or modification) of the Computational Threshold Adversary introduced by Bitcoin, which bounds the proportion of the computational power owned by parties. Byzantine users can deviate from the protocol. They are modeled by an adversary. The adversary can perfectly coordinates all malicious users. It can learn the messages sent by honest users (*i.e.* non malicious users), delay them, and then chooses messages sent by malicious ones. Further the adversary is weakly adaptive: it can select at any time which users to corrupt in replacement of corrupted ones (*i.e.* corruptions are "moving"), however a corruption becomes effective T blocks after the adversary has selected the user to be corrupted. The adversary is computationally bounded so that it can neither forge honest nodes' signatures nor break the hash function and the signature scheme. Finally, we assume that all users (honest and malicious) share an initial knowledge that we call *genesis block* which contains an initial arbitrary UTXO set. We assume this block also shares the same properties as regular blocks. How to setup the genesis block is out of the scope of this paper.

4   The Addressed Problem

STAKECUBE aims at allowing any honest user i to locally maintain a sequence of blocks $B_0^i, B_1^i, \ldots, B_h^i$, where h represents the index (or the height) of the block in the sequence. This sequence of blocks represents i's copy of the distributed ledger, and satisfies both Safety and Liveness properties. In addition, the orchestration of the shards allows STAKECUBE to satisfy both Scalability and Efficiency properties. STAKECUBE is parametrized with an arbitrary security parameter κ, so that all its properties are guaranteed with probability at least $1 - e^{-O(\kappa)}$.

Property 1 (Safety). If honest user i accepts a block B_h^i at height h in its copy of the ledger then, for any honest user j that accepts a block at height h in its copy ledger, $B_h^j = B_h^i$.

Property 2 (Liveness). If a honest user submits transaction tx, then eventually tx appears in a block accepted in the copy of all honest users.

In STAKECUBE, participation of honest users is conditional to the possession of UTXOs. Participation is voluntary: Any honest user can join a shard (determined by the protocol), whenever she wishes, with the objective of eventually being involved in the Byzantine resilient protocols executed in this shard. Participation is temporary: The sojourn time of an honest user in a shard is defined by the time it takes for STAKECUBE to create T blocks. Once she leaves, she can participate again by joining another shard, and does so until she spends her UTXO. As users may own multiple UTXOs, they can simultaneously and verifiably sit in different shards. In the following, a user that issues a join request with its current credential is called an *active* user. STAKECUBE satisfies Scalability and Efficiency properties. This is achieved due to the properties of the block creation process. Adding a new block takes two Byzantine fault tolerant protocols to be run in parallel within each shard, one network wide diffusion by each shard, one inter-shard byzantine agreement, and finally one broadcast for the block (more details will be given in Sect. 6.3).

Property 3 (Scalability). All Byzantine fault tolerant protocols we rely on have an (overall) $O(n^3)$ message complexity. However in STAKECUBE these protocols are executed by committees whose size is small and fixed. Because the number of shard is $O(\sqrt{N})$, the overall communication cost is $O(NC_1^3 + C_2^3)$, with C_1 and C_2 some constants depending on κ. Thus, each participant's average communication cost is sublinear in N.

Property 4 (Efficiency). All Byzantine fault tolerant protocols we rely on use a constant number of rounds. Thus adding a new block also takes a constant number of rounds. Because a transaction, once diffused, will be included in the next block and blocks are permanently attach to the blockchain, it takes at most two blocks to include a newly received transaction.

5   A Set of Ingredients

To solve the addressed problem, StakeCube relies on the orchestration of the following ingredients.

Cryptographic Primitives. Digital signature together with random hash functions allow the implementation of verifiable random functions (VRF) [21]. In a VRF, a secret key sk allows the evaluation y of hash function $\mathfrak{h}$ on input x as well as the computation of a non-interactive proof that shows that the secret key sk is the only one that can compute y. Verification of the proof is done with respect to the public key pk only. The proof must remain sound even when pk is computed maliciously and $\mathfrak{h}(sk, x)$ must remain pseudorandom even when an adversary can query values of $\mathfrak{h}$ and proofs for them for any input value x'.

Byzantine Vector Consensus. A vector consensus protocol [12] is a Byzantine resilient protocol where n participants agree on a vector representing the input value of each participant. Validity condition states that in presence of $f \leq \lfloor (n-1)/3 \rfloor$ Byzantine nodes, the vector contains at least $f + 1$ non-null values, and for each non-null value $v_i \neq \perp, 1 \leq i \leq n$, this value was initially proposed by participant i.

Random Beacon. A Random beacon is a service that provides a public source of randomness. It was first proposed by Rabin [24] in the context of contract signing. In our case, we need the random beacon to be emulated by a distributed protocol without trusted third parties, that is, a protocol that satisfies the following security properties:

1. *Guaranteed output delivery.* All honest participants eventually output a value.
2. *Unpredictable.* Any adversary's ability to predict any information about the beacon prior to it being published is negligible.
3. *Unbiased.* For all adversarial strategies, the output is statistically close to a uniformly random string.
4. *Publicly verifiable.* The protocol also produces a proof that can be verified by third parties to be convinced that a beacon is indeed the output of the protocol.

Suitable instantiations for the distributed setting includes SCRAPE [9] and RandHerd [25]. In the following we denote by μ_{core} the minimum of the fractional resiliency of the vector consensus and random beacon protocols.

Verifiable Byzantine Agreement. We use a verifiable Byzantine agreement in order to agree on the next signed block despite corrupted shards. Our main requirement for this algorithm is to be optimistic, *i.e.* efficient in the absence of faults. Indeed, the analysis in Sect. 7 shows that the probability for a shard to be corrupted exponentially decreases with shards core size. Any verifiable Byzantine algorithm satisfying our assumptions can be used. We rely on the solution proposed by Shen et al. [11] since it is leader-based, efficient and tolerant to temporary partitions. The fractional resiliency of this protocol is noted $\mu_{corrupted}$.

Distributed Hash Table (DHT). Distributed hash tables (DHTs) build their topology according to structured graphs, and for most of them, the following principles hold: each node of the system has an assigned identifier, and the identifier space, *e.g.*, the set of 256-bit strings, is partitioned among all the nodes of the system. Nodes self-organize within the graph according to a distance function based on the identifier space.

Sharded DHT. The notion of Sharded DHT is similar to a regular DHT, except that each vertex of the DHT is a set of nodes instead of a single node. That is, nodes gather together into shards, and shards self-organize into a DHT graph topology. Sharded DHTs can be made robust to adversarial strategies as achieved in SChord [15], and PeerCube [3], and robust to high churn as achieved in PeerCube [3] by running Byzantine tolerant algorithms within each shard. For these reasons, we rely on PeerCube architecture, while weakening its model by removing the assumption of a global trusted party supplying verifiable random identifier, and by removing the assumption of a static adversary. For self-containment reasons, we now recall the main design features of PeerCube. Briefly, this is a DHT that conforms to an hypercube. Each vertex (*i.e.* shard) of the hypercube is dynamically formed by gathering nodes that are logically close to each other according to a distance function applied on the identifier space. Shards are built so that the respective common prefix of their members is never a prefix of one-another. This guarantees that each shard has a unique common prefix, that in turn serves as a shard's *label*. The shard's label characterizes the position of the shard in the overall hypercubic topology, as in a regular DHT. Shards size is upper and lower bounded. Whenever the size of shard S exceeds a given value s_{max}, S splits into two shards such that the label of each of these two new shards is prefixed by S label, and whenever the size of S falls under a given value s_{min}, S merges with another shard to give rise to a new shard whose label is a prefix of S label. Each shard self-organizes into two sets, the core set and the spare set. The core set is a fixed-size random subset of the whole shard. It is responsible for running the Byzantine agreement protocols in order to guarantee that each shard behaves as a single and correct entity (by for example forwarding all the join and lookup requests to their destination) despite malicious participants [4]. Members of the spare set merely keep track of shard state. Joining the core set only happens when some existing core member leaves, in which case the new member of the core set is randomly elected among the spare set. By doing this, nodes joining the system weakly impact the topology of the hypercube [3].

6   Design Principles of STAKECUBE

STAKECUBE allows the creation of a permissionless distributed ledger in a PoS setting. The key idea of STAKECUBE is to organise users (*i.e.* stakeholders) into shards—such that the number of shards increases sub-linearly with the total number of active UTXOs—and within each shard, to randomly choose a constant size committee in charge of executing the distributed algorithms that contribute to the creation of blocks.

The randomization of shards members gives a statistical bound the number of malicious participants sitting at each shards, ensuring the correct execution of the agreement primitives. More precisely, we compute bounds that may still cause some shards to have too much malicious participants (*i.e.* they become *corrupted shards*), but the overall number of corrupted shards is bounded. This technique allows us to fix a small shard size while keeping the ability to make security-efficiency trade-offs.

Each block at height h in the blockchain is unique, and is obtained by running an inter-shard agreement procedure among a sub-committee of shards.

To be able to tolerate the presence of a Byzantine adversary, we must guarantee that the adversary cannot predict the shards in which users will sit, and that the sojourn time of users in their shard is limited. To achieve this, we introduce the notion of unpredictable and perishable users' credentials in Sect. 6.1. Then to cope with this induced churn, we show how to update, sign a install the shards' views in Sect. 6.2. This process occurs right before the acceptance of a new block. Finally, as described in Sect. 6.3 the creation of blocks is efficiently handled by an agreement among a verifiable sub-committee of shards.

6.1   Unpredictable and Perishable Users' Credentials

As described in Sect. 5, Peercube critically relies on a (global) trusted party supplying verifiable random identifiers to nodes. In this section, we detail how to construct those in our decentralized setting, using the already known public keys and some randomness present in each block. For each unspent public key, *i.e.* for each UTXO, owned by a user, a sequence of unpredictable and perishable credentials are tightly assigned to her. Validity of a credential spans T blocks, with T some positive integer. The credential σ assigned to user i for its UTXO (pk_i, sk_i) is computed as follows. Let B_{h_0} be the block at height h_0 of the blockchain such that pk_i was created in B_{h_0}, *i.e.*, it exists a transaction in B_{h_0} such that pk_i appears in the output list of that transaction. For any blockchain height $h \geq h_0 + T$, such that UTXO (pk_i, sk_i) still exists when B_h is accepted in the blockchain,

$$\sigma_{pk_i}(h) := \mathfrak{h}(pk_i || B_{h'}.\rho), \quad \text{where} \quad h' := h_0 + \lfloor \frac{h - h_0}{T} \rfloor T, \tag{1}$$

with $B_{h'}.\rho$ a random number whose computation is detailed in Sect. 6.3. Suppose that i's UTXO (pk_i, sk_i) is created in block B_h. Then by Relation 1, i's first credential for UTXO (pk_i, sk_i) is computed based on the content of block B_{h+T} and perishes at block B_{h+2T}. Then, i's second credential for (pk_i, sk_i) is computed based on the content of block B_{h+2T} and perishes at block B_{h+3T}, and so on until i spends (pk_i, sk_i). User i's credential uniquely characterizes the shard to which user i is allowed to sit, and this shard is the one whose label prefixes i's current credential $\sigma_{pk_i}(h)$. By the non-inclusion property of PeerCube [3], there does not exist a shard whose label is the prefix of another shard, and thus, there is a unique shard whose label prefixes credential $\sigma_{pk_i}(h)$. When her current credential expires, i leaves the shard she is in, and if she wants to continue to participate to STAKECUBE, joins a new shard based on her new credential.

There are a couple of details that should be noted.

1. User i does not need to participate in STAKECUBE for the entire life of her UTXO (pk_i, sk_i). She can join STAKECUBE ($i.e.$ join a shard) at any time h under credential $\sigma_{pk_i}(h)$, however once a user joins her shard, she must stay online (and actively participates if she is a core member) until $\sigma_{pk_i}(h)$ expires. As a result, there does not exist any explicit leave request. A leave simply consists in not issuing a join request upon credential renewal. A consequence of this rule is that, in case user i participates under credential $\sigma_{pk_i}(h)$ and spends her UTXO (pk_i, sk_i) before $\sigma_{pk_i}(h)$ expires, then i continues to participate under $\sigma_{pk_i}(h)$ until $\sigma_{pk_i}(h)$ expires. Note that because a transaction only grants credentials after a delay, this rule does not allow a user to simultaneously own multiple credentials for the same stake. Note also that if i is disconnected for a small amount of time this does not jeopardized the safety of the shard only its liveness.

2. Recall that the adversary has a bounded fraction μ of $stake$ in STAKECUBE. To defend STAKECUBE against Sybil attacks ($i.e.$, the fact that the adversary creates a considerable number of UTXOs with the objective of overpopulating each shard with malicious owners of those UTXOs), we require that each UTXO cannot be credited with more than M stake, with M some predefined constant. Consequently, by the fact that for any $h > 0$ one credential $\sigma(h)$ represents exactly one UTXO, there is a bound $\mu_{cred} > \mu$ on the fraction of malicious credentials in STAKECUBE, which is reached when all malicious UTXOs have 1 stake and all honest ones maximize their stake, $i.e.$, each honest UTXO has M stake. Note that UTXOs with M' stake, such that $M' > M$ may be handled by granting them $\lceil M'/M \rceil$ credentials, although we do not treat this case explicitly. Section 7 analyzes the distribution of malicious credentials among shards.

Regarding the behavior of the adversary, there are a couple of remarks to note.

1. At any time, the adversary might spend some selected UTXOs in order to create new ones and thus new credentials with the objective of targeting some shards. However, because of the initial T blocks delay required to obtain the first credential for an UTXO (see Relation 1), any newly created UTXO will give rise to a credential only after all existing credentials are renewed as well. Therefore, the adversary has no preferred strategy regarding transactions and forced renewal.

2. Each block B_h contains a random seed, denoted by $B_h.\rho$, which cannot, by construction, be either biased or predictable before the block is created (how such seeds are generated is detailed in Sect. 6.3). Thus by Relation 1, the adversary cannot determine nor influence the value of renewed credentials. Consequently, for any blockchain height $h \geq 0$ and for any pk_i, $\sigma_{pk_i}(h + T)$ is unpredictable while for any $0 \leq h' \leq h$, the sequence $(\sigma_{pk_i}(h' + T))_{0 \leq h' \leq h}$ is computable and verifiable from the blockchain.

6.2   Shard Membership

As described above, during the period of time that elapses between the creation of an UTXO to its spending, the UTXO owner can participate to the blockchain construction by successively joining a series of shards. In practice this may give rise to a voluminous amount of join requests, which might be highly prejudicial to STAKECUBE's scalability and efficiency if each joining request led to the insertion of the newcomer in the core which run the distributed operations. Rather, by relying on PeerCube design (see Sect. 5), a newcomer joins the spare set of the shard and not its core set. This newcomer will be a candidate for being elected as a member of the core set whenever the core set will undergo a membership modification. Management of the view composition, and election in the core set is the purpose of the remaining of the section.

View of a Shard. The view of a shard S reflects the composition of both its core and spare sets, denoted respectively by S_c and S_s. Update of the view is strongly correlated to blockchain events: any block appended to the blockchain is preceded, in each shard, by the update and the installation of the shard view. In the following, the view of shard S installed right before block B_h is appended to the blockchain is denoted by $view_S(h)$. We have $view_S(h) = (S_c(h), S_s(h))$, where $S_c(h)$ (resp. $S_s(h)$) represent the composition of S's core set (resp. spare set) at time h.

Update of the Shard View. When a newcomer (*i.e.* a user under a valid credential) issues a request to join her shard S, her request is propagated and broadcast to the members of S_c. Core members i locally store the join request in their buffer b_i of pending requests. Note that expiration of credentials do not need to be locally memorized, prior to being handled by the view update algorithm, since by Relation 1, credentials can only expire when a new block is appended to the blockchain. Let $view_S(h - 1)$ be the current view of S when a (honest) core member $i \in S_c(h-1)$ receives some valid block B_h (Sect. 6.3 details the creation of blocks). The following three steps are successively executed:

1. A Byzantine vector agreement protocol is run among $S_c(h - 1)$ members to decide on the set of newcomers: core members i propose their local buffer b_i, and the outcome of the protocol is a vector $v(h)$ of newcomers such that non-null values for honest core members i are equal to their buffer b_i. Each honest core member i replaces its local buffer b_i with the union of the users of the decided vector. We have $b_i = \cup_{b_j \in v(h), b_j \neq \perp} b_j$.
2. Each user $i \in S_c(h-1)$ removes from b_i the set $r_S(h)$ of users whose credential expires with B_h. User i initializes a new spare set $S_s(h)$ with $S_s(h) = b_i \cup S_s(h - 1) \setminus r_S(h)$, and orders $S_s(h)$.
3. Each user $i \in S_c(h - 1)$ initializes a new core set $S_c(h)$ with $S_c(h) = S_c(h - 1) \setminus r_S(h)$. If $S_c(h-1) \cap r_S(h) \neq \emptyset$, some previous core members $i \in S_c(h-1)$ have credential that expire with B_h. As a consequence, an election among the

users of $\mathcal{S}_s(h)$ is carried out for i's replacement, so as to keep $|\mathcal{S}_c(h)| = s_{\min}$. The core election works as follows:

(a) A random beacon protocol is run among $\mathcal{S}_c(h-1)$ members to decide on a common random seed ρ.
(b) A pseudo-random number generator $PRG(\rho)$ is initialized with ρ as seed.
(c) $PRG(\rho)$ is used to draw a random number $j \in [\![1, |S_s(h)|]\!]$. The j-th member of $\mathcal{S}_s(h)$ is removed from $\mathcal{S}_s(h)$ and added to $\mathcal{S}_c(h)$. This process is repeated until $|\mathcal{S}_c(h)| = s_{\min}$.

Once these steps are completed, each core member j installs her new view $view_{\mathcal{S}}^j(h)$ with the new values of $S_c(h)$ and $S_s(h)$, signs it, and sends it to the spare members. Once a spare receives $\mu_{core}s_{\min} + 1$ signatures on the same view, it installs it. In the meantime, each core member j resets its buffer $b_j = \emptyset$. Note that multiple join requests may lead a shard $\mathcal{S}$ to split into two shards, or, on the contrary, may lead two shards $\mathcal{S}'$ and $\mathcal{S}''$ to merge within a single one $\mathcal{S}$. The treatment of such topological changes are omitted in the above procedure for space reasons, but can be derived from [2].

To summarize, the shard membership procedure ensures that, for any shard $\mathcal{S}$ of STAKECUBE, all members of $\mathcal{S}$ install the same view $view_{\mathcal{S}}(h)$ before appending block B_h to their copy of the blockchain.

Diffusing Views. Merely installing the new view for each shard is not sufficient. We need the other shards of STAKECUBE to maintain this knowledge to be able to verify any signed information exchanged during inter-shard communication (*e.g.* during the block proposal procedure, see Sect. 6.3). Therefore, whenever a new view $view_{\mathcal{S}}(h)$ is installed along with its $\mu_{core}s_{\min} + 1$ signatures, it is also broadcast to the whole network as a notification of the view update. Note that shards only store the last view $view_{\mathcal{S}'}(h)$ of any other shard $\mathcal{S}'$ and not the whole history of $\mathcal{S}'$ views. Moreover, a new view $view_{\mathcal{S}'}(h+1)$, can be verified against the last view $view_{\mathcal{S}'}(h)$, so that corrupted shards can only lie on their core members and omit newcomers.

6.3   Construction of the Next Block of the Blockchain

We propose a Byzantine resilient cross-shard mechanism to agree on a unique valid block, despite the presence of at most f_{shard} corrupted shards (see Sect. 7 for f_{shard} computation). Indeed, the presence of an adaptive adversary may compromise the safety of some shards by succeeding in having more than a proportion μ_{core} of malicious users sitting in their core set. Although the probability of such event can be made arbitrarily low (see the analysis in Sect. 7), we must handle it. The presence of corrupted shards put us in the same situation as in a consensus protocol: given the same initial chain, any shard is able to create the next block, and the decision must be a unique block, despite malicious users lying or not responding. As will be shortly described, agreeing on a unique valid block is efficiently and robustly achieved by running a Verifiable Byzantine Agreement among a subset of the shards of STAKECUBE randomly selected.

Reaching Consensus on the Next Block. The process of creating a new block B_h starts right after B_{h-1} has been accepted. A committee of shards, denoted in the sequel by $\mathbb{C}$, is elected among the shards of STAKECUBE. The election of each of these shards relies on the seed of block B_{h-1}, derived from the random beacon protocol. Once elected, committee $\mathbb{C}$ executes a verifiable Byzantine agreement to decide on the unique block B_h to be appended to the blockchain. The main steps of this process are as follows:

1. All shards $\mathcal{S}$ compute the elected committee $\mathbb{C}$, similarly to the core election procedure (see Sect. 6.2), i.e.,
   (a) Let $\mathbb{L}$ be the set of all the shards' labels (recall from Sect. 6.2 that each shard diffuses its new view $views_\mathcal{S}(h)$). $\mathbb{L}$ is then ordered through a canonical order.
   (b) A pseudo-random number generator $PRG(B_{h-1}.\rho)$ is initialized, where $B_{h-1}.\rho$ is the seed of the last block B_{h-1}.
   (c) $PRG(B_{h-1}.\rho)$ is used to draw a random number $j \in [\![1, |\mathbb{L}|]\!]$. The j-th member of $\mathbb{L}$ is removed from $\mathbb{L}$ and added to $\mathbb{C}$ (initially initialized to $\emptyset$). This process is repeated until $\mathbb{C}$ contains $s_\mathbb{C}$ shards, with $s_\mathbb{C} = (f_{shard}/\mu_{corrupted}) + 1$. Recall that f_{shard} is the maximal number of corrupted shards in STAKECUBE (whose computation is presented in Sect. 7), and $\mu_{corrupted}$ is the fraction of malicious nodes tolerated by the Verifiable Byzantine Agreement protocol (see Sect. 5).
2. Members of committee $\mathbb{C}$ run the verifiable Byzantine Agreement protocol, with their proposed block B_h as input (the construction of the proposed block is described in the next paragraph). Finally the decision is a block $B_{h'}$ signed by $2f_{shard} + 1$ shards.
3. Block b_h is broadcast in STAKECUBE and appended to STAKECUBE users' copy of the blockchain.

Security Remark: By definition of $s_\mathbb{C}$, committee $\mathbb{C}$ cannot be corrupted, independently of the shards selected by the election. Committee $\mathbb{C}$ is still chosen randomly for two reasons. First, it naturally spreads the load of creating a block across the whole network. Second, it prevents corrupted shards from trying to manipulate the election process to get in the committee and slow it down. Note that at this stage a random seed is already available from the last block and thus there is no need to run a distributed random beacon.

Efficiency Remark: We rely on a leader-based Byzantine Agreement algorithm to benefit from its optimistic efficiency. Indeed, since f_{shard} can be made arbitrarily small (see Sect. 7), and the members of committee $\mathbb{C}$ are randomly selected, we expect the first leader to almost always be an honest shard.

Construction of the Proposed Block. We finally describe how each shard $\mathcal{S}$ of $\mathbb{C}$ constructs its block B_h (see the above case 2). The construction results from an agreement on the content of block B_h among the core members of $\mathcal{S}$ and on the generation of the seed of B_h. Let $views_\mathcal{S}(h) = (\mathcal{S}_c(h), \mathcal{S}_s(h))$ be the current view of shard $\mathcal{S}$.

1. Each core member in $\mathcal{S}_c(h)$ proposes *(i)* its list of pending transactions and *(ii)* its VRF value seeded with $B_{h-1}.\rho$ together with the VRF proof, to the Byzantine Vector consensus protocol. The decision value is a vector of input values, such that non-null values for honest core members are equal to their list of pending transactions and their VRF value and VRF proof.
2. Construction of block B_h is then realized as follows.
   - The hash of the previous block B_{h-1} is inserted in B_h's header.
   - The union of transactions from the decided vector defines B_h's body.
   - The hash of the concatenation of the VRF values of the decided vector defines the seed $B_h.\rho$ of B_h.
   - The list of VRF proofs of the decided vector is inserted in B_h's header as a proof of randomness for seed $B_h.\rho$.

The reason why the random beacon protocol is not reused is because it is supposed to be run within a non corrupted shard. For the We have different requirements. First, we want the seed to be close to random even in the case of corrupted shards. This does come at the cost of giving the adversary a bounded number of choices for the seed. Second, we do not mind that a corrupted shard may decide to abort the computation of the seed, because we cannot prevent it from not proposing a block anyway.

7   Security Analysis

We analyze the probability that some of the shards of STAKECUBE are corrupted, that is that their core set contain more than $\mu_{core}s_{\min}$ malicious users. In the following we denote by ν the fraction of corrupted shards. To conduct such an analysis, we examine a simplified scenario. We approximate the behavior of STAKECUBE by taking the amortized execution over one period of T blocks. That is, we study the corruption probability when all the shards are built and the cores are elected over one period. This is equivalent to the scenario in which all credentials are synchronously renewed at the same block. Note that, for a fixed number of active users, the number of credential renewals, core election, and topological changes is statistically the same for every period of length T.

7.1   Corruption Probability of a Core Set During a Period of T Blocks

Let s be the size of shard $\mathcal{S}$, μ_{shard} be a bound on the ratio of malicious users within $\mathcal{S}$, and μ_{core} be the fractional resiliency of both the Vector Agreement protocol and Random Beacon one. We assume that $0 \leq \mu_{shard} < \mu_{core} \leq \mu$. We compute an upper bound on the probability that the fraction of malicious users in the core set is higher than μ_{core} by the end of the period. As described in Sect. 6.2, the core set is elected by randomly taking $s_{\min}$ credentials from shard $\mathcal{S}$, without replacement. Let Y be the random variable equal to the number of malicious credentials within the core, *i.e.*, Y follows an hypergeometric distribution whose probability mass function is given by

$$\forall k \in [\![0, s_{\min}]\!], \mathbb{P}[Y = k] = \binom{\lfloor s\mu_{shard} \rfloor}{k} \binom{\lfloor s(1 - \mu_{shard}) \rfloor}{s_{\min} - k} \binom{s}{s_{\min}}^{-1}. \quad (2)$$

We are interested in deriving the probability that after T core renewals the core set $\mathcal{S}$ is corrupted. The core set corruption refers to the situation where the proportion of malicious credentials in the core exceeds μ_{core}. Applying the Hoeffding bound [17] on Relation (2) leads to the following bound

$$\mathbb{P}[Y/s_{\min} \geq \mu_{core}] \leq e^{-2(\mu_{core} - \mu_{shard})^2 s_{\min}}.$$

Thus, assuming that the fraction of malicious users in a shard is below μ_{shard}, the corruption probability over T blocks exponentially decreases when $s_{\min}$ increases.

7.2 Distribution of Malicious Credentials Among All Shards

The above section assumes that the fraction of malicious users in all the shards is below μ_{shard}. In this section we compute an upper bound on the probability that this assumption does not hold. We make simplification assumptions on how the shards are formed. First, we assume that there are K shards of size S, giving rise to *i.e.* $N := SK$ credentials in total. Second, we assume that shards configuration in STAKECUBE during the concerned period results from a random credential assignment to all the shards. Recall that μ_{cred} is the overall ratio of malicious credentials. Let X_i be the random variable representing the number of malicious credentials in the i-th shard, with $1 < i < K$. And finally, we note $\mathbf{X} = (X_1, \ldots, X_k) \in \{0, S\}^K$ be the vector made of these K random variables. Random variable $\mathbf{X}$ represents the distribution of malicious credentials in STAKECUBE. It follows a multivariate hypergeometric distribution, *i.e.*, each of the $N = SK$ credentials is assigned to a shard. We analyse the shard assignment of a random sample of size $N\mu_{cred}$. Let I be the set of vectors representing STAKECUBE when $N\mu_{cred}$ credentials are malicious. We have

$$I = \{\mathbf{x} \in [0, S]^K \mid \sum_{i=1}^{K} x_i = N\mu_{cred}\}$$

and

$$\forall \mathbf{x} \in I, \mathbb{P}[\mathbf{X} = \mathbf{x}] = \binom{N}{N\mu_{cred}}^{-1} \prod_{i=1}^{K} \binom{S}{x_i}.$$

We are interested in computing the probability that a given shard j among the K ones contains more than m malicious credentials, that is, let $I_{m,j}$ be defined as follows

$$I_{m,j} = \{\mathbf{x} \in I \mid x_j \geq m\}.$$

We have:

$$\mathbb{P}[X_j \geq m] = \mathbb{P}[\mathbf{X} \in I_{m,j}]$$

$$= \sum_{x \in I_{m,j}} \binom{N}{N\mu_{cred}}^{-1} \prod_{i=1}^{K} \binom{S}{x_i}$$

$$= \sum_{k=m}^{S} \binom{S}{k} \binom{N}{N\mu_{cred}}^{-1} \sum_{\substack{x_1,\dots,x_{K-1}\in[0,S] \\ \sum_{1\leq i\leq K-1} x_i = N\mu_{cred}-k}} \prod_{1\leq i\leq K, i\neq j} \binom{S}{x_i}.$$

Knowing that $\sum_{1\leq i\leq K-1} x_i = N\mu_{cred} - k$ and $\sum_{1\leq i\leq K-1} S = N - S$, we can apply Vandermonde's identity:

$$\forall j, \mathbb{P}[\mathbf{X} \in I_{m,j}] = \sum_{k=m}^{S} \binom{N}{N\mu_{cred}}^{-1} \binom{S}{k} \binom{N-S}{N\mu_{cred}-k}.$$

We now get our result by applying first the (univariate) Hoeffding bound, and then the union bound.

$$\forall j, \mathbb{P}[\mathbf{X} \in I_{S\mu_{shard},j}] \leq e^{-2(\mu_{shard}-\mu_{cred})^2 S}.$$

Thus the probability that at least one shard of the system contains more than $\mu_{shard}S$ malicious credentials is bounded by

$$\mathbb{P}[\mathbf{X} \in \cup_{j=1}^{K} I_{S\mu_{shard},j}] \leq K e^{-2(\mu_{shard}-\mu_{cred})^2 S}$$

$$= e^{-(2(\mu_{shard}-\mu_{cred})^2 S - \ln K)}.$$

Term $\cup_{j=1}^{K} I_{S\mu_{shard},j}$ is the set of shards assignations to malicious credentials, such that at least one shard has a fraction greater than or equal to μ_{shard} of malicious credentials. Moreover, due to the union bound, this upper bound also holds if the shards have different sizes and S is the minimum, hence, we can simply use $S := s_{min}$. As for K, the worst case is reached when there is a maximal number of shards, *i.e.* $K := N/s_{min}$.

7.3   Putting it All Together

In the previous subsection we got exponentially decreasing bounds on the probability that at least one shard is corrupted, *i.e.*, proving security when the bound on the number of malicious shards f_{shard} is set to 0. We let for future work the generalization of this calculation with arbitrary values of f_{shard}, which would give us tighter parameters.

The adversary has a fraction μ of stake. Requiring each credential to be associated to at most M stake gives us the following (worst case) ratio of malicious credentials, which is reached when each malicious UTXOs has 1 stake and each honest one maximizes its stake, *i.e.*, has M stake. We then have:

$$\mu_{cred} = \frac{1}{1 + M^{-1}(\mu^{-1} - 1)}.$$

Thus M should be as small as possible to decrease the adversary effective stake. However low values of M may require users to participate with a large number of credentials in parallel, increasing the communication cost for individual users. Knowing μ and security parameter κ, the parameters μ_{shard} and $s_{\min}$ can be obtained by solving the following inequalities

$$\mu_{shard} \leq \mu_{cred} + \sqrt{\frac{\kappa - \ln \frac{N}{s_{\min}}}{2s_{\min}}} \quad \text{and} \quad s_{\min} \geq \frac{\kappa}{2(\mu_{core} - \mu_{shard})^2}.$$

8   Conclusion and Future Work

In this paper we have presented STAKECUBE a new blockchain protocol which aims at improving scalability of the block-wise Byzantine agreement approach by combining sharding techniques, users presence and stake transfer to operate in a PoS setting. Each block at height h in the blockchain is by design unique (no fork), and once a block is accepted in the blockchain, the next one is created by a sub-committee of shards whose selection depends on the random seed of the last accepted block.

The next step is to take into account the stake associated with each credential as weights into both the core election and the election of the shard in charge of creating the next block. This will allow us to get rid of the $\mu_{cred} - \mu$ gain in adversarial power, while keeping the remaining of the security arguments similar. More generally, refinements of the security analysis will give us the ability to instantiate STAKECUBE with better parameters while keeping the same security level.

We also plan to implement a prototype of STAKECUBE to demonstrate its efficiency and scalability properties, and to showcase some possible applications.

Acknowledgements. We are thankful to Gérard Memmi (LTCI Telecom ParisTech), and David Leporini, Guillaume Hebert and Thomas Domingos (Atos BDS) for their fruitful discussions. This work was carried as part of the Blockchain Advanced Research & Technologies (BART) Initiative and the Institute for Technological Research SystemX, and therefore granted with public funds within the scope of the French Program *Investissements d'Avenir*.

References

1. Abraham, I., Malkhi, D.: The blockchain consensus layer and BFT. Bull. Eur. Assoc. Theor. Comput. Sci. **3**(123) (2017)
2. Anceaume, E., Sericola, B., Ludinard, R., Tronel, F.: Modeling and evaluating targeted attacks in large scale dynamic systems. In: International Conference on Dependable Systems and Networks (DSN) (2011)
3. Anceaume, E., Ludinard, R., Ravoaja, A., Brasileiro, F.: PeerCube: a hypercube-based P2P overlay robust against collusion and churn. In: IEEE International Conference on Self-Adaptive and Self-Organizing Systems (SASO) (2008)

4. Anceaume, E., Ludinard, R., Sericola, B.: Performance evaluation of large-scale dynamic systems. ACM SIGMETRICS Perform. Eval. Rev. **39**(4), 108–117 (2012)
5. Ateniese, G., Bonacina, I., Faonio, A., Galesi, N.: Proofs of space: when space is of the essence. In: Abdalla, M., De Prisco, R. (eds.) SCN 2014. LNCS, vol. 8642, pp. 538–557. Springer, Cham (2014). https://doi.org/10.1007/978-3-319-10879-7_31
6. Awerbuch, B., Scheideler, C.: Towards scalable and robust overay networks. In: International Workshop on Peer-to-Peer Systems (IPTPS) (2007)
7. Badertscher, C., Gaži, P., Kiayias, A., Russell, A., Zikas, V.: Ouroboros genesis: composable proof-of-stake blockchains with dynamic availability. In: ACM SIGSAC Conference on Computer and Communications Security (CCS) (2018)
8. David, B., Gaži, P., Kiayias, A., Russell, A.: Ouroboros praos: an adaptively-secure, semi-synchronous proof-of-stake blockchain. In: Nielsen, J.B., Rijmen, V. (eds.) EUROCRYPT 2018. LNCS, vol. 10821, pp. 66–98. Springer, Cham (2018). https://doi.org/10.1007/978-3-319-78375-8_3
9. Cascudo, I., David, B.: SCRAPE: scalable randomness attested by public entities. In: Gollmann, D., Miyaji, A., Kikuchi, H. (eds.) ACNS 2017. LNCS, vol. 10355, pp. 537–556. Springer, Cham (2017). https://doi.org/10.1007/978-3-319-61204-1_27
10. Chaum, D.: Untraceable electronic mail, return addresses, and digital pseudonyms. Commun. ACM **24**(2), 84–90 (1988)
11. Chen, J., Gorbunov, S., Micali, S., Vlachos, G.: Algorand agreement: Super Fast and Partition Resilient Byzantine Agreement. Technical report (2018). https://eprint.iacr.org/2018/377
12. Correia, M., Neves, N.F., Veríssimo, P.: From consensus to atomic broadcast: time-free byzantine-resistant protocols without signatures. Comput. J. **49**(1), 82–96 (2006)
13. Daian, P., Pass, R., Shi, E.: Snow White: Provably Secure Proofs of Stake. Cryptology ePrint Archive, Report 2016/919 (2016). https://eprint.iacr.org/2016/919
14. EOS.IO: Technical white paper v2 (2019). https://github.com/EOSIO/Documentation/blob/master/TechnicalWhitePaper.md. Accessed 03 Oct 2019
15. Fiat, A., Saia, J., Young, M.: Making chord robust to byzantine attacks. In: Brodal, G.S., Leonardi, S. (eds.) ESA 2005. LNCS, vol. 3669, pp. 803–814. Springer, Heidelberg (2005). https://doi.org/10.1007/11561071_71
16. Gilad, Y., Hemo, R., Micali, S., Vlachos, G., Zeldovich, N.: Algorand: scaling byzantine agreements for cryptocurrencies. In: Symposium on Operating Systems Principles (SOSP) (2017)
17. Hoeffding, W.: Probability Inequalities for sums of bounded random variables. In: Fisher, N.I., Sen, P.K. (eds.) The Collected Works of Wassily Hoeffding. Springer Series in Statistics (Perspectives in Statistics). Springer, New York (1994). https://doi.org/10.1007/978-1-4612-0865-5_26
18. Intel: Hyperledger Sawtooth description (2019). https://sawtooth.hyperledger.org/docs/core/releases/latest/architecture/poet.html. Accessed 03 Oct 2019
19. Kiayias, A., Russell, A., David, B., Oliynykov, R.: Ouroboros: A Provably Secure Proof-of-Stake Blockchain Protocol. Cryptology ePrint Archive, Report 2016/889 (2016). https://eprint.iacr.org/2016/889
20. Kokoris-Kogias, E., Jovanovic, P., Gasser, L., Gailly, N., Syta, E., Ford, B.: Omniledger: a secure, scale-out, decentralized ledger via sharding. In: IEEE Symposium on Security and Privacy (SSP) (2018)
21. Micali, S., Rabin, M.O., Vadhan, S.P.: Verifiable random functions. In: IEEE Symposium on Foundations of Computer Science (1999)
22. Moran, T., Orlov, I.: Proofs of space-time and rational proofs of storage. In: Cryptology ePrint Archive, Report 2016/035 (2016)

23. Nakamoto, S.: Bitcoin: A peer-to-peer electronic cash system (2008). https://bitcoin.org/bitcoin.pdf
24. Rabin, M.O.: Transaction protection by beacons. J. Comput. Syst. Sci. **27**(2), 256–267 (1983)
25. Syta, E., et al.: Scalable bias-resistant distributed randomness. In: IEEE Symposium on Security and Privacy (SSP) (2017)

Dissecting Tendermint

Yackolley Amoussou-Guenou[1,2(✉)], Antonella Del Pozzo[1],
Maria Potop-Butucaru[2], and Sara Tucci-Piergiovanni[1]

[1] CEA LIST, PC 174, 91191 Gif-sur-Yvette, France
`yackolley.amoussou-guenou@cea.fr`
[2] Sorbonne Université, CNRS, LIP6, 75005 Paris, France

Abstract. In this paper we analyze Tendermint, proposed in [12], one of the most popular blockchains based on PBFT Consensus. Our methodology consists in identifying the algorithmic principles of Tendermint necessary for a specific system model. The current paper dissects Tendermint under two communication models: synchronous and eventually synchronous ones. This methodology allowed to identify bugs in preliminary versions of the protocol and to prove its correctness under the most adversarial conditions: an eventually synchronous communication model under Byzantine faults. The message complexity of Tendermint is $O(n^3)$.

Keywords: BFT Consensus · Blockchain · Tendermint · Complexity

1 Introduction

A blockchain is a distributed ledger implementing an append-only list of blocks chained to each other, it serves as an immutable and non repudiable ledger in a system composed of untrusted processes. The append operation needs to preserve the chain shape of the data structure, leading to the necessity to have a mechanism allowing processes to agree on the next block to append. Bitcoin blockchain, for example, employs the proof-of-work mechanism [19], that is, processes willing to append a new block have to solve a crypto-puzzle and the winning process will append the new block. While this mechanism does not require a real coordination between the processes participating to the Bitcoin system, it might lead to inconsistencies. Indeed, if more than one process solves the crypto-puzzle to extend the same last block then processes may have blockchains with different suffix as long as the conflict is unsolved.

In blockchain systems area the recent tendency is to privilege solutions based on distributed agreement than proof-of-work. This is motivated by the fact that the majority of proof-of-work based solutions such as Bitcoin or Ethereum are energetically not viable when efficiency is targeted. Moreover proof of work solutions guarantee the existence of an unique chain only with high probability which is the major drawback for using blockchains in industrial applications. That is, forks even though they are rare do still happen with an impact on the consistency guarantees offered by the system and consensus algorithms play an important role to prevent inconsistencies. In [8] the authors proved that consensus [27] is

© Springer Nature Switzerland AG 2019
M. F. Atig and A. A. Schwarzmann (Eds.): NETYS 2019, LNCS 11704, pp. 166–182, 2019.
https://doi.org/10.1007/978-3-030-31277-0_11

necessary in order to avoid forks. Therefore, alternatives to proof-of-work have been recently considered and interestingly, the research in blockchain systems revived a branch of distributed systems research: Byzantine fault-tolerant protocols having PBFT consensus protocol as ambassador. It should be noted that PBFT solutions cannot be used in permissionless settings if the number of participants to the agreement is not known in advance. That is, in permissionless settings, for each block, a subset of processes (called validators in Tendermint) runs a Byzantine fault-tolerant consensus algorithm to propose the next block to be appended to the blockchain. All the existing solutions for PBFT consensus use the number of validators as hardcore information in their algorithm.

Related Work. In the blockchain realm, there exist several Byzantine Fault Tolerant Consensus based blockchain proposals (e.g., [3,9,16,17], and [23]).

The consensus problem, as proved in the seminal FLP paper [21], cannot be solved in an asynchronous message-passing system (when there are no upper bounds on the message delivery delay) in the presence of one faulty (crash) process. Moreover, in [27], the authors prove that consensus cannot be solved in presence of f Byzantine faulty processes if the overall number of processes n is less than $3f + 1$ in a synchronous message-passing system (where the message delivery delay is upper bounded). In between those impossibility results, it is still possible to solve consensus in an asynchronous setting, either adding randomness [11] (which also proved the impossibility result for $n \leq 3f$ for any asynchronous solution) or partial synchrony as in Dwork et al. [18] (DLS) where BFT Consensus is solved an eventual synchronous message-passing system (there is a time τ after which there is an upper bound on the message delivery delay). DLS preserves safety during the asynchronous period and the termination only after τ, when the message transfer delay becomes bounded. The message complexity of this protocol is $O(n^4)$ per epoch and it needs $O(n)$ epochs before deciding. Finally, Castro and Liskov proposed PBFT [14], a leader-based protocol that optimizes the performances of the previous solution. If the leader is correct the complexity boils down to $O(n^2)$. Otherwise, a view change mechanism takes place, to change the leader and resume the computation. The view-change is used to avoid that, in case of faulty leader, if some correct process decides on a value v, the other correct processes cannot decide on a value $v' \neq v$ when the new leader proposes a new value. Such mechanism implies that when a leader is suspected to be faulty, all processes have to collect enough evidences for the view-change. That is, the view-change message contains at least $2f + 1$ signed messages and these messages are sent from at least $2f + 1$ processes which yields a message complexity of $O(n^2)$. These messages are then sent to all processes, the view-change has then $O(n^3)$ message complexity. Since the protocol terminates when there is a correct leader, which may happen for the first time in epoch $f + 1$, then in the worst case scenario it has a message complexity of $O(n^4)$. Interestingly, Tendermint as well as similar recent approaches e.g. [2] use an alternative mechanism for leader replacement that allows to drop message complexity to $O(n^3)$. Basically, processes instead of exchanging all the messages they already delivered (used previously to trigger a view change), locally keep track of potentially decided values.

Our Contribution. In this paper we analyze Tendermint proposed in [12] as one of the most promising but not fully analyzed blockchain protocols that implements Byzantine fault tolerant consensus. Tendermint targets an eventual synchronous system [18], which means that safety has to be guaranteed in the asynchronous periods and liveness in synchronous ones, when a subset of processes can be affected by Byzantine failures. To analyze the protocol, we dissect Tendermint identifying the techniques used to address different challenges in the considered system model: synchronous round-based communication model and eventual synchronous communication model. For each type of model we provide the corresponding algorithm (a variant of Tendermint [12]) and compute its complexity. Interestingly, and contrary to the classical view-changed based approaches, message complexity in the worst case scenario is $O(n^3)$. This is because processes, instead of exchanging all the messages they already delivered, locally keep track of potentially decided values to preserve the safety, hence reducing the message complexity. In the same spirit, HotStuff [2] (a concurrent proposal) incurs the same message complexity, sharing with Tendermint a linear proposer replacement. Note as well that the proposed methodology allowed us to identify bugs (see [5]) in the preliminary versions of the protocol ([12, 26]).

This paper and [6] target two different consensus algorithms that are core of two different releases of Tendermint blockchain. In [6] the authors reverse-engineered and then formalized the Tendermint blockchain protocol implemented initially by the Tendermint Foundation [31]. [6] allowed to identify several bugs in the initial version of Tendermint implementation (see [5]). Moreover, we proved that the termination property cannot be guaranteed in general, and hence an additional assumption on the execution is needed to solve Consensus. After the publication of our findings, Tendermint foundation proposed a new algorithm, [12], that is currently implemented as consensus-core for the new release of Tendermint. The new version of the protocol claimed to include new mechanisms that removed the need of additional assumptions in order to guarantee the termination. The pseudo-code proposed in [12] and further implemented by Tendermint foundation still had some bugs at the time when we started to analyse it, which we reported [30].

In order to help practitioners, and in particular Tendermint foundation, to detect easily their errors and compare with the existing state of the art, in this paper we decided to have a bottom up approach by identifying the minimal building blocks a PBFT-like protocol should include in order to solve consensus function on the considered system and communication model (going from synchronous to eventually synchronous) and the behavior of Byzantine nodes. We used Tendermint as case study and identified the mechanisms needed by the protocol in order to be correct. Our study resulted in three variants of the protocol for which we analyzed the correctness and the complexity. In this paper, we included two of the three algorithms (we decided to left aside the trivial one where Byzantines have a symmetrical behavior and the communication is synchronous). Moreover, the complexity analysis proposed in our paper may help both practitioners and academics to compare Tendermint to the state of the art which was an open question so far.

2   Model

The system is composed of an infinite set Π of sequential processes, namely $\Pi = \{p_1, \dots\}$; *Sequential* means that a process executes one step at a time. This does not prevent it from executing several threads with an appropriate multiplexing. As local processing time are negligible with respect to message transfer delays, they are considered as equal to zero.

Arrival Model. We assume a *finite arrival model* [4], i.e. the system has infinitely many processes Π but each run has only finitely many. The size of the set $\Pi_\rho \subset \Pi$ of processes that participate in each system run is not a priori-known. We also consider a finite subset $V \subseteq \Pi_\rho$ of validators. The set V may change during any system run and its size n is a-priori known. A process is promoted in V based on a so-called merit parameter, which can model for instance its stake in proof-of-stake blockchains. Note that in the current Tendermint implementation, it is a separate module included in the Cosmos project [25] that is in charge of implementing the selection of V.

Failure Model. There is no bound on processes that can exhibit a Byzantine behaviour [29] in the system, but up to f validators can exhibit a Byzantine behaviour at each point of the execution. A Byzantine process is a process that behaves arbitrarily. A process (or validator) that exhibits a Byzantine behaviour is called *faulty*. Otherwise, it is *non-faulty* or *correct* or *honest*. To be able to solve the consensus problem, we assume that $f < n/3$ and more precisely we consider $n = 3f + 1$.

Communication Model. Processes communicate by exchanging messages through an eventually synchronous network [18]. *Eventually Synchronous* means that after a finite unknown time $\tau > 0$ there is a bound δ on the message transfer delay. When $\tau = 0$ the network is *synchronous*.

In the following we assume the presence of a *broadcast primitive*. A process p_i by invoking the primitive broadcast($\langle TAG, m \rangle$) broadcasts a message, where TAG is the type of the message, and m its content. To simplify the presentation, it is assumed that a process can send messages to itself. The primitive broadcast() is a best effort broadcast, which means that when a correct process broadcasts a value, eventually all the correct processes deliver it. A process p_i receives a message by executing the primitive delivery(). Messages are created with a digital signature, and we assume that digital signatures cannot be forged. When a process p_i delivers a message, it knows the process p_j that created the message.

Let us note that the assumed broadcast primitive in an open dynamic network can be implemented through *gossiping*, i.e. each process sends the message to current neighbors in the underlying dynamic network graph. In these settings the finite arrival model is a necessary condition for the system to show eventual synchrony. Intuitively, a finite arrival implies that message losses due to topology changes are bounded, so that the propagation delay of a message between two processes not directly connected can be bounded [10, 28].

Round-Based Execution Model. We assume that each correct process evolves in rounds. A *round* consists of three phases, in order: (i) a *Send* phase, where the process broadcasts messages computed during the last round, or a default messages for the first round; (ii) a *Delivery* phase where the process collects messages sent during the current and previous rounds; and (iii) a *Compute* phase where the process uses the messages delivered to change its state. At the end of a round a process exits from the current round and starts the next round. Each round has a finite duration, we consider the Send and the Compute phase as being atomic, they are executed instantaneously, but not the Delivery phase. In a synchronous network, we assume the duration of the Delivery phase, and so of the round is δ. We assume that processes have no access to a global clock but have access to local clocks, these clocks might not be synchronized with each other but are allowed to have bounded clock skew.

Problem Definition. In this paper we analyze the correctness of Tendermint protocol with respect to the consensus specification: **Termination**, every correct process eventually decides some value; **Integrity**, no correct process decides twice; **Agreement**, if there is a correct process that decides a value v, then eventually all the correct processes decide v; **Validity** [13,15], a decided value is valid, it satisfies the predefined predicate denoted valid().

3   Tendermint Algorithms

Tendermint BFT Consensus protocol [12,26,31] is a variant of PBFT consensus, at the core layer of the Tendermint blockchain.

The algorithm follows the rotating coordinator paradigm i.e., for each new block to be appended there is a proposer, chosen among the validators, that proposes the block. If the block is not decided then a new proposer is selected and so on, until a block is decided by all the correct validators and consensus terminates. In the following we present variants of [12] in synchronous and eventual synchronous communication models.

Basic Principles of the Protocol. Each block in the blockchain is characterized by its height h, which is the distance in terms of blocks from the genesis block, which is at height 0. For each new height, the two protocols (Algorithm 2 for the synchronous case and Algorithm 4 for the eventual synchronous case) share a common algorithmic structure, they proceed in *epochs*, and each epoch e consists in three rounds: the *PRE-PROPOSE* round; the *PROPOSE* round; and the *VOTE* round. During the PRE-PROPOSE round, the proposer pre-proposes a value v to all the other validators. During the PROPOSE round, if a validator accepts v then it proposes such value. If a validator receives *enough* proposals for the same value v then it votes for v during the VOTE round. Finally, if a validator receives *enough* votes for v, it decides on v. In this case, *enough* means at least $2f+1$ occurrences of the same value from $2f+1$ different validators and from each validator only the first value delivered for each round is considered, (cf. Algorithm 1).

If the proposer is correct then it pre-proposes the same value to all the $2f + 1$ correct validators. All the $2f + 1$ correct validators propose such value, it follows that all the $2f + 1$ correct validators vote for such value and decide for it. If the proposer is Byzantine it can pre-propose different values to different correct validators, creating a partition in the proposal value set collected by validators. Depending on what the remaining Byzantine validators do, some correct validators may decide on a value v and some other may not[1], then a new epoch starts. In order to not violate the agreement property, validators that have not decided yet in the previous epoch must only decide for v, for this reason validators, before vote for some value v, lock on that value, i.e., they will refuse to propose a further pre-proposed value different than v.

Information from One Epoch to the Next. *lockedValue* and *validValue* variables[2] carry the potentially decided value from one epoch to the next one. The *lockedValue* idea is the following. If one correct validator decides on v, it means that it collected $2f + 1$ votes for v during the VOTE phase, since there are at most f Byzantine validators thus there are at least $f + 1$ correct validators that voted for v and those validators must not vote for any other different value than v. For this reason if a validator delivers $2f + 1$ proposals for v during the PRO-POSE round it sets its *lockedValue* to v. Since each new pre-proposed value v' is proposed if v' is equal to *lockedValue* or *validValue* (not true for at lest $f + 1$ correct validators that set *lockedValue* to v), then there can be at most $2f$ possible proposals for v' that are not enough to lock and vote for v', i.e., it is not possible to decide for any value different than v. On the other side, if no correct validator decided yet, Byzantine faulty validators may force different correct validators to lock on different values. Let us consider a scenario where the proposer is Byzantine and proposes v to $f + 1$ correct validators and then f Byzantine validators make $x \leq f$ of them lock on v and a similar scenario can happen with another value v' so that we can have different correct validators, let us say $y \leq f$ locked on a different value. If any new pre-proposal is checked only against the *lockedValue* then a correct validator locked on a value v refuses (does not propose) all values different from v, it means that when some correct validator is locked, the proposer needs to propose some of the value on which the correct validators are locked on, but such value, in order to be accepted cannot be checked only against the *lockedValue* because we may never have enough correct validators proposing such value. For this reason validators keep track of the *validValue* and by construction of the algorithm all correct validators have the same *validValue* at the end of the epoch (in the synchronous period). Such value is then used to set the value to pre-propose and it is further used along with *lockedValue* to accept or not a pre-proposed value.

---

[1] Since there are $3f + 1$ validators, there cannot be two different values that collect $2f + 1$ distinct votes in the same epoch.

[2] *validValue* was not present in the previous version of Tendermint [26], that was suffering from the Live Lock bug [1].

Algorithm 1. Messages management for validator p_i

1: **upon** $\langle \text{TYPE}, h, e, \text{message} \rangle$ **from** validator p_j **do**
2:   **if** $\nexists c : (\langle \text{TYPE}, h, e, c \rangle, p_j) \in messagesSet$ **then**
3:     $messagesSet_i \leftarrow messagesSet_i \cup (\langle \text{TYPE}, h, e, \text{message} \rangle, p_j)$

Messages Syntax. When the validator p_i broadcasts a message $\langle TAG, h, e, m \rangle$, where m contains a value v, we say that p_i pre-proposes, proposes or votes v if TAG=PRE-PROPOSE, TAG=PROPOSE, TAG=VOTE, respectively.

Variables and Data Structures. h is an integer representing the consensus instance the validator is currently executing. e_i is an integer representing the epoch where the validator p_i is, we note that for each height, a validator may have multiple epochs. $decision_i$ is the decision of validator p_i for the consensus instance h. $proposal_i$ is the value the validator p_i proposes. $vote_i$ is the value the validator p_i votes. $lockedValue_i$ stores a value which is potentially decided by some other validator. If validator p_i delivers more than $2f + 1$ proposes for the same value v during its PROPOSE round, it sets $lockedValue_i$ to v. $validValue_i$ stores a value which is potentially decided by some other validator. If the validator p_i delivers at least $2f + 1$ proposes for the same value v (from different validators) whether during its PROPOSE round or its VOTE round, it sets $validValue_i$ to v. $validValid_i$ is the last value that a validator delivered at least $2f + 1$ times, and can be different than $lockedValue_i$. The latter two variables are used as follows: if p_i is the next proposer then p_i pre-proposes $validValid_i$ if different from nil. Otherwise, if p_i is a validator, it checks the new pre-proposal against $lockedValue_i$ and $validValid_i$ if those are different from nil.

Functions. We denote as $Value$ the set containing all blocks, as $MemPool$ the set containing all the transactions, and as $Messages$ the set containing all messages.

- proposer : $Height \times Epoch \rightarrow V \subseteq \Pi_\rho$ is a deterministic function which gives the proposer out of the validators set for a given epoch at a given height in a round robin fashion.
- valid : $Value \rightarrow Bool$ is an application dependent predicate that is satisfied if the given value is valid w.r.t. the blockchain. If there is a value v such that valid(v) = true, we say that v is valid. Note that we set valid(nil) = false.
- getValue() return a valid value.
- sendByProposer : $Height \times Epoch \times Value \rightarrow Bool$ is an predicate that gives true if the given value has been pre-proposed by the proposer of the given height during the given epoch.
- $2f + 1$: $\mathcal{P}(\text{Messages}) \rightarrow Bool$: checks if there are at least $2f + 1$ proposals (resp. votes) in the given set of messages.

Everything defined above is common to the two algorithms. In each section we specify the data structures relative to a specific version of the algorithm.

Algorithm 2. Simplified Algorithm part 1 for height h executed at validator p_i

```
 1: Initialization:
 2:    e_i := 0                                          /* This current epoch number */
 3:    decision_i := nil        /* This variable stocks the decision of the validator p_i */
 4:    lockedValue_i := nil; validValue_i := nil
 5:    proposal_i := getValue() /* This variable stocks the value the validator will (pre-)propose */
 6:    v_i := nil                   /* Local variable stocking the pre-preposal if delivered */
 7:    vote_i := nil

 8: Round PRE-PROPOSE(e_i):
 9:    Send phase:
10:       if decision_i ≠ nil then
11:          ∀v, p_j : (⟨VOTE, h, e_i, v⟩, p_j) ∈ messagesSet_i, broadcast⟨VOTE, h, e_i, v⟩
12:          return
13:       if proposer(h, e_i) = p_i then
14:          broadcast ⟨PRE − PROPOSE, h, e_i, proposal_i⟩ to all validators
15:    Delivery phase:
16:       while (timerPrePropose not expired) do
17:          if ∃v : sendByProposer(h, e_i, v) then
18:             v_i ← v                            /* v is the value sent by the proposer */
19:    Compute phase:
20:       if !valid(v_i) then
21:          proposal_i ← nil                   /* Note that valid(nil) is set to false */
22:       else
23:          if validValue_i = nil ∨ v_i ∈ {lockedValue_i, validValue_i} then
24:             proposal_i ← v_i
25:          else
26:             proposal_i ← nil
```

3.1 Byzantine Synchronous System

In Algorithms 1, 2 and 3 we describe the algorithm to solve consensus in a synchronous system in presence of Byzantine failures. The algorithm proceeds in 3 rounds for any given epoch at height h:

- Round PRE-PROPOSE (lines 8–26, Algorithm 2): If the validator p_i is the proposer of the epoch, it pre-proposes its proposal value, otherwise, it waits for the proposal from the proposer. The proposal value of the proposer is its $validValue_i$ if $validValue_i \neq nil$. If a validator p_j delivers the pre-proposal from the proposer of the epoch, p_j checks the validity of the pre-proposal and if to accept it with respect to the values in $validValue_i$ and $lockedValue_i$. If the pre-proposal is accepted and valid, p_j sets its proposal $proposal_j$ to the pre-proposal, otherwise it sets it to nil.
- Round PROPOSE (lines 1–13, Algorithm 3): During the PROPOSE round, each validator broadcasts its proposal, and collects the proposals sent by the other validators. After the Delivery phase, validator p_i has a set of proposals, and checks if v, pre-proposed by the proposer, was proposed by at least $2f + 1$ different validators, if it is the case, and the value is valid, then p_i sets $vote_i, validValue_i$ and $lockedValue_i$ to v, otherwise it sets $vote_i$ to nil.
- Round VOTE (lines 14–32, Algorithm 3): In the round VOTE, a correct validator p_i votes $vote_i$ and broadcasts all the proposals it delivered during the current epoch. Then p_i collects all the messages that were broadcast. First p_i checks if it has delivered at least $2f + 1$ of proposal for a value v' pre-proposed by the proposer of the epoch, in that case, it sets $validValue_i$

Algorithm 3. Simplified Algorithm part 2 for height h executed at validator p_i

```
1:  Round PROPOSE(e_i):
2:     Send phase:
3:        if proposal_i ≠ nil then
4:           broadcast ⟨PROPOSE, h, e_i, proposal_i⟩ to all validators
5:     Delivery phase:
6:        while (timerPropose not expires) do{}              /* Collect messages */
7:     Compute phase:
8:        if ∃v : 2f + 1⟨PROPOSE, h, e_i, v⟩ ∧ valid(v) ∧ sendByProposer(h, e_i, v) then
9:           lockedValue_i ← v
10:          validValue_i ← v
11:          vote_i ← v
12:       else
13:          vote_i ← nil

14: Round VOTE(e_i):
15:    Send phase:
16:       ∀v, p_j : (⟨PROPOSE, h, e_i, v⟩, p_j) ∈ messagesSet_i, broadcast⟨PROPOSE, h, e_i, v⟩
17:       if vote_i ≠ nil then
18:          broadcast ⟨VOTE, h, e_i, vote_i⟩
19:    Delivery phase:
20:       while (timerVote not expires) do{}                 /* Collect messages */
21:    Compute phase:
22:       if ∃v' : 2f + 1⟨PROPOSE, h, e_i, v'⟩ ∧ valid(v') ∧ sendByProposer(h, e_i, v') then
23:          validValue_i ← v'
24:       if ∃v_d, e_d : 2f + 1⟨VOTE, h, e_d, v_d⟩ ∧ valid(v_d) ∧ decision_i = nil then
25:          decision_i ← v_d
26:       else
27:          e_i ← e_i + 1
28:          v_i ← nil
29:          if validValue_i ≠ nil then
30:             proposal_i ← validValue_i
31:          else
32:             proposal_i ← getValue()
```

to that value then it checks if a value v' pre-proposed by the proposer of the current epoch is valid and has at least $2f + 1$ votes, if it is the case, then p_i decides v' and goes to the next height; otherwise it increases the epoch number and updates the value of $proposal_i$ with respect to $validValue_i$.

3.2 Byzantine Eventual Synchronous System

This section presents the Algorithm 1, and Algorithms 4, 5 that solve Consensus in an eventually synchronous model in presence of Byzantine faulty validators. This algorithm has been reported in an early version of [12] with the bugs fixed in [30]. To achieve the consensus in this setting two additional variables need to be used, (i) $lockedEpoch_i$ is an integer representing the last epoch where validator p_i updated $lockedValue_i$, and (ii) $validEpoch_i$ is an integer which represents the last epoch where p_i updates $validValue_i$. These two new variables are used to not violate the agreement property during the asynchronous period. During such period different epochs may overlap at different validators, then it is needed to keep track of the relative epoch when a validator locks in order to not accept "outdated" information generated during a previous epoch. Moreover, a round

Algorithm 4. Tendermint Consensus part 1 for height h executed by p_i

```
1:  Initialization:
2:     e_i := 0                                              /* Current epoch number */
3:     decision_i := nil        /* This variable stocks the decision of the validator p_i */
4:     lockedValue_i := nil; validValue_i := nil
5:     lockedEpoch_i := -1; validEpoch_i := -1
6:     proposal_i := getValue() /* This variable stocks the value the validator will (pre-)propose */
7:     v_i := nil                   /* Local variable stocking the pre-preposal if delivered */
8:     validEpoch_j := nil           /* Local variable stocking the proposer's validEpoch */
9:     vote_i := nil            /* This variable stock the value the validator will vote for */
10:    timeoutPrePropose := Δ_Pre-propose; timeoutPropose := Δ_Propose; timeoutVote := Δ_Vote

11: Round PRE-PROPOSE:
12:    Send phase:
13:       if decision_i ≠ nil then
14:          ∀v, p_j : (⟨VOTE, h, e_i, v⟩, p_j) ∈ messagesSet_i, broadcast⟨VOTE, h, e_i, v⟩
15:          return
16:       if proposer(h, e_i) = p_i then
17:          broadcast ⟨PRE − PROPOSE, h, e_i, proposal_i, validEpoch_i⟩
18:    Delivery phase:
19:       set timerPrePropose to timeoutPrePropose
20:       while (timerPrePropose not expired) ∧ ¬(∃v_j, e_j : sendByProposer(h, e_i, v_j, e_j)) do
21:          if ∃v_j, e_j : sendByProposer(h, e_i, v_j, e_j) then
22:             v_i ← v_j                      /* v_j is the value sent by the proposer */
23:             validEpoch_j ← e_j             /* e_j is the validEpoch sent by the proposer */
24:       if ¬(∃v, epochProp : sendByProposer(h, e_i, v, epochProp)) then
25:          timeoutPrePropose ← timeoutPrePropose + 1
26:    Compute phase:
27:       if 2f + 1 ⟨PROPOSE, h, validEpoch_j, v_i⟩ ∧ validEpoch_j ≥ lockedEpoch_i ∧ validEpoch_j < e_i ∧ valid(v_i) then
28:          proposal_i ← v_i
29:       else
30:          if !valid(v_i) ∨ (lockedEpoch_i > validEpoch_j ∧ lockedValue_i ≠ v_i) then
31:             proposal_i ← nil                    /* Note that valid(nil) is set to false */
32:          if valid(v_i) ∧ (lockedEpoch_i = -1 ∨ lockedValue_i = v_i) then
33:             proposal_i ← v_i
```

duration management mechanism needs to be introduced, i.e. increasing time-outs. In the previous algorithm, rounds were lasting δ, the known message delay. In an eventually synchronous system such approach is not feasible, since during the asynchronous period messages may take unbounded delay before being delivered. It follows that, since there are at most f Byzantine faulty validators, when a validator delivers messages from $n - f$ different validators it can terminate the delivery phase, but such phase may last an unbounded time. On the contrary, in the PRE-PROPOSE round only the proposer is sending a message, and generally messages may take a lot of time before being delivered, for such reasons timeouts need to be used in order to manage the rounds duration and adapted to message delays, such that once the system enters in the synchronous period, rounds last enough for messages send during the round to be delivered before the end of it.

The algorithm proceeds in 3 rounds for any given epoch e at height h. The description is mainly the same as in Sect. 3.1, thus in the following we underline just the differences:

– Round PRE-PROPOSE (lines 11–33, Algorithm 4): The description of this round is mainly the same as before. We highlight the fact that a correct

---

Algorithm 5. Tendermint Consensus part 2 for height h executed by p_i

---

1: **Round PROPOSE:**
2:   **Send phase:**
3:     **if** $proposal_i \neq nil$ **then**
4:       **broadcast** $\langle$PROPOSE, $h, e_i, proposal_i\rangle$
5:     **broadcast** $\langle$HeartBeat, PROPOSE, $h, e_i\rangle$
6:   **Delivery phase:**
7:     set $timerPropose$ to timeoutPropose
8:     **while** $(timerPropose$ not expires$) \wedge \neg(2f + 1\langle$HeartBeat, PROPOSE, $h, e_i\rangle)$ **do**$\{\}$ /* Note that the HeartBeat messages should be from different validators */
9:     **if** $\neg(2f + 1\langle$HeartBeat, PROPOSE, $h, e_i\rangle)$ **then**
10:       timeoutPropose $\leftarrow$ timeoutPropose $+ 1$
11:   **Compute phase:**
12:     **if** $\exists v' : 2f + 1\langle$PROPOSE, $h, e_i, v'\rangle \wedge valid(v') \wedge$ sendByProposer(h, e_i, v') **then**
13:       $lockedValue_i \leftarrow v'$
14:       $lockedEpoch_i \leftarrow e_i$
15:       $validValue_i \leftarrow v'$
16:       $validEpoch_i \leftarrow e_i$
17:       $vote_i \leftarrow v'$
18:     **else**
19:       $vote_i \leftarrow nil$

20: **Round VOTE:**
21:   **Send phase:**
22:     $\forall v, p_j : (\langle$PROPOSE, $h, e_i, v\rangle, p_j) \in messagesSet_i$, **broadcast**$\langle$PROPOSE, $h, e_i, v\rangle$
23:     **if** $vote_i \neq nil$ **then**
24:       **broadcast** $\langle$VOTE, $h, e_i, vote_i\rangle$
25:     **broadcast** $\langle$HeartBeat, VOTE, $h, e_i\rangle$
26:   **Delivery phase:**
27:     set $timerVote$ to timeoutVote
28:     **while** $(timerVote$ not expires$) \wedge \neg(2f + 1\langle$HeartBeat, VOTE, $h, e_i\rangle)$ **do**$\{\}$
29:     **if** $\neg(2f + 1\langle$HeartBeat, VOTE, $h, e_i\rangle)$ **then**
30:       timeoutVote $\leftarrow$ timeoutVote $+ 1$
31:   **Compute phase:**
32:     **if** $\exists v'' : 2f + 1\langle$PROPOSE, $h, e_i, v''\rangle \wedge valid(v'') \wedge$ sendByProposer(h, e_i, v'') **then**
33:       $validValue_i \leftarrow v''$
34:       $validEpoch_i \leftarrow e_i$
35:     **if** $\exists v_d, e_d : 2f + 1\langle$VOTE, $h, e_d, v_d\rangle \wedge valid(v_d) \wedge decision_i = nil$ **then**
36:       $decision_i \leftarrow v_d$
37:     **else**
38:       $e_i \leftarrow e_i + 1$
39:       $v_i \leftarrow nil$
40:       **if** $validValue_i \neq nil$ **then**
41:         $proposal_i \leftarrow validValue_i$
42:       **else**
43:         $proposal_i \leftarrow getValue()$

---

validator p_i takes into account also $lockedEpoch_i$ in order to accept a pre-proposed value.

- Round PROPOSE (lines 1–19, Algorithm 5): When a correct validator p_i updates $lockedValue_i$ (resp. $validValue_i$), it also update $lockedEpoch_i$ (resp. $validEpoch_i$) to the current epoch.
- Round VOTE (lines 20–43, Algorithm 5): If a correct validator p_i delivered at least $f + 1$ same type of messages from an epoch higher than the current one, p_i moves directly to the PRE-PROPOSE round of that epoch and when a correct validator p_i updates $validValue_i$, it also update $validEpoch_i$ to the current epoch.

We recall that each validator has a time-out for each round. If during a round validator p_i does not deliver at least $2f+1$ messages sent during that round (or the pre-proposal for the PRE-PROPOSE round), the corresponding time-out is increased. Those messages can be values or heartbeats, in the case in which a correct validator has not a value to propose or vote.

3.3   Correctness Proof of Tendermint Algorithm in a Byzantine Eventual Synchronous Setting

In this section, we prove the correctness of Algorithms 4 and 5 (Tendermint) in an eventual synchronous system. Due to the lack of space, the missing proofs can be found in the technical report [7].

Lemma 1 (Validity). *In an eventual synchronous system, Tendermint verifies the following property: A decided value satisfies the predefined predicate denoted as* valid().

Lemma 2 (Integrity). *In an eventual synchronous system, Tendermint verifies the following property: No correct validator decides twice.*

Lemma 3. *Let v be a value, e an epoch, and the set $L^{v,e} = \{p_j : p_j$ correct $\wedge$ lockedValue$_j = v \wedge$ lockedEpoch$_j = e$ at the end of epoch $e\}$. In an eventual synchronous system, Tendermint verifies the following property: If $|L^{v,e}| \geq f+1$ then no correct validator p_i will have lockedValue$_i \neq v \wedge$ lockedEpoch$_i \geq e$, at the end of each epoch $e' > e$, moreover a validator in $L^{v,e}$ only proposes v or nil for each epoch $e' > e$.*

Lemma 4 (Agreement). *In an eventual synchronous system, Tendermint verifies the following property: If there is a correct validator that decides a value v, then eventually all the correct validators decide v.*

Lemma 5 (Termination). *In an eventual synchronous system, Tendermint verifies the following property: Every correct validator eventually decides some value.*

Proof. By construction, if a correct validator does not deliver more than $2f+1$ messages (or 1 from the proposer in the PRE-PROPOSE round) from different validators during the corresponding round, it increases the duration of its round, so eventually during the synchronous period of the system all the correct validators will deliver the pre-proposal, proposals and votes from correct validators respectively during the PRE-PROPOSE, PROPOSE and the VOTE round. Let e be the first epoch after that time.

If a correct validator decides before e, by Lemma 4 all correct validators decide which ends the proof. Otherwise at the beginning of epoch e, no correct validator decides yet. Let p_i be the proposer of e. We assume that p_i is correct and pre-propose v; v is valid since getValue() always return a valid value (lines 6, Algorithm 4 & line 43, Algorithm 5), and validValue$_i$ is always valid (lines 12 & 32, Algorithm 5). We have 2 cases:

– Case 1: At the beginning of epoch e, $|\{p_j : p_j \text{ correct} \wedge (lockedEpoch_j \leq validEpoch_i \vee lockedValue_j = v)\}| \geq 2f + 1$.
  Let p_j be a correct validator where the condition $lockedEpoch_j \leq validEpoch_i \vee lockedValue_j = v$ holds. After the delivery of the pre-proposal v from i, p_j will update $proposal_j$ to v (lines 27–33, Algorithm 4). During the PROPOSE round, p_j proposes v (line 4, Algorithm 5), and since there are at least $2f + 1$ similar correct validators they will all propose v, and all correct validators will deliver at least $2f + 1$ proposals for v (line 7, Algorithm 5).
  Correct validators will set their $vote$ to v (lines 12–4, Algorithm 5), will vote v, and will deliver these votes, so at least $2f + 1$ of votes (lines 24 & 26, Algorithm 5). Since we assume that no correct validators decided yet, and since they deliver at least $2f + 1$ votes for v, they will decide v (lines 35–36, Algorithm 5).
– Case 2: At the beginning of epoch e, $|\{p_j : p_j \text{ correct} \wedge (lockedEpoch_j \leq validEpoch_i \vee lockedValue_j = v)\}| < 2f + 1$.
  Let p_j be a correct validator where the condition $lockedEpoch_j > validEpoch_i \wedge lockedValue_j \neq v$ holds. When p_i will make the pre-proposal, p_j will set $proposal_j$ to nil (line 31, Algorithm 4) and will propose nil (line 4, Algorithm 5).
  By counting only the propose value of the correct validators, no value will have at least $2f + 1$ proposals for v. There are two cases:
  • No correct validator delivers at least $2f + 1$ proposals for v during the PROPOSE round, so they will all set their $vote$ to nil, vote nil and go to the next epoch without changing their state (lines 19 & 24–26 & 37–43, Algorithm 5).
  • If there are some correct validators that delivers at least $2f + 1$ proposals for v during the PROPOSE round, which means that some Byzantine validators send proposals for v to those validators.
    As in the previous case, they will vote for v, and since there are $2f + 1$ of them, all correct validators will decide v. Otherwise, there are less than $2f + 1$ correct validators that deliver at least $2f + 1$ proposals for v. Only them will vote for v (line 24, Algorithm 5). Without Byzantine validators, there will be less than $2f + 1$ vote for v, no correct validator will decide (lines 35–36, Algorithm 5) and they will go to the next epoch, if Byzantine validators send votes for v to a correct validator such as it delivers at least $2f + 1$ votes for v during VOTE round, then it will decide (lines 35–36, Algorithm 5), and by Lemma 4 all correct validators will eventually decide.
    Let p_k be one of the correct validators that delivers at least $2f + 1$ proposals for v during PROPOSE round, it means that $lockedValue_k = v$ and $lockedEpoch_k = e$. It follows that at the end of epoch e, all correct validators will have $validValue = v$ and $validEpoch = e$.
If there is no decision, either no correct validator changes its state, otherwise all correct validators change their state and have the same $validValue$ and $validEpoch$, eventually a proposer of an epoch will satisfy the case 1, and that ends the proof.

If p_i, the proposer of epoch e, is Byzantine and more than $2f+1$ correct validators delivered the same message during PRE-PROPOSE round, and the pre-proposal is valid, the situation is like p_i was correct. Otherwise, there are not enough correct validators that delivered the pre-proposal, or if the pre-proposal is not valid, then there will be less than $2f+1$ correct validators that will propose that value, which is similar to the case 2.

Since the proposer is selected in a round robin fashion, a correct validator will eventually be the proposer, and correct validators will decide. $\square_{Lemma\,5}$

Theorem 1. *In an eventual synchronous system, Tendermint implements the consensus specification.*

3.4   Complexity of Tendermint Algorithm in a Byzantine Eventual Synchronous Setting

Let us consider the following scenario after the asynchronous period (i.e., after τ), in which in the first f epochs, $e_{i+1}, \ldots, e_{i+f}$, there are f Byzantine proposers that make lock only one correct validator at each epoch on f different values with different $lockedEpoch$, $e_{i+1}, \ldots, e_{i+f}$. Let p_j be the last correct validator that locked, and let v such value ($lockedValue_j = v$) with $lockedEpoch_j = e_{i+f}$. Then all the other correct validators have $validValue$ set to v and $validEpoch$ set to e_{i+f}. This happens thanks to the fact that when a correct validator locks on a value then at the end of the epoch every correct validator sets its $validValue$ to that value. The algorithm terminates when a pre-proposal is proposed and voted by more than $2f$ correct validators, i.e, when the pre-proposed value has $validEpoch$ greater equal than the validator $lockedEpoch$. Thus, during the period of synchrony, the first correct proposer that proposes leads the algorithm to terminate in $f+1$ rounds. Let us consider the case in which there f correct validators locked on f different values with different $lockedEpoch$ before τ. Let us assume that p_j is the last correct validator that locked on a value v, thus it has the highest $lockedEpoch$ but not all the correct validators have their $validValue$ set to v (due to the asynchronous communication). Let us now consider that after τ the first f proposers are Byzantines and stay silent. The following proposers are correct but their pre-propose value might not be accepted by enough correct validators as long as p_j, with the highest $validEpoch$ and $lockedEpoch$ proposes. Which eventually happens due to the round robin selection function. Thus, the protocol terminates in a number of epochs proportional to the number of validators $O(n)$, while the lower bound to solve BFT Consensus in the worst case scenario is $f+1$ [20]. As for message complexity, since at each epoch, all validators broadcast messages, it follows that during one epoch the protocol uses $O(n^2)$ messages, thus in the worst case scenario the message complexity is $O(n^3)$.

In the following we address the bit complexity of Tendermint. In Tendermint, each message is composed as follow:

- PRE-PROPOSE: The marker that the message is from the round PRE-PROPOSE; two integers one for the current height, and the second for the current epoch; the proposed value; and an integer representing the epoch on which the proposer last updated its *validValue*.
- PROPOSE: The marker that the message is from the round PROPOSE; two integers representing the current height and the current epoch; and a value which is the proposed block.
- VOTE: The marker that the message is from the round VOTE; two integers representing the current height and the current epoch; and a value which is the voted block.
- HeartBeat: The marker that the HeartBeat is from the round VOTE or PROPOSE; two integers representing the current height and the current epoch.

A correct validator keeps in memory, for each epoch for a given height, one message for each type (PROPOSE, VOTE) and at most 2 messages of type HeartBeat from each validator, and only one PRE-PROPOSE. A correct validator may have at most 1 message from PRE-PROPOSE, n messages from PROPOSE, n messages from VOTE, and $2n$ messages of type HeartBeat. Hence, for each epoch at any given height, a validator stores at most $4n+1$ messages of size $O(\log n)$. In the worst case, for the whole execution, a validator may store $O(n^2)$ messages. Therefore, the bit complexity in the worst case is $O(n^2 \log n)$.

Note that [24] proposes a bit complexity of $O(n^3 \log n)$ for an optimal round complexity using a variant of the tree structure of the Exponential Information Gathering protocol introduced in [22]. Clearly, there is a tradeoff between the bit complexity and the round complexity of the Byzantine agreement.

4 Conclusion

The contribution of this work is twofold. First, it analyzes Tendermint consensus protocol and provides detailed proof of its correctness and complexity. Second, it dissects such protocol in order to link the algorithmic techniques to the considered system model. We believe that this methodology can contribute in making Byzantine-tolerant consensus algorithms more understandable for developers and practitioners.

Acknowledgment. The authors would like to thank the reviewers of NETYS 2019 for their insightful comments. The authors also thank Zaynah Dargaye for numerous discussions, and in particular for the consistency of this work.

References

1. Livelock scenario. https://github.com/tendermint/tendermint/wiki/0.7-Livelock-Scenario. Accessed 14 Mar 2019
2. Abraham, I., Gueta, G., Malkhi, D.: Hot-stuff the linear, optimal-resilience, one-message BFT devil. CoRR abs/1803.05069 (2018). http://arxiv.org/abs/1803.05069
3. Abraham, I., Malkhi, D., Nayak, K., Ren, L., Spiegelman, A.: Solidus: An incentive-compatible cryptocurrency based on permissionless byzantine consensus. CoRR, abs/1612.02916 (2016)
4. Aguilera, M.K.: A pleasant stroll through the land of infinitely many creatures. ACM Sigact News **35**(2), 36–59 (2004)
5. Amoussou-Guenou, Y., Del Pozzo, A., Potop-Butucaru, M., Tucci-Piergiovanni, S.: Correctness and Fairness of Tendermint-core Blockchains. CoRR abs/1805.08429 (2018)
6. Amoussou-Guenou, Y., Del Pozzo, A., Potop-Butucaru, M., Tucci-Piergiovanni, S.: Correctness of tendermint-core blockchains. In: 22nd International Conference on Principles of Distributed Systems, OPODIS 2018, 17–19 December 2018, Hong Kong, China. pp. 16:1–16:16 (2018)
7. Amoussou-Guenou, Y., Del Pozzo, A., Potop-Butucaru, M., Tucci-Piergiovanni, S.: Dissecting Tendermint. Research report, LIP6, Sorbonne Université, CNRS, UMR 7606; CEA List (2018). https://hal.archives-ouvertes.fr/hal-01881212v2
8. Anceaume, E., Del Pozzo, A., Ludinard, R., Potop-Butucaru, M., Tucci-Piergiovanni, S.: Blockchain abstract data type. In: SPAA 2019 (2019, to appear)
9. Androulaki, E., et al.: Hyperledger fabric: a distributed operating system for permissioned blockchains. In: Proceedings of the Thirteenth EuroSys Conference, EuroSys 2018, Porto, Portugal, 23–26 April 2018, pp. 30:1–30:15 (2018)
10. Baldoni, R., Bertier, M., Raynal, M., Tucci-Piergiovanni, S.: Looking for a definition of dynamic distributed systems. In: Malyshkin, V. (ed.) PaCT 2007. LNCS, vol. 4671, pp. 1–14. Springer, Heidelberg (2007). https://doi.org/10.1007/978-3-540-73940-1_1
11. Ben-Or, M.: Another advantage of free choice (extended abstract): completely asynchronous agreement protocols. In: Proceedings of the Second Annual ACM Symposium on Principles of Distributed Computing, pp. 27–30. ACM (1983)
12. Buchman, E., Kwon, J., Milosevic, Z.: The latest gossip on BFT consensus. Technical report, Tendermint (2018). https://arxiv.org/abs/1807.04938
13. Cachin, C., Kursawe, K., Petzold, F., Shoup, V.: Secure and efficient asynchronous broadcast protocols. In: Kilian, J. (ed.) CRYPTO 2001. LNCS, vol. 2139, pp. 524–541. Springer, Heidelberg (2001). https://doi.org/10.1007/3-540-44647-8_31
14. Castro, M., Liskov, B.: Practical byzantine fault tolerance. In: Proceedings of the Symposium on Operating Systems Design and Implementation (OSDI) (1999)
15. Crain, T., Gramoli, V., Larrea, M., Raynal, M.: (Leader/Randomization/Signature)-free Byzantine Consensus for Consortium Blockchains (2017). http://csrg.redbellyblockchain.io/doc/ConsensusRedBellyBlockchain.pdf. Accessed 22 May 2018
16. Crain, T., Gramoli, V., Larrea, M., Raynal, M.: DBFT: Efficient byzantine consensus with a weak coordinator and its application to consortium blockchains. arXiv preprint arXiv:1702.03068 (2017)
17. Decker, C., Seidel, J., Wattenhofer, R.: Bitcoin meets strong consistency. In: Proceedings of the 17th International Conference on Distributed Computing and Networking Conference (ICDCN) (2016)

18. Dwork, C., Lynch, N.A., Stockmeyer, L.J.: Consensus in the presence of partial synchrony. J. ACM **35**(2), 288–323 (1988)
19. Dwork, C., Naor, M.: Pricing via processing or combatting junk mail. In: Brickell, E.F. (ed.) CRYPTO 1992. LNCS, vol. 740, pp. 139–147. Springer, Heidelberg (1993). https://doi.org/10.1007/3-540-48071-4_10
20. Fischer, M.J., Lynch, N.A.: A lower bound for the time to assure interactive consistency. Inf. Process. Lett. **14**(4), 183–186 (1982)
21. Fischer, M.J., Lynch, N.A., Paterson, M.S.: Impossibility of distributed consensus with one faulty process. J. ACM **32**(2), 374–382 (1985)
22. Garay, J.A., Moses, Y.: Fully polynomial byzantine agreement in t+1 rounds. In: Proceedings of the Twenty-Fifth Annual ACM Symposium on Theory of Computing, 16–18 May 1993, San Diego, CA, USA, pp. 31–41 (1993)
23. Kokoris-Kogias, E., Jovanovic, P., Gailly, N., Khoffi, I., Gasser, L., Ford, B.: Enhancing bitcoin security and performance with strong consistency via collective signing. In: Proceedings of the 25th USENIX Security Symposium (2016)
24. Kowalski, D.R., Mostéfaoui, A.: Synchronous byzantine agreement with nearly a cubic number of communication bits: synchronous byzantine agreement with nearly a cubic number of communication bits. In: ACM Symposium on Principles of Distributed Computing, PODC 2013, Montreal, QC, Canada, 22–24 July 2013, pp. 84–91 (2013)
25. Kwon, J., Buchman, E.: Cosmos: A Network of Distributed Ledgers. https://cosmos.network/resources/whitepaper. Accessed 22 May 2018
26. Kwon, J., Buchman, E.: Tendermint. https://tendermint.readthedocs.io/en/master/specification.html. Accessed 22 May 2018
27. Lamport, L., Shostak, R., Pease, M.: The byzantine generals problem. ACM Trans. Programm. Lang. Syst. **4**(3), 382–401 (1982)
28. Muñoz-Escoí, F.D., de Juan-Marín, R.: On synchrony in dynamic distributed systems. Open Comput. Sci. **8**(1), 154–164(2018). https://doi.org/10.1515/comp-2018-0014
29. Pease, M., Shostak, R., Lamport, L.: Reaching agreement in the presence of faults. J. ACM **27**(2), 228–234 (1980)
30. Tendermint: correctness issues. https://github.com/tendermint/spec/issues. Accessed 24 Sept 2018
31. Tendermint: Tendermint Core (BFT Consensus) in Go. https://github.com/tendermint/tendermint/blob/e88f74bb9bb9edb9c311f256037fcca217b45ab6/consensus/state.go. Accessed 22 May 2018

CUDA-DTM: Distributed Transactional Memory for GPU Clusters

Samuel Irving[1], Sui Chen[1], Lu Peng[1(✉)], Costas Busch[1], Maurice Herlihy[2], and Christopher J. Michael[1]

[1] Louisiana State University, Baton Rouge, LA 70803, USA
lpeng@lsu.edu
[2] Brown University, Providence, RI 02912, USA

Abstract. We present CUDA-DTM, the first ever Distributed Transactional Memory framework written in CUDA for large scale GPU clusters. Transactional Memory has become an attractive auto-coherence scheme for GPU applications with irregular memory access patterns due to its ability to avoid serializing threads while still maintaining programmability. We extend GPU Software Transactional Memory to allow threads across many GPUs to access a coherent distributed shared memory space and propose a scheme for GPU-to-GPU communication using CUDA-Aware MPI. The performance of CUDA-DTM is evaluated using a suite of seven irregular memory access benchmarks with varying degrees of compute intensity, contention, and node-to-node communication frequency. Using a cluster of 256 devices, our experiments show that GPU clusters using CUDA-DTM can be up to 115x faster than CPU clusters.

Keywords: Distributed Transactional Memory · GPU cluster · CUDA

1 Introduction

Because today's CPU clock speeds are increasing slowly, if at all, some computationally intensive applications are turning to specialized hardware accelerators such as graphics processing units. Originally developed for graphics applications, GPUs have become more versatile, and are now widely used for increasingly complex scientific and machine learning applications. Though traditional GPU applications required little or no coordination among concurrent threads, GPUs are now routinely used for irregular applications that often require complex synchronization schemes to ensure the integrity of data shared by concurrent threads.

Conventional synchronization approaches typically rely on locking: a coherence strategy in which a thread must acquire an exclusive lock before accessing shared data. Though conceptually simple, locking schemes for irregular memory access applications are notoriously difficult to develop and debug on traditional systems due to well-known pitfalls: Priority Inversion occurs when a lower-priority thread holding a lock is preempted by a higher-priority thread;

© Springer Nature Switzerland AG 2019
M. F. Atig and A. A. Schwarzmann (Eds.): NETYS 2019, LNCS 11704, pp. 183–199, 2019.
https://doi.org/10.1007/978-3-030-31277-0_12

Convoying occurs when a thread holding a lock is delayed, causing a queue of waiting threads to form; and most importantly, a deadlock, in which overall progress halts indefinitely, can occur if multiple threads attempt to acquire a set of locks in different orders. These pitfalls are especially difficult to avoid in GPU and cluster computing applications, where the degree of parallelism is orders-of-magnitude higher than traditional applications.

Transactional Memory (TM) [8] is an increasingly popular alternative synchronization model in which programmers simply mark the beginning and end of critical sections so the system can treat those regions as "Transactions", which appear to execute atomically with respect to other transactions. At runtime, a complex conflict-detection system, invisible to the programmer, guarantees forward progress and that deadlocks cannot arise. The allure of Transactional Memory is that it commonly achieves performance comparable to that of custom lock-based solutions despite requiring only minimal effort. The programmability advantages of Transactional Memory are magnified in situations where high degrees of parallelism make lock-based solutions difficult to design and debug.

This paper investigates the performance of the first scalable Distributed Transactional Memory (DTM) [9] system for large-scale clusters of GPUs. Individual GPU threads are granted access to a coherent distributed shared memory space and can perform fine-granularity remote memory operations without halting the kernel or halting other threads within the same warp. Inter-node communication is achieved using active support from the host CPU, which sends and receives messages on behalf of the GPU. Coherence is automatically ensured using Transactional Memory, which guarantees lock-freedom, serializability, and forward progress while requiring minimal effort from programmers.

2   Related Work

There exists much prior work on the use of STM for single-device irregular memory access applications on the GPU. Cederman *et al.* [2] first proposed the use of STM on GPUs and evaluate two STM protocols. Xu *et al.* [17] proposed GPUSTM with encounter-time lock sorting to avoid deadlocks. Holey *et al.* [10] propose and evaluate multiple single-device GPU STM protocols. Shen *et al.* [15] propose a priority-rule based STM system for GPUs in which ownership of data objects can be stolen from other threads. Villegas *et al.* [16] propose APUTM, an STM design in which transactions are simultaneously executed on the GPU and host CPU. STM has been also used to maintain NVRAM persistence for GPUs [5].

There also exists much prior work in the hardware acceleration of TM on GPUs. Kilo TM [6] is a hardware-based GPU transactional memory system that supports weakly-isolated transactions in GPU kernel code; this work has been extended many times including by Chen et al. who recently described how to relax read-write conflicts with multi-version memory and Snapshot Isolation [4] and two early conflict resolution schemes [3].

There is much ongoing research in DTM for CPU clusters where it is most commonly implemented using a data-flow model, in which transactions are immobile and shared memory objects are dynamically moved between nodes [9]. DTM has been implemented in many software languages, most notably C++ [12]. There is ongoing research on how best to scale DTM to very large numbers of threads [14].

3   Design

CUDA-DTM provides an API that allows GPU programmers to treat all GPUs as a single unified compute resource and all storage resource as a single unified memory space. Individual GPU threads across all devices are assigned unique global thread IDs and allowed to access shared virtual memory space using unique global virtual memory addresses. CUDA-DTM is designed for clusters with heterogeneous nodes, each containing one or more GPU accelerators that can access the network vicariously through the host processor.

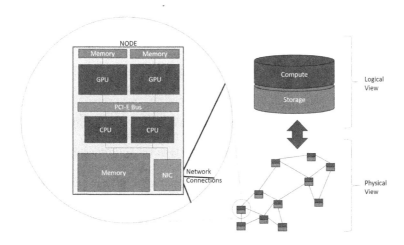

Fig. 1. Cluster-level overview of CUDA-DTM.

A lightweight STM coherence protocol allows programmers to ensure deadlock-free coherence automatically. CUDA-DTM uses custom GPU-to-GPU communication on top of CUDA-Aware MPI. A cluster level overview of CUDA-DTM is shown in Fig. 1.

CUDA-DTM is designed for heterogeneous clusters in which nodes are equipped with GPU accelerators, which are the only devices executing transactions, and host CPUs, which facilitate communication between GPUs. As shown in Fig. 1, the current CUDA-DTM design assumes only the CPU has direct access to the Network Interface Card (NIC) and thus must be responsible for all network communication. Node-to-Node communication is achieved using MPI. The stages for communication between devices and the network via the host in a CUDA-DTM cluster are shown in Fig. 2. Only local threads are allowed to access

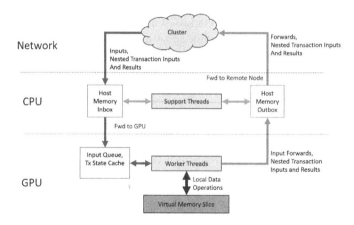

Fig. 2. Node-level overview of CUDA-DTM showing the control-flow cycle.

the local virtual memory slice directly. A system of message passing, shared data structures, and active support from host threads enable transactions to move to the node containing the requisite data.

Slices of the shared memory space are stored in each GPUs memory. GPU worker threads perform local data operations directly on the slice of virtual memory. CUDA-DTM uses a control-flow model, in which objects are immobile and remote procedure calls are used to move work between nodes. When a transaction accesses a virtual memory address that does not resolve locally, a remote procedure call is used to create a new sub-transaction on the remote node, termed a Remote Nested Transaction [13], by passing transaction inputs and an abbreviated execution history; this process is repeated each time transaction execution accesses data outside the local memory slice, resulting in a hierarchy structure in which top-level transactions may be comprised of many nested transactions, each detecting its own conflicts and capable of being aborted and restarted independently described in [13]. The entire hierarchy of nested transactions must be committed simultaneously.

This control-flow Remote Nested Transaction strategy only requires remote communication when transaction execution leaves the local memory slice, thereby avoiding the frequent broadcasts required by some data-flow models [9] and eliminating the need for a global clock, which can also have a significant communication overhead.

In the current design, shared memory is evenly distributed between nodes, and thus the owner of any virtual address can be found using the most-significant 8 bits of the 32-bit virtual address. Remote Nested Transaction creations and forwarded inputs, for which the critical section has not yet started, are sent to remote nodes by support threads on the host CPU. Outgoing messages are first accumulated on device before a "ready to send" message is passed into pinned host memory. A host support thread then uses CUDA-Aware MPI to send a batch of messages to the correct destination.

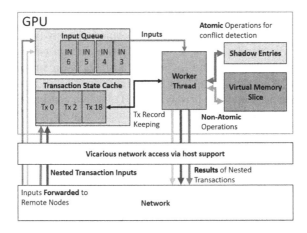

Fig. 3. Device-level overview of CUDA-DTM showing the two core data structures facilitating transaction control-flow.

Support threads on the host processor ensure that incoming messages accumulate in an "inbox" in GPU global memory. GPU worker threads pull work assignments out of the inbox and perform work depending on the contents of the message; types of messages in the system and the two data structures that function as an inbox are shown in Fig. 3. The inbox consists of (1) an Input Queue, which accumulates the parameters for un-started transactions, and (2) the Transaction State Cache which is used to store the current state and access history of transactions that have entered the critical section on the current node. Host support threads are capable of accessing these structures during kernel execution using asynchronous CUDA memcpys.

Communication between GPUs is facilitated by two structures stored in global memory: the Input Queue and the Transaction State Cache, as shown in Fig. 3. The input queue receives blocks of inputs, each containing the parameters for an un-started transaction; the size and usage of each input is application specific. The Transaction State Cache is used to store undo-logs for Transactions that are waiting for the result of a Remote Nested Transactions. Each working thread on the GPU has a Transaction State Cache Set that it is responsible for which is regularly polled when no other work is available.

During the execution of a transaction, a transaction state is created and maintained in local memory; the active transaction state is modified when performing atomic operations to the shadow entries stored locally using the conflict detection rules described in Sect. 3.1. When execution of a transaction accesses a virtual memory address outside of the current node and must create a Remote Nested Transaction, an entry is created in the Transaction State Cache; the entry contains the unique transaction ID, created using the unique thread ID shifted and then added to a private counter, the largest address accessed so far, the undo-log, and state variable indicating the transaction has not yet been aborted nor committed. Remote Nested Transactions are created directly in the remote

Transaction State Cache of the node containing the desired data; Transaction State entries are stored such that they can be copied directly from memory using CUDA-Aware MPI. Similarly, the results of a transaction can be sent directly into the Transaction State cache – overwriting the state variable so working threads can see that a transaction has been committed or aborted. Serialization and deserialization are handled entirely by CUDA when communicating between device and host and entirely by MPI when communicating between nodes.

3.1   Transactional Memory Model

CUDA-DTM detects and resolves conflicts using a modified version of the Pessimistic Software Transactional Memory (PSTM) protocol described in [10] built on top of the virtual memory system described above. The use of a distributed memory space is invisible to the transactional memory protocol as a new remote nested transaction is created each time execution moves between nodes.

Ownership is tracked via 32-bit Shadow Entries that store the unique virtual transaction id number for the transaction that is accessing the corresponding object; shadow entries are all initialized to be 0. This design uses a single-copy model in which there is only one write-able copy of each object in the system; while this forces the serialization of accesses to individual objects, it also minimizes the storage and compute overheads of the system, allowing the working data set size to be very large.

Threads in the same warp are allowed to execute simultaneous transactions using a private state variable, which masks off threads that have been aborted or are waiting for work. Live-locks are prevented using exponential back-off, in which transactions that are aborted multiple times are forced to wait an exponentially increasing length of time before restarting.

PSTM was chosen for our design due to its simplicity, low overheads, and its eager conflict detection – which aborts transactions early and can help reduce the number of remote messages.

When a transaction begins execution or is restarted: its local state is set to ACTIVE and its local undo log is cleared, as shown in Algorithm 1. Each transaction maintains a private undo log in local memory which can be used to reverse changes to local shadow entries and shared memory in the event of an abortion. A single transaction may create several Remote Nested Transactions, each with its own private undo log on its respective node.

Algorithm 1 TX_begin(i)

$T_i.state = ACTIVE$;
$T_i.undoLog \leftarrow \emptyset$;

Algorithm 2 TX_validate(i)

---

if $T_i.state = ACTIVE$ **then**
    TX_commit(i);
else
    TX_abort(i);

Algorithm 3 TX_commit(i)

---

foreach $u \in T_i.undoLog$ **do**
    $shadow[u.addr] \leftarrow 0$;
if $T_i.parent$!= null **then**
    send commit result to parent;

Algorithm 4 TX_abort(i)

---

foreach $u \in T_i.undoLog$ **do**
    $data[u.addr] \leftarrow u.value$;
    $shadow[u.addr] \leftarrow 0$;
if $T_i.parent$!= null **then**
    send abort result to parent;

Algorithm 5 TX_access(i,addr)

---

if $T_i.state$!= ACTIVE **then**
    return;
if addr is not local **then**
    Create remote nested Tx;
    $T_i.state = WAITING$;
    return;
if $addr \notin T_i.undoLog$ **then**
    if $addr > T_i.maxAddr$ **then**
        while(!tryLock(addr,i))
    else
        if !tryLock(addr,i) **then**
            $T_i.state = ABORTED$;
        return;
    add   (addr,objects[addr])   to $T_i.undoLog$;

Algorithm 6 tryLock(i,addr)

---

if $shadow[addr] \neq 0$ **then**
    return false;
return CAS(shadow[addr],i,0));

At validation, any transaction whose state is still ACTIVE is ready to be committed, as shown in Algorithm 2. A thread's state is only set to ABORTED after failing to acquire exclusive control over a specific shared memory address. Setting the state to ABORTED effectively masks off threads when other threads in the same warp are still ACTIVE.

If still ACTIVE at validation time, all changes performed by the transaction must be made permanent by simply releasing all locks acquired during execution, as shown in Algorithm 3. If this transaction is a Remote Nested Transaction that was created by a parent transaction on another node, then a result message must be sent to the parent node.

In the event of an abort, a thread must iterate through the undo log, restore the original object values, and reset ownership of the corresponding shadow entries as shown in Algorithm 4. If this transaction is a Remote Nested Transaction, then a result message must be sent to the parent node indicating that all transactions must be restarted; otherwise, the transaction will resume execution when the thread warp re-executes TX_begin.

For simplicity, we combine TX_read and TX_write into TX_access, as shown in Algorithm 5, because PSTM does not distinguish between read and write operations when detecting conflicts. PSTM pessimistically assumes that any address touched by a transaction will eventually be modified, and thus a transaction should immediately be aborted if it fails to acquire exclusive control over a specific shared memory address.

Although transactions can perform speculative writes to shared memory, other threads cannot read these values until the transaction commits and the corresponding shadow entry is released.

When TX_access is called using a virtual address that is mapped to a different node, execution of the current transaction must be suspended and a Remote Nested Transaction created. Execution of the parent transaction is suspended by first storing the undo-log into the local Transaction State Cache and, if the transaction originated on the current node, assigning it a unique ID. The working thread indicates the target node when creating a Remote Nested Transaction Start message, along with variables required to begin execution on the remote node, and includes the largest address accessed so far. This message is inserted into the appropriate remote GPU Transaction State Cache where a new transaction state is created including a new local-only undo-log and a reference to the originating node that will ultimately receive a message indicating the result of the transaction. The process of creating a Remote Nested Transaction, suspending, and resuming transactions is handled entirely by the CUDA-DTM system and is invisible to the programmer.

To gain ownership of an object, a thread will perform an Atomic Compare-and-Swap operation (CAS) on the object's corresponding shadow entry, as shown in Algorithm 6. This CAS operation attempts to atomically exchange the current shadow entry value with the thread's unique, non-zero id. This exchange is only performed if the expected value of "0" is found; otherwise, the function returns the value discovered before the exchange. If the function returns a non-zero value, then the current transaction has failed to gain ownership and may abort. If the exchange is successful, the transaction is allowed to proceed.

Our modified PSTM allows transactions to use blocking atomic operations when accessing addresses in increasing order; this is tracked by storing the max-address-locked-so-far (termed "maxAddr" in Algorithm 5). This strategy reduces the total number of abortions, as a transaction is only aborted when trying and failing to acquire a lock out of order. Transactions can proceed as normal if an out of order lock is successfully acquired on the first try. After successfully accessing a shared memory object, its address and current value are inserted into the undo log so that speculative changes can be reversed in the event of an abortion (referred to as (addr, objects[addr]) in Algorithm 5).

3.2   Communication

GPU worker threads provide virtual memory addresses to the CUDA-DTM API, which performs the necessary communication operations under-the-hood. Operations using virtual addresses that are mapped to local physical addresses resolve quickly because the object and shadow entry are stored in local global memory. However, when a virtual address is mapped to a remote physical address, the API automatically creates a Remote Nested Transaction that continues execution on the remote device that contains the requisite data.

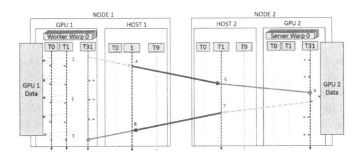

Fig. 4. Timing of the communication protocol stages showing the execution of a Remote Nested Transaction (Color figure online).

The CUDA-DTM communication protocol uses three asynchronous messages passes, as shown in Fig. 4: (1) the originating thread writes a message to an outbox in global memory (orange dashed arrow) and then sets a "ready" Boolean in host memory to "true"; (2) a support thread on the host detects that the "ready" Boolean is true for a outbox and sends the message to the correct node using an asynchronous MPI write to remote host memory (thick blue arrow); (3) support threads in the remote node's host receive the incoming message and place it in the correct thread's inbox using an asynchronous cudaMemCpy (green line with circle on the end).

Depending on how aggressively messages are batched, all threads may have a designated inbox in global device memory and a designated outbox in pinned host memory.

After creating a Remote Nested Transaction, worker threads are allowed to begin execution of a new transaction; worker threads cycle between responsibilities when blocked waiting for remote communication by polling the transaction state cache and input queue (purple double-sided arrow).

Figure 4 shows the timing of GPU-to-GPU communication for transactions that have already begun the critical section of a transaction that increments multiple addresses. (1) Warp 0 is initially un-diverged and all threads begin virtual memory increments using different virtual memory addresses. Of the threads shown, only thread 31's virtual memory address is mapped to a physical address on a remote node. Threads 0 and 1 are forced to wait while Thread 31 enters its transaction state into the transaction state cache, builds a Remote Nested Transaction creation message and notifies the host that a message is waiting to send. Finally, the rest of the warp quickly make copies of the desired objects from global memory. (2) In this example, the transaction state cache and input queue have no available work for Thread 31 to begin, so Threads 0 and 1 continue to perform virtual memory operations while Thread 31 is masked off. When other threads in the warp use the CUDA-DTM API, thread 31 polls the input queue and checks the state of its suspended transaction waiting for work. (3) After five memory operations, the warp finally re-converges when thread 31 receives the Nested Transaction Result.

(4) In this example, ten host threads are responsible for supporting the local GPU worker threads. Responsibility for checking outboxes for readiness is evenly divided among host threads, and thus support thread 1 sees outbox 31 is ready, uses the message's address to calculate its destination, and sends the message to node 2 using an asynchronous MPI write operation. (5) On node 2, host support thread 1 checks thread 31's inbox, discovers a new message, and copies the message into device memory using an asynchronous CUDA copy. (6) Thread 31 on Node 2, having been polling its inbox for incoming work, receives the result of the Nested Transaction from Node 1-Thread 31, begins execution of the Nested Transaction on the new node using a fresh-undo log. Here, the desired virtual memory address resolves locally and the increment is completed successfully. Having reached the end of the Nested Transaction, Node 2's thread 31 commits the transaction by releasing ownership of local shadow entries and destroying the corresponding entry in the transaction state cache. Thread 31 creates a new Nested Transaction Result message indicating the transaction is complete and sends it to the originating Node 0. (7) Support thread 1 on host 2 detects an outgoing message is ready and sends the message back to host 1 where (8) support thread 1 on host 1 copies the final transaction result into the inbox of the originating worker thread using CUDA asynchronous copy to device.

CUDA-Aware MPI is used in cases where outgoing messages can be batched together in global memory, all bound for the same destination. In these cases, only the owner of the final message added to the batch is forced to notify the host that the batch is ready to send. The protocol is achieved using single-writer, single-reader arrays when possible, avoiding the need for atomic operations that increase overheads.

4   Experimental Analysis

For this experiment, we use a set of seven irregular memory access benchmarks commonly used for studying TM; the benchmarks differ in length, composition, contention, and shared data size. A 128-node cluster featuring two CPUs and two GPUs per node is used for this experiment using a 56 GB/s Infiniband oversubscribed mesh; each CPU is a 2.8 GHz E5-2689v2 Xeon processor with 64 GB RAM; each GPU is a NVIDIA Tesla K20x connected via an Intel 82801 PCIe bridge. CUDA-DTM is compiled using CUDA v9.2.148 and MVAPICH2 version 2.2.

Coherence protocols are detailed in Table 1. Transactions are only executed by GPU threads in the GPU and CUDA-DTM configurations.

For this work we use seven benchmarks commonly used to profile TM performance: Histogram (HIST) [1], in which the results of a random number generator are stored in a shared array; two variants of the Hash Table benchmark [7]: one in which each transaction inserts a single element (HASH-S), and one where each transaction inserts four elements simultaneously (HASH-M), as described in [10]; Linked-List (LL) [7], in which elements are inserted into a sorted List; KMeans [11]; and two graph algorithms: Single-Source Shortest Path (SSSP) [1] and Graph-Cut (GCut), which finds the minimum cut of a graph using Karger's algorithm [4].

Table 1. Coherence protocols

Cluster	Protocol	Devices	Max threads per device
CPU	Single-CPU STM using std::threads	1	10
GPU	Single-GPU STM	1	4096 × 1024
CPU DTM	Hybrid-MPI DTM using std::threads	256	10
CUDA DTM	DTM for GPUs, supported by Hybrid MPI	256	4096 × 1024 + 10 on Host

Using 128 nodes, CUDA-DTM achieves a harmonic mean speedup of 1,748x over the single-node, multi-threaded CPU baseline across the 10 benchmarks used in this study, as shown in Fig. 5. Similarly, CUDA-DTM achieves a harmonic mean speedup of 6.9x over a CPU cluster of the same size due to the performance advantages of the GPU architecture. CPU DTM achieves slightly less than a 256x speedup over a single CPU due to the high parallelizability of all seven benchmarks and long run times hiding network latencies. The near-ideal speedup of CPU DTM suggests that the 56 Gb/s bandwidth of the network is never saturated with messages.

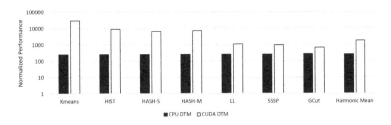

Fig. 5. The performances of CUDA-DTM and CPU DTM on a 128 node cluster normalized by single-node CPU performance.

The speedups achieved by CUDA-DTM are best explained by the execution time breakdown shown in Fig. 6. Using Figs. 5 and 6, we see that CUDA-DTM

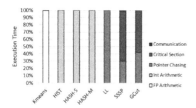 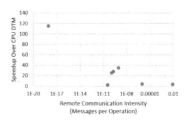

Fig. 6. (Left) CUDA-DTM execution time breakdown and (Right) CUDA-DTM Speedup over CPU DTM vs. remote communication intensity.

achieves a speedup of 25 to 115x over the CPU for compute intensive benchmarks, in which execution time is dominated by arithmetic operations, consistent with the ∼70x higher theoretical peak throughput of the GPU. Similarly, we see CUDA-DTM achieves a speedup of 2.5 to 4.2x for memory intensive benchmarks, in which execution time is mostly spent chasing pointers through shared memory, similar to the ∼4.2x higher theoretical bandwidth of the GPU (250 GB/s vs 59.7 GB/s). Finally, we see the smallest speedup for benchmarks with high contention, as the advantages of the massive number of GPU threads is limited by blocking atomic operations during the critical section. Remote communication is only a very small percentage of the execution time despite varying degrees of remote-communication intensity.

CUDA-DTM's sensitivity to the remote-communication intensity of the workload is visualized in Fig. 6. Here we see benchmarks with the most infrequent remote communications generally show the largest speedup over the CPU, though the magnitude of the speedup is heavily impacted by the type of operations used between remote communication. Benchmarks with the highest communication intensity are also memory-intensive, limiting the potential speedup to the ∼4.2x higher memory bandwidth of the GPU. The best performing benchmark, KMeans, is very FLOP intensive, benefiting from both the high volume of operations between remote messages and the ∼70x higher computational throughput of the GPU. CUDA-DTM's speedup will converge on 1x as the remote intensity increases, because the GPU has no communication advantages over the CPU.

Figure 7 shows the average number of messages generated per committed transaction for each benchmark. GCut generates the fewest messages per transaction while showing the smallest speedup over the CPU while HIST, HASH-S, and HASH-M all show largest speedups despite delivering at least one message per transaction. LL generates over 100 messages per transaction while searching the shared List for the proper data insertion point; we use this graph to suggest that the bottleneck of each benchmark is not the inter-node bandwidth, as the GPU has no inter-node bandwidth advantages over the CPU. KMeans generates very few messages, as centroids are only globally averaged after long spans of intra-node averaging. Similarly, GCut runs isolated instances of Karger's algorithm on each node, only generating messages when a new lowest-min-cut-so-far is discovered.

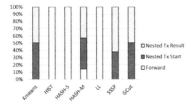 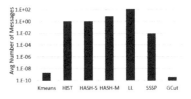

Fig. 7. (Left) Avg number of remote messages generated per transaction showing varying degrees of network intensity. (Right) Breakdown of remote message types.

The types of remote messages generated by each transaction are profiled in Fig. 7. HIST, HASH-S, and LL almost never have critical sections that span multiple nodes; nearly all messages are Forwards. HASH-M is similar to its -S counterpart, except the critical section almost always spans multiple nodes; in HASH-M threads will likely perform many non-atomic operations after locking shadow entries but since the critical section has started the transaction must always created Remote Nested Transactions. The remaining benchmarks generate Remote Nested Transaction Start- and Result- messages in nearly equal number, due to low abortion rates and only using the network during the critical section.

Compute intensive workloads have the potential for the largest speedup on GPU clusters due to the ~70x higher theoretical computational throughput. Figure 8 shows that KMeans, HIST, and both HASH benchmarks have a much higher compute intensity than the remaining benchmarks.

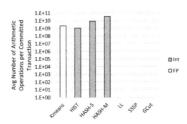

Fig. 8. Average number of arithmetic operations per committed transaction.

The KMeans benchmark exhibits nearly ideal behavior for the GPU and thus show the best performance improvements over the CPU in our experiments, as shown in Fig. 8. In these benchmarks, each transaction performs a long series of distance calculations before acquiring a single lock for a brief critical section. The computation intensity, and thus the magnitude of the GPU advantage, of the benchmark is proportional to the number of dimensions for each data point. Remote communication is minimal, as each node effectively runs in isolation before using a binary-tree style reduction and time between these synchronizations is long. KMeans achieves more than the expected ~70x speedup, and closer to the ideal ∼140x higher FLOPS reported in the K20x specifications due to the very infrequent usage of remote communication and shared memory and comparatively higher FLOP density.

The Histogram, HASH-S, and HASH-M benchmarks show large improvements over the CPU in our experiments, though not as large as KMeans, as shown in Figure 8. These benchmarks perform a long series of shift and XOR operations on integers to produce random keys to be inserted into a shared data structure using an Xorshift random number generating algorithm. Performance is again compute-bound, this time dominated by shift and XOR operations, and thus the GPU has a large advantage. The large volume of integer operations is again sufficient to hide the time spent searching for the linked-list insertion points in both HASH benchmarks and the remote memory access resulting from each transaction. Similarly, the increased contention of the HASH-M benchmark has little impact on performance due to the compute intensity of the random key calculations. Histogram outperforms HASH-S and HASH-M because it requires no memory operations outside of the critical section; HASH-S and HASH-M require long searches through linked lists, though HASH-M benefits from requiring 4x as many integer operations as HASH-S.

We profile the number of non-atomic virtual memory operations per committed transaction and show the results in Fig. 9. Memory intensive applications can benefit from the ∼4.2x higher bandwidth of GPU global memory and the increased parallelism of cluster computing. We observe the LL benchmark has the largest volume of memory accesses and recall from Fig. 6 that execution time is overwhelmingly spent performing memory accesses.

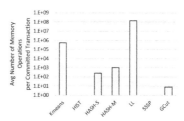

Fig. 9. Average number of local memory accesses per transaction.

Figure 9 shows benchmarks that still benefit from the GPU's higher global memory bandwidth, despite the remote communication overheads. CUDA-DTM shows a 4.2x speedup over the CPU DTM baseline, though performance is limited by irregular memory access patterns, the overheads of transaction record keeping, and warp divergence. Execution time is dominated by long searches through memory, which hides the large average number of messages sent per transaction. The expected speedup for memory-intensive applications is calculated using the CPUs reported 59.7 GB/s max memory bandwidth and the GPUs reported 250 GB/s global memory bandwidth, as the much faster GPU shared memory cannot be used for atomic operations nor is it sufficiently large to store the virtual memory slice.

We measure the contention of each benchmark using the average number of shadow entries modified per transaction and the average time required to gain data ownership. KMeans and HIST require a single lock, as their critical sections make changes to one shared object.

Benchmarks that require changes to dynamic data structures require two locks per insertion: one for allocating a new object and one for updating the pointer on an existing object; as such, HASH-S and LL require exactly two locks for each transaction and HASH-M, which inserts four objects simultaneously, requires exactly eight. Contention in these benchmarks is low because changes are diluted in a very large number of shared objects.

GCut requires exactly two locks to merge two lists together by updating a pointer, though contention increases during execution as vertices are merged and the number of shared objects decreases; as result, the amount of time required to acquire each lock increases as shown in Fig. 10. SSSP is the only benchmarks in this study which require a variable number of locks, though the average in each is low. The average and maximum transaction length, 32 in each case, is determined by the topology of the graph. The minimum, only one in each benchmark, is used when the propagation rules do not require visiting any neighbors.

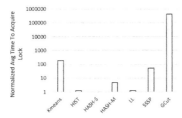

Fig. 10. Normalized wait time per lock.

Figure 10 shows the average amount of time required to successfully complete a CAS operation on a single shadow entry. Times are normalized by that of the HASH-S benchmark, in which contention is the lowest due to the large number of shared objects and short amount of time spent in the critical section. GCut has the longest wait time by far, due to the decreasing shared data size and thus the increasing contention. Despite KMeans high performance, the time spent acquiring locks is second highest due to very small shared memory size and the large number of threads; KMeans performance is still dominated by FLOPs and the impact of the high contention is hidden. However, SSSP and GCut are unable to hide lock-acquisition latency using global memory accesses or arithmetic operations, and their performance suffers as shown in Fig. 10, in which they achieve only a fraction of the theoretical $\sim$4.2x speedup from higher bandwidth.

SSSP and Min-Cut are both graph based benchmarks where a subset of the graph must be locked and modified by each transaction; performance is limited by longer transactions (2 to 32 shadow entries each) resulting in high contention (35x higher than the average of all benchmarks), which limits the advantages of the GPUs high parallelism.

5   Conclusion

We propose CUDA-DTM, the first implementation of a coherent distributed shared memory system for GPU clusters using Distributed Transactional Memory. This paper demonstrates that a GPU cluster can outperform a CPU cluster in non-network intensive workloads despite irregular memory accesses and the overheads of accessing virtual memory. We also demonstrate that the strengths of the GPU, namely the high arithmetic operation throughput and higher memory bandwidth, offer large performance advantages over the CPU despite the large number of moving pieces required to support irregular distributed memory access. Our design allows programmers to use coherent remote memory operations without worrying about deadlocks from thread-divergence or lock competition.

References

1. Burtscher, M., Nasre, R., Pingali, K.: A quantitative study of irregular programs on GPUS. In: 2012 IEEE International Symposium on Workload Characterization (IISWC), pp. 141–151. IEEE (2012)
2. Cederman, D., Tsigas, P., Chaudhry, M.T.: Towards a software transactional memory for graphics processors. In: EGPGV, pp. 121–129 (2010)
3. Chen, S., Peng, L.: Efficient GPU hardware transactional memory through early conflict resolution. In: 2016 IEEE International Symposium on High Performance Computer Architecture (HPCA), pp. 274–284. IEEE (2016)
4. Chen, S., Peng, L., Irving, S.: Accelerating GPU hardware transactional memory with snapshot isolation. In: 2017 ACM/IEEE 44th Annual International Symposium on Computer Architecture (ISCA), pp. 282–294. IEEE (2017)
5. Chen, S., Zhang, F., Liu, L., Peng, L.: Efficient GPU NVRAM persistent with helper warps. In: ACM/IEEE International Conference on Design Automation (DAC). ACM/IEEE (2019)
6. Fung, W.W., Singh, I., Brownsword, A., Aamodt, T.M.: Hardware transactional memory for GPU architectures. In: Proceedings of the 44th Annual IEEE/ACM International Symposium on Microarchitecture, pp. 296–307. ACM (2011)
7. Gramoli, V.: More than you ever wanted to know about synchronization: synchrobench, measuring the impact of the synchronization on concurrent algorithms. In: ACM SIGPLAN Notices, vol. 50, pp. 1–10. ACM (2015)
8. Herlihy, M., Moss, J.E.B.: Transactional memory: architectural support for lock-free data structures, vol. 21. ACM (1993)
9. Herlihy, M., Sun, Y.: Distributed transactional memory for metric-space networks. Distrib. Comput. **20**(3), 195–208 (2007)

10. Holey, A., Zhai, A.: Lightweight software transactions on GPUs. In: 2014 43rd International Conference on Parallel Processing (ICPP), pp. 461–470. IEEE (2014)
11. Minh, C.C., Chung, J., Kozyrakis, C., Olukotun, K.: Stamp: stanford transactional applications for multi-processing. In: 2008 IEEE International Symposium on Workload Characterization, pp. 35–46. IEEE (2008)
12. Mishra, S., Turcu, A., Palmieri, R., Ravindran, B.: HyflowCPP: a distributed transactional memory framework for c++. In: 2013 12th IEEE International Symposium on Network Computing and Applications (NCA), pp. 219–226. IEEE (2013)
13. Moss, J.E.B.: Nested transactions: an approach to reliable distributed computing. Technical report, Massachusetts Institute of Tech Cambridge Lab for Computer Science (1981)
14. Sharma, G., Busch, C.: Distributed transactional memory for general networks. Distrib. Comput. **27**(5), 329–362 (2014)
15. Shen, Q., Sharp, C., Blewitt, W., Ushaw, G., Morgan, G.: PR-STM: priority rule based software transactions for the GPU. In: Träff, J.L., Hunold, S., Versaci, F. (eds.) Euro-Par 2015. LNCS, vol. 9233, pp. 361–372. Springer, Heidelberg (2015). https://doi.org/10.1007/978-3-662-48096-0_28
16. Villegas, A., Navarro, A., Asenjo, R., Plata, O.: Toward a software transactional memory for heterogeneous CPU-GPU processors. J. Supercomput. 1–16 (2017). https://link.springer.com/article/10.1007/s11227-018-2347-0#citeas
17. Xu, Y., Wang, R., Goswami, N., Li, T., Gao, L., Qian, D.: Software transactional memory for GPU architectures. In: Proceedings of Annual IEEE/ACM International Symposium on Code Generation and Optimization, p. 1. ACM (2014)

Towards Synthesis of Distributed Algorithms with SMT Solvers

Carole Delporte-Gallet, Hugues Fauconnier, Yan Jurski,
François Laroussinie, and Arnaud Sangnier[(⊠)]

IRIF, Univ Paris Diderot, CNRS, Paris, France

sangnier@irif.fr

Abstract. We consider the problem of synthesizing distributed algorithms working on a specific execution context. We show it is possible to use the linear time temporal logic in order to both specify the correctness of algorithms and their execution contexts. We then provide a method allowing to reduce the synthesis problem of finite state algorithms to some model-checking problems. We finally apply our technique to automatically generate algorithms for consensus and epsilon-agreement in the case of two processes using the SMT solver Z3.

1 Introduction

On the Difficulty to Design Correct Distributed Algorithms. When designing distributed algorithms, researchers have to deal with two main problems. First, it is not always possible to find an algorithm which solves a specific task. For instance, it is known that there is no algorithm for distributed consensus in the full general case where processes are subject to failure and communication is asynchronous [6]. Second, they have to prove that their algorithms are correct, which can sometimes be very tedious due to the number of possible executions to consider. Moreover distributed algorithms are often designed by assuming a certain number of hypothesis which are sometimes difficult to properly formalize.

Even though most distributed algorithms for problems like leader election, consensus, set agreement, or renaming, are not very long, their behavior is difficult to understand due to the numerous possible interleavings and their correctness proofs are extremely intricate. Furthermore these proofs strongly depend on the specific assumptions made on the *execution context* which specifies the way the different processes are scheduled and when it is required for a process to terminate. In the case of distributed algorithms with shared registers, interesting execution contexts are for instance the *wait-free* model which requires that each process terminates after a finite number of its own steps, no matter what the other processes are doing [8] or the *obstruction-free* model where every process that eventually executes in isolation has to terminate [9]. It is not an easy task to describe formally such execution context and the difference between contexts

---

Supported by ANR FREDDA (ANR-17-CE40-0013).

M. F. Atig and A. A. Schwarzmann (Eds.): NETYS 2019, LNCS 11704, pp. 200–216, 2019.
https://doi.org/10.1007/978-3-030-31277-0_13

can be crucial when searching for a corresponding distributed algorithm. As a matter of fact, there is no wait-free distributed algorithm to solve consensus [10], even with only two processes, but there exist algorithms in the obstruction-free case.

Proving Correctness vs Synthesis. When one has designed a distributed algorithm for a specific execution context, it remains to prove that it behaves correctly. The most common way consists in providing a 'manual' proof hoping that it covers all the possible cases. The drawback of this method is that manual proofs are subject to bugs and they are sometimes long and difficult to check. It is often the case that the algorithms and their specification are described at a high-level point of view which may introduce some ambiguities in the expected behaviors. Another approach consists in using automatic or partly automatic techniques based on formal methods. For instance, the tool TLA+ [3] provides a language to write proofs of correctness which can be checked automatically thanks to a proof system. This approach is much safer, however finding the correct proof arguments so that the proof system terminates might be hard. For finite state distributed algorithms, another way is to rely on model-checking [2,14]. Here, a model for the algorithm together with a formula specifying its correctness, expressed for example in temporal logics like LTL or CTL [5], are given, and checking whether the model satisfies the specification is then automatic. This is the approach of the tool SPIN [11] which has allowed to verify many algorithms.

These methods are useful when they succeed in showing that a distributed algorithm is correct, but when it appears that the algorithm does not respect its specification, then a new algorithm has to be conceived and the tedious work begins again. One way to solve this issue is to design distributed algorithms which are correct by construction. In other words, one provides a specification and then an automatic tool synthesizes an algorithm for this specification. Synthesis has been successfully applied to various kinds of systems, in particular to design reactive systems which have to take decisions according to their environment: in such cases, the synthesis problem consists in finding a winning strategy in a two player games (see for instance [7]). In a context of distributed algorithms, some recent works have developed some synthesis techniques in order to obtain automatically some thresholds bounds for fault-tolerant distributed algorithms [12]. The advantage of such methods is that the synthesis algorithm can be used to produce many distributed algorithms and there is no need to prove that they are correct, the correctness being ensured (automatically) by construction.

Our Contributions. In this work, we first define a simple model to describe distributed algorithms for a finite number of processes communicating thanks to shared registers. We then show that the correctness of these algorithms can be specified by a formula of the linear time temporal logic LTL [13,15] and more interestingly we show that classical execution contexts can also be specified in LTL. We then provide a way to synthesize automatically distributed algorithms from a specification. Following SAT-based model-checking approach [1], we have furthermore implemented our method in a prototype which relies on the SMT-solver Z3 [4] and for some specific cases synthesizes non-trivial algorithms. Of course the complexity is high and we can at present only generate algorithms for two processes but they are interesting by themselves and meet their specification w.r.t. several execution contexts.

2 Distributed Algorithms and Specification Language

2.1 Distributed Algorithms with Shared Memory

We begin by defining a model to represent distributed algorithms using shared memory. In our model, each process is equipped with an atomic register that it is the only one to write but that can be read by all the others processes (*single writer-multiple readers registers*).

The processes manipulate a data set $\mathcal{D}$ including a set of input values $\mathcal{D}_\mathcal{I} \subseteq \mathcal{D}$, a set of output values $\mathcal{D}_\mathcal{O} \subseteq \mathcal{D}$ and a special value $\perp \in \mathcal{D} \setminus (\mathcal{D}_\mathcal{I} \cup \mathcal{D}_\mathcal{O})$ used to characterize a register that has not yet been written. The actions performed by the processes are of three types, they can either write a data in their register, read the register of another process or decide a value. For a finite number of processes n, we denote by $Act(\mathcal{D}, n) = \{\mathbf{wr}(d), \mathbf{re}(k), \mathbf{dec}(o) \mid d \in \mathcal{D} \setminus \{\perp\}, k \in [1, n], o \in \mathcal{D}_\mathcal{O}\}$ where $\mathbf{wr}(d)$ stands for "write the value d to the register", $\mathbf{re}(k)$ for "read the register of process k", and $\mathbf{dec}(o)$ for "output (or decide) the value o".

The action performed by a process at a specific instant depends on the values it has read in the registers of the other processes, we hence suppose that each process stores a local copy of the shared registers that it modifies when it performs a read or a write. Furthermore, in some cases, a process might perform different actions with the same local copy of the registers, because for instance it has stored some information on what has happened previously. This is the reason why we equip each process with a local memory as well. A process looking at its copy of the registers and at its memory value decides to perform an unique action on its local view and to update its memory. According to this, we define the code executed by a process in a distributed algorithm as follows.

Definition 1 (Process algorithm). *A* process algorithm *P for an environment of n processes over the data set $\mathcal{D}$ is a tuple (M, δ) where:*

1. *M is a finite set corresponding to the local memory values of the process;*
2. *$\delta : \mathcal{D}_\mathcal{I} \cup (\mathcal{D}^n \times M) \mapsto Act(\mathcal{D}, n) \times M$ is the action function which determines the next action to be performed and the update of the local memory, such that if $\delta(s) = (\mathbf{dec}(o), m')$ then $s = (\mathbf{V}, m) \in \mathcal{D}^n \times M$ and $m = m'$.*

A pair $(a, m) \in Act(\mathcal{D}, n) \times M$ is called a *move*. The last condition ensures that a process first move cannot be to decide a value (this is only to ease some definitions) and when a process has decided then it cannot do anything else and its decision remains the same. Note that the first move to be performed by the process from an input value i in $\mathcal{D}_\mathcal{I}$ is given by $\delta(i)$.

A process state s for a process algorithm P is either an initial value in $\mathcal{D}_\mathcal{I}$ or a pair $(\mathbf{V}, m) \in \mathcal{D}^n \times M$ where the first component corresponds to the local view of the processes and m is the memory value. Let $\mathcal{S}_P \subseteq \mathcal{D}_\mathcal{I} \cup (\mathcal{D}^n \times M)$ the states associated to P. An initial state belongs to $\mathcal{D}_\mathcal{I}$. We now define the behavior of a process when it has access to a shared memory $\mathbf{R} \in \mathcal{D}^n$ and its identifier in the system is $i \in [1, n]$. For this we define a transition relation $\xrightarrow{i} \subseteq (\mathcal{S}_P \times \mathcal{D}^n) \times (Act(\mathcal{D}, n) \times M) \times (\mathcal{S}_P \times \mathcal{D}^n)$ such that $(s, \mathbf{R}) \xrightarrow{i, (a, m')} (s', \mathbf{R}')$ iff for all $j \in [1, n]$ if $i \neq j$ then $\mathbf{R}[j] = \mathbf{R}'[j]$, and we are in one of the the following cases:

1. if $a = \mathbf{wr}(d)$ then $\mathbf{R}'[i] = d$ and $s' = (\mathbf{V}', m')$ such that $\mathbf{V}'[i] = d$ and, for all $j \in [1, n] \setminus \{i\}$, if $s = (\mathbf{V}, m)$ (i.e. $s \notin \mathcal{D}_\mathcal{I}$) then $\mathbf{V}'[j] = \mathbf{V}[j]$ and otherwise $\mathbf{V}'[j] = \bot$ i.e. the write action updates the corresponding shared register as well as the local view.
2. if $a = \mathbf{re}(k)$ then $\mathbf{R}' = \mathbf{R}$, and $s' = (\mathbf{V}', m')$ (i.e. $s \notin \mathcal{D}_\mathcal{I}$) with $\mathbf{V}'[k] = \mathbf{R}[k]$ and, for all $j \in [1, n] \setminus \{k\}$, if $s = (\mathbf{V}, m)$ then $\mathbf{V}'[j] = \mathbf{V}[j]$ and otherwise $\mathbf{V}'[j] = \bot$, i.e. the read action copies the value of the shared register of process k in the local view.
3. if $a = \mathbf{dec}(o)$ then $\mathbf{R}' = \mathbf{R}$ and $s' = s$, i.e. the decide action does not change the local state of any process, neither the shared registers.

The transition relation $\xrightarrow{i}_P \subseteq (\mathcal{S}_P \times \mathcal{D}^n) \times (\mathcal{S}_P \times \mathcal{D}^n)$ associated to the process algorithm P is defined by: $(s, \mathbf{R}) \xrightarrow{i}_P (s', \mathbf{R}')$ iff $(s, \mathbf{R}) \xrightarrow{i, \delta(s)} (s', \mathbf{R}')$. Different process algorithms can then be combined to form a distributed algorithm.

Definition 2 (Distributed algorithm). *A n processes distributed algorithm A over the data set $\mathcal{D}$ is given by $P_1 \otimes P_2 \otimes \ldots \otimes P_n$ where P_i is a process algorithm for an environment of n processes over the data set $\mathcal{D}$ for all $i \in [1, n]$.*

We now define the behavior of such a n processes distributed algorithm $P_1 \otimes P_2 \otimes \ldots \otimes P_n$. We call a *configuration* of A a pair of vectors $C = (\mathbf{S}, \mathbf{R})$ where $\mathbf{S}$ is a n dimensional vector such that $\mathbf{S}[i] \in \mathcal{S}_{P_i}$ represents the state for process i and $\mathbf{R} \in \mathcal{D}^n$ represents the values of the shared registers. We use $\mathcal{C}_A$ to represent the set of configurations of A. The initial configuration for the vector of input values $\mathbf{In} \in \mathcal{D}_\mathcal{I}^n$ is then simply $(\mathbf{In}, \mathbf{R})$ with $\mathbf{R}[i] = \bot$ for all $i \in [1, n]$. Given a process identifier $i \in [1, n]$ and a pair (a, m) where $a \in Act(\mathcal{D}, n)$ and m is a memory value for process i, we define the transition relations $\xrightarrow{i, (a, m)}$ over configurations as $(\mathbf{S}, \mathbf{R}) \xrightarrow{i, (a, m)} (\mathbf{S}', \mathbf{R}')$ iff we have $(\mathbf{S}[i], \mathbf{R}) \xrightarrow{i, (a, m)} (\mathbf{S}'[i], \mathbf{R}')$ and for every $j \neq i$: $\mathbf{S}'[j] = \mathbf{S}[j]$. The execution step $\xRightarrow{i}_A$ of process i for the distributed algorithm A is defined by $(\mathbf{S}, \mathbf{R}) \xRightarrow{i}_A (\mathbf{S}', \mathbf{R}')$ iff $(\mathbf{S}[i], \mathbf{R}) \xrightarrow{i}_{P_i} (\mathbf{S}'[i], \mathbf{R}')$, note that in that case we have $(\mathbf{S}, \mathbf{R}) \xrightarrow{i, \delta_i(S[i])} (\mathbf{S}', \mathbf{R}')$ if δ_i is the action function of P_i.

2.2 Example

Algorithm 1 provides a classical representation of a tentative distributed algorithm to solve consensus with two processes. Each process starts with an input value V and the consensus goal is that both processes eventually decide the same value which must be one of the initial values. It is well known that there is no wait-free algorithm to solve consensus [6,8] hence this algorithm will not work for any set of executions, in particular one could check that if the two processes start with a different input value and if they are executed in a round-robin manner (i.e. process 1 does one step and then process 2 does one and so on) then none of the process will ever decide and they will exchange their value for ever. We shall see however later that under some restrictions on the set of considered executions this algorithm solves consensus.

Algorithm 1. Consensus algorithm for process i with i ∈ {1, 2}

Require: V: the input value of process i
1: **while** true **do**
2:     r[i]:=V
3:     tmp:=r[3-i]
4:     **if** tmp=V or tmp = ⊥ **then**
5:         Decide(V)
6:         Exit()
7:     **else**
8:         V:=tmp
9:     **end if**
10: **end while**

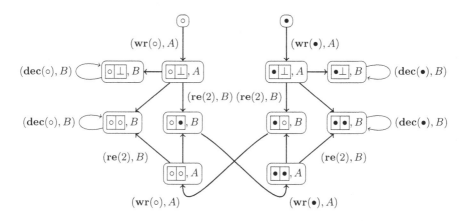

Fig. 1. View of a process algorithm P for a process with identifier 1

Figure 1 gives a visual description of the process algorithm corresponding to the Algorithm 1 supposing that the corresponding process has identifier 1.

In this graph, each nodes represents a process state, the memory is the set $\{A, B\}$ and the data belongs to $\{\circ, \bullet\}$. From each node, we have some edges labeled with the action to perform according to the process state. The first action consists in writing the input data in the register, which leads to a state where the local view contains the data in the first register and $\bot$ in the local copy of the second register and the local memory cell is A. Afterwards, the process reads the second register and on Fig. 1, we represent all the possible data that could be in this register (i.e either $\circ$, $\bullet$ or $\bot$) in the local view and the memory cell evolves to B. Hence, the elements A and B of the memory set are used to represent the local state of the algorithm: when the local memory is A it means that the last action performed by the process was the write action corresponding to the Line 2 of Algorithm 1 and when its value is B, it means that the Algorithm has performed the read action corresponding to the Line 3. We only need these two values for the memory, because in our setting after having read the memory, the read value is stored in the local copy of the register and according to it, the algorithm either decides or goes back to Line 2. Note that when we leave one of the state at the bottom of the figure by reading the second register, we take into account that $\bot$ cannot be present in this register, since at this stage this register has necessarily been written.

3   Using *LTL* to Reason on Distributed Algorithms

3.1   Kripke Structures and *LTL*

We specify distributed algorithms with the Linear time Temporal Logic (*LTL*). We recall here some basic definitions concerning this logic and how its formulae are evaluated over Kripke structures labeled with atomic propositions from a set AP.

Definition 3 (Kripke structure). *A Kripke structure $\mathcal{K}$ is a 4-tuple (Q, E, ℓ, q_{init}) where Q is a countable set of states, $q_{init} \in Q$ is the initial state, $E \subseteq Q^2$ is a total[1] relation and $\ell \colon Q \to 2^{AP}$ is a labelling function.*

A path (or an execution) in $\mathcal{K}$ from a state q is an infinite sequence $q_0 q_1 q_2 \cdots$ such that $q_0 = q$ and $(q_i, q_{i+1}) \in E$ for any i. We use $\mathsf{Path}_{\mathcal{K}}(q)$ to denote the set of paths from q. Given a path ρ and $i \in \mathbb{N}$, we write ρ^i for the path $q_i q_{i+1} q_{i+2} \cdots$ (the i-th suffix of ρ) and $\rho(i)$ for the i-th state q_i.

In order to specify properties over the execution of a Kripke structure, we use the Linear time Temporal Logic (*LTL*) whose syntax is given by the following grammar $\phi, \psi ::= p \mid \neg\phi \mid \phi \vee \psi \mid \mathbf{X}\phi \mid \phi\mathbf{U}\psi$ where p ranges over AP. We use standard abbreviations: $\top, \bot, \vee, \Rightarrow \ldots$ as well as the classical temporal modalities $\mathbf{F}\phi \overset{\text{def}}{=} \top\mathbf{U}\phi$ and $\mathbf{G}\phi \overset{\text{def}}{=} \neg\mathbf{F}\neg\phi$. Given a path ρ of a Kripke structure $\mathcal{K} = (Q, E, \ell, q_{init})$, the satisfaction relation $\models$ for *LTL* is defined inductively by:

---

[1] *I.e., for all $q \in Q$, there exists $q' \in Q$ s.t. $(q, q') \in E$.*

$$\rho \models p \text{ iff } p \in \ell(\rho(0))$$
$$\rho \models \neg \phi \text{ iff } \rho \not\models \phi$$
$$\rho \models \phi \vee \psi \text{ iff } \rho \models \phi \text{ or } \rho \models \psi$$
$$\rho \models \mathbf{X}\phi \text{ iff } \rho^1 \models \phi$$
$$\rho \models \phi \mathbf{U}\psi \text{ iff } \exists i \geq 0.\ \rho^i \models \psi \text{ and } \forall 0 \leq j < i.\ \rho^j \models \phi$$

We then write $\mathcal{K} \models \phi$ iff $\rho \models \phi$ for any $\rho \in \mathsf{Path}_{\mathcal{K}}(q_{\text{init}})$. Since we quantify over all the paths, we speak of universal model-checking.

3.2   Specifying Distributed Algorithms

We will now see how to use LTL formulae for specifying the correctness of distributed algorithms under specific execution contexts. We consider distributed algorithms for n processes working over a data set $\mathcal{D}$. The set of atomic propositions that we will use in this context will then be : $\mathsf{AP}_{\mathcal{D}}^n = \{\mathsf{active}_i, \mathsf{D}_i\}_{1 \leq i \leq n} \cup \{\mathsf{In}_i^d\}_{1 \leq i \leq n, d \in \mathcal{D}_\mathcal{I}} \cup \{\mathsf{Out}_i^d\}_{1 \leq i \leq n, d \in \mathcal{D}_\mathcal{O}}$ where active_i represents the fact that process i has been the last one to execute an action, D_i that process i has decided, In_i^d that the initial value of process i is d and Out_i^d that the output value of process i is d. Note that we always have: $\mathsf{D}_i \Leftrightarrow \bigvee_d \mathsf{Out}_i^d$.

We shall now see how we associate a Kripke structure labeled with these propositions with a distributed algorithm. Let $A = P_1 \otimes P_2 \otimes \ldots \otimes P_n$ be a n process distributed algorithm over the data set $\mathcal{D}$. The states of the Kripke structures contain configurations of A together with information on which was the last process to perform an action as well as the output value for each process (set to $\perp$ if the process did not output any value yet). Formally, we define $\mathcal{K}_A = (Q_A, E_A, \ell_A, q_{\text{init}}^A)$ with:

- $Q_A = \{q_{\text{init}}^A\} \cup (\mathcal{C}_A \times [0, n] \times (\mathcal{D}_\mathcal{O} \cup \{\perp\})^n)$, the first component is a configuration of A, the second is the identifier of the last process which has performed an action (it is set to 0 at the beginning), the third contains the output value;
- E_A is such that:
  - $(q_{\text{init}}^A, ((\mathbf{In}, \perp), 0, \perp)) \in E$ for all initial configurations $(\mathbf{In}, \perp)$ of A (here $\perp$ stands for the unique vector in $\{\perp\}^n$), i.e. the initial configurations are the one accessible from the initial state q_{init} after one step,
  - $(((\mathbf{S}, \mathbf{R}), i, \mathbf{O}), ((\mathbf{S}', \mathbf{R}'), j, \mathbf{O}')) \in E_A$ iff $(\mathbf{S}, \mathbf{R}) \xrightarrow{j}_A (\mathbf{S}', \mathbf{R}')$ and if the action performed by process j (from $\mathbf{S}[j]$ to $\mathbf{S}'[j]$) is $\mathbf{dec}(o)$ then $\mathbf{O}'[j] = o$ and $\mathbf{O}'[k] = \mathbf{O}[k]$ for all $k \in [1, n] \setminus \{j\}$, otherwise $\mathbf{O} = \mathbf{O}'$.
- the labelling function ℓ_A is such that:
  - $\ell_A(q_{\text{init}}^A) = \emptyset$,
  - $\mathsf{active}_i \in \ell_A((\mathbf{S}, \mathbf{R}), i, \mathbf{O})$ and $\mathsf{active}_j \notin \ell((\mathbf{S}, \mathbf{R}), i, \mathbf{O})$ if $j \neq i$, i.e the last process which has performed an action is i,
  - $\mathsf{In}_j^d \in \ell_A((\mathbf{S}, \mathbf{R}), i, \mathbf{O})$ iff $\mathbf{S}[j] \in \mathcal{D}_\mathcal{I}$ and $d = \mathbf{S}[j]$, i.e. process j is still in its initial configuration with its initial value d,
  - $\mathsf{D}_j \in \ell_A((\mathbf{S}, \mathbf{R}), i, \mathbf{O})$ iff $\mathbf{O}[j] \neq \perp$, i.e. process j has output its final value;
  - Out_j^d iff $\mathbf{O}[j] = d$, i.e. the value output by process j is d.

For a LTL formula ϕ over $\mathsf{AP}_\mathcal{D}^n$, we say that the distributed algorithm A satisfies ϕ, denoted by $A \models \phi$, iff $\mathcal{K}_A \models \phi$.

The LTL formulae over $\{\mathsf{In}_i^d\}_{1 \leq i \leq n, d \in \mathcal{D}_\mathcal{I}} \cup \{\mathsf{Out}_i^d\}_{1 \leq i \leq n, d \in \mathcal{D}_\mathcal{O}}$ will be typically used to state some correctness properties about the link between input and output values. The strength of our specification language is that it allows to specify execution contexts thanks to the atomic propositions in $\{\mathsf{active}_i, \mathsf{D}_i\}_{1 \leq i \leq n}$.

Even if this is not the main goal of this research work, we know that given a n processes distributed algorithm A over a finite data set $\mathcal{D}$ and a LTL formula Φ over $\mathsf{AP}_\mathcal{D}^n$, one can automatically verify whether $A \models \Phi$ and this can be done in polynomial space. Indeed model-checking an LTL formula Φ over a Kripke structure can be achieved in polynomial space [15]: the classical way consists in using a Büchi automaton corresponding to the negation of the formula Φ (which can be of exponential size in the size of the formula) and then checking for intersection emptiness *on the fly* (the automaton is not built but traveled). The same technique can be applied here to verify $A \models \Phi$ without building explicitly $\mathcal{K}_A$. Therefore we have the following result which is a direct consequence of [15]:

Proposition 1. *Given a n processes distributed algorithm A over a finite data set $\mathcal{D}$ and a LTL formula Φ over $\mathsf{AP}_\mathcal{D}^n$, verifying whether $A \models \Phi$ is in* PSPACE.

3.3   Examples

Specification for Consensus Algorithms. We recall that the consensus problem for n processes can be stated as follows: each process is equipped with an initial value and then all the processes that decide must decide the same value (*agreement*) and this value must be one of the initial one (*validity*). We do not introduce for the moment any constraints on which process has to propose an output, this will come later. We assume that the consensus algorithms work over a data set $\mathcal{D}$ with $\mathcal{D}_\mathcal{I} = \mathcal{D}_\mathcal{O}$, i.e. the set of input values and of output values are equal. The agreement can be specified by the following formula:

$$\Phi_{\text{agree}}^c \overset{\text{def}}{=} \mathbf{G} \bigwedge_{1 \leq i \neq j \leq n} \left((\mathsf{D}_i \wedge \mathsf{D}_j) \Rightarrow (\bigwedge_{d \in \mathcal{D}_\mathcal{O}} \mathsf{Out}_i^d \Leftrightarrow \mathsf{Out}_j^d) \right)$$

We state here that if two processes have decided a value, then this value is the same. For what concerns the validity, it can be expressed by:

$$\Phi_{\text{valid}}^c \overset{\text{def}}{=} \mathbf{X} \bigwedge_{1 \leq i \leq n} \bigwedge_{d \in \mathcal{D}_\mathcal{I}} \left(\left(\mathbf{F}\, \mathsf{Out}_i^d \right) \Rightarrow \left(\bigvee_{1 \leq j \leq n} \mathsf{In}_j^d \right) \right)$$

In this case, the formula simply states that if eventually a value is output, then this value was the initial value of one the processes. Note that this formula begins with the temporal operator $\mathbf{X}$ because in the considered Kripke structure the initial configurations are reachable after one step from q_{init}.

We are now ready to provide specifications for the execution context, i.e. the formulae which tell when processes have to decide. First we consider a *wait-free* execution context, each process produces an output value after a finite number of its own steps, independently of the steps of the other processes [8]. This can be described by the LTL formula:

$$\Phi_{\mathrm{wf}} \stackrel{\text{def}}{=} \bigwedge_{1 \leq i \leq n} \left((\mathbf{G}\,\mathbf{F}\,\mathsf{active}_i) \Rightarrow (\mathbf{F}\,\mathsf{D}_i) \right)$$

This formula states that for each process, if it is regularly (infinitely often) active, then at some point (i.e. after a finite number of steps) it must decide. Consequently if a distributed algorithm A is such that $A \models \Phi^c_{\mathrm{agree}} \wedge \Phi^c_{\mathrm{valid}} \wedge \Phi_{\mathrm{wf}}$, then A is a wait-free distributed algorithm for consensus. However we know that even for two processes such an algorithm does not exist [6,8]. But, when considering other execution contexts, it possible to have an algorithm for consensus.

An another interesting execution context is the *obstruction-free* context. Here, every process that eventually executes in isolation has to produce an output value [9]. This can be ensured by the following LTL formula which exactly matches the informal definition.

$$\Phi_{\mathrm{of}} \stackrel{\text{def}}{=} \bigwedge_{1 \leq i \leq n} \left((\mathbf{F}\,\mathbf{G}\,\mathsf{active}_i) \Rightarrow (\mathbf{F}\,\mathsf{D}_i) \right)$$

The distributed algorithm $A^c_{of} = P_1 \otimes P_2$, where P_1 is the process algorithm described by Fig. 1 and P_2 is the symmetric of P_1 obtained by replacing the action $\mathbf{re}(2)$ actions by $\mathbf{re}(1)$, is such that $A^c_{of} \models \Phi^c_{\mathrm{agree}} \wedge \Phi^c_{\mathrm{valid}} \wedge \Phi_{\mathrm{of}}$.

Finally, another interesting context is the one corresponding to a round-robin scheduling policy. This context is given by the LTL formula, which basically states that if the n processes behave in a round-robin fashion, i.e. there are active one after another, then they all have to decide.

$$\Phi_{\mathrm{rr}} \stackrel{\text{def}}{=} \left[\mathbf{G}\Big(\bigwedge_{1 \leq i \leq n} (\mathsf{active}_i \Rightarrow \mathbf{X}\,\mathsf{active}_{(1+i\%n)}) \Big) \right] \Rightarrow \left[\bigwedge_{1 \leq i \leq n} \big(\mathbf{F}\,\mathsf{D}_i \big) \right]$$

For the previously mentioned algorithm, we have $A^c_{of} \not\models \Phi_{\mathrm{rr}}$, in fact as said in Sect. 2.2, if the processes are scheduled in a round-robin fashion and if their input values are different, then they will exchange their value forever and never decide. Note that we could easily define some Φ^k_{rr} formula to specify a round-robin policy where every process performs exactly k successive moves (instead of 1).

Specification for ε-Agreement Algorithms. We assume that the data set $\mathcal{D}$ is such that $\mathcal{D}_\mathcal{I}$ and $\mathcal{D}_\mathcal{O}$ are finite subset of $\mathbb{Q}$. We now present a variant of the ε-agreement. As for consensus, each process receives an initial value and the output values must respect the following criteria: (1) they should be between the smallest input value and the greatest one (*validity*) and (2) the outputs values all stand in an interval whose width is less or equal to ε (*agreemeent*). For instance, if we take $\mathcal{D}_\mathcal{I} = \{0,1\}$ and $\mathcal{D}_\mathcal{O} = \{0,\frac{1}{2},1\}$, then if the two processes have input 0 and 1 respectively, the sets of accepted output values for $\frac{1}{2}$-agreement is

$\{\{0\}, \{1\}, \{\frac{1}{2}\}, \{0, \frac{1}{2}\}, \{\frac{1}{2}, 1\}\}$. In this case, we can rewrite the formula for validity and agreement as follows:

$$
\Phi_{\text{valid}}^{\varepsilon} \stackrel{\text{def}}{=} \mathbf{X} \left[\bigvee_{d_m \leq d_M \in \mathcal{D}_{\mathcal{I}}} \left[\left(\bigvee_{1 \leq i \leq n} \text{In}_i^{d_m} \right) \wedge \left(\bigvee_{1 \leq i \leq n} \text{In}_i^{d_M} \right) \wedge \right. \right.
$$
$$
\left. \left. \mathbf{G}\left[\left(\bigwedge_{d < d_m \in \mathcal{D}_{\mathcal{O}}} \bigwedge_{1 \leq i \leq n} \neg \text{Out}_i^d \right) \wedge \left(\bigwedge_{d > d_M \in \mathcal{D}_{\mathcal{O}}} \bigwedge_{1 \leq i \leq n} \neg \text{Out}_i^d \right) \right] \right] \right]
$$

And:

$$
\Phi_{\text{agree}}^{\varepsilon} \stackrel{\text{def}}{=} \mathbf{G} \bigwedge_{1 \leq i \neq j \leq n} \left((\text{D}_i \wedge \text{D}_j) \Rightarrow \left(\bigvee_{d, d' \in \mathcal{D}_{\mathcal{O}} \, s.t. \, |d'-d| \leq \varepsilon} \text{Out}_i^d \wedge \text{Out}_j^{d'} \right) \right)
$$

For what concerns the specification of the execution context, we can take the same formulae Φ_{wf}, Φ_{of} and Φ_{rr} introduced previously for the consensus.

4 Synthesis

4.1 Problem

We wish to provide a methodology to synthesize automatically a distributed algorithm satisfying a specification given by a LTL formula. In this matter, we fix the number of processes n, the considered data set (which contains input and output values) $\mathcal{D}$ and the set of memory values M for each process. A process algorithm P is said to use memory M iff $P = (M, \delta)$. A distributed algorithm $A = P_1 \otimes ... \otimes P_n$ uses memory M if for $i \in [1, n]$, the process P_i uses memory M. The **synthesis problem** can then be stated as follows:

Inputs: A number n of processes, a data set $\mathcal{D}$, a set of memory values M and a LTL formula Φ over $\text{AP}_{\mathcal{D}}^n$
Output: Is there a n processes distributed algorithm A over $\mathcal{D}$ which uses memory M and such that $A \models \Phi$?

We propose a method to solve this decidability problem and in case of positive answer we are able to generate as well the corresponding distributed algorithm.

4.2 A Set of Universal Kripke Structures for the Synthesis Problem

We show here how the synthesis problem boils down to find a specific Kripke structure which satisfies a specific LTL formula. In the sequel, we fix the parameters of our synthesis problem: a number n of processes, a data set $\mathcal{D}$, a set of memory values M and a LTL formula Φ_{spec} over $\text{AP}_{\mathcal{D}}^n$. We build a Kripke structure $\mathcal{K}_{n, \mathcal{D}, M}$ similar to the Kripke structure $\mathcal{K}_A$ associated to a distributed algorithm A but where the transition relation allows all the possible behaviors (all the possible move for every process in any configuration).

First, note that each process algorithm P for an environment of n processes over the data set $\mathcal{D}$ which uses memory M has the same set of process states $\mathcal{S}_P$. We denote $\mathcal{S} = \mathcal{D}_{\mathcal{I}} \cup (\mathcal{D}^n \times M)$ this set. Similarly each n processes distributed algorithm A over $\mathcal{D}$ which uses memory M has the same set of configurations $\mathcal{C}_A$ that we will denote simply $\mathcal{C}$. We recall that these configurations are of the form $(\mathbf{S}, \mathbf{R})$ with $S \in \mathcal{S}^n$ is a vector of n processes states and $\mathbf{R} \in \mathcal{D}^n$.

The Kripke structure $\mathcal{K}_{n,\mathcal{D},M}$ uses the set of atomic propositions $\mathsf{AP}_{\mathcal{D}}^n \cup \mathsf{AP}_{\mathcal{C},\mathcal{O}}$ where $\mathsf{AP}_{\mathcal{C},\mathcal{O}} = \{\mathsf{P}_{C,\mathbf{O}} \mid C \in \mathcal{C}, \mathbf{O} \in (\mathcal{D}_{\mathcal{O}} \cup \{\bot\})^n\}$ contains one atomic proposition for every pair made by a configuration C and vector of output values $\mathbf{O}$. Its states will be the same as $\mathcal{K}_A$ but for every possible actions there will be an outgoing edge. Formally, we have $\mathcal{K}_{n,\mathcal{D},M} = (Q, E, \ell, q_{\text{init}})$ with:

- $Q = \{q_{\text{init}}\} \cup (\mathcal{C} \times [0, n] \times (\mathcal{D}_{\mathcal{O}} \cup \{\bot\})^n)$ (as for $\mathcal{K}_A$)
- E is such that:
  - $\big(q_{\text{init}}, ((\mathbf{In}, \bot), 0, \bot)\big) \in E$ for all initial configurations $(\mathbf{In}, \bot)$ in $\mathcal{D}_{\mathcal{I}}^n \times \{\bot\}^n)$, (as for $\mathcal{K}_A$),
  - $\big(((\mathbf{S}, \mathbf{R}), i, \mathbf{O}), ((\mathbf{S}', \mathbf{R}'), j, \mathbf{O}')\big) \in E$ iff $(\mathbf{S}, \mathbf{R}) \xRightarrow{j,(a,m)} (\mathbf{S}', \mathbf{R}')$ for some $(a, m) \in Act(\mathcal{D}, n) \times M$. And:
    * if $a = \mathbf{dec}(o)$ then $\mathbf{S}[j] = (\mathbf{V}, m)$ for $\mathbf{V} \in \mathcal{D}^n$ and $\mathbf{O}'[j] = o$ and $\mathbf{O}'[k] = \mathbf{O}[k]$ for all $k \in [1, n] \setminus \{j\}$, otherwise $\mathbf{O} = \mathbf{O}'$ (the memory cells does not change once the decision is fixed),
    * if $\mathbf{O}[j] \neq \bot$, then $a = \mathbf{dec}(\mathbf{O}[j])$ (the decision cannot change, no other action can be performed).
- the labelling function ℓ is defined the same way as in $\mathcal{K}_A$ for the atomic propositions in $\mathsf{AP}_{\mathcal{D}}^n$ and $\mathsf{P}_{C,O} \in \ell((\mathbf{S}, \mathbf{R}), i, \mathbf{O})$ iff $C = (\mathbf{S}, \mathbf{R})$ and $O = \mathbf{O}$.

Hence the relation E simulates all the possible moves from any configuration $(\mathbf{S}, \mathbf{R})$ and the Kripke structure $\mathcal{K}_{n,\mathcal{D},M}$ contains all possible executions of any n processes algorithms over $\mathcal{D}$ using memory M.

Defining an algorithm consists in selecting exactly one action for each process in every configuration. Here we do this by adding to the structure extra atomic propositions $\mathsf{P}_{(a,m)}^i$ with $1 \leq i \leq n$ and $(a, m) \in Act(\mathcal{D}, n) \times M$ which specifies for each configuration what should be the next move of process i. We denote by $\mathsf{AP}_{Act,M}^n$ this set of new atomic propositions. An *algorithm labelling* for $\mathcal{K}_{n,\mathcal{D},M}$ is then simply a function $\ell' : Q \mapsto 2^{\mathsf{AP}_{Act,M}^n}$. We denote by $\mathcal{K}_{n,\mathcal{D},M}^{\ell'}$ the Kripke structure obtained by adding to $\mathcal{K}_{n,\mathcal{D},M}$ the extra labelling provided by ℓ'. When defining such an algorithm labelling, we need to be careful that it corresponds effectively to a distributed algorithm: our processes are deterministic (only one action is allowed for P_i in some configuration) and a process has to choose the same action when its local view is identical. Such an algorithm labelling ℓ' is said to be *consistent* iff the following conditions are respected:

1. $\ell'(q_{\text{init}}) = \emptyset$,
2. for all $((\mathbf{S}, \mathbf{R}), i, \mathbf{O}) \in Q$, for all $j \in [1, n]$ there exists a unique $\mathsf{P}_{(a,m)}^j \in \ell'((\mathbf{S}, \mathbf{R}), i, \mathbf{O})$, each process has exactly one move in each configuration,

3. for all $((\mathbf{S},\mathbf{R}), i, \mathbf{O}), ((\mathbf{S}',\mathbf{R}'), j, \mathbf{O}') \in Q$, if $\mathbf{S}[k] = \mathbf{S}'[k]$ and if $\mathsf{P}^k_{(a,m)} \in$ $\ell'((\mathbf{S},\mathbf{R}), i, \mathbf{O})$ then $\mathsf{P}^k_{(a,m)} \in \ell'((\mathbf{S}',\mathbf{R})', j, \mathbf{O}')$, i.e. in all configuration with the same state of process k, the moves of process k must be the same.

A consistent algorithm labelling ℓ' induces then a distributed algorithm $A^{\ell'} = P_1 \otimes \ldots \otimes P_n$ where for all $j \in [1, n]$, we have $P_i = (M, \delta_i)$ and $\delta_i(s) = (a, m)$ iff for all configurations $((\mathbf{S},\mathbf{R}), j, \mathbf{O}) \in Q$ such that $\mathbf{S}[i] = s$, we have $\mathsf{P}^i_{(a,m)} \in \ell'(((\mathbf{S},\mathbf{R}), j, \mathbf{O}))$. Conditions 1. to 3. ensure that this definition is well-founded.

To check by the analysis of the Kripke structure $\mathcal{K}^{\ell'}_{n,\mathcal{D},M}$ whether the algorithm $A^{\ell'}$ induced by a consistent algorithm labelling satisfies the specification Φ_{spec}, we have to find a way to extract from $\mathcal{K}^{\ell'}_{n,\mathcal{D},M}$ the execution corresponding to $A^{\ell'}$. This can be achieved by the following LTL formula:

$$\Phi_{\mathrm{out}} \overset{\mathrm{def}}{=} \mathbf{X}\,\mathbf{G}\left[\bigvee_{C \in \mathcal{C}} \bigvee_{\mathbf{O} \in \mathcal{O}} \bigvee_{i,a,m} \left(\mathsf{P}^i_{(a,m)} \wedge \mathsf{P}_{C,\mathbf{O}} \wedge \mathbf{X}(\mathrm{active}_i \Rightarrow \mathsf{P}_{\mathrm{Next}(C,\mathbf{O},i,a,m)})\right)\right]$$

where $\mathrm{Next}(C, \mathbf{O}, i, a, m)$ is the (unique) extended configuration $(C', \mathbf{O}')$ such that $C \xRightarrow{i,(a,m)} C'$ and $\mathbf{O}[j] = \mathbf{O}'[j]$ for all $j \neq i$ and $\mathbf{O}'[i] = o$ if $a = \mathbf{dec}(o)$ otherwise $\mathbf{O}'[i] = \bot$. We can then combine Φ_{out} with the correctness specification Φ_{spec} to check in $\mathcal{K}^{\ell'}_{n,\mathcal{D},M}$ whether the executions of $A^{\ell'}$ (which are the executions of $\mathcal{K}_{A^{\ell'}}$) satisfy Φ_{spec}.

Proposition 2. *Given a consistent algorithm labelling ℓ' and its induced distributed algorithm $A^{\ell'}$,*

$$A^{\ell'} \models \Phi_{spec} \quad iff \quad \mathcal{K}^{\ell'}_{n,\mathcal{D},M} \models \Phi_{out} \Rightarrow \Phi_{spec}$$

Sketch of Proof. To prove this it is enough to see that the control states of $\mathcal{K}_{A^{\ell'}}$ and of $\mathcal{K}^{\ell'}_{n,\mathcal{D},M}$ are the same and that any infinite sequence of such states ρ beginning in q_{init} is an execution in $\mathcal{K}_{A^{\ell'}}$ iff it is an execution in $\mathcal{K}^{\ell'}_{n,\mathcal{D},M}$ verifying Φ_{out}. □

Consequently, to solve the synthesis problem it is enough to find a consistent algorithm labelling ℓ' such that $\mathcal{K}^{\ell'}_{n,\mathcal{D},M} \models \Phi_{\mathrm{out}} \Rightarrow \Phi_{\mathrm{spec}}$. Note that as explained before this produces exactly the correct algorithm $A^{\ell'}$. We have hence a decision procedure for the synthesis problem: it reduces to some instances of model-checking problem for LTL formulae.

5   Experiments

We have implemented a prototype to automatically synthesize algorithms for consensus and ε-agreement problems. For this we use the SMT solver Z3 [4]: it is now classical to use SAT solver for model-checking [1] and it was natural to consider this approach especially because we need to add an existential quantification over the atomic propositions encoding the moves of the processes[2]. Our prototype is however a bit different from the theoretical framework explained in Sect. 4 and we explain here the main ideas behind its implementation.

First, the implementation does not consider general (quantified) LTL formulas but encodes directly the considered problem (consensus or ε-agreement) for a set of parameters provided by the user into a Z3-program, and the result provided by the SMT solver Z3 is then *automatically* analysed in order to get algorithms for processes.

We now sketch the main aspects of the reduction to Z3. The code starts by existentially quantifying over the action functions for each process: an action function δ^p for a process p is encoded as an integer value δ^p_s for every process state s which gives the next action to performed. In Z3, such a δ^p_s is a bitvector (whose size is $\log_2(|Act(\mathcal{D}, n) \times M| + 1)$). It remains to encode the different properties we want to ensure (depending on the considered problem). Here are several examples:

– To deal with the formula Φ^c_{agree} for the consensus, we use a set of Boolean constants (one for every global configuration C). Their truth value can be easily defined as true when all processes in C have terminated and decided the same value, or as false when at least two processes have decided different values in C. For the other cases, we add constraints stating that the value associated with C equals true when for every successor (here a successor is any configuration reachable after an action (a, m) of some process p such that this action (a, m) corresponds to the value δ^p_s where s is the state of p in C). It remains to add a last constraint: for every initial configuration C_0, the constant associated with Φ^c_{agree} has to be true. Note that this definition is based on the fact that the property is an invariant: we want to ensure that no reachable configuration violates a local property.

– Encoding the formula Φ^c_{valid} follows the same approach: we use a boolean value for every configuration C and for every input data d, and define their truth value in such a way that it is true iff the value d cannot be decided in the next configurations. If some process has already decided d in C, the constant equals to false. If all processes have decided and no one choose d, it is true. Otherwise a positive value requires that for every successor C', the constants are also true. Finally we add constraints specifying for every initial configuration C_0 the values d that cannot be chosen by requiring that their corresponding values are true.

– The obstruction free context Φ_{of} is encoded as follows: we need two sets of constants for every process p. The first set contains one integer value (encoded as a bitvector in Z3) for every configuration and it is defined in order to be the number of moves that process p has to perform (alone) to decide (and terminate). This distance is bounded by the number of states nb_{state} of process p (and we use the value nb_{state} to represent the non-termination

---

[2] We do not describe here the reduction: it uses standard techniques for encoding LTL formulae to SAT instance.

of the process). In addition, we consider a set of boolean values (one for every configuration) which are defined in order to equal to true iff for every reachable configuration from C, the computed distance is strictly less than nb_{loc}.

- Encoding the wait-free context uses the same idea. We have to verify that from every reachable configuration, every process will terminate (for this we use the fact that when a process decides a value, it does not perform action anymore, and then other processes progress). Note that in this case, the bound on the distance is the number of *global* configurations.

In addition to this encoding, we can also use standard techniques of bounded model-checking by fixing a smaller bound for the computation of the distances described above. When this is done, the program may provide an algorithm, or answer that an algorithm **with this bound** does not exist (it remains to try with a greater bound). This heuristic is crucial to synthesize algorithms in many cases (the computation of distances is quite expensive since it is connected to the number of states or configurations).

The parameters of our prototype are then: (1) the number of processes: n, (2) the range of initial values and the range of possible values in registers, (3) the size of the processess memory, (4) the types of scheduling policy (wait free, obstruction free, round-robin, or a combination of them), and (5) the value of ε for the ε-agreement problem. Finally one can ask for symmetric programs (each process has the same action function) and in the following we only consider symmetric solutions.

State Explosion Problem. As explained in previous sections, we are faced with a huge complexity. For example, with 2 processes, two possible initial values and a memory size equals to 2, there are more than 450 configurations for the distributed algorithms. If we consider 3 processes, 2 initial values et a memory size equals to 3, we get more than 240 *thousands* configurations! This gap explains why our prototype only provides algorithms for 2 processes. Note that even for the case $n = 2$, the complete encoding of the problem may use several thousands of variables in the Z3 code, and the SMT solver succeeds in providing a result. Of course, the implementation of our prototype in its current form is quite naive and some efficiency improvements are possible.

Moreover note that our prototype is often more efficient for finding algorithms when they exist than for proving that no algorithm within the resource fixed by the parameters[3] exists. First it is often easier to find a valuation than verifying that no valuation exists, and secondly we can use heuristics to accelerate the procedure (for example by bounding the length of computations: in this case, if a valuation is found, we can stop, otherwise we have to try again with different settings). This fact can be seen as a variant of a well-known

---

[3] Note that we cannot prove that no algorithm exists, but only that no algorithm *with this memory bound* exists if the corresponding SAT instance has no solution.

phenomenon in sat-based model-checking: it is usually very efficient to find a bug (that is an execution satisfying or not a formula), but it is not the case to prove full verification.

Consensus. For 2 components, 2 initial and final values, a memory of size 2 and the obstruction free policy, we get the algorithm of Sect. 2.2 (Fig. 1) except that the processes use their register to write the value they *do not* plan to decide (it is clearly symmetric to the previous algorithm). Note that the size of memory is important: there is no algorithm with memory of size 1: indeed we need to distinguish the configuration $(0,0)$ (the proper register equals to 0 and the last read value of the register of other process is 0) when it is reached after a Read (both process agree on the value to decide) and when it is reached after a Write(0) performed by the process to update its register in order to agree with the other process. This absence of algorithm with a memory of size 1 corresponds to an UNSAT result for the program: the formula Φ_{synth} with these parameters is not satisfiable. When we tried to look for algorithms for wait-free case, we found no solution with our program: indeed we know that there is no such algorithms!

More interestingly we can ask for a program correct w.r.t. several execution contexts. For example, we can ask for program correct w.r.t. obstruction free, round-robin for one step and also round-robin for two steps. The program generates[4] the algorithm depicted in Fig. 2 (we follow the same presentation as in Sect. 2 for the algorithm and since we have only two processes, we use $(\mathbf{re}, -)$ instead of $(\mathbf{re}(1), -)$: a read operation always deals with the other process).

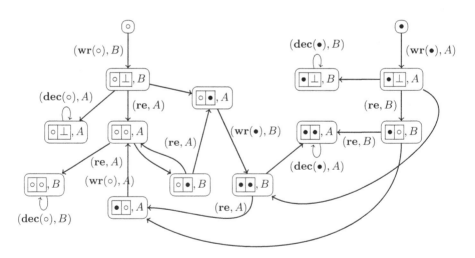

Fig. 2. View of a process algorithm P for consensus, w.r.t. to obstruction free and round-robin 1 and 2.

---

[4] It takes few seconds to produce the algorithm on a standard laptop.

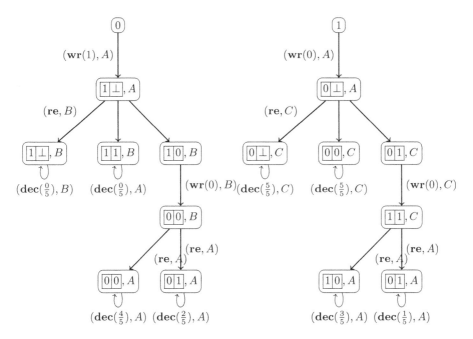

Fig. 3. View of a process algorithm P for $\frac{1}{5}$-agreement, w.r.t. wait free scheduling.

ε-agreement. For this problem, we have to fix ε. In Fig. 3, we present an algorithm for $\frac{1}{5}$-agreement for 2 processes, with initial values $\{0, 1\}$ and memory 3. The set of possible decision values is $\{0, \frac{1}{5}, \frac{2}{5}, \frac{3}{5}, \frac{4}{5}, 1\}$. Note that this algorithm works for the wait-free execution context, and therefore also for round-robin (for any step) and for obstruction free. Here the memory size equals to 3: this is illustrated by the fact that the configuration $(0, 0)$ (the register's value is 0 and the last read value from the other process is 0) appears in three nodes.

6   Conclusion

We have shown here that in theory it is possible to solve the synthesis problem for distributed algorithm as soon as we fix the set of data that can be written in the registers and the memory needed by each process in the algorithm. However even if this problem is decidable, our method has to face two different problems: first, it does not scale and second, when the answer to the synthesis problem is negative, we cannot conclude that there is no algorithm at all. In the future, we will study more intensively whether for some specific cases we can decide the existence of a distributed algorithm satisfying a given specification without fixing any restrictions on the exchanged data or on the size of the algorithms. We believe that for some specific distributed problems, this is in fact feasible.

References

1. Clarke, E.M., Biere, A., Raimi, R., Zhu, Y.: Bounded model checking using satisfiability solving. Formal Methods Syst. Des. **19**(1), 7–34 (2001)
2. Clarke, E.M., Emerson, E.A.: Design and synthesis of synchronization skeletons using branching time temporal logic. In: Kozen, D. (ed.) Logic of Programs 1981. LNCS, vol. 131, pp. 52–71. Springer, Heidelberg (1982). https://doi.org/10.1007/BFb0025774
3. Cousineau, D., Doligez, D., Lamport, L., Merz, S., Ricketts, D., Vanzetto, H.: TLA + Proofs. In: Giannakopoulou, D., Méry, D. (eds.) FM 2012. LNCS, vol. 7436, pp. 147–154. Springer, Heidelberg (2012). https://doi.org/10.1007/978-3-642-32759-9_14
4. de Moura, L., Bjørner, N.: Z3: an efficient SMT solver. In: Ramakrishnan, C.R., Rehof, J. (eds.) TACAS 2008. LNCS, vol. 4963, pp. 337–340. Springer, Heidelberg (2008). https://doi.org/10.1007/978-3-540-78800-3_24
5. Emerson, E.A.: Temporal and modal logic. In: Leeuwen, J.V. (ed.) Handbook of Theoretical Computer Science, vol. B, Chapter 16, pp. 995–1072. Elsevier (1990)
6. Fischer, M.J., Lynch, N.A., Paterson, M.: Impossibility of distributed consensus with one faulty process. J. ACM **32**(2), 374–382 (1985)
7. Grädel, E., Thomas, W., Wilke, T. (eds.): Automata, Logics, and Infinite Games: A Guide to Current Research [outcome of a Dagstuhl seminar, February 2001]. LNCS, vol. 2500. Springer, Heidelberg (2002). https://doi.org/10.1007/3-540-36387-4
8. Herlihy, M.: Wait-free synchronization. ACM Trans. Program. Lang. Syst. **13**(1), 124–149 (1991)
9. Herlihy, M., Luchangco, V., Moir, M.: Obstruction-free synchronization: double-ended queues as an example. In: ICDCS 2003, pp. 522–529 (2003)
10. Herlihy, M., Shavit, N.: The Art of Multiprocessor Programming. Morgan Kaufmann, Burlington (2008)
11. Holzmann, G.J.: The SPIN Model Checker - Primer and Reference Manual. Addison-Wesley, Boston (2004)
12. Lazic, M., Konnov, I., Widder, J., Bloem, R.: Synthesis of distributed algorithms with parameterized threshold guards. In: OPODIS 2017, vol. 95. LIPIcs, pp. 32:1–32:20. Schloss Dagstuhl - Leibniz-Zentrum fuer Informatik (2017)
13. Pnueli, A.: The temporal logic of programs. In: Proceedings of the 18th Annual Symposium on Foundations of Computer Science (FOCS 1977), pp. 46–57. IEEE Computer Society Press, October–November 1977
14. Queille, J.P., Sifakis, J.: Specification and verification of concurrent systems in CESAR. In: Dezani-Ciancaglini, M., Montanari, U. (eds.) Programming 1982. LNCS, vol. 137, pp. 337–351. Springer, Heidelberg (1982). https://doi.org/10.1007/3-540-11494-7_22
15. Vardi, M.Y., Wolper, P.: An automata-theoretic approach to automatic program verification (preliminary report). In: LICS 1986, pp. 332–344. IEEE Computer Society (1986)

Recoverable Mutual Exclusion
with Abortability

Prasad Jayanti and Anup Joshi[⊠]

Dartmouth College, Hanover, NH 03755, USA
anupj@cs.dartmouth.edu

Abstract. In light of recent advances in non-volatile main memory technology, there has been a flurry of research in designing algorithms that are resilient to process crashes. As a result of main memory non-volatility, a process is allowed to crash any time during the execution, without affecting the state of the data stored in the main memory. With the assumption that a process eventually restarts after a crash, prior works have focused on designing mutual exclusion algorithms that use the non-volatile main memory to recover from such crashes. Such mutual exclusion algorithms that provide multiple processes with a mutually exclusive access to a shared resource in the presence of process crashes are called Recoverable Mutual Exclusion (RME) algorithms. We present the first RME algorithm where a process has the ability to abort executing the algorithm, if it decides to give up its request for a shared resource before being granted access to that resource. With n being the maximum number of processes for which the algorithm is designed, in the absence of a crash our algorithm guarantees a worst-case remote memory references (RMR) complexity of $O(\log n)$ per passage on the Distributed Shared Memory (DSM) machines, and a complexity of $O(\log n)$ or $O(n)$ on Cache Coherent (CC) machines, depending on how caches are managed.

Keywords: Concurrent algorithm · Synchronization ·
Mutual exclusion · Recoverable algorithm · Fault tolerance ·
Non-volatile main memory · Shared memory · Multi-core algorithms

1 Introduction

Recent advances in non-volatile main memory (NVMM) technology [1–3] have given rise to designing algorithms that are resilient to process crashes. These memory technologies allow interfacing the processor directly with the non-volatile main memory. Therefore, in the event of a process crash, the system restarts the crashed process and the process then recovers from the crash by consulting the contents of the NVMM.

The first author is grateful to the Frank family and Dartmouth College for their support through James Frank Family Professorship of Computer Science.
The second author is grateful for the support from Dartmouth College.

M. F. Atig and A. A. Schwarzmann (Eds.): NETYS 2019, LNCS 11704, pp. 217–232, 2019.
https://doi.org/10.1007/978-3-030-31277-0_14

To leverage this advantage given by the NVMM, there has been a keen interest recently in designing algorithms for such systems. A starting point is to design a variant of the classical mutual exclusion problem [4] in which the objective is to protect access to a shared resource in a manner that atmost one process has access to the resource at any point in time. Thus, it began with Golab and Ramaraju [5] reformulating the classical mutual exclusion problem into the novel *Recoverable Mutual Exclusion* (RME) problem in 2016. After which there has been a flurry of research in designing algorithms for the RME problem [6–10]. The main interest in these works has been in designing algorithms with various desirable properties while maintaining the remote memory reference (RMR) complexity for Cache-Coherent (CC) multiprocessors and Distributed Shared Memory (DSM) multiprocessors to a minimum.

A straightforward approach to recover from process crashes would be to shut down the entire system and restart it. However, a motive behind designing RME algorithms is to make the crashes less disruptive to other processes which do not crash. Therefore, repairing the damage due to a crash by using the NVMM is far less demanding to a process that did not crash since it does not suffer from such a full-system restart. However, prior works on RME fall short in a crucial aspect when compared to solutions to the classical mutual exclusion problem. Imagine a real-time system with multiple threads that uses one of these RME algorithms to secure access to a critical shared resource. In the event of a crash the waiting time of a non-crashing thread would still be increased by the time it takes for the crashing process to recover from its crash. This issue is further amplified when the crashes are frequent and the system is operating under tight deadlines. Hence, it makes sense for a waiting thread to be able to abort its attempt to acquire access to the shared resource, and not miss any of its other deadlines. Although classical mutual exclusion algorithms are amenable to support the ability to abort, unfortunately, none of the prior works on the RME problem support such an ability to abort.

In this paper, we present the first RME algorithm that provides the abort functionality. Our algorithm has a bounded RMR on the CC and DSM machines besides possessing some additional desirable properties.

Related Research. All of the prior work on RME has focused on designing algorithms that do not provide abortability as a capability. Golab and Ramaraju [5] formalized the RME problem and designed several algorithms by adapting traditional mutual exclusion algorithms. Ramaraju [11], Jayanti and Joshi [7], and Jayanti et al. [9] designed RME algorithms that support the First-Come-First-Served property [12]. Golab and Hendler [6] presented an algorithm that has sub-logarithmic RMR complexity on CC machines. In another work, Golab and Hendler [8] presented an algorithm that has the ideal $O(1)$ passage complexity, but this result assumes that *all* processes in the system crash *simultaneously*. Recently, Jayanti et al. [10] presented a unified algorithm that has a sub-logarithmic RMR complexity on both CC and DSM machines. For works not on RME but on the theme of crash-restart systems using non-volatile main-memory, Attiya et al. [13] present linearizable implementations of recoverable objects.

When it comes to abortability for classical mutual exclusion problem, Scott [14] and Scott and Scherer [15] designed abortable algorithms that build on the queue-based algorithms [16,17]. Jayanti [18] designed an algorithm based on read, write, and comparison primitives having $O(\log n)$ RMR complexity which is also optimal [19]. Lee [20] designed an algorithm for CC machines that uses the Fetch-and-Add and Fetch-and-Store primitives. Alon and Morrison [21] designed an algorithm for CC machines that has a sub-logarithmic RMR complexity and uses the read, write, Fetch-And-Store, and comparison primitives. Recently, Jayanti and Jayanti [22] designed an algorithm for the CC and DSM machines that has a constant amortized RMR complexity and uses the read, write, and Fetch-And-Store primitives. While the works mentioned so far have been deterministic algorithms, randomized versions of classical mutual exclusion with abortability exist. Pareek and Woelfel [23] give a sublogarithmic RMR complexity randomized algorithm and Giakkoupis and Woelfel [24] give an $O(1)$ expected amortized RMR complexity randomized algorithm.

Our Contribution. We show that, as with classical mutual exclusion, the recoverable mutual exclusion problem is amenable to abortability with a reasonable RMR complexity. We present the first abortable RME algorithm for the CC and DSM machines using only read, write, and comparison primitives. We design our algorithm by developing on ideas from a prior RME algorithm by Jayanti and Joshi [7]. Our algorithm has an RMR complexity of $O(f + \log n)$ when used on DSM machines and certain type of CC machines, but it has $O(f + n)$ RMR complexity on another type of CC machines (see Sect. 3.4 for full details), where n is the number of processes for which the algorithm is designed and f is the number of times a process crashes between the time it invokes and exits the algorithm. Attiya et al. [19] proved a lower bound that the RMR complexity is $\Omega(\log n)$ for even classical mutual exclusion algorithms that use read, write, and comparison primitives. Therefore, our algorithm adds only $O(1)$ RMR per crash on the DSM machines. In addition to the above, our algorithm satisfies the First-Come-First-Served [12] property. It would be interesting if it is possible to bring down the RMR complexity to $O(f + \log n)$ for all CC machines.

2   Model and Problem Specification

Our system consists of n asynchronous processes named $1, 2, \ldots, n$ and atomic persistent variables (which include shared variables and variables used by a single process). The persistent variables support the operations *read*, *write*, and *compare&swap* (CAS). The CAS operation has the signature: $\mathrm{CAS}(X, old, new)$, where X is a variable name, and old and new are some values. A $\mathrm{CAS}(X, old, new)$ operation atomically changes X's value to new, if X contained the value old, and returns $true$; otherwise, it returns $false$ and leaves X unchanged. The persistent variables are assumed to reside in the non-volatile main memory (NVMM) [1–3], which allows them to retain their values in the event of a process crash. Note, our algorithm also uses process local variables, which are assumed to be stored in the process registers (we clarify in the description of the algorithm the nature of variables used). A *configuration* of the system is specified by the values of all shared variables and the states of the n processes, where the state of a process p is in turn specified by the value of PC_p, p's program counter, and the values of p's local variables. The configuration changes when a process takes a step. Any process can execute either a *normal step* or a *crash step* at any time. In a normal step of p, p executes the instruction pointed by its program counter PC_p. A crash step models the crash of a process and can occur regardless of what portion of code the process is executing.

The Abortable RME Problem. In the RME problem, each process repeatedly cycles through four sections of code—Remainder, Try, Critical, and Exit sections. An *algorithm* for RME specifies the code for the Try and Exit sections of each process. If a process p executes a normal step when in Remainder, p moves to Try; and if p executes a normal step when in CS, p moves to Exit (therefore, we encapsulate the CS of p with one normal step). A crash step of p sets PC_p to point to its Remainder section and sets all other registers of p to $\perp$. In addition, in the Abortable RME problem, p can receive an external signal to *abort* continuing to the CS while inside Try, in which case p may execute Exit without executing CS to go back to the Remainder[1]. A *run* of an algorithm is an infinite sequence of steps. We assume every run satisfies the following conditions: (i) if a process is in Try, Critical, or Exit sections, it later executes a (normal or crash) step, and (ii) if a process enters Remainder because of a crash step, it later executes a normal step.

RMR Complexity and Passages. In a CC machine each process has a cache. A read operation by a process p on a shared variable X fetches a copy of X from shared memory to p's cache, if a copy is not already present. Any non-read operation on X by any process invalidates copies of X at all caches. An operation on X by p counts as a *remote memory reference* (RMR) if either the operation is not a read or X's copy is not in p's cache. When a process crashes, we assume that its cache contents are lost. In a DSM machine, instead of caches, shared memory is partitioned, with one partition residing at each process, and each shared variable resides in exactly one partition. Any operation (read or non-read) by a process on a shared variable X is counted as an RMR if X is not in p's partition.

A *passage* of a process p in a run starts when p enters Try (from Remainder) and ends at the earliest later time when p returns to Remainder (either because p crashes or because p completes Exit and moves back to Remainder). A *superpassage* of a process p in a run starts when p either enters Try for the first

---

[1] p might have already set itself up to enter the CS, or could be executing the CS, in which case it executes Exit after completing the CS.

time in the run or when p enters Try for the first time after the previous super-passage has ended, and it ends when p returns to Remainder not by a crash step but by completing the Exit section. Note that p's super-passage can contain an unbounded number of p's passages because of its repeated crashes during the super-passage. The *passage RMR complexity* (respectively, *super-passage RMR complexity*) of an RME algorithm is the worst-case number of RMRs that a process incurs in a passage (respectively, in a super-passage). We express this RMR complexity in terms of n and f, where n is the number of processes for which the algorithm is designed and f is the number of times the process crashes during the super-passage.

Problem Statement. The goal is to design an algorithm (i.e., code for Try and Exit sections) for the Abortable RME problem, such that, all of the following conditions are met in every run of the algorithm. Conditions P1, P4, P5 are from Golab and Ramaraju [5], and P2, P6, P7, P8 are from Jayanti and Joshi [7]. The additional property P3 and the modifications needed for other properties to accomodate abortability are emphasized in italics.

P1. <u>Mutual Exclusion</u>: At most one process is in the CS at any point.

P2. <u>Bounded Exit</u>: There is a bound b such that, if a process p is in the Exit section and it executes steps without crashing, it enters the Remainder section in atmost b of its own steps.

P3. <u>Bounded Abort</u>: *There is a bound b such that, if a process p receives the abort signal and p executes steps without crashing, then p enters the CS or the Remainder section in b of its own steps.*
    This property captures the intuition that a process frees itself from all waiting once it receives the abort signal.

P4. <u>Starvation Freedom</u>: If the total number of crashes in the run is finite and a process p has infinite number of steps, then p enters the CS in each super-passage *in which it does not receive an abort signal.*

P5. <u>Critical Section Reentry (CSR) [5]</u>: If a process p crashes while in the CS, then no other process enters the CS during the interval from p's crash to the point in the run when p next enters the CS.

P6. <u>Wait-Free Critical Section Reentry (Wait-Free CSR) [7]</u>: There is a bound b such that, if a process p crashes while in the CS, then p reenters the CS before completing b consecutive normal steps.

P7. <u>First-Come-First-Served (FCFS) [7]</u>: There is a bound b such that, if a process p performs b contiguous normal steps in its super-passage s before another process p' initiates its super-passage s' *and p does not receive an abort signal in s,* then p' does not enter the CS in super-passage s' before p first enters the CS in super-passage s'.

P8. <u>Well-formedness</u>: Let s be a normal step by p in which p completes the Try section, and s' be the latest step by p before s in which p starts a super-passage or p crashes outside of the Try section in CS, or Exit. *Well-formedness* stipulates where the control moves to after step s, as follows:

- If s' is a step when the super-passage starts, then s moves control to CS, *Exit section or Remainder section.*
- If s' is a crash step while p is in Try section, then s moves control to CS, *Exit section or Remainder section.*
- If s' is a crash step while p is in CS, then s moves control to CS.
- If s' is a crash step while p is in Exit, then s moves control to CS, Exit section, or Remainder section.

3   The Algorithm

We present our abortable RME algorithm in Fig. 1. The algorithm is designed for n processes, with each process getting a distinct name from the set $\{1, 2, \ldots, n\}$. All the persistent variables used by our algorithm are stored in the non-volatile main memory. Variables with names in small letters and a subscript of p to their name are variables local to the process p, and are stored in p's registers. We assume that the CS is an idempotent block of code, which allows a process to re-execute it from start even if the process crashes in the middle of the CS. We assume that the external signal to an arbitrary process p asking it to abort is made available at ABORTSIGNAL$[p]$ as a boolean value, with a value of *true* indicating that the signal is active and a value of *false* indicating otherwise. Our algorithm is obtained by expanding on ideas of Jayanti and Joshi's [7] algorithm. Therefore, like their algorithm, our algorithm relies on a special object called *min-array*. For more details about the min-array, please read the description of REGISTRY in Sect. 3.1.

3.1   Shared Variables and Their Purpose

We describe below the role played by each shared variable used in the algorithm.

GO$[p]$: This is a flag that process p waits on before entering the CS and supports the read, write, and CAS operations. To achieve the local-spin property, GO$[p]$ is allocated to p's memory module on DSM machines. This variable is set to a non-zero integer value by p inside the Try Section. A process q makes p the owner of the CS first, and then q releases p from its wait loop by assigning 0 to GO$[p]$. In our algorithm it is also possible that a process $r \neq q$ notices that p is the owner of the CS and hence may try to set GO$[p]$ to 0 by attempting a CAS operation on this variable. Hence, in such cases a different process r, instead of q who captured CS for p, releases p from its wait.

TOKEN: TOKEN is an integer variable supporting read and CAS operations. TOKEN is used to implement a counter so that its values can be used to assign token numbers to processes requesting the CS: in the Try section, a process reads TOKEN to get its token number and then increments TOKEN. The token thus obtained by a process is used for the entirety of its super-passage.

Persistent variables (stored in NVMM)
REGISTRY : A min-array, initially empty.
CSSTATUS $\in \{0,1\} \times \mathcal{P} \times \mathbb{N}$, initially $(0,1,0)$.
$\forall p$, GO$[p]$ is an integer initialized to 0.
$\forall p$, EXITING$[p]$ is a boolean initialized to $false$.
TOKEN is an integer initialized to 1.

    Try Section
1. if EXITING$[p]$ **then go to Exit Section** (Line **12**)
2. $tok_p \leftarrow$ GO$[p]$
3. **if** CSSTATUS $== (1, p, *) \wedge tok_p == 0$ **then go to Critical Section** (Line **11**)
    else if $tok_p \neq 0$ **then go to** Line **7**
4. $tok_p \leftarrow$ TOKEN
5. CAS(TOKEN, $tok_p, tok_p + 1$)
6. GO$[p] \leftarrow tok_p$
7. REGISTRY.write($p, (p, tok_p)$)
8. promote()
9. **while** GO$[p] \neq 0$
10.   **if** ABORTSIGNAL$[p]$ **then go to Exit Section** (Line **12**)
    end Try Section

11. **Critical Section**
    Exit Section
12. EXITING$[p] \leftarrow true$
13. REGISTRY.write($p, (p, \infty)$)
14. $tok_p \leftarrow$ GO$[p]$
15. **if** $tok_p \neq 0$ **then**
16. $(bit_p, peer_p, peertok_p) \leftarrow$ CSSTATUS
17.   **if** $bit_p == 0$ **then** CAS(CSSTATUS, $(bit_p, peer_p, peertok_p), (0, p, tok_p)$)
18.   GO$[p] \leftarrow 0$
19. $(bit_p, peer_p, peertok_p) \leftarrow$ CSSTATUS
20. **if** $bit_p == 1 \wedge peer_p == p$ **then** CAS(CSSTATUS, $(1, p, peertok_p), (0, p, peertok_p)$)
21. promote()
22. EXITING$[p] \leftarrow false$
    end Exit Section

    procedure promote()
23. $(bit_p, peer_p, peertok_p) \leftarrow$ CSSTATUS
24. **if** $bit_p == 0$ **then**
25. $(succ_p, succtok_p) \leftarrow$ REGISTRY.findmin()
26.   **if** $succtok_p \neq \infty$ **then** CAS(CSSTATUS, $(bit_p, peer_p, peertok_p), (1, succ_p, succtok_p)$)
27. $(bit_p, peer_p, peertok_p) \leftarrow$ CSSTATUS
28. **if** $bit_p == 1$ **then** CAS(GO$[peer_p], peertok_p, 0$)
    end procedure

Fig. 1. Abortable RME Algorithm. Code for process p.

REGISTRY: REGISTRY is a min-array that has the same purpose as the one in Jayanti and Joshi's [7] work, which we reiterate here for clarity. The min-array, henceforth referred only as REGISTRY, is an array and has n locations, one per process. It supports two operations: write() and findmin(). REGISTRY.write(p, v), when executed by p, sets REGISTRY$[p]$ to v. The operation REGISTRY.findmin() returns the minimum value in the array. Like in [7],

REGISTRY acts like a queue by holding the names of processes waiting to enter the CS, and orders them according to their token numbers. p inserts in REGISTRY an element (p, tok_p) (Line **7**), where tok_p holds p's token number (we call this step by p as "registering" its super-passage). When exiting or aborting, p deletes this element (Line **13**) by writing (p, ∞) (we call this step by p as "unregistering" its super-passage). The elements in REGISTRY are ordered according to their token numbers: $(p, t) < (q, t')$ if $t < t'$ or $t = t' \wedge p < q$. Thus, the findmin() operation returns (p, t), where p is the process in REGISTRY with the smallest token. If REGISTRY is empty (i.e., every location in the array is empty), findmin() returns a value (q, ∞), with some process name q. We require that the two operations satisfy wait-freedom and idempotence, which allows the algorithm to repeatedly execute these operations in presence of a crash. As mentioned in Sect. 4 of [7], the implementation given in Appendix A of [7] does satisfy these properties. We therefore use that implementation in our algorithm. Their implementation of REGISTRY uses read, write, and CAS and is adapted from f-arrays [25].

CSSTATUS: This variable is a record with three fields: $(bit, peer, peertok)$. The first field, bit, is a single bit field denoting whether the CS is occupied or not. A value of 0 in the bit indicates the CS is free and in that case $peer$ denotes the process that last wrote to CSSTATUS while using $peertok$ as the token for its super-passage. If the value of the bit is 1, it indicates the CS is occupied and in that case, $peer$ denotes the name of the process that currently owns the CS and $peertok$ is the token used by the process with name $peer$ for its current super-passage. The operations supported by CSSTATUS are read and CAS.

EXITING$[p]$: This is a boolean variable that supports the read and write operations. p might crash while executing the Exit section, so we use the EXITING$[p]$ variable to remind p that it was executing the Exit section. Hence, EXITING$[p] = true$ indicates that p should be executing the Exit section after restarting from a crash; EXITING$[p] = false$ indicates p is yet to execute the Exit section in the current super-passage.

A Remark on Wrap-Around of Token Numbers. In our algorithm the bit size of the token numbers generated using TOKEN is constrained by the $peertok$ field of CSSTATUS. Assuming a word length of 64-bits, a reasonable assumption on modern multiprocessor systems, we argue as follows that wrap-around of token numbers is not a practical concern. Assume that the system consists of $16,384$ processes, it would therefore need 14 bits to represent each process. Accounting for the bit field from CSSTATUS, we are left with 49 bits to represent a token number. For the token number to wrap around, there must be 2^{49} passages. If there are 2^{20} (a million) passages per second, it would take 17 years for the token number to wrap around. Therefore, wrap-around is not a practical concern.

3.2   Informal Description

In this section we informally describe the working of our algorithm presented in Fig. 1. We first describe how a process p would execute the Try and Exit section in absence of a crash or an abort signal, and then proceed to explain the algorithm if a crash is encountered anywhere or an abort signal is activated.

Crash-Free and Abort-Free Super-Passage. When p wants to enter the CS from the Remainder section, it starts executing the Try section. Lines **1–3** perform a check if the preceding passage by p ended in a crash. Our algorithm maintains the invariant that whenever p is starting a super-passage, the following holds about the shared variables: CSSTATUS $\neq (1, p, *)$ (i.e., CSSTATUS says that p is not the owner of CS), EXITING$[p] = false$, and GO$[p] = 0$. Therefore, after reading the above shared variables, none of the **if** conditions from Lines **1–3** are met, hence, p proceeds execution from Line **4**. At Line **4** p obtains a token for itself and then increments the global counter (Line **5**). It then saves the obtained token into GO$[p]$ (Line **6**) for its own use so that in the event of a crash it does not obtain a different token. Then, at Line **7**, it inserts its name, tagged with its token, into the REGISTRY (i.e., p "registers" its super-passage). If p executes normal steps upto Line **7** in super-passage s before another process q initiates its super-passage s' and p does not receive an abort signal in s, then q does not enter the CS in s' before p first enters the CS in s (this is useful for the FCFS property). After executing Line **7**, p executes the `promote()` procedure (Line **8**) whose job is to capture the CS for the longest waiting process q registered in REGISTRY and inform q that it no longer needs to wait (we describe the procedure in detail shortly). Following this, p waits until it is informed that it no longer needs to wait (Line **9**) all the while simultaneously checking if it received an abort signal (Line **10**). If p reads that ABORTSIGNAL$[p] = true$ at Line **10**, it has received the external signal to abort continuing to the CS, hence, it starts executing the Exit section at Line **12**. Upon being informed about its turn to enter the CS (i.e., GO$[p] = 0$), p enters the CS. Note, we assume that starting when p enters the CS and so long as it is executing the CS PC_p remains **11**, except after crashes where for a brief while p executes some code from Try to get back to CS and PC_p changes back to **11**. When p leaves the CS, it first sets a checkpoint at Line **12** signifying that it has started executing the Exit section by writing $true$ into EXITING$[p]$, so that in the event of a crash it comes back to Exit section. At Line **13**, it removes its own name from the REGISTRY (i.e., it "unregisters" its own super-passage). Following that it executes Lines **14–15** whose job is to check if p entered Exit section upon receiving an abort signal. Since at present we are considering a super-passage in absence of a crash or an abort signal, p entered the CS on noticing GO$[p] = 0$. Hence, at Line **14** p takes note of the current value of GO$[p]$ and at Line **15** it checks if that value is 0. By the above, the **if** condition at Line **15** is not met, hence, p resumes execution from Line **19**. At Line **19** p reads the current content of CSSTATUS. Our algorithm maintains the invariant that so long as p has ownership of the CS, CSSTATUS has the value $(1, p, tok_p)$, where tok_p is the value of p's token for current super-passage.

Therefore, the **if** condition at Line **20** is met, hence p marks the CS as available by performing the CAS at Line **20**. Following this, p tries to capture the CS for the longest waiting process by executing `promote()` (Line **21**). Whether p lets another process into the CS or not, it completes its own super-passage by setting EXITING[p] to *false* (Line **22**) to indicate that it has completed executing the Exit Section.

Executing `promote()`. We describe the `promote()` procedure as follows. This procedure identifies a process that has been waiting the longest to enter the CS, and lets that process into the CS, if the CS is free. To this purpose, at Line **23**, p reads the contents of CSSTATUS. If the first bit of CSSTATUS is 0, it means the CS is free, therefore, p performs this check at Line **24**. If p finds that the bit is 0, at Line **25** p retrieves the information of the longest waiting process q from REGISTRY (i.e., the name of that process and its token). It then checks if q has a valid token at Line **26** (if an invalid token number denoted by ∞ is received, it means the REGISTRY is empty). If so, then p tries to install q as the new owner of the CS. p does this by performing a CAS at Line **26** that attempts to write into CSSTATUS the information of q. A successful CAS will indicate that q is the one who is going to occupy the CS now. Note, while p is executing Lines **24–26** in the manner described above, another process might be executing the same lines and could execute Line **26** before p. This would result in p's CAS at Line **26** to fail. It is also possible that p succeeded in doing the CAS at Line **26**, but crashed immediately. Our algorithm ensures that if p crashes while performing the `promote()` procedure, it will come back to re-execute the procedure from start. And in that re-execution of `promote()`, p will notice that the **if** condition at Line **24** does not meet (although, it had captured the CS for q prior to the crash). In either of the two cases described above, in Lines **27–28** p takes the responsibility to "wake" any process that is currently occupying the CS. Hence, at Line **27**, p again reads CSSTATUS to identify the process r whose name was last written into CSSTATUS. If p finds that the first bit of CSSTATUS is 1, it does a CAS on GO[r] to write a 0 (Line **28**). If r was not woken up already, this CAS ensures that it is woken up now. Otherwise, p's CAS is bound to fail because either GO[r] = 0 already or r started a new super-passage with a different token in GO[r] (which was written at Line **6**).

Servicing an Abort Signal. Next we describe how p services an abort when it notices that an abort signal has been activated after reading ABORTSIGNAL[p]. p notices the abort signal when it reads ABORTSIGNAL[p] at Line **10** and as a result it starts executing the Exit section at Line **12**. At Line **12** p first sets a checkpoint to signify that it has started executing the Exit section by writing *true* into EXITING[p], so that in the event of a crash it comes back to Exit section. At Line **13**, it unregisters its own super-passage by removing its name from the REGISTRY. Following that it executes Lines **14–15** whose job is to check if p entered Exit section upon receiving an abort signal from the Remainder. Suppose it finds that $tok_p = 0$ (i.e., GO[p] = 0), which is possible because some other process captured the CS for p while p left the Try section for aborting. In that case, it executes the remaining Exit section as described above. This is because the case is as if p entered the CS and then is completing its super-passage by executing Exit section. Assume otherwise that it finds $tok_p \neq 0$ (i.e., $\mathrm{Go}[p] \neq 0$). It then reads the contents of CSSTATUS at Line **16** and checks if the CS is free by checking the first bit of CSSTATUS (Line **17**). If it finds that the CS is free, p attempts to update the content of CSSTATUS by writing its own name and token into it by performing a CAS at Line **17**. This updating of the content of CSSTATUS in spite of CS being free might not be intuitive, but it is one of the subtle features of our algorithm which we will explain shortly. p then clears its own token from its $\mathrm{Go}[p]$ variable to prepare itself for the next super-passage (Line **18**). Note, when aborting $\mathrm{Go}[p]$ might hold a token value p obtained for its current super-passage. If $\mathrm{Go}[p]$ is not explicitly wiped, on its next super-passage p might re-use its old token due to Lines **2–3**. This will lead to a violation of FCFS property, hence, clearing its own token from $\mathrm{Go}[p]$ at Line **18** is important. From Line **19** onwards p executes the Exit section as described above. However, it is important to note that having to do Lines **19–20** is another subtle feature of our algorithm, whose discussion we defer for later.

Recovery from a Crash. When p begins a passage after the preceding passage ended in a crash, p starts by reading EXITING$[p]$ at Line **1**. If it finds that EXITING$[p] = true$, then p crashed while executing the Exit section in the previous passage. p could be executing the Exit section in the previous passage as a result of an abort or due to p coming out of CS prior to crash. In any case, p executes the Exit section from Line **12**. Our Exit section is designed to be idempotent, i.e., if p crashes in the middle of Exit section and re-executes it from the start multiple times, then it would appear to take effect once. Hence, it allows us to execute the Exit section from Line **12** after a crash in the Exit section. If EXITING$[p] = false$, then p reads the contents of $\mathrm{Go}[p]$ and CSSTATUS (Lines **2–3**). If p finds that CSSTATUS $== (1, p, *)$ (i.e., p has ownership of the CS with a certain token) and $\mathrm{Go}[p] = 0$, then p has exclusive access to the CS. Hence, p moves to the CS at Line **11**. Otherwise, p checks if $tok_p \neq 0$ at Line 3, which implies that it has obtained a token prior to the crash, stored it in $\mathrm{Go}[p]$, but does not have the ownership of CS yet. In that case p goes on to continue with the super-passage from Line **7**, where it starts with registering the super-passage and continuing as described above. If p finds that $tok_p = 0$, it means p is yet to even get a token for itself. In that case p starts from Line **4** as if it started a new super-passage (see description above).

3.3   Subtle Features of the Algorithm

In the description of the algorithm given above, we deferred the discussion of a few subtle features of the algorithm. We discuss those subtle features in this section, namely, (A) Maintaining $\mathrm{Go}[p]$ as an integer variable instead of a boolean, (B) why does a process p perform a blind CAS on $\mathrm{Go}[peer_p]$ at Line **28**,

(C) updating the content of CSSTATUS at Line **17** in spite of CS being free, and (D) performing Lines **19–20** even when servicing an abort. We demonstrate below the reason behind performing these operations as follows.

The Need for Feature A. In local-spin mutual exclusion algorithms (e.g., [7,16]) it is generally the case that the spin variable is a boolean flag. However, in our algorithm a process spins on an integer for a specific reason which we describe as follows. Suppose a boolean flag was used instead of an integer, the following scenario shows that it would result in violating mutual exclusion property. Suppose process p is in the CS in a configuration where every other process is in the Remainder section. A process q from the Remainder section needs access to the CS and hence executes the Try section and eventually makes a call to the `promote()` procedure at Line **8** in the Try. q executes the `promote()` procedure upto but not including Line **27**, where it is supposed to wake up the current owner of the CS. At this point p comes out of the CS and starts executing the Exit section so that it eventually calls the `promote()` procedure. p executes Lines **23–27** to make q the new owner of CS, reads the content of CSSTATUS into bit_p $(= 1)$ and $peer_p$ $(= q)$ at Line **27**, and at Line **28** p stops (i.e., just before letting q into the CS). At this point q resumes execution from Line **27**, notes that it itself is now the owner of the CS and hence sets its own Go flag to *true* at Line **28**. Therefore, q enters the CS, completes executing it, and then eventually finishes its super-passage. Now assume that another process r executes the Try section, finds the CS to be free and hence puts itself into the CS. After this q again decides to enter the CS, hence it starts a new super-passage. It executes the Try section to find the CS to be occupied by r, hence it waits for its turn by looping at Lines **9–10**. At this moment, p which had stopped at Line **28** resumes its execution and since it read the first bit of CSSTATUS to be 1 with $peer_p = q$, p lets q into the CS by writing *true* into Go[q]. q reads the Go[q] flag and enters the CS. Since in the next configuration q and r are in the CS, mutual exclusion is violated. To avoid this issue we use the Go flag as an integer variable so that Go[q] either stores 0 or the token q uses for its current super-passage. This way when p resumes later as described in the scenario above, it tries to CAS into Go[q] with a token that q used in its earlier super-passage. Such a CAS is bound to fail in the scenario above since Go[q] would use a new token in the next super-passage.

The Need for Feature B. Our algorithm is based on a previous RME algorithm by Jayanti and Joshi [7] in which the delegation of ownership of the CS to a process and writing to the spin variable of that process is done by a single process. However, in our algorithm from this paper a process p performs a blind CAS on Go[$peer_p$] at Line **28**, if it finds that a process $peer_p$ occupies the CS, although p might not have made $peer_p$ the owner of the CS. The reason behind designing the algorithm this way is as follows. Suppose a process p is executing the `promote()` procedure such that it executes Lines **23–27**, where it is makes a process q the owner of the CS. However, p crashes just before writing 0 to Go[q] at Line **28**. When p restarts, it cannot tell by reading any of the shared variables if it was the one who made q the owner of the CS (unlike in [7], where reading the CSOWNER variable would give this information). Hence, regardless of whether p made q the owner of CS or not, p assumes the responsibility of waking q from its wait loop and performs the CAS at Line **28**.

The Need for Feature C. When p is aborting from its super-passage by executing the Exit section, at Line **17** it performs a CAS on CSSTATUS to declare that the CS is free in spite of noticing that the CS is free and the first bit of CSSTATUS is 0 already. As we describe below, if this step is not performed, p could be made the owner of CS even though p has aborted its super-passage and is in the Remainder section. Assume that the CAS at Line **17** is not performed and the **if** block at Lines **15–18** contains only one step to write the value 0 to GO[p]. Assume there is a process q in the CS and all other processes including p are in the Remainder section. p decides to acquire access to CS, therefore, it executes the Try section and waits for its turn by looping at Lines **9–10**. q then comes out of the CS and starts executing the Exit section. q executes the Exit section all the way calling the promote() procedure and right upto Line **25** and stops at Line **26**. Therefore, the value of CSSTATUS $= (0, q, tok_q)$ and q has read p's entry from REGISTRY such that q is enabled to perform the CAS at Line **26** and would succeed in doing so. At this moment p decides to abort its super-passage and hence it starts executing the Exit section. p first removes its entry from REGISTRY at Line **13** (therefore, REGISTRY becomes empty now). Since p was not woken up by q to go into the CS, GO[p] $= tok_p$, hence p writes 0 to GO[p] at Line **18**. The **if** condition at Line **20** is not met (since CSSTATUS $= (0, q, tok_q)$), therefore, p calls the promote() procedure at Line **21**. Inside the call to promote(), p finds that the REGISTRY is empty at Line **25**, and the **if** condition at Line **28** is not met because CSSTATUS $= (0, q, tok_q)$. Hence, p completes promote() without modifying any shared variable, goes back to Exit where it writes *false* to EXITING[p] and then goes back to Remainder. At this point q resumes execution and performs the CAS at Line **26**. Since CSSTATUS is unchanged in the meantime, q succeeds in doing the CAS thus making p the owner of the CS. This situation is undesirable because p is in the Remainder section and is made the owner of the CS. If instead the CAS at Line **18** is performed by p, then q's CAS at Line **26** would not succeed and hence the undesirable situation is avoided.

The Need for Feature D. When p aborts from its super-passage, it is possible that p is made the owner of the CS even though it is aborting. In such a scenario it is necessary that p relinquishes its ownership of the CS and continues with the abort. We demonstrate below (with an argument similar to the above) that not performing Lines **19–20** when p is aborting leads to an undesirable scenario. Like above, assume there is a process q in the CS and all other processes including p are in the Remainder section. p decides to acquire access to CS, therefore, it executes the Try section and waits for its turn by looping at Lines **9–10**. q then comes out of the CS and starts executing the Exit section. q executes the

Exit section all the way calling the promote() procedure and right upto Line **27** and stops at Line **28**. Therefore, the value of CSSTATUS $= (1, p, tok_p)$ and q is enabled to perform the CAS at Line **28**. At this moment p decides to abort its super-passage and hence it starts executing the Exit section. p first removes its entry from REGISTRY at Line **13** (therefore, REGISTRY becomes empty now). Since p was not woken up by q to go into the CS, $\mathrm{GO}[p] = tok_p$, hence p writes 0 to $\mathrm{GO}[p]$ (the **if** condition at Line **17** fails due to the value of CSSTATUS). By our assumption p does not perform Lines **19–20** but executes promote() procedure at Line **21** where it sets its own $\mathrm{GO}[p]$ variable to 0 at Line **28** (because CSSTATUS $= (1, p, tok_p)$). It then goes back to the Remainder after updating EXITING[p]. At this moment q starts taking steps and is unsuccessful at the CAS at Line **28**. q then goes back to the Remainder after updating EXITING[q]. It follows that CSSTATUS $= (1, p, tok_p)$, where tok_p is the token p used in previous super-passage, although p is in Remainder. Had p performed Lines **19–20**, it would have updated CSSTATUS to $(0, p, tok_p)$ denoting that the CS should be kept free.

3.4   RMR Complexity

We discuss the RMR complexity a process incurs per passage as follows. As described in Lemma 2 of Jayanti and Joshi's work [7], the REGISTRY.write() operation incurs $O(\log n)$ RMRs and the REGISTRY.findmin() operation incurs $O(1)$ RMRs on both CC and DSM machines. On DSM machines, where we host the variables $\mathrm{GO}[p]$ and EXITING[p] in p's memory partition, p's operations on these variables incur zero RMRs. Therefore, on DSM machines our algorithm incurs $O(\log n)$ RMR per passage.

On CC machines, similarly, it would be tempting to believe that all these other operations incur constant RMRs, however, it depends on the way the cache is managed in the machine. Therefore, for this discussion we divide CC machines into two categories: (1) *strict* CC machines and (2) *relaxed* CC machines, which we describe below and discuss how the RMR is calculated in each category. On *strict* CC machines, a process will incur an RMR when a failed CAS is performed on a variable it is about to read even though the process had a cached copy of the variable prior to the CAS. On *relaxed* CC machines a process will not incur an RMR if a CAS operation fails on a variable it is about to read. Note, this behavior of incurring RMRs on CC machines is in addition to our discussion from Sect. 2. Therefore, the RMR complexity remains $O(\log n)$ on the relaxed CC machines (similar to DSM machines), but shoots up to $O(n)$ on strict CC machines for the following reason. Assume a process p is waiting to enter the CS at Line **9**, $n/2 - 1$ processes are in the Remainder section and there are $n/2$ processes that are about to execute Line **28** to perform a CAS on $\mathrm{GO}[p]$. Out of these processes only one performs the CAS, goes back to the Remainder while letting p into the CS due to the CAS, and the rest $n/2 - 1$ process have still not executed Line **28**. Now there are $n/2$ processes in the Remainder section, p in the CS, and $n/2 - 1$ processes that are about to execute Line **28** to perform a CAS on $\mathrm{GO}[p]$. Assume p completes the CS, executes the Exit section, and goes back to Remainder section. Meanwhile the $n/2$ processes from Remainder come out of the Remainder for a new passage and queue up. p then queues up behind these processes with a new token and starts waiting at Line **9** to enter the CS. At this moment those $n/2 - 1$ processes that had stopped at Line **28** execute a step causing a failed CAS. This causes p to incur an RMR for every failed CAS incurring $O(n)$ RMRs. Therefore, on strict CC machines our algorithm incurs $O(n)$ RMRs per passage. To summarize, the algorithm incurs $O(\log n)$ RMRs per passage on DSM and relaxed CC machines, and $O(n)$ RMRs per passage on strict CC machines. Likewise, it incurs $O(f + \log n)$ RMRs per super-passage on DSM and relaxed CC machines, and $O(f + n)$ RMRs per super-passage on strict CC machines.

3.5   Main Theorem

The theorem below summarizes the result of our paper.

Theorem 1. *The algorithm in Fig. 1 is an abortable recoverable mutual exclusion algorithm for n processes and satisfies properties P1-P8 described in Sect. 2. The algorithm incurs $O(\log n)$ RMRs per passage on DSM and relaxed CC machines and $O(n)$ RMRs per passage on strict CC machines.*

References

1. Raoux, S., et al.: Phase-change random access memory: a scalable technology. IBM J. Res. Dev. **52**(4/5), 465 (2008)
2. Strukov, D.B., Snider, G.S., Stewart, D.R., Williams, R.S.: The missing memristor found. Nature **453**(7191), 80 (2008)
3. Tehrani, S., et al.: Magnetoresistive random access memory using magnetic tunnel junctions. Proce. IEEE **91**(5), 703–714 (2003)
4. Dijkstra, E.W.: Solution of a problem in concurrent programming control. Commun. ACM **8**(9), 569 (1965)
5. Golab, W., Ramaraju, A.: Recoverable mutual exclusion: [extended abstract]. In: Proceedings of the 2016 ACM Symposium on Principles of Distributed Computing, PODC 2016, pp. 65–74. ACM, New York (2016)
6. Golab, W., Hendler, D.: Recoverable mutual exclusion in sub-logarithmic time. In: Proceedings of the ACM Symposium on Principles of Distributed Computing, PODC 2017, pp. 211–220. ACM, New York (2017)
7. Jayanti, P., Joshi, A.: Recoverable FCFS mutual exclusion with wait-free recovery. In: 31st International Symposium on Distributed Computing, DISC 2017, pp. 30:1–30:15 (2017)
8. Golab, W., Hendler, D.: Recoverable mutual exclusion under system-wide failures. In: Proceedings of the 2018 ACM Symposium on Principles of Distributed Computing, PODC 2018, pp. 17–26. ACM, New York (2018)
9. Jayanti, P., Jayanti, S., Joshi, A.: Optimal recoverable mutual exclusion using only FASAS. In: Podelski, A., Taïani, F. (eds.) NETYS 2018. LNCS, vol. 11028, pp. 191–206. Springer, Cham (2019). https://doi.org/10.1007/978-3-030-05529-5_13

10. Jayanti, P., Jayanti, S., Joshi, A.: Recoverable Mutual Exclusion with Sublogarithmic RMR Complexity on CC and DSM machines. In: Accepted for publication in PODC 2019 (2019)
11. Ramaraju, A.: RGLock: recoverable mutual exclusion for non-volatile main memory systems. Master's thesis, University of Waterloo (2015)
12. Lamport, L.: A new solution of Dijkstra's concurrent programming problem. Commun. ACM **17**(8), 453–455 (1974)
13. Attiya, H., Ben-Baruch, O., Hendler, D.: Nesting-safe recoverable linearizability: modular constructions for non-volatile memory. In: Proceedings of the 2018 ACM Symposium on Principles of Distributed Computing, pp. 7–16. ACM (2018)
14. Scott, M.L.: Non-blocking timeout in scalable queue-based spin locks. In: Proceedings of the Twenty-First Annual Symposium on Principles of Distributed Computing, PODC 2002, pp. 31–40. ACM, New York (2002)
15. Scott, M.L., Scherer, W.N.: Scalable queue-based spin locks with timeout. In: Proceedings of the Eighth ACM SIGPLAN Symposium on Principles and Practices of Parallel Programming, PPoPP 2001, pp. 44–52. ACM, New York (2001)
16. Mellor-Crummey, J.M., Scott, M.L.: Algorithms for scalable synchronization on shared-memory multiprocessors. ACM Trans. Comput. Syst. **9**(1), 21–65 (1991)
17. Craig, T.S.: Building FIFO and priority-queuing spin locks from atomic swap. Technical report TR-93-02-02, Department of Computer Science, University of Washington, February 1993
18. Jayanti, P.: Adaptive and efficient abortable mutual exclusion. In: Proceedings of the Twenty-Second Annual Symposium on Principles of Distributed Computing, PODC 2003, pp. 295–304. ACM, New York (2003)
19. Attiya, H., Hendler, D., Woelfel, P.: Tight RMR lower bounds for mutual exclusion and other problems. In: Proceedings of the Fortieth ACM Symposium on Theory of Computing, STOC 2008, pp. 217–226. ACM, New York (2008)
20. Lee, H.: Fast local-spin abortable mutual exclusion with bounded space. In: Lu, C., Masuzawa, T., Mosbah, M. (eds.) OPODIS 2010. LNCS, vol. 6490, pp. 364–379. Springer, Heidelberg (2010). https://doi.org/10.1007/978-3-642-17653-1_27
21. Alon, A., Morrison, A.: Deterministic abortable mutual exclusion with sublogarithmic adaptive RMR complexity. In: Proceedings of the 2018 ACM Symposium on Principles of Distributed Computing, PODC 2018, pp. 27–36. ACM, New York (2018)
22. Jayanti, P., Jayanti, S.V.: Constant amortized RMR complexity deterministic abortable mutual exclusion algorithm for CC and DSM models. In: Accepted for publication in PODC 2019 (2019)
23. Pareek, A., Woelfel, P.: RMR-efficient randomized abortable mutual exclusion. In: Aguilera, M.K. (ed.) DISC 2012. LNCS, vol. 7611, pp. 267–281. Springer, Heidelberg (2012). https://doi.org/10.1007/978-3-642-33651-5_19
24. Giakkoupis, G., Woelfel, P.: Randomized abortable mutual exclusion with constant amortized RMR complexity on the CC model. In: Proceedings of the ACM Symposium on Principles of Distributed Computing, PODC 2017, pp. 221–229. ACM, New York (2017)
25. Jayanti, P.: f-arrays: implementation and applications. In: Proceedings of the Twenty-First Symposium on Principles of Distributed Computing, PODC 2002, pp. 270–279. ACM, New York (2002)

Security

An Efficient Network IDS for Cloud Environments Based on a Combination of Deep Learning and an Optimized Self-adaptive Heuristic Search Algorithm

Zouhair Chiba$^{(\boxtimes)}$, Noreddine Abghour, Khalid Moussaid,
Amina El Omri, and Mohamed Rida

LIMSAD Labs, Faculty of Sciences Ain Chock,
Hassan II University of Casablanca, 20100 Casablanca, Morocco
`chiba.zouhair@gmail.com`, {`NOREDDINE.ABGHOUR,`
`KHALID.MOUSSAID, AMINA.ELOMRI, MOHAMED.RIDA`}`@univh2c.ma`

Abstract. Nowadays, Cloud Computing (CC) is one of the fastest emerging core technologies in the current information era. It is leading a new revolution on the ways of data storage and calculation. CC remains gaining traction among organizations thanks to its appealing features like pay-per-use model for billing customers, elasticity, ubiquity, scalability and availability of resources for businesses. Hence, many organizations are moving their workloads or processes to cloud due to its inherent advantages. Nevertheless, several security issues arise with the transition to this computing paradigm including intrusion detection. Attackers and intruders developed new sophisticated tools defeating traditional Intrusion Detection Systems (IDS) by huge amount of network traffic data and dynamic behaviors. The existing Cloud IDSs suffer from low detection accuracy and high false positive rate. To overcome this issue, we propose a smart approach using a self-adaptive heuristic search algorithm called "Improved Self-Adaptive Genetic Algorithm" (ISAGA) to build automatically a Deep Neural Network (DNN) based Anomaly Network Intrusion Detection System (ANIDS). ISAGA is a variant of standard Genetic Algorithm (GA), which is developed based on GA improved through an Adaptive Mutation Algorithm (AMA) and optimization strategies. The optimization strategies carried out are Parallel Processing and Fitness Value Hashing that reduce execution time, convergence time and save processing power. Our approach consists of using ISAGA with the goal of searching the optimal or near optimal combination of most relevant values of the parameters included in construction of DNN based IDS or impacting its performance, like feature selection, data normalization, architecture of DNN, activation function, learning rate and Momentum term, which ensure high detection rate, high accuracy and low false alarm rate. CloudSim 4.0 simulator platform and CICIDS2017 dataset were used for simulation and validation of the proposed system. The implementation results obtained have demonstrated the ability of our ANIDS to detect intrusions with high detection accuracy and low false alarm rate, and have indicated its superiority in comparison with state-of-the-art methods.

© Springer Nature Switzerland AG 2019
M. F. Atig and A. A. Schwarzmann (Eds.): NETYS 2019, LNCS 11704, pp. 235–249, 2019.
https://doi.org/10.1007/978-3-030-31277-0_15

Keywords: Cloud computing · Anomaly detection ·
Network intrusion detection system · Deep Neural Network · Optimization ·
Genetic algorithm · Adaptive Mutation Algorithm · Heuristic search algorithm ·
Parallel processing · Fitness value hashing · CICIDS2017 dataset

1   Introduction

In the recent decade, adoption of Cloud Computing is increasing at an unprecedented pace. There is a steady rise in the number of companies adopting and moving their workloads to cloud. On demand elasticity, and other benefits including diversity of resources, reliability and cost flexibility have led enterprises to pursue the development and operations of their applications in a "cloud-first" fashion [1]. Cloud computing (CC) can be defined in many manners. There is no universal definition for it. NIST's (National Institute of Standards and Technology) definition of CC is considered as the de facto definition. According to NIST, "Cloud computing is a model for enabling ubiquitous, convenient, on-demand network access to a shared pool of configurable computing resources (e.g., networks, servers, storage, applications and services) that can be rapidly provisioned and released with minimal management effort and or service provider interaction" [2]. The key characteristics of cloud computing are; On-demand self-service, Broad network access, Resource pooling, Rapid elasticity and Measured service. Moreover, CC provides mainly three delivery models, namely Infrastructure as a Service (IaaS), Platform-as a Service (PaaS), Software as a Service (SaaS), which can be used by various organizations to solve their data storage and processing needs. Nowadays, everyone is using cloud computing in our day to day life in one form or another without realizing it, like Microsoft Office 365, Gmail and Dropbox etc. There are many advantages of using cloud computing such as anytime-anywhere accessibility, better geographic coverage with the fastest time, less investment on infrastructure, etc., but there are also challenges using cloud computing like data security, lack of resources and expertise etc. Among the challenges, data security stands very tall [3]. In fact, based on the survey conducted by a leading SaaS provider, RightScale, one of the major challenge in the adoption of CC is security as shown in Fig. 1.

In any business or Cloud Computing data are exceptionally prominent, data leaking or corruption can shatter the confidence of the people and can lead to the collapse of that business. Currently cloud computing is used directly or indirectly in many businesses and if any data breaching has happened in cloud computing, that will affect the cloud computing as well as the company's business. This is one of the principal reasons for cloud customers and cloud services provides give more attention to data security [3]. Mostly, the leakage and damage of important information has occurred frequently in some cloud services because of network intrusion [4]. Intrusion and attack tools have become more sophisticated challenging existing network Cloud IDSs by large volumes of network traffic data, dynamic and complex behaviors and new types of attacks. It is obvious that a network Cloud IDS should analyze large volumes of network traffic data, detect efficiently the new attack behaviors and reach high accuracy with low false. However, preprocessing, analyzing and detecting intrusions in Cloud environments using traditional techniques have become very costly in terms of computation, time and budget. Therefore, efficient intrusions detection in Cloud environments requires adoption of new intelligent techniques such as Machine Learning techniques [5].

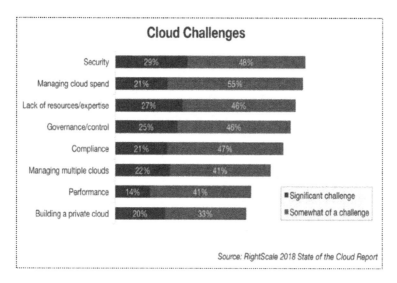

Fig. 1. Cloud challenges in 2018

In this work, we propose an intelligent approach using a self-adaptive heuristic search algorithm called "Improved Self-Adaptive Genetic Algorithm (ISAGA)" to build automatically a Deep Neural Network (DNN) based anomaly Network IDS (NIDS). DNN has been widely studied in machine learning research field and amply used for practical applications in image processing computer vision and speech recognition, etc. Hence, DNN is adopted in this study as it shows prominent classification performance [6]. ISAGA is a variant of standard Genetic Algorithm (GA), which is developed based on GA, improved through an Adaptive Mutation Algorithm (AMA) [7] and optimization strategies. AMA allows to automatically adjust the mutation rate should be applied for any given individual from the population of ISAGA, in order to augment the chance of preserving individuals that are performing well versus the optimization problem in hand and reduce the chance of preserving individuals that don't perform well. That tuning or adjustment of mutation rate takes place while ISAGA is running, hopefully resulting in the best parameters being used at any specific time during execution. It is this continuous adaptive adjustment of ISAGA parameters that will often result in its performance improvement. Further, ISAGA is optimized through optimization strategies, like Parallel Processing and Fitness Value Hashing, which reduce execution time, convergence time and save processing power. As the fitness function is typically the most computationally expensive component, and it is often going to be the bottleneck of GA, this makes it an ideal candidate for multi-core optimization (Parallel Processing). By using multiple cores, it is possible to compute the fitness of numerous individuals simultaneously. Besides, Fitness Value

Hashing is another strategy that can reduce the amount of time spent computing fitness values by storing previously calculated fitness values in a hash table. Thereby, when a previously visited solution (chromosome) is revisited, its fitness value can be retrieved from the hash table, avoiding the need to recalculate it.

Our approach consists of using ISAGA with the goal of searching the optimal or near-optimal combination of most relevant values of the parameters included in construction of DNN based IDS or impacting its performance, like feature selection, data normalization, architecture of DNN, activation function, learning rate and momentum term, which ensure high detection rate, high accuracy and low false alarm rate. In addition, the proposed IDS is designed to be deployed in both front-end and back-end of the cloud. Consequently, that helps to detect attacks from external network of the cloud and also internal attacks either in internal physical network or virtual network within hypervisors.

The rest of this paper is organized as follows: Sect. 2 introduces previous research works. Section 3 presents positions of the proposed system in a Cloud Network. Section 4 provides the necessary background to understand operation of AMA and the role of the optimization strategies incorporated to ISAGA. Next, Sect. 5 explains our proposed approach. Experimental results and analysis are given in Sect. 6. Finally, Sect. 7 ends with conclusions.

2   Literature Review

Mehmood et al. [8] have proposed a Distributed Intrusion Detection System using Mobile Agents in Cloud Computing (DIDMACC) to detect distributed attacks in Cloud. They have used mobile agents to carry intrusion alerts collected from different VMs where Suricata NIDS is deployed to the management server. In this server, the correlation module (Open Source Security Information Management (OSSIM) correlation engine) correlates intrusion alerts to generate high level alerts that correspond to a distributed attack. Then, the management server sends the signature of a detected attack to all virtual machines monitored, to update the signature database of local Suricata IDS to avoid such intrusions in future. The results show that the use of mobile agents to carry intrusion-related data and code reduces network load, and correlation of intrusive events collected by those mobile agents by means of a correlation engine helps in detection of distributed intrusions. However, the proposed system can't detect zero-day attacks or unknown attacks.

Mehibs and Hachim [9] have proposed Back Propagation Artificial Neural Network to build network intrusion detection system with the goal to detect intruders and suspicious activities in and around the cloud environment. The proposed module consists of two stages, the learning stage and the test stage. In the first stage, this model is trained with back propagation algorithm using KDD 99 dataset to classify normal behavior and the other four types of attack (DOS, Probe, U2R, and R2L). In the second stage, the trained module is evaluated with three datasets to predict the class label of test samples. The topology adopted for neural network of proposed IDS consists of three layers (input layer, hidden layer, output layer); the number of neurons in input layer is equal to 41 which is the number of feature in KDD99 dataset. The number of neurons in hidden layer is equal to 20, which is determined after trial and error. In the output layer, the number of neuron is equal to 5 which correspond to the normal behavior and the four types of attack. The experimental result demonstrates effectiveness of the proposed NIDS characterized by high detection rate and low false alarm.

Saljoughi et al. [10] have presented a network intrusion detection system (NIDS) for Cloud environment using Multilayer Perceptron Neural Network (MLP) and Particle Swarm Optimization Algorithm (PSO) to detect intrusions and attacks. The PSO algorithm was utilized to find the best weights and biases of the neural network (MLP), which is then trained by trained data and the obtained optimal weights. In order to have the most efficiency and security, the proposed NIDS is placed in the network, and it is connected directly to the router of the Cloud, and the others similar NIDS are installed on the processing servers. All NIDS send attack incidents to a central server with a large storage space; and if necessary, this data will be used by the proposed system. The results obtained from optimization of the neural network using the Particle Swarm algorithm showed a substantial improvement in the function of the NIDS based on MLP, in terms of the precision of detecting attacks faced by the networks and reduction of time complexities.

Navimipour and Hajimirzaei [11] have developed new intrusion detection system (IDS) based on a combination of a multilayer perceptron (MLP) network, and artificial bee colony (ABC) and Fuzzy C-means (FCM) clustering algorithm. An ANN can operate alone in an IDS, but the combination of ANN, ABC, and fuzzy clustering makes an IDS more powerful and efficient. The proposed method involves three phases, which are training, validation, and testing. The homogeneous subsets of training data are prepared with fuzzy clustering. Consequently, the training speed rate is enhanced by separating the dataset into uniform subsets. During training phase, after performing the clustering, MLP network with backpropagation (BP) algorithm is used to build and train the IDS model. The steepest descent method is adapted to the BP learning rule. The weight and threshold value of the network are adjusted by BP to reach a low-error sum of squares. With BP, the gradient descent method is used to balance the weight values of all layers. Generally, the initial weights of the network are generated in random way within a certain interval; the training starts with this starting point and proceeds step by step to a minimum error. The ABC helps the MLP to determine ideal/optimal values for linkage weights and biases more rapidly. The performance of the system is precisely assessed in the validation phase. Finally, in the testing phase, intrusion detection is processed by passing the test data through the previously-trained model. The CloudSim simulator and NSL-KDD dataset are used to verify the proposed model. Various evaluation criteria, such Mean absolute error (MAE), root mean square error (RMSE), and the kappa statistic are used to compare similar IDSs with the proposed method. The obtained results have demonstrated the superiority of the proposed method in comparison with other state-of-the-art methods.

Ghosh et al. [12] have designed a network intrusion detection system to detect attacks and malicious activities in Cloud environment. The proposed IDS includes two stages. The first stage consists of creation of a feature subset by using a novel algorithm called BCS-GA which combines the advantages of Binary Cuckoo search algorithm (BCS) and Genetic Algorithm (GA). The proposed BCS-GA algorithm was applied on NSL-KDD training dataset to remove several irrelevant features, in order to reduce the training time and memory storage space required for such high dimensional dataset. Thus, initial NSL-KDD dataset contains 41 features, but after applying BCS-GA algorithm, it successfully reduced to 16 features. In the second stage, Neural Network classifier was trained by the reduced training dataset using 16 features. Thereafter, classification accuracy of that classifier was tested by means of a separate reduced testing dataset. Experimental results indicate that the proposed IDS produces 78.229% of accuracy.

3   Positioning of the Proposed System in a Cloud Network

The aim of our proposed IDS is to detect intruders and suspicious activities in and around the Cloud Computing environment by monitoring network traffic, while maintaining confidentiality, availability, integrity and performance of cloud resources and offered services. It allows detecting and stopping attacks in real time impairing the security of the Cloud Datacenter.

As shown in Fig. 2, we propose to place our NIDS on two strategic positions:

1. **Front-End of Cloud:** Placing NIDS on front end of Cloud helps to detect network intrusions or attacks coming from external network of Cloud, launched from zombie hosts or by hackers connected to the Internet who attempt to bypass the firewall in order to access the internal cloud, which can be a private one. Therefore, NIDS plays the role of the second line of defense behind the firewall to overcome its limitations and acts as an additional preventive layer of security.

2. **Back-End of Cloud:** Positioning NIDS sensors on processing servers located at back end of the Cloud helps to detect intrusions occurring on its internal network. In a virtual environment, we have many virtual machines on the same physical server, and they can inter-communicate through the virtual switch without leaving the physical server. Thus, network security devices on the LAN can't monitor this network traffic; if the traffic does not need to pass through security appliances primarily a firewall, therefore, a loophole for all kinds of security attacks will be opened. Hence, the starting point of an attacker/hacker is compromising only one VM, and using it as a springboard to take control of the other VMs within the same hypervisor. This is generally done without being monitored or detected, giving the attacker a huge hack domain. Moreover, the virtual environment is exposed to various threats and risks, centered mostly on the hypervisor; Hyper jacking, VM escape, VM migration, VM theft and Inter-VM traffic.

Our NIDS is designed to monitor that virtual traffic, and also the flow of traffic from or to the processing server on the physical network. We haven't chosen to install the NIDS on each virtual machine because it will be an additional burden; it will weigh down the work of the VM. Further, such configuration requires multiple instances of NIDS, which makes complex management of NIDS, whereas VMs are dynamically migrated, provisioned or de-provisioned.

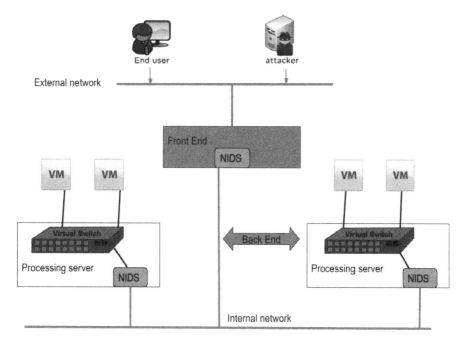

Fig. 2. Positions of proposed ANIDS-DNNISAGA in a cloud network

4   Related Background

As mentioned previously, ISAGA used in this work is a variant of standard Genetic Algorithm (GA), which is developed based on GA, improved through an Adaptive Mutation Algorithm (AMA) and optimization strategies. Hence, this section provides the necessary background to understand operation of AMA and the role of those optimization strategies. First subsection briefly presents Adaptive Genetic Algorithms, especially Adaptive Mutation Algorithm (AMA). While, the second subsection introduces and explains the role of the optimization strategies applied to GA, namely Parallel Processing and Fitness Value Hashing.

4.1   Adaptive Genetic Algorithms: Adaptive Mutation Algorithm

Adaptive Genetic Algorithms (AGA) [7] are a popular subset of genetic algorithms, which can provide significant performance improvements over standard implementations when utilized in the suitable circumstances. A key factor that determines how well a genetic algorithm (GA) will perform is the manner in which its parameters are configured. Thus, finding the right values for the mutation rate and crossover rate plays in substantial role when building an efficient and effective GA. Typically, configuring the parameters will require some trial and error, together with some intuition, before eventually attaining a satisfactory configuration. AGA are useful because they can help in the tuning of these parameters automatically by adjusting them based on the state of the algorithm. These parameter adjustments take place while GA is running, hopefully resulting in the best parameters being used at any specific time during execution. It is this continuous adaptive adjustment of GA parameters that will often result in its performance improvement. AGA used in this work uses information such as the average population fitness and the population's current best fitness to calculate and update its parameters in a way that best suits its present state. For example, by comparing any specific individual to the current fittest individual in the population, it's possible to gauge how well that individual is performing in relation to the current best. Typically, we want to augment the chance of preserving individuals that are performing well and reduce the chance of preserving individuals that don't perform well. One way we can do this is by allowing the algorithm to adaptively update the *mutation rate*. We can determine if the algorithm has started to converge by calculating the difference between the current best fitness and the average population fitness. When the average population fitness is close to the current best fitness, we know the population has started to converge around a small area of the search space. When calculating what the mutation rate should be for any given individual, two of the most important factors/characteristics to consider are how well the current individual is performing and how well the entire population is performing as a whole. The algorithm we had used in this work to assess these two characteristics and update the mutation rate is called **Adaptive Mutation Algorithm**, and it is defined by Eqs. (1) and (2).

f_i: Is the fitness value (score) of the current individual identified by the index i.

f_{max}: Is the best fitness from the population.

f_{avg}: Is the average population fitness.

m: Is the mutation rate that was set during initialization of GA.

p_m: Is the new mutation rate that should be applied for the current individual.

$$p_m = (f_{max} - f_i)/(f_{max} - f_{avg}) \times m, \ f_i > f_{avg} \tag{1}$$

$$p_m = m, \ f_i \leq f_{avg} \tag{2}$$

As shown by the Eq. 1, when the individual's fitness (f_i) is higher than the population's average fitness (f_{avg}), firstly, we calculate the difference between f_{max} and f_i. Afterwards, we compute the difference between f_{max} and f_{avg} and perform the division of the two resulted values. At last, we use the quotient of previous division to scale the mutation rate (m) that was set during initialization. Otherwise, as indicated by Eq. 2, if the individual's fitness is the same or less than the population's average fitness, we simply use the mutation rate as set during initialization. Adaptive genetic algorithm can be employed to adjust more than just the mutation rate however. Similar technique can be applied to adjust other parameters of the genetic algorithm like the crossover rate to get further improvements as needed.

4.2   Optimization Strategies for Genetic Algorithm

With the fitness function, typically being the most processing demanding component of genetic algorithm (GA), it makes sense to focus on improvement of the fitness function to see the best return in performance. In this section, we will explore two optimization strategies that are used in this work to improve performance of GA by optimizing the fitness function, namely **Parallel Processing** and **Fitness Value Hashing**.

Parallel Processing

One of the easiest approaches to achieve a performance enhancement of GA is by optimizing the fitness function. The fitness function is typically the most computationally expensive component; and it is often going to be the bottleneck of GA. This makes it an ideal candidate for multi-core optimization. By using multiple cores, it is possible to compute the fitness of numerous individuals simultaneously, which makes a tremendous difference when there are often hundreds of individuals to evaluate per population. Java 8 provides some very useful libraries that make supporting parallel processing in our GA much easier. Using *Java's IntStream*, we can implement parallel processing in our fitness function without worrying about the fine details of parallel processing (such as the number of cores we need to support); it will instead create an optimal number of threads depending on the number of cores available in our multi-core system. Hence, by using parallel processing, fitness function will be able to run across multiple cores of the computer. Consequently, it is possible to considerably reduce the amount of time the GA spends evaluating individuals and, so reduce the overall time of execution of GA, and accelerate convergence process [7].

Fitness Value Hashing

Fitness Value Hashing is another strategy that can reduce the amount of time spent computing fitness values by storing previously calculated fitness values in a hash table [7]. During running of GA, solutions found previously will occasionally be revisited due to the random mutations and recombinations of individuals. This occasional revisiting of solutions becomes more common as GA converges and begins to find solutions in an increasingly smaller area of the search space. Each time a solution is revisited its fitness value needs to be recalculated, wasting processing power on recurrent, duplicate computations. Luckily, this can be easily fixed by storing fitness values in a hash table after they have been computed. When a previously visited solution is revisited, its fitness value can be retrieved from the hash table, avoiding the need to recalculate it.

5 The Proposed System

Our approach consists of using a self-adaptive heuristic search algorithm called "Improved Self-Adaptive Genetic Algorithm (ISAGA)" to build automatically a Deep Neural Network (DNN) based anomaly Network IDS (NIDS). ISAGA is a variant of standard Genetic Algorithm (GA), which is developed based on GA, improved through an Adaptive Mutation Algorithm (AMA) (Subsect. 4.1) and optimization strategies (Subsect. 4.2). Our DNN is a Back Propagation Neural network (BPNN) with one input layer, two hidden layers and one output layer. The number of nodes in the input layer corresponds to the number of attributes/features in the vector of connection instance from IDS datasets received by DNN, while the number of nodes in each hidden layer will be generated by ISAGA. Whereas, the output layer comprises one node, which gives a value of 1 in case of classification of input pattern by DNN as normal traffic, otherwise, it provides a value of 0 to indicate an intrusion. Our approach includes mainly four stages. In two first stages, we have studied deeply several works related to intrusion detection systems based on BPNN or DNN.

The first stage was focused on the determination of the most relevant parameters employed to construct that type of classifier or that affect its performance. As shown by Table 1, at the end of our study, we have concluded that the most important parameters are [13]: The number of selected features/attributes, that corresponds to the number of nodes in the input layer, Normalization of data, Architecture of Neural Network, specifically the number of nodes in the hidden layer(s), Activation function or transfer function, Learning rate and Momentum term.

The second stage consists of comparison of studied works in order to select for each parameter cited above, between two and four relevant and pertinent values, which have given the best results in terms of intrusion detection.

Table 1. List of parameters influencing the performance of a BPNN or a DNN based IDS and their different values

Parameters	Different values
Number of attributes	10 attributes CIDDS-001 [14]
	70 attributes CICIDS2017 [15]
	14 attributes Kyoto 2006+ [16]
	12 attributes NSL-KDD [13, 17]
Normalization	Min-max normalization [13]
	Statistical normalization [13]
Activation function	Hyperbolic tangent [13]
	Sigmoid [13]

In our work, ISAGA will generate randomly the number of nodes of both hidden layers of DNN and the values of Learning rate and Momentum term. Through genetic operations such selection, elitism, crossover and mutation, ISAGA algorithm is able to found the ideal values of those parameters. The most of the existing network traffic datasets that are publicly available are either outdated, unlabelled or unreliable. Some of these suffer from lack of traffic diversity and volume, some do not cover the variety of known attacks, while others are missing or hiding features that are present in the most common network protocols. However, the CICIDS2017 dataset [15] generated in 2017 by the Canadian Institute of Cybersecurity overcomes those issues. It represents a dataset that satisfy the eleven indispensable characteristics of a valid IDS dataset, namely Anonymity, Attack Diversity, Complete Capture, Complete Interaction, Complete Network Configuration, Available Protocols, Complete Traffic, Feature Set, Metadata, Heterogeneity and Labelling [18]. Thus, for the purpose of training and evaluating our proposed system, the CICIDS2017 dataset was primarily used. Thereby, the number of inputs in our DNN is fixed at 70 inputs, which corresponds to the number of features selected in [15] from CICIDS2017 dataset.

The third stage: For successful use of ISAGA, two key elements must be well defined; the representation/encoding of chromosomes and the Fitness Function.

- **Chromosome encoding/representation:** In our study, we have chosen the binary representation for chromosomes. Each chromosome is a possible combination of values of the pertinent parameters mentioned previously, that will be used to construct an instance of IDS based DNN. Each parameter constitutes a gene in the chromosome, as indicated by Table 2. Hence, each chromosome takes the form of a binary string of 58 bits. Binary substrings corresponding to learning rate and Momentum term genes of a chromosome are converted into decimal values, then normalized using the Min-Max normalization technique to get values between 0 and 1, which will be serve as Learning rate and Momentum term of the IDS generated based on that chromosome.

- **Fitness Function or Evaluation Function:** We have chosen the AUC metric [13] as a score (fitness function) of individuals of ISAGA to assess their adaptability to the optimization problem. The AUC is a performance metric of IDSs, that represents the ability to avoid misclassifications of network packets. From our point of view, it is a good trade-off between DR (Detection Rate) metric and FPR (False Positive Rate) metric. In effect, this is due to the fact that AUC is the arithmetic mean of DR and TNR (1-FPR) as shown by Eq. 3 of the AUC. As it is known, a good IDS is one that achieves a high detection rate (DR) and low false positive rate (FPR). As demonstrated by Eq. 3, as the value of DR increases and that of FPR decreases, consequently, the value of AUC increases. Therefore, from our point of view, AUC is the best metric for evaluating an IDS. That is the reason of choice of AUC as fitness function.

$$AUC = (DR + TNR)/2 = (DR + (1 - FPR))/2 \qquad (3)$$

The fourth stage: As shown by Fig. 3, ISAGA process begins with a randomly generated population of 1000 individuals (potential solutions) represented by their chromosomes; each chromosome takes the form of a binary string of 58 bits. Then, this population evolves through several generations by means of genetic operations such elitism, selection, recombination (crossover) and mutation until stopping or optimization criterion of ISAGA is met. At each generation, for each chromosome, the Fitness Hash Table (FHT) is checked to verify if this chromosome is already visited, in this case, its fitness value is pulled from FHT. Otherwise, this chromosome is used to create an instance of an IDS based on DNN. Afterwards, this IDS firstly goes through the learning phase, then passes to the test/evaluation phase and returns the values of performance metrics calculated at the end of last phase. Among those performance metrics, we select the pertinent of them, namely AUC metric to serve as "Fitness Function" for evaluation of goodness of chromosomes, then AUC (fitness value) value is stored in FHT. From one generation to the next, ISAGA converges towards the global optimum through genetic operations cited previously. Finally, the best individual (chromosome) is picked out as the final result once the optimization criterion is met. In our work, termination condition adopted for ISAGA is production of 200 generations. Hence, the best chromosome resulted corresponds to the optimal or near-optimal values of parameters used to build an ideal IDS based DNN, which yields high detection rate and low false alarm rate.

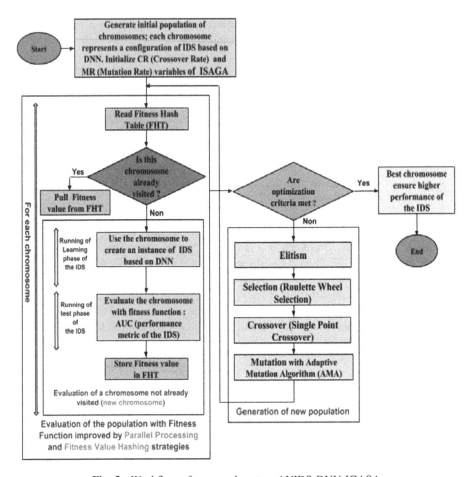

Fig. 3. Workflow of proposed system ANIDS DNN-IGASA

Table 2. Chromosome used by Improved ISAGA

Genes	Number of bits to encode the gene	Possible/Number of values
Normalization	01	**0** (Min-Max normalization) or **1** (Statistical normalization)
Activation function	01	**0** (Hyperbolic tangent) or **1** (Sigmoid)
Nb of nodes in hidden layer 01	08	256
Nb of nodes in hidden layer 02	08	256
Learning rate	20	2^{20} values
Momentum term	20	2^{20} values

6   Experimental Results and Analysis

The experiments were carried out on a Windows 10–64 bits PC with 32 GB RAM and CPU Intel(R) Core-i7 2700 K CPU. For simulation, we have used CloudSim simulator 4.0 and CICIDS2017 dataset. From CICIDS2017, we have extracted two independents subsets, namely training dataset and testing dataset, following the approach adopted by Ahmin et al. in [15]. Thus, among the 80 features of CICIDS2017, 71 relevant features are selected (70 features as input features for DNN plus 01 feature represents Label feature). Whereas, for data preprocessing, numericalization or categorical encoding is used for qualitative feature, namely feature Label, while Min-Max normalization or Statistical normalization (Z-score) are applied to other 70 quantitative features. Table 3 summarizes the distribution and size of these subsets.

Table 3. Distribution and size of training and testing datasets

Dataset	Attack records	Normal records	Total
Training dataset	20000	20000	40000
Testing dataset	20000	20000	40000

The experiments conducted on our proposed system show that at the end of ISAGA process that is to say after 200 generations, the best individual (chromosome) is found. That fittest chromosome allows building the best ANIDS-DNNISAGA. Table 4 shows parameters of the best ANIDS-DNNISAGA obtained and its performances. As indicated by Table 5, our proposed IDS yields best results that other state-of-art methods. Further, optimization strategies incorporated to ISAGA, namely Parallel Processing and Fitness Value Hashing have brought several benefits; 88% reduction of execution time compared to a standard GA, acceleration of the ISAGA convergence process and save of processing power.

Table 4. Parameters and performance of best IDS based DNN obtained using ISAGA

Parameters	Value	Performance metric	Value
Number of nodes in input layer	70	Accuracy	99.88%
Number of nodes in hidden layer 01	45	Precision	99.99%
Number of nodes in hidden layer 02	21	Detection Rate (DR)	99.88%
Number of nodes in output layer	1	False Negative Rate (FNR)	0.12%
Activation function	Sigmoid function	False Positive Rate (FPR)	0.11%
Data normalization	Min-Max normalization	True Negative Rate (TNR)	99.89%
Learning rate	8.754557301698653E-7	F-score	0.99
Momentum rate	1.294012698456624E-4	AUC	99.89%

Table 5. Comparison of performances of our ANIDS-DNNISAGA and other research works

Work	[5]	[9]	[10]	[11]	[12]	[19]	[20]	[21]	Our Proposed IDS: ANIDS-DNNISAGA
Accuracy (%)	98	97.02	99.44	98.42	78.23	93.88		96.53	**99.88**
Precision (%)					96.50		97.2	95.23	**99.99**
FPR (%)	2	0.21			3.07	18.8	1.7	0.56	**0.11**
FNR (%)					35.92				**0.12**
TPR (DR) (%)	99				64.08	96.29	97.3	76.50	**99.88**
TNR (%)		99.79			96.93				**99.89**
F-score					77.02		0.972	0.8484	**0.99**
AUC (%)	98.5				80.50	88.75	87.97	87.97	**99.89**

7 Conclusions and Future Work

In order to develop a powerful ANIDS for detection and prevention of both inside and outside assaults in cloud environments with high detection precision and low false warnings, we have adopted a smart approach to build automatically such IDS based on Deep Neural network (DNN). Our method consists of using Improved Self-Adaptive Genetic Algorithm (ISAGA), with the purpose of searching the optimal values of the parameters included in construction of IDS based DNN (IDSDNN). As result, at the end ISAGA process, the optimal or near-optimal values of parameters used to build an ideal IDSDNN are found, which allows constructing a powerful Anomaly IDS called "ANIDS-DNNISAGA" reaching high detection rate and low false positive rate. Experimental results conducted using CloudSim 4.0 and CICIDS2017 dataset demonstrate that our ANIDS-DNNISAGA outperforms several recent works. More-over, performance improvement strategies integrated in ISAGA have reduced execution time, convergence time and saved processing power. Moreover, we have chosen to place our proposed IDS on Front-End and Back-End of the Cloud, to detect and stop attacks in real time impairing the security of the Cloud Datacenter.

We plan to use other meta-heuristic algorithms such particle swarm optimization, artificial bee colony (ABC) algorithm, ant colony optimization (ACO), crow search algorithm or whale optimization algorithm to compare them with the Optimized Self-Adaptive Heuristic Search Algorithm employed in this paper.

References

1. Verizon, State of the Market: Enterprise Cloud. http://www.verizonenterprise.com/resources/reports/rp_state-of-the-marketenterprise-cloud-2016_en_xg.pdf. Accessed 17 Feb 2019
2. Hogan, M., Sokol, A.: NIST cloud computing standards roadmap. Version 2. NIST Cloud Computing Standards Roadmap Working Group. NIST Special Publications 500-291, NIST, Gaithersburg, MD, pp. 1–113 (2013)
3. Kumar, P.R., Raj, P.H., Jelciana, P.: Exploring data security issues and solutions in cloud computing. Procedia Comput. Sci. **125**, 691–697 (2018)

4. Wang, W., Ren, L., Chen, L., Ding, Y.: Intrusion detection and security calculation in industrial cloud storage based on an improved dynamic immune algorithm. Inf. Sci. **501**, 543–557 (2018)
5. Idhammad, M., Afdel, K., Belouch, M.: Distributed intrusion detection system for cloud environments based on data mining techniques. Procedia Comput. Sci. **127**(C), 35–41 (2018)
6. Krizhevsky, A., Sutskever, I., Hinton, G.E.: ImageNet classification with deep convolutional neural networks. In: Advances in Neural Information Processing Systems, pp. 1097–1105. Curran Associates, Inc., Lake Tahoe (2012)
7. Jacobson, L., Kanbe, B.: Genetic Algorithms in Java Basics, pp. 143–144. Apress, New York (2015)
8. Mehmood, Y., Shibli, M.A., Kanwal, A., Masood, R.: Distributed intrusion detection system using mobile agents in cloud computing environment. In: 2015 Conference on Information Assurance and Cyber Security (CIACS), pp. 1–8. IEEE (2015)
9. Mehibs, S.M., Hashim, S.H.: Proposed network intrusion detection system in cloud environment based on back propagation neural network. J. Univ. Babylon Pure Appl. Sci. **26**(1), 29–40 (2018)
10. Saljoughi, A.S., Mehrvarz, M., Mirvaziri, H.: Attacks and intrusion detection in cloud computing using neural networks and particle swarm optimization algorithms. Emerg. Sci. J. **1**(4), 179–191 (2018)
11. Hajimirzaei, B., Navimipour, N.J.: Intrusion detection for cloud computing using neural networks and artificial bee colony optimization algorithm. ICT Expr. **5**, 56–59 (2018)
12. Ghosh, P., Jha, S., Dutta, R., Phadikar, S.: Intrusion detection system based on BCS-GA in cloud environment. In: Shetty, N.R., Patnaik, L.M., Prasad, N.H., Nalini, N. (eds.) ERCICA 2016, pp. 393–403. Springer, Singapore (2018). https://doi.org/10.1007/978-981-10-4741-1_35
13. Chiba, Z., Abghour, N., Moussaid, K., El Omri, A., Rida, M.: A novel architecture combined with optimal parameters for back propagation neural networks applied to anomaly network intrusion detection. Comput. Secur. **75**, 36–58 (2018)
14. Tama, B.A., Rhee, K.: Attack classification analysis of IoT network via deep learning approach. Res. Briefs Inf. Commun. Technol. Evol. (ReBICTE) **3**, 1–9 (2017)
15. Ahmim, A., Maglaras, L., Ferrag, M.A., Derdour, M., Janicke, H.: A novel hierarchical intrusion detection system based on decision tree and rules-based models. arXiv preprint arXiv:1812.09059 (2018)
16. Musbau, D.A, Alhassan, J.K.: Ensemble learning approach for the enhancement of performance of intrusion detection system. In: International Conference on Information and Communication Technology and its Applications (ICTA 2018), pp. 1–8. CEUR-WS, Minna (2018)
17. The NSL-KDD data set. http://nsl.cs.unb.ca/NSL-KDD. Accessed 17 Feb 2019
18. Gharib, A., Sharafaldin, I., Lashkari, A.H., Ghorbani, A.A.: An evaluation framework for intrusion detection dataset. In: 2016 International Conference on Information Science and Security (ICISS), pp. 1–6. IEEE, Pattaya (2016)
19. Sharma, P., Sengupta, J., Suri, P.K.: WLI-FCM and artificial neural network based cloud intrusion detection system. Int. J. Adv. Network. Appl. **10**(1), 3698–3703 (2018)
20. Aslahi-Shahri, B.M., et al.: A hybrid method consisting of GA and SVM for intrusion detection system. Neural Comput. Appl. **27**(6), 1669–1676 (2016)
21. Hamamoto, A.H., Carvalho, L.F., Sampaio, L.D.H., Abrão, T., Proença Jr., M.L.: Network anomaly detection system using genetic algorithm and fuzzy logic. Expert Syst. Appl. **92**, 390–402 (2018)

Efficient Security Policy Management Using Suspicious Rules Through Access Log Analysis

Maryem Ait El Hadj[1]([✉]), Ahmed Khoumsi[2], Yahya Benkaouz[3],
and Mohammed Erradi[1]

[1] ITM Team, ENSIAS, Mohammed V University in Rabat, Rabat, Morocco
maryem_aitelhadj@um5.ac.ma, mohamed.erradi@gmail.com
[2] Department of Electrical and Computer Engineering, University of Sherbrooke,
Sherbrooke, Canada
ahmed.khoumsi@usherbrooke.ca
[3] Conception and Systems Laboratory, FSR, Mohammed V University in Rabat,
Rabat, Morocco
y.benkaouz@um5s.net.ma

Abstract. Logs record the events and actions performed within an organization's systems and networks. Usually, log data should conform with the security policy in use. However, access logs may show the occurrence of unauthorized accesses which may be due to security breaches, such as intrusions or conflicting rules in security policies. Due to the huge amount of log data generated every day and presumed to grow over time, analyzing access logs becomes a hard task that requires enormous computational resources. In this paper, we suggest a method that analyses an access log, and uses the obtained results to determine whether an Attribute-Based Access Control (ABAC) security policy contains conflicting rules. This access log-based approach allows to obtain an efficient conflict detection method, since conflicts are searched among suspicious rules, instead of all the rules of the policy. Those suspicious rules are identified by analyzing the access log. To improve efficiency even more, the access log is decomposed into clusters which are analyzed separately. Furthermore, cluster representatives make the proposed approach scalable for continuous access log case. The scalability is confirmed by experiment results, and our approach effectively identifies conflicts with an average recall of 95.65%.

Keywords: ABAC policies · Access log clustering and analysis ·
Cluster representative · Suspicious rule · Conflict detection

1 Introduction

Logs contain useful information regarding actions performed within an organization's systems and networks. For instance, when a service fails, logs are

© Springer Nature Switzerland AG 2019
M. F. Atig and A. A. Schwarzmann (Eds.): NETYS 2019, LNCS 11704, pp. 250–266, 2019.
https://doi.org/10.1007/978-3-030-31277-0_16

examined to gain insights into the failure and potential problems (i.e. identify the problem source). Among the various categories of logs, we consider more particularly access logs, that keep track of access requests to existing resources and corresponding decisions to accept or reject these requests.

Traditionally, to identify a failure, a simple keyword search within logs (e.g. "warning", "error") is performed. However, such an approach is often time consuming. Due to the huge amount of access log data generated every day and presumed to grow over time, analyzing access logs becomes a hard task that requires enormous computational resources, and sophisticated procedures. Thus, it is interesting to offer adequate and efficient techniques for access logs analysis. Usually, access logs should conform with the security policy in use. However, access logs may show the occurrence of unauthorized accesses, which may be due to security breaches, such as intrusions or conflicting rules in security policies. In this paper, we suggest a method that decomposes an access log into clusters which are analyzed separately, and uses the obtained results to determine whether an Attribute-Based Access Control (ABAC) [24] security policy contains conflicting rules. The latter are searched among suspicious rules, instead of all the rules of the policy. Those suspicious rules are obtained by analyzing the access log.

The remainder of this paper is structured as follows: We begin in Sect. 2 by presenting the motivation and methodology of using access logs analysis for detecting security conflicts. Section 3 presents our method to analyze an access log. In Sect. 4, we present how we detect conflicting rules of a security policy, based on the access log analysis results. Section 5 reports and discusses experimental results. Related work are given in Sect. 6. Finally, the conclusion and expected future work are presented in Sect. 7.

2 Motivation and Methodology

A (security) policy is specified by a set of rules that describe authorized accesses as well as unauthorized ones. Detecting conflicts in a policy can be naturally be done by analyzing all the rules of the policy. Let us consider the case of an evolutive policy, i.e. a policy to which rules are added from time to time. Since adding a new rule may generate conflicts with other rules of the policy [5], evolutive policies should therefore be analyzed regularly. The question that arises is then:

– Since just a few rules are added between two analyses, is it possible to analyze the policy by considering only some of its rules, instead of all its rules?

To answer the above question which is motivated by the desire of efficiency, we suggest to use an access log, with the idea that conflicting rules in the policy should cause contradictory access records in the access log. Consider a policy P and an access log L. Our approach is then to detect contradictory access records in L, from which we deduce suspicious rules in P that could have caused the contradictions. Then, conflicts are searched only among suspicious rules, instead of all rules.

Let us illustrate our idea with a policy P where rules are added like in a stack, i.e. the last added rule in P is the first rule of P. Also, we assume that P uses $First\text{-}Applicable$ strategy, i.e. when an access request rq occurs, P applies the first rule that matches rq (i.e. the first rule whose conditions are satisfied by rq). Let the following r_1 be the current first rule of P:

– r_1: $Permit_{\{read\}}$ (IpAdressSRC = 10.1.1.122, DepartmentSRC = Production, IpAdressDST = 10.1.1.120, DepartmentDST = Production)

Intuitively, this rule indicates that the machine belonging to the production department with IP address "10.1.1.122" has the right to read in the service having IP address "10.1.1.120". Consider an access request rq, where a service with IP address "10.1.1.122" requests to read the resource with IP address "10.1.1.120" that belongs to the production department. Since r_1 authorizes the access requested by rq, the following access record is written in the access log:

– ρ_1: Access allowed to 10.1.1.122 to read in 10.1.1.120.

Consider that the following new rule r_2 is then added to P:

– r_2: $Deny_{\{read\}}$ (IpAdressSRC = 10.1.1.122, DepartmentSRC = Production, IpAdressDST = 10.1.1.120, DepartmentDST = Production)

Note that now r_2 and r_1 are the first and second rules of P, respectively. If the same access request rq arrives a second time, rq is refused by P, because it is refused by r_2 (which is the first rule of P). Hence, the following access record is written in the access log:

– ρ_2: Access prohibited to 10.1.1.122 to read in 10.1.1.120.

Therefore, the access log contains two contradictory access records (ρ_1 and ρ_2), which report that two identical access requests have been accepted and refused, respectively.

Then, the objective is to search in P the rules that match the two contradictory ρ_1 and ρ_2 (i.e. the rules whose conditions are satisfied by the values of ρ_1 or ρ_2). The result is that r_1 and r_2 match ρ_1 and ρ_2, and hence are considered as suspicious. Then, conflict detection in P should be applied considering uniquely suspicious rules (i.e. r_1 and r_2) instead of all rules of P.

As we have explained, our approach is motivated by an improvement in efficiency, since a security policy is analyzed considering only some of its rules (qualified as suspicious), instead of all its rules. However, the approach necessitates to analyze an access log. So the question that arises is:

– Is it worth analyzing only a small part of a policy instead of all the policy, if on the other hand we have to add the analysis of an access log?

Our answer is Yes, from the fact that on average a rule of a security policy contains significantly more attributes than an access record. Hence, analyzing a rule takes significantly more time than analyzing an access record. Our answer is confirmed by experiment results in Sect. 5 (Fig. 3).

Since access records are generated every day and presumed to grow over time (i.e. continuous access logs, where access records are added periodically), analyzing the access log arises the following question:

– Is it possible making the proposed approach scalable for a large amount of log data, and for continuous access logs?

To answer the above question which is motivated by the desire to make the proposed approach scalable, while considering continuous access logs, we suggest decomposing the access log into clusters which are analyzed separately, and then select a representative for each cluster. The idea is that instead of analyzing all access records (which are previously analyzed), cluster representatives would allow for a more efficient approach, where one compares the newly added access records with cluster representatives. Then, the analysis procedure is applied only within the cluster(s) where the new access records were inserted, instead of analyzing the new access records with the whole access log. This motivation is confirmed by experiment results in Sect. 5 (Table 2).

3   Access Log Analysis

A complex computing system is usually composed of several modules that communicate with each other. To be able to identify a posteriori access problems of such system, it is common that each of its modules generates a local access log, i.e. a log that keeps track of access requests to the module and corresponding decisions to accept or reject these requests. Before presenting access log analysis, we first give some formal definitions that we consider throughout the paper.

Definition 1. (*Access Record*)
An access record ρ_i is formally specified by an action (e.g. read, write), a decision X (Permit or Deny), and one or more expressions "$att_k = v_k$", where att_k is an attribute name and v_k is a value of att_k. Such access record ρ_i is expressed as follows, where m_i is the number of attributes in ρ_i:

$$\rho_i : X_a(att_1 = v_1, \cdots, att_{m_i} = v_{m_i}) \tag{1}$$

Intuitively, $X_a(att_1 = v_1, \cdots, att_{m_i} = v_{m_i})$ records the occurrence of a request to execute the access action a and for which the decision X (Permit or Deny) has been taken. This access record also indicates the respective values $v_1, \cdots, v_{m_i}$ of the attributes $att_1, \cdots, att_{m_i}$ during the access request.

Example 1. $Deny_{read}$(IpAdressSRC = 10.1.1.122,   DepartmentSRC = Production, IpAdressDST = 10.1.1.120, HostTypeDST = service). This access record indicates that the machine belonging to the production department with IP address "10.1.1.122" tried to read the service with IP address "10.1.1.120", but the access was denied to it.

We define an access log as a finite set of access records: $L = \{\rho_1, \rho_2, \cdots, \rho_l\}$, where ρ_i is an access record, and l is the number of access records.

3.1 Access Log Preprocessing

Due to the diversity of access log sources, we have configured a Syslog Server[1] that aims to receive and collect log data from all relevant nodes in the system over the syslog protocol, and group them into a single global access log. The latter is then parsed in order to recognize, extract and reformulate each of its access records using the above formulation (1).

Example 2. Consider the following access record written in Syslog format [11]:
   ρ: *Oct 02 20:08:41 _gateway %ASA-6-302016: Teardown UDP connection 14 denied to read for 10.1.1.122-90-service-UDP-Production to 10.1.1.120-96-service-UDP-Production duration 0:02:05 bytes 156.*

After recognition, extraction and reformulation of the above access record, we obtain the following equivalent access record:

– $Deny_{read}$ (IpAdressSRC = 10.1.1.122, SRCAdminID = 90, HostTypeSRC = service, ProtocolSRC = UDP, DepartmentSRC = Production, IpAdressDST = 10.1.1.120, DSTAdminID = 96, HostTypeDST = service, ProtocolDST = UDP, DepartmentDST = Production).

3.2 Access Log Clustering

To deal with the huge amount of generated access logs, we suggest to apply a clustering method to group similar access records in the same cluster, based on computed similarity measures. The similarity measure is a function S_{log} that assigns a similarity score $S_{log}(\rho_i, \rho_j)$ to any given pair of access records ρ_i and ρ_j. Such a score reflects the degree of similarity between ρ_i and ρ_j, with respect to their attributes values. The similarity score is a value between 0 and 1. In particular, a score 1 means that ρ_i and ρ_j could be distinguished uniquely by their decisions and actions, while they are indistinguishable by their attributes. The similarity score function S_{log} is formally defined as follows:

Definition 2. *(Access Record Similarity)*
   Consider two access records $\rho_i : X_a(att_1 = u_1, \cdots, att_{m_i} = u_{m_i})$ *and* $\rho_j : Y_b(att'_1 = v_1, \cdots, att'_{m_j} = v_{m_j})$. *Let* $m_{i,j}$ *be the number of attributes that are common to* ρ_i *and* ρ_j *(hence* $m_{i,j} \leq m_i$, $m_{i,j} \leq m_j$). *Let* $\mu_{i,j}$ *be the number of common attributes that have the same value in* ρ_i *and* ρ_j *(hence* $\mu_{i,j} \leq m_{i,j}$). *The similarity between* ρ_i *and* ρ_j *is noted* $S_{log}(\rho_i, \rho_j)$ *and defined as follows:*

$$S_{log}(\rho_i, \rho_j) = \frac{\mu_{i,j}}{m_i + m_j - m_{i,j}} \tag{2}$$

Note that for $i = j$, we obtain $m_i = m_{i,i} = \mu_{i,i}$, and hence $S_{log}(\rho_i, \rho_i) = 1$.

---
[1]   https://www.linuxjournal.com/content/creating-centralized-syslog-server.

Example 3. Consider the following access records ρ_1 and ρ_2:

- $\rho_1 : Deny_{read}$ (IpAdressSRC = 10.1.1.122, SRCAdminID = 90, HostTypeSRC = service, ProtocolSRC = UDP, DepartmentSRC = Production, IpAdress-DST = 10.1.1.120, DSTAdminID = 96, HostTypeDST = service, Proto-colDST = UDP, DepartmentDST = Production)
- $\rho_2 : Permit_{read}$ (IpAdressSRC = 10.1.1.120, SRCAdminID = 91, Host-TypeSRC = service, ProtocolSRC = UDP, DepartmentSRC = Production, IpAdressDST = 10.1.1.120, DSTAdminID = 96, HostTypeDST = service, ProtocolDST = UDP, DepartmentDST = Production)

ρ_1 and ρ_2 have the same ten attributes: IpAdressSRC, SRCAdminID, Host-TypeSRC, ProtocolSRC, DepartmentSRC, IpAdressDST, DSTAdminID, Host-TypeDST, ProtocolDST and DepartmentDST. Eight of these attributes have the same value in both ρ_1 and ρ_2. Therefore, $m_1 = m_2 = m_{1,2} = 10$, and $\mu_{1,2} = 8$. By using Eq. (2), we get the similarity score: $\frac{8}{(10+10-10)} = \frac{8}{10} = 0.8$.

The results obtained in the similarity measures are used to group access records into clusters. Given an access log $L = \{\rho_1, \rho_2, \cdots, \rho_l\}$, clustering L consists in partitioning L into several subsets (or clusters): $C_1, C_2, \cdots$, where each C_i contains access records that are similar. Two access records ρ_i and ρ_j are considered similar if their similarity score $S_{log}(\rho_i, \rho_j)$ is greater than a given threshold. The value of the threshold is set to 0.8, based on [7]. Note that the clusters satisfy the following two properties:

- each cluster contains at least one access record;
- each access record belongs to exactly one cluster.

It is worth noting that some existing clustering techniques need that the number of clusters be given as an input parameter. For example, k-Means and its variants need the number of clusters as a parameter to run [3]. Density-based clustering and its extensions require the neighborhood size to be passed as a variable [13]. Which is not the case in this paper.

Selecting Cluster Representative: Clusters of access records are created in the first access log analysis (i.e. the first time we analyze an access log). For each created cluster, we select a representative, which is the access record that has the greatest average similarity with the other access records in the same cluster. Such representative is the access record that minimizes the following score, where m is the cluster size (i.e. its number of access records):

$$Score(\rho_i) = \frac{1}{m} \sum_{j=1}^{m} (1 - S_{log}(\rho_i, \rho_j)) \qquad (3)$$

The cluster representatives are used to determine in which cluster every access record should be inserted. More precisely, if $\rho_1, \rho_2, \cdots$ are cluster representatives of clusters $C_1, C_2, \cdots$, an access record ρ is inserted in C_i whose representative ρ_i is the most similar to ρ, i.e. in C_i that maximizes $S_{log}(\rho_i, \rho)$, for $i = 1, 2, \cdots$.

3.3 Access Log Contradiction Detection

Once a cluster is constructed from scratch and when it is modified (by the addition of new access records), we need to verify if the new version of the cluster contains contradictory access records (or more simply: contradictions). We say that two access records are contradictory, if they have recorded the same attribute values but different decisions on the same action, e.g. an access record permits to read a resource, while the other one denies it. Formally, an access record contradiction is defined as follows:

Definition 3. *(Access Record Contradiction)*
    Consider two access records $\rho_i : X_a(att_1 = u_1, \cdots, att_{m_i} = u_{m_i})$ *and* $\rho_j :$ $Y_b(att'_1 = v_1, \cdots, att'_{m_j} = v_{m_j})$. ρ_i *and* ρ_j *are contradictory iff:*
    1 - $X \neq Y$
    2 - $a = b$, *and*
    3 - $S_{log}(\rho_i, \rho_j) = 1$

Points 1 and 2 mean that ρ_1 and ρ_2 take different decisions ($X \neq Y$) on the same action ($a = b$). Point 3 means that ρ_1 and ρ_2 use exactly the same attributes, and that each attribute has the same value in both ρ_1 and ρ_2. In other words, ρ_i and ρ_j are distinguished uniquely by their actions and decisions.

Example 4. Consider the following access records ρ_1 and ρ_2:

- $\rho_1 : Deny_{read}$ (IpAddressSRC = 10.1.1.122, ProtocolSRC = UDP, DepartmentSRC = Production, IpAdressDST = 10.1.1.120, ProtocolDST = UDP, DepartmentDST = Production)
- $\rho_2 : Permit_{read}$ (IpAddressSRC = 10.1.1.122, ProtocolSRC = UDP, DepartmentSRC = Production, IpAdressDST = 10.1.1.120, ProtocolDST = UDP, DepartmentDST = Production)

ρ_1 and ρ_2 are contradictory, because $S_{log}(\rho_1, \rho_2) = 1$ (ρ_1 and ρ_2 are similar), while the action read is denied in ρ_1 and permitted in ρ_2.
    Contradiction access records will be used in the next step (Sect. 4) to identify suspicious rules among which we will search conflicting rules.

4 Security Policy Verification

Errors in the policy rules specification may compromise the system security by leading to unauthorized access or denying authorized ones. Therefore, it is important to detect conflicts within a security policy. In this direction, for each detected contradiction within an access log, we search conflicting rules in the policy if any, that could have caused the contradiction. Intrusions can be another possible cause of contradictions in an access log. However, in this paper, we only consider the case of conflicting rules, while intrusion detection is beyond the scope of this paper. We first give some definitions related to security policy and security conflict.

4.1   Security Policy Structure

A policy P is a non-empty set of rules $P = \{r_1, r_2, ..., r_n\}$. Each rule $r_i \in P$ is specified by a condition and an action decision. The condition of a rule is defined as a conjunction of one or more "$att \in V_{att}$", where att is an attribute name and V_{att} is a set of possible values of att. The action decision of a rule is noted X_{act}, where X is the decision *Permit* or *Deny*, and act is a set of actions. $Permit_{read}$ and $Deny_{write}$ are two examples of action decisions. A rule $r_i \in P$ will be written as follows:

$$r_i : X_{act}(att_1 \in V_{att_1}, \cdots , att_{p_i} \in V_{att_{p_i}}) \tag{4}$$

Example 5. $Permit_{\{read, write\}}$ (IpAdressSRC $\in \{$ 10.1.1.122$\}$, DepartmentSRC $\in \{$Production$\}$, IpAdressDST $\in \{$10.1.1.120$\}$, HostTypeDST $\in \{$service$\})$.

Intuitively, this rule indicates that the machine belongs to the production department with IP address "10.1.1.122" has the right to read and write in the service having IP address "10.1.1.120".

The formulations of the access records and the rules (i.e. formulation (1) and (4)) might look similar, whereas the main difference is : in a rule, we define a set of actions and each attribute name may have a set of attribute values, while in an access record, we have only one action and for each attribute name we only have one value. In order to define a security conflict, we reformulate equivalently a rule in access domain. The definition of access domain is given below:

Definition 4. *(Access Domain)*
    Given a rule r_i defined as : $X_{act}(att_1 \in V_{att_1}, att_2 \in V_{att_2}, ..., att_{p_i} \in V_{att_{p_i}})$, we reformulate equivalently r_i in the following form: $r_i : X_{act}((att_1, att_2, ..., att_{p_i}) \in V_{att_1} \times V_{att_2} \times ... \times V_{att_{p_i}})$. That is, instead of specifying separately a set of values for each attribute att_k, we specify a unique set of values for the p_i-tuple $(att_1, att_2, ..., att_{p_i})$ of all attributes. Such a set is called access domain of r_i and noted AD_{r_i}. So the rule r_i can be expressed in the form $r_i = X_{act}((att_1, att_2, ..., att_n) \in AD_{r_i})$. For simplicity, we note $r_i = X_{act}(AD_{r_i})$.

4.2   Security Policy Conflicts

A security conflict occurs when an access request matches more than two rules in a policy, leading to contradictory decisions. We say that an access request R matches a rule r_i, if every attribute value of R satisfies the attribute values of r_i. Suppose that a rule r_1 states that a subject s is permitted to read the resource r and another rule r_2 states that the same subject s is denied to read the same resource with the same attribute values. Therefore, we say that r_1 and r_2 are conflicting. The formal definition of security conflict is given below:

Definition 5. *Security Conflict*

Consider two rules $r_i = X_a(AD_{r_i})$ and $r_j = Y_b(AD_{r_j})$, r_i and r_j present a conflict (or are conflicting) iff:

1. $AD_{r_i} \cap AD_{r_j} \neq \emptyset$
2. $X \neq Y$, and
3. $a \cap b \neq \emptyset$.

Example 6. Consider the following rules r_1 and r_2:

- r_1 : $Deny_{read}$ (IpAdressSRC, ProtocolSRC, DepartmentSRC, IpAdressDST, ProtocolDST, DepartmentDST) $\in \{$ 10.1.1.121, 10.1.1.122$\} \times \{$UDP$\} \times \{$Production$\} \times \{$10.1.1.119, 10.1.1.120$\} \times \{$UDP$\} \times \{$Production$\}$
- r_2 : $Permit_{\{read,write\}}$ (IpAdressSRC, ProtocolSRC, DepartmentSRC, IpAdressDST, ProtocolDST, DepartmentDST) $\in \{$ 10.1.1.122$\} \times \{$UDP$\} \times \{$Production$\} \times \{$10.1.1.120$\} \times \{$UDP$\} \times \{$Production$\}$

Since $AD_{r_i} \cap AD_{r_j} = AD_{r_2} \neq \emptyset$, and r_1 and r_2 have the common action *read* and different decisions *Deny* and *Permit*, we deduce that they are conflicting. Intuitively, r_1 forbids that the machine with IP address "10.1.1.122" read the resource given in the service with IP address "10.1.1.120", while r_2 permits it.

4.3   Security Conflict Detection

In this section, we show how to use access record contradictions to detect suspicious rules, and check if they are conflicting. Before continuing, we need the following definition:

Definition 6. *(Rule matching an access record)*

Consider a rule $r = X_{act}(att_1 \in V_{att_1}, \cdots, att_p \in V_{att_p})$ and an access record $\rho = Y_b(att'_1 = v_1, \cdots, att'_m = v_m)$. We say that r matches ρ (and also ρ matches r), iff

1 - Every attribute att'_i of ρ is an attribute of r noted att_{p_i},
2 - $v_{att'_i} \in V_{att_{p_i}}$, for $i = 1 \cdots m$,
3 - $X = Y$, and
4 - $b \in act$.

The suggested method to detect conflicting rules from contradictory access records is depicted in Algorithm 1. The input is a list of contradictory access records CL, as well as the security policy SP, and the output is a list of conflicting rules. The idea is that, for each pair of contradictory access records (ρ_i, ρ_j) in CL, we search the sets R_{ρ_i} and R_{ρ_j} of suspicious rules that match ρ_i and ρ_j respectively (Function *Search* lines 13–22 of Algorithm 1). Then, we verify in the list of retrieved rules (i.e., $R_{\rho_i} \times R_{\rho_j}$), if there exist pairs of conflicting rules (i.e., pair of rules $(r_1, r_2) \in R_{\rho_i} \times R_{\rho_j}$ that satisfy points 1, 2 and 3 of Definition 5).

Algorithm 1. Verifying the Existence of Conflicts in a Security Policy

---

Input: Set CL of pairs of contradictory access records.
   SP: security policy
Output: Set CR of pairs of conflicting rules of SP, which is initialized to empty.
 1: **procedure** CONFLICTVERIFICATION(CL, SP)
 2:   **for** every pair of contradictory access records (ρ_i, ρ_j) of CL **do**
 3:     $R_{\rho_i} \times R_{\rho_j} =$ SEARCH$((\rho_i, \rho_j), SP)$ ▷ Function SEARCH is defined in lines 12-21
 4:     **for** every pair of rules $(r, r') \in R_{\rho_i} \times R_{\rho_j}$ **do**
 5:       **if** r and r' are conflicting (i.e. points 1, 2, 3 of Def. 5 are satisfied) **then**
 6:         Insert (r, r') in CR
 7:       **end if**
 8:     **end for**
 9:   **end for**
10:   **return** CR
11: **end procedure**
12: **function** SEARCH$((\rho_i, \rho_j), SP)$ ▷ Search the sets R_{ρ_i} and R_{ρ_j} of rules of SP that match ρ_i
                                        and ρ_j respectively.
13:   **for** every rule $r_k \in SP$ **do**
14:     **if** r_k matches ρ_i (i.e. points 1, 2, 3 and 4 of Def. 6 are satisfied) **then**
15:       Insert r_k in R_{ρ_i}
16:     **else if** r_k matches ρ_j **then**
17:       Insert r_k in R_{ρ_j}
18:     **end if**
19:   **end for**
20:   **return** $R_{\rho_i} \times R_{\rho_j}$
21: **end function**

The time complexity for verifying the existence of conflicts in a security policy is in $O(2|CL| \times n^2 \times p \times q)$, where $|CL|$ is the size of the set CL, n is the policy size, p is the maximum number of attributes in the log records, and q is the maximum number of attributes in the rules of the policy. $|CL|$ and n^2 are due to the fact that for each contradiction in CL, we must check $\frac{n \times (n-1)}{2}$ pairs of rules. $p \times q$ is for searching r that matches ρ (line 17 and 18 in Algorithm 1). If we assume that $|CL|$ is proportional to l (which seems realistic to us), we can approximate the time complexity by $O(l \times n^2 \times p \times q)$.

5   Experimental Results

To evaluate the proposed approach, we have implemented our method with Java and the experiments were made using a laptop with a 2.7 GHz Intel Core i5 CPU, 8 GB RAM. For testing purposes, we have applied our method to access logs generated by monitoring a system traffic from the architecture depicted in Fig. 1. An ASA^2 firewall was configured to control the network traffic with respect to the Access Control Lists (ACLs) in the matrix flow shown in Table 1. ACLs consists of a list of rules, each rule defines the action to take when a packet arrives at the firewall. For example, when the firewall receives a packet from INTERNET to destination INTRANET, the firewall denies it. Therefore, a rule can be interpreted in the form $(Condition, X)$, where $Condition$ is predicates

---

[2] https://www.cisco.com/c/en_ca/products/security/asa-5500-series-next-generation-firewalls/index.html.

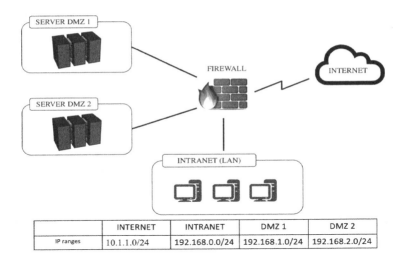

IP ranges	INTERNET	INTRANET	DMZ 1	DMZ 2
	10.1.1.0/24	192.168.0.0/24	192.168.1.0/24	192.168.2.0/24

Fig. 1. Architecture design

Table 1. Firewall matrix flow

$\vec{r}$	INTERNET	INTRANET	DMZ 1	DMZ 2
INTERNET	Permit	Deny	Permit	Deny
INTRANET	Permit	Permit	Permit	Permit
DMZ 1	Permit	Deny	Permit	Deny
DMZ 2	Permit	Deny	Deny	Permit

describing what packets are matched by this rule and X is the decision performed on the matched packets (e.g., Permit, Deny). Since we consider ABAC model to specify the security policy, the ACLs are transformed into ABAC rules, which are specified by a condition and an action decision. Therefore, an ABAC policy can be trivially constructed by creating a separate rule corresponding to each ACL rule, simply using *Condition* and X to identify the relevant condition and an action decision. Of course, such an ABAC policy is a verbose version of the original ACL policy. The verbosity can be for example by adding some actions (e.g., read, write) to the decision X and some attributes describing the system (e.g., Host name, department...). More details about mining ABAC policies is given in [21].

In order to collect different access logs from various components of the system into a single global access log, we used a Syslog Server. We have chosen Syslog protocol, because it is supported by a wide range of devices and can be used to log different types of events. Furthermore, Syslog provides a very high flexibility for log generators, which can place whatever information they deem important within the content field [11]. To analyze our results, we have considered the

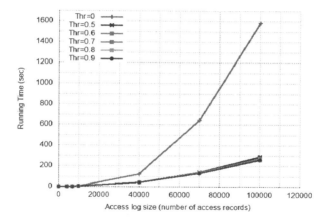

Fig. 2. Running time vs. threshold

overall execution time (i.e. of both *Access Log Analysis* and *Security Policy Verification*). More precisely, we have analyzed how the running time is influenced by the threshold used in the clustering step (0.8 by default, see Sect. 3.2). This parameter influences the result of clustering (i.e. the number of clusters) which in turn influences the execution times of both access log analysis and security policy verification. We also consider the size of the analyzed access log, as well as the size of the newly added access log (for continuous access logs).

Figure 2 shows the running time of our method as a function of the access log size for different thresholds and for a policy with 1088 rules. The curves explicitly show that the running time increases with the number of access records in a quadratic way. The obtained curves in Fig. 2, demonstrate the impact of the threshold values (i.e., 0, 0.5, 0.6, 0.7, 0.8 and 0.9) on the performance (running time). The obtained results can be explained by the fact that when the *threshold* decreases, the sizes of the obtained clusters increase, and hence the running time also increases. In the extreme case where *threshold* = 0 (i.e., similar to applying our method without clustering), we obtain the worst running time. These results demonstrate the time gained from the clustering step. On the average, the best running time is obtained from the threshold 0.8. Thus, the default value of the selected threshold for our experiments is set to 0.8.

As already explained, the use of access logs is justified by the fact that conflicts are searched among suspicious rules (which are deduced from contradictory access records) instead of all rules. We have compared the efficiency (in execution time) of our approach with an approach without access log (i.e. that searches conflicts among all rules of P, instead of only suspicious rules). Figure 3 presents the running time for the two approaches for different samples size $S_i(n, l)$, where n is the policy size and l is the access log size. The figure shows that the execution time of our approach is lower than the execution time of the approach without access log analysis, which confirms our motivation.

Let us recall that the use of clustering is motivated by the desire to improve the scalability of the proposed approach in the case of continuous access log (i.e. where access records are added periodically). Table 2 presents the running time of two approaches to analyzing an access log after the addition of new access records. *Approach 1*: analysis based on the whole access log. *Approach 2*: analysis based on cluster representatives. The execution time of *Approach 2* is very lower than the execution time of *Approach 1* (since the newly added access records are compared to a few access records instead of all access records), which furthermore confirms the relevance of using clustering, and cluster representatives.

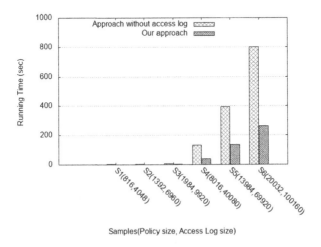

Fig. 3. Our approach vs. an approach without access log analysis

Table 2. Running time of two approaches to analyzing an access log after the addition of new access records

Access log size	Running time (msec)	
	Analysis based on the whole access log	Analysis based on cluster representatives
101	3199	1
304	3696	4
631	4471	7
6960	45070	77

In order to evaluate the proposed method performance, we use *recall* measurement. This later measures the percentage of conflict in the data set being detected. To compute this value, we need to compute the *true positives* (TP), which reflect the correctly detected conflicts using access log analysis, and *false negatives* (FN) are conflicts that we failed to correctly detected. Using these values, recall is calculated using $Recall = \frac{TP}{TP+FN}$. To have an effective model, a high value of recall is required, where lower recall means the approach could more likely miss conflicts. Experimental results show that the proposed method effectively identifies policy conflicts with an average recall of 95.65% on all datasets.

6   Related Work

6.1   Related Work on Log Analysis

In the past decade, Log analysis is widely used for system management tasks and problem diagnosis, such as anomaly detection [4,20,22], security failure analysis [6,9] and performance monitoring [16,23], etc. State of the art concerning log data analysis can be widely summarized into three categories. The first category addresses the problem of log format normalization that fits existing common log formats [17]. The second category considers the importance of finding an efficient log parsing [8]. The last category is about the use of data mining and machine learning in log analysis [15,22]. To the best of our knowledge, this paper presents the first attempt that aims to detect conflicts in ABAC policies using logs analysis, which none of the existing solutions addresses.

Within big data environments, analyzing log files becomes complex and hard to manage. Therefore, several works propose using data mining and machine learning techniques to analyze the logs for different objectives. For example, in [15], Lou et al. mine invariants from unstructured console logs. An anomaly occurs during the system execution if a new log breaks certain invariants. The authors in [4] present DeepLog, a network for modeling system logs using Long Short-Term Memory (LSTM). By training on normal logs, it learns log patterns and detects anomalies in new logs if they deviate from the learned patterns. Breier et al. [2] propose a method for anomaly detection using data mining algorithms. Anomaly profiles are made from rules extracted by testing data sets. Lin et al. [14] propose LogCluster that makes use of agglomerative hierarchical clustering on vectors extracted from log messages. For each cluster, they extract a representative log sequence which they compare to previously extracted sequences to see if the sequence is new and a possible anomaly. However, both [2] and [14] depend on training data (Data Discover knowledge) to decide if the log message is an anomaly. The work presented in [20] focuses on access control violation. The authors transform raw log into a graph and then cluster the graph using an improved MajorClust technique. Then, they conduct anomaly calculation on the clustering results based on a score considering several properties that characterize each cluster. To decide whether or not a cluster is an anomaly, they estimate a threshold to provide a recommendation for the forensic investigator. Although, this intervention of forensic investigators when suspicious behavior is detected makes the solution has limited usability regarding full automation.

In addition to the above work that has focused on logs analysis for problem diagnosis, there exist work conducted to understand the meaning of log messages. For example, Zhu et al. [25] proposed a "learning to log" framework, which aims to provide informative guidance on logging. In order to facilitate the understanding of log messages, Shang et al. [18] proposed an approach which associates the development knowledge (e.g., source code, commits, issue reports) present in various software repositories with the log lines in order to assist users in log understanding.

6.2 Related Work on Policy Analysis

Access control protects the system's resources against unauthorized access via a set of policies. When it comes to distributed systems, multiple policies may overlap, which results to conflicting and redundant rules. These kinds of anomalies may lead to both safety problems (allowing unauthorized accesses) and availability problems (denying an access in emergencies). Khoumsi et al. [12] categorize the anomalies into conflicting anomalies and non-conflicting ones. The first category occurs when a request matches several rules that have different actions (conflicts), whereas the second occurs when the same request matches several rules that have the same action (redundancies). The authors of [12] model a security policy by a finite state automaton, which is then used to analyze the policy, for example to verify if it is complete and if it contains conflicting rules. Several other conflicts detection strategies have been presented in the literature including decision trees, automaton and graph [1,10,19]. For example, Hu et al. [10] consider representing policies as decision trees to detect conflicts. In [1], Ayache et al. propose the verification of access control policies based on Finite State Machines (FSM) to detect anomalies.

Compared to related work on policy analysis, we analyze more efficiently a security policy, by detecting conflicts among suspicious rules of the policy, instead of all its rules. Suspicious rules are deduced from an access log analysis. To make our approach even more efficient, the access log is decomposed into clusters which are analyzed separately. Such a clustering is very relevant in the presence of very large access logs (big data context), as well as for continuous access logs, where new access records are added periodically.

7 Conclusion

We have presented an approach to detect efficiently conflicting rules in a security policy. Our contribution is three-fold: firstly, the method is made efficient by searching conflicts among suspicious rules of the policy, instead of all its rules. Those suspicious rules are determined by analyzing an access log. The second contribution is that the scalability of the method for very large access logs is ensured by decomposing the access log into several clusters which are analyzed separately. Finally, after every modification of an access log, it is analyzed using only a single access record (called representative) per cluster, instead of considering all access records. Efficiency of our method is confirmed by experiment results. As future work, a work in progress is to realize a parallel implementation of the method based on *MapReduce* to support distributed data processing.

We also aim to integrate the conflict resolution towards building a complete environment for verifying and correcting security policies.

References

1. Ayache, M., Erradi, M., Khoumsi, A., Freisleben, B.: Analysis and verification of XACML policies in a medical cloud environment. Scalable Comput. Pract. Experience **17**(3), 189–206 (2016)
2. Breier, J., Branišová, J.: A dynamic rule creation based anomaly detection method for identifying security breaches in log records. Wireless Pers. Commun. **94**(3), 497–511 (2017). https://doi.org/10.1007/s11277-015-3128-1
3. Celebi, M.E., Kingravi, H.A., Vela, P.A.: A comparative study of efficient initialization methods for the k-means clustering algorithm. Expert Syst. Appl. **40**(1), 200–210 (2013)
4. Du, M., Li, F., Zheng, G., Srikumar, V.: DeepLog: anomaly detection and diagnosis from system logs through deep learning. In: Proceedings of the 2017 ACM SIGSAC Conference on Computer and Communications Security, pp. 1285–1298 (2017)
5. Dunlop, N., Indulska, J., Raymond, K.: Dynamic conflict detection in policy-based management systems. In: Proceedings Sixth International Enterprise Distributed Object Computing Conference, 2002, EDOC 2002, IEEE, pp. 15–26 (2002)
6. Gu, Z., Pei, K., Wang, Q., Si, L., Zhang, X., Xu, D.: LEAPS: detecting camouflaged attacks with statistical learning guided by program analysis. In: 2015 45th Annual IEEE/IFIP International Conference on Dependable Systems and Networks (DSN), IEEE, pp. 57–68 (2015)
7. Guo, S.: Analysis and Evaluation of Similarity Metrics in Collaborative Filtering Recommender System. Master's thesis, Lapland University of Applied Sciences (2014)
8. He, P., Zhu, J., Zheng, Z., Lyu, M.R.: Drain: an online log parsing approach with fixed depth tree. In: 2017 IEEE International Conference on Web Services (ICWS), IEEE, pp. 33–40 (2017)
9. Hong, J., Liu, C.C., Govindarasu, M.: Integrated anomaly detection for cyber security of the substations. IEEE Trans. Smart Grid **5**(4), 1643–1653 (2014)
10. Hu, H., Ahn, G.J., Kulkarni, K.: Discovery and resolution of anomalies in web access control policies. IEEE Trans. Dependable Secure Comput. **10**(6), 341–354 (2013)
11. Kent, K., Souppaya, M.: Guide to computer security log management. NIST special publication 92 (2006)
12. Khoumsi, A., Erradi, M., Krombi, W.: A formal basis for the design and analysis of firewall security policies. J. King Saud Univ. Comput. Inf. Sci. **30**(1), 51–66 (2016)
13. Kriegel, H.P., Kröger, P., Sander, J., Zimek, A.: Density-based clustering. Wiley Interdisc. Rev. Data Min. Knowl. Discov. **1**(3), 231–240 (2011)
14. Lin, Q., Zhang, H., Lou, J.G., Zhang, Y., Chen, X.: Log clustering based problem identification for online service systems. In: Proceedings of the 38th International Conference on Software Engineering Companion, ACM, pp. 102–111 (2016)
15. Lou, J.G., Fu, Q., Yang, S., Xu, Y., Li, J.: Mining invariants from console logs for system problem detection. In: USENIX Annual Technical Conference (2010)
16. Nagaraj, K., Killian, C., Neville, J.: Structured comparative analysis of systems logs to diagnose performance problems. In: Proceedings of the 9th USENIX Conference on Networked Systems Design and Implementation, USENIX Association, p. 26 (2012)

17. Sapegin, A., Jaeger, D., Azodi, A., Gawron, M., Cheng, F., Meinel, C.: Hierarchical object log format for normalisation of security events. In: 9th International Conference on Information Assurance and Security, IEEE, pp. 25–30 (2013)
18. Shang, W., Nagappan, M., Hassan, A.E., Jiang, Z.M.: Understanding log lines using development knowledge. In: 2014 IEEE International Conference on Software Maintenance and Evolution (ICSME), IEEE, pp. 21–30 (2014)
19. St-Martin, M., Felty, A.P.: A verified algorithm for detecting conflicts in XACML access control rules. In: Proceedings of the 5th ACM SIGPLAN Conference on Certified Programs and Proofs, ACM, pp. 166–175 (2016)
20. Studiawan, H., Payne, C., Sohel, F.: Graph clustering and anomaly detection of access control log for forensic purposes. Digit. Invest. **21**, 76–87 (2017)
21. Xu, Z., Stoller, S.D.: Mining attribute-based access control policies. IEEE Trans. Dependable Secure Comput. **12**(5), 533–545 (2015)
22. Yagoub, I., Khan, M.A., Jiyun, L.: IT equipment monitoring and analyzing system for forecasting and detecting anomalies in log files utilizing machine learning techniques. In: 2018 International Conference on Advances in Big Data, Computing and Data Communication Systems (icABCD), IEEE, pp. 1–6 (2018)
23. Yuan, D., et al.: Be conservative: enhancing failure diagnosis with proactive logging. OSDI **12**, 293–306 (2012)
24. Yuan, E., Tong, J.: Attributed based access control (ABAC) for web services. In: IEEE International Conference on Web Services (ICWS 2005), IEEE (2005)
25. Zhu, J., He, P., Fu, Q., Zhang, H., Lyu, M.R., Zhang, D.: Learning to log: helping developers make informed logging decisions. In: Proceedings of the 37th International Conference on Software Engineering, IEEE Press, vol. 1, pp. 415–425 (2015)

A Vaccination Game for Mitigation Active Worms Propagation in P2P Networks

Mohamed Amine Rguibi[(⊠)] and Najem Moussa[(⊠)]

LAROSERI, Department of Computer Science, Faculty of Sciences,
University of Chouaib Doukkali, El Jadida, Morocco
{rghibi.m,moussa.n}@ucd.ac.ma

Abstract. The spread of computer active worms is usually modeled by epidemic diffusion processes and widely applied to peer-to-peer computing and social networks. Many protective interventions are recommended to restrain the electronic epidemic, such as immunization strategies or the installation of anti-virus software. In real-world networks, a natural framework for game theory is created where each player (internet user) decides on his own strategy: to secure his host by paying the cost of antivirus software or to remain unsecured, and then takes the risk of being infected later. We introduce this issue by presenting an agent-based model for simulating a vaccination game. In this work, we study the neighbor's impact including the imitation behavior effects on vaccination behavior, which may help to relieve the severity of active worms in peer to peer networks. The simulation results show that imitation behavior works well only when the network initially have more than 20% of vaccinated peers. Moreover, the higher the cost of vaccination, the more players tend to imitate the strategy of neighbors.

Keywords: Epidemic · Game theory · Peer-to-peer

1 Introduction

The widespread use of peer-to-peer networks puts almost all Internet users at a security risk. Because of the architecture of these types of networks, the communication between peer to peer users does not require a central server to manage it. This computer architecture by its very nature is vulnerable to security breaches. A lot of researches have been done over the past 20 years, confirming that there is a mean disadvantage of using peer-to-peer networks and it is the problem of user/data security. And presenting too many solutions to resolve it. For example, applying the game theory to solve this kind of issues was very recommended [1–3].

Active worms become one of the main problem since the early days of the Internet [4,5]. A worm is a program that replicates itself and spreads through network connections to infect other machines, eating up bandwidth and storage

© Springer Nature Switzerland AG 2019
M. F. Atig and A. A. Schwarzmann (Eds.): NETYS 2019, LNCS 11704, pp. 267–274, 2019.
https://doi.org/10.1007/978-3-030-31277-0_17

space, which makes infected computers down. Today and with the growth of the Internet, there are more potential targets to infect. This encourages growth in the number of active worms, as well as their ways of spreading. This can still be attributed to the rapid growth of the Internet; realize that more systems on the Internet lead to higher connectivity resulting in higher propagation speeds.

In recent years, although various models and algorithms have been realized to identify the mechanism of propagation of active worms, as well as to try to catch and stop the propagation of active worms [6–10]. In order to prevent the spread of active worms and mitigate its negative impact on the Internet and especially on peer-to-peer networks, we need to have a detailed understanding of how an active worm propagates.

To define the characteristic of security issues, we applied a vaccination game theory at a peer to peer network. In this paper, we developed a vaccination game in order to evaluate its performance versus the active propagation on unstructured peer to peer network. First, we present our proposed vaccination game model in the Sect. 2. Next, in Sect. 3 we examine the effect that varying a number of model parameters has on the steady state behaviour of the network. Finally, in Sect. 4 we conclude our work and summarizes the paper with some future works.

2   Model

This section presents our model for simulating propagation of active worm in a peer to peer network. Before the active worm spread in the network, peers make a decision whether to get vaccinated or not based on their vaccination strategy. A vaccinated peer in our context means that peer has installed a new version of antivirus or has updated its antivirus software. The decision is affected by the payoff of others (imitation strategy) or the social impact, which is controlled by the probability α. Then, propagation of active worm takes place based on the standard susceptible–infectious–recovered (SIR) model as in the Fig. 1. To summarise our model, we consider two stages: the decision-making stage and active worm propagation stage. The detail of each dynamic is the following.

2.1   Decision-Making Stage

At this point, each peer makes the decision to get vaccinated or not. We assume that the vaccination process confers a perfect immunization against active worm propagation to vaccinated peers in the network. If a peer decides to change its strategy to get vaccinated - e.g: take preventive measures, such as installing new antivirus software or updating an older version of its antivirus-. The peer payoff will be $-C$ as the vaccination cost $(0 \leq C \leq 1)$. So the peer must pay the cost of the vaccination from its calculated payoff.

There are only two situations, when a peer chooses not to change its strategy to be vaccinated:

– If the peer is infected, then its payoff is -1.

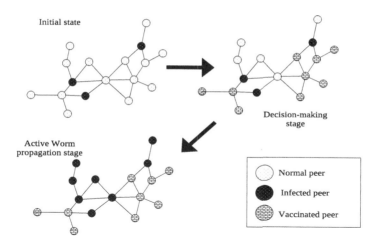

Fig. 1. Decentralised unstructured P2P Network. Vaccinated peers, Malicious and infected peers and other normal peers

– If the peer is not infected, the payoff is 0.

We also calculate the payoffs of the neighbors of peer i in the same way. The probability $P(s_i \leftarrow s_j)$ that the peer i with the strategy s_i imitates the peer $j's$ strategy s_j is given by a pairwise comparison according to the Fermi function [11,12].

$$P(s_i \leftarrow s_j) = \frac{1}{1 + exp[\frac{\pi_i - \pi_j}{K}]} \tag{1}$$

With probability $1-\alpha$, the focal peer i compares its payoff with one randomly selected neighbor, $j's$ payoff, and then makes the decision to get vaccinated or not based on Eq. 1 (payoff-based decision strategy). Then again, with probability α, the focal peer i ignores his payoff and neighbors payoffs and counts the number of its neighbors strategies, and then imitate $j's$ strategy based on Eq. 2 (popularity-based imitation strategy).

$$P(s_i \leftarrow s_j) = \begin{cases} \frac{1}{1+exp[\frac{N_{non(i)} - N_{vac(i)}}{K}]} & (N_{non(i)} \geq N_{vac(i)}) \\ \frac{1}{1+exp[\frac{N_{vac(i)} - N_{non(i)}}{K}]} & (otherwise) \end{cases} \tag{2}$$

Where K is a measure of noise and controls the strength of selection ($0 < K < \infty$). In our model, we fixed the value of K to be $K = 0.1$ to be the same as the typical studies [13–15]. α controls the intensity between the payoff factor and the network factor ($0 \leq \alpha \leq 1$). $N_{vac(i)}(N_{non(i)})$ is the number of the vaccinated (non-vaccinated) neighbors of i.

On the other hand, we calculate peer i payoff π_i as follows:

$$\pi_i = \begin{cases} N_{non(i)}L + \tau_i - N_{non(i)}C & \lambda < T \\ N_{non(i)}L_e + \tau_i - N_{non(i)}C & \lambda \geq T \end{cases}$$

Where $N_{non(i)}$ is the number of neighbors of peer i that choose to not get vaccinated, τ_i is the number of neighbors of peer i and μ is a parameter of our model. As described in reference [16], $T = \gamma/\beta$ is a threshold and λ denote the first eigenvalue of the graph $G[\tau_i - S_i^n]$. $L_e > \mu$ and $L < \mu$ represent the payoffs in the former and latter cases, respectively.

2.2 Active Worm Propagation Stage

In this stage the active worm spreading takes place. Of course after the peers have been or not have not been vaccinated by the above decision-process, The dynamics are described by the standard SIR model in which the network is divided into three types: Susceptible (S), Infectious (I) and Recovered (R) peers as described in the Fig. 2.

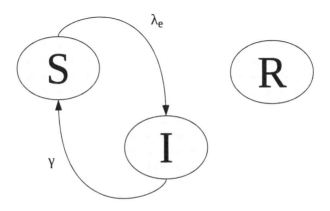

Fig. 2. State transition diagram of active worm propagation.

First, we randomly select I_0 malicious peers are already infected by the active worm. After the active worm propagation spreads out, each non-vaccinated peer i gets infected with the probability $\lambda_e = 1 - (1 - \beta)^{\tau_{inf(i)}}$, where $\tau_{inf(i)}$ is the number of infected neighbors and β is the transmission rate per step t. There is no risk of infection for the vaccinated peers because the vaccination provides perfect immunity. In our model, all vaccinated peers remain in the recovery state R during the active worm propagation stage. Once each peer is infected, it recovers from the infection and changes its state to susceptible state with rate γ per step t. Since it is difficult to mathematically describe the dynamics of structured populations, we numerically simulate the epidemic dynamics by building a custom-built simulator and using the Gillespie algorithm [6,17].

3   Simulation Results and Discussion

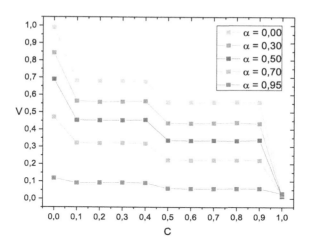

Fig. 3. Impact of α on the vaccination behavior.

Each simulation experiment is performed over a generated Barabasi-Albert graph [18] that represents the P2P overlaying network, where $m_0 = 9$ and $m = 6$. The network size is then determined by the number of users $N_{users} = 1000$. In order to help readers to reproduce our experiments, we present how to set the parameter settings of our model in detail.

We suppose that initially 10% randomly selected peers are malicious. Simulations were initially carried out with $I_0 = 10$ randomly selected peers that are in the infected state and $V_0 = 10$ randomly selected peers are initially get vaccinated, while the others peers are all in the susceptible state. In this paper, we aimed to evaluate the neighbor's impact including the imitation behavior effects on vaccination behavior (the effect of α and μ) and the vaccination cost C. Other parameters that stay constant throughout our experiments, were $\beta = \gamma = 0.1$, $\mu = 0.9$, $L_e = 2$ and $L = 0$.

We consistently varied values of α to know the effect on the vaccination coverage. Figure 3, shows vaccination coverage as the functions of the vaccination cost C and the value of α. First, we focus on $\alpha = 0$, which means that a peer i compares its payoff only with one randomly selected neighbor j and ignore the popularity of its neighbors. The peer i will get vaccinated, if its payoff is greater then μ ($\pi_i > \mu$). In this case, the peer i calculates its payoff based on the vaccination cost and the neighbor's impact, then it makes its own decision to get immunity its self or not. The results show that payoff-based decision strategy with the neighbor's impact outperforms popularity-based imitation strategy. On the other hand, we can notice that the fraction of vaccinated peers decreases with the decreasing of α. It means that when peers choose to imitate neighbors strategies, only a small fraction of peers choose to get vaccinated ($\alpha = 0.95$). This is mainly due to the small initially fraction of vaccinated peers $V_0 = 1\%$. Popularity-based imitation strategy can only yield better results if the majority of peers are initially get vaccinated. Of course, the both strategies can not provide good results if the vaccination cost C is high.

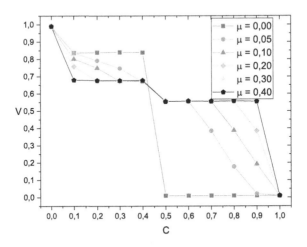

Fig. 4. Impact of μ on the vaccination behavior.

Now, we focus on how vaccination cost C and our model parameter μ affects vaccination behavior. We fixed $\alpha = 0.0$ in order to evaluate the performance of payoff-based decision strategy with the neighbor's impact. In Fig. 4, we show the fraction of vaccinated peers in terms C and we varied μ. As we can see, if the vaccination cost is low ($C < 0.5$), the payoff-based decision strategy with the neighbor's impact positively facilitates making the decision to get the vaccination because the payoffs of peers are also low ($\pi < 0.1$). Conversely, the payoff-based decision strategy with the neighbor's impact has the reverse effect when the vaccination cost is high ($C \geq 0.5$) and the peers payoffs' are low ($\pi < 0.1$). Thus, we can conclude that the neighbor's impact has a positive and negative effect on the vaccination process, when the vaccination cost is low ($C < 5$), it is better to ignore the neighbor's impact. In contrast, when the vaccination is high ($0.5 \geq C \geq 0.9$), we must take the neighbor's impact into consideration.

4   Conclusion

In this paper, we proposed a vaccination game to evaluate its performances on active worm propagation in the peer to peer unstructured networks. Here, we present two strategies for peers to calculate payoff:

– Popularity-based imitation strategy.
– Payoff-based decision strategy.

Our simulations results show that we must not only reliance on popularity-based imitation strategy. Especially, when the number of initially vaccinated peers is low compared to the size of the peer to peer network. On the other hand, we found that when peers calculate its payoffs with neighbor's impact, and then take the decision to get vaccinated or remain unsafe has both positive and negative effects depending on the vaccination cost and the peer payoff's.

To conclude, this model we have presented has been developed for unstructured P2P networks and we hope that this model can work as well for interconnected structured P2P networks such as Chord and Pastry.

References

1. Mavronicolas, M., Papadopoulou, V., Philippou, A., Spirakis, P.: Network game with attacker and protector entities. In: Deng, X., Du, D.-Z. (eds.) ISAAC 2005. LNCS, vol. 3827, pp. 288–297. Springer, Heidelberg (2005). https://doi.org/10.1007/11602613_30
2. Mavronicolas, M., Papadopoulou, V., Philippou, A., Spirakis, P.: A graph-theoretic network security game. In: Deng, X., Ye, Y. (eds.) WINE 2005. LNCS, vol. 3828, pp. 969–978. Springer, Heidelberg (2005). https://doi.org/10.1007/11600930_98
3. Mavronicolas, M., Monien, B., Papadopoulou, V.G.: How many attackers can selfish defenders catch? In: Proceedings of the 41st Annual Hawaii International Conference on System Sciences (HICSS 2008), p. 470, IEEE, January 2008
4. Wang, Y., Wen, S., Xiang, Y., Zhou, W.: Modeling the propagation of worms in networks: a survey. IEEE Commun. Surv. Tutorials **16**(2), 942–960 (2014)
5. Jafarabadi, A., Azgomi, M.A.: A stochastic epidemiological model for the propagation of active worms considering the dynamicity of network topology. Peer-to-Peer Network. Appl. **8**(6), 1008–1022 (2015)
6. Fu, F., Rosenbloom, D.I., Wang, L., Nowak, M.A.: Imitation dynamics of vaccination behaviour on social networks. Proc. R. Soc. B Biol. Sci. **278**(1702), 42–49 (2010)
7. Liu, C., Zhang, Z.K.: Information spreading on dynamic social networks. Commun. Nonlinear Sci. Numer. Simul. **19**(4), 896–904 (2014)
8. Mishra, B.K., Pandey, S.K.: Dynamic model of worm propagation in computer network. Appl. Math. Model. **38**(7–8), 2173–2179 (2014)
9. Wang, Q., Chen, Z., Chen, C., Pissinou, N.: On the robustness of the botnet topology formed by worm infection. In: 2010 IEEE Global Telecommunications Conference GLOBECOM 2010, IEEE, pp. 1–6, December 2010
10. Yu, W., Wang, X., Calyam, P., Xuan, D., Zhao, W.: Modeling and detection of camouflaging worm. IEEE Trans. Dependable Secure Comput. **8**(3), 377–390 (2011)
11. Szabó, G., Tőke, C.: Evolutionary prisoner's dilemma game on a square lattice. Phys. Rev. E **58**(1), 69 (1998)
12. Traulsen, A., Pacheco, J.M., Nowak, M.A.: Pairwise comparison and selection temperature in evolutionary game dynamics. J. Theor. Biol. **246**(3), 522–529 (2007)
13. Fukuda, E., et al.: Risk assessment for infectious disease and its impact on voluntary vaccination behavior in social networks. Chaos Solitons Fractals **68**, 1–9 (2014)
14. Han, D., Sun, M.: Can memory and conformism resolve the vaccination dilemma? Physica A Stat. Mech. Appl. **415**, 95–104 (2014)

15. Ichinose, G., Kurisaku, T.: Positive and negative effects of social impact on evolutionary vaccination game in networks. Physica A Stat. Mech. Appl. **468**, 84–90 (2017)
16. Saha, S., Adiga, A., Vullikanti, A.K.S.: Equilibria in epidemic containment games. In: Twenty-Eighth AAAI Conference on Artificial Intelligence, June 2014
17. Gillespie, D.T.: Exact stochastic simulation of coupled chemical reactions. J. Phys. Chem. **81**(25), 2340–2361 (1977)
18. Barabási, A.L., Albert, R.: Emergence of scaling in random networks. Science **286**(5439), 509–512 (1999)

How to Choose Its Parents in the Tangle

Vidal Attias[1] and Quentin Bramas[2(✉)]

[1] ENS Rennes, Rennes, France
[2] ICUBE, Strasbourg University, CNRS, Strasbourg, France
bramas@unistra.fr

Abstract. The Tangle is a data structure mainly used to store transactions in the IOTA cryptocurrency. It has similarities with the blockchain structure of Bitcoin but in the Tangle, a block contains only one transaction and has not one, but two parents. The security and the stability of this distributed data structure is highly dependent on the algorithm used to select the parents of a new block.

Previous work showed that the current parents selection algorithms are insecure, not stable or have low performances. And we propose a new algorithm that combines all these properties.

Keywords: Blockchain · Distributed ledger · Security · Performances evaluation

1 Introduction and Model

A Distributed Ledger Technology (DLT) is (i) an append-only data structure and (ii) a protocol that defines how the agents in a network agree to append new data. The Bitcoin is the most famous example. It uses the blockchain to store the transactions and the Proof of Work (PoW) to elect a node in the network responsible for writing a new block. In this paper, we are interested in the data structure called *Tangle*, used to store transactions in the IOTA cryptocurrency, and especially in the algorithm used to append new data. We present a new algorithm and show it offers better performances compared to existing algorithms.

The Tangle. We consider a set of connected agents generating transactions. The transactions are stored in a Directed Acyclic Graph (DAG) called *Tangle*. Each agent has a local copy of the Tangle. A vertex of the Tangle, called *site*, represents a transaction and has two parents (potentially the same one) in the Tangle. A site is said to *directly confirm* its parents and *indirectly confirm* its other ancestors in the Tangle. A *tip* of the Tangle is a site which has no child, i.e which isn't confirmed by any site. The *genesis* is the only site with no parents.

In order to include a transaction in the Tangle, an agent must perform a proof of work, i.e, solving a cryptographic puzzle requiring a certain amount of computational power. The *weight* of a site represents this work and we assume

© Springer Nature Switzerland AG 2019
M. F. Atig and A. A. Schwarzmann (Eds.): NETYS 2019, LNCS 11704, pp. 275–280, 2019.
https://doi.org/10.1007/978-3-030-31277-0_18

each site has a weight of 1. Then, the *cumulative weight* of a site is defined [Pop16] as the sum of its own weight with the weight of its descendants (the sites which confirm it). See Fig. 1 for an illustration.

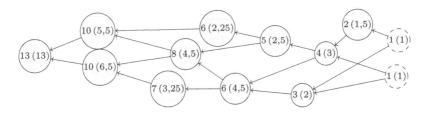

Fig. 1. An example of a Tangle. In each site is written its cumulative weight and in bracket its real cumulative weight (see Sect. 2).

Tips Selection Algorithm (TSA). When a site is added to the Tangle, its parents are selected by a *Tip Selection Algorithm* (TSA). The TSA must select two tips (unconfirmed sites) that are not conflicting. The TSA is a fundamental component of the protocol because it implicitly indicates what is the current view of the agent generating the new site. Indeed, if two tips are conflicting, the TSA indicates which one is considered correct (and should be extended by appending a new site to it) or orphaned (by ignoring it).

Each site in the Tangle has two parents but a site can have multiple children, because of the local versions of the Tangle can be different for two agents in the network, due to the latency. The TSA could chose a site which is a tip in the local version on the Tangle, but that is already confirmed in another one.

The whitepaper [Pop16] presents two TSA[1]:

- Uniform TSA: Each parent is chosen uniformly at random among all the tips.
- Markov Chain Monte Carlo (MCMC): the selection of each parent is done by using a random walk. A walker starts from a given site (eg, the genesis), moves from site to child site, and stops when it reaches a tip. At each site, it uses a transition function depending of the site's cumulative weight denoted by w. In a site v, the probability of going to a child $u \in C(v)$ is:

$$p_{v,u} = \exp(-\alpha(w(v) - w(u))) / \sum_{c \in C(v)} \exp(-\alpha(w(v) - w(c)))$$

where $\alpha > 0$ is a parameter of the algorithm. This TSA is currently used in production in the IOTA cryptocurrency with the parameter $\alpha = 0.001$. We denote this TSA MCMC($\alpha = 0.001$) in the remainder. One may notice that as we send two random walks, we must enforce that the two tips are not in conflict.

---

[1] A third one is briefly presented but is actually just a variation of the MCMC that we present here.

The Double Spending Problem. The double spending attack in a DLT consists in generating two transactions using the same funding source but with two distinct recipients. The aim for the attacker is to persuade each recipient that the transaction it receives is valid and that the other one is not.

In order to simplify, one recipient can be a car seller and the second one the attacker himself. The attacker broadcasts the first transaction and then waits for the car seller to be convinced of the validity of its transaction and to give the car's keys. Then, the attacker broadcasts the second transaction, and generates multiple other transactions to make the first one invalid. When all the network's agents consider the first transaction as invalid, the seller will have given its car without having got the money.

To prevent a double spend attack in the Tangle, it is necessary that computational power used by the honest agents to generate their sites[2] is greater than the computational power of the adversary [Bra18].

Contributions. In this article, we presents a new way to compute the cumulative weight and a new TSA using this new weight. Then, we analyse theoretically and with simulations our new TSA and show that it improves the MCMC currently used in production by IOTA on some points, while being as good on other points: (i) it gets executed much more quickly, which is a real advantage for the network's nodes generating a great number of transactions, (ii) it doesn't leave unconfirmed transactions, even in high load and (iii) it is secure.

2   A New Way to Compute the Cumulative Weight

The main issue of the cumulative weight as defined previously is that for a given site, its children's cumulative weight does not give any indications on the real weight of the subtangles 4confirming them. Let us consider a site with two children, each having a cumulative weight of 10. Then, there is no way to differentiate between the case (a) where 9 sites are confirming both children and the case (b) where 9 sites are confirming the first child and 9 other sites are confirming the second child. In the first case, the corresponding cumulative weight should be lower since it is easier to generate the 11 sites in the first case compared to the 20 sites in the second one. When the cumulative weight is used in a random walk, the probability to move toward a subtangle should not depend on the number of children connected to this subtangle.

We define the *real cumulative weight* $R(u)$ of a site u as one plus half the sum of its children's real cumulative weights:

$$R(u) = 1 + \sum_{c \in C(u)} R(c)/2 \tag{1}$$

---

[2] Observe here that the computational power *used* by the honest agents is not the same as the computational power of the honest agent. Indeed, the former could be much lower than the latter.

$$p_{v,u} = R(u) / \sum_{c \in C(v)} R(c) \qquad (2)$$

This makes sense because half of each site's weight contributes to each of its parent[3]. Also, one can notice that the sum of real cumulative weights of any subset of children correspond exactly to the amount of power used to confirm those children. We also decided to change the formula used to compute probabilities in the random walk. Thus, a walker located at a site v has a probability $p_{v,u}$, given by (2), to move toward a child u. An algorithm that computes all the real weights consists in iterating over all the sites, from the tips to the genesis, applying the Eq. (1). We will denote this TSA *MCMC-new* in the remaining of the paper.

3   Analyse

Complexity. The TSA is executed each time a transaction is issued by an agent, thus it should be efficient.

During its execution, the MCMC($\alpha = 0.001$) algorithm must first compute the cumulative weight of each site and then perform two random walks from the genesis to a tip. The complexity of a random walk is in $O(n)$ where n is the amount of sites in the Tangle, assuming the average number of child per site is constant. Computing the cumulative weight, however, is far from efficient, as existing algorithms are in $\Theta(n^2)$ [Gal18] with a space complexity also in $\Theta(n^2)$ (Fig. 2).

Computing the real cumulative weight only requires $O(n)$ operations. Indeed, a depth-first iteration of the Tangle is sufficient. For each site u we compute $R(u)$ in function of the value $R(c)$ of its children: $R(u) = 1 + \sum_{c \in C(u)} R(c)/2$. Figure 2 shows the evolution of the executing time of the MCMC($\alpha = 0.001$) and MCMC-new in function of the size of the Tangle.

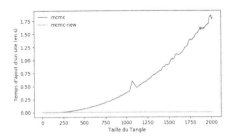
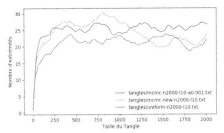

Fig. 2. Execution time in second of the TSA in function of size of the Tangle

Fig. 3. Number of tips in function of the size of the Tangle

---

[3] This can easily be generalized to the case where each site has k parents, by dividing by k instead of 2 in Eq. (1).

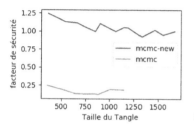

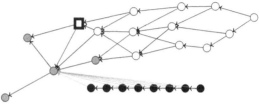

Fig. 4. Security factor in function of the number of sites confirming the target.

Fig. 5. Generation of a *feather* parasite Tangle. The rectangle is the target site, white sites are honest and black sites are parasite ones.

Stability of the Number of Tips. We define the stability of a TSA as a property to maintain a constant amount of tips in average. Formally, with a perfectly stable TSA, the average number of tips is a Markov chain with a non-null stationary distribution [Bra18]. We know [Pop16] that the uniform TSA is stable and the average number of tips is 2λ in average with λ being the average numbers of sites generated per time unit. By simulations, we can observe that MCMC ($\alpha = 0.001$) and MCMC-new are also stable with an average amount of tips around 2λ, similarly to the uniform TSA.

Security. In order to analyse the security of a TSA, we measure the amount of sites required to create a parasite Tangle. For a certain Tangle T and a target site t, a *parasite Tangle* is a set of sites P connected to T such as *(i)* each site of P does not confirm the target site t and *(ii)* the probability for the TSA to chose a tip in P is greater than $1/2$. The security factor is then the ratio between the number of sites confirming the target site and the number of sites in the parasite Tangle. Intuitively, the parasite tangle represents the sites an attacker has to generate to perform a double spend on the target, and the security factor is the proportion of the computational power an attack should own to do so.

Figure 4 shows the security factor of $MCMC(\alpha = 0.001)$ and MCMC-new in function of the number of sites confirming the target site. These results are obtained by generating Tangles of variable sizes. In order to generate our parasite Tangle, we use a feather attack (shown in Fig. 5), which consists in generating sites such as each one confirms the previous one and a site confirmed by the target site. In the MCMC($\alpha = 0.001$) case, the attack is slightly different as each parasite site confirms the previous parasite site and a site among a set of sites confirmed by the target site (and not only a single site).

We observe that the security factor of MCMC-new is near 1 and is much lower for the MCMC($\alpha = 0.001$). However, we conjecture that the security factor of MCMC($\alpha = 0.001$) tends to 1 as the number n of sites that confirm the target tends to infinity. Indeed, for really big values of n, the random walk depends almost only on the subtangle's weight. One can show that in the best cast (for the adversary), the parasite Tangle is a feather and gets attached to the Tangle on a site s which has only one child in the Tangle t. When the parasite Tangle is sufficiently big, every random walk must step by s and the probability for a random walk in s to chose to go to the parasite Tangle is greater then $1/2$ if:

$$\exp(-\alpha(w_s - w_t)) < \sum_{i=1}^{k} \exp(-\alpha(w_s + i))$$

Where k is the size of the parasite Tangle and w_s, resp. w_t, is the site cumulative weight of s, resp. of the target site. The sum on the right part of the inequation is the contribution from each site of the parasite tangle, because in a feather parasite Tangle, each site is a child of s. We are interested by finding the smallest k verifying this inequation, *i.e.* such as n/k is the security factor. By calculus, we find that for n tending to infinity, this n/k tends to 1.

We showed that our algorithm performs better than the one currently used in production in the IOTA cryptocurrency, considering computational complexity and security and is equivalent in terms of stability.

References

[Bra18] Bramas, Q.: The Stability and the Security of the Tangle. Working paper or preprint, April 2018. https://hal.archives-ouvertes.fr/hal-01716111

[Gal18] Gal, A.: Algorithm for calculating cumulative weight (2018). https://github.com/alongalky/iota-docs/blob/master/cumulative.md

[Pop16] Popov, S.: The Tangle. White paper (2016). https://iota.org/IOTA_Whitepaper.pdf

Bitcoin Security with Post Quantum Cryptography

Meryem Cherkaoui Semmouni[1(✉)], Abderrahmane Nitaj[2],
and Mostafa Belkasmi[1]

[1] SIME, Mohammed V University, ENSIAS Rabat, Rabat, Morocco
{meryem.semmouni,m.belkasmi}@um5s.net.ma
[2] University of Caen Normandie, Caen, France
abderrahmane.nitaj@unicaen.fr

Abstract. In a future quantum world with a large quantum computer, the security of the digital signatures used for Bitcoin transactions will be broken by Shor's algorithm. Bitcoin has to switch to post-quantum cryptography. In this paper, we show that the post quantum signatures based on LWE and ring LWE are the most promising to use in the presence of large quantum computers running Shor's algorithm.

Keywords: Bitcoin · Elliptic curve · Lattice · Learning with error

1 Introduction

The influence of new technologies on the economy and individuals has given birth to a new interpretation of money that makes life more easier. This new interpretation aims to emigrate from cash to an electronic money recorded in electronic devices. The use of electronic money is encouraged in several countries. It also has a lot of benefits, so transactions have become easy, cheap, more reliable and can be done anywhere and at anytime. The increase of frauds and the different attacks launched by the hackers, gave birth to the privacy and authentication problem for this kind of electronic system with this kind of danger. In this context cryptography offers multiple solutions to overcome these sensitive data protection issues in e-commerce.

An important application of cryptography is to secure Bitcoin. Bitcoin is a peer-to-peer network without any central authority such as banks or governments. It was presented in 2008 by Satoshi Nakomoto [17]. To authorize payments or transfers, Bitcoin uses the Elliptic Curve Digital Signature Algorithm (ECDSA) [12] with the hash function SHA-256 [13], and the Koblitz curve secp256k1 with the equation:

$$secp256k1 : \ y^2 = x^3 + 7 \pmod{p_1}, \ p_1 = 2^{256} - 2^{32} - 2^9 - 2^8 - 2^7 - 2^6 - 2^4 - 1.$$

The curve secp256k1 was proposed in 2000 by the Standards for Efficient Cryptography Group of Certicom in the standards for efficient cryptography SEC2

© Springer Nature Switzerland AG 2019
M. F. Atig and A. A. Schwarzmann (Eds.): NETYS 2019, LNCS 11704, pp. 281–288, 2019.
https://doi.org/10.1007/978-3-030-31277-0_19

and is used in Bitcoin since 2009. The Koblitz curve has many advantages when used in industrial applications, especially efficiency, security and shortness of the key, but the main problem is its weakness in front of quantum attacks.

In this paper, we study the possibility of using the digital signature TESLA# [8] (pronounced "Tesla Sharp") for Bitcoin system. TESLA# has many advantages.

- TESLA# is based on the Ring Learning with Errors (R-LWE) assumption which makes it a prominent candidate for a post-quantum digital signature.
- TESLA# improves all its predecessors such as Ring-Tesla [3] and Tesla.
- TESLA# has a fast key generation, signing and verification.
- TESLA# has highly secure parameters at the level of both pre-quantum and post-quantum cryptography.
- TESLA# has a secure implementation against timing and cache attacks.

We show that TESLA# is an efficient signature scheme in the context of Bitcoin which avoids quantum attacks. We recommend to use it in the future: it is better to use Momentum proof of work which is better than the standard proof of work [2] used todays on Bitcoin Blockchain transaction.

The rest of this paper is organized as follows. In Sect. 2, we recall some facts on Bitcoin and secp256k1. In Sect. 3, we introduce lattices and describe the digital signature scheme TESLA#. In Sect. 4 we study its security. In Sect. 5 we describe the use of TESLA# in Bitcoin. We conclude the paper in Sect. 6.

2 Description of the Cryptography Used in Bitcoin

Bitcoin is a peer-to-peer decentralized digital currency based on asymmetric cryptography. It was first proposed by Satoshi Nakamoto [17] in 2008 and exploited since 2009. It is a proof of work based on cryptocurrency which makes miners able to mining on Bitcoin, and users to transfer directly without the use of an intermediary such as a bank or a government, using just their addresses. Bitcoin is implemented using the Elliptic Curve Digital Signature Algorithm (ECDSA) to verify ownership transactions on the network, with the Koblitz curve Secp256k1. This curve Secp256k1 is define over a finite field $\mathcal{F}_p$ as follows:

- The prime number is $p = 2^{256} - 2^{32} - 2^9 - 2^8 - 2^7 - 2^6 - 2^4 - 1$.
- The equation curve is $y^2 \equiv x^3 + 7 \pmod{p}$.
- The maximum length of the keys is $\lceil \log_2(p) \rceil = 256$.

The hard problem upon which the security is based is the Elliptic Curve Logarithm Problem ECDLP. Unfortunately, the problem can be solved by a quantum computer running Shor's algorithm [19]. For 256 bits, Shor's algorithm needs only 3848 seconds to solve ECDLP.

3 The Digital Signature Scheme TESLA#

In this section, we show how to avoid quantum attacks on Bitcoin with ECDSA by using the lattice-based signature TESLA# [8].

3.1 Lattice

The arithmetic used in TESLA# is based on lattices.

Definition 1. *Let* $B = \{b_1, \ldots, b_n\}$, $b_i \in \mathbb{R}^m$ *be a set of n linearly independent vectors of m coordinates with $n \leq m$. The lattice $\mathcal{L}$ associated to B is the discrete additive subgroup of $\mathbb{R}^m$ containing all integer linear combinations of the vectors of B:*

$$\mathcal{L}(B) = \left\{ \sum_{i=1}^{n} x_i b_i \mid x_i \in \mathbb{Z} \right\}.$$

The integer n is the dimension of the lattice and m is the rank. When $m = n$, the lattice is called full-rank. The basis B can be represented as a matrix $B = [b_1, \ldots, b_n]$. The determinant of the lattice is defined by $\det(\mathcal{L}) = \sqrt{B^T \cdot B}$ where B is considered here as the matrix of the vectors $b_1, \ldots, b_n$. In the theory of lattices, several problems are considered hard and are resistant to quantum computers. Lattice-based cryptography is based on the hardness of some lattice problems such as SVP, CVP, and LWE. We list below the main hard problems.

1. **The Shortest Vector Problem (SVP):** Given a lattice basis B, find the shortest nonzero vector in $\mathcal{L}(B)$.
2. **The Closest Vector Problem (CVP):** Given a lattice basis B and a target vector v_0 not in the lattice $\mathcal{L}(B)$, find $v \in \mathcal{L}(B)$, the closest vector to v_0.
3. **Learning With Errors Problem (LWE):** Let A be a $n \times n$ matrix which is uniformly distributed in $\mathbb{Z}/q\mathbb{Z}$. Let s and e be two unknown vectors. The LWE problem is to find s and e using A and $As + e$ with the shortest non-zero vector for the Euclidean norm.
4. **Ring-Learning With Errors Problem (Ring-LWE):** Ring-LWE problem is similar than the LWE problem where the unknown parameters s and e are vectors from a the ring of polynomials $\mathcal{R}_q = \mathbb{Z}_q[x]/(x^n + 1)$.

3.2 The Digital Signature Scheme TESLA#

Tesla# [8] is a candidate for post-quantum digital signatures. It is provably secure with a security reduction to the Ring Learning With Errors (Ring-LWE) problem. The digital signature scheme TESLA# is composed by three algorithms: the key generation algorithm, the signing algorithm, and the verification algorithm.

4   The Security of TESLA#

The Ring-LWE problem is a hard assumption, that was introduced in [16] together with a (quantum) worst case to average-case reduction to certain problems over ideal lattices.

The security of TESLA# stems from the hardness of the Ring Learning with Errors (Ring-LWE) problem. The Ring-LWE problem can be seen as an instantiation of the LWE problem. In this section we present the main attacks against Tesla# signature and countermeasures to avoid these attacks.

4.1   The Decoding Attack

An LWE instance $(A, As + e)$ is seen as an instance of the bounded distance decoding problem (BDDP). The most basic way of solving a BDD instance is using Babai's Nearest Plane algorithm [6]. This method can be described as follows: First Suppose that there is multiple samples $(A, As + e)$ of an LWE instance parameterized by n, α and q. Second, perform lattice reduction basis on the lattice $\mathcal{L}(A^T)$ to obtain a new basis B, where A^T is the transpose of A. Babai's Nearest Plane algorithm works by recursively computing the closest vector on the sublattice spanned by subsets of the the reduced basis. This attack is based on reducing the lattice by lattice reduction techniques such as LLL [15].

The probability to recover the vector s by Babai's Nearest Plane algorithm is approximated by

$$\prod_{i=1}^{m} erf\left(\frac{\|b_i^*\|\sqrt{\pi}}{2\alpha q}\right),$$

where $\{b_1^*, ..., b_m^*\}$ is the Gram-Schmidt orthogonal basis. To ovoid the attack by Baba's technique, the probability must be small, that is $\prod_{i=1}^{m} erf\left(\frac{\|b_i^*\|\sqrt{\pi}}{2\alpha q}\right) < \epsilon$ for a small parameter ϵ .

On the other hand, the complexity of the LLL algorithm is $\mathcal{O}\left(e^{n^3 C} \log M\right)$ where $C > (2/\sqrt{3})^{1/6}$ and M is maximum length of the basis vectors $\{b_1, ..., b_n\}$, that is $M = \max_{i=1}^{n} \|b_i\|$. As a consequence, to ovoid the LLL algorithm attack, the dimension n of the lattice should be large.

4.2   Lattice Reduction

Lattice reduction is to find short vectors in the scaled dual lattice. We construct this lattice from a given $A \in \mathbb{Z}_q^{m \times n}$ by computing a basis for the nullspace of A^T over $\mathbb{Z}_q$, lift to $\mathbb{Z}$ and extend by $qI \in \mathbb{Z}_q^{m \times m}$ to make it q-ary and compute a basis for $\mathcal{L}$, we obtain at the end the scaled dual lattice $\mathcal{L} = \{x \in \mathbb{Z}_q^m | xA \equiv 0 \mod q\}$. Lattice reduction will return the shortest non-zero vector b_0 which by definition is a short vector in $\mathcal{L}$, so that $b_0 A \equiv 0 \mod q$ which is exactly solving the Short Integer Solutions problem.

So $\langle b_0, As + e \rangle = \langle b_0, e \rangle$, which follows a Gaussian distribution and it often returns small samples for both b_0 and e.

Given an LWE instance characterised by n, α, q and a vector b_0 of length $\|b_0\|$ in the scaled dual lattice $\mathcal{L}^T = \{x \in \mathbb{Z}_q^m | xA \equiv 0 \mod q\}$, the advantage of distinguishing $\langle b_0, e \rangle$ from random is close to $e^{-\pi(\|b_0\|\alpha)^2}$. So if $\|b_0\|$ is too large then the (Gaussian) distribution of $\langle b_0, e \rangle$ will be too flat to distinguish from random. To avoid this attacks $\|b_0\|\alpha$ must be large enough.

4.3   Non-lattice Attacks

There are two non-lattice approaches to solve LWE, namely the attack based on the algorithm by Blum, Kalai, and Wassermann (BKW) [7] and the algorithm by Arora and Ge [5]. Both algorithms require a large number of LWE samples to be applied efficiently.

BKW solves LWE via the SIS strategy, given m samples (A, c) following D_σ^n, we require short vectors u_i in the scaled dual lattice of the lattice generated by the rows of A. BKW creates these vectors by adding elements from a tables with q^b entries each, where each table is used to find collisions on b components of a (a row of A). The BKW algorithm shows that subexponential algorithms exist for learning parity functions in the presence of noise: the BKW algorithm solves the Learning Parity with Noise problem in time $2^{O(n/log n)}$ [1].

An alternative approach, proposed by Arora and Ge, is used to solve LWE by setting up a system of noise-free non-linear polynomials of which the secret s is a root [5]. Polynomials are constructed from the observation that the error, when falling in the range $[-t, t]$ (for some $t \in \mathbb{Z}$ such that $2t + 1 < q$), is always a root of the polynomial $P(x) = x \prod_{i=1}^{t}(x + i)(x - i)$. Then, we know that the secret s is a root of $P(a \cdot x - c)$ constructed from LWE samples. Arora and Ge, offer an algorithm for solving LWE in time $2^{O(n^{2\xi})}$ where ξ is a constant such that $\alpha q = n^\xi$.

Both algorithms require a (very) large number of LWE samples to be applied efficiently. TESLA# inherits the property from Ring-TESLA that Gaussian sampling is only needed for key pair generation. Instances for [3] are given far less LWE samples, so TESLA# also will give less LWE samples. TESLA# is resistant to such attacks.

4.4   Timing Attacks

Tesla# uses an isochronous (Constant time) Gaussian sampler [8] that improve the Gaussian sampler proposed first by Ducas et al. [10]. This improved Gaussian sampler is used to speed up the computation of TESLA#'s key generation and to protect against timing attacks by taking the "same time" of execution regardless of the private data. The design of new algorithm consists to sample according to the Bernoulli distribution $B_{e^{-t/2\sigma^2}}$ with t is an l-bit integer.

4.5   Parameters Recommendation

For hardness guarantees [9], the ring R_q must be instantiated so that $q \equiv 1$ mod $2n$, and the Gaussian parameter $\sigma\sqrt{2\pi}$ must be greater than or equal to two. The parameters presented in [8] provide 128-bit post-quantum security and 256-bit classical security for TESLA#.

5   Using TESLA# for Bitcoin

In this section, we show how to provide more security for Bitcoin systems in the presence of quantum computers.

5.1 Hash Function

In the Bitcoin, the Koblitz curve secp256k1 is combined with the hash function SHA-256 in the ECDSA signature process while TESLA# uses BLAKE2 [4] and the more recent and more secure hash function SHA-3 [11].

5.2 Authentication Process

An efficient quantum algorithm to solve ECDLP problem was given by Shor. Since Bitcoin signature scheme is ECDSA based on ECDLP problem, these attack will impact Bitcoin authentication system security. The bitcoin signature used for authentication is generated by signing the hash of the transaction and the public key belongs to the payer. Both the signature and public key prove the transaction is created by the owner of the bitcoin address.

In Bitcoin system, authentication with cryptographic digital signature is used to secure and authorize payments or transfers. In this paper we demonstrate that TESLA# is a secure signature against the quantum attacks and gives a fast signing and verifying signing, also private key will not be revelated from the public key so the address and transactions will become secure. TESLA# is an efficient signature in the context of Bitcoin to avoid quantum attacks, it could be used to replace the ECDSA digital signature based on Elliptic curve Discret Logarithm Problem which is breakable by a Shor's algorithm.

5.3 Bitcoin Mining

The security of Bitcoin is based on mining with Proof Of Work, in this phase the most important parameter is the hash function. For the present architecture of Bitcoin, the hash function is SHA-256.

Thanks to Grover's quantum search algorithm [14], it is now possible to perform the Bitcoin proof of work using a quadratical fewer hashes needed in standard proof of work using SHA-256, so the use of another type of hash fuction is recommended. To enhance the secuity of mining, it is better to use Momentum proof of work which is better than the standard proof of work [2] which is used for Bitcoin transaction.

6 Conclusion

We have studied and compared the digital signature ECDSA based on the Koblitz elliptic curve secp256k1 and the digital signature TESLA# based on lattices and the Learning with error problem for use in Bitcoin. Our analysis shows that the signature TESLA# is more secure than ECDSA, especially for Shor's quantum attack on the elliptic discrete lograrithm problem. We conclude that TESLA# is more suitable and secure for use in the Bitcoin, especially for long term applications.

References

1. Albrecht, M.R., Player, R., Scott, S.: On the concrete hardness of learning with errors. J. Math. Cryptol. **9**(3), 169–203 (2015)
2. Aggarwal, D., Brennen, G.K., Lee, T., Santha, M., Tomamichel, M.: Quantum attacks on Bitcoin, and how to protect against them. arXiv preprint arXiv:1710.10377 (2017)
3. Akleylek, S., Bindel, N., Buchmann, J., Krämer, J., Marson, G.A.: An efficient lattice-based signature scheme with provably secure instantiation. In: Pointcheval, D., Nitaj, A., Rachidi, T. (eds.) AFRICACRYPT 2016. LNCS, vol. 9646, pp. 44–60. Springer, Cham (2016). https://doi.org/10.1007/978-3-319-31517-1_3
4. Aumasson, J.-P., Neves, S., Wilcox-O'Hearn, Z., Winnerlein, C.: BLAKE2: simpler, smaller, fast as MD5. In: Jacobson, M., Locasto, M., Mohassel, P., Safavi-Naini, R. (eds.) ACNS 2013. LNCS, vol. 7954, pp. 119–135. Springer, Heidelberg (2013). https://doi.org/10.1007/978-3-642-38980-1_8
5. Arora, S., Ge, R.: New algorithms for learning in presence of errors. In: Aceto, L., Henzinger, M., Sgall, J. (eds.) ICALP 2011. LNCS, vol. 6755, pp. 403–415. Springer, Heidelberg (2011). https://doi.org/10.1007/978-3-642-22006-7_34
6. Babai, L.: A las vegas-NC algorithm for isomorphism of graphs with bounded multiplicity of eigenvalues. In: 27th FOCS, pp. 303–312. IEEE Computer Society Press, Toronto, 27–29 October 1986
7. Blum, A., Kalai, A., Wasserman, H.: Noise-tolerant learning, the parity problem, and the statistical query model. In: 32nd ACM STOC, pp. 435–440. ACM Press, Portland, 21–23 May 2000
8. Barreto, P.S., Longa, P., Naehrig, M., Ricardini, J.E., Zanon, G.: Sharper ring-LWE signatures. Cryptology ePrint Archive, Report 2016/1026 (2016)
9. Chopra, A.: Improved parameters for the ring-TESLA digital signature scheme. IACR Cryptology ePrint Archive 2016, p. 1099 (2016)
10. Ducas, L., Durmus, A., Lepoint, T., Lyubashevsky, V.: Lattice signatures and bimodal Gaussians. In: Canetti, R., Garay, J.A. (eds.) CRYPTO 2013. LNCS, vol. 8042, pp. 40–56. Springer, Heidelberg (2013). https://doi.org/10.1007/978-3-642-40041-4_3
11. Dworkin, M.J.: SHA-3 standard: permutation-based hash and extendable-output functions. National Institute of Standards and Technology (NIST), Gaithersburg (MD), USA, August 2015
12. FIPS PUB 186–4, Digital Signature Standard (DSS), July 2013. http://nvlpubs.nist.gov/nistpubs/FIPS/NIST.FIPS.186-4.pdf
13. FIPS PUB 180–4, Secure Hash Standard (SHS). https://nvlpubs.nist.gov/nistpubs/fips/nist.fips.180-4.pdf
14. Grover, L.K.: A fast quantum mechanical algorithm for database search. In: Proceedings of the ACM STOC 1996, pp. 212–219. ACM, May 1996
15. Lenstra, A.K., Lenstra, H.W., Lovasz, L.: Factoring polynomials with rational coefficients. Math. Ann. **261**, 513–534 (1982)
16. Lyubashevsky, V., Peikert, C., Regev, O.: On ideal lattices and learning with errors over rings. In: Gilbert, H. (ed.) EUROCRYPT 2010. LNCS, vol. 6110, pp. 1–23. Springer, Heidelberg (2010). https://doi.org/10.1007/978-3-642-13190-5_1

17. Nakamoto, S.: Bitcoin: a peer-to-peer digital cash system, 24 May 2009. https:// bitcoin.org/bitcoin.pdf
18. Rivest, R.L., Shamir, A., Adleman, L.: A method for obtaining digital signatures and public-key cryptosystems. Commun. ACM **21**(2), 120–126 (1978)
19. Shor, P.W.: Polynomial-time algorithms for prime factorization and discrete logarithms on a quantum computer. SIAM J. Comput. **26**, 1484–1509 (1997)

Concurrency

Achieving Starvation-Freedom in Multi-version Transactional Memory Systems

Ved P. Chaudhary[1(✉)], Chirag Juyal[1(✉)], Sandeep Kulkarni[2(✉)],
Sweta Kumari[1(✉)], and Sathya Peri[1(✉)]

[1] CSE Department, IIT Hyderabad, Sangareddy, India
{cs14mtech11019,cs17mtech11014,cs15resch01004,sathya_p}@iith.ac.in
[2] CSE Department, Michigan State University, East Lansing, MI, USA
sandeep@cse.msu.edu

Abstract. Software Transactional Memory systems (STMs) have gar-
nered significant interest as an elegant alternative for addressing synchronization and concurrency issues with multi-threaded programming
in multi-core systems. Client programs use STMs by issuing transactions.
STM ensures that transaction either commits or aborts. A transaction
aborted due to conflicts is typically re-issued with the expectation that
it will complete successfully in a subsequent incarnation. However, many
existing STMs fail to provide starvation freedom, i.e., in these systems,
it is possible that concurrency conflicts may prevent an incarnated transaction from committing. To overcome this limitation, we systematically
derive a novel starvation free algorithm for multi-version STM. Our algorithm can be used either with the case where the number of versions is
unbounded and garbage collection is used or where only the latest K versions are maintained, *KSFTM*. We have demonstrated that our proposed
algorithm performs better than existing state-of-the-art STMs.

Keywords: Software Transactional Memory System ·
Concurrency control · Starvation-freedom · Opacity · Local opacity ·
Multi-version

1 Introduction

STMs [1,2] are a convenient programming interface for a programmer to access
shared memory without worrying about consistency issues. STMs often use an
optimistic approach for concurrent execution of *transactions* (a piece of code
invoked by a thread). In optimistic execution, each transaction reads from the
shared memory, but all write updates are performed on local memory. On completion, the STM system *validates* the reads and writes of the transaction. If any

---

Author sequence follows lexical order of last names.

© Springer Nature Switzerland AG 2019
M. F. Atig and A. A. Schwarzmann (Eds.): NETYS 2019, LNCS 11704, pp. 291–310, 2019.
https://doi.org/10.1007/978-3-030-31277-0_20

inconsistency is found, the transaction is *aborted*, and its local writes are discarded. Otherwise, the transaction is committed, and its local writes are transferred to the shared memory. A transaction that has begun but has not yet committed/aborted is referred to as *live*.

A typical STM is a library which exports the following methods: *stm-begin* which begins a transaction, *stm-read* which reads a *transactional object* or *t-object*, *stm-write* which writes to a *t-object*, *stm-tryC* which tries to commit the transaction. Typical code for using STMs is as shown in Algorithm 1 which shows how an insert of a concurrent linked-list library is implemented using STMs.

Correctness: Several *correctness-criteria* have been proposed for STMs such as opacity [3], local opacity [4,5]. All these *correctness-criteria* require that all the transactions including the aborted ones appear to execute sequentially in an order that agrees with the order of non-overlapping transactions. Unlike the correctness-criteria for traditional databases, such as serializability, strict-serializability [6], the correctness-criteria for STMs ensure that even aborted transactions read correct values. This ensures that programmers do not see any undesirable side-effects due to the reads by transaction that get aborted later such as divide-by-zero, infinite-loops, crashes etc. in the application due to concurrent executions. This additional requirement on aborted transactions is a fundamental requirement of STMs which differentiates STMs from databases as observed by Guerraoui & Kapalka [3]. Thus in this paper, we focus on optimistic executions with the *correctness-criterion* being *local opacity* [5].

Algorithm 1. Insert(LL, e): Invoked by a thread to insert an element e into a linked-list LL. This method is implemented using transactions.

```
1: retry = 0;                                    8:    ...
2: while (true) do                               9:      ret = stm-tryC(id); /* stm-tryC can return
3:    id = stm-begin (retry);                          commit or abort */
4:    ...                                        10:     if (ret == commit) then break;
5:    v = stm-read(id, x); /* reads value of x as v */  11:     else retry++;
6:    ...                                        12:     end if
7:    stm-write(id, x, v'); /* writes a value v' to x */ 13: end while
```

Starvation Freedom: In the execution shown in Algorithm 1, there is a possibility that the transaction which a thread tries to execute gets aborted again and again. Every time, it executes the transaction, say T_i, T_i conflicts with some other transaction and hence gets aborted. In other words, the thread is effectively starved because it is not able to commit T_i successfully.

A well known blocking progress condition associated with concurrent programming is starvation-freedom [7, chap. 2], [8]. In the context of STMs, starvation-freedom ensures that every aborted transaction that is retried infinitely often eventually commits. It can be defined as: an STM system is said to be *starvation-free* if a thread invoking a transaction T_i gets the opportunity to retry T_i on every abort (due to the presence of a fair underlying scheduler with bounded termination) and T_i is not *parasitic*, i.e., T_i will try to commit given a chance then T_i will eventually commit. Parasitic transactions [9] will not commit even when given a chance to commit possibly because they are caught in an infinite loop or some other error.

Wait-freedom is another interesting progress condition for STMs in which every transaction commits regardless of the nature of concurrent transactions and the underlying scheduler [8]. But it was shown by Guerraoui and Kapalka [9] that it is not possible to achieve *wait-freedom* in dynamic STMs in which data sets of transactions are not known in advance. So in this paper, we explore the weaker progress condition of *starvation-freedom* for transactional memories while assuming that the data sets of the transactions are *not* known in advance.

Related Work on the Starvation-Free STMs: Starvation-freedom in STMs has been explored by a few researchers in literature such as Gramoli et al. [10], Waliullah and Stenstrom [11], Spear et al. [12]. Most of these systems work by assigning priorities to transactions. In case of a conflict between two transactions, the transaction with lower priority is aborted. They ensure that every aborted transaction, on being retried a sufficient number of times, will eventually have the highest priority and hence will commit. We denote such an algorithm as *single-version starvation-free STM* or *SV-SFTM*.

Although *SV-SFTM* guarantees starvation-freedom, it can still abort many transactions spuriously. Consider the case where a transaction T_i has the highest priority. Hence, as per *SV-SFTM*, T_i cannot be aborted. But if it is slow (for some reason), then it can cause several other conflicting transactions to abort and hence, bring down the efficiency and progress of the entire system.

Figure 1 illustrates this problem. Consider the execution: $r_1(x,0)r_1(y,0)$ $w_2(x,10)w_2(z,10)w_3(y,15)w_1(z,7)$. It has three transactions T_1, T_2 and T_3. Let T_1 have the highest priority. After reading y, suppose T_1 becomes slow. Next T_2 and T_3 want to write to x, z and y respectively and *commit*. But T_2 and T_3's write operations are in conflict with T_1's read operations. Since T_1 has higher priority and has not committed yet, T_2 and T_3 have to *abort*. If these transactions are retried and again conflict with T_1 (while it is still live), they will have to *abort* again. Thus, any transaction with priority lower than T_1 and conflicts with it has to abort. It is as if T_1 has locked the t-objects x, y and does not allow any other transaction, write to these t-objects and to *commit*.

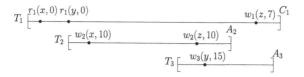

Fig. 1. Limitation of single-version starvation free algorithm

Multi-version Starvation-Free STM: A key limitation of single-version STMs is limited concurrency. As shown above, it is possible that one long transaction conflicts with several transactions causing them to abort. This limitation can be overcome by using multi-version STMs where we store multiple versions of the data item (either unbounded versions with garbage collection, or bounded versions where the oldest version is replaced when the number of versions exceeds the bound).

Several multi-version STMs have been proposed in the literature [13–16] that provide increased concurrency. But none of them provide starvation-freedom. Suppose the execution shown in Fig. 1 uses multiple versions for each t-object. Then both T_2 and T_3 create a new version corresponding to each t-object x, z and y and return commit while not causing T_1 to abort as well. T_1 reads the initial value of z, and returns commit. So, by maintaining multiple versions all the transactions T_1, T_2, and T_3 can commit with equivalent serial history as $T_1T_2T_3$ or $T_1T_3T_2$. Thus multiple versions can help with starvation-freedom without sacrificing on concurrency. This motivated us to develop a multi-version starvation-free STM system.

Although multi-version STMs provide greater concurrency, they suffer from the cost of garbage collection. One way to avoid this is to use bounded-multi-version STMs, where the number of versions is bounded to be at most K. Thus, when $(K + 1)^{th}$ version is created, the oldest version is removed. Furthermore, achieving starvation-freedom while using only bounded versions is especially challenging given that a transaction may rely on the oldest version that is removed. In that case, it would be necessary to abort that transaction, making it harder to achieve starvation-freedom.

This paper addresses this gap by developing a starvation-free algorithm for bounded MVSTMs. Our approach is different from the approach used in *SV-SFTM* to provide starvation-freedom in single version STMs (the policy of aborting lower priority transactions in case of conflict) as it does not work for MVSTMs. As part of the derivation of our final starvation-free algorithm, we consider an algorithm *PKTO* (*Priority-based K-version Timestamp Order*) that considers this approach and show that it is insufficient to provide starvation freedom.

Contributions of the Paper:

– We propose a multi-version starvation-free STM system as *K-version starvation-free STM* or *KSFTM* for a given parameter K. Here K is the number of versions of each t-object and can range from 1 to ∞. To the best of our knowledge, this is the first starvation-free MVSTM. We develop *KSFTM* algorithm in a step-wise manner starting from MVTO [13] *(Multi-Version Timestamp Order)* as follows:
   • First, in Subsect. 3.3, we use the standard idea to provide higher priority to older transactions. Specifically, we propose priority-based K-version STM algorithm *Priority-based K-version MVTO* or *PKTO*. algorithm guarantees the safety properties of strict-serializability and local opacity. However, it is not starvation-free.
   • We analyze *PKTO* to identify the characteristics that will help us to achieve preventing a transaction from getting aborted forever. This analysis leads us to the development of *starvation-free K-version TO* or *SFKTO* (Subsect. 3.4), a multi-version starvation-free STM obtained by revising *PKTO*. But SFKTO does not satisfy correctness, i.e., strict-serializability, and local opacity.

- Finally, we extend SFKTO to develop *KSFTM* (Subsect. 3.5) that preserves the starvation-freedom, strict-serializability, and local opacity. Our algorithm works on the assumption that any transaction that is not deadlocked, terminates (commits or aborts) in a bounded time.

– Our experiments (Sect. 4) show that *KSFTM* gives an average speedup on the worst-case time to commit of a transaction by a factor of 1.22, 1.89, 23.26 and 13.12 times over *PKTO*, *SV-SFTM*, NOrec STM [17] and ESTM [18] respectively for counter application. *KSFTM* performs 1.5 and 1.44 times better than *PKTO* and *SV-SFTM* but 1.09 times worse than NOrec for low contention KMEANS application of STAMP [19] benchmark whereas *KSFTM* performs 1.14, 1.4 and 2.63 times better than *PKTO*, *SV-SFTM* and NOrec for LABYRINTH application of STAMP benchmark which has high contention with long-running transactions.

2   System Model and Preliminaries

Following [5,20], we assume a system of n processes/threads, $p_1, \ldots, p_n$ that access a collection of *transactional objects* (or *t-objects*) via atomic *transactions*. Each transaction has a unique identifier. Within a transaction, processes can perform *transactional operations or methods*: *stm-begin*() that begins a transaction, *stm-write*(x, v) operation that updates a t-object x with value v in its local memory, the *stm-read*(x) operation tries to read x, *stm-tryC*() that tries to commit the transaction and returns *commit* $\mathscr{C}$ if it succeeds. Otherwise, *stm-tryA*() that aborts the transaction and returns *abort* $\mathscr{A}$. For the sake of presentation simplicity, we assume that the values taken as arguments by *stm-write*() are unique.

Operations *stm-read*() and *stm-tryC*() may return $\mathscr{A}$, in which case we say that the operations *forcefully abort*. Otherwise, we say that the operations have *successfully* executed. Each operation is equipped with a unique transaction identifier. A transaction T_i starts with the first operation and completes when any of its operations return $\mathscr{A}$ or $\mathscr{C}$. We denote any operation that returns $\mathscr{A}$ or $\mathscr{C}$ as *terminal operations*. Hence, operations *stm-tryC*() and *stm-tryA*() are terminal operations. A transaction does not invoke any further operations after terminal operations.

For a transaction T_k, we denote all the t-objects accessed by its read operations as $rset_k$ and t-objects accessed by its write operations as $wset_k$. We denote all the operations of a transaction T_k as $T_k.evts$ or $evts_k$.

History: A *history* is a sequence of *events*, i.e., a sequence of invocations and responses of transactional operations. The collection of events is denoted as $H.evts$. For simplicity, we only consider *sequential* histories here: the invocation of each transactional operation is immediately followed by a matching response. Therefore, we treat each transactional operation as one atomic event, and let $<_H$ denote the total order on the transactional operations incurred by H. With this assumption, the only relevant events of a transaction T_k is of the types: $r_k(x, v)$, $r_k(x, \mathscr{A})$, $w_k(x, v)$, *stm-tryC*$_k(\mathscr{C})$ (or c_k for short), *stm-tryC*$_k(\mathscr{A})$, *stm-tryA*$_k(\mathscr{A})$ (or a_k for short). We identify a history H as tuple $\langle H.evts, <_H \rangle$.

Let $H|T$ denote the history consisting of events of T in H, and $H|p_i$ denote the history consisting of events of p_i in H. We only consider *well-formed* histories here, i.e., no transaction of a process begins before the previous transaction invocation has completed (either *commits* or *aborts*). We also assume that every history has an initial *committed* transaction T_0 that initializes all the t-objects with value 0.

The set of transactions that appear in H is denoted by $H.txns$. The set of *committed* (resp., *aborted*) transactions in H is denoted by $H.committed$ (resp., $H.aborted$). The set of *incomplete* or *live* transactions in H is denoted by $H.incomp = H.live = (H.txns - H.committed - H.aborted)$.

For a history H, we construct the *completion* of H, denoted as $\overline{H}$, by inserting $stm\text{-}tryA_k(\mathscr{A})$ immediately after the last event of every transaction $T_k \in H.live$. But for $stm\text{-}tryC_i$ of transaction T_i, if it released the lock on first t-object successfully that means updates made by T_i is consistent so, T_i will immediately return commit.

Due to lack of space, we define other useful notions used in this paper such as opacity [3], local opacity [4,5], strict-serializability [6] formally in technical report [21].

3   The Working of *KSFTM* Algorithm

In this section, we propose *K-version starvation-free STM* or *KSFTM* for a given parameter K. Here K is the number of versions of each t-object and can range from 1 to ∞. When K is 1, it boils down to single-version starvation-free STM. If K is ∞, then *KSFTM* uses unbounded versions and needs a separate garbage collection mechanism to delete old versions like other MVSTMs proposed in the literature [13,14]. We denote *KSFTM* using unbounded versions as *UVSFTM* and the version with garbage collection as *UVSFTM-GC*.

To explain the intuition behind the *KSFTM* algorithm, we start with the modification of MVTO [13,22] algorithm and then make a sequence of modifications to it to arrive at *KSFTM* algorithm. The rest of the section is organized as follows. In Subsect. 3.1, we define starvation freedom and identify assumptions made in the paper. Subsection 3.2 discusses data structures for all the algorithms developed in this section. Subsection 3.3 develops *PKTO* that adds the approach of providing priority to older transactions in MVTO algorithm. We show why this is insufficient to provide starvation freedom in multi-version setting. Subsection 3.4 identifies a key idea that can help in providing starvation freedom. Unfortunately, using this idea alone is insufficient as it can violate strict-serializability and consequently local opacity. Subsection 3.5 describes *KSFTM* algorithm that simultaneously maintains correctness, strict-serializability and local opacity while providing starvation-freedom.

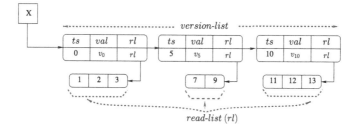

Fig. 2. Data structures for maintaining versions

3.1 Starvation-Freedom Explanation

This section starts with the definition of starvation-freedom. Then we describe the assumption that we make about the scheduler for our algorithm to satisfy starvation-freedom.

Definition 1. Starvation-Freedom: *A STM system is said to be starvation-free if a thread invoking a non-parasitic transaction T_i gets the opportunity to retry T_i on every abort, due to the presence of a fair scheduler, then T_i will eventually commit.*

As explained by Herlihy & Shavit [8], a fair scheduler implies that no thread is forever delayed or crashed. Hence with a fair scheduler, we get that if a thread acquires locks then it will eventually release the locks. Thus a thread cannot block out other threads from progressing.

Assumption About Scheduler: In order for starvation-free algorithm *KSFTM* (described in Subsect. 3.5) to work correctly, we make the following assumption about the fair scheduler:

Assumption 1. Bounded-Termination: *For any transaction T_i, invoked by a thread Th_x, the fair system scheduler ensures, in the absence of deadlocks, Th_x is given sufficient time on a CPU (and memory etc.) such that T_i terminates (either commits or aborts) in bounded time.*

While the bound for each transaction may be different, we use L to denote the maximum bound. In other words, in time L, every transaction will either abort or commit due to the absence of deadlocks.

There are different ways to satisfy the scheduler requirement. For example, a round-robin scheduler which provides each thread equal amount of time in any window satisfies this requirement as long as the number of threads is bounded. In a system with two threads, even if a scheduler provides one thread 1% of CPU and another thread 99% of the CPU, it satisfies the above requirement. On the other hand, a scheduler that schedules the threads as '$T_1, T_2, T_1, T_2, T_2, T_1, T_2,$ $T_2, T_2, T_2, \ T_1, T_2, T_2, \ T_2, T_2, T_2, T_2, T_2, T_2, T_1, T_2 (16\, times)$' does not satisfy the above requirement. This is due to the fact that over time, thread 1 gets infinitesimally smaller portion of the CPU and, hence, the time required for it to complete (commit or abort) will continue to increase over time.

In our algorithm, we will ensure that it is deadlock free using standard techniques from the literature. In other words, each thread is in a position to make progress. We assume that the scheduler provides sufficient CPU time to complete (either commit or abort) within a bounded time.

3.2 Algorithm Preliminaries

In this sub-section, we describe the invocation of transactions by the application. Next, we describe the data structures used by the algorithms.

Transaction Invocation: Transactions are invoked by the threads. Suppose a thread Th_x invokes a transaction T_i. If this transaction T_i gets *aborted*, Th_x will reissue it, as a new *incarnation* of T_i, say T_j. The thread Th_x will continue to invoke new incarnations of T_i until an incarnation commits.

When the thread Th_x invokes a transaction, say T_i, for the first time then the STM system assigns T_i a unique timestamp called *current timestamp or CTS*. If it aborts and retries again as T_j, then its CTS will be different. However, in this case, the thread Th_x will also pass the CTS value of the first incarnation (T_i) to the STM system. By this, Th_x informs the STM that, T_j is not a new invocation but is an incarnation of T_i. The CTS values are obtained by incrementing a global atomic counter G_tCntr.

We denote the CTS of T_i (first incarnation) as *Initial Timestamp or ITS* for all the incarnations of T_i. Thus, the invoking thread Th_x passes cts_i to all the incarnations of T_i (including T_j). Thus for T_j, $its_j = cts_i$. The transaction T_j is associated with the timestamps: $\langle its_j, cts_j \rangle$. For T_i, which is the initial incarnation, its ITS and CTS are the same, i.e., $its_i = cts_i$. For simplicity, we use the notation that for transaction T_j, j is its CTS, i.e., $cts_j = j$.

We now state our assumptions about transactions in the system.

Assumption 2. *We assume that in the absence of other concurrent conflicting transactions, every transaction will commit. In other words, (a) if a transaction T_i is executing in a system where other concurrent conflicting transactions are not present then T_i will not self-abort. (b) Transactions are not parasitic (explained in Sect. 1).*

If transactions self-abort or behave in parasitic manner then providing starvation-freedom is impossible.

Common Data Structures and STM Methods: Here we describe the common data structures used by all the algorithms proposed in this section.

In all our algorithms, for each t-object, the algorithms maintain multiple versions in form of *version-list* (or *vlist*). Similar to MVTO [13], each version of a t-object is a tuple denoted as *vTuple* and consists of three fields: (1) timestamp characterizing the transaction that created the version, (2) value, and (3) a list, *read-list* (or *rl*) consisting of transaction ids (or CTSs) that read from this version.

Figure 2 illustrates this structure. For a t-object x, we use the notation $x[t]$ to access the version with timestamp t. Depending on the algorithm considered, the fields of this structure change.

We assume that the STM system exports the following methods for a transaction T_i: (1) $stm\text{-}begin(t)$ where t is provided by the invoking thread, Th_x. From our earlier assumption, it is the CTS of the first incarnation or $null$ if Th_x is invoking this transaction for the first time. This method returns a unique timestamp to Th_x which is the CTS/id of the transaction. (2) $stm\text{-}read_i(x)$ tries to read t-object x. It returns either value v or $\mathscr{A}$. (3) $stm\text{-}write_i(x, v)$ operation that updates a t-object x with value v locally. It returns ok. (4) $stm\text{-}tryC_i()$ tries to commit the transaction and returns $\mathscr{C}$ if it succeeds. Otherwise, it returns $\mathscr{A}$.

Correctness Criteria: For ease of exposition, we initially consider strict-serializability as *correctness-criterion* to illustrate the correctness of the algorithms. Subsequently, we consider a stronger property, local opacity that is more suitable for STMs.

3.3   Priority-Based MVTO Algorithm

In this subsection, we describe a modification to the multi-version timestamp ordering (MVTO) algorithm [13, 22] to ensure that it provides preference to transactions that have low ITS, i.e., transactions that have been in the system for a longer time. We denote the basic algorithm which maintains unbounded versions as *Priority-based MVTO* or *PMVTO* (akin to the original MVTO). We denote the variant of *PMVTO* that maintains K versions as *PKTO* and the unbounded versions variant with garbage collection as *PMVTO-GC*.

While providing higher priority to older transactions suffices to provide starvation-freedom in *SV-SFTM*, we note that *PKTO* is not starvation free. The reason that demonstrates why *PKTO* is not starvation free forms our basis of designing SFMVTO that provides starvation-freedom (described in Subsect. 3.4).

We now describe *PKTO*. This description can be trivially extended to *PMVTO* and *PMVTO-GC* as well.

$stm\text{-}begin(t)$: A unique timestamp ts is allocated to T_i which is its CTS (i from our assumption). The timestamp ts is generated by atomically incrementing the global counter G_tCntr. If the input t is null, then $cts_i = its_i = ts$ as this is the first incarnation of this transaction. Otherwise, the non-null value of t is assigned as its_i.

$stm\text{-}read(x)$: Transaction T_i reads from a version of x in the shared memory (if x does not exist in T_i's local buffer) with timestamp j such that j is the largest timestamp less than i (among the versions of x), i.e., there exists no version of x with timestamp k such that $j < k < i$. After reading this version of x, T_i is stored in $x[j]$'s read-list. If no such version exists then T_i is *aborted*.

$stm\text{-}write(x, v)$: T_i stores this write to value x locally in its $wset_i$. If T_i ever reads x again, this value will be returned.

stm-tryC : This operation consists of three steps. In Step 1, it checks whether T_i can be *committed*. In Step 2, it performs the necessary tasks to mark T_i as a *committed* transaction and in Step 3, T_i return commits.

1. Before T_i can commit, it needs to verify that any version it creates does not violate consistency. Suppose T_i creates a new version of x with timestamp i. Let j be the largest timestamp smaller than i for which version of x exists. Let this version be $x[j]$. Now, T_i needs to make sure that any transaction that has read $x[j]$ is not affected by the new version created by T_i. There are two possibilities of concern:
   (a) Let T_k be some transaction that has read $x[j]$ and $k > i$ (k = CTS of T_k). In this scenario, the value read by T_k would be incorrect (w.r.t strict-serializability) if T_i is allowed to create a new version. In this case, we say that the transactions T_i and T_k are in *conflict*. So, we do the following: (i) if T_k has already *committed* then T_i is *aborted*; (ii) Suppose T_k is live and its_k is less than its_i. Then again T_i is *aborted*; (iii) If T_k is still live with its_i less than its_k then T_k is *aborted*.
   (b) The previous version $x[j]$ does not exist. This happens when the previous version $x[j]$ has been overwritten. In this case, T_i is *aborted* since *PKTO* does not know if T_i conflicts with any other transaction T_k that has read the previous version.
2. After Step 1, we have verified that it is ok for T_i to commit. Now, we have to create a version of each t-object x in the *wset* of T_i. This is achieved as follows:
   (a) T_i creates a $vTuple$ $\langle i, wset_i.x.v, null\rangle$. In this tuple, i (CTS of T_i) is the timestamp of the new version; $wset_i.x.v$ is the value of x is in T_i's *wset*, and the read-list of the $vTuple$ is *null*.
   (b) Suppose the total number of versions of x is K. Then among all the versions of x, T_i replaces the version with the smallest timestamp with $vTuple$ $\langle i, wset_i.x.v, null\rangle$. Otherwise, the $vTuple$ is added to x's *vlist*.
3. Transaction T_i is then *committed*.

The algorithm described here is only the main idea. The actual implementation will use locks to ensure that each of these methods are linearizable [23]. It can be seen that *PKTO* gives preference to the transaction having lower ITS in Step 1a. Transactions having lower ITS have been in the system for a longer time. Hence, *PKTO* gives preference to them. The detailed pseudocode along with the description can be found in the technical report [21]. We have the following property on the correctness of *PKTO*.

Property 1. Any history generated by the *PKTO* is strict-serializable.

Consider a history H generated by *PKTO*. Let the *committed* sub-history of H be $CSH = H.subhist(H.committed)$. It can be shown that CSH is opaque with the equivalent serialized history SH' is one in which all the transactions of CSH are ordered by their CTSs. Hence, H is strict-serializable.

While *PKTO* (and *PMVTO*) satisfies strict-serializability, it fails to prevent starvation. The key reason is that if transaction T_j conflicts with T_k and T_k has already committed, then T_j must be aborted. This is true even if T_j is the oldest transaction in the system. Furthermore, next incarnation of T_j may have to be aborted by another transaction T_k'. This cannot be prevented as conflict between T_j and T_k' may not be detected before T_k' has committed. A detailed illustration of starvation in *PKTO* is shown in the technical report [21].

3.4   Modifying *PKTO* to Obtain SFKTO: Trading Correctness for Starvation-Freedom

Our goal is to revise *PKTO* algorithm to ensure that *starvation-freedom* is satisfied. Specifically, we want the transaction with the lowest ITS to eventually commit. Once this happens, the next non-committed transaction with the lowest ITS will commit. Thus, from induction, we can see that every transaction will eventually commit.

Key Insights for Eliminating Starvation in *PKTO*: To identify the necessary revision, we first focus on the effect of this algorithm on two transactions, say T_{50} and T_{60} with their CTS values being 50 and 60 respectively. Furthermore, for the sake of discussion, assume that these transactions only read and write t-object x. Also, assume that the latest version for x is with ts 40. Each transaction first reads x and then writes x (as part of the *stm-tryC* operation). We use r_{50} and r_{60} to denote their read operations while w_{50} and w_{60} to denote their *stm-tryC* operations. Here, a read operation will not fail as there is a previous version present.

Now, there are six possible permutations of these statements. We identify these permutations and the action that should be taken for that permutation in Table 1. In all these permutations, the read operations of a transaction come before the write operations as the writes to the shared memory occurs only in the *stm-tryC* operation (due to optimistic execution) which is the final operation of a transaction.

From this table, it can be seen that when a conflict is detected, in some cases, algorithm *PKTO* *must* abort T_{50}. In case both the transactions are live, *PKTO* has the option of aborting either transaction depending on their ITS. If T_{60} has

Table 1. Permutations of operations

S. No.	Sequence	Possible actions by *PKTO*
1	$r_{50}, w_{50}, r_{60}, w_{60}$	T_{60} reads the version written by T_{50}. No conflict
2	$r_{50}, r_{60}, w_{50}, w_{60}$	Conflict detected at w_{50}. Either abort T_{50} or T_{60}
3	$r_{50}, r_{60}, w_{60}, w_{50}$	Conflict detected at w_{50}. Hence, abort T_{50}
4	$r_{60}, r_{50}, w_{60}, w_{50}$	Conflict detected at w_{50}. Hence, abort T_{50}
5	$r_{60}, r_{50}, w_{50}, w_{60}$	Conflict detected at w_{50}. Either abort T_{50} or T_{60}
6	$r_{60}, w_{60}, r_{50}, w_{50}$	Conflict detected at w_{50}. Hence, abort T_{50}

lower ITS then in no case, $PKTO$ is required to abort T_{60}. In other words, it is possible to ensure that the transaction with the lowest ITS and the highest CTS is never aborted. Although in this example, we considered only one t-object, this logic can be extended to cases having multiple operations and t-objects.

Next, consider Step 1b of stm-tryC in $PKTO$ algorithm. Suppose a transaction T_i wants to read a t-object but does not find a version with a timestamp smaller than i. In this case, T_i has to abort. But if T_i has the highest CTS, then it will certainly find a version to read from. This is because the timestamp of a version corresponds to the timestamp of the transaction that created it. If T_i has the highest CTS value then it implies that all versions of all the t-objects have a timestamp smaller than CTS of T_i. This reinforces the above observation that a transaction with the lowest ITS and highest CTS is not aborted.

To summarize the discussion, algorithm $PKTO$ has an in-built mechanism to protect transactions with lowest ITS and highest CTS value. However, this is different from what we need. Specifically, we want to protect a transaction T_i, with lowest ITS value. One way to ensure this: if transaction T_i with lowest ITS keeps getting aborted, eventually it should achieve the highest CTS. Once this happens, $PKTO$ ensures that T_i cannot be further aborted. In this way, we can ensure the liveness of all transactions.

The Working of Starvation-Free Algorithm: To realize this idea and achieve starvation-freedom, we consider another variation of MVTO, *Starvation-Free MVTO* or *SFMVTO*. We specifically consider SFMVTO with K versions, denoted as *SFKTO*.

A transaction T_i instead of using the current time as cts_i, uses a potentially higher timestamp, *Working Timestamp - WTS* or wts_i. Specifically, it adds $C * (cts_i - its_i)$ to cts_i, i.e.,

$$wts_i = cts_i + C * (cts_i - its_i); \tag{1}$$

where, C is any constant greater than 0. In other words, when the transaction T_i is issued for the first time, wts_i is same as $cts_i (= its_i)$. However, as transaction keeps getting aborted, the drift between cts_i and wts_i increases. The value of wts_i increases with each retry.

Furthermore, in SFKTO algorithm, CTS is replaced with WTS for *stm-read*, *stm-write* and *stm-tryC* operations of $PKTO$. In SFKTO, a transaction T_i uses wts_i to read a version in *stm-read*. Similarly, T_i uses wts_i in *stm-tryC* to find the appropriate previous version (in Step 1b) and to verify if T_i has to be aborted (in Step 1a). Along the same lines, once T_i decides to commit and create new versions of x, the timestamp of x will be same as its wts_i (in Step 3). Thus the timestamp of all the versions in *vlist* will be WTS of the transactions that created them.

SFKTO algorithms ensures starvation-freedom in presence of a fair scheduler that satisfies Assumption 1 (bounded-termination). While the proof of this property is somewhat involved, the key idea is that the transaction with lowest ITS value, say T_{low}, will eventually have highest WTS value than all the other transactions in the system. Then it cannot be aborted. But SFKTO and its variant SFMVTO do not satisfy strict-serializability which is illustrated in the technical report [21].

3.5   Design of *KSFTM*: Regaining Correctness While Preserving Starvation-Freedom

In this section, we discuss how principles of *PKTO* and SFKTO can be combined to obtain *KSFTM* that provides both correctness (strict-serializability and local opacity) as well as starvation-freedom. To achieve this, we first understand why the initial algorithm, *PKTO* satisfies strict-serializability. This is because CTS was used to create the ordering among committed transactions. CTS is based on real-time ordering. In contrast, SFKTO uses WTS which may not correspond to the real-time, as WTS may be significantly larger than CTS as shown by history $H1$ in Fig. 3.

One straightforward way to modify SFKTO is to delay a committing transaction, say T_i with WTS value wts_i until the real-time (G_tCntr) catches up to wts_i. This will ensure that the value of WTS will also become the same as the real-time thereby guaranteeing strict-serializability. However, this is unacceptable, as in practice, it would require transaction T_i locking all the variables it plans to update and wait. This will adversely affect the performance of the STM system.

We can allow the transaction T_i to commit before its wts_i has caught up with the actual time if it does not violate the real-time ordering. Thus, to ensure that the notion of real-time order is respected by transactions in the course of their execution in SFKTO, we add extra time constraints. We use the idea of timestamp ranges. This notion of timestamp ranges was first used by Riegel et al. [24] in the context of multi-version STMs. Several other researchers have used this idea since then such as Guerraoui et al. [25], Crain et al. [26] etc.

Thus, in addition to ITS, CTS and WTS, each transaction T_i maintains a timestamp range: *Transaction Lower Timestamp Limit* or $tltl_i$, and *Transaction Upper Timestamp Limit* or $tutl_i$. When a transaction T_i begins, $tltl_i$ is assigned cts_i and $tutl_i$ is assigned the largest possible value which we denote as infinity. When T_i executes a method m in which it reads a version of a t-object x or creates a new version of x in *stm-tryC*, $tltl_i$ is incremented while $tutl_i$ gets decremented[1].

We require that all the transactions are serialized based on their WTS while maintaining their real-time order. On executing a method m, T_i is ordered w.r.t to other transactions that have created a version of x based on increasing order of WTS. For all transactions T_j which also have created a version of x and whose wts_j is less than wts_i, $tltl_i$ is incremented such that $tutl_j$ is less than $tltl_i$. Note that all such T_j are serialized before T_i. Similarly, for any transaction T_k which has created a version of x and whose wts_k is greater than wts_i, $tutl_i$ is

---

[1] Technically ∞, which is assigned to $tutl_i$, cannot be decremented. But here as mentioned earlier, we use ∞ to denote the largest possible value that can be represented in a system.

decremented such that it becomes less than $tltl_k$. Again, note that all such T_k are serialized after T_i.

If T_i reads a version x created by T_j then T_i is serialized after T_j and before any other T_k that also created a version of x such that $wts_j < wts_k$. The algorithm ensures that $wts_j < wts_i < wts_k$. For correctness, we again increment $tltl_i$ and decrement $tutl_i$ as above. After the increments of $tltl_i$ and the decrements of $tutl_i$, if $tltl_i$ turns out to be greater than $tutl_i$ then T_i is aborted. Intuitively, this implies that T_i's WTS and real-time orders are out of *synchrony* and cannot be reconciled.

Finally, when a transaction T_i commits: T_i records its commit time (or $comTime_i$) by getting the current value of G_tCntr and incrementing it by $incrVal$ which is any value greater than or equal to 1. Then $tutl_i$ is set to $comTime_i$ if it is not already less than it. Now suppose T_i occurs in real-time before some other transaction, T_k but does not have any conflict with it. This step ensures that $tutl_i$ remains less than $tltl_k$ (which is initialized with cts_k).

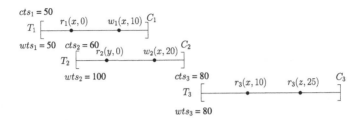

Fig. 3. Correctness of *KSFTM* algorithm

We illustrate this technique with the history $H1$ shown in Fig. 3. When T_1 starts its $cts_1 = 50, tltl_1 = 50, tutl_1 = \infty$. Now when T_1 commits, suppose G_tCntr is 70. Hence, $tutl_1$ reduces to 70. Next, when T_2 commits, suppose $tutl_2$ reduces to 75 (the current value of G_tCntr). As T_1, T_2 have accessed a common t-object x in a conflicting manner, $tltl_2$ is incremented to a value greater than $tutl_1$, say 71. Next, when T_3 begins, $tltl_3$ is assigned cts_3 which is 80 and $tutl_3$ is initialized to ∞. When T_3 reads 10 from T_1, which is $r_3(x, 10)$, $tutl_3$ is reduced to a value less than $tltl_2(= 71)$, say 70. But $tltl_3$ is already at 80. Hence, the limits of T_3 have crossed and thus causing T_3 to abort. The resulting history consisting of only committed transactions $T_1 T_2$ is strict-serializable.

Based on this idea, we next develop a variation of SFKTO, *K-version Starvation-Free STM System* or *KSFTM*. To explain this algorithm, we first describe the structure of the version of a t-object used. It is a slight variation of the t-object used in *PKTO* algorithm. It consists of: (1) timestamp, ts which is the WTS of the transaction that created this version (and not CTS like *PKTO*); (2) the value of the version; (3) a list, called read-list, consisting of transactions ids (could be CTS as well) that read from this version; (4) version real-time timestamp or **vrt** which is the tutl of the transaction that created this version. Thus a version has information of WTS and tutl of the transaction that created it.

Now, we describe the main idea behind *stm-begin*, *stm-read*, *stm-write* and *stm-tryC* operations of a transaction T_i which is an extension of *PKTO*. Note that as per our notation i represents the CTS of T_i.

stm-begin(t): A unique timestamp ts is allocated to T_i which is its CTS (i from our assumption) which is generated by atomically incrementing the global counter G_tCntr. If the input t is null then $cts_i = its_i = ts$ as this is the first incarnation of this transaction. Otherwise, the non-null value of t is assigned to its_i. Then, WTS is computed by Eq. 1. Finally, tltl and tutl are initialized as: $tltl_i = cts_i$, $tutl_i = \infty$.

stm-read(x): Transaction T_i reads from a version of x with timestamp j such that j is the largest timestamp less than wts_i (among the versions x), i.e. there exists no version k such that $j < k < wts_i$ is true. If no such j exists then T_i is aborted. Otherwise, after reading this version of x, T_i is stored in j's *rl*. Then we modify tltl, tutl as follows:

1. The version $x[j]$ is created by a transaction with wts_j which is less than wts_i. Hence, $tltl_i = max(tltl_i, x[j].\text{vrt} + 1)$.
2. Let p be the timestamp of smallest version larger than i. Then $tutl_i = min(tutl_i, x[p].\text{vrt} - 1)$.
3. After these steps, abort T_i if tltl and tutl have crossed, i.e., $tltl_i > tutl_i$.

stm-write(x, v): T_i stores this write to value x locally in its $wset_i$.

stm-tryC : This operation consists of multiple steps:

1. Before T_i can commit, we need to verify that any version it creates is updated consistently. T_i creates a new version with timestamp wts_i. Hence, we must ensure that any transaction that read a previous version is unaffected by this new version. Additionally, creating this version would require an update of tltl and tutl of T_i and other transactions whose read-write set overlaps with that of T_i. Thus, T_i first validates each t-object x in its $wset$ as follows:
   (a) T_i finds a version of x with timestamp j such that j is the largest timestamp less than wts_i (like in *stm-read*). If there exists no version of x with a timestamp less than wts_i then T_i is aborted. This is similar to Step 1b of the *stm-tryC* of *PKTO* algorithm.
   (b) Among all the transactions that have previously read from j suppose there is a transaction T_k such that $j < wts_i < wts_k$. Then (i) if T_k has already committed then T_i is aborted; (ii) Suppose T_k is live, and its_k is less than its_i. Then again T_i is aborted; (iii) If T_k is still live with its_i less than its_k then T_k is aborted.
   This step is similar to Step 1a of the *stm-tryC* of *PKTO* algorithm.
   (c) Next, we must ensure that T_i's tltl and tutl are updated correctly w.r.t to other concurrently executing transactions. To achieve this, we adjust tltl, tutl as follows: (i) Let j be the ts of the largest version smaller than wts_i. Then $tltl_i = max(tltl_i, x[j].\text{vrt} + 1)$. Next, for each reading transaction,

T_r in $x[j].read\text{-}list$, we again set, $tltl_i = max(tltl_i, tutl_r + 1)$. (ii) Similarly, let p be the ts of the smallest version larger than wts_i. Then, $tutl_i = min(tutl_i, x[p].\texttt{vrt} - 1)$. (Note that we don't have to check for the transactions in the read-list of $x[p]$ as those transactions will have tltl higher than $x[p].\texttt{vrt}$ due to $stm\text{-}read$.) (iii) Finally, we get the commit time of this transaction from G_tCntr: $comTime_i = G\_tCntr.add\&Get(incrVal)$ where $incrVal$ is any constant ≥ 1. Then, $tutl_i = min(tutl_i, comTime_i)$. After performing these updates, abort T_i if tltl and tutl have crossed, i.e., $tltl_i > tutl_i$.

2. After performing the tests of Step 1 over each t-objects x in T_i's $wset$, if T_i has not yet been aborted, we proceed as follows: for each x in $wset_i$ create a vTuple $\langle wts_i, wset_i.x.v, null, tutl_i \rangle$. In this tuple, wts_i is the timestamp of the new version; $wset_i.x.v$ is the value of x is in T_i's $wset$; the read-list of the $vTuple$ is $null$; $\texttt{vrt}$ is $tutl_i$ (actually it can be any value between $tltl_i$ and $tutl_i$). Update the $vlist$ of each t-object x similar to Step 2 of $stm\text{-}tryC$ of $PKTO$.

3. Transaction T_i is then committed.

Step 1c.(iii) of $stm\text{-}tryC$ ensures that real-time order between transactions that are not in conflict. It can be seen that locks have to be used to ensure that all these methods to execute in a linearizable manner (i.e., atomically). The detailed pseudo code along with the description can be found in accompanying technical report [21]. We get the following nice properties on $KSFTM$ with the complete details in [21]. For simplicity, we assumed C and $incrVal$ to be 0.1 and 1 respectively in our analysis. But the proof and the analysis holds for any value greater than 0.

Theorem 1. *Any history generated by KSFTM is strict-serializable and locally-opaque.*

Theorem 2. *KSFTM algorithm ensures starvation-freedom.*

4   Experimental Evaluation

For performance evaluation of $KSFTM$ with the state-of-the-art STMs, we implemented the the algorithms $PKTO$, $SV\text{-}SFTM$ [10–12] along with $KSFTM$ in C++[2] We used the available implementations of NOrec STM [17], and ESTM [18] developed in C++. Although, only $KSFTM$ and $SV\text{-}SFTM$ provide starvation-freedom, we compared with other STMs as well, to see its performance in practice.

Experimental System: The experimental system is a 2-socket Intel(R) Xeon(R) CPU E5-2690 v4 @ 2.60 GHz with 14 cores per socket and 2 hyperthreads (HTs) per core, for a total of 56 threads. Each core has a private 32KB L1 cache and 256 KB L2 cache. The machine has 32 GB of RAM and runs Ubuntu

---

[2] Code is available here: https://github.com/PDCRL/KSFTM.

16.04.2 LTS. In our implementation, all threads have the same base priority and we use the default Linux scheduling algorithm. This satisfies the Assumption 1 (bounded-termination) about the scheduler. We ensured that there no parasitic transactions [27] in our experiments.

Methodology: Here we have considered two different applications: (1) Counter application - In this, each thread invokes a single transaction which performs 10 reads/writes operations on randomly chosen t-objects. A thread continues to invoke a transaction until it successfully commits. To obtain high contention, we have taken large number of threads ranging from 50–250 where each thread performs its read/write operation over a set of 5 t-objects. We have performed our tests on three workloads stated as: (W1) Li - Lookup intensive: 90% read, 10% write, (W2) Mi - Mid intensive: 50% read, 50% write and (W3) Ui - Update intensive: 10% read, 90% write. This application is undoubtedly very flexible as it allows us to examine performance by tweaking different parameters (refer to the technical report [21] for details). (2) Two benchmarks from STAMP suite [19] - (a) We considered KMEANS which has low contention with short running transactions. The number of data points as 2048 with 16 dimensions and total clusters as 5. (b) We then considered LABYRINTH which has high contention with long running transactions. We considered the grid size as 64x64x3 and paths to route as 48.

To study starvation in the various algorithms, we considered *max-time*, which is the maximum time taken by a transaction among all the transactions in a given experiment to commit from its first invocation. This includes time taken by all the aborted incarnations of the transaction to execute as well. To reduce the effect of outliers, we took the average of max-time in ten runs as the final result for each application.

Results Analysis: Fig. 4 illustrates max-time analysis of *KSFTM* over the above mentioned STMs for the counters application under the workloads $W1$, $W2$ and $W3$ while varying the number of threads from 50 to 250. For *KSFTM* and *PKTO*, we chose the value of K as 5 and C as 0.1 as the best results were obtained with these parameters (refer to the technical report [21] for details). We can see that *KSFTM* performs the best for all the three workloads. *KSFTM* gives an average speedup on max-time by a factor of 1.22, 1.89, 23.26 and 13.12 over *PKTO*, *SV-SFTM*, NOrec STM and ESTM respectively.

Figure 5(a) shows analysis of max-time for KMEANS while Fig. 5(b) shows for LABYRINTH. In this analysis we have not considered ESTM as the integrated STAMP code for ESTM is not publicly available. For KMEANS, *KSFTM* performs 1.5 and 1.44 times better than *PKTO* and *SV-SFTM*. But, NOrec is performing 1.09 times better than *KSFTM*. This is because KMEANS has short running transactions have low contention. As a result, the commit time of the transactions is also low.

On the other hand for LABYRINTH, *KSFTM* again performs the best. It performs 1.14, 1.4 and 2.63 times better than *PKTO*, *SV-SFTM* and NOrec respectively. This is because LABYRINTH has high contention with long running transactions. This result in longer commit times for transactions.

Figure 5(c) shows the stability of *KSFTM* algorithm over time for the counter application. Here we fixed the number of threads to 32, K as 5, C as 0.1, t-objects as 1000, along with 5 s warm-up period on $W1$ workload. Each thread invokes transactions until its time-bound of 60 s expires. We performed the experiments on number of transactions committed over time in the increments 5 s. The experiment shows that over time *KSFTM* is stable which helps to hold the claim that *KSFTM*'s performance will continue in same manner if time is increased to higher orders.

We have executed several experiments to study various parameters such as average case analysis, number of aborts, effect of garbage-collection, best value of K and optimal value of C. These are explained in detail in the technical report [21].

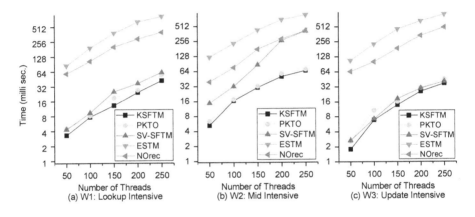

Fig. 4. Performance analysis on workload $W1$, $W2$, $W3$

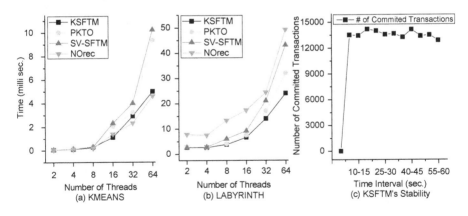

Fig. 5. Performance analysis on KMEANS, LABYRINTH and KSFTM's Stability

5   Conclusion

In this paper, we proposed *KSFTM* which ensures starvation-freedom while maintaining K versions for each t-objects. It uses two insights to ensure starvation-freedom in the context of MVSTMs: (1) using ITS to ensure that older transactions are given a higher priority, and (2) using WTS to ensure that conflicting transactions do not commit too quickly before the older transaction could commit. We show *KSFTM* satisfies strict-serializability [6] and local opacity [4,5]. Our experiments show that *KSFTM* performs better than starvation-free state-of-the-arts STMs as well as non-starvation free STMs under long running transactions with high contention workloads.

Acknowledgments. We are thankful to the anonymous reviewers for carefully reading the paper and providing us valuable suggestions.

References

1. Herlihy, M., Moss, J.E.B.: Transactional memory: architectural support for lock-free data structures. SIGARCH Comput. Archit. News **21**(2) (1993)
2. Shavit, N., Touitou, D.: Software transactional memory. In: PODC (1995)
3. Guerraoui, R., Kapalka, M.: On the correctness of transactional memory. In: PPoPP (2008)
4. Kuznetsov, P., Peri, S.: Non-interference and local correctness in transactional memory. In: ICDCN (2014) 197–211
5. Kuznetsov, P., Peri, S.: Non-interference and local correctness in transactional memory. Theor. Comput. Sci. **688**, 103–116 (2017)
6. Papadimitriou, C.H.: The serializability of concurrent database updates. J. ACM **26**(4) (1979)
7. Herlihy, M., Shavit, N.: The Art of Multiprocessor Programming, Revised Reprint, 1st edn. Morgan Kaufmann Publishers Inc., San Francisco (2012)
8. Herlihy, M., Shavit, N.: On the nature of progress. In: Fernàndez Anta, A., Lipari, G., Roy, M. (eds.) OPODIS 2011. LNCS, vol. 7109, pp. 313–328. Springer, Heidelberg (2011). https://doi.org/10.1007/978-3-642-25873-2_22
9. Bushkov, V., Guerraoui, R., Kapalka, M.: On the liveness of transactional memory. In: ACM Symposium on PODC (2012)
10. Gramoli, V., Guerraoui, R., Trigonakis, V.: TM2C: a software transactional memory for many-cores. In: EuroSys (2012)
11. Waliullah, M.M., Stenström, P.: Schemes for avoiding starvation in transactional memory systems. Concurr. Comput. Pract. Exp. **21**(7), 859–873 (2009)
12. Spear, M.F., Dalessandro, L., Marathe, V.J., Scott, M.L.: A comprehensive strategy for contention management in software transactional memory (2009)
13. Kumar, P., Peri, S., Vidyasankar, K.: A TimeStamp based multi-version STM algorithm. In: Chatterjee, M., Cao, J., Kothapalli, K., Rajsbaum, S. (eds.) ICDCN 2014. LNCS, vol. 8314, pp. 212–226. Springer, Heidelberg (2014). https://doi.org/10.1007/978-3-642-45249-9_14
14. Lu, L., Scott, M.L.: Generic multiversion STM. In: Afek, Y. (ed.) DISC 2013. LNCS, vol. 8205, pp. 134–148. Springer, Heidelberg (2013). https://doi.org/10.1007/978-3-642-41527-2_10

15. Fernandes, S.M., Cachopo, J.: Lock-free and scalable multi-version software transactional memory. In: PPoPP (2011)
16. Perelman, D., Byshevsky, A., Litmanovich, O., Keidar, I.: SMV: selective multi-versioning STM. In: Peleg, D. (ed.) DISC 2011. LNCS, vol. 6950, pp. 125–140. Springer, Heidelberg (2011). https://doi.org/10.1007/978-3-642-24100-0_9
17. Dalessandro, L., Spear, M.F., Scott, M.L.: NOrec: streamlining STM by abolishing ownership records. In: PPoPP (2010)
18. Felber, P., Gramoli, V., Guerraoui, R.: Elastic transactions. J. Parallel Distrib. Comput. **100**(C), 103–127 (2017)
19. Minh, C.C., Chung, J., Kozyrakis, C., Olukotun, K.: STAMP: stanford transactional applications for multi-processing. In: IISWC (2008)
20. Guerraoui, R., Kapalka, M.: Principles of Transactional Memory, Synthesis Lectures on Distributed Computing Theory. Morgan and Claypool, San Rafael (2010)
21. Chaudhary, V.P., Juyal, C., Kulkarni, S.S., Kumari, S., Peri, S.: Starvation freedom in multi-version transactional memory systems. CoRR abs/1709.01033 (2017)
22. Bernstein, P.A., Goodman, N.: Multiversion concurrency control: theory and algorithms. ACM Trans. Database Syst **8**, 465–483 (1983)
23. Herlihy, M.P., Wing, J.M.: Linearizability: a correctness condition for concurrent objects. ACM Trans. Program. Lang. Syst. **12**(3), 463–492 (1990)
24. Riegel, T., Felber, P., Fetzer, C.: A lazy snapshot algorithm with eager validation. In: Dolev, S. (ed.) DISC 2006. LNCS, vol. 4167, pp. 284–298. Springer, Heidelberg (2006). https://doi.org/10.1007/11864219_20
25. Guerraoui, R., Henzinger, T.A., Singh, V.: Permissiveness in transactional memories. In: Taubenfeld, G. (ed.) DISC 2008. LNCS, vol. 5218, pp. 305–319. Springer, Heidelberg (2008). https://doi.org/10.1007/978-3-540-87779-0_21
26. Crain, T., Imbs, D., Raynal, M.: Read invisibility, virtual world consistency and probabilistic permissiveness are compatible. In: Xiang, Y., Cuzzocrea, A., Hobbs, M., Zhou, W. (eds.) ICA3PP 2011. LNCS, vol. 7016, pp. 244–257. Springer, Heidelberg (2011). https://doi.org/10.1007/978-3-642-24650-0_21
27. Bushkov, V., Guerraoui, R.: Liveness in transactional memory. In: Guerraoui, R., Romano, P. (eds.) Transactional Memory. Foundations, Algorithms, Tools, and Applications. LNCS, vol. 8913, pp. 32–49. Springer, Cham (2015). https://doi.org/10.1007/978-3-319-14720-8_2

Mutex-Based De-anonymization
of an Anonymous Read/Write Memory

Emmanuel Godard[1], Damien Imbs[1], Michel Raynal[2,3(✉)],
and Gadi Taubenfeld[4]

[1] LIS, Université d'Aix-Marseille, Marseille, France
[2] Univ Rennes IRISA, Rennes, France
`raynal@irisa.fr`
[3] Department of Computing, Polytechnic University, Hung Hom, Hong Kong
[4] The Interdisciplinary Center, 46150 Herzliya, Israel

Abstract. Anonymous shared memory is a memory in which processes use different names for the same shared read/write register. As an example, a shared register named A by a process p and a shared register named B by another process q can correspond to the very same register X, and similarly for the names B at p and A at q which can correspond to the same register $Y \neq X$. Hence, there is a permanent disagreement on the register names among the processes. This new notion of anonymity was recently introduced by G. Taubenfeld (PODC 2017), who presented several memory-anonymous algorithms and impossibility results.

This paper introduces a new problem, that consists in "de-anonymizing" an anonymous shared memory. To this end, it presents an algorithm that, starting with a shared memory made up of m anonymous read/write atomic registers (i.e., there is no a priori agreement on their names), allows each process to compute a local addressing mapping, such that all the processes agree on the names of each register. The proposed construction is based on an underlying deadlock-free mutex algorithm for $n \geq 2$ processes (recently proposed in a paper co-authored by some of the authors of this paper), and consequently inherits its necessary and sufficient condition on the size m of the anonymous memory, namely m must belong to the set $M(n) = \{m : \text{ such that } \forall \ell : 1 < \ell \leq n : \gcd(\ell, m) = 1\} \setminus \{1\}$. This algorithm, which is also symmetric in the sense process identities can only be compared by equality, requires the participation of all the processes; hence it can be part of the system initialization. Last but not least, the proposed algorithm has a noteworthy first-class property, namely, its simplicity.

Keywords: Anonymity · Anonymous shared memory ·
Asynchronous system · Atomic read/write register ·
Concurrent algorithm · Deadlock-freedom · Local memory ·
Mapping function · Mutual exclusion · Simplicity · Synchronization

© Springer Nature Switzerland AG 2019
M. F. Atig and A. A. Schwarzmann (Eds.): NETYS 2019, LNCS 11704, pp. 311–326, 2019.
https://doi.org/10.1007/978-3-030-31277-0_21

1 Introduction

Read/Write Registers. *Read/write registers* are the basic objects of sequential
computing. From a theoretical point of view, they constitute the cells of a Turing
machine tape, and from a programming point of view, they are the memory
locations on top of which are built high-level objects such as stacks, queues, and
trees (to cite a few of the most common).

In a concurrent programming context, a read/write register can be shared
(accessed) by several processes to coordinate their actions or progress to a common goal. The most popular consistency condition for registers is *atomicity*,
which states that all its read and write operations appear as if they have been
executed sequentially, this sequence S being such that, if an operation op1 terminates before operation op2 starts, op1 appears before op2 in S, and a read
operation returns the value written by the closest preceding write in S [13].

A register is said to be single-reader (SR) or multi-reader (MR) according to
the number of processes that are allowed to read it. Similarly, a register can be
single-writer (SW) or multi-writer (MW). A lot of algorithms have been proposed
(e.g., see the textbooks [19,22]), which build MWMR registers from SWSR or
SWMR registers in the presence of asynchrony and process crashes. In the other
direction, an adaptive construction of SWMR registers from MWMR registers
is described in [7].

Anonymous Memory. While the notion of *process anonymity* has been studied
for a long time from an algorithmic and computability point of view, both in
message-passing systems (e.g., [2,5,24]) and shared memory systems (e.g., [4,6,
11]), the notion of *memory anonymity* has been introduced only very recently
in [23]. (See [21] for an introductory survey on process and memory anonymity).

Let us consider a shared memory SM made up of m atomic read/write registers. Such a memory can be seen as an array with m entries, namely $SM[1..m]$.
In a non-anonymous memory system, for any index x, $1 \leq x \leq m$, if two or
more processes invoke the address $SM[x]$ they access the very same register. As
stated in [23], in the classical system model, there is an a priori agreement on the
names of the shared registers. This a priori agreement facilitates the implementation of the coordination rules the processes have to follow to progress without
violating the safety (consistency) properties associated with the application they
solve [19,22].

This a priori agreement does no longer exist in a memory-anonymous system.
In such a system the very same address identifier $SM[x]$ invoked by a process
p_i and invoked by a different process p_j does not necessarily refer to the same
atomic read/write register. More precisely, a memory-anonymous system is such
that:

– for each process p_i an adversary defined, over the set $\{1, 2, \cdots, m\}$, a permutation $f_i()$ such that when p_i uses the address $SM[x]$, it actually accesses
  $SM[f_i(x)]$, and
– no process knows the permutations.

Let us notice that the read/write registers of a memory-anonymous system are necessarily MWMR.

Results on Anonymous Memory. In [23], mutual exclusion, consensus, and renaming, problems are addressed, and memory-anonymous algorithms and impossibility results are presented. Concerning deadlock-free mutual exclusion in failure-free asynchronous read/write systems, the following results are presented:

- A symmetric deadlock-free algorithm for two processes ("symmetric" means process identifiers are not ordered and can only be compared for equality, see Sect. 2.2).
- A theorem stating there is no deadlock-free algorithm if the number of processes n is not known.
- A condition on the size m of the anonymous memory which is necessary for any symmetric deadlock-free algorithm. More precisely, given an n-process system where $n \geq 2$, there is no deadlock-free mutual exclusion algorithm if the size m does not belong to the set $M(n) = \{\, m \text{ such that } \forall\, \ell : 1 < \ell \leq n\text{:} \gcd(\ell, m) = 1 \,\} \setminus \{1\}$.

Let us observe that the previous condition implies that it is not possible to design a symmetric deadlock-free mutex algorithm when the size of the anonymous memory m is an even integer greater than 2. As symmetric deadlock-free mutex algorithms suited to a non-anonymous memory do not require a parity-related property on the number of registers they use, it follows that, when the size of the memory m is an even integer greater than 2, non-anonymous read/write registers are computationally stronger than anonymous registers.

In the conclusion of [23], a few open problems are presented, one of them being "the existence of a symmetric starvation-free mutual exclusion algorithm for two processes", another one being "the existence of a symmetric deadlock-free mutual exclusion algorithm for more than two processes". This second problem was recently solved in [3] where an algorithm is presented, which assumes $m \in M(n)$. It follows that the very existence of this algorithm shows that the condition $m \in M(n)$ is also a sufficient condition for symmetric deadlock-free mutual exclusion in read/write anonymous memory systems.

Content of the Paper. As shown in [3, 23], the design of memory-anonymous algorithms is not a trivial task. We started this work with an attempt to design a starvation-free memory-anonymous mutual exclusion algorithm. This drove us to the observation that the fact "there is currently a competition among processes" must be memorized in one way or another to prevent a process from always defeating other processes, and thereby ensure starvation-freedom.

Finally, considering an n-process system, after many attempts, this work ended with a relatively simple symmetric *de-anonymization* algorithm, namely, an algorithm that transforms an anonymous read/write memory into a non-anonymous read/write memory. This algorithm requires the participation of all the processes, and assumes that processes do not fail. Once memory de-anonymization is obtained (e.g., at system initialization), it becomes possible to use algorithms based on a non-anonymous memory on top of anonymous memory.

The proposed construction relies on an underlying memory-anonymous symmetric deadlock-free mutual exclusion algorithm (the one introduced in [3]). Hence, it inherits its requirement on m, namely, $m \in M(n)$. It follows that, when m satisfies this condition, m anonymous registers and m non-anonymous registers have the same computability power from an anonymous/non-anonymous mutual exclusion point of view. Let us also notice that, if a non-anonymous memory algorithm executed on top of the proposed construction requires m' registers where m' does not belong to the set $M(n)$ defined above, it is sufficient to select the first integer greater than m' belonging to $M(n)$ as the value of m, and, at the non-anonymous memory upper layer, $(m - m')$ registers are ignored. Let us notice that the proposed construction is *universal* in the sense any concurrent non-anonymous memory algorithm can be executed on top of it.

On the Difficulty of the Problem. In a non-anonymous memory system, there is no ambiguity on the read/write registers used by the processes. As already said, its identifiers are unambiguously shared by all processes, and no other algorithm is concurrently using these registers. Differently, as, in an anonymous memory system, $SM[x]$ can denote different registers for distinct processes, a process must (in one way or another) write "enough" registers to transmit information to other processes. This is a direct consequence of the fact that there is no a priori agreement on the identities of the shared atomic read/write registers and the fact that – due to its very nature – no anonymous register can be a single-writer register.

Hence, the difficulty in the construction of a memory de-anonymization algorithm comes from the fact that, due to memory anonymity, it concurrently uses the same registers like the ones used by the underlying mutex algorithm it uses as a subroutine. As we will see, to circumvent this issue, the proposed memory de-anonymization algorithm will use (in a very simple way) the local memory of each process to store the value of an increasing counter, which simulates a shared non-anonymous register on which the processes agree and can consequently use to coordinate their local progress.

The de-anonymization problem addressed in this paper may seem of theoretical interest only (as many other problems appeared first). As long as its practical interest is concerned, we do not have to forget that, as nicely expressed by the physicist Niels Bohr "prediction is very difficult, especially when it about the future!". Nevertheless, the results presented in this paper shows that, from a computability point of view, there are cases where – in a failure-free context– anonymous read/write registers are as strong as non-anonymous registers.

Let us also notice that a similar problem (but much simpler, even trivial) appears in message-passing systems, where any two nodes (processes) are connected by a communication channel, locally known as internal ports by each process, $port_i[x]$ being the local name of the channel connecting process p_i to some process p_j. In this context, it is possible that for any two processes p_i and p_k, the local names $port_i[x]$ and $port_k[x]$ denote channels connecting them to two different processes, while $port_i[x]$ and $port_k[y]$, $x \neq y$, connect them to the same process. Differently, from process identities, values stored in ports are purely local and have no global meaning. Moreover, it is straightforward for a process to learn the name of the process it is connected to when it uses a given local port.

Simplicity is a First Class Property. The simplicity of the proposed algorithm does not mean it was simple to obtain. This was not a trivial task as simplicity is rarely obtained for free. As said by A.J. Perlis (the first Turing Award recipient) "Simplicity does not precede complexity, but follows it" [16]. Let us also remember the following sentence written by the mathematician/philosopher Blaise Pascal at the end of a letter to a friend: "I apologize for having written such a long letter, I had not enough time to write a shorter one". The implication "simple $\Rightarrow$ easy" is rarely true for non-trivial problems [1]. Simplicity requires effort, but is very rewarding. It is a first class scientific property which participates in the beauty of science [9].

Roadmap. The paper is composed of 7 sections. Section 2 introduces the computing model, the notion of a symmetric algorithm, and mutual exclusion. Section 3 defines the de-anonymization problem. A first de-anonymization algorithm is presented in Sect. 4 and proved in Sect. 5. This algorithm requires each register of the de-anonymized memory to forever contain $1 + \log_2 m$ bits of control information. Then, the previous algorithm is enriched in Sect. 6 to obtain an algorithm which associates a single bit of permanent control information with each register of the de-anonymized memory. Section 7 concludes the paper.

Remark. On a practical side, it appears that the concept of an anonymous memory allows us to model epigenetic cell modifications [18]. Hence, it could be useful in biologically inspired distributed systems [14,15].

2 System Model, Symmetric Algorithm, and Mutex Algorithm

2.1 Process and Communication Model

Processes. The system is composed of a finite set of $n \geq 2$ asynchronous processes denoted $p_1, .., p_n$. The subscript i in p_i is only a notational convenience, which is not known by the processes. *Asynchronous* means that each process proceeds to its own speed, which can vary with time and remains always unknown to the other processes. Each process p_i knows its identity id_i and the total number of processes n. No two processes have the same identity.

Anonymous Shared Memory. The shared memory is made up of m atomic anonymous read/write registers denoted $SM[1...m]$. Hence, *all* registers are anonymous. As indicated in the Introduction, when p_i uses the address $SM[x]$, it actually uses $SM[f_i(x)]$, where $f_i()$ is a permutation defined by an external adversary. We will use the notation $SM_i[x]$ to denote $SM[f_i(x)]$, to stress the fact that no process knows the permutations.

It is assumed that all the registers are initialized to the same value. Otherwise, thanks to their different initial values, it would be possible to distinguish different registers, which consequently will no longer be fully anonymous.

To Summarize: Which Adversaries? The adversaries considered in the paper are consequently asynchrony and memory anonymity. There are no process failures (this assumption is motivated by the fact that the proposed construction is based on a mutual exclusion algorithm, and mutual exclusion algorithms are impossible to build from read/write registers in the presence of process failures). Furthermore, unlike the mutual exclusion model where a process may never leave its remainder region, we assume that all the processes must participate in the algorithm.

2.2 Symmetric Algorithm

The notion of a *symmetric algorithm* dates back to the eighties [10,12]. Here, as in [23], a *symmetric algorithm* is an "algorithm in which the processes are executing exactly the same code and the only way for distinguishing processes is by comparing identifiers. Identifiers can be written, read, and compared, but there is no way of looking inside an identifier. Thus it is not possible to know whether an identifier is odd or even".

Moreover, symmetry can be restricted by considering that the only comparison that can be applied to identifiers is equality. In this case, there is no order structuring the identifier name space. In the following, we consider the more restricting definition, namely, "symmetric" means "symmetric with comparison limited to equality".

Let us notice that, as all the processes have the same code and all the registers are initialized to the same value, process identities become a key element when one has to design an algorithm in such a constrained context.

2.3 One-Shot Mutual Exclusion

One-Shot Mutual Exclusion. Mutual exclusion is the oldest and certainly the most important of the synchronization problems. Formalized by E.W. Dijkstra in the mid-sixties [8], it consists in building what is called a lock (or mutex) object, defined by two operations, denoted acquire() and release(). (Recent textbooks including mutual exclusion and variants of it are [19,22].)

The invocation of these operations by a process p_i always follows the following pattern: "acquire(); *critical section*; release()", where "critical section" is any sequence of code. Moreover, "one-shot" means that a process invokes at most once the operations acquire() and release(). The mutex object satisfying the deadlock-freedom progress condition is defined by the following two properties.

- Mutual exclusion. No two processes are simultaneously in their critical section.

– Deadlock-freedom progress condition. If there is a process p_i that has a pending operation acquire(), there is a process p_j (maybe $p_j \neq p_i$) that eventually executes its critical section.

As already mentioned, a memory-anonymous symmetric deadlock-free mutual exclusion algorithm is presented in [3]. This algorithm assumes that size m of the anonymous memory belongs to the set $M(n) = \{\ m\ $ such that $\forall \ell :\ 1 < \ell \leq n$: $\gcd(\ell, m) = 1\} \setminus \{1\}$. Hence, the mutex-based read/write memory de-anonymization algorithm presented in Sect. 4 is optimal with respect to the values of m for which deadlock-free mutual exclusion can be built despite memory anonymity.

3 The De-anonymization Problem

Definition. Given an n-process asynchronous system, in which the processes communicate via a set of m anonymous read/write registers $SM[1..m]$, the aim is for each process p_i to compute an addressing function $\mathsf{map}_i()$, which is a permutation over the set of the memory indexes $\{1, \cdots, m\}$, such that the two following properties are satisfied. It is assumed that all processes participate in the de-anonymization.

– Safety. For any $y \in \{1, \cdots, m\}$ and any process p_i, we have $SM_i[\mathsf{map}_i(y)] = SM[y]$.
– Liveness. There is a finite time after which all the processes have computed their addressing function $\mathsf{map}_i()$.

The safety property states that, once a process p_i has computed $\mathsf{map}_i()$, its local anonymous memory address $SM_i[x]$, where $x = \mathsf{map}_i(y)$, denotes the shared register $SM[y]$.

Accessing the De-anonymized Memory. Once de-anonymized, the way the memory is accessed by the processes is illustrated in Fig. 1. For any index y, $1 \leq y \leq m$, the processes access the same register as follow: $SM_i[\mathsf{map}_i(y)]$ used by p_i and $SM_j[\mathsf{map}_j(y)]$ used by p_j denote the same register.

4 A Symmetric De-anonymization Algorithm

4.1 Memory De-anonymization in an n-Process Read/Write System

Underlying Principle. The principle that underlies the design of the read/write memory de-anonymization algorithm (Algorithm 1) is based on an *competition/elimination* process, at the end of which a single winner process imposes its adversary-defined index permutation to all the processes, which becomes the shared names of the anonymous read/write registers, on which all processes agree.

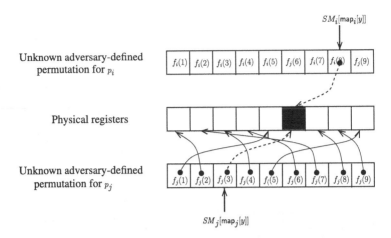

$SM_i[\mathsf{map}_i[y]]$

Unknown adversary-defined permutation for p_i

| $f_i(1)$ | $f_i(2)$ | $f_i(3)$ | $f_i(4)$ | $f_i(5)$ | $f_j(6)$ | $f_i(7)$ | $f_i(8)$ | $f_j(9)$ |

Physical registers

Unknown adversary-defined permutation for p_j

| $f_j(1)$ | $f_j(2)$ | $f_j(3)$ | $f_j(4)$ | $f_j(5)$ | $f_j(6)$ | $f_j(7)$ | $f_j(8)$ | $f_j(9)$ |

$SM_j[\mathsf{map}_j[y]]$

Fig. 1. Accessing the memory after de-anonymization

The competition/elimination process uses an underlying mutual exclusion algorithm. Each process invokes acquire() and is eliminated when it leaves the critical section. The last process to enter the critical section is the winner.

Challenges. In order to detect which process is the last, the processes needs to collaborate to increase a counter whose value will reach n when the last process will enter the critical section. We stress that because the memory is anonymous there is no straightforward way to leverage a critical section. Since there is no agreement on the resources (here the anonymous registers themselves), we underline that being in critical section does not grant any restricted access to the memory. In the following, properties of the underlying algorithm are described, which are used to build the required shared resource, namely a shared counter.

Properties of the Underlying Mutex Algorithm that Are Used. In addition to the fact it solves mutual exclusion, the underlying mutex algorithm has behavioral properties that are implicitly used in the design of the de-anonymization algorithm and explicitly used in its proof.

- Property Mutex-1. A process writes only its identity or $\perp$ in an anonymous register.
- Property Mutex-2. When a process invokes acquire(), it reads all anonymous registers.
- Property Mutex-3. When a process is allowed to enter the critical section, all registers contain its identity.
- Property Mutex-4. After a process is allowed to enter the critical section and before it invokes release(), any other competing process can issue at most one write operation. It follows that, when a process p_i is inside the critical section, and x processes are inside their invocations of acquire(), at least $(m-x)$ anonymous registers contain its identity id_i. Moreover, when a process releases the critical section (operation release()), it writes $\perp$, in all the registers

which contain its identity. Hence, at least $(m - x)$ such registers are reset to their initial value $\perp$.

Enriching the Underlying Mutex Algorithm to Share a Counter. As can be seen from the previous properties, even when a process is alone in the critical section, it could happen that some of its writes are overwritten by another process. Property Mutex-4 states that a process, which is not in the critical section, may erase what was written by the process in critical section only once. That is no more than $(n - 1)$ registers can be erased. As $m - (n - 1) > 0$, by copying the value in *all* the anonymous registers, the process currently in the critical section ensures that at least one copy will not be overwritten. From property Mutex-2, the next process to enter the critical section will learn the correct value of the counter.

Sharing the counter in such a way is more easily done by integrating these operations within each read and write operation on the anonymous registers, issued by the underlying mutual exclusion algorithm. These basic operations are consequently enriched as described in Algorithm 2. These modifications are safe for the mutual exclusion algorithm since they do not interfere with operations and variables of this algorithm.

Let us remark that a similar technique, based on appropriate broadcast abstraction and quorums, is used in message-passing systems to update the local copies of a shared register [20]. Here the read and write operations issued by the underlying mutex algorithm are enriched to play the role of a broadcast abstraction.

Local Variables. Each process s p_i manages three local variables.

- ct_i is a local counter initialized to 0, which will increase inside the integer interval $[0..n]$. The set of the n local variables ct_i implement a shared counter CT which increases by step 1 from its initial value 0 to n (line 2). (Actually, the set of the final values of the n local variables ct_i will be the set $\{1, 2, \ldots, n\}$.)
- $sm_i[1..m]$ is used to store a local copy of the anonymous memory $SM_i[1..m]$. A process p_i reads the anonymous memory by invoking SM_i.scan(), which is an asynchronous (non-atomic) reading of all the anonymous registers.
- $last1_i$ is a Boolean, initialized to false, which will be set to true only by the last process that will access the critical section.

Each Register Contains a Tag and a Value. In order not to confuse the values written in anonymous registers by processes executing statements of Algorithm 1 (not including the operations acquire() and release()), and the values written by other processes executing the underlying mutex algorithm, all the values written in the anonymous memory are prefixed by a tag. More explicitly, the tag MUTEX is used by the mutex algorithm, while the tag DESA is used by the de-anonymization algorithm.

Each anonymous read/write register is initialized to MUTEX$\langle 0, \perp \rangle$. The first value (0) is the initial value of the global counter CT, while the second value ($\perp$) is the initial value used by the mutex algorithm.

---

operation SM_i.scan() **returns** $([SM_i[1], \cdots, SM_i[m]])$.

operation de-anonymize(id_i) **is**   % code for process p_i
(1) acquire(id_i);
(2) $ct_i \leftarrow ct_i + 1$;
      % ct_i is the local representation of the global counter CT. It is updated at each process
      % by the read and write operations of the underlying mutex algorithm (see Algorithm 2)
(3) $last1_i \leftarrow (ct_i = n)$;
(4) release(id_i); % realizes an implicit broadcast of ct_i %
(5) **if** $(last1_i)$
(6) **then for each** $x \in \{1, \cdots, m\}$ **do** $SM_i[x] \leftarrow$ DESA(x) **end for**
        % the permutation for p_i is: $\forall\, y \in \{1, \cdots, m\}$: map$_i(y) = y$ %
(7) **else repeat** $sm_i \leftarrow SM_i$.scan() **until** $(\forall\, x : sm_i[x]$ is tagged DESA$)$ **end repeat**;
(8) **for each** $x \in \{1, \cdots, m\}$ **do** map$_i(y) \leftarrow x$ where $sm_i[x]=$DESA(y) **end for**
        % the perm. for p_i is: $\forall\, y \in \{1, \cdots, m\}$: map$_i(y) = x$, where $sm_i[x] =$ DESA(y) %
(9) **end if**.

Algorithm 1: Memory de-anonymization in an n-process read/write system

Behavior of a Process p_i: First Invoke the Mutex Algorithm. All the
processes invoke the operation de $-$ anonymize(id_i). When a process p_i invokes
it, it first acquires the critical section (line 1). The code inside the critical section
is a simple increase of the shared counter CT globally implemented by the local
variables ct_i (line 2). Hence, if p_i is the ℓth process to access the critical section,
ct_i is updated from $\ell - 1$ to ℓ, and p_i will inform the other processes of this
increase when it will invoke release() (line 4). Let us notice that, at line 3, p_i sets
to true its local Boolean variable $last1_i$ only if it is the last process to execute
the critical section. Then, the behavior of p_i depends on the fact it is or not the
last process to enter the critical section (see below).

**Behavior of a Process p_i: The Read and Write Operations Used by the
Mutex Algorithm.** As already indicated, to ensure correct dissemination of the
last increase of CT (update of the local variable ct_j at a process p_j), the read
and write operations that allow the mutex algorithm to access the anonymous
registers are modified as described in Algorithm 2.

---

operation read of $SM_i[x]$ executed by the mutex algorithm **is**
(1) $\langle ct, val \rangle \leftarrow SM_i[x]$;
(2) $ct_i \leftarrow$ max(ct_i, ct);
(3)   return(val).

operation write of v in $SM_i[x]$ executed by the mutex algorithm **is**
(4) $SM_i[x] \leftarrow$ MUTEX$\langle ct_i, v \rangle$;
(5)   return(ok).

Algorithm 2: Modified read and write operations (code for p_i)

As the operation release() of the mutex algorithm writes $\perp$ (i.e., the
MUTEX$\langle CT, \perp \rangle$) in at least $(m - (n - 1))$ anonymous registers (Property Mutex-

4), it follows that if a process p_i accesses later the critical section, it updated its local counter ct_i when it executed acquire(), which reads all anonymous registers (Property Mutex-1).

Behavior of a Process p_i: The Winner Imposes its Addressing Permutation to All. The de-anonymization is done at lines 5–9. The $(n-1)$ processes that won the first $(n-1)$ critical sections execute line 7, in which they loop until they see all the registers tagged DESA.

Let p_ℓ be the last process that entered the critical section (hence, $ct_\ell = n$ and $last1_\ell$ is the only Boolean equal to true). This process imposes its adversary-defined addressing permutation as the common addressing, which realizes a non-anonymous memory. To this end, for any $x \in \{1, \cdots, m\}$, p_ℓ writes DESA(x) in $SM_\ell[x]$ (line 6). Hence, for any x we have $\mathsf{map}_\ell(x) = x$.

Let p_i be any other process that is looping at line 7 until it sees all the registers tagged DESA. When this occurs, it computes $\mathsf{map}_i()$, which is such that for any $x \in \{1, \cdots, m\}$, if $sm_i[x] =$DESA(y) then $\mathsf{map}_i(x) = y$ (line 7).

4.2 Using the De-anonymized Memory

It follows from the de-anonymization algorithm that when a process has written the tag DESA in all registers, thanks to their local mapping function $\mathsf{map}_i()$, all the processes share the same indexes for the same registers.

When this occurs, process p_k could start executing its local algorithm defined by the upper layer application, but if it writes an application-related value in some of these registers, this value can overwrite a value DESA() stored in a register not yet read by other processes. To prevent this problem from occurring, all the values written by a process at the application level are prefixed by the tag APPL, and include a field containing the common index y associated with this register. In this way, any process p_i will be able to compute its local mapping function $\mathsf{map}_i()$, and can start its upper layer application part, as soon as it has computed $\mathsf{map}_i()$.

Let us notice that one bit is needed to distinguish the tag DESA and the tag APPL. Hence, each of a value DESA(x) and a value APPL$(x, -)$ requires $(1+\log_2 m)$ control bits.

5 Proof of the Algorithm

Lemma 1. *Each process exits* acquire() *and, denoting i_k the index of the kth process that enters the critical section, when p_{i_k} invokes* release(), *it writes the value* MUTEX$\langle k, \perp \rangle$ *in at least $(m - (n-1))$ anonymous registers.*

Proof. Let us first observe that, as (i) the underlying mutex algorithm is independent of the values of the local variables ct_i, (ii) is deadlock-free, and (iii) each process invokes acquire() only once, it is actually starvation-free.

Let p_{i_1} be the first process that enters the critical section. As $ct_{i_1} = 0$, it follows that after line 2 we have $ct_{i_1} = 1$. Then, when p_{i_1} invokes release(), it writes MUTEX$\langle 1, \perp \rangle$ in at least $(m - (n - 1))$ anonymous registers (Property Mutex-4 and line 4 of Algorithm 2). It follows then (i) from Property Mutex-2 and lines 1–2 of Algorithm 2), and (ii) Property Mutex-1, Property Mutex-3, and line 4 of Algorithm 2, that when another process p_{i_2} enters the critical section, p_{i_2} has previously read and written all registers, from which we conclude from lines 1–5 of Algorithm 2 that $ct_{i_2} = 1$. It follows that p_{i_2} increases ct_{i_2} from 1 to 2 at line 2 of Algorithm 1.

The previous reasoning being repeated n times, we eventually have: $ct_{i(x)} = x$ at each process $p_{i(x)}$, $1 \leq x \leq n - 1$, and $ct_{i_n} = n$ at process p_{i_n}. It follows that no process blocks forever when it executes the lines 1–4 of Algorithm 1. $\square_{Lemma}$ 1

Lemma 2. *The local mapping function* map$_i()$ *computed by each process p_i is a permutation over the set of register indexes $\{1, \cdots, m\}$. Moreover, for any index $y \in \{1, \cdots, m\}$ and any pair of processes p_i and p_j, $SM_i[\mathsf{map}_i(y)]$ and $SM_j[\mathsf{map}_j(y)]$ address the very same register.*

Proof. Let us assume that a process p_i executes line 6. From Lemma 1 there is a single such process p_i. Let p_j be any other process that executes lines 7–8. Due to the "repeat" loop of line 7, p_j executes line 8 only after all registers contain the tag DESA. Only p_i writes the registers with this tag, and (at line 6) wrote DESA(y) inside $SM_i[y]$, for each $y \in \{1, ..., m\}$. Hence, when p_j reads DESA(y) from $SM_j[x]$, it learns that this register is known by p_i as $SM_i[y]$. At line 8, p_j consequently considers x as the value of map$_j(y)$. It follows that $SM_j[\mathsf{map}_j(y)]$ (i.e., $SM_j[x]$) and $SM_i[\mathsf{map}_i(y)]$ (which is $SM_i[y]$) denote the very same read/write register. As this is true for any process $p_j \neq p_i$, the lemma follows. $\square_{Lemma}$ 2

Lemma 3. *Any process p_i terminates the operation* de-anonymize$()$.

Proof. The proof follows from Lemma 1, which states that all processes enter and leave the critical section. Moreover, as p_{i_n} executes line 6 of Algorithm 1, it follows that no other process can block forever at line 7 of this algorithm, which concludes the proof of the lemma. $\square_{Lemma}$ 3

Theorem 1. *Algorithm   1 is a symmetric algorithm that solves the de-anonymization problem in a system made up of n asynchronous processes communicating by reading and writing m anonymous read/write atomic registers, where m belongs to the set $M(n) = \{m$ such that $\forall \ell : 1 < \ell \leq n$: $\gcd(\ell, m) = 1\} \setminus \{1\}$.*

Proof. A simple examination of the code shows that process identities are compared only by equality, from which follows the "symmetry" property. The rest of the proof follows from Lemma 2 and Lemma 3. $\square_{Theorem}$ 1

6   Reducing the Size of Control Information

Algorithm 1 requires that, once de-anonymized, each register must contain forever $1 + \log_2 m$ bits of control information. This section shows that this information can be reduced to a single bit.

Revisiting the Shared Memory. Each read/write register $SM[x]$ is now assumed to be composed of two parts $SM[x].BIT$ and $SM[x].RM$, more precisely, we have $SM[x] = \langle SM[x].BIT, SM[x].RM \rangle$. $SM[x].BIT$ is for example the leftmost bit of $SM[x]$, and $SM[x].RM$ the other bits. The meaning and the use of $SM[x].RM$ are exactly the same as $SM[x]$ in Algorithm 1 and Algorithm 2. For each x, $SM[x].BIT$ is initialized to 0, while (as in Algorithm 1) $SM[x].RM$ is initialized to MUTEX$\langle 0, \perp \rangle$.

To simplify both the writing and the reading of the improved algorithm, we write

- "$SM_i[x] \leftarrow$ DESA(x)" when the first bit of $SM_i[x]$ is not modified by the write (line 6),
- "SM_i.scan() when we are interested in the $SM_i.RM$" part of the registers only (line 7),
- "$BIT_i[x] \leftarrow 1$" when the remaining part of $SM_i[x]$ is not modified by the write (line 15),
- "BIT_i.scan()" when we are interested in the bits $SM_i.BIT$ only (line 16).

---

operation SM_i.scan() **returns** $([SM_i[1], \cdots, SM_i[m]])$.

operation de-anonymize2(id_i) **is**   % code for p_i
     % the lines 1-9 are the same as in Algorithm 1; the lines 10-17 are new
(1)   acquire(id_i);
(2) $ct_i \leftarrow ct_i + 1$;
(3) $last1_i \leftarrow (ct_i = n)$;
(4)   release(id_i); % realizes an implicit broadcast of ct_i %
(5)   **if** $(last1_i)$
(6)   **then for each** $x \in \{1, \cdots, m\}$ **do** $SM_i[x] \leftarrow$ DESA(x) **end for**
                % the permutation for p_i is: $\forall y \in \{1, \cdots, m\}$: map$_i(y) = y$ %
(7)   **else repeat** $sm_i \leftarrow SM_i$.scan() **until** $(\forall x : sm_i[x]$ is tagged DESA) **end repeat**;
(8)   **for each** $x \in \{1, \cdots, m\}$ **do** map$_i(y) \leftarrow x$ where $sm_i[x]=$DESA(y) **end for**
                % perm. for p_i is $\forall y \in \{1, \cdots, m\}$: map$_i(y) = x$, where $sm_i[x] =$ DESA(y)
(9)   **end if**;
(10) acquire(id_i);
(11) $ct_i \leftarrow ct_i + 1$;
(12) $last2_i \leftarrow (ct_i = 2n)$;
(13) release(id_i); % realizes an implicit broadcast of ct_i %
(14) **if** $(last2_i)$
(15)   **then for each** $x \in \{1, \cdots, m\}$ **do** $BIT_i[x] \leftarrow 1$ **end for**
(16)   **else repeat** $bit_i \leftarrow BIT_i$.scan() **until** $(\exists x : bit_i[x] = 1)$ **end repeat**
(17) **end if**.

Algorithm 3: Algorithm with a single bit of control information

Behavior of a Process p_i. Algorithm 3 is the improved algorithm. It is Algorithm 1 (lines 1–9), followed by a second global synchronization phase (lines 10–17), which is similar to the one at lines 1–9.

After the processes have executed line 9 (end of the first global synchronization phase), each of them knows its mapping function map$_i()$, but no process knows that all the other processes know their own mapping function. This motivates the second use of the mutual exclusion algorithm, which, as the left bit of any register $SM[x].BIT$ still contains its initial value 0, ensures that when the last process (say p_k) that entered the second critical section exits it, it knows that all the processes have computed their mapping function, and no process that executes the "repeat" loop of line 16 can exit it.

To identify the last process that entered the (second) critical section, when a process p_i is inside the critical section it increases the abstract register CT (line 11), and sets $last2_i$ to **true** only if it discovers it is the last process that accessed the critical section (line 12), More precisely, we have the following.

- If p_i is not the last process to increase CT (locally represented by ct_i), $last2_i$ is equal to **false**, and consequently p_i waits until it sees at least one register whose bit $SM_i[x].BIT$ is equal to 1 (line 16). When this occurs p_i learns that the second phase is terminated (hence it knows that all the processes have computed their mapping function), and it can proceed to execute an upper layer non-anonymous register algorithm.
- Differently, if p_i is the last process to increase CT, it changes to 1 the left bit of all the registers (line 15), which unblocks all the other processes. As the bits $SM_i[x].BIT$ are never reset to 0, eventually all the processes know that each of them knows its mapping function.

As they follow the same synchronization pattern, the proof of the second part of Algorithm 3 (lines 10–17) is the same as the one of its first global synchronization phase (lines 1–9), which is the same as the one of Algorithm 1.

7   Conclusion

In addition to introducing the memory de-anonymization problem, this paper has shown that, in an n-process system where $n \geq 2$ and process identities can only be compared with equality, a shared memory made up of m anonymous read/write registers and a shared memory made up of m non-anonymous read/write registers have the same computability power for the values of m satisfying the necessary condition for deadlock-free anonymous mutex algorithms from [23], namely m must belong to the set $M(n) = \{ m \mid$ such that $\forall \ell : 1 < \ell \leq n: \gcd(\ell, m) = 1 \} \setminus \{1\}$. Let us observe that, as it includes an infinite sequence of prime numbers, $M(n)$ is infinite. It follows that, once de-anonymization (in which all processes participate) is obtained, it becomes possible to use a symmetric starvation-free mutex algorithm, thereby obtaining a symmetric starvation-free mutex algorithm working on top of an anonymous memory[1].

We emphasize that the above construction (of running a starvation-free mutex algorithm on top of a de-anonymization layer), does not solve the original

---

[1] Peterson's mutual exclusion algorithm is such a symmetric algorithm [17]. As it requires $2n - 1$ non-anonymous atomic registers, we need to have both $m \in M(n)$ and $m \geq 2n - 1$.

open problem from [20], regarding the existence of a memory-anonymous two-process starvation-free mutex algorithm. In the definition of the mutex problem participation is not required (a process may never leave its remainder code), while our implementation of the de-anonymization layer, assumes that participation is required, or, equivalently, that the number of participants is known by all processes.

As stated in [23], the memory-anonymous communication model "enables us to understand better the intrinsic limits for coordinating the actions of asynchronous processes". It consequently enriches our knowledge of what can be (or cannot be) done when an adversary replaced a common addressing function, by individual and independent addressing functions, one per process.

Among problems that remain open, there are the design of de-anonymization algorithms (symmetric with equality only, or symmetric with equality, greater than, and lower than) not based on an underlying memory anonymous mutex algorithm, and the statement of a necessary and sufficient condition on the value of m (size of the anonymous memory) for which de-anonymization is possible (for each type of symmetry).

Acknowledgments. This work was partially supported by the French ANR project DESCARTES (16-CE40-0023-03) devoted to layered and modular structures in distributed computing. The authors want to thank the referees for their constructive comments.

References

1. Aigner, M., Ziegler, G.: Proofs from THE BOOK. Springer, Heidelberg (2010). 274 p. ISBN 978-3-642-00856-6
2. Angluin D.: Local and global properties in networks of processes. In: Proceedings of the 12th Symposium on Theory of Computing (STOC 1980). ACM Press, pp. 82–93 (1980)
3. Aghazadeh Z., Imbs D., Raynal M., Taubenfeld G., Woelfel P.: Optimal memory-anonymous symmetric deadlock-free mutual exclusion. In: Proceedings of the 38th ACM Symposium on Principles of Distributed Computing (PODC 2019), 10 p. ACM Press (2019)
4. Attiya, H., Gorbach, A., Moran, S.: Computing in totally anonymous asynchronous shared-memory systems. Inf. Comput. **173**(2), 162–183 (2002)
5. Bonnet, F., Raynal, M.: Anonymous asynchronous systems: the case of failure detectors. Distrib. Comput. **26**(3), 141–158 (2013)
6. Bouzid, Z., Raynal, M., Sutra, P.: Anonymous obstruction-free (n, k)-set agreement with $(n-k+1)$ atomic read/write registers. Distrib. Comput. **31**(2), 99–117 (2018)
7. Delporte-Gallet, C., Fauconnier, H., Gafni, E., Lamport, L.: Adaptive register allocation with a linear number of registers. In: Afek, Y. (ed.) DISC 2013. LNCS, vol. 8205, pp. 269–283. Springer, Heidelberg (2013). https://doi.org/10.1007/978-3-642-41527-2_19
8. Dijkstra, E.W.: Solution of a problem in concurrent programming control. Commun. ACM **8**(9), 569 (1965)
9. Dijkstra, E.W.: Some beautiful arguments using mathematical induction. Algorithmica **13**(1), 1–8 (1980)

10. Garg V.K., Ghosh J.: Symmetry in spite of hierarchy. In: Proceedings of the 10th International Conference on Distributed Computing Systems (ICDCS 1990), pp. 4–11. IEEE Computer Press (1990)
11. Guerraoui, R., Ruppert, E.: Anonymous and fault-tolerant shared-memory computations. Distrib. Comput. **20**, 165–177 (2007)
12. Johnson R.E., Schneider F.B.: Symmetry and similarity in distributed systems. In: Proceedings off the 4th ACM Symposium on Principles of Distributed Computing (PODC 1985), pp. 13–22, ACM Press (1985)
13. Lamport, L.: On interprocess communication, part I: basic formalism. Distrib. Comput. **1**(2), 77–85 (1986)
14. Navlakha, S., Bar-Joseph, Z.: Algorithms in nature: the convergence of systems biology and computational thinking. Mol. Syst. Biol. **7**(546), 1–11 (2011)
15. Navlakha, S., Bar-Joseph, Z.: Distributed information processing in biological and computational systems. Commun. ACM **58**(1), 94–102 (2015)
16. Perlis, A.J.: Epigrams on programming. ACM SIGPLAN Not. **17**(1), 7–13 (1982)
17. Peterson, G.L.: Myths about the mutual exclusion problem. Inform. Process. Lett. **12**(3), 115–116 (1981)
18. Rashid S., Taubenfeld G., Bar-Joseph Z.: Genome wide epigenetic modifications as a shared memory consensus. In: 6th Workshop on Biological Distributed Algorithms (BDA 2018), London (2018)
19. Raynal, M.: Concurrent Programming: Algorithms, Principles and Foundations. Springer, Heidelberg (2013). https://doi.org/10.1007/978-3-642-32027-9. 515 p. ISBN 978-3-642-32026-2
20. Raynal, M.: Fault-Tolerant Message-passing Distributed Systems: An Algorithmic Approach. Springer, Heidelberg (2018). https://doi.org/10.1007/978-3-319-94141-7. 492 p. ISBN 978-3-319-94140-0
21. Raynal, M., Cao, J.: Anonymity in distributed read/write systems: an introductory survey. In: Podelski, A., Taïani, F. (eds.) NETYS 2018. LNCS, vol. 11028, pp. 122–140. Springer, Cham (2019). https://doi.org/10.1007/978-3-030-05529-5_9
22. Taubenfeld, G.: Synchronization Algorithms and Concurrent Programming. Pearson Education/Prentice Hall, London (2006). 423 p. ISBN 0-131-97259-6
23. Taubenfeld G.: Coordination without prior agreement. In: Proceedings of the 36th ACM Symposium on Principles of Distributed Computing (PODC 2017), pp. 325–334. ACM Press (2017)
24. Yamashita, M., Kameda, T.: Computing on anonymous networks: part I - characterizing the solvable cases. IEEE Trans. Parallel Distrib. Syst. **7**(1), 69–89 (1996)

A Pragmatic Non-blocking Concurrent Directed Acyclic Graph

Sathya Peri[1(✉)], Muktikanta Sa[1(✉)], and Nandini Singhal[2(✉)]

[1] Department of Computer Science and Engineering,
Indian Institute of Technology Hyderabad, Sangareddy, India
{sathya_p,cs15resch11012}@iith.ac.in
[2] Microsoft (R&D) Pvt. Ltd., Bangalore, India
nandini12396@gmail.com

Abstract. In this paper, we have developed two non-blocking algorithms for maintaining acyclicity in a concurrent directed graph. The first algorithm is based on a *wait-free reachability* query and the second one on *partial snapshot-based obstruction-free reachability* query. Interestingly, we are able to achieve the acyclic property in a dynamic setting without (1) making use of helping descriptors by other threads, or (2) clean double collect mechanism. We present a proof to show that the graph remains acyclic at all times in the concurrent setting. We also prove that the acyclic graph data-structure operations are linearizable. We implement both the algorithms in C++ and test through several micro-benchmarks. Our experimental results illustrate an average of 7x improvement over the sequential and global-lock implementation.

Keywords: Acyclic graph · Concurrent data structure · Linearizability · Lock-freedom

1 Introduction

A graph is a common data-structure that can model many real-world objects and pairwise relationships among them. Graphs have a huge number of applications in various fields like social networking, VLSI design, road networks, graphics, blockchains and many more. Usually, these graphs are *dynamic* in nature, that is, they undergo dynamic changes like addition and removal of vertices and/or edges [9]. These applications also need data-structure which supports dynamic changes and can expand at run-time depending on the availability of memory in the machine.

Nowadays, multi-core systems have become ubiquitous. To fully harness the computational power of these systems, it has become necessary to design efficient data-structures which can be executed by multiple threads concurrently. In the

This work is partly funded by a research grant from Intel, USA.
N. Singhal—Work done while a student at IITH.

M. F. Atig and A. A. Schwarzmann (Eds.): NETYS 2019, LNCS 11704, pp. 327–344, 2019.
https://doi.org/10.1007/978-3-030-31277-0_22

past decade, there have been several efforts to port sequential data-structures to a concurrent setting, like stacks [12], queues [2,16], sets [10,11,17,23], trees [5,19].

Most of these data-structure use locks to handle mutual exclusion while doing any concurrent modifications. However, in an asynchronous shared-memory system, where an arbitrary delay or a crash failure of a thread is possible, a lock-based implementation is vulnerable to arbitrary delays or deadlock. For instance, a thread could acquire a lock and then sleep (or get swapped out) for a long time, or the thread could get involved in a deadlock with the other threads while obtaining locks, or even crash after obtaining a lock.

On the other hand, in a lock-free data-structure, threads do not acquire locks. Instead, they use atomic hardware instructions such as compare-and-swap, test-and-set etc. These instructions ensure that at least one non-faulty thread is guaranteed to finish its operation in a finite number of steps. Therefore, lock-free data-structures are highly scalable and naturally fault-tolerant.

Although several concurrent data-structures have been developed, concurrent graph data-structures and the related operations are still largely unexplored. In several graph applications, one of the crucial requirements is preserving *acyclicity*. Acyclic graphs are often applied to problems related to databases, data processing, scheduling, finding the best route during navigation, data compression, blockchains etc. Applications relying on graphs mostly use a sequential implementation and the accesses to the shared data-structures are synchronized through the global-locks, which causes serious performance bottlenecks.

A relevant application is *Serialization Graph Testing (SGT)* in Databases [24, Chap 4] and Transactional Memory (TM) [22]. SGT requires maintaining an acyclic graph on all concurrently executing (database or TM) transactions with edges between the nodes representing conflicts among them. In a concurrent scenario, where multiple threads perform different operations, maintaining acyclicity without using locks is not a trivial task. Indeed, it requires every shared memory access to be checked for the violation of the acyclic property, which necessitates that all the operations be efficient.

Apart from SGT, several popular blockchains maintain acyclic graphs such as tree structure (Bitcoin [3,18], Ethereum [4] etc.) or general DAGs (Tangle [21]).

1.1   Contributions

In this paper, we present an efficient non-blocking concurrent acyclic directed graph data-structure. Its operations are similar to the concurrent graph proposed by Chatterjee et al. [6] with some non-trivial modifications. The contributions of our work are summarized below:

1. We describe an Abstract Data Type (ADT) that maintains an acyclic directed graph $G = (V, E)$. It comprises of the following methods on the sets V and E: (1) Add Vertex: AcyAddV (2) Remove Vertex: AcyRemV, (3) Contains Vertex: AcyConV (4) Add Edge: AcyAddE (5) Remove Edge: AcyRemE

and (6) Contains Edge: ACYCONE. The ADT remains acyclic after completion of any of the above operations in G. The acyclic graph is represented as an adjacency list.

2. We present an efficient concurrent non-blocking implementation of the ADT (Sect. 3). We present two approaches for maintaining acyclicity: the first one is based on a wait-free reachability query(SCR: Single Collect Reachable) and the second one is based on obstruction-free reachability query (DCR: Double Collect Reachable) similar to the GETPATH method of Chatterjee et al. [6] (Sect. 4).

3. We prove the correctness by showing the operations of the concurrent acyclic graph data-structure are linearizable [14]. We also prove the non-blocking progress guarantee, specifically we prove: (a) The operations ACYCONV and ACYCONE are wait-free, only if the vertex keys are finite; (b) Among the two algorithms for maintaining acyclicity, we show that the first algorithm based on searchability is wait-free, whereas the second algorithm based on reachability queries is obstruction-free and (c) The operations ACYADDV, ACYREMV, ACYCONV, ACYADDE, ACYREME, and ACYCONE are lock-free Sect. 5.

4. We implemented the non-blocking algorithms in C++ and evaluated over a number of micro-benchmarks. Our experimental results depict on an average of 7x improvement over the sequential and global lock implementation (Sect. 6).

1.2   Related Work

Kallimanis and Kanellou [15] presented a concurrent graph that supports wait-free edge updates and traversals. They use an adjacency matrix representation for the graph, with a bounded number of vertices. As a result, their data-structure does not allow any insertion or deletion of vertices after initialization of the graph. This may not be adequate for many real-world applications which need dynamic modifications of vertices as well as unbounded graph size.

A recent work by Chatterjee et al. [6] proposed a non-blocking concurrent graph data-structure which allows multiple threads to perform dynamic insertion and deletion of vertices & edges. Our paper extends this data-structure to maintain acyclicity of a directed graph.

1.3   Overview of the Algorithm Design

Before getting into the technical details (in Sect. 3) of the algorithm, we first provide an overview of the design. We implement an acyclic concurrent unbounded directed graph as a concurrent list of linked lists [11] also used by Chatterjee et al. [6]. The *vertex-nodes* are placed in a sorted linked-list and the neighboring vertices of each vertex-node are placed in a rooted sorted linked-list of *edge-nodes*. To achieve efficient graph traversal, we maintain a pointer from each edge-node to its corresponding vertex-node. Each vertex-node's edge-list and vertex-list are lock-free with respect to concurrent update and lookup operations.

As we know that lock-freedom is not composable [8] and our algorithm is a composition of lock-free operations, we prove the liveness of our algorithm independent of the lock-free list arguments. In addition to that, we also propose some refined optimizations for the concurrent acyclic graph operations that not only enhance the performance but also simplify the design.

Our main requirement is preserving *acyclicity* and one can see that a cycle is created only after inserting an edge to the graph. So, after the insertion of a new edge to the graph, we verify if the resulting graph is acyclic or not. If it creates a cycle, we simply delete the inserted edge from the graph. However, the challenge is that these intermediate steps must be oblivious to the user and the graph must always appear to be acyclic. We ensure this by adding a *transit* field to the edges that are temporarily added. To verify the acyclic property of the graph, we propose two efficient algorithms: first one based on a wait-free reachability query and the second one based on obstruction-free reachability query similar to the GET-PATH operation of [6]. Both the reachability algorithms perform breadth-first search (BFS) traversal. For the sake of efficiency, we implement BFS traversal in a non-recursive manner. However, in order to achieve overall performance, we do not make use of *helping descriptors* for the reachability queries.

2   System Model and Preliminaries

The Memory Model. We consider an asynchronous shared-memory model with a finite set of p processors accessed by a finite set of n threads. The non-faulty threads communicate with each other by invoking methods on the shared objects. We run our acyclic graph data-structure on a shared-memory multi-core system with multi-threading enabled which supports atomic `read`, `write`, `fetch-and-add` (FAA) and `compare-and-swap` (CAS) instructions.

Correctness. We consider *linearizability* proposed by Herlihy and Wing [14] as the correctness criterion for the graph operations. We assume that the execution generated by a data-structure is a collection of method invocation and response events. Each invocation of a method call has a subsequent response. An execution is linearizable if it is possible to assign an atomic event as a *linearization point* (*LP*) inside the execution interval of each method such that the result of each of these methods is the same as it would be in a sequential execution in which the methods are ordered by their LPs [14].

Progress. The *progress* properties specify when a thread invoking operations on the shared memory objects completes in the presence of other concurrent threads. In this context, we present an acyclic graph implementation with operations that satisfies *lock-freedom*, based on the definitions in Herlihy and Shavit [13].

3   The Data Structure

3.1   Abstract Data Type

An acyclic graph is defined as a directed graph $G = (V, E)$, where V is the set of vertices and E is the set of directed edges. Each edge in E is an ordered pair of vertices belonging to V. Every vertex has an immutable unique key. The vertex represented by the key k is denoted k. A directed edge from the vertex k to l is denoted as $e(k, l) \in E$.

For a concurrent acyclic graph, we define following ADT operations:

1. ACYADDV(k) adds a vertex k to V, only if $k \notin V$ and then returns **true**, otherwise it returns **false**.
2. ACYREMV(k) deletes a vertex k from V, only if $k \in V$ and then returns **true**, otherwise it returns **false**. Once a vertex k is deleted successfully, all its outgoing and incoming edges are also removed.
3. ACYCONV(k) returns **true** only if $k \in V$, otherwise it returns **false**.
4. ACYADDE(k, l) operation is slightly involved and works as follows.
   (a) It adds an edge $e(k, l)$ to E, if (i) $k \in V$ and $l \in V$ (ii) $e(k, l) \notin E$ and adding it does not create a cycle in the graph. If either of the conditions (i) or (ii) are not satisfied, the edge is not added to E and it returns **false** along with an indicative strings VERTEX NOT PRESENT, EDGE ALREADY PRESENT or CYCLE DETECTED depending on execution.
   (b) If both (i) and (ii) conditions mentioned above are true and there is no concurrent edge addition, then this method adds the edge $e(k, l)$ to E and returns **true** along with an indicative string EDGE ADDED.
   (c) If both (i) and (ii) conditions, mentioned in Step 4a, are true and there is a concurrent edge addition (such as $e(u, v)$) then the edge $e(k, l)$ may or may not get added to E. In case, $e(k, l)$ gets added to E, then the method returns **true** along with an indicative string EDGE ADDED. Otherwise, it returns **false** along with CYCLE DETECTED.
   There is an inherent non-determinism in this edge addition procedure. It can be seen from Step 4c that this method may return **false** in presence of other concurrent edge additions. But if the primary requirement is to ensure that the graph remains acyclic such as in SGT or blockchains, then this behaviour is acceptable.
5. ACYREME(k, l) deletes the edge $e(k, l)$ from E, only if $e(k, l) \in E$ and $k \in V$ and $l \in V$ then it returns **true** along with an indicative string EDGE REMOVED. If $k \notin V$ or $l \notin V$, it returns **false** along with a string VERTEX NOT PRESENT. If $e(k, l) \notin E$, it returns **false** along with a string EDGE NOT PRESENT.
6. ACYCONE(k, l) if $e(k, l) \in E$ and $k \in V$ and $l \in V$ then it returns **true** along with a string EDGE PRESENT, otherwise it returns **false** along with a string VERTEX OR EDGE NOT PRESENT.

3.2   The Data-Structures

The algorithm uses three kinds of nodes structures: VNode, ENode and BFSNode. These structures and the adjacency list representation of an acyclic graph are shown in Fig. 1. The VNode structure has five fields, two pointers vnext and enext, an immutable key k, an atomic counter ecount, and a VisitedArray array. The use of ecount and VisitedArray are described in the later section. The pointer vnext is an atomic pointer pointing to the next VNode in the vertex-list, whereas, an enext pointer points to the edge head of the edge-list of a VNode. Similarly, an ENode structure has three fields, two pointers enext and pointv and an immutable key l. The enext is an atomic pointer pointing to the next ENode in the edge-list and pointv points to the corresponding VNode, which helps direct access to its VNode while performing any traversal like BFS, DFS, etc. We assume that all the VNodes have a unique identification key k and all the adjacency ENodes of a VNode have also a unique key l.

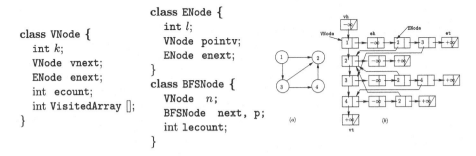

```
class VNode {
    int k;
    VNode vnext;
    ENode enext;
    int ecount;
    int VisitedArray [];
}
```

```
class ENode {
    int l;
    VNode pointv;
    ENode enext;
}
class BFSNode {
    VNode  n;
    BFSNode  next, p;
    int lecount;
}
```

Fig. 1. Node structures used in the acyclic graph data-structure: ENode, VNode and BFSNode. (a) An acyclic graph (b) The concurrent acyclic graph representation of data-structure for (a).

A BFSNode has three pointers n, next and p, and a counter lecount. The pointer n holds the corresponding VNode's address, next points to the next BFSNode in the BFS-list and p points to the corresponding parent. The local counter lecount stores n's ecount value which is used in the COMPARETREE and COMPAREPATH methods.

We initialize the vertex-list with dummy head(vh) and tail(vt) (called sentinels) with values $-\infty$ and ∞ respectively. Similarly, each edge-lists is also initialized with dummy head (eh) and tail (et) (refer Fig. 1).

Our acyclic graph data-structure maintains some *invariants*: (a) the vertex-list is sorted based on the VNode's key value k and each unmarked VNode is reachable from vh, (b) also each of the edge-lists are sorted based on the ENode's key value l and unmarked ENodes are reachable from eh of the corresponding VNode and (c) the concurrent graph always stays *acyclic*.

4   Working of the Non-blocking Algorithm

In this section, we describe the technical details of all the acyclic graph operations.

Pseudo-code Convention: The acyclic graph algorithm is depicted in Figs. 2, 3, 4, 6. We use $p.x$ to access the member field x of a class object pointer p. To return multiple variables from an operation, we use $\langle x_1, x_2, \ldots, x_n \rangle$. To avoid the overhead of another field in the node structure, we use bit-manipulation: we use last two significant bits of a pointer p. We define six methods that manipulate these bits: (a) ISMARKED(p) and ISTRANSIT(p), return **true** if the last two significant bits of pointer p are set to 01 and 10, respectively, else, both return **false**, (b) MARKEDREF(p), UNMARKEDREF(p), ADDEDREF(p) and TRANSITREF(p) sets the last two significant bits of the pointer p to 01, 00, 11 and 10, respectively. An invocation of ACYCVNODE(k) creates a new **VNode** with key k. Similarly, an invocation of ACYCENODE(k) creates a new **ENode** with key k in **TRANSIT** state (explained below). Whereas, an invocation of ACYCBNODE(k) creates a new **BFSNode** with vertex k. For a newly created **VNode**, the pointer fields are **NULL**. Similarly, a newly created **ENode** initialises its pointer fields to **NULL** as well. In case of a new **BFSNode**, the pointer field n, **next** and p are initialized with k, **NULL** and parent node, respectively. Each slot of a **VisitedArray** in each **VNode** is initialized to 0 and the counter **ecount** is also initialized to 0.

To ensure acyclicity, we use a operation descriptor with a pointer in a single memory-word with *bit-masking*. In case of an x86-64 bit architecture, memory has a 64-bit boundary and the last three least significant bits are unused. So, our operator descriptor uses the last two significant bit of the pointer. If the last two bits are set to: (a) 01 then the pointer is **MARKED**, (b) 10 indicates the pointer is in **TRANSIT**, (c) 11 value of the pointer indicates **ADDED** and (d) 00 indicates the pointer is unused and unmarked.

We next describe the vertex and edge operations. We use the term method and operation interchangeably in the rest of this document.

4.1   Acyclic Vertex Operations

The acyclic vertex operations ACYADDV, ACYREMV and ACYCONV are depicted in Fig. 2. The ACYCONV method does not help other threads in the process of traversal from the vertex head **vh** to the destination vertex. If the keys in the vertex set are finite, then the ACYCONV operation is wait-free.

An ACYADDV(key) operation is invoked by passing the key to be inserted, in Lines 1 to 14. It first traverses the vertex-list in a lock-free manner starting from **vh** using LOCV procedure (Line 3) until it finds a vertex with its key greater than or equal to key. In the process of traversal, it physically deletes all logically deleted **VNodes** using **CAS** operation for helping previously pending ACYREMV operations. Once it reaches the appropriate location, say $currv$ and has identified its predecessor, say $predv$, it checks if the key is already present. If the key is not present, it attempts to add the new **VNode**, say $newv$ in between the $predv$ and $currv$ (Line 9) using **CAS** operation. If the **CAS** is unsuccessful, then these steps are retried. On the other hand, if key is already present then the method returns **false**.

Like an ACYADDV, an ACYREMV(key) operation is invoked by passing the key to be deleted, in Lines 15 to 31. It traverses the vertex-list in a lock-free manner starting from vh using LOCV procedure (Line 17) until it finds a vertex with its key greater than or equal to *key*. Similar to the ACYADDV, during the traversal it physically deletes all logically removed VNodes using CAS operations for helping other pending ACYREMV operations. Once it reaches the appropriate location, say *currv* and its predecessor, say *predv*, it checks to see if *key* is already present. If present, it attempts to remove *currv* in two steps (like [11]), (a) atomically marking the vnext of *currv* using a CAS (Line 23), and (b) atomically updating the vnext of the *predv* to point to the vnext of *currv* using a CAS (Line 24). On any unsuccessful CAS, these steps are reattempted. If the *key* is not present then, this method returns false.

```
1:  Operation AcyAddV(key)            32: Operation AcyConV(key)
2:    while (1) do                    33:   currv ← vh.vnext;
3:      ⟨predv, currv⟩ ← LocV (vh, key);  34:   while (currv.k < key) do
4:      if (currv.k = key) then       35:     currv ← UnMarkedRef
5:        return false;                     (currv.vnext);
6:      else                          36:   end while
7:        newv ← AcyCVnode (key);     37:   if (currv.k = key ∧ ¬ isMarked
8:        newv.vnext ← currv;              (currv)) then
9:        if (CAS (predv.vnext, currv, newv)) then  38:   return true;
                                       39:   else
10:         return true;               40:     return false;
11:       end if                       41:   end if
12:     end if                         42: end Operation
13:   end while
14: end Operation                      43: Operation AcyConE(k, l)
                                       44:   ⟨ u, v, st ⟩ ← ConCPlus(k, l);
15: Operation AcyRemV(key)             45:   if (st = false) then
16:   while (1) do                     46:     return ⟨false, "VERTEX NOT PRESENT"⟩;
17:     ⟨predv, currv⟩ ← LocV (vh, key);  47:   end if
18:     if (currv.k ≠ key) then        48:   curre ← u.enext;
19:       return false;                49:   while (curre.l < l) do
20:     end if                         50:     curre ← UnMarkedRef
21:     cnext ← currv.vnext;                (curre.enext);
22:     if (¬ isMarked (cnext)) then   51:   end while
23:       if (CAS (currv.vnext, cnext, MarkedRef  52:   if (curre.l = l ∧ ¬ isMarked (u) ∧ ¬
          (cnext))) then                   isMarked (v) ∧ ¬ isMarked (curre) ∧ ¬
24:         if (CAS (predv.vnext, currv, cnext))    isTransit (curre)) then
          then                         53:     return ⟨true, "EDGE PRESENT"⟩;
25:           break;                    54:   else
26:         end if                      55:     return ⟨false, "VERTEX OR EDGE NOT
27:       end if                           PRESENT"⟩;
28:     end if                          56:   end if
29:   end while                         57: end Operation
30:   return true;
31: end Operation
```

Fig. 2. Pseudo-codes of ACYADDV, ACYREMV, ACYCONV and ACYCONE

When a vertex is deleted from a graph, all its incoming and outgoing edges should also get removed. Once a CAS at Line 23 is successful, the vertex is logically deleted from the vertex-list and its outgoing edges are deleted atomically. Notice that, all the incoming edges are logically deleted from the corresponding ENodes of any edge-lists. This is because each ENode has a direct pointer pointv to its vertex node and calls ISMARKED to validate the deleted VNode. Finally, these ENodes are physically deleted using CAS operation by any other helping edge operation (which is described later).

An ACYCONV(*key*) operation, first traverses the vertex-list in a wait-free manner skipping all the logically marked VNodes until it finds a vertex with its key greater than or equal to *key* (in Lines 32 to 42). Once it reaches the appropriate VNode, it checks if its key value is equal to the *key* and if it is unmarked, then it returns **true** otherwise returns **false**. ACYCONV method does not help other threads during the traversal.

4.2 Acyclic Edge Operations

The acyclic edge operations ACYADDE and ACYREME are depicted in Fig. 3 and ACYCONE is depicted in Fig. 2.

```
58: Operation ACYADDE(k, l)
59:   ⟨ u, v, st ⟩ ← ACYCONVPLUS(k, l);
60:   if (st = false) then
61:     return ⟨ false, VERTEX NOT PRESENT ⟩ ;
62:   end if
63:   while (1) do
64:     if (ISMARKED (u) ⋁ ISMARKED (v)) then
65:       return ⟨ false, VERTEX NOT PRESENT ⟩ ;
66:     end if
67:     ⟨prede, curre⟩ ← LOCE (u.enext, l);
68:     if (curre.l = l) then
69:       return ⟨ false, EDGE ALREADY PRESENT ⟩ ;
70:     end if
71:     newe ← ACYCENODE (l);
72:     newe.enext ← TRANSITREF (curre);
73:     newe.pointv ← v;
74:     nnext ← newe.enext;
75:     if (CAS (prede.enext, curre, newe )) then
76:       if (¬SCR(v, u)) then // SCR or DCR is invoked
77:         newe.enext ← ADDEDREF(nnxt);
78:         u.ecount.FetchAndAdd(1); // only if DCR is invoked
79:         return ⟨ true, EDGE ADDED ⟩ ;
80:       else
81:         newe.enext ← MARKEDREF(nnxt);
82:         return ⟨ false, CYCLE DETECTED ⟩ ;
83:       end if
84:     end if
85:   end while
86: end Operation
```

```
87:  Operation ACYREME(k, l)
88:    ⟨ u, v, st ⟩ ← ACYCONVPLUS(k, l);
89:    if (st = false) then
90:      return ⟨false, "VERTEX NOT PRESENT"⟩ ;
91:    end if
92:    while (1) do
93:      if (ISMARKED (u) ⋁ ISMARKED (v)) then
94:        return ⟨false, "VERTEX NOT PRESENT"⟩;
95:      end if
96:      ⟨prede, curre⟩ ← LOCE (u.enext, l);
97:      if (curre.l ≠ l) then
98:        return ⟨false, "EDGE NOT PRESENT"⟩;
99:      end if
100:     cnt ← curre.enext;
101:     if (¬ ISMARKED (cnt)) then
102:       if (CAS (curre.enext, cnt, MARKEDREF (cnt))) then
103:         u.ecount.FetchAndAdd(1);// only if DCR is invoked
104:         if (CAS (prede.enext, curre, cnt)) then
105:           break;
106:         end if
107:       end if
108:     end if
109:   end while
110:   return ⟨true, "EDGE REMOVED"⟩;
111: end Operation
```

Fig. 3. Pseudo-codes of ACYADDE and ACYREME.

An ACYADDE(*k*, *l*) operation, begins in Lines 58 to 86 by validating the presence of the *k* and *l* in the vertex-list by invoking ACYCONVPLUS (Line 59) and validating that both the vertices are unmarked (Line 64). If the validations fail, it returns **false** along with an indicative string VERTEX NOT PRESENT. Once the validation succeeds, LOCE is invoked(Line 67) to find the location to insert $e(k, l)$ in the edge-list of the *k*. The operation LOCE works similar to the helping method LOCV; except that in the traversal phase, it physically deletes two kinds of logically deleted ENodes (to help a pending incompleted ACYADDE or ACYREME operations): (a) ENodes whose VNode has already been logically deleted using a CAS, and (b) the logically deleted ENodes using a CAS. The operation LOCE traverses the edge-list until it finds an ENode with its key greater than or equal to l. Once it reaches the appropriate location, say *curre* and its predecessor, say *prede*, it checks if the key l is already present. If the key is already present, it simply returns false along with an indicative string EDGE ALREADY PRESENT. Otherwise, it attempts a CAS to add a new $e(k, l)$ with TRANSIT state in between *prede* and *curre* (Line 75). On an unsuccessful CAS, the operation is re-tried.

Once the edge $e(k, l)$ is inserted in a transit state, it invokes the reachability method to test whether this edge has created a cycle. As explained earlier, this method returns false if adding this edge creates a cycle. Further, the reachability method can return false even if this edge does not create a cycle in presence of other concurrent ACYADDEmethods.

As mentioned earlier, we have proposed two algorithms to maintain the acyclicity property. First one is the wait-free reachable algorithm SCR, and the second one is the obstruction-free reachable algorithm DCR. The detailed working of these algorithms is given in the subsequent subsections. If the edge $e(k, l)$ creates a cycle, we delete it by setting its state from TRANSIT to MARKED (Line 81) and return false along with an indicative string CYCLE DETECTED. Otherwise, we set the state from TRANSIT to ADDED (Line 77) and return true along with an indicative string EDGE ADDED. Like ACYADDE, an ACYREME(k, l) operation (Lines 87 to 111), first validates the presence of the corresponding VNodes and check if they are unmarked. If the validations fail, it returns false along with an indicative string VERTEX NOT PRESENT. Once the validation succeeds, it finds the location to delete the $e(k, l)$ in the edge-list of the k. Similar to ACYADDE, in the traversal phase, it also physically deletes two kinds of logically deleted ENodes: (a) ENodes whose VNode has been logically deleted, and (b) the logically deleted ENodes. It traverses the edge-list until it finds an ENode with its key greater than or equal to l. Once it reaches the appropriate location, say *curre* and its predecessor, say *prede*, it checks if the key l is already present. If the key is not present, it returns false along with a string EDGE NOT PRESENT; otherwise it attempts to remove *curre* in two steps: (a) atomically marking the enext of *curre* using a CAS (Line 102), and then (b) atomically updating the enext of *prede* to point to the enext of *curre* using a CAS (Line 104). On any unsuccessful CAS, it reattempts this process. After a successful CAS, it returns true along with a string EDGE REMOVED.

Similarly, an ACYCONE(k, l) operation, in Lines 43 to 57, validates the presence of the corresponding VNodes. Then it traverses the edge-list of k in a wait-free manner skipping all logically marked ENodes until it finds an edge with its key greater than or equal to l. Once it reaches the appropriate ENode, checks its key value equal to l and it is unmarked and not in TRANSIT state and also k and l are unmarked, then it returns true along with a string EDGE PRESENT otherwise it returns false along with a sting VERTEX OR EDGE NOT PRESENT. Like ACYCONV, we also do not allow ACYCONE for any helping thread in the process of traversal.

4.3   Wait-Free Single Collect Reachable Algorithm

In this subsection, we describe one of our algorithms to detect the cycle of a concurrent graph in a wait-free manner. As mentioned earlier, a cycle can be only be formed on adding an edge to the graph. The SCR (k,l) operation, in Lines 112 to 137, performs non-recursive BFS traversal starting from the vertex k. Reader can refer [7] to know the working of the BFS traversals in graphs. In the process of BFS traversal, it explores VNodes which are reachable from k and unmarked. If it reaches l, then it terminates by returning true to the AcyAddE operation. Then AcyAddE deletes $e(k,l)$ by setting enext pointer from the TRANSIT state to MARKED state and returns false along with an indicative string CYCLE DETECTED. If it is unable to reach l from k after exploring all reachable VNodes through TRANSIT or ADDED or unmarked ENodes, then it terminates by returning false to the AcyAddE operation. Now AcyAddE adds $e(l)$ by setting enext pointer from the TRANSIT state to ADDED state and then it returns true along with an indicative string EDGE ADDED, which preserves the acyclic property after AcyAddE (Figs. 4 and 5).

In the process of BFS traversal, we have used a VisitedArray (with size as that of the number of threads) to put all the visited VNodes locally. This is because multiple threads repeatedly invoke reachable operation concurrently, a boolean variable or a boolean array would not suffice like in case of sequential execution. We have used a thread local variable cnt as a counter for the number

```
112: Operation SCR (k, l)
113:    tid ← this_thread.get_id();
114:    queue <VNode > Q;
115:    cnt ← cnt + 1;
116:    k.visitedArray[tid] ← cnt ;
117:    Qe.enque(k);
118:    while (¬Q.empty()) do
119:       VNode cvn ← Q.deque();
120:       eh ← cvn.enext;
121:       for (ENode itn ← eh.enext to et) do
122:          if (¬isMARKED (itn)) then
123:             VNode adjn ← itn.pointv;
124:             if (¬isMARKED (adjn)) then
125:                if (adjn = l) then
126:                   return true;
127:                end if
128:                if (adjn[tid] ≠ cnt) then
129:                   adjn.VisitedArray [tid] ← cnt;
130:                   Q.enque(adjn);
131:                end if
132:             end if
133:          end if
134:       end for
135:    end while
136:    return false;
137: end Operation
```

```
138: Operation BFSTreeCollect (k, l)
139:    queue <BFSNode > Q; cnt ← cnt + 1;
140:    k.visitedArray[tid] ← cnt ;
141:    bNode ← AcyCBnode (k, NULL, NULL, k.ecount);
142:    bTree.Insert(bNode); Q.enque(bNode);
143:    while (¬Q.empty()) do
144:       BFSNode cvn ← Q.deque();
145:       eh ← cvn.n.enext;
146:       for (ENode itn ← eh.enext to et) do
147:          if (¬isMARKED (itn)) then
148:             VNode adjn ← itn.pointv;
149:             if (¬isMARKED (adjn)) then
150:                if (adjn = l) then
151:                   bNode ← AcyCBnode (adjn, cvn, NULL, adjn.ecount);
152:                   bTree.Insert(bNode);
153:                   return ⟨bTree, true⟩;
154:                end if
155:                if (adjn[tid] ≠ cnt) then
156:                   adjn.VisitedArray [tid] ← cnt;
157:                   bNode ← AcyCBnode (adjn, cvn, NULL, adjn.ecount);
158:                   bTree.Insert(bNode);
159:                   Q.enque(bNode);
160:                end if
161:             end if
162:          end if
163:       end for
164:    end while
165:    return ⟨bTree, false⟩;
166: end Operation
```

Fig. 4. Pseudo-codes of SCR and BFSTreeCollect.

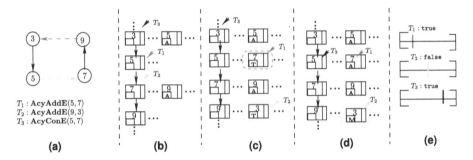

Fig. 5. An example working of the methods while preserving acyclicity. (a) The initial graph, T_1, T_2 and T_3 are concurrently performing operations. The corresponding data-structure is shown in (b). In (c), T_3 is traversing the vertex list, while T_1 and T_2 have added their corresponding edges in TRANSIT, T state and performing cycle detection. (d) T_1 has succeeded; and changed the status to ADDED, A. However, T_2 failed; it changes the status to MARKED, M. Meanwhile, T_3 finds the respective edge. (e) One possible linearization of this concurrent execution.

of repeated traversals by a thread. So, a `VisitedArray` slot maintains cnt value (see Line 116).

However, an ENode in TRANSIT state cannot be removed by any other concurrent thread other than the thread that added it, only if it creates a cycle. The threads which are performing cycle detection can see all the ENodes in TRANSIT or ADDED state. Further, a concurrent AcyConE operation will ignore all the ENodes with TRANSIT state. This ensures that when an ENode is in the ADDED state, an AcyAddE operation will return **true** along with a string EDGE ADDED.

However, it is to be noted that with this algorithm, it is possible that an edge may not get added to the graph even though it does not create a cycle. This can happen in the following scenario; two threads T_1 and T_2 are adding edges lying in the path of a single cycle. In this case, both the threads detect that the newly added ENode (in TRANSIT state) has led to the formation of a cycle and both may delete their respective edges. However, in a sequential execution, only one of the edges would be removed. But, this implementation is correct w.r.t our sequential specification (thereby preserving our correctness criteria, linearizability) as the graph at the end of each operation remains acyclic. The proof of the acyclicity is given in the technical report [20].

Although the wait-free SCR algorithm does not add an edge at times even when it does not create a cycle, it can be seen its working is non-trivial. A trivial algorithm can always return **false** for AddEdge while not violating the specification and hence satisfying linearizability. SCR algorithm is much stronger and allows insertion of edges even in the presence of concurrent updates, as explained in the working.

4.4   Obstruction-Free Double Collect Reachable Algorithm

In this subsection, we present an obstruction-free reachability, DCR algorithm, which is designed based on the atomic snapshot algorithm by Afek et al. [1] and reachable algorithm by Chatterjee et al. [6]. There is no non-determinism in the DCR algorithm. It never fails to add an edge if the edge does not create a cycle. However, unlike wait-free SCR, DCR is obstruction-free. It returns only in the absence of any other concurrent updates.

The DCR (k,l) algorithm, in Lines 167 to 175, performs a SCAN starting from k. It checks whether l is reachable from k. This reachable information is returned to the ACYADDE operation and then ACYADDE decides whether to add $e(k,l)$ (is in the TRANSIT state) to the edge-list of k.

The SCAN method, in Lines 176 to 191, first creates two BFS-trees, *otree* and *ntree* to hold the VNodes in two consecutive BFS traversal. It performs repeated BFS-tree collection by invoking BFSTREECOLLECT until two consecutive collects are the same. The BFSTREECOLLECT procedure, in Lines 138 to 166, performs a non-recursive BFS traversal starting from the vertex k. In the process of BFS traversal, it explores all the reachable and unmarked VNodes through adjacent ENodes which are in the TRANSIT or ADDED or unmarked state. However, it keeps adding all these VNodes in the $bTree$(see Line 142, 152, 158). If it reaches l, then it terminates by returning $bTree$ and a reachable status true (Line 153) to the SCAN method. If it is unable to reach l from k after exploring all reachable VNodes, then it terminates by returning $bTree$ and a reachable status false (Line 165) to the SCAN method.

```
167: Operation DCR (k, l)
168:    tid ← this_thread.get_id();
169:    status ← SCAN (k, l, tid);
170:    if (status = true) then
171:       return true;
172:    else
173:       return NULL;
174:    end if
175: end Operation

176: procedure SCAN (u, v, tid)
177:    list < BFSNode > otree, ntree ;
178:    ⟨otree, of⟩ ← BFSTREECOLLECT (u, v, tid);
179:    while (true) do
180:       ⟨ntree, nf⟩ ← BFSTREECOLLECT (u, v, tid);
181:       if (of = true ∧ nf = true ∧ COMPAREPATH (otree, ntree)) then
182:          return nf;
183:       else
184:          if (of = false ∧ nf = false ∧ COMPARETREE (otree, nt)) then
185:             return nf;
186:          end if
187:       end if
188:       of ← nf;
189:       otree ← ntree;
190:    end while
191: end procedure
```

```
192: procedure COMPARETREE (otree, ntree)
193:    if (otree = NULL ∨ ntree = NULL) then
194:       return false ;
195:    end if
196:    BFSNode oit ← otree.Head, nit ← ntree.Head;
197:    do
198:       if (oit.n ≠ nit.n ∨ oit.lecount ≠ nit.lecount ∨ oldit.p ≠ newit.p) then return false;
199:       end if
200:       oit ← oit.next; nit ← nit.next;
201:    while (oit ≠ ot.Tail ∧ nit ≠ nt.Tail );
202:    if (oit.n ≠ nit.n ∨ oit.lecount ≠ nit.lecount ∨ oit.p ≠ nit.p) then return false;
203:    else return true ;
204:    end if
205: end procedure

206: procedure COMPAREPATH (otree, ntree)
207:    if (otree = NULL ∨ ntree = NULL) then
208:       return false ;
209:    end if
210:    BFSNode oit ← otree.Tail, nit ← ntree.Tail;
211:    do
212:       if (oit.n ≠ nit.n ∨ oit.lecount ≠ nit.lecount ∨ oldit.p ≠ newit.p) then return false;
213:       end if
214:       oit ← oit.p; nit ← nit.p;
215:    while (oit ≠ ot.Head ∧ nit ≠ nt.Head );
216:    if (oit.n ≠ nit.n ∨ oit.lecount ≠ nit.lecount ∨ oit.p ≠ nit.p) then return false;
217:    else return true;
218:    end if
219: end procedure
```

Fig. 6. Pseudo-codes of DCR, SCAN, COMPARETREE and COMPAREPATH.

If two consecutive BFSTREECOLLECT method return the same boolean status value `true`, then we invoke COMPAREPATH to compare if the two `BFS-trees` are same. If both the trees are same, then the SCAN method returns `true` to DCR operation, which means that l is reachable from k. Then DCR returns `true` to the ACYADDE operation and subsequently ACYADDE deletes $e(k, l)$ by setting `enext` pointer from the `TRANSIT` state to the `MARKED` state and returns `false` (this is because $e(k, l)$ created a cycle). However, if two consecutive BFSTREECOLLECT methods return the same status value `false`, then we invoke COMPARETREE to compare if the two `BFS-trees` are same. If they are, the SCAN method returns `false` to the DCR operation which implies that l is not reachable from k. Then DCR returns `false` to the ACYADDE operation and then ACYADDE adds $e(l)$ by setting the `enext` pointer from the `TRANSIT` state to `ADDED` state and then it returns `true`, which confirms the acyclic property after ACYADDE. If two consecutive BFSTREECOLLECT methods return the same boolean status value `true` or `false` but do not match in the COMPAREPATH or COMPARETREE, then we discard the older `BFS-tree` and restart the BFSTREECOLLECT.

The COMPAREPATH method, in Lines 206 to 219, compares two `BFS-tree` based on the path along with the `lecount` values. It starts from the last `BFSNode` and follows the parent pointer p until it reaches to the starting `BFSNode` or any mismatch that occurred at a `BFSNode`. It returns `false` for any mismatch occurred, otherwise returns `true`. Similarly, the COMPARETREE method, in Lines 192 to 205, compares two `BFS-tree` based on all explored `VNodes` in the process of BFS traversal and along with the `lecount` values. It starts from the starting `BFSNode` and follows with the next pointer `next` until it reaches the last `BFSNode` or any mismatch that occurred at a `BFSNode`. It returns `false` for any mismatch occurred and otherwise returns `true`.

To capture the modifications along the path of BFS-traversal, we have an atomic counter `ecount` associated with each vertex. During any edge update operation, before $e(k, l)$ gets physically deleted, the counter `ecount` of the source vertex k is certainly incremented at Line 78 or 103 either by the operation that logically deleted the $e(k, l)$ or any edge helping operations. To verify the double collect, we compare the `BFS-tree` along with the counter.

It is to be noted that even though the DCR algorithm is better than SCR as the specification of ACYADDE operation does not exhibit any non-determinism, it does not exploit as much concurrency as the SCR algorithm. As explained, the SCR algorithm is wait-free without using helping descriptors, whereas DCR is obstruction-free. In Sect. 6, we compared the performance of both these algorithms and as expected observed that SCR performs better.

5   Correctness and Progress Guarantee

In this section, we prove the correctness of our concurrent acyclic graph data-structure based on LP [14] events inside the execution interval of each of the operations.

Theorem 1. The non-blocking concurrent acyclic graph operations are linearizable.

Theorem 2. For the presented concurrent acyclic graph algorithm, (1). The operations AcyConV, AcyConE and SCR are wait-free, if the vertex keys are finite, (2). The operation DCR is obstruction-free and, (3). The operations AcyAddV, AcyRemV, AcyConV, AcyAddE, AcyRemE, and AcyConE are lock-free.

The proof of Theorems 1 and 2 can be referred to from the technical report [20].

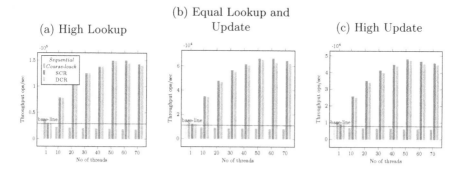

(a) High Lookup   (b) Equal Lookup and Update   (c) High Update

Fig. 7. Acyclic graph data-structure.

6   Experimental Evaluation

We performed our tests on 56 cores machine with Intel Xeon (R) CPU E5-2630 v4 running at 2.20 GHz frequency. Each core supports 2 logical threads. Every core's L1 cache has 64k, L2 has 256k cache memory private to that core; L3 cache (25 MB) is shared across all cores of a processor. The tests were performed in a controlled environment, where we were the sole users of the system. The implementation[a] has been done in C++ (without any garbage collection) and threading is achieved by using Posix threads. All the programs were optimized at -O3 level.

We start our experiments by creating an initial directed graph with 1000 vertices and nearly $\binom{1000}{2}/4 \approx 125000$ edges added randomly. Then we create a fixed number of threads with each thread randomly performing a set of operations chosen by a particular workload distribution. We evaluate the number of operations finished their execution in unit time and then calculate the throughput. We run each experiment for 20 seconds and the final data point values are collected after taking an average of 7 iterations. We present the results for the following workload distributions for acyclic directed graph over the ordered set of operations {AcyAddV, AcyRemV, AcyConV, AcyAddE, AcyRemE, AcyConE}

---

[a] The source code is available on https://github.com/PDCRL/ConcurrentGraphDS.

as: (1) *High Lookup*: (2.5%, 2.5%, 45%, 2.5%, 2.5%, 45%), see the Fig. 7a. (2) *Equal Lookup and Update*: (12.5%, 12.5%, 25%, 12.5%, 12.5%, 25%), see the Fig. 7b. (3) *High Update*: (22.5%, 22.5%, 5%, 22.5%, 22.5%, 5%), Fig. 7c.

From Fig. 7, we notice that both SCR and DCR algorithms perform well with the number of threads in comparison with sequential and coarse-lock based version. The wait-free single collect reachable algorithm performs better than the obstruction-free double collect reachable algorithm. However, we notice that the performance of the coarse lock-based algorithm decreases with the number of threads. Moreover also, it performs worse than even the sequential implementation. On average, both the non-blocking algorithms are able to achieve nearly 7× times higher throughput over the sequential implementation.

7   Conclusion

In this paper, we presented two efficient non-blocking concurrent algorithms for maintaining acyclicity in a directed graph where vertices & edges are dynamically inserted and/or deleted. The first algorithm is based on a wait-free reachability query, SCR, and the second one is based on partial snapshot-based obstruction-free reachability query, DCR. Both these algorithms maintain the acyclic property of the graph throughout the concurrent execution. We prove that the acyclic graph data-structure operations are linearizable. We also present a proof to show that the graph remains acyclic at all times in the concurrent setting. We evaluated both the algorithms in C++ implementation and tested through a number of micro-benchmarks. Our experimental results show that our proposed algorithms obtain an average of 7x improvement over the sequential implementation and the coarse lock based ones.

In spite of the performance of the SCR, it suffers from the non-determinism during concurrent addition of edges. It can be seen that DCR gets rid of the non-determinism and makes sure that an edge surely gets added if it does not create a cycle. In the future, we plan to measure the number of false positives incurred by the SCR algorithm on varying workloads and suggest ways to reduce them.

Acknowledgements. We would like to thank the anonymous reviewers and our shepherd, C. Aiswarya for their useful suggestions and comments. Following their suggestions, we made several improvements to the manuscript. This research was funded by MediaLab Asia for funding Graduate Scholarship.

References

1. Afek, Y., Attiya, H., Dolev, D., Gafni, E., Merritt, M., Shavit, N.: Atomic snapshots of shared memory. J. ACM **40**(4), 873–890 (1993)
2. Barnes, G.: A method for implementing lock-free shared-data structures. In: Proceedings of the Fifth Annual ACM Symposium on Parallel Algorithms and Architectures, SPAA 1993, pp. 261–270. ACM, New York (1993)

3. Brito, J., O'Sullivan, A.: Bitcoin: A Primer for Policymakers. Mercatus Center at George Mason University (2013)
4. Buterin, V.: Ethereum: a next generation smart contract and decentralized application platform (2013). https://github.com/ethereum/wiki/wiki/white-paper
5. Chatterjee, B., Nguyen, N., Tsigas, P.: Efficient lock-free binary search trees. In: Proceedings of the 2014 ACM Symposium on Principles of Distributed Computing, PODC 2014, pp. 322–331. ACM, New York (2014)
6. Chatterjee, B., Peri, S., Sa, M., Singhal, N.: A simple and practical concurrent non-blocking unbounded graph with linearizable reachability queries. In: ICDCN 2019, pp. 168–177 (2019)
7. Cormen, T.H., Leiserson, C.E., Rivest, R.L., Stein, C.: Introduction to Algorithms. MIT Press, Cambridge (2009)
8. Dang, N.N., Tsigas, P.: Progress guarantees when composing lock-free objects. In: Jeannot, E., Namyst, R., Roman, J. (eds.) Euro-Par 2011. LNCS, vol. 6853, pp. 148–159. Springer, Heidelberg (2011). https://doi.org/10.1007/978-3-642-23397-5_15
9. Demetrescu, C., Finocchi, I., Italiano, G.F.: Dynamic graphs. In: Handbook of Data Structures and Applications, Chapman and Hall/CRC (2004)
10. Fomitchev, M., Ruppert, E.: Lock-free linked lists and skip lists. In: Proceedings of the Twenty-Third Annual ACM Symposium on Principles of Distributed Computing, PODC 2004, St. John's, Newfoundland, Canada, 25–28 July 2004, pp. 50–59 (2004)
11. Harris, T.L.: A pragmatic implementation of non-blocking linked-lists. In: Welch, J. (ed.) DISC 2001. LNCS, vol. 2180, pp. 300–314. Springer, Heidelberg (2001). https://doi.org/10.1007/3-540-45414-4_21
12. Hendler, D., Shavit, N., Yerushalmi, L.: A scalable lock-free stack algorithm. In: Proceedings of the Sixteenth Annual ACM Symposium on Parallelism in Algorithms and Architectures, SPAA 2004, pp. 206–215. ACM, New York (2004)
13. Herlihy, M., Shavit, N.: On the nature of progress. In: Fernàndez Anta, A., Lipari, G., Roy, M. (eds.) OPODIS 2011. LNCS, vol. 7109, pp. 313–328. Springer, Heidelberg (2011). https://doi.org/10.1007/978-3-642-25873-2_22
14. Herlihy, M.P., Wing, J.M.: Linearizability: a correctness condition for concurrent objects. ACM Trans. Program. Lang. Syst. **12**(3), 463–492 (1990)
15. Kallimanis, N.D., Kanellou, E.: Wait-free concurrent graph objects with dynamic traversals. In: OPODIS 2015, pp. 27:1–27:17 (2015)
16. Ladan-Mozes, E., Shavit, N.: An optimistic approach to lock-free FIFO queues. Distrib. Comput. **20**(5), 323–341 (2008)
17. Michael, M.M.: High performance dynamic lock-free hash tables and list-based sets. In: SPAA, pp. 73–82 (2002)
18. Nakamoto, S.: Bitcoin: a peer-to-peer electronic cash system (2008). http://bitcoin.org/bitcoin.pdf
19. Natarajan, A., Mittal, N.: Fast concurrent lock-free binary search trees. In: ACM SIGPLAN Symposium on Principles and Practice of Parallel Programming, PPoPP 2014, Orlando, FL, USA, 15–19 February 2014, pp. 317–328 (2014)
20. Peri, S., Sa, M., Singhal, N.: A pragmatic non-blocking concurrent directed acyclic graph. CoRR, abs/1611.03947 (2016)
21. Serguei Popov. The tangle (2018). https://iota.org/iotawhitepaper.pdf
22. Sinha, A., Malik, S.: Runtime checking of serializability in software transactional memory. In: IPDPS 2010, pp. 1–12 (2010)

23. Valois, J.D.: Lock-free linked lists using compare-and-swap. In: Proceedings of the Fourteenth Annual ACM Symposium on Principles of Distributed Computing, Ottawa, Ontario, Canada, 20–23 August 1995, pp. 214–222 (1995)
24. Weikum, G., Vossen, G.: Transactional Information Systems: Theory, Algorithms, and the Practice of Concurrency Control and Recovery. Morgan Kaufmann, Burlington (2002)

Networks

The Fake News Vaccine

A Content-Agnostic System for Preventing Fake News from Becoming Viral

Oana Balmau[3], Rachid Guerraoui[1], Anne-Marie Kermarrec[2],
Alexandre Maurer[1(✉)], Matej Pavlovic[1], and Willy Zwaenepoel[3]

[1] École Polytechnique Fédérale de Lausanne, Lausanne, Switzerland
{rachid.guerraoui,alexandre.maurer,matej.pavlovic}@epfl.ch
[2] Mediego, Cesson-Sévigné, France
anne-marie.kermarrec@mediego.com
[3] University of Sydney, Camperdown, Australia
{oana.balmau,willy.zwaenepoel}@sydney.edu.au

Abstract. While spreading fake news is an old phenomenon, today social media enables misinformation to instantaneously reach millions of people. Content-based approaches to detect fake news, typically based on automatic text checking, are limited. It is indeed difficult to come up with general checking criteria. Moreover, once the criteria are known to an adversary, the checking can be easily bypassed. On the other hand, it is practically impossible for humans to check every news item, let alone preventing them from becoming viral.

We present CREDULIX, the first content-agnostic system to prevent fake news from going viral. CREDULIX is implemented as a *plugin* on top of a social media platform and acts as a *vaccine*. Human fact-checkers review a *small* number of popular news items, which helps us estimate the inclination of each user to share fake news. Using the resulting information, we automatically estimate the probability that an unchecked news item is fake. We use a *Bayesian* approach that resembles *Condorcet's Theorem* to compute this probability. We show how this computation can be performed in an *incremental*, and hence *fast* manner.

1 Introduction

The expression "fake news" has become very popular after the 2016 presidential election in the United States. Both political sides accused each other of spreading false information on social media, in order to influence public opinion. Fake news have also been involved in Brexit and seem to have played a crucial role in the French election. The phenomenon is considered by many as a threat to democracy, since the proportion of people getting their news from social media is significantly increasing.

We present CREDULIX, the first content-agnostic system to prevent fake news from getting *viral*. From a software perspective, CREDULIX is a plugin to a social media platform. From a more abstract perspective, it can also be viewed as a

© Springer Nature Switzerland AG 2019
M. F. Atig and A. A. Schwarzmann (Eds.): NETYS 2019, LNCS 11704, pp. 347–364, 2019.
https://doi.org/10.1007/978-3-030-31277-0_23

vaccine for the social network. Assuming the system has been exposed to some (small) amount of fake news in the *past*, CREDULIX enables it to prevent *future* fake news from becoming viral. It is important to note that our approach does not exclude other (e.g. content-based) approaches, but *complements* them.

CREDULIX retains the idea of using a team of certified human fact-checkers. However, we acknowledge that they cannot review *all* news items. Such an overwhelming task would possibly require even more fact-checkers than users. Here, the fact-checkers only check a *few viral* news items, i.e., ideally news items that have been shared and seen the most on the social network[1]. Many such fact-checking initiatives already exist all around the world (e.g., [2,3]). Such checks enable us to build *user credulity records*: records of which fact-checked items a user has seen and shared.

We use a *Naive Bayes* approach[2] to estimate the credibility of news items based on which users shared them and how these users treated fake news in the past. News items considered fake with a sufficiently high probability can then be prevented from further dissemination, i.e., from becoming viral. Our result is in the spirit of *Condorcet's jury Theorem* [15], which states that a very high level of reliability can be achieved by a large number of weakly reliable individuals. To determine the probability of falsehood of a news item X, we look at the behavior of users towards X. This particular behavior had a certain a priori probability to happen. We compute this probability based on the previously constructed user credulity records. Then, after determining the average fraction of fake news on the social network, we apply Laplace's Rule of Succession [35] and then Bayes' Theorem [25] to obtain the desired probability.

When this probability goes beyond a threshold (say 99.9999%), the social network can react accordingly. E.g., it may stop showing the news item in other users' news feeds. It is important to note that our approach does not require any users to share a large amount of fake news. It suffices that some users share more fake news than others.

Also note that CREDULIX does not completely eliminate the spreading of all fake news—unpopular items only seen by very few users might pass undetected, since it is the user interactions with an item that contribute to its detection. However, CREDULIX does prevent fake items from going viral—once a sufficient (but still low) number of users were exposed to a fake item, CREDULIX takes the

---

[1] Some news items are indeed seen by millions, and are easy to check a posteriori. For instance, according to CNN [1], the following fake news items were read by millions: *"Thousands of fraudulent ballots for Clinton uncovered"*; *"Elizabeth Warren endorsed Bernie Sanders"*; *"The NBA cancels 2017 All-Star Game in North Carolina"*.

[2] Naive Bayes approaches [32,36] assume that the random variables are independent, even if they are not totally independent in practice. This enables to simplify a problem that, otherwise, would be far too complex to tackle. Naive Bayes approaches work surprisingly well in many complex real-world situations, and are also very robust [32] ([36] explains some possible theoretical reasons for this). Here, the imprecision of the probability we compute is compensated by the fact that we choose a threshold which is extremely close to 1 (i.e., $1 - 10^{-6}$, or 99.9999%). Thus, even with an error of $\times 100$, the actual probability would be $1 - 10^{-4}$, with does not change much from our perspective.

appropriate action. Thus, fake news items that would otherwise become popular (arguably the most harmful ones) are always detected by CREDULIX.

Our approach is *generic* in the sense that it does not depend on any specific criteria. Here, for instance, we look at what users *share* to determine if a news item is *fake*. However, the approach is independent of the precise meanings of "share" and "fake": they could respectively be replaced by ("like" or "report") and ("funny", "offensive", "politically liberal" or "politically conservative").

In some sense, CREDULIX shares similarities with recommender systems, since the news items are being classified into categories based on users' reactions. However, the purpose of CREDULIX is fundamentally different from that of recommender systems. While recommenders aim to provide personalized content based on users' preferences, CREDULIX' classification of news items being true or fake is independent of the requesting user. The aim is to prevent the spread of fake news, not to provide users with a personalized selection of news articles.

Turning the theory behind CREDULIX into a system deployable in practice is a non-trivial task. In this paper we address these challenges as well. In particular, we present a practical approach to computing news item credibility in a *fast*, incremental manner.

We implement CREDULIX as a standalone Java plugin and connect it to Twissandra [14] (an open source Twitter clone), which serves as a baseline system. CREDULIX interferes very little with the critical path of users' operations and thus has a minimal impact on user request latency. We evaluate CREDULIX in terms of its capacity to detect fake news as well as its performance overhead when applied to a real social network of over 41M users [27]. After fact-checking the 1024 most popular news items (out of a total of over 35M items), over 99% of unchecked fake news items are correctly detected by CREDULIX. We also show that CREDULIX does not incur significant overhead in terms of throughput and latency of user operations (sharing items and viewing the news feed): average latency increases by at most 5%, while average throughput decreases by at most 8%.

2   Theoretical Foundations

In this section we give an intuition of the theoretical result underlying CREDULIX, followed by its formalization as a theorem. We finally show how to restate the problem in a way that allows efficient, fast computation of news item credibility.

2.1   Intuition

The context is a social network where users can post news items, such as links to newspapers or blog articles. Users exposed to these news items can in turn share them with other users (Twitter followers, Facebook friends etc.). The social network has a fact-checking team

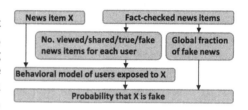

Fig. 1. News item falsehood probability computation.

whose role is to determine whether certain news items are fake (according to some definition of fake)[3]. The news items that the fact-checking team needs to check is very low compared to the total number of items in the social network.

The Main Steps. Our approach goes through the following three main steps:

1. The fact-checking team reviews few news items (ideally those that have been the most viral ones in the past). This is considered the ground truth in our context.
2. CREDULIX creates a probabilistic model of each user's sharing behavior based on their reactions (share/not share) to the fact-checked items in Step (1). This captures the likelihood of a user to share true (resp. fake) items in the future.
3. For a new, unchecked news item X, we use the behavior models generated in Step (2) to determine the probability that X is fake, based on who viewed and shared X.

A high-level view of our technique is depicted in Fig. 1. We use a Bayesian approach. For example, if an item is mostly shared by users with high estimated probabilities of sharing fake items, while users with high estimated probabilities of sharing true items rarely share it, we consider the item likely to be fake (see Fig. 2).

The above-mentioned main steps happen *continuously and in parallel*, as the system is running. Over time, fresh news items are created, new users join the system and users interact with news items. Step (1) happens peri-

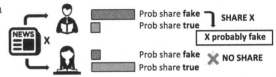

Fig. 2. Users reacting to new item X.

odically, as the fact-checking team reviews more articles and increases the number of news articles that are part of the ground truth. Step (2) and (3) happen continuously, as users are interacting with news items. Updates in users' sharing behavior (Step (2)) trigger updates in the likelihood of an unchecked news item being classified as true or fake (Step (3)).

In order to initialize CREDULIX, the fact-checking team needs to review a low number of news items. The required number of reviewed items depends on their relative popularity, but not on the overall number of items in the system. In our evaluation, reviewing 1024 most popular news items is sufficient for fast and accurate fake news detection. To work with real-world item popularity, we use a corpus of 35M real tweets to select our items. Regardless of the overall number of items, we would still only need to review 1024 of them. We consider that this number of items is still easy to fact-check through non-automated techniques, e.g. by making use of existing fact-checking initiatives [2–6].

---

[3] Our truth and falsehood criteria here are as good as the fact-checking team. CREDULIX trusts the fact-checking team to correctly identify true and false news items.

Preventing the Spread of Fake News. Once we estimate the probability of a news item X being fake, preventing its spread becomes easy. Let p_0 be any cutoff probability threshold. Each time a user views or shares X, we compute p, the probability of X being fake, which we detail below. If $p \geq p_0$ (i.e., X has a probability at least p_0 to be fake), CREDULIX stops showing X in the news feed of users, preventing X from spreading and becoming viral.

2.2   Basic Fake News Detection

User Behavior. We model the behavior of a user u using the two following probabilities:

- $P_T(u)$: probability that u shares a news item if the item is true.
- $P_F(u)$: probability that u shares a news item if the item is fake.

The probabilities $P_T(u)$ and $P_F(u)$ are assumed to be independent between users. In practice, this is the case if the decision to share a news item X is mainly determined by X itself (Fig. 3).

We obtain estimates of $P_T(u)$ and $P_F(u)$ for each user based on the user's behavior (share/not share) with respect to fact-checked items. For any given user u, let $v_T(u)$ (resp. $s_T(u)$) denote the

$v_T(u)$	Number of fact-checked *true* items *viewed* by u
$s_T(u)$	Number of fact-checked *true* items *shared* by u
$v_F(u)$	Number of fact-checked *false* items *viewed* by u
$s_F(u)$	Number of fact-checked *false* items *shared* by u

Fig. 3. User Credulity Record (UCR).

number of fact-checked true news items *viewed* (resp. *shared*) by u, and $v_F(u)$ (resp. $s_F(u)$) the number of fact-checked fake news items *viewed* (resp. *shared*) by u. We call the tuple $(v_T(u), s_T(u), v_F(u), s_F(u))$ the *User Credulity Record* (UCR) of u.

Probability of a News Item Being Fake. Let X be a news item (not fact-checked). Let V and S be any two sets of users that have *viewed* and *shared* X, respectively. In the following, we define a function $p(V, S)$. We then show (Theorem 1) that $p(V, S)$ is the probability that X is fake.

Let g be the estimated *global fraction* of fake news items in the social network, with $g \in (0, 1)$. The fraction g can be estimated by fact-checking a set of news items picked uniformly at random from the whole social network.

We now define the 6 following functions (based on the UCR). Note that these functions do not correspond to anything in particular. We only use them as intermediary steps to simplify notation when defining define $p(V, S)$, and to make the following proofs simpler.

- $\beta_1(u) = (s_T(u) + 1)/(v_T(u) + 2)$
- $\beta_2(u) = (s_F(u) + 1)/(v_F(u) + 2)$
- $\beta_3(u) = (v_T(u) - s_T(u) + 1)/(v_T(u) + 2)$
- $\beta_4(u) = (v_F(u) - s_F(u) + 1)/(v_F(u) + 2)$
- $\pi_T(V, S) = \prod_{u \in S} \beta_1(u) \prod_{u \in V-S} \beta_3(u)$
- $\pi_F(V, S) = \prod_{u \in S} \beta_2(u) \prod_{u \in V-S} \beta_4(u)$

We now define $p(V, S)$ as follows (at this point, this is just an arbitrary definition; in Theorem 1, we show that $p(V, S)$ actually is the probability that X is fake):

$$p(V, S) = \frac{g\pi_F(V, S)}{g\pi_F(V, S) + (1 - g)\pi_T(V, S)} \tag{1}$$

Let g^* be the real fraction of fake news items in the social network (of which g is an estimate). We first show that, if $g = g^*$, then the probability that X is fake is $p(V, S)$ (Theorem 1). Then, we consider the case where we can only assume that $g \leq g^*$ (i.e. we only have a lower bound of g^*). We then show that the probability that X is fake is at least $p(V, S)$, which gives us a conservative estimate (Theorem 2).

Theorem 1. *Let $g = g^*$. A news item viewed by a set of users V and shared by a set of users S is fake with probability $p(V, S)$.*

Proof. According to Laplace's Rule of Succession [35], we have $P_T(u) = \beta_1(u)$ and $P_F(u) = \beta_2(u)$. Consider a news item X that has not been fact-checked. Consider the following events: (1) E: X viewed by a set of users V and shared by a set of users S; (2) F: X is fake; (3) T: X is true. Our goal is to evaluate $P(F|E)$: the probability that X is fake knowing E.

- If X is true, $P(E|T) = \prod_{u \in S} P_T(u) \prod_{u \in V-S}(1 - P_T(u)) = \pi_T(V, S)$.
- If X is fake, $P(E|F) = \prod_{u \in S} P_F(u) \prod_{u \in V-S}(1 - P_F(u)) = \pi_F(V, S)$.

The probability that X is fake (independently of E) is $P(F) = g^*$, and the probability that X is true (independently of E) is $P(T) = 1 - g^*$. Thus, we can determine the probability that E is true: $P(E) = P(E|T)P(T) + P(E|F)P(F) = (1 - g^*)\pi_T(V, S) + g^*\pi_F(V, S)$. $P(F|E) = P(E|F)P(F)/P(E)$ according to Bayes' Theorem [25]. Then, $P(F|E) = g^*\pi_F(V, S)/(g^*\pi_F(V, S) + (1 - g^*)\pi_T(V, S)) = p(V, S)$. Thus, the result.

If g^* is unknown, we assume that g is a lower bound of g^*. We get in this case the following theorem.

Theorem 2. *For $g \leq g^*$, a news item viewed by a set of users V and shared by a set of users S is fake with probability at least $p(V, S)$.*

Proof. First, note that $\pi_T(V, S)$ and $\pi_F(V, S)$ are strictly positive by definition. Thus, the ratio $\pi_T(V, S)/\pi_F(V, S)$ is always strictly positive. $\forall x \in (0, 1)$, let $g(x) = x\pi_F(V, S)/(x\pi_F(V, S) + (1 - x)\pi_T(V, S))$. Then, $p(V, S) = h(g)$, and according to Theorem 1, the news item is fake with probability $h(g^*)$. Written differently, $g(x) = 1/(1 + k(x))$, with $k(x) = (1/x - 1)\pi_T(V, S)/\pi_F(V, S)$. As $g \leq g^*$, $1/g \geq 1/g^*$, $1 + k(g) \geq 1 + k(g^*)$ and $h(g) \leq h(g^*)$. Thus, the result.

2.3   Fast Fake News Detection

CREDULIX' measure of credibility of a news item X is the probability $p(V, S)$ that X is fake. An obvious way to compute this probability is to recalculate $p(V, S)$ using Eq. (1) each time X is viewed or shared by a user. Doing so, however, would be very expensive in terms of computation. Below, we show an efficient method for computing news item credibility. We first describe the computation of UCRs, and then present our fast, incremental approach for computing news item credibility using *item ratings* and *UCR scores*. This is crucial for efficiently running CREDULIX in practice.

Computing User Credulity Records (UCRs). Recall that the four values $(v_T(u), s_T(u), v_F(u), s_F(u))$ constituting a UCR only concern *fact-checked* news items. We thus update the UCR of user u (increment one of these four values) in the following two scenarios.

1. When u views or shares a news item that has been fact-checked (i.e., is known to be true or fake).
2. Upon fact-checking a news item that u had been exposed to.

   In general, the more fact-checked news items a user u has seen and shared, the more *meaningful* u's UCR. Users who have not been exposed to any fact-checked items cannot contribute to CREDULIX.

Item Rating. In addition to $p(V, S)$, we introduce another measure of how confident CREDULIX is about X being fake: the *item rating* $\alpha(V, S)$, whose role is equivalent to that of $p(V, S)$. We define it as $\alpha(V, S) = \pi_T(V, S)/\pi_F(V, S)$, V and S being the sets of users that viewed and shared X, respectively. If we also define $\alpha_0 = (1/p_0 - 1)/(1/g - 1)$ as the rating threshold corresponding to the probability threshold p_0, then, $p(V, S) \geq p_0$ is equivalent to $\alpha(V, S) \leq \alpha_0$.

   We have $p(V, S) = g\pi_F(V, S)/(g\pi_F(V, S) + (1 - g)\pi_T(V, S)) = g/(g + (1 - g)(\pi_T(V, S)/\pi_F(V, S))) = g/(g + (1 - g)\alpha(V, S))$. We have $p(V, S) \geq p_0$ if and only if $g/p(V, S) \leq g/p_0$, that is: $g + (1 - g)\alpha(V, S) \leq g/p_0$, which is equivalent to $\alpha(V, S) \leq (1/p_0 - 1)/(1/g - 1)$, that is: $\alpha(V, S) \leq \alpha_0$.

   When the item X with $\alpha(V, S) \leq \alpha_0$ is about to be displayed in a user's news feed, CREDULIX suppresses X. Note that α_0 can be a fixed constant used throughout the system, but may also be part of the account settings of each user, giving users the ability to control how "confident" the system needs to be about the falsehood of an item before suppressing it.

According to the definition of $\pi_T(V, S)$ and $\pi_F(V, S)$, each time X is viewed (resp. shared) by a new user u, we can update X's rating $\alpha(V, S)$ by multiplying it by $\gamma_v(u) = \beta_1(u)/\beta_2(u)$ (resp. $\gamma_s(u) = \beta_3(u)/\beta_4(u)$). We call $\gamma_v(u)$ and $\gamma_s(u)$ respectively the *view score* and *share score* of u's UCR, as their value only depends on u's UCR. Consequently, when a user views or shares X, we only need to access a single UCR in order to update the rating of X. This is what allows CREDULIX to update news item credibility fast, without recomputing Eq. (1) each time the item is seen by a user.

In what follows, we refer to $\gamma_v(u)$ and $\gamma_s(u)$ as u's *UCR score*. The more a UCR score differs from 1, the stronger its influence on an item rating (which is computed as a product of UCR scores). We consider a UCR score to be *useful* if it is different from 1 (as item ratings are products of UCR scores).

3   Credulix as a Social Media Plugin

CREDULIX can be seen as a plugin to an existing social network, like, for instance, Facebook's translation feature. The translator observes the content displayed to users, translating it from one language to another. Similarly, CREDULIX observes news items about to be displayed to users and tags or suppresses those considered fake.

Despite the fast computation described in Sect. 2.3, there are still notable challenges posed by turning an algorithm into a practical system. In order for the CREDULIX plugin to be usable in practice, it must not impair user experience. In particular, its impact on the latency and throughput of user operations (retrieving news feeds or tweeting/sharing articles) must be small. Our design is motivated by minimizing CREDULIX' system resource overhead.

Selective Item Tracking. Every second, approximately 6000 new tweets appear on Twitter and 50000 new posts are created on Facebook [7]. Monitoring the credibility of all these items would pose significant resource overhead. With CREDULIX, each view/share event requires an additional update to the news item's metadata. However, we do not need to keep track of all the items in the system, but just the ones that show a potential of becoming viral.

CREDULIX requires each item's metadata to contain an additional bit indicating whether that item is *tracked*. The rating of item X is only computed and kept up to date by CREDULIX if X is tracked.

We set the *tracked* bit for item X when X is shared by an *influential user*. We define influential users as users who have a high number of followers. The intuition behind this approach is that a news item is more likely to become viral if it is disseminated by a well-connected user [23]. The follower threshold necessary for a user to be considered influential is a system parameter.

Interaction with the Social Media Platform. We consider two basic operations a user u can perform:

- *Sharing* a news item and
- *Viewing* her own news feed.

Sharing is the operation of disseminating a news item to all of u's followers (e.g., tweeting, sharing, updating Facebook status etc.). *Viewing* is the action of requesting the news feed, to see new posts shared by users that u follows.

Baseline Sharing. A schema of the *Share* operation is shown in Fig. 4. The regular flow of the operation is shown in blue and CREDULIX is shown in orange. User u shares an item X (1). First, the social graph is queried to retrieve

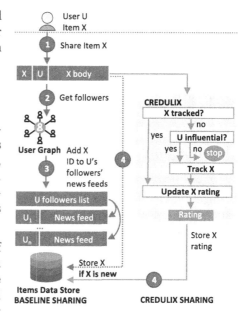

Fig. 4. Sharing a news item

u's followers (2). The system then appends the ID of X to the news feeds of u's followers (3). Finally, if X is a new item, the body of X is stored in a data store (4).

Sharing with Credulix. If u is not an influential user, the flow of the share operation described above stays the same. If u is influential, we mark X as tracked and associate an item rating with X, because we expect X to potentially become viral. If X is tracked, CREDULIX updates the rating of X using u's UCR share score. Thus, for tracked items, CREDULIX may require one additional write to the data store compared to the Baseline version, in order to store the updated item rating. This is done off the critical path of the user request, hence not affecting request latency.

Baseline News Feed Viewing. A schema of the *View* operation is shown in Fig. 5. User u requests her news feed (1). For each item ID in u's news feed (stored in memory), the system retrieves the corresponding item body from the data store (2) and sends all of them back to the user (3).

Viewing News Feed with Credulix. CREDULIX augments the *View* operation in two ways.

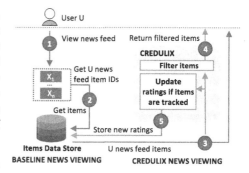

Fig. 5. Viewing news feed

First, after the news feed articles are retrieved from the data store, CREDULIX checks the ratings of the items, filtering out the items with a high probability of being fake. Second, if u's news feed contains tracked items, CREDULIX updates the rating of those items using u's UCR view score. Hence, a supplementary write to the data store is necessary, compared to the Baseline version, for storing the items' updated ratings. Again, we do this in the background, not impacting user request latency.

4   Evaluation

In this section, we evaluate our implementation of CREDULIX as a stand-alone Java plugin. We implement a Twitter clone where the *share* and *view* operation executions are depicted in Figs. 4 and 5. We refer to the Twitter clone as *Baseline* and we compare it to the variant with CREDULIX plugged in, which we call CREDULIX. For the data store of the Baseline we use Twissandra's data store [14], running Cassandra version 2.2.9 [11]. The main results of our evaluation are the following.

1. CREDULIX efficiently stops the majority of fake news from becoming viral, with no false positives. CREDULIX reduces the number of times a viral fake news item is viewed from hundreds of millions to hundreds of thousands (in Sect. 4.2).
2. CREDULIX' impact on system performance is negligible for both throughput and latency (in Sect. 4.3).

4.1   Experimental Setup and Methodology

We perform our evaluation using a real Twitter graph of over 41M users [27]. We consider users to be influential if they are among the 5% most followed users.

   We use a set of tweets obtained by crawling Twitter to get a distribution of item popularity. Out of over 35M tweets we crawled, the 1024 (0.003%) most popular tweets are retweeted almost 90 million times, which corresponds to over 16% of all the retweets. Two key values influence CREDULIX' behavior:

- r: The number of fact-checked news items during UCR creation (i.e., the number of news items constituting the ground truth). We use $r = 1024$, which causes one third of the user population to have useful UCR scores.
- msp: The max share probability models users' intrinsic sharing behavior: how likely users are to share news items they are exposed to. This models how users react to news items. It is *not* a system parameter of CREDULIX. We expect msp to be different for different news items, as some items become viral (high msp) and some do not (low msp). Since we do not know the real-world value of msp, we do use it as a parameter of our experiments (not a parameter of CREDULIX itself), in order to explore the behavior of our system in all situations. As our evaluation shows, regardless of what the real value of msp is, CREDULIX effectively prevents fake items from going viral.

While the network and the tweets come from real data sets, we generate the user behavior (i.e., probability to share fake and true news items), as we explain below. We proceed in two steps:

1. *UCR creation*: determining the UCR (i.e., v_T, s_T, v_F, s_F) for each user based on propagation of fact-checked news items.
2. *Fake item detection*: using the UCRs obtained in the previous step, we use CREDULIX to detect fake news items and stop them from spreading.

This separation is only conceptual, for clarity of the presentation. As CREDULIX is running in a social network, both UCR creation (or UCR updates) and fake item detection happen *continuously and in parallel.*

UCR Creation. For each user u, we set $P_T(u)$ and $P_F(u)$ (see Sect. 2) to values chosen uniformly at random between 0 and msp. The likelihood of a user to share true or fake news is the main user characteristic used by CREDULIX.

We take a subset of **r** popular tweets from our tweet dataset and consider this subset the ground truth, randomly assigning truth values to items. This phase of our experiments simulates the human fact-checking process.

In practice, the true news items on real social media still greatly outnumber the fake news items. Thus, it might look intuitive to make the ratio between fake and true items generated this way correspond to the (rather small) fraction of fake items present in real social networks. However, contrary to the intuition, this is not necessary. CREDULIX works best if the ratio between true and fake items that constitute the ground truth is balanced, i.e., the fraction of fake news items is one half.[4] To achieve balance in the ground truth, it suffices to bias the fact-checking process towards items that are likely to be fake. Indeed, even many of the already existing fact-checking initiatives [2–6] tend to focus on fake items and their output is balanced, if not biased towards fake items. In order to stay conservative in our evaluation, we set this ratio to 1/4, meaning that each item in our generated ground truth is fake with probability 1/4 and true with probability 3/4.

To create the UCRs, we propagate these **r** ground-truth items through the social graph. We assign each of the **r** items a target share count, which corresponds to its number of retweets in our dataset. The propagation proceeds by exposing a random user u to the propagated item X and having u decide (based on $P_T(u)$ and $P_F(u)$) whether to share X or not. If u shares X, we show X to all u's followers that have not yet seen it. During item propagation, we keep track of how many true/fake items each user has seen/shared and update the UCRs accordingly.

We repeat this process until one of the following conditions is fulfilled: (1) The target number of shares is reached, or (2) At least 80% of users have been exposed to X, at which point we consider the network saturated.

---

[4] One half as the optimal fraction of fake items in the ground truth is confirmed by our experiments.

At the end of the UCR creation step, each user has an updated UCR, tracking how many true/false items that user has seen/shared. These UCRs are used in the next phase for detecting which (not fact-checked) news items are fake.

Fake Item Detection. After creating the UCRs, we measure how effectively these can be leveraged to detect fake news. To this end, in the second step of the evaluation, we propagate news items through the social graph. We consider these items not fact-checked. One such experiment consists of injecting an item in the system, by making a random user u share it. The propagation happens as in the previous phase, with two important differences. First, we do not update u's UCR. Instead, whenever u is exposed to an item, we update that item's rating using u's UCR score. We use the share score if u shares the item, otherwise we use the view score (see Sect. 2). Second, we only propagate the item once, continuing until the propagation stops naturally, or until the probability of an item being fake reaches $p_0 = 0.999999$.

In the evaluation, we are interested in whether (and how fast) CREDULIX reacts to fake items, and whether the propagation of true items stays unaffected. To this end, we repeat this experiment 500 times with a fake news item and 500 times with a true news item to obtain the results presented later in this section.

We conduct the experiments on a 48-core machine, with four 12-core Intel Xeon E7-4830 v3 processors operating at 2.1 GHz, 512 GB of RAM, running Ubuntu 16.04.

4.2   Stopping Fake News from Becoming Viral

This experiment presents the end-to-end impact of CREDULIX on the number of times users are exposed to fake news. To this end, we measure the number of times a user is exposed to a fake news item in the baseline case and compare it to a case with CREDULIX in place.

Figure 6 conveys results for items with varying rates of virality, modeled by our `msp` parameter. It shows how many times a user has been exposed to a fake item, cumulatively over the total number of fake items that we disseminate.

We can see that regardless of how viral the items would naturally become, CREDULIX is able to timely detect the fake items before they spread to too' many users. CREDULIX restricts the number of views from hundreds of millions to tens or hundreds of thousands.

None of our experiments encountered false positives (i.e., true items being incorrectly labeled as fake). Considering the increasing responsibility being attributed to social

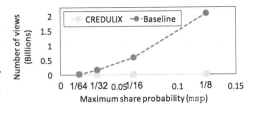

Fig. 6. Fake news spreading as a function of `msp` (lower is better). For low `msp`, news items do not become viral. For high `msp`, CREDULIX blocks the majority of fake news items.

network providers as mediators of information, it is crucial that true news items are not accidentally marked as fake.

In Fig. 7 we plot the percentage of fake items displayed with CREDULIX for two graph sizes. On a smaller graph of 1M users generated with the SNAP generator [28], CREDULIX achieves a lower fake item detection rate. This is because

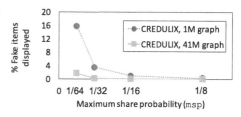

Fig. 7. Fake news spreading with CREDULIX, as a function of msp, for different social graph sizes (lower is better).

the impact of fact-checked items is smaller on a small graph, leading to fewer users with relevant UCR scores. This result suggests that on a real social graph that is larger than the one we use, CREDULIX would be more efficient than in our experiments.

Figure 7 also shows how the detection rate depends on the tendency of users to share news items. The more viral the items get (the higher the msp value), the more effective CREDULIX becomes at fake item detection. Intuitively, the more items users share, the more precisely we are able to estimate their sharing behavior. The lower detection rate for small msp values does not pose a problem in practice, as a low msp

Table 1. Workload characteristics. The only parameter we vary is msp, from which the view/share ratio follows.

msp value	% views, % shares
1/8	94% views, 6% shares
1/16	97% views, 3% shares
1/32	99% views, 1% shares
1/64	99.9% views, 0.1% Shares

also means that items naturally do not become viral (Table 1).

While not visible in the plot, it is worth noting that not only the relative amount of viewed fake items decreases, but also the *absolute* one. For example, while for msp = 1/32 a fake news item has been displayed almost 3k times (out of over 84k for Baseline), for msp = 1/16 a fake item has only been displayed 1.2k times (out of over 128k Baseline) in the 1M graph.

Interestingly, with increasing tendency of items to go viral (i.e. increasing msp), even the *absolute* number of displayed fake items decreases. The relative decrease effect is not due to an absolute increase for Baseline. Instead, it is due to a higher msp value ensuring more spreading of (both true and fake) news items in our UCR creation phase. This in turn produces better UCRs, increasing CREDULIX' effectiveness.

4.3   Credulix Overhead

We evaluate CREDULIX' impact on user operations' (viewing and sharing) *throughput* and *latency*. We present our results for four workloads, each corresponding to a value of msp used above (Fig. 6). Note that the msp values (1/8, 1/16, 1/32, and 1/64) also determine the ratio of view operations (respectively ca. 94%, 97%, 99%, and 99.9%). We present results for two social graph sizes:

41M users, and 1M users, with 16 worker threads serving user operations, showing that the CREDULIX' overhead in terms of throughput and latency is low.

Figure 8 shows the throughput comparison between CREDULIX and Baseline, for the four workloads. The throughput penalty caused by CREDULIX is at most 8%. The impact on throughput is predominantly caused by CREDULIX' background tasks, as detailed in Sect. 3. Moreover, CREDULIX does not add significant overhead relative to the Baseline as

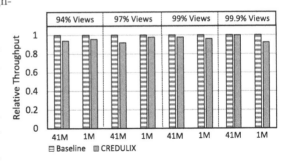

Fig. 8. CREDULIX' throughput overhead

the graph size increases. The throughput differences between the two graph sizes are not larger than 10%. This is due to our design which relies on selective item tracking.

Figure 9 shows view and share latencies for the 99.9% views workload. The latency values for the other workloads are similar and we omit them for brevity. For the 41M User Twitter graph, the average and 90th percentile latencies are roughly the same for CREDULIX and for Baseline. We notice, however, heavier fluctuations for the 1M User graph. Overall,

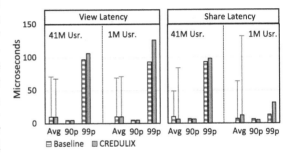

Fig. 9. CREDULIX' latency overhead: 99.9% views

latency increases by at most 17%, at the 90th percentile, while the median latency is the same for both operations, for both systems (4 ms per operation). The low overhead in latency is due to CREDULIX keeping its computation outside the critical path. Standard deviation of latencies is high both for the Baseline and for CREDULIX, for both share and view operations.

The high variation in latency is caused by the intrinsic differences between the users; share operations of a user with more followers need to propagate to more users than posts of users with few or no followers. The high 99th percentile latency for both systems results from Twissandra (our Baseline) being implemented in Java, a language (in)famous for its garbage collection breaks. Operations running concurrently with the GC thus experience high latencies. The impact of garbage collection is stronger with CREDULIX than with Baseline, as CREDULIX creates more short-lived objects in memory to orchestrate its background tasks. In addition to the intrinsic differences between users discussed above, garbage collection also significantly contributes to the high standard deviation observed in all latencies.

5 Discussion and Limitations

We believe that CREDULIX is a good step towards addressing the fake news problem, but we do not claim it to be the ultimate solution. CREDULIX is one of many possible layers of protection against fake news and can be used independently of other mechanisms. It is the combination of several approaches that can create a strong defense. This section discusses the limitations of CREDULIX.

News Propagation. CREDULIX does not prevent users from actively pulling any (including fake) news stories directly from their sources. CREDULIX *identifies* fake news on a social media platform and, if used as we suggest, prevents users from being notified about other users sharing fake news items. CREDULIX could easily be used to even remove items from users' timelines once identified as fake. As this may raise questions about freedom of speech and censorship, CREDULIX does not focus on completely removing items.

Manual Fact-Checking. CREDULIX relies on manual fact-checking and thus can only be as good as the fact-checkers. Only users who have been exposed to manually fact-checked items can be leveraged by CREDULIX. However, fact-checking a small number of popular news items is sufficient to obtain enough users with usable UCRs. Fact-checking a small number of news items is feasible, especially given the recent upsurge of fact-checking initiatives [2–6].

User Behavior. CREDULIX' algorithm is based on the assumption that among those users exposed to fact-checked news items, some share more fake items than others. Analogous assumptions are commonly used in other contexts such as recommender systems. For example, a user-based recommender system would not be useful if all users behaved the same way, i.e. everybody giving the same ratings to the same items.

Our approach shines when the inclination of most users to share fake news does not change too quickly over time. Many systems that are being successfully applied in practice (e.g. reputation systems, or systems based on collaborative filtering) fundamentally rely on this same assumption.

Malicious Attacks. The assumption that users do not change their behavior too quickly could, however, potentially be exploited by a malicious adversary. Such an adversary controlling many machine-operated user accounts could deceive the system by breaking this assumption. For example, all accounts controlled by the adversary could be sharing only true reviewed news items for an extended period of time and then suddenly share an un-reviewed fake one (or do the opposite, if the goal is to prevent a truthful news item from being disseminated). Even then, a successful attack would only enable the spread of the news item, without guaranteeing its virality. Moreover, the adversary runs a risk that the fake item will later be fact-checked and thus will appear in their

UCRs, reducing the chances of repeating this attack with another fake item. In fact, the more popular such an item becomes (which is the likely goal of the adversary), the higher the chance of it being fact-checked. The trade-off between false positives and false negatives is expressed by the p_0 parameter (see Sect. 2), i.e. the certainty required to flag an item as fake. A high value of p_0 might make it easier for the adversary to "smuggle" fake items in the system, but makes it more difficult to prevent true news items from spreading.

Updating of the Ground Truth. Like any vaccine, CREDULIX relies on a fraction of fake news to exist in the social network in order to be efficient. If CREDULIX stops the fake news from becoming viral, then the system might lack the ground truth to make future predictions. Hence, there might be periods when fake news can appear again. To avoid such fluctuations, CREDULIX' ground truth should be continuously updated with some of the most current fake news items. CREDULIX' evolution in time, including changes in user behavior as well as updating of the ground truth related to system dynamics, are research directions we are considering for future work.

Filtering News. One could argue that removing some news items from users' news feeds might be seen as a limitation, even as a form of censorship. But social media already take that liberty as they display to users only about 10% of the news that they could show. Rather than censorship, CREDULIX should be viewed as an effort to ensure the highest possible quality of the items displayed, considering the credibility of an item to be one of the quality criteria.

6   Related Work

CREDULIX shares similarities with *reputation systems* [30], in creating profiles for users (UCRs in CREDULIX) and in assuming that the future behavior of users will be similar to their past behavior. In our approach, however, users are not rated directly by other users. Instead, we compute users' UCRs based on their reaction to what we consider ground truth (fact-checked items).

CREDULIX also resembles *recommender systems* [31] in the sense that it preselects items for users to see. Unlike in recommender systems, however, the pre-selection is independent of the requesting user. Our goal is not to provide a personalized selection.

Another approach to detect fake news is to *automatically check content* [17]. Content analysis can also help detect machine-generated fake blogs [26] or social spam using many popular tags for irrelevant content [29]. Another line of research has been motivated by the role of social networks for fake news dissemination in the case of catastrophic events such as hurricanes and earthquakes [21,22].

News item credibility can also be inferred by applying *machine learning* techniques [18], by using a set of reliable content as a training set [33], or by analyzing a set of predetermined features [20]. Other parameters of interest are linguistic quantifiers [34], swear words, pronouns or emoticons [19]. Yet, a malicious agent knowing these specific features could use them to spread fake news.

Facebook received much media attention concerning their politics about fake news. Their first approach was to *assess news sources' reliability* in a centralized way [8]. Recently, Facebook launched *community-based* assessment experiment [9] asking the users to evaluate the reliability of various news sources. The idea is to give more exposure to news sources that are "broadly trusted". Our approach is finer-grained and goes to the level of news *items*. Facebook also used third-party fact checkers to look at articles flagged by users. Very recent work [10] suggests that Facebook started implementing a technique for stopping misinformation which assigns trustworthiness ratings to its users.

Fact-checking tools help to annotate documents and to create knowledge bases [12,13]. Curb [24] focuses on the problem of which items to fact-check and when, relying on users to manually flag items. These tools facilitate the fact-checking process that CREDULIX relies on. Like CREDULIX, it leverages the crowd to detect and reduce the spread of fake news and misinformation and assumes a very similar user behavior model. Curb, however, focuses on the problem of which items to fact-check and when, relying on users to manually flag items. Curb only prevents the spreading of items that have been fact-checked. In addition, it assumes fact-checking to happen instantaneously, without taking into account the considerable fact-checking delay.

7 Conclusions

We presented CREDULIX, the first content-agnostic system to detect and limit the spread of fake news on social networks with a very small performance overhead. For a more detailed version of the work, including more experiments, explanations and references, see [16].

References

1. http://money.cnn.com/2016/11/02/media/fake-news-stories/
2. http://www.politifact.com/
3. https://www.snopes.com/
4. https://www.washingtonpost.com/news/fact-checker/
5. https://www.truthorfiction.com/
6. https://fullfact.org/
7. http://www.zettasphere.com/mind-boggling-stats-for-1-second-of-internet-activity/
8. https://www.washingtonpost.com/news/the-switch/wp/2018/01/19/facebook-will-now-ask-its-users-to-rank-news-organizations-they-trust
9. https://techcrunch.com/2018/01/19/facebooks-news-feed-update-trusted-sources
10. https://www.washingtonpost.com/technology/2018/08/21/facebook-is-rating-trustworthiness-its-users-scale-zero-one
11. Cassandra. http://cassandra.apache.org/
12. Documentcloud. https://www.documentcloud.org/
13. Open calais. http://opencalais.com/

14. Twissandra Twitter clone, build on top of cassandra. https://github.com/twissandra/twissandra/
15. Austen-Smith, D., Banks, J.S.: Information aggregation, rationality, and the condorcet jury theorem (1996)
16. Balmau, O., Guerraoui, R., Kermarrec, A.M., Maurer, A., Pavlovic, M., Zwaenepoel, W.: Limiting the spread of fake news on social media platforms by evaluating users' trustworthiness. arXiv preprint arXiv:1808.09922 (2018)
17. Ciampaglia, G.L., Shiralkar, P., Rocha, L.M., Bollen, J., Menczer, F., Flammini, A.: Computational fact checking from knowledge networks. PLoS One **10**, e0128193 (2015)
18. Dewan, P., Kumaraguru, P.: Towards automatic real time identification of malicious posts on facebook. In: PST (2015)
19. Gupta, A., Kumaraguru, P.: Credibility ranking of tweets during high impact events. In: PSOSM (2012)
20. Gupta, A., Kumaraguru, P., Castillo, C., Meier, P.: TweetCred: real-time credibility assessment of content on Twitter. In: Aiello, L.M., McFarland, D. (eds.) SocInfo 2014. LNCS, vol. 8851, pp. 228–243. Springer, Cham (2014). https://doi.org/10.1007/978-3-319-13734-6_16
21. Gupta, A., Lamba, H., Kumaraguru, P., Joshi, A.: Faking sandy: characterizing and identifying fake images on twitter during hurricane sandy. In: WWW (2013)
22. Imran, M., Castillo, C., Diaz, F., Vieweg, S.: Processing social media messages in mass emergency: a survey. ACM CSUR (2015)
23. Jenders, M., Kasneci, G., Naumann, F.: Analyzing and predicting viral tweets. In: WWW Companion (2013)
24. Kim, J., Tabibian, B., Oh, A., Schölkopf, B., Gomez Rodriguez, M.: Leveraging the crowd to detect and reduce the spread of fake news and misinformation. In: WSDM (2018)
25. Koch, K.R.: Bayes' theorem. In: Bayesian Inference with Geodetic Applications (1990)
26. Kolari, P., Java, A., Finin, T., Oates, T., Joshi, A.: Detecting spam blogs: a machine learning approach. In: AAAI (2006)
27. Kwak, H., Lee, C., Park, H., Moon, S.: What is Twitter, a social network or a news media? In: WWW (2010)
28. Leskovec, J., Krevl, A.: SNAP datasets: stanford large network dataset collection. http://snap.stanford.edu/data (2014)
29. Markines, B., Cattuto, C., Menczer, F.: Social spam detection. In: AIRWeb (2009)
30. Resnick, P., Kuwabara, K., Zeckhauser, R., Friedman, E.: Reputation systems. Commun. ACM **43**, 45–48 (2000)
31. Resnick, P., Varian, H.R.: Recommender systems. Commun. ACM **40**, 56–59 (1997)
32. Rish, I.: An empirical study of the naïve bayes classifier. In: IJCAI 2001 Workshop on Empirical Methods in Artificial Intelligence, vol. 3, January 2001
33. Saikaew, K.R., Noyunsan, C.: Features for measuring credibility on facebook information. Int. Sch. Sci. Res. Innov. **9**, 174–177 (2015)
34. Viviani, M., Pasi, G.: A multi-criteria decision making approach for the assessment of information credibility in social media. In: Petrosino, A., Loia, V., Pedrycz, W. (eds.) WILF 2016. LNCS (LNAI), vol. 10147, pp. 197–207. Springer, Cham (2017). https://doi.org/10.1007/978-3-319-52962-2_17
35. Zabell, S.L.: The rule of succession. Erkenntnis **31**, 283–321 (1989)
36. Zhang, H.: The optimality of naive bayes. In: Proceedings of the Seventeenth International Florida Artificial Intelligence Research Society Conference, pp. 562–567 (2004)

Distributed Online Data Aggregation in Dynamic Graphs

Quentin Bramas[1]([✉]), Toshimitsu Masuzawa[3], and Sébastien Tixeuil[2]

[1] University of Strasbourg, ICUBE, CNRS, Strasbourg, France
bramas@unistra.fr
[2] Sorbonne University, LIP6, CNRS, Paris, France
[3] Osaka University, Suita, Japan

Abstract. We consider the problem of aggregating data in a dynamic graph, that is, aggregating the data that originates from all nodes in the graph to a specific node, the sink. We are interested in giving lower bounds for this problem, under different kinds of adversaries.

In our model, nodes are endowed with unlimited memory and unlimited computational power. Yet, we assume that communications between nodes are carried out with pairwise interactions, where nodes can exchange control information before deciding whether they transmit their data or not, given that each node is allowed to transmit its data at most once. When a node receives a data from a neighbor, the node may aggregate it with its own data.

We consider three possible adversaries: the online adaptive adversary, the oblivious adversary, and the randomized adversary that chooses the pairwise interactions uniformly at random. For the online adaptive and the oblivious adversaries, we give impossibility results when nodes have no knowledge about the graph and are not aware of the future. Also, we give several tight bounds depending on the knowledge (be it topology related or time related) of the nodes. For the randomized adversary, we show that the Gathering algorithm, which always commands a node to transmit, is optimal if nodes have no knowledge at all. Also, we propose an algorithm called Waiting Greedy, where a node either waits or transmits depending on some parameter, that is optimal when each node knows its future pairwise interactions with the sink.

1 Introduction

Dynamic graphs, that is, graphs that evolve over time, can conveniently model dynamic networks, which recently received a lot of interest from the academic community (*e.g.* mobile sensor networks, vehicular networks, disruption tolerant networks, interaction flows, etc.). Depending on the problem considered, various

This work was performed within the Labex SMART supported by French state funds managed by the ANR within the Investissements d'Avenir program under reference ANR-11-IDEX-0004-02. **A preliminary 2 pages poster of this work appeared in IEEE ICDCS 2016** [4].

© Springer Nature Switzerland AG 2019
M. F. Atig and A. A. Schwarzmann (Eds.): NETYS 2019, LNCS 11704, pp. 365–380, 2019.
https://doi.org/10.1007/978-3-030-31277-0_24

models were used: among others, static graphs can be used to represent a snapshot in time of a dynamic graph, functions can be used to define continuously when an edge appears over time, and sequences of tuples can represent atomic interactions between nodes over time.

The problem we consider in this paper assumes an arbitrary dynamic network, such as sensors deployed on a human body, cars evolving in a city that communicate with each other in an ad hoc manner, etc. We suppose that initially, each node in the network originates some data (*e.g.* that originates from a sensor, or from computation), and that these data must be aggregated at some designated node, the *sink*. To this goal, a node may send its data to a communication neighbor at a given time (the duration of this communication is supposed to be one time unit). We assume that there exists an aggregation function that takes two data as input and gives one data as output (the function is aggregating in the sense that the size of the output is supposed to be the same as a single input, such functions include min, max, etc.).

The main constraint for communications between nodes is that a node is allowed to send its data (be it its original data, or aggregated data) exactly once (*e.g.* to keep energy consumption low). A direct consequence of this constraint is that a node must aggregate data anytime it receives some, provided it did not send its data previously. It also implies that a node cannot participate in the data aggregation protocol once it has transmitted its data. A nice property of any algorithm implementing this constraint is that the number of communications is minimum. The problem of aggregating all data at the sink with minimum duration is called the *minimum data aggregation time problem* [6]. The essence of such a data aggregation algorithm is to decide whether or not to send a node's data when encountering a given communication neighbor: by waiting, a node may be able to aggregate more data, while by sending a node disseminates data but excludes itself for the rest of the computation.

In this paper, we consider that nodes may base their decision on their initial knowledge and past experience (past interactions with other nodes) only. Then, an algorithm accommodating those constraints is called an *online distributed data aggregation* algorithm. The existence of such an algorithm is conditioned by the (dynamic) topology, initial knowledge of the nodes (*e.g.* about their future communication neighbors), etc.

For simplicity, we assume that interactions between the nodes are carried out through pairwise operations. Anytime two nodes a and b are communication neighbors (or, for short, are interacting), either no data transfer happens, or one of them sends its data to the other, that executes the aggregation function on both its previously stored data and the received data, the output is then stored in the (new) stored data of the receiver. In the sequel, we use the term *interaction* to refer to a pairwise interaction.

We assume that an adversary controls the dynamics of the network, that is, the adversary decides which are the interactions. As we consider atomic interactions, the adversary decides what sequence of interactions is to occur in a given execution. Then, the sequence of static graphs to form the evolving graph can be seen as a sequence of single edge graphs, where the edge denotes the interaction that is chosen by the scheduler at this particular moment. Hence, the time when an interaction occurs is exactly its index in the sequence. Our model of dynamic graphs as a sequence of interactions differs from existing models on several points. First, general models like *Time-varying-graph* [8] make use of continuous time, which adds a lot of complexity. Also, discrete time general models such as *evolving graph* [8] capture the network evolution as a sequence of static graphs. Our model is a simplification of the evolving graph model where each static graph has a single edge. *Population protocols* [2] also consider pairwise interactions, but focus on finite state anonymous nodes with limited computational power and unlimited communication power (a given node can transmit its information many times), while we consider powerful nodes (that can record their past interactions) that are communication limited (they can send their data only once). Finally, *Dynamic edge-relabeling* [7] is similar to population protocols, but the sequence of pairwise interactions occurs inside an evolving graph. This model shares the same differences as population protocols with our model.

Related Work. The problem of data aggregation has been widely studied in the context of wireless sensor networks. The literature on this problem can be divided in two groups depending on the assumption made about the collisions being handled by an underlying MAC layer.

In the case when collisions are not handled by the MAC layer, the goal is to find a collision-free schedule that aggregates the data in minimum duration. The problem was first studied by Annamalai *et al.* [3], and formally defined by Chen *et al.* [9], which proved that the problem is NP-complete. Then, several papers [12–14,16] proposed centralized and distributed approximation algorithms for this problem. The best known algorithm is due to Nguyen *et al.* [12]. More recently, Bramas *et al.* [6] considered the generalization of the problem to dynamic wireless sensor networks (modeled by evolving graphs). Bramas *et al.* [6] show that the problem remains NP-complete even when restricted to dynamic WSNs of degree at most 2 (compared to 3 in the static case).

When collisions are handled by the MAC layer, various problems related to data aggregation have been investigated. The general term *in-network aggregation* includes several problems such as gathering and routing information in WSNs, mostly in a practical way. For instance, a survey [11] relates aggregation functions, routing protocols, and MAC layers with the objective of reducing resource consumption. *Continuous aggregation* [1] assumes that data have to be aggregated, and that the result of the aggregation is then disseminated to all participating nodes. The main metric is then the delay before aggregated data is delivered to all nodes, as no particular node plays the role of a sink. Most related to our concern is the work by Cornejo *et al.* [10]. In their work, each node starts with a token, the time is finite and no particular node plays the role of a sink node. Then, the topology evolves with time, and at each time instant, a node has at most one neighbor with whom it can interact and send or not its token. The goal is to minimize the number of nodes that own at least one token. Assuming an algorithm does not know the future, Cornejo *et al.* [10] prove that its competitive ratio is $\Omega(n)$ with high probability (w.r.t. the optimal offline algorithm) against an oblivious adversary.

Our Contributions. In this paper we define the problem of distributed online data aggregation in dynamic graphs, and study its complexity. It turns out that the problem difficulty strongly depends on the power of the adversary (that chooses which interactions occur in a given execution).

For the oblivious and the online adaptive adversaries, we give several impossibility results when nodes have no knowledge about the future evolution of the dynamic graph, nor about the topology. Also, when nodes are aware of the underlying graph (where an edge between two nodes exists if those nodes interact at least once in the execution), the data aggregation is impossible in general. To examine the possibility cases, we define a cost function whose purpose is to compare the performance of a distributed online algorithm to the optimal offline algorithm for the same sequence of interactions. Our results show that if all interactions in the sequence occur infinitely often, there exists a distributed online data aggregation algorithm whose cost is finite. Moreover, if the underlying graph is a tree, we present an optimal algorithm.

For the randomized adversary, we first present tight bounds when nodes have full knowledge about the future interactions in the whole graph. In this case, the best possible algorithm terminates in $\Theta(n\log(n))$ interactions, in expectation and with high probability. Then, we consider nodes with restricted knowledge, and we present two optimal distributed online data aggregation algorithms that differ in the knowledge that is available to nodes. The first algorithm, called *Gathering*, assumes nodes have no knowledge whatsoever, and terminates in $O(n^2)$ interactions on average, which we prove is optimal with no knowledge. The second one, called *Waiting Greedy*, terminates in $O\left(n^{3/2}\sqrt{\log(n)}\right)$ interactions with high probability, which we show is optimal when each node only knows the time of its next interaction with the sink (the knowledge assumed by Waiting Greedy).

We believe our research paves the way for stimulating future researches, as our proof arguments present techniques and analysis that can be of independent interest for studying dynamic networks.

2   Model

A dynamic graph is modeled as a couple (V, I), where V is a set of nodes and $I = (I_t)_{t\in\mathbb{N}}$ is a sequence of pairwise interactions (or simply interactions). An interaction occurs when two nodes in the network can exchange information. A special node in V is the *sink* node, and is denoted by s in the sequel. In the sequence $(I_t)_{t\in\mathbb{N}}$, the index t of an interaction also refers to its *time of occurrence*. In the sequel V always denotes the set of nodes, $n \geq 3$ its size, and $s \in V$ the sink node.

In general, we consider that nodes in V have unique identifiers, unlimited memory and unlimited computational power. However, we sometimes consider nodes with no persistent memory between interactions; those nodes are called *oblivious*.

Initially, each node in V receives a data. Nodes have different data and a node can transmit its data at most once. Formally, during an interaction $I_t = \{u, v\}$, if both nodes have not yet transmitted their data, then one of the node has the possibility to transmit its data to the other node. The receiver aggregates the received data with its own data. The transmission and the aggregation take exactly one time unit. If a node decides to transmit its data, then it does not own any data, and is not able to receive other's data anymore.

Problem Statement. The data aggregation problem consists in choosing at each interaction whether a node transmits (and which one) or not so that after a finite number of interactions, the sink is the only node that owns data. In this paper we study distributed and online algorithms that solve this problem. Such algorithms are called *distributed online data aggregation* (DODA) algorithms.

A DODA is an algorithm that takes as input an interaction $I_t = \{u, v\}$, and its time of occurrence $t \in \mathbb{N}$, and outputs either u, v or $\perp$. If a DODA outputs a node, this node is the receiver of the other node's data. In more details, if u is the output, this means that before the interaction both u and v own data, and the algorithm orders v to transmit its data to u. The algorithm is able to change the memory of the interacting nodes, for instance to store information that can be used in future interactions. In the sequel, $\mathcal{D}_{\text{ODA}}$ denotes the set of all DODA algorithms. And $\mathcal{D}_{\text{ODA}}^\emptyset$ denotes the set of DODA algorithms that only require oblivious nodes. Executing a DODA algorithm A on a sequence of interactions I correspond to executing A on each interaction $I_t \in I$, and the duration of the execution is the first time of occurrence of the interaction when the sink becomes the only node that owns data.

A DODA can require some knowledge to work. A knowledge is a function (or just an attribute) given to every node that gives some information about the future, the topology or anything else. By default, a node $u \in V$ has two pieces of information: its identifier $u.ID$ and a boolean $u.isSink$ that is true if u is the sink, and false otherwise. A DODA algorithm may use additional functions associated with different knowledge. $\mathcal{D}_{\text{ODA}}(i_1, i_2, \ldots)$ denotes the set of DODA algorithms that use the functions $i_1, i_2, \ldots$, representing the *knowledge* of the nodes. The first function we define for a node $u \in V$ in a dynamic graph (V, I), is the function $u.meetTime$ that maps a time $t \in \mathbb{N}$ with the smallest time $t' > t$ such that $I_{t'} = \{u, s\}$ *i.e.*, the time of the next interaction with the sink (for $u = s$, we define $s.meetTime$ as the identity, $t \mapsto t$). Then $\mathcal{D}_{\text{ODA}}(meetTime)$ refers to the set of DODA algorithms that use the information $meetTime$.

Adversary Models. In this paper we consider three models of adversaries:

- *The oblivious adversary.* This adversary knows the algorithm's code, and must construct the sequence of interactions before the execution starts.
- *The adaptive online adversary.* This adversary knows the algorithm's code and can use the past execution of the algorithm to construct the next interaction. However, it must make its own decision as it does not know in advance

the decision of the algorithm. In the case of deterministic algorithms, this adversary is equivalent to the oblivious adversary.
- *The randomized adversary.* This adversary constructs the sequence of interactions by picking pairwise interactions uniformly at random.

Section 3 presents our results with the oblivious and the adaptive online adversaries. The results with the randomized adversary are given in Sect. 4.

Definition of Cost. To study and compare different DODA algorithms, we use a tool slightly different from the competitive analysis that is generally used to study online algorithms. The competitive ratio of an algorithm is the ratio between its performance and the optimal offline algorithm's performance. However, one can hardly define objectively the performance of an algorithm. For instance, if we just consider the number of interactions before termination, then an oblivious adversary can construct a sequence of interactions starting with the same interaction repeated an arbitrary number of time. In this case, even the optimal algorithm has infinite duration. Moreover, the adversary can choose the same interaction repeatedly after that the optimal offline algorithm terminates. This can prevent any non optimal algorithm from terminating and make it have an infinite competitive-ratio.

To prevent this we define the cost of an algorithm. Our cost is a way to define the performance of an algorithm, depending on the performance of the optimal offline algorithm. We believe our definition of cost is well-suited for a lots of problems where the adversary has a strong power, especially in dynamic networks. One of its main advantages is that it is invariant by trivial transformation of the sequence of interactions, like inserting or deleting duplicate interactions.

For the sake of simplicity, the execution of an offline optimal data aggregation algorithm, having minimum duration, is called a *convergecast*. Consider a sequence of interactions I. Let $opt(t)$ be the ending time of a convergecast on I, starting at time $t \in \mathbb{N}$. If the ending time is infinite (if the optimal offline algorithm does not terminate) we write $opt(t) = \infty$. Let $T : \mathbb{N}_{\geq 1} \mapsto \mathbb{N} \cup \{\infty\}$ be the function defined as follows:

$$T(1) = opt(0), \qquad \forall i \geq 1 \quad T(i+1) = opt(T(i)+1)$$

$T(i)$ is the duration of i successive convergecasts (two convergecasts are consecutive if the second one starts just after the first one completes).

Let $duration(A, I)$ be the termination time of algorithm A executed on the sequence of interactions I. Now, we define the cost $cost_A(I)$ of an algorithm A on the sequence I, as the smallest integer i such that $duration(A, I) \leq T(i)$:

$$cost_A(I) = \min\{i \mid duration(A, I) \leq T(i)\}$$

This means that $cost_A(I)$ is an upper bound on the number of successive convergecasts we can perform during the execution of A, on the sequence I. It follows from the definition that an algorithm performs an optimal data aggregation if and only if $cost_A(I) = 1$.

Also, if $duration(A, I) = \infty$, then it is possible that $cost_A(I) < \infty$. Indeed, if $i_{max} = \min_i\{i \mid T(i) = \infty\}$ is well-defined, then $cost_A(I) = i_{max}$, otherwise $cost_A(I) = \infty$.

3   Oblivious and Online Adaptive Adversaries

In this section we give several impossibility results when nodes have no knowledge, and then show several results depending on the amount of knowledge. We choose to limit our study to some specific knowledge, but one can be interested in studying the possible solutions for different kind of knowledge.

3.1   Impossibility Results when Nodes Have No Knowledge

Theorem 1. *For every algorithm $A \in \mathcal{D}_{\mathsf{ODA}}$, there exists an adaptive online adversary generating a sequence of interactions I such that $cost_A(I) = \infty$.*

Proof. Let I be the sequence of interactions among 3 nodes a, b, and the sink s, defined as follows. $I_0 = \{a, b\}$. If a transmits, then $\forall i > 0$, $I_{2i+1} = \{a, s\}$ and $I_{2i+2} = \{a, b\}$ so that b is never able to transmit. Symmetrically if b transmits the same thing happens. If no node transmits, then $I_1 = \{b, s\}$. If b transmits, then $\forall i > 0$, $I_{2i+2} = \{a, b\}$ and $I_{2i+3} = \{b, s\}$ so that a is never able to transmit. Otherwise $I_2 = \{a, b\}$ and we continue as in the first time. A never terminates, and a convergecast is always possible for the offline optimal algorithm, so that $cost_A(I) = \infty$. □

In the case of deterministic algorithms, the previous theorem is true even with an oblivious adversary. However, for a randomized algorithm, the problem is more complex. The following theorem states that the impossibility results for oblivious randomized algorithm, leaving the case of general randomized algorithms against oblivious adversary as an open question.

Theorem 2. *For every randomized algorithm $A \in \mathcal{D}^{\emptyset}_{\mathsf{ODA}}$, there exists an oblivious adversary generating a sequence of interactions I such that $cost_A(I) = \infty$ with high probability[1].*

Proof. Let $V = \{s, u_0, \ldots, u_{n-2}\}$. In the sequel, indexes are modulo $n-1$ i.e., $\forall i, j \geq 0$, $u_i = u_j$ with $i \equiv j \mod (n-1)$. Let I^{∞} defined by, for all $i \in \mathbb{N}$, $I_i^{\infty} = \{u_i, s\}$. Let I^l be the finite sequence, prefix of length $l > 0$ of I^{∞}. For every $l > 0$, the adversary can compute the probability P_l that no node transmits its data when executing A on I^l. $(P_l)_{l>0}$ is a non-increasing sequence, it converges to a limit $\mathcal{P} \geq 0$. For a given l, if $P_l \geq 1/n$, there is at least two nodes whose probability not to transmit when executing A on I^l is at least $n^{-\frac{1}{n-2}} = 1 - O\left(\frac{1}{\sqrt{n}}\right)$. To prove this, we can see the probability P_l as the product of $n-1$ probabilities p_0, p_1, $\ldots$, p_{n-2} where p_i is the probability that node u_i

---

[1] An event A occurs with high probability if $P(A) > 1 - O(1/\log(n))$.

does not transmit during I^l. Those events are independent since the algorithm is oblivious. Let $p_d \geq p_{d'}$ be the two greatest probabilities in $\{p_i\}_{0 \leq i \leq n-2}$, we have:

$$\left(\prod_{i=0}^{n-2} p_i \geq \frac{1}{n}\right) \Rightarrow \left(\sum_{i=0}^{n-2} \log(p_i) \geq \log\left(\frac{1}{n}\right)\right)$$

$$\Rightarrow \left((n-2)\log(p_{d'}) \geq \log\left(\frac{1}{n}\right)\right) \Rightarrow \left(p_{d'} \geq n^{-\frac{1}{n-2}}\right)$$

This implies that, if $\mathcal{P} \geq 1/n$, then A does not terminate on the sequence I^∞ with high probability.

Otherwise, let l_0 be the smallest index such that $P_{l_0} < 1/n$. So that with high probability, at least one node transmits when executing A on I^{l_0}. Also, $P_{l_0-1} \geq 1/n$ so that the previous argument implies that there is at least two nodes u_d and $u_{d'}$ whose probability to still have a data (after executing A on I^{l_0-1}) is at least $n^{-\frac{1}{n-2}}$. If $l_0 = 0$ we can choose $\{u_d, u_{d'}\} = \{u_1, u_2\}$. We have $u_d \neq u_{l_0}$ or $u_{d'} \neq u_{l_0}$. Without loss of generality, we can suppose $u_d \neq u_{l_0}$, so that the probability that u_d transmits is the same in I^{l_0-1} and in I^{l_0}.

Now, u_d is a node whose probability not to transmit when executing A on I^{l_0} is at least $n^{-\frac{1}{n-2}} = 1 - O\left(\frac{1}{\sqrt{n}}\right)$. Let I' be the sequence of interactions defined as follows:

$$\forall i \in [0, n-2] \setminus \{d-1\}, \ I'_i = \{u_i, u_{i+1}\}, \ I'_{d-1} = \{u_{d-1}, s\}$$

I' is constructed such that u_d (the node that has data with high probability) must send its data along a path that contains all the other nodes in order to reach the sink. But this path contains a node that does not have a data.

Let I be the sequence of interaction starting with I^{l_0} and followed by I' infinitely often. We have shown that with high probability, after l_0 interactions, at least one node transmits its data and the node u_d still has a data. The node that does not have data prevents the data owned by u_d from reaching s. So that A does not terminate, and since a convergecast is always possible for the offline optimal algorithm, then $cost_A(I) = \infty$.   □

3.2 When Nodes Know the Underlying Graph

Let $\bar{G}$ be the underlying graph i.e., $\bar{G} = (V, E)$ with $E = \{(u, v) \mid \exists t \in \mathbb{N}, I_t = \{u, v\}\}$. The following results assume that the underlying graph is given initially to every node.

Theorem 3. If $n \geq 4$, then, for every algorithm $A \in \mathcal{D}_{ODA}(\bar{G})$, there exists an online adaptive adversary generating a sequence of interactions I such that $cost_A(I) = \infty$.

Proof. $V = \{s, u_1, u_2, u_3\}$. We create a sequence of interactions with the underlying graph $\bar{G} = (V, \{(s, u_1), (u_1, u_2), (u_2, u_3), (u_3, s)\})$. We start with the following interactions:

$$(\{u_1, s\}, \{u_3, s\}, \{u_2, u_1\}, \{u_2, u_3\}). \tag{1}$$

If u_2 transmits to u_1 in I_2, then we repeat infinitely often the three following interactions:

$$(\{u_1, u_2\}, \{u_2, u_3\}, \{u_3, s\}, ...).$$

Else, if u_2 transmits to u_3 in I_3, then we repeat infinitely often the three following interactions:

$$(\{u_3, u_2\}, \{u_2, u_1\}, \{u_1, s\}, ...).$$

Otherwise, we repeat the four interactions (1), and apply the previous reasoning. Then, A never terminates, and a convergecast is always possible, so that $cost_A(I) = \infty$. □

Theorem 4. *If the interactions occurring at least once, occur infinity often, then there exists $A \in \mathcal{D}^{\emptyset}_{ODA}(\bar{G})$ such that $cost_A(I) < \infty$ for every sequence of interactions I. However, $cost_A(I)$ is unbounded.*

Theorem 5. *If $\bar{G}$ is a tree, there exists $A \in \mathcal{D}^{\emptyset}_{ODA}(\bar{G})$ that is optimal.*

3.3 If Nodes Know Their Own Future

For a node $u \in V$, $u.future$ denotes the future of u i.e., the sequence of interactions involving u, with their times of occurrences. In this case, according to the model, two interacting nodes exchange their future and non-oblivious nodes can store it. This may seem contradictory with the motivation of the problem (that aims to reduce the number of transmissions). However, it is possible that the data must be sent only once for reasons not related to energy (such as data that cannot be duplicated, tokens, etc.). So, even if, in general, oblivious algorithms should be favored, we still investigated this case for the sake of completeness.

Theorem 6. *There exists $A \in \mathcal{D}_{ODA}(future)$ such that $cost_A(I) \leq n$ for every sequence of interactions I.*

Proof. One can show that the duration of $n - 1$ successive convergecasts is sufficient to perform a broadcast from any source. So every node broadcast its future to the other nodes. After that, all the nodes are aware of the future of every nodes and can compute an optimal data aggregation schedule. So that it takes only one convergecast to aggregate the data of the whole network. In total, n successive convergecasts are sufficient. □

4   Randomized Adversary

The randomized adversary constructs the sequence of interactions by picking a couple of nodes among all possible couples, uniformly at random. Thus, the underlying graph is a complete graph of n nodes (including the sink) and every interaction occurs with the same probability $p = \frac{2}{n(n-1)}$.

In this section, the complexity is computed on expectation (because the adversary is randomized) and no more "in the worst case" as previously. In this case, considering the number of interactions is sufficient to represent the complexity of an algorithm. We see in Theorem 8 that an offline algorithm terminates in $\Theta(n \log(n))$ interactions w.h.p. This bound gives a way to convert the complexity in term of number of interaction to a cost. Indeed, if an algorithm $\mathcal{A}$ terminates in $O(n^2)$ interactions, then it performance is $O(n/\log(n))$ times worse than the offline algorithm and $cost_A(I) = O(n/\log(n))$ for a randomly generated sequence of interactions I. For the sake of simplicity, in the remaining of the section, we give the complexity in terms of number of interactions.

Since an interaction does not depend on previous interactions, the algorithms we propose here are oblivious i.e., they do not modify the memory of the nodes. In more details, the output of our algorithms depends only on the current interaction and on the information available in the node.

First, we introduce three oblivious DODA algorithms. For the sake of simplicity, we assume that the output is ignored if the interacting nodes do not both have a data. Also, to break symmetry, we suppose the nodes that interact are given as input ordered by their identifiers.

- Waiting ($\mathcal{W} \in \mathcal{D}_{\mathsf{ODA}}^{\emptyset}$): A node transmits only when it is connected to the sink s: $\mathcal{W}(u_1, u_2, t)$ equals u_i if $u_i = s$, and $\bot$ otherwise.
- Gathering ($\mathcal{GA} \in \mathcal{D}_{\mathsf{ODA}}^{\emptyset}$): A node transmits its data when it is connected to the sink s or to a node having data: $\mathcal{GA}(u_1, u_2, t)$ equals u_2 if $u_2 = s$, otherwise it equals u_1
- Waiting Greedy with parameter $\tau \in \mathbb{N}$ ($\mathcal{WG}_\tau \in \mathcal{D}_{\mathsf{ODA}}^{\emptyset}(meetTime)$): The node with the greatest meet time transmits, if its meet time is greater than τ:

$$\mathcal{WG}_\tau : (u_1, u_2, t) = \begin{cases} u_1 & \text{if } m_1 \le m_2 \wedge \tau < m_2 \\ u_2 & \text{if } m_1 > m_2 \wedge \tau < m_1 \\ \bot & \text{otherwise} \end{cases} \quad \text{with} \quad \begin{array}{l} m_1 = u_1.meetTime(t) \\ m_2 = u_2.meetTime(t) \end{array}$$

One can observe that after time τ, the algorithm acts as the Gathering algorithm.

4.1   Lower Bounds

We show a lower bound $\Omega(n^2)$ on the number of interactions required for DODA against the randomized adversary. The lower bound holds for all algorithms (including randomized ones) that do not have knowledge about future of the evolving network. The lower bound matches the upper bound of the *Gathering* algorithm given in the next subsection. This implies that this bound is tight.

Theorem 7. *The expected number of interactions required for DODA is $\Omega(n^2)$.*

Proof. We show that the last data transmission requires $\Omega(n^2)$ interactions in expectation.

We consider any (randomized) algorithm A and its execution for DODA. Before the last transmission (from some node, say v, to the sink s), only v has data except for s.

The probability that v and s interacts in the next interaction is $\frac{2}{n(n-1)}$. Thus, the expected number EI of interactions required for v to transmit to s is:

$$EI = \frac{n(n-1)}{2}$$

So that the whole aggregation requires at least $EI = \Omega(n^2)$.   □

We also give a tight bound for algorithms that know the full sequence of interactions.

Theorem 8. *The best algorithm in $\mathcal{D}_{ODA}^{\emptyset}$ (full knowledge) terminates in $\Theta(n\log(n))$ interactions, in expectation and with high probability.*

Proof. First, we show that the expected number of interactions of a broadcast algorithm is $\Theta(n \log n)$. The first data transmission occurs when the source node (say v_0) interacts with another node. The probability of occurrence of the first data transmission is $\frac{2(n-1)}{n(n-1)}$. After the $(i-1)$-th data transmission, i nodes (say $V_{i-1} = \{v_0, v_1, \ldots, v_{i-1}\}$) have the data and the i-th data transmission occurs when a node in V_{i-1} interacts with a node not in V_{i-1}. This happens with probability $\frac{2i(n-i)}{n(n-1)}$.

Thus, if X is the number of interactions required to perform a broadcast, then we have:

$$E(X) = \sum_{i=1}^{n-1} \frac{n(n-1)}{2i(n-i)} = \frac{n(n-1)}{2} \sum_{i=1}^{n-1} \frac{1}{i(n-i)} = \frac{n(n-1)}{2n} \sum_{i=1}^{n-1} \left(\frac{1}{i} + \frac{1}{n-i}\right)$$

$$= (n-1) \sum_{i=1}^{n-1} \frac{1}{i} \in \Theta(n \log n).$$

And the variance is

$$Var(X) = \sum_{i=1}^{n-1} \left(1 - \frac{2i(n-i)}{n(n-1)}\right) \Big/ \left(\frac{2i(n-i)}{n(n-1)}\right)^2 = n(n-1) \sum_{i=1}^{n-1} \frac{n(n-1) - 2i(n-i)}{(2i(n-i))^2}$$

$$= O\left(n^4 \sum_{i=1}^{\lfloor n/2\rfloor - 1} \left(\frac{1}{i(n-i)}\right)^2\right)$$

The last sum is obtained from the previous one by observing that it is symmetric with respect to the index $i = n/2$, and the removed elements ($i = \lfloor n/2\rfloor$ and possibly $i = \lceil n/2 \rceil$) are negligible. We define $f : x \mapsto \frac{1}{x^2(n-x)^2}$. Since f is increasing between 1 and $n/2$, we have

$$\sum_{i=1}^{\lfloor n/2 \rfloor - 1} f(i) \leq \int_1^{n/2} f(x)dx = \frac{\frac{(n-2)n}{n-1} + 2\log(n-1)}{n^3} = O\left(\frac{1}{n^2}\right)$$

So that the variance is in $O(n^2)$. Using the Chebyshev's inequality, we have

$$P(|X - E(X)| > n\log(n)) = O\left(\frac{1}{\log^2(n)}\right)$$

Therefore, a sequence of $\Theta(n\log(n))$ interactions is sufficient to perform a broadcast with high probability. By reversing the order of the interactions in the sequence of interactions, this implies that a sequence of $\Theta(n\log(n))$ interactions is also sufficient to perform a convergecast with the same probability. Aggregating data along the convergecast tree gives a valid data aggregation schedule.   □

Corollary 1. *The best algorithm in $\mathcal{D}_{\mathsf{ODA}}(future)$ terminates in $\Theta(n\log(n))$ interactions, in expectation and with high probability.*

Proof. If each node starts with its own future, $O(n\log(n))$ interactions are sufficient to retrieve with high probability the future of the whole network. Then $O(n\log(n))$ interactions are sufficient to aggregate all the data with the full knowledge.   □

4.2   Algorithm Performance Without Knowledge

Without any knowledge, we show that the Gathering algorithm is optimal.

Theorem 9. *The expected number of interactions the Waiting requires to terminate is $O(n^2 \log(n))$. The expected number of interactions the Gathering requires to terminate is $O(n^2)$.*

4.3   Algorithm Performance with *meetTime*

In this subsection we study the performance of our algorithm Waiting Greedy, find the optimal value of the parameter τ and prove that this is the best possible algorithm with only the *meetTime* information (even if nodes have unbounded memory). We begin by a lemma to find how many interactions are needed to have a given number of nodes interacting with the sink.

Lemma 1. *If f is a function such that $f(n) = o(n)$ and $f(n) = \omega(\log(n))$ then, in $nf(n)$ interactions, $\Theta(f(n))$ nodes interact with the sink w.h.p.*

Now we can state our theorem about the performance of Waiting Greedy depending on the parameter τ. To prove this Theorem, we partition the set of nodes in two important subsets, L that contains the nodes that interact with the sink between time $\tau/2$ and τ and L^c its complementary. We show that the duration of our algorithm comes from two phases, one before time $\tau/2$ when the nodes in L^c have a high probability to meet another node in L, and one after $\tau/2$ when the nodes in L meet the sink directly.

Theorem 10. *Let f be a function such that $f(n) = o(n)$ and $f(n) = \omega(\log(n))$. The algorithm Waiting Greedy with $\tau = \Theta\left(\max\left(nf(n), n^2\log(n)/f(n)\right)\right)$ terminates in τ interactions w.h.p.*

Proof. To have an upper bound on the number of interactions needed by Waiting Greedy to terminate, we decompose the execution in two phases, one between time 0 and a time t_1 and the other between time t_1 and a time $t_2 = \tau$ (for simplicity, one can take $t_1 = \tau/2$). In the last phase, a set of nodes $L \subset V$ interacts at least once directly with the sink. Nodes in L do not transmit to anyone in the first phase by definition of the algorithm (they have a meetTime smaller than τ). Nodes in L help the other nodes (in $L^c = V\backslash L$) to transmit their data in the first phase. Maybe nodes in L^c can transmit to L in the second phase, but we do not take this into account, that is why it is an upper bound.

If a node u in L^c interacts with a node in L in the first phase, either it transmits its data, otherwise (by definition of the algorithm) it has a meetTime smaller than τ (and smaller than t_1 because it is not in L). In every case, a node in L^c that meets a node in L in the first phase, transmits its data. To prove the theorem i.e., in order for the algorithm to terminates before τ with high probability, we prove two claims: (a) the number of nodes in L is $f(n)$ with high probability if $t_2 - t_1 = nf(n)$ and (b) all nodes in L^c interact with a node in L before t_1 with high probability if $t_1 = \Theta(n^2\log(n)/f(n))$. The first claim is implied by Lemma 1. Now we prove the second claim.

Let X be the number of interactions required for the nodes in L^c to meet a node in L. The probability of the i-th interaction between a node in L^c (with a data) and a node in L, after $i - 1$ such interactions already occurred, is $2f(n)(n - f(n) - i)/n(n - 1)$. Then we have:

$$E(X) = \sum_{i=1}^{n-f(n)-1} \frac{n(n-1)}{2f(n)(n-f(n)-i)} = \frac{n(n-1)}{2f(n)} \sum_{i=1}^{n-f(n)-1} \frac{1}{n-f(n)-i}$$

$$\sim_{+\infty} \frac{n^2}{2f(n)}\log(n-f(n)) = \frac{n^2}{2f(n)}\log(n(1-f(n)/n)) \sim_{+\infty} \frac{n^2\log(n)}{2f(n)}$$

$$Var(X) = \sum_{i=1}^{n-f(n)-1} \frac{\left(1 - \frac{2f(n)(n-f(n)-i)}{n(n-1)}\right)}{\left(\frac{2f(n)(n-f(n)-i)}{n(n-1)}\right)^2} \sim \sum_{i=1}^{n-f(n)-1} \frac{n^4}{4f(n)^2n^2} \sim \frac{n^3}{4f(n)^2}$$

Like previously, using the Chebyshev's inequality, this implies that $X = O\left(\frac{n^2\log(n)}{f(n)}\right)$ w.h.p.   □

Corollary 2. *The algorithm Waiting Greedy, with* $\tau = \Theta(n^{3/2}\sqrt{\log(n)})$ *termi- nates in* τ *interactions with high probability.*

Proof. In the last theorem, the bound $O\left(\max\left(nf(n), n^2\log(n)/f(n)\right)\right)$ is mini- mized by the function $f\colon n \mapsto \sqrt{n\log(n)}$. $\qquad\square$

From the previous corollary, we maximize the performance of our algorithm by chosing $\tau = \Theta(n^{3/2}\sqrt{\log(n)})$. To prove that no other algorithm has better performance, we show that, if an algorithm terminates before $\Theta(n^{3/2}\sqrt{\log(n)})$ interactions, then the number of nodes that do no meet the sink is so big that they cannot aggregate their data quickly enough. Indeed, when two nodes do not meet the sink before $\Theta(n^{3/2}\sqrt{\log(n)})$, then their *meetTime* information is useless for deciding which one should transmit, so we can analyze the aggregation speed of a large subset of the node.

Theorem 11. *Waiting Greedy with* $\tau = \Theta(n^{3/2}\sqrt{\log(n)})$ *is optimal in* $\mathcal{D}_{\mathrm{ODA}}(meetTime)$.

Proof. For the sake of contradiction, we suppose the existence of an algorithm $A \in \mathcal{D}_{\mathrm{ODA}}(meetTime)$ that terminates in $T(n)$ interactions with high probabil- ity, with $T(n) = o\left(n^{3/2}\sqrt{\log(n)}\right)$. Without loss of generality we can suppose that A does nothing after $T(n)$ interactions. Indeed, the algorithm A' that exe- cutes A up to $T(n)$ and does nothing afterward has the same upper bound (since the bound holds with high probability).

Let L be the set of nodes that interact directly with the sink during the first $T(n)$ interactions. Let L^c be its complementary in $V\backslash\{s\}$. We know from Lemma 1 that $\#L = O(T(n)/n) = o\left(\sqrt{n\log(n)}\right)$ w.h.p.

We can show that $T(n)$ interactions are not sufficient for all the nodes in L^c to interact with nodes in L. If nodes in L^c want to send their data to the sink, some data must be aggregated among nodes in L^c, then the remaining nodes in L^c that still own data must interact with a node in L before $T(n)$ interactions (this is not even sufficient to perform the DODA, but is enough to reach a contradiction).

When two nodes in L^c interact, their meetTime (that are greater than $T(n)$) and the previous interactions are independent with the future interactions occur- ring before $T(n)$. This implies that when two nodes in L^c interact, using those information to decide which node transmits is the same as choosing the sender randomly. From Theorem 9, this implies that the optimal algorithm to aggregate data in L^c is the Gathering algorithm.

Now, we show that, even after the nodes in L^c use the Gathering algorithm, there is with high probability at least one node in L^c that still owns data and that does not interact with any node in L. This node prevents the termina- tion of the algorithm before $T(n)$ interactions with high probability, which is a contradiction.

Formally, we have the following lemmas. Due to space constraints, the proofs can be found in a technical report [5].

Lemma 2. *Let $g(n)$ be the number of nodes in L^c. After using the Gathering algorithm during $T(n)$ interactions, the number of nodes in L^c that still own data is in $\omega(\sqrt{n/\log(n)})$ w.h.p.*

Lemma 3. *Let $H \subset L^c$ be the nodes in L^c that still own data after the gathering. Then, $T(n)$ interactions are not sufficient for all the nodes in H to interact with nodes in L, w.h.p.*

End of the Proof of Theorem 11. We have shown that $T(n)$ interactions are not sufficient for the nodes in L^c to transmit their data (directly or indirectly) to the nodes in L. Indeed, we have shown that the nodes in L^c can apply the gathering algorithm so that $\omega(\sqrt{n\log(n)})$ nodes in L^c still own data with high probability. But, with high probability, one of the $\omega(\sqrt{n\log(n)})$ remaining nodes does not interact with a node in L in $T(n)$ interactions. This implies that, with high probability, at least one node cannot send its data to the sink in $T(n)$ interactions and an algorithm A with such a bound T does not exist. ☐

5   Concluding Remarks

We defined and investigated the complexity of the distributed online data aggregation problem in dynamic graphs where interactions are controlled by an adversary. We obtained various tight complexity results for different adversaries and node knowledge, that open several scientific challenges:

1. What knowledge has a real impact on the lower bounds or algorithm efficiency?
2. What results can be generalized to a model where nodes can transmit a constant number of times instead of only once?
3. Can randomized adversaries that use a non-uniform probabilistic distribution alter significantly the bounds presented here in the same way as in the work by Yamauchi *et al.* [15]?

References

1. Abshoff, S., Meyer auf der Heide, F.: Continuous aggregation in dynamic ad-hoc networks. In: Halldórsson, M.M. (ed.) SIROCCO 2014. LNCS, vol. 8576, pp. 194–209. Springer, Cham (2014). https://doi.org/10.1007/978-3-319-09620-9_16
2. Angluin, D., Aspnes, J., Eisenstat, D., Ruppert, E.: The computational power of population protocols. Distrib. Comput. **20**(4), 279–304 (2007)
3. Annamalai, V., Gupta, S.K.S., Schwiebert, L.: On tree-based convergecasting in wireless sensor networks. In: 2003 IEEE Wireless Communications and Networking, WCNC 2003, vol. 3, pp. 1942–1947. IEEE (2003)
4. Bramas, Q., Masuzawa, T., Tixeuil, S.: Distributed online data aggregation in dynamic graphs. In: 36th IEEE International Conference on Distributed Computing Systems, ICDCS 2016, Nara, Japan, 27–30 June 2016, pp. 747–748. IEEE Computer Society (2016)

5. Bramas, Q., Masuzawa, T., Tixeuil, S.: Distributed online data aggregation in dynamic graphs. arXiv preprint arXiv:1602.01065 (2016)
6. Bramas, Q., Tixeuil, S.: The complexity of data aggregation in static and dynamic wireless sensor networks. In: Pelc, A., Schwarzmann, A.A. (eds.) SSS 2015. LNCS, vol. 9212, pp. 36–50. Springer, Cham (2015). https://doi.org/10.1007/978-3-319-21741-3_3
7. Casteigts, A., Chaumette, S., Ferreira, A.: Characterizing topological assumptions of distributed algorithms in dynamic networks. In: Kutten, S., Žerovnik, J. (eds.) SIROCCO 2009. LNCS, vol. 5869, pp. 126–140. Springer, Heidelberg (2010). https://doi.org/10.1007/978-3-642-11476-2_11
8. Casteigts, A., Flocchini, P., Quattrociocchi, W., Santoro, N.: Time-varying graphs and dynamic networks. In: Frey, H., Li, X., Ruehrup, S. (eds.) ADHOC-NOW 2011. LNCS, vol. 6811, pp. 346–359. Springer, Heidelberg (2011). https://doi.org/10.1007/978-3-642-22450-8_27
9. Chen, X., Hu, X., Zhu, J.: Minimum data aggregation time problem in wireless sensor networks. In: Jia, X., Wu, J., He, Y. (eds.) MSN 2005. LNCS, vol. 3794, pp. 133–142. Springer, Heidelberg (2005). https://doi.org/10.1007/11599463_14
10. Cornejo, A., Gilbert, S., Newport, C.: Aggregation in dynamic networks. In: Proceedings of the 2012 ACM Symposium on Principles of Distributed Computing, pp. 195–204. ACM (2012)
11. Fasolo, E., Rossi, M., Widmer, J., Zorzi, M.: In-network aggregation techniques for wireless sensor networks: a survey. IEEE Wirel. Commun. 14(2), 70–87 (2007)
12. Nguyen, T.D., Zalyubovskiy, V., Choo, H.: Efficient time latency of data aggregation based on neighboring dominators in WSNs. In: 2011 IEEE Global Telecommunications Conference (GLOBECOM 2011), pp. 1–6. IEEE (2011)
13. Ren, M., Guo, L., Li, J.: A new scheduling algorithm for reducing data aggregation latency in wireless sensor networks. Int. J. Commun. Netw. Syst. Sci. 3(8), 679 (2010)
14. XiaoHua, X., Li, M., Mao, X.F., Tang, S., Wang, S.G.: A delay-efficient algorithm for data aggregation in multihop wireless sensor networks. IEEE Trans. Parallel Distrib. Syst. 22(1), 163–175 (2011)
15. Yamauchi, Y., Tixeuil, S., Kijima, S., Yamashita, M.: Brief announcement: probabilistic stabilization under probabilistic schedulers. In: Aguilera, M.K. (ed.) DISC 2012. LNCS, vol. 7611, pp. 413–414. Springer, Heidelberg (2012). https://doi.org/10.1007/978-3-642-33651-5_34
16. Yu, B., Li, J., Li, Y.: Distributed data aggregation scheduling in wireless sensor networks. In: IEEE INFOCOM 2009, pp. 2159–2167. IEEE (2009)

A Multi-criteria Group Decision Making Method for Big Data Storage Selection

Jabrane Kachaoui[(✉)] and Abdessamad Belangour

Faculty of Science Ben M'Sik, Hassan II University, Casablanca, Morocco
jabrane2005@gmail.com, belangour@gmail.com

Abstract. The terms Data Lake and Data Warehouse are very commonly used to talk about Big Data storage. The two concepts are providing opportunities for businesses to better strengthen data management and achieve competitive advantages. Evaluating and selecting the most suitable approach is however challenging. These two types of data storage are often confused, whereas they have many more differences than similarities. In fact, the only real similarity between them is their ability to store data. To effectively deal with this issue, this paper analyses these emerging Big Data technologies and presents a comparison of the selected data storage concepts. The main aim is then to propose and demonstrate the use of an AHP model for the Big Data storage selection, which may be used by businesses, public sector institutions as well as citizens to solve multiple criteria decision-making problems. This multi-criteria classification approach has been applied to define which of the two models is better suited for data management.

Keywords: Data Lake · Data Warehouse · Big Data · AHP model · Data storage platforms · Decision-making

1 Introduction

In today's highly competitive business environment, companies are increasingly rushed to use Big Data for processing and analyzing data of all kinds in order to make better decisions in a short delay [1]. This objective is still complicated due to the huge quantity of data to treat to reach this objective [2]. As a result, endorsing and implementing the appropriate Big Data storage approach, which is able to (a) quickly find and analyze data, and (b) display information in a timely and relevant manner for efficient decision making becomes crucial.

The data storage and analysis technology is improving rapidly due to technological evolution [3]. Nevertheless; challenges differ for different applications as they have various requirements of consistency, usability or compatibility [4]. Thus, to perform any type of analysis on such large and complex data, the expansion of hardware platforms is imminent and the choice of the appropriate platform becomes a decisive decision [5]. The primary purpose of this paper is to provide an Analytic Hierarchy Process (AHP) model for the big data storage selection. Some of the various Big Data storage platforms are discussed in detail and their application are represented.

© Springer Nature Switzerland AG 2019
M. F. Atig and A. A. Schwarzmann (Eds.): NETYS 2019, LNCS 11704, pp. 381–386, 2019.
https://doi.org/10.1007/978-3-030-31277-0_25

2 Literature Review

2.1 Data Storage Solution and Selection Problem

Various studies have been conducted on determining the relevant criteria for evaluating and selecting Big Data storage approaches. This evaluation requires a series of decisions based on a wide range of factors and then each of these decisions have considerable impact on the evaluation of performance, usability and maintainability for overall success of the most suitable data storage selection [10].

The evaluation has a great impact on the quality of attributes. Valacich, George, and Hoffer proposed several the most common criteria to choose the right platform. These are: cost, functionality, efficiency, vendor support, viability of vendor, response time, flexibility, documentation and ease of installation [9]. Lake and Drake emphasize the importance of the computational complexity factor and the increased efficiency of algorithms in the big data era [3]. Marakas and O'Brien propose a lot of evaluation factors like performance, cost, reliability, availability, compatibility, modularity, technology, ergonomics, scalability, and support characteristics [11].

2.2 Multiple Criteria Decision-Making Approach

Real-world decision-making problems are complex and no structures are to be considered through the examination of a single criterion, our point of view that will lead to the optimum and informed decision [8, 12]. MCDM offers a lot of methods that can help in problem structuring and tackling the problem complexity because of the multidimensionality of the sustainability goal and the complexity of socio-economic, environment and government systems [10, 13].

The AHP is a MCDM tool that has been used in almost all the applications related with decision making [8]. The AHP is a powerful, flexible and widely used method for complex problems, which consider the numeric scale for the measurement of quantitative and qualitative performances in a hierarchical structure [6]. This is an Eigenvalue approach to the pairwise comparisons.

3 Criteria Description

Based on this literature review, these criteria are selected and favored to choose the most appropriate platform responding to the requirements of various big data storage challenges. They are classified into three categories:

1. technical (hardware and resources configuration requirements) perspective:
    1.1 availability and fault tolerance – this criterion has the values of: Poor (1)/Fair (2)/Good (3)/Very Good (4)/Excellent (5), these values will be used for others criteria thereafter.
    1.2 scalability and flexibility – 1, 2, 3, 4, 5,
    1.3 data type and metadata – 1, 2, 3, 4, 5,
    1.4 data security – 1, 2, 3, 4, 5,

1.5 performance (latency) – 1, 2, 3, 4, 5,

1.6 distributed storage capacity –centralized storage system (1)/distributed storage (2),

1.7 data processing modes –Transaction processing (1)/Real-time processing (2)/ Batch processing (3),

2. Social (people skills and knowledge) perspective:

2.1 ease of installation and maintenance – 1, 2, 3, 4, 5,

2.2 Heterogeneous tooling – 1, 2, 3, 4, 5,

2.3 deployment experience – 1, 2, 3, 4, 5,

3. Cost and policy perspective,

3.1 sustainability –Low (1)/Medium (2)/High (3),

3.2 policy and regulation–1, 2, 3, 4, 5,

3.3 Data governance–1, 2, 3, 4, 5,

3.4 cost–Open source (1)/Trial version (2)/Commercial release (3),

Based on the literature review of the possible Strengths and Weaknesses of various big data storages platforms, two approaches were selected as alternatives to be compared [15]. these alternatives are Data Lake and Data Warehouse. A decision table with the values for the selected alternatives can be seen in the Table 1. The data used are from 2018. The AHP model's structure is a hierarchy of four levels constituting goal, criteria, sub-criteria and alternatives.

Table 1. Decision table for the Big Data storage selection, Source: Author.

Alternatives	Criteria and their type													
	1.1	1.2	1.3	1.4	1.5	1.6	1.7	2.1	2.2	2.3	3.1	3.2	3.3	3.4
	Max	Max	Max	Max	Max	Max	Max	Max	Max	Max	Max	Max	Max	Max
Data Lake	5	5	5	2	5	2	3	2	4	2	1	2	2	1
Data Warehouse	3	2	2	5	3	1	1	5	2	5	3	4	4	3

To analyze business challenges and to meet users need, three use cases were designed for a logical application. These use cases are focused only on the storage approaches, which offer data analysis tools. However, these approaches can be integrated with several data transfer and search platforms to support the whole Big Data life cycle and related phases.

Use case 1 – scientist or advanced user

Integrating and exploring data from various sources and building blocks for creating a solution to a data science problem is required. Batch processing platform is more important than real-time processing. Data security is not required, because data are used overall for testing purposes. User has a very good knowledge and programming skills. The selected approach has to be open source with no data security, no policy and regulation.

Use case 2 – medium-sized business

The business needs scalable, flexible, available, and fault tolerance approach with a good computational complexity for the purpose of storing a big amount of data. a real-time processing platform is most suitable for this use case without overlooking data security aspect and data governance to ensure security and accuracy. The Platform has to be an easy software deployment with a wide technical support.

Use case 3 – public sector institution

For this use case, a flexible, available and fault tolerance approach which is able to offer a high variety and flexibility of computational complexity extensions is needed. Batch processing and open source platform with an ease of use is preferred. This platform should be easy to be deployed. Security tools must be available. good documentation and reference manual are required for maintenance needs.

4   Results and Discussion

In all the cases, the technical perspective is the most important item. For a second stage, Use case 1 and 3 prefer the social perspective. For the use case 2 (medium-sized business), the cost and policy perspective is the second most important perspective (Fig. 1).

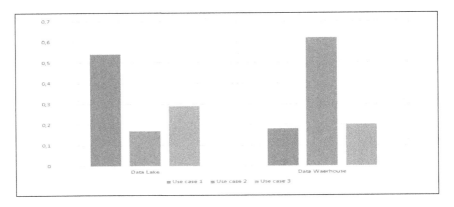

Fig. 1. Weights of the alternatives for each use case. Source: Author.

Based on the needs of the user defined in the use case 1, Data Lake is the most suitable big data storage approach (58%). For the use case 2, the choice is Data Warehouse (62%). For the use case 3, the choice is Data Lake (29%) and Data Warehouse (20%). Decision-makers precisions may provide a paired comparison which is restricted by their experience and knowledge, as well as by the complexity of the big data storage selection problem in terms of setting up these concepts. To deal with this problem, the decision-makers must understand the details, strengths, and limitations of the AHP method as well as the related platforms [14].

5 Conclusion

Big data storage tools offer organizations new ways to improve their ability to grasp information hiding in their data. The evaluation and selection of the most suitable big data storage tool is however challenging due to multidimensional nature of the decision making problem, and the subjectiveness and imprecision of the decision making process.

To effectively deal with these issues, this paper has presented a multi-criteria group decision making method for evaluating the performance of big data storage tool alternatives, and has studied The impact of the AHP method in Big Data storage selection. The proposal model was made based on the literature review in order to provide an overview of the Big Data storage approach, which offers a simple but efficient evaluation method that can help scientists, businesses and public sector institutions in selecting the most suitable storage platform. The aim from a such analytics study to Big Data storage, valuable information will be extracted and exploited with a better way.

This paper is a first step of a study to deal with all kind of data with a better analysis way. A new architecture will be rolled in our future work which merged Data Lake and Data Warehouse to deal with all these use cases described in this paper for a better data management.

References

1. Tsuchiya, S., Sakamoto, Y., Tsuchimoto, Y., Lee, V.: Big data processing in cloud environments. FUJITSU Sci. Technol. **48**(2), 159–168 (2012)
2. Peer Research, Big data analytics: intel's it manager survey on how organizations are using big data, Intel (2012). http://www.triforce.com.au/pdf/data-insights-peer-research-report.pdf
3. Lake, P., Drake, R.: Information Systems Management in the Big Data Era. Springer, London (2014)
4. Shamsi, J., Khojaye, M.A., Qasmi, M.: A data-intensive cloud computing: requirements, expectations, challenges, and solutions. J. Grid Comput. **11**(2), 281–310 (2013). https://doi.org/10.1007/s10723-013-9255-6
5. Singh, D., Reddy, C.K.: A survey on platforms for big data analytics. J. Big Data **1**(8), 1–20 (2014). https://doi.org/10.1186/s40537-014-0008-6
6. Saaty, T.L.: How to make a decision: the analytic hierarchy process. Eur. J. Oper. Res. **48**(1), 9–26 (1990). https://doi.org/10.1016/0377-2217(90)90057-I
7. Saaty, T.L.: Decision making with the analytic hierarchy process. Int. J. Serv. Sci. **1**(1), 83–98 (2008). https://doi.org/10.1504/IJSSCI.2008.017590
8. Vaidya, O.S., Kumar, S.: Analytic hierarchy process: an overview of applications. Eur. J. Oper. Res. **169**(1), 1–29 (2006). https://doi.org/10.1016/j.ejor.2004.04.028
9. Valacich, J., Schneider, C.: Information Systems Today: Managing in the Digital World, 6th edn. Pearson Education Limited, Australia (2011)
10. Lnenicka, M.: AHP model for the big data analytics platform selection. Acta Inform. Pragnesia **4**(2), 108–121 (2015)

11. Marakas, G.M., O'Brien, J.A.: Introduction to Information Systems. New York: McGraw-Hill/Irwin. Wei, C.C., Chien, C.F., Wang, M.J.J.: An AHP-based approach to ERP system selection. Int. J. Prod. Econ. **96**(1), 47–62 (2013)https://doi.org/10.1016/j.ijpe.2004.03.004

12. Zavadskas, E.K., Turskis, Z.: Multiple criteria decision making (MCDM) methods in economics: an overview. Technol. Econ. Dev. Econ. **17**(2), 397–427 (2011). https://doi.org/10.3846/20294913.2011.593291

13. Liou, J.J.H., Tzeng, G.-H.: Comments on "Multiple criteria decision making (MCDM) methods in economics: an overview". Technol. Econ. Dev. Econ. **18**(4), 672–695 (2012). https://doi.org/10.3846/20294913.2012.753489

14. Wei, C.C., Chien, C.F., Wang, M.J.J.: An AHP-based approach to ERP system selection. Int. J. Prod. Econ. **96**(1), 47–62 (2005). https://doi.org/10.1016/j.ijpe.2004.03.004

15. Kachaoui, J., Belangour, A.: Challenges and Benefits of Deploying Big Data Storage Solution (2019). https://doi.org/10.1145/3314074.3314097

Author Index

Printed in the United States
By Bookmasters